Thaipusam in Malaysia

The **ISEAS – Yusof Ishak Institute** (formerly Institute of Southeast Asian Studies) was established as an autonomous organization in 1968. It is a regional centre dedicated to the study of socio-political, security and economic trends and developments in Southeast Asia and its wider geostrategic and economic environment. The Institute's research programmes are the Regional Economic Studies (RES, including ASEAN and APEC), Regional Strategic and Political Studies (RSPS), and Regional Social and Cultural Studies (RSCS).

ISEAS Publishing, an established academic press, has issued more than 2,000 books and journals. It is the largest scholarly publisher of research about Southeast Asia from within the region. ISEAS Publishing works with many other academic and trade publishers and distributors to disseminate important research and analyses from and about Southeast Asia to the rest of the world.

Thaipusam in Malaysia: A Hindu Festival in the Tamil Diaspora

Carl Vadivella Belle

ISEAS YUSOF ISHAK INSTITUTE

First published in Singapore in 2017 by ISEAS Publishing
30 Heng Mui Keng Terrace
Singapore 119614

E-mail: publish@iseas.edu.sg
Website: <http://bookshop.iseas.edu.sg>

ISEAS Library Cataloguing-in-Publication Data

Belle, Carl Vadivella.
   Thaipusam in Malaysia : A Hindu Festival in the Tamil Diaspora.
   1. Thaipusam—Malaysia.
   2. Fasts and feasts—Hinduism.
   3. Murugan (Hindu deity)—Cult—Singapore.
BL1239.82 T43B43   2017

ISBN 978-981-4695-75-6 (soft cover)
ISBN 978-981-4695-83-1 (e-book PDF)

Typeset by Superskill Graphics Pte Ltd
Printed in Singapore by Mainland Press Pte Ltd

Contents

Acknowledgements

This book would not be possible without the generous assistance and encouragement of many people. I must offer my most sincere thanks to Dr Gauri Krishnan, formerly of the Asian Civilizations Museum, and now of the National Heritage Board, Singapore, who made the initial suggestion that I should write a book on this subject. I am deeply grateful to Ambassador K. Kesavapany, former Director of ISEAS, who offered enthusiastic support and encouragement, and who also suggested lines of inquiry. Others at ISEAS who gave much support included Dr Ooi Kee Beng, Dr Lee Hock Guan, Dr Hui Yew-Foong and Professor A. Mani. Mr Stephen Logan and Mr Ng Kok Kiong offered continuing warm and friendly editorial advice, and Mrs Y.L. Lee provided prompt and efficient administrative support.

Academics in Malaysia and elsewhere who provided assistance included Dr K. Anbalakan of Universiti Sains Malaysia; Dr S. Nagarajan of Wawasan Open University whose help and friendship over many years has been invaluable; Dr Andrew Willford of Cornell University, USA; the late Dr S.M. Ponniah whose kindness and insights were legendary; and Mr Patrick Harrigan whose advice over many years has been extremely helpful. I must offer a special tribute to Toh Puan Uma Sambathan whose sage advice, counsel and generous assistance over years has been incalculable. I should record my appreciation for the helpful comments made by the two anonymous peer reviewers, both of whom offered sound and constructive criticism and whose advice saved me from several very elementary mistakes.

The photographs which appear in these pages were kindly supplied by Mr Kahan Singh Gill, Mr V. Chockalingam, Mr Jayaganesan Kangris and

Mr Ganesh Kolandaveloo, all of Malaysia; Mr Eric Lafforgue of France; and
Sri C. Balasubramaniam of Gujarat, India. I am deeply indebted for their
permission to use these photographs within this book.

There are many people to whom I owe thanks for advice, friendship,
support and encouragement. These include Mr and Mrs V. Thanapal
who have provided accommodation and assistance for many years,
and indeed who in many ways have helped make this book possible;
Mrs T. Pushpharani, Mrs T. Rukmani, Dr T. Mohanaraj and
Dr N. Parameswary, all of whom have provided much appreciated practical
assistance and advice; Mr Kumar and Mrs Nui Menon; Mr K. and Mrs Ah
Leng Thuruvan; Dr S. Yoga Bhavani and Mr Jeyakumar Rajaratnam;
Datuk A. Vaithilingam, former President of the Malaysian Hindu Sangam;
Mr Pathmarajah Nagalingam; Mr K. and Mrs Gomathi Thiruvasagam;
Ms Khoo Salma Nasution and Mr Abdur-Razzak Lubis and the staff of
Areca Books whose warm generosity and helpful suggestions were greatly
appreciated; Mr A.J. and Mrs Pooranam Lakshminarayanan and family;
Mr and Mrs N. Selva; the late Mr N.S. Sundrasekaran and Mrs Kasi
Sundrasekaran; Mr Arj and Mrs Veronica Athimulam; Ms A. Thanam;
Mr V. Chockalingam who provided a generous and fulsome introduction to
Hinduism in Melaka; Mr Kumaresh Batumalai; Mr and Mrs R. Kurunathan;
Mr S. Lakshmannan; Mr and Mrs P. Chandrasegaran; Sister Deva Kunjari
Sambanthan; Mr S. Somasandharam; Mr K.P. Mathivanan; and Dr Hari
Ram Ramayya, Mr Ramayya Narasamullo Naidu and Mrs Susila Appu
Nair, all of whom showed me much kindness during my trips to Kangar.
I must also acknowledge the openness and generosity of the hundreds of
devotees who were so willing to answer my questions, as well as those
who provided moral and practical support during my field research.
I should also express my gratitude to religious scholars of other traditions
who were willing to discuss philosophies and beliefs, and in particular
Muslim and Buddhist scholars in Kuala Lumpur, Penang and Singapore.
My former colleagues at Flinders University, Mr Geoff Boyce, Mrs Maureen
Howland, Dr Abul Farooqe, Sri Thong Phap and Ms Kiley Doherty provided
a friendly and accommodating environment which encouraged discussion
and the exchange of ideas. Finally, I must thank Ms Jenelle Davies,
Mr Wes Kilham and the late, and much missed, Professor David S. Dolan
who offered support at a time when it was most needed.

I offer my special thanks and eternal gratitude to my wife, Wendy
Valli Belle, who has helped in so many ways throughout the compilation

of this book, and whose sound advice, humour and plain commonsense has seen me through numerous writer's crises, both real and imagined.

This book is dedicated to the memory of Guru Doraisamy, who served as an inspiration to so many, and whose generosity, compassion, wisdom and profundity continue to live on in the community he founded.

Introduction

In the Beginning

My first experience of Thaipusam occurred on 24 January 1978. Encouraged by Indian contacts who suggested that the festival might be of some general interest, I rose at 4 a.m., and accompanied by my wife, Wendy, four visitors from Australia, and a young Tamil man who had agreed to act as our guide, we made our way to Batu Caves, about thirteen kilometres north of Kuala Lumpur. Despite the early hour the area around the caves was already crowded and we had to park some distance from the main site. (Press reports calculated the 1978 attendance at 500,000 and I was later to find that many people had spent the night at the caves.) We threaded our way through the concourse to the very foot of the steps leading to the main cave (known as the Temple Cave), which would, we hoped, provide us with a privileged view of the festival and its participants.

Since our arrival in Malaysia we had been fed a diet of highly dramatic (some might say sensationalist) stories of the Thaipusam festival. We had heard accounts of the numerous *kavadi* (ritual burden) bearers, their bodies pierced with skewers and hooks, carrying their loads up the sharp incline of the stairway leading to the main shrine within the Temple Cave; of the immense crowds; of the auditory overload, consisting of the chants and shouts of devotees, the constant drumming, the loudspeakers relaying amplified religious music as well as the droning speeches of visiting political dignitaries. And this festival was dedicated to the deity Murugan, a South Indian god so seemingly obscure and generally unknown that he earned but a brief paragraph in one of the putatively authoritative texts which had provided my background reading into Hinduism, and no entries at all in the remainder. Most of what we had heard about Thaipusam had comprised the impressions of the few expatriates who had visited the festival, and who tended to view it as a curiosity, a form of local colour, an incidental divertissement which provided a suitable touch of the "mysterious East" to round out their stay in "oriental" Malaysia. None of our informants had looked upon Thaipusam as a meaningful religious observance of deep significance to devotees and the wider Hindu community; in other words, as a festival worthy of consideration in its own right. We were advised that should we wish to venture into the immense crowds we would witness a series of amazing exhibitions; devotees who performed miraculous yet grotesque acts in the name of religion. We were also warned that Thaipusam could prove stomach churning, and was not a spectacle for the faint-hearted.

These rather cursory and impressionistic accounts provided no real insights to what Thaipusam betokened as a religious observance, nor did they even begin to prepare me for what I was to experience. But then the fifteen months I had spent in Malaysia had been a continual exposure to the unexpected. Prior to my posting as an Attaché to the Australian High Commission, Kuala Lumpur, in late 1976, I had been furnished with a schedule of pre-departure briefings which had adumbrated in nebulous and often misleading detail some of the supposed social and political realities of the country in which I now found myself. As a consequence I found myself poorly equipped to deal with the complex realities of Malaysian life, in particular the plethora of ethnic, religious, socio-economic, educational and linguistic issues which dominated Malaysian political discourse, and to which my work daily exposed me. In particular I possessed but a rudimentary understanding of the great religious traditions which informed and enlivened the worldviews of the component ethnicities of Malaysia. I had attempted to remedy my ignorance with a programme of focused reading, supplemented wherever possible with exploration of local cultures, or at least those cultural aspects which were both open and accessible to expatriates. My expressions of interest were rewarded with warm Malaysian hospitality, generosity and encouragement. As a result I visited mosques, churches, temples, weddings, initiations, firewalkings and cultural performances, as well as the open houses which marked the great festivals of each community — Hari Raya Puasa, which concluded the Muslim fasting month of Ramadan; Chinese New Year; the Hindu festival of Deepavali and the Christian commemoration of Good Friday and Christmas. As I gradually gained the confidence of my Malaysian colleagues, I began to receive invitations to functions and ceremonies that were normally closed to expatriate "Europeans". These included a kampong *silat* training session, family religious observances and temple and mosque related activities. These explorations boosted my general understanding of the dynamics of Malaysian life and assisted me to piece together the complex three-dimensional jigsaw which constitutes Malaysian culture and society.

And therein lay a further reason behind my visit to Batu Caves that January morning. Hindu associates, aware of my growing interest in the various forms of religious expression in Malaysia, had suggested that Thaipusam, and in particular the disciplined austerities surrounding the kavadi ritual, might provide a general introduction to some of the traditions of South Indian Hinduism, in particular those relating to the deity Murugan, as well as the fundamental philosophy of *bhakti* (devotional) worship which underscored Hinduism in Malaysia.

Our arrival at Batu Caves coincided with a temporary lull in proceedings. We stood in the preternatural darkness of the predawn cool, orienting ourselves to our surroundings, and commenting upon the curiously charged atmosphere we had all detected; a singular amalgam of muted exultation and anticipatory enthusiasm. To our right the looming bulk of Batu Caves was etched against the setting full moon and the still night sky. The steps leading to the Temple Cave were gently illuminated by strings of coloured light globes. To our left, hundreds of onlookers, nearly all ethnic Indians, waited patiently on either side of the roped lane reserved for kavadi bearers and their followers. Soldiers and police, all armed, and nearly all Malay, were stationed at regular intervals along the lane; practising Muslims detailed to guard a Hindu festival.

Our reveries were fractured by a sudden commotion. Several drummers preceded a group of chanting, dancing devotees who made their way towards our vantage point, their progress animated by a tangible wave of excitement. This group surrounded a young man who appeared to be anchored below a kind of mobile tower, largely consisting of a decorated platform incorporating an image of the deity whom I had learned to recognize as Murugan, son of the supreme deity, Siva. The votary's torso was laced with hooks, each of which was attached to a fine silver chain which hung from the platform. A "skewer" protruded from his tongue, another penetrated his cheeks. The entire group radiated an emphatic, compelling and ecstatic energy, a form of intense exhilaration which fell well beyond the parameters of anything I had hitherto understood to constitute religious expression.

For the next eight hours we remained at Batu Caves, and as recalled in my personal diary, "witnessed some of the most amazing sights one could hope to see". Throughout the morning hundreds of kavadi bearers, often clustered in groups, made their way to the stairs and up into the caves. All were accompanied by retinues of drummers and were surrounded by circles of supporters chanting and singing. While many of the kavadi bearers bore burdens similar to that of the devotee we had seen earlier, others restricted themselves to small wooden arches; some devotees had their cheeks transfixed by long spears; young men danced on huge upturned knives borne by their friends; couples conveyed babies in slings suspended from sugar cane; both men and women carried vessels full of milk. Most devotees radiated that same mysterious and unfathomable rapture, almost overpowering in its intensity, which had so astonished me earlier that morning.

Throughout the course of the morning we shifted from place to place within the Batu Caves complex. We visited the sites along the *Sungai Batu* (Rocky River) where most devotees began their journey, and watched the aspirants bathing, achieving trance, undergoing piercings, and having their kavadis fitted. We shuffled up the congested stairways to the shrine in the Temple Cave where the kavadi bearers terminated their pilgrimages.

Like so many "foreign" observers of Thaipusam, I was intensely curious about what I had seen and experienced during the festival. I had not been prepared either for the sheer size of the crowd that had gathered at Batu Caves that morning, or the large number of active participants — pilgrims, musicians and supporting attendants — who had made their way to the main shrine within the Temple Cave. Nor had I even remotely anticipated the ecstatic devotion of those who had elected to bear kavadis. Like many "Westerners" I was puzzled by the absence of pain or evidence of blood among devotees, and the unaccountable exultation of the pilgrims, especially in view of the ritual privations they had endured.

In February 1979, a mere six weeks prior to my scheduled return to Australia, a close Hindu friend, Ramasamy (not his real name), informed me that several of his relatives intended to take kavadis under the direction of his uncle, a recognized medium. He invited me to observe the group as it prepared for and fulfilled the kavadi ritual. We arrived at our destination slightly after nightfall on Thaipusam Eve, and ascended the steps to the Temple Cave. The interior of the cave was suffused with the liquid light thrown by dozens of candles and lamps, and the air was heavily laden with the commingled scents of incense and burning camphor. Ramasamy and his cousins offered their obeisance, firstly to Lord Ganesha, the elephant-headed deity whom they described as the Remover of Obstacles, and then to Lord Murugan. We left the cave and made our way to the riverbank where the group of devotees known to Ramasamy had assembled. The group leader welcomed me, and although he worked almost non-stop in overseeing the purificatory rituals, supervising trance states and fitting kavadis, made time to provide me with abbreviated explanatory comments about his own actions and those of each kavadi bearer. In the main, the group, numbering about twenty-five people, consisted of working-class Tamils, drawn from the rubber and palm oil estates adjacent to Kuala Lumpur, but also included two Chinese university students, and a Eurasian Catholic lawyer who informed me that he divided his worship between Jesus and Murugan. The group contained a wide spread of ages ranging from teenagers to votaries in their fifties. Although predominantly male, the group included several women, most in their early twenties, and one much older woman who had dedicated herself to Murugan. At about 12:30 a.m. the party set off for the caves. I followed them, observing the ascent to the caves, the ecstatic dancing culminating before the main shrine, the termination of the trance state, the dismantling of the kavadis. Later that morning I breakfasted with the devotees at a nearby enclosure set aside for this purpose.

My sojourn in Malaysia and in particular the festival of Thaipusam had affected me in ways that I had not envisaged. From the very outset of my posting I had found Malaysia vital and compelling, a country visibly grappling with the residual problems bequeathed by colonialism, struggling to come to terms with the legacy of its immediate history, and to reconcile the sometimes contradictory diversity of cultures, traditions and worldviews under the overarching umbrella of nationhood. Throughout my years in Malaysia I had made a number of deep and enduring friendships; my family and I had been welcomed into numerous homes where we had been received with warmth and hospitality. My return to Australia was accompanied by a wholly unanticipated and quite profound culture shock, and sustained "homesickness" for the society I had left behind. It appeared obvious that in certain respects my departure had been premature; there were still lessons to learn, and mysteries, both intellectual and personal, that I needed to penetrate. Within six months of my return I had shocked myself (but neither my wife, nor my Malaysian friends), by announcing my "conversion"[1] to Saivite Hinduism, and my concomitant vow to bear a succession of kavadis at the festival of Thaipusam at Batu Caves.

My first kavadi was taken on 20 January 1981, and was followed by regular pilgrimages which have continued until the present day. Each of these pilgrimages exposed me to new and often profound experiences, and both widened and deepened my knowledge of Thaipusam, Murugan worship and Hinduism in Malaysia. In 1989 I was invited to address the Fifth Malaysian National Hindu Conference held in Petaling Jaya, Selangor. Senior Hindus suggested that I write a book about my religious experiences. The resultant volume, a highly personal account of the "confessional" genre, and entitled *Towards Truth: An Australian Spiritual Journey*,[2] was published in February 1992 in Kuala Lumpur. Although this book was well received by Hindus within Malaysia and Singapore, and in other parts of the world, my later studies made me painfully aware of its many and varied scholarly limitations. I have therefore declined offers made over several years to reprint this work.

Routes Travelled

In 1993, while working as Australian correspondent for the U.S.-based journal *Hinduism Today*, I was invited to apply for admission to an off-campus and part-time Master of Arts programme at Deakin University in the Australian state of Victoria. To this date my interest in Thaipusam had been shaped by two major influences — firstly my role as a privileged "insider", albeit that of a "Western" pilgrim, and secondly, the spirit of scholarly inquiry. To that point my knowledge of Thaipusam had been largely moulded by the philosophies and rituals of the so-called "great tradition" school of Saiva Siddhanta, especially the more esoteric conventions of Murugan worship as they related to and enmeshed with that tradition. While this background was sufficient to provide an interpretative paradigm for my own participation in Thaipusam, it proved too narrow to sustain any detailed analysis of the collocation of behaviours and belief structures which collectively comprise this complex and multifaceted festival. In particular the terms of my personal engagement with Thaipusam neither provided me with the breadth of perspective necessary to discern the intricate and often fluid web of relationships which permeate the supposedly inviolable boundaries of *Agamic* and "village" Hinduism, nor allowed me to appreciate how these relationships catalyse the negotiation, reformulation and transmission of concepts within the broader context of Hindu society. Scholarly inquiry thus insisted that I move beyond the conventions of "great tradition" learning and plunge into a wider study embracing the agglomeration of castes, sub-ethnic and religious discourses which cumulatively make up the body of beliefs generally classified under the rubric of Hinduism.

Integral to my research for my dissertation (which was subsequently upgraded to doctoral level), were periods of fieldwork, including several trips to Malaysia, one extended over three months (1995), and supplementary trips, each of six weeks duration (1997, 2000 and 2004), interspersed by a ten-week trip to South India in 1998 funded by a research grant awarded by Deakin University. My 1995 travel incorporated a six-week stay in London, which not only enabled me to interact with other scholars, but also included one-month's research into colonial documents, reports, and related materials held within the official collection of the Oriental and Indian Office Library. These papers yielded much valuable information and occasionally rare and illustrative vignettes on the Indian experience in British Malaya.

Malaysia. The focal points of my Malaysian visits, which have continued to the present day, have been the close observation of the festival of Thaipusam as conducted at Batu Caves and in Penang, as well as similar and related festivals at Melaka, Kangar and other locations. My presence at these festivals has provided openings which have enabled me to arrange extended interviews with kavadi bearers and their attendants. Over the years I have met with several hundred such devotees, as well as members of their families and supporting retinues. The process of organizing interviews has undoubtedly been advanced by respondents' awareness of my own history of kavadi pilgrimage, and by my standing as a devotee who has written a "confessional" book about these experiences. My interviewees have represented the entire gamut of kavadi worshippers in terms of ethnicity, sex, age and vocational status, and have included participants who have borne kavadis for non-*Agamic* deities.

My knowledge of local conditions and the assistance of friends and erstwhile colleagues have also enabled me to interview a range of people who hold or have held prominent positions within the Indian and Hindu communities. These included temple officials as well as a large number of individuals whose impressions and recollections have done much to deepen and embellish my own perspectives. Similarly, Malay and Chinese friends and contacts provided me with introductions to religious scholars and officiates, many of whom provided invaluable and illuminating information, and whose warmth and generosity always proved enlightening. Many interviewees made their availability conditional upon their guaranteed anonymity. Accordingly, where I have made reference to the views or recollections of an individual, I have footnoted these with the initials of the interviewee.

In preparing this study I have been careful to contextualize the views of self-proclaimed "reformers". Many of those who fall within this category are Western educated, of professional standing, modernist in outlook and fluent in English. One could thus be easily led to form the impression that the views of the "reformers" represent an authoritative perspective on what constitutes "correct" Hindu philosophies and rituals. In fact, it has been my experience that most reformers subscribe to a textual Hinduism which is both rarefied and "rational" (and often "disenchanted" in the Weberian sense), and thus largely stripped of its *Puranic* traditions, its emotional content, and the ritual modes of expression which infuse most forms of the South Indian *bhakti* tradition. Many reformers who propound Vedantic philosophies, or who pursue an idealized "philosophical" Hinduism largely isolated from its ritualized expressions, are often but sparsely informed, and hold grossly simplified and stereotypical views about such subjects as *Agamic* beliefs, the scope of Murugan worship and its relationship to didactic philosophy, or the belief structures undergirding village/popular Hinduism. Most are acutely sensitive to imagined Western perceptions of Hinduism. I have been constantly queried, sometimes aggressively, about the need to research village/popular Hinduism in Malaysia. Indeed in 1995 one academic insistently counselled me to overlook the "uncivilized" views and beliefs of the majority of the Hindu population in order to provide a more "acceptable" (even if bowdlerized) portrayal of Malaysian Hinduism. While I have noted the views of the "reformers" as belonging to a small, albeit highly visible minority of Malaysian Hindus, I have not permitted them to unduly bias my overall findings.

Over the past three decades I have undertaken trips to major temples and noted pilgrimage sites throughout Peninsular Malaysia, especially those related to Murugan worship and the kavadi ritual. These necessarily involved visits to the entire spectrum of Hindu places of worship, ranging from orthodox *Agamic* temples (exemplified by well-managed Jaffna Tamil and Chettiar temples), to small village structures fashioned of plank and zinc. I have observed the conduct of many different rituals, including several examples of mediumship, and met a number of religious figures, many self-educated, others possessing the dubious imprimatur of self-anointment.[3] Requests to research temple records within Malaysia were invariably declined, generally with the polite rebuttal that these were off limits to any person other than properly elected officials and trustees. However, in many, if not most instances, the need to view temple records was circumvented by prolonged interviews with older devotees.

During my extended 1995 visit, I was invited to spend time on a coconut/rubber estate in northern Perak. This provided me with opportunities to visit several adjoining coconut, rubber and oil palm estates. My stay permitted me to gain insights into the "plantation" ethos which has played such a formative role in shaping Indian culture and society in Malaysia. My time on the estate also brought the unexpected bonus of interaction with nearby Telegu communities, and the opportunity to inspect several estate-based Vaishnaivite temples.

India. My fieldwork in India in 1998 furnished me with an invaluable opportunity to examine the Murugan cultus within its metropolitan setting, to visit many of the regions from which Tamil immigrants to Malaysia had been drawn, and to observe as much as possible in a ten-week trip of "village" Hinduism in South India.

Undoubtedly the focal point of my visit was my participation in a weeklong 120-kilometres *pada yatra* (foot pilgrimage) which commenced in Palakkad (Kerala) and culminated in the festival of Thaipusam at the major pilgrimage centre of Palani, Tamil Nadu. (This is described in Chapter 7.) The pilgrimage group was predominantly composed of *Smartha* Brahmans. The pilgrimage enabled me to note daily rituals, to record the behaviour patterns of pilgrims, to hold a series of in-depth discussions with members of the party, and finally to observe pilgrimage traditions and the kavadi ritual at Palani.

My visits to major temples and pilgrimage sites connected with the Murugan cultus not only provided me with an introduction to centres pivotal to the traditions of Murugan worship, but also allowed me to explore a number of destinations I had previously only read about in books, heard in discourses, conversations or songs within Malaysia, or viewed as the idealized offerings of temple artists. Conversations with temple priests, pilgrims and devotees often supplied me with incisive and valuable insights. A prolonged discussion over lunch with the head priest at the major seashore temple and pilgrimage centre of Tiruchendur dispelled in one succinct session several of the more spurious claims made by Hindu reformers and other observers regarding kavadi rituals and behaviour at Thaipusam in Malaysia.

In addition my trip to India included stays at several *asrama*, mainly, but not exclusively, linked to the Murugan cultus. These visits supplied an introduction to institutions of spiritual teaching and thought, and in some cases the traditions of the *guru/sishya* (master/disciple) relationship. These institutions and traditions are largely unavailable in Malaysia. In each centre I was treated with extraordinary kindness and generosity, and I was encouraged to question swamis, itinerant *sadhus*, officials and pilgrims, both Indian and international.

Contextualizing Thaipusam

Thaipusam is a Saivite festival dedicated to the worship of the deity Murugan, the son of the supreme deity, Siva, and held to be the *Mahadeva* (god) of spiritual disciplines, austerities and yogic powers, and thus capable of bestowing *mukti* (final liberation) upon those who engage in concentrated worship of him. While the deity has absorbed a complex amalgam of Sanskrit and Tamil influences, in pre-modern and modern India he has been increasingly identified as a Dravidian and specifically Tamil deity, who through a prolonged process of syncretization has accumulated a wide variety of motifs, attributes and belief structures which render him acceptable and accessible to all segments of Tamil Hindu society. Murugan worship in Malaysia is widespread among Tamils of both Indian and Sri Lankan descent.

In essence, Thaipusam celebrates the bestowal of the *Sakti Vel* (cosmic spear or *Vetrivel*) upon Murugan, by Parvati, consort of Siva, at the outset of Murugan's campaign to defeat Surapadman, head of the *asuras* (demonic forces or lower astral beings). A substantial corpus of *Puranic*[4] mythology informs the Murugan cultus. At the *cosmological* level the Murugan mythology may be interpreted to embrace themes of phenomenological atrophy and dissolution, as well as subsequent reconstitution and renewal. At the *human* level Murugan's battle with Surapadman is internalized and the *Vel* becomes a key to spiritual liberation. My field research suggests that many devotees view Thaipusam — the commemoration of Murugan's acquisition of the *Vel* — as a highly propitious occasion in which to resolve personal karmic difficulties, or to "repay" the deity for major adjustments or transformations in family and social life. Thaipusam is thus marked by individual acts of devotion involving austerity and sacrifice, often taking the form of bodily mortification, accompanied by trance states, and the bearing of kavadis.

While Thaipusam is consciously formulated upon the mythology, traditions and modes of worship celebrated at the great pilgrimage centre of Palani, Tamil Nadu, the processes of relocation and adaptation within Malaysia have in certain respects endowed the festival with a uniquely Malaysian orientation. In the years since I first witnessed Thaipusam, both the social context in which Thaipusam is celebrated and the overall conduct of the festival have altered considerably. The crowds attending the festival have continued to increase by the year (the Malaysian press estimated that in 2011 approximately 1.3 million people attended Thaipusam at Batu Caves, while 300,000 gathered at the Penang festival), the number of kavadi pilgrims has more than doubled, the publicity surrounding the festival has gained greater prominence, and Thaipusam has been declared a public holiday in several states, and more recently (2008) in the Federal Territory. Thaipusam is not only the most popular and prominent Hindu festival in Malaysia, it is also the most visible and powerful assertion of Hindu identity. Recent studies reveal that Indians constitute only 7.4 per cent of Peninsular Malaysia's population of approximately thirty million people, with Hindus comprising about 84.1 per cent of that figure.[5] Yet, Thaipusam at Batu Caves has become the largest single religious festival in Malaysia, and is generally believed to be the most significant Hindu festival outside India. While Thaipusam is dedicated to Murugan, kavadis are borne for nearly all Hindu deities worshipped in Malaysia, including those belonging to non-*Agamic* and Vaishnavite traditions.

The literature dealing with the Indian experience in Malaya/Malaysia is considerable, ranging from accounts of the establishment and later abolition of migratory systems of labour through to the formation and consolidation of Indian political and cultural organizations, and including investigations into the contemporary Indian situation within multi-ethnic

Malaysia.⁶ Until comparatively recently the availability of literature describing or analysing Hinduism in Malaysia was far more problematic. As Ramanathan Kalimuthu has pointed out in his comprehensive 1995 doctoral dissertation, *Hindu Religion in an Islamic State: The Case of Malaysia*, many of the studies of Indian society which have focused on the phenomena of Indian ethnicity have provided detailed political, economic, social and linguistic analyses while all but neglecting religion or religious issues.⁷ However, over the past few years this dearth has been at least partially remedied with the publication of four detailed and illuminating studies. Alexandra Kent's *Divinity and Diversity: A Hindu Revitalization Movement in Malaysia*⁸ explores the following of godman Sathya Sai Baba in Malaysia. This was followed in 2005 by Vineeta Sinha's fine and well-constructed study of the deity Muneeswaran.⁹ While Sinha's focus is mainly upon Singapore, her work overlaps with the more generic sphere of Hinduism in Peninsular Malaysia. Finally, Andrew Willford's two penetrating and well researched works, namely *Cage of Freedom: Tamil Identity and the Ethnic Fetish in Malaysia* (2006) and, in conjunction with S. Nagarajan, *Tamils and the Haunting of Justice: History and Recognition in Malaysia's Plantations* (2014), detail many aspects of Hinduism within the context of a nation highly charged with the politics of religio-ethnic communalism.¹⁰ In addition, noted scholar of Murugan, Fred W. Clothey, has dedicated a chapter of his 2006 work, *Ritualising on the Boundaries: Continuity and Innovation in the Tamil Diaspora*, to Thaipusam at Batu Caves.¹¹ My own chapter, "Hindu Resurgence in Malaysia", a contribution to a wider volume, *Rising India and Indian Communities in East Asia* (2008), while modest in comparison, seeks to provide an overview of the current state of Hinduism in Malaysia.¹²

The body of available literature on Thaipusam is rather sparse. Few studies have attempted to view Thaipusam in its own terms rather than as an object of "orientalist"¹³ speculation and theorizing. Notable exceptions are Lawrence Babb's 1976 work on Thaipusam in Singapore which explores the role of the individual in Hindu ritual,¹⁴ and Raymond Lee's 1989 study which furnishes a well-constructed phenomenological overview of Thaipusam at Batu Caves.¹⁵ Ervin et al.¹⁶ provide a detailed and empathetic description of the role of trance as a mode of spiritual transformation at Thaipusam, but do not attempt any detailed analysis of the festival in terms of Hindu categories.

It is my contention that Thaipusam, a major, highly colourful and extremely complex festival, has been seriously misunderstood by most

Western observers. In essence, Western interpretations of Thaipusam fall into three major, albeit overlapping schools:

1. **The Exotic Malaysia/Mysterious East School.** This consists of the frankly sensationalist descriptions which exploit both the festival and its participants as objects of curiosity, a diversion or source of potential entertainment, most typically for other Westerners. These accounts are invariably written from a generalist perspective, are undisguisedly orientalist, and while sometimes ostensibly sympathetic their underlying leitmotif remains the cultural distance of the writer from "the Other".[17] The most objectionable accounts of Thaipusam comprise those which might be termed the "benighted native" approach, cast in terms of implied cultural superiority of the writer, openly condescending or contemptuous,[18] or in some cases simply unconscionable.[19]

2. **The Lost Village Tradition/Social Deprivation School.** This is perhaps the most common interpretation, and strongly encouraged by certain Hindu reformist groups who are supposedly arguing from the privileged and sanctioned perspective of "Great Tradition" Hinduism, and who are interested in recasting Malaysian Hinduism in terms of a modernist agenda. This viewpoint contends that Thaipusam constitutes the debased remnants of a decayed and perhaps lost village tradition, somehow transplanted to Malaya/Malaysia (invariably by Hindus of the lowest castes), and asserts that these rituals find no justification within *Agamic* or classical Hindu belief structures. The festival is thus sustained by illiterate and ignorant members of a chronically deprived working class/lower caste Hindu population (Chinese participation is rarely mentioned, let alone explained), who use Thaipusam as a cathartic outlet to relieve the unmitigated harshness which characterizes their oppression. These accounts often repeat the common fallacy that Thaipusam as practised in Malaysia is banned in India.[20]

3. **The Psychoanalytic School.** This genre, largely conducted within the framework of Neo-Freudian psychoanalytic theory, tends to view the raw materials of Thaipusam in terms of the abreacted impulses and dispositions of repressed sexuality combined with social protest. Thus the spectacle of young men (these accounts invariably marginalize and downplay the participation of women and older devotees), piercing their flesh with skewers and steel rods, transported by the rapture of

orgiastic trance, and penetrating into the interiors of temples and caves, are fulfilling a ritual whose inner meanings and significance — the "real" motives which impel their public performances — somehow elude the participants themselves, but may be carefully decoded by privileged (usually Western) scholars accoutred with the appropriate armoury of psychoanalytic techniques.[21]

Each of the interpretations grouped under categories (1) and (2), written by scholars and observers who in the main have experienced Thaipusam as a largely sociological phenomenon, suggests its own rationale for the construction and inner dynamics of the festival, and argued on the basis of readily observable and purely Malaysian evidence may achieve a deceptive plausibility. It is relatively simple to trace the origins of such interpretations. A large percentage of Malaysia's ethnic Tamil population *does* consist of an oppressed and marginalized underclass, and it may seem axiomatic to many Western scholars to link the esoteric rituals of Thaipusam to the traumas of subjugation, and to the intense need for recognition in a society which neither cares to remember the historic achievements of Indian labour nor values or respects their current contributions. Similarly, it would be easy to accept the views of a numerically insignificant but disproportionately vocal group of self-proclaimed Hindu "reformers" as authoritative. As previously related, many of those who fall within this category are Western educated, of professional standing, fluent in English, modernist in outlook, and immediately accessible to any field worker conducting research into Hinduism in Malaysia. This group is more than prepared to diminish the experiences and practices of those whose perspectives do not accord with their own, especially Hindus who are working class and poorly educated.

My research, fieldwork and experiences over many Thaipusams suggest that these interpretations are based upon incomplete ethnographies, which fail to locate Thaipusam, the kavadi ritual and Malaysian Hinduism within a sufficiently broad or comprehensive framework. Nicholas Dirks has warned of the dangers of translating specific observations based on restricted fieldwork into universalistic generalizations.[22] The limitations of the approaches outlined above are revealed by wider research, including analyses of metropolitan Tamil Hindu traditions,[23] studies of Thaipusam and the kavadi ritual within the broader Tamil diaspora, close readings of the modern Indian migration to and history within Malaya/Malaysia,[24] and the intense fieldwork which must be undertaken if one is to disentangle the layers of meaning embedded in a festival as involved and as multifaceted as Thaipusam.[25]

Many of the previous interpretations have thus reached conclusions which will not withstand the scrutiny of close inquiry. As I will show, Thaipusam has its roots in continuing traditions and philosophies readily located in both popular and *Agamic* Hinduism, and those aspects considered objectionable, exotic or bizarre by Western observers have precedents, and nearly always equivalents, within metropolitan Tamil Hindu culture. Nor is the kavadi ritual restricted to lower caste Hindus or younger males; participants are drawn from nearly all sectors of Malaysian Hindu society and include considerable numbers of women. I have uncovered no evidence to suggest that the dynamics of Thaipusam are influenced by inter-caste rivalry; this is not to suggest that caste distrust or friction is non-existent, but rather that it is not a major causative factor in the overall construction of the festival. My fieldwork and personal experiences dispel the notion that the trance state at Thaipusam axiomatically produces amnesia;[26] the majority of devotees whom I interviewed were able to provide compelling and often vivid descriptions of their trance experiences. Moreover, comparative studies dispel the "social deprivation" theory of Thaipusam; they demonstrate that the kavadi ritual is a common diaspora phenomenon and that this occurs within societies where Tamil practitioners are neither politically or socially disadvantaged. Indeed, these studies clearly reveal that Thaipusam, Murugan worship and kavadi rituals have typical normative elements which manifest at the festivals commemorated in both Batu Caves and Penang. The book will argue, inter alia, that Thaipusam festivals at both locations, while in some senses uniquely Malaysian,[27] are "orthodox" in the sense that they reproduce worship rituals and behavioural patterns which owe their origins to Tamil Murugan traditions that continue to be practised in India.

This book will explore the festival of Thaipusam in terms of its own inner dynamics — the traditions and belief structures which ensure the festival's continuing relevance to Malaysian Hindus. It will argue that Thaipusam in Malaysia reflects a growing sense of Hindu identity in Malaysia, and an as yet inchoate unity. It will contend that while the kavadi ritual provides profound meaning at the individual and group level, Thaipusam furnishes a public arena for and gives expression to a powerful Hindu resurgence, largely, though not exclusively, fuelled by

Dravidian assertiveness. Over time, Thaipusam has developed its own paradigmatic impulses which have stimulated and continue to promote the expression, aggregation and negotiation of Hindu identity in Malaysia. This book will thus demonstrate that the festival incorporates competing discourses — based on caste, the multiplicity of sects and traditions ranging from village to *Agamic* — within the generic rituals and received frameworks associated with Murugan worship. Thaipusam thus provides a public arena for the open articulation and assertion of the concatenation of diverse and often competing discourses which fall under the rubric of Malaysian Hinduism.

In investigating the catalytic forces which are reformulating Hinduism in Malaysia, the book will examine the crucial role played by the deity Murugan as the quintessential Tamil deity, and thus a powerful symbol of the Dravidian renaissance. This analysis will necessarily involve exploration of the history and traditions of the metropolitan culture from which Malaysian Hinduism has arisen, and the continuing applicability of its major tenets and impulses among Malaysian Hindus.

In situating the festival within the context of a Malaysia dominated by Malay and Islamic power brokers, a society in which both the Indian community and Hinduism are relegated to the margins, the book will explore the festival of Thaipusam as a vehicle for mobilization of religious symbols and values which not only simultaneously articulate ethnicity and thus resist the forces which threaten cultural and religious integrity, but which also ultimately signal wider allegiances to the broader politico-cultural world of an imagined, immeasurably rich, and enduring Indo-Hindu civilization.

Structure

The book is organized as follows. Chapter 1 provides an essential overview of the social and political context in which the Indian community within Malaysia is situated. This traces migratory streams and the post-*Merdeka* (independence) trajectory of Indians as a minority community within a society dominated by communally infused discourses structured upon "race" and religion. Chapter 2 explores the history and development of Tamil institutions and belief structures, including kingship, temples, *bhakti* Hinduism and Saiva Siddhanta. In essence this chapter argues that the Hindu institutions which developed through the period of the great dynasties — the Pallava, Pandya, Chola and Vijayanagara — indelibly shaped the Hinduism which continues to obtain today. Chapter 3 examines the impact of British colonialism upon Indian and specifically South Indian society, and demonstrates how "colonial knowledge" helped create and sustain contemporary Hindu reform movements. Chapter 4 looks at the relocation and development of Hinduism in Malaya/Malaysia, including the modification of caste, the construction and management of temples, and the continuing negotiation of Hindu identity within modern Malaysia. In Chapter 5 I explore the Murugan cultus in some detail, tracing his evolution as a "Tamil" deity, outlining the rich corpus of *Puranic* mythology (including that which underpins both the commemoration of, and ritual behaviour at, Thaipusam). This chapter also examines the continuing influence of the Murugan cultus and its multifaceted appeal to a society characterized by enduring diversity. Chapter 6 provides a phenomenological exploration of Thaipusam at Batu Caves. This looks at the founding and development of Batu Caves as a pilgrimage centre, the kingship rituals and chariot procession which establish the overall parameters of the festival, and the formal acts of vow fulfilment which constitute the kavadi ritual. Chapter 7 consists of a comparative study on Thaipusam and the kavadi ritual within Penang, metropolitan India, as well as a number of diaspora locations. This demonstrates that both the festival and the modes of worship found within Malaysia are observed by Tamil Hindus within many societies and among many castes and classes. In Chapter 8 I examine the kavadi ritual within the context of the Tamil Hindu pilgrimage ritual, that is as a *tirtha yatra* ("divine crossing") in which the devotee moves from the periphery of quotidian life to the sacred centre (*axis mundi*) within the context of vow fulfilment. This chapter will show that the pilgrimage ritual at Thaipusam is saturated with and dominated by a logic drawn from Murugan cosmology but also from wider Tamil belief structures. Finally, in Conclusions I look at the continuing and expanding significance of Thaipusam, its central role in providing a forum for the redefinition of Hinduism in Malaysia, and its multivocality in terms of the messages it sends to a variety of audiences.

Presentation

Throughout this book I have employed the most common Malaysian Romanized spelling of Tamil and Sanskrit terms, and following the

example of C.J. Fuller,[28] I have omitted diacritical marks. This has been
largely prompted by the varied spellings of Tamil words which appear in
different contexts in Malaysia, and are almost invariably offered without
diacritics. Thus, for example, the term *kovil* for temple is often spelled
koyil or even *koil*; *aluga* (beautiful) kavadis are often rendered as *alaku* or
alahu; while Murugan may be offered as *Murukan* or *Muruhan*. Sometimes
multiple spellings of the same word appear within the one work. Within
Malaysia, both spelling and meaning are complicated by the fact that many
Tamil and Sanskrit words have found their way into the Bahasa Malaysia
vocabulary, where they often assume meanings which are marginally or
markedly different from their original currency in India. Thus, in Malay a
guru is a teacher or instructor (with or without religious overtones), whereas
the Sanskrit *swami* becomes the Malay *suami* (husband). Over time some
of these Bahasa Malaysia meanings have been transplanted or returned to
the Tamil lexicon. In addition, several words relevant to this study, such
as "Thaipusam" (alternatively offered as *Thaipoosam* or *Tai Pucam*) and
"kavadi" have passed into the common Malaysian English vocabulary, and
their English spellings are the most widely circulated among Malaysians
generally. My aim has to been achieve consistency as well as clarity. I have
italicized Tamil and Sanskrit terms with the exceptions of proper nouns
and the two terms just listed, i.e., "Thaipusam" and "kavadi".

Notes

1. This is described in my book, *Towards Truth: An Australian Spiritual Journey*
   (Kuala Lumpur: Pacific Press, 1992).
2. Ibid.
3. Several of this latter group were obvious frauds. One such "swami", attended
   by a retinue of strong-arm thugs, complete with minatory body language,
   proudly showed me photos of his visit to Australia. One of these disclosed
   that he had visited a prominent Sydney massage parlour, an establishment
   which had gained nationwide notoriety in the 1980s during a well-publicized
   Australian political scandal.
4. The role and nature of *Puranas* will be discussed in Chapters 2 and 4. *Puranas*
   are books of mythology both extolling and describing the deeds of the
   great deities, but simultaneously conveying underlying metaphorical and
   metaphysical subtexts.
5. P. Uthayakumar, *Indian Marginalization of the Indians in Malaysia*, emailed to
   the author on 6 April 2010. In the 2000 census, Hindus accounted for 84.1 per

cent of the Indian population, while Christians numbered 7.8 per cent, and Muslims 4.1 per cent (Saw Swee-Hock, "Population Trends and Patterns in Multi-Racial Malaysia", in *Malaysia: Recent Trends and Challenges*, edited by Saw Swee-Hock and K. Kesavapany [Singapore: Institute of Southeast Asian Studies, 2006], p. 19). Recent discussions suggest that the Hindu percentage of the Indian population remains at this level.

6. Recent examples include Carl Vadivella Belle, *Tragic Orphans; Indians in Malaysia* (Singapore: Institute of Southeast Asian Studies, 2015); Janakey Raman Manickam, *The Malaysian Indian Dilemma: The Struggles and Agony of the Indian Community in Malaysia* (Klang: Janakey Raman, 2010); Muzafar Desmond Tate, *The Malaysian Indians: History, Problems and Future* (Petaling Jaya, Strategic Information and Research Development Centre, 2008); and the Malaysian section in *Rising India and Indian Communities in East Asia*, edited by K. Kesavapany, A. Mani, and P. Ramasamy (Singapore: Institute of Southeast Asian Studies, 2008). My reservations regarding *The Malaysian Indians* can be found at Carl Vadivella Belle, "Malaysian Indians: An Incomplete History", *Malaysiakini*, 25 June 2009 <http://www.malaysiakini.com/opinions/107202> (accessed 26 June 2009).

7. Ramanathan Kalimuthu, "Hindu Religion in an Islamic State: The Case of Malaysia" (PhD dissertation, Universiteit van Amsterdam, 1995), p. 11.

8. Alexandra Kent, *Divinity and Diversity: A Hindu Revitalization Movement in Malaysia* (Singapore and Copenhagen: Institute of Southeast Asian Studies/ NIAS Press, 2004).

9. Vineeta Sinha, *A New God in the Diaspora? Muneeswaran Worship in Contemporary Singapore* (Singapore and Copenhagen: Singapore University Press/NIAS Press, 2005).

10. Andrew C. Willford, *Cage of Freedom: Tamil Identity and the Ethnic Fetish in Malaysia* (Ann Arbor: University of Michigan Press, 2006); Andrew Willford (in collaboration with S. Nagarajan), *Tamils and the Haunting of Justice: History and Recognition in Malaysia's Plantations* (Singapore: NUS, 2014).

11. Fred W. Clothey, *Ritualising on the Boundaries: Continuity and Innovation in the Tamil Diaspora* (Columbia: University of South Carolina Press, 2006).

12. Carl Vadivella Belle, "Hindu Resurgence in Malaysia", in *Rising India and Indian Communities in East Asia*, edited by K. Kesavapany, A. Mani, and P. Ramasamy (Singapore: Institute of Southeast Asian Studies, 2008).

13. The term "orientalist" is used throughout this book in the sense developed by Edward Said. In basic terms, orientalism consists of Western portrayals of a given "third world" subject which both represent it and fix it as inherently "oriental". This portrayal is hegemonic in that it appropriates and speaks for the "other", and in various ways, often subtle, seeks to dominate the other by, inter alia, demonstrating the irrefragable differences and distance — social,

racial and cultural — between the observer and the observed. Edward Said, *Orientalism: Western Conceptions of the Orient* (London: Penguin, 1991).

14. Lawrence A. Babb, *Thaipusam in Singapore: Religious Individualism in a Hierarchical Culture* (Singapore: University of Singapore, Department of Sociology Working Paper No. 49, 1976).

15. Raymond L.M. Lee, "Taipucam in Malaysia: Ecstasy and Identity in a Tamil Hindu Festival", *Contributions to Indian Sociology* 23, no. 2 (1989).

16. Frank C. Ervin et al., "The Psychobiology of Trance: Physiological and Endocrine Coordinates", *Transcultural Psychiatric Review* 25 (1988).

17. Examples of this school include Arthur Hullett, "Thaipusam and the Cult of Subramaniam", *Geo* 3, no. 4 (1981). Hullett's article actually displays a photo of statuary of the *avatars* of Vishnu, which he claims to be "Kartikkeya, a manifestation of Subramaniam or Murugan" (pp. 72–73), and has worshippers chanting "Wai, wai, wai" instead of "Vel, Vel, Vel" (p. 77); <http://www. LonelyPlanet.com.destinations/south_east-asia/Singapore/printable.htm>. This website, showing a complete misunderstanding of the festival, describes Thaipusam as "masochistic" and perpetrates the myth that Thaipusam is banned in India (accessed 25 November 2003).

18. An example of this genre is provided in Blanche D'Alpuget, *Turtle Beach* (Ringwood: Penguin, 1981). The pejorative comments about Malaysia's component ethnic groups which litter this book are apparently justified by the heroine's admission of inherent racism (p. 53). Thaipusam becomes an "orgy", an "abomination", with the priests chanting "mumbo-jumbo" (p. 147). The book contains the falsehood that the festival is banned in India (p. 144). It is difficult to dispute D'Cruz and Steele's assertion that *Turtle Beach* is, at the very least, implicitly racist (J.V. D'Cruz and William Steele, *Australia's Ambivalence towards Asia* [Clayton: Monash University Press, 2003] p. 26). For a close discussion of the racism conveyed by *Turtle Beach*, see pages 199–287 of this work.

19. A rancid and truly offensive example of this genre is offered by Gail Saari, whose fanciful and frankly sensationalist description of Thaipusam proclaims it "like Halloween in Greenwich Village with more S&M". Later she states, "It is more disturbing to see women in trances than to see men similarly affected. The women in the throes of religious ecstasy — with their hair unbound and uncombed, tongues artificially reddened with saffron powder (*sic*) and lewdly flitting in and out of their mouths, crazy sensual smiles, eyes rolling and breasts and hips undulating — *violate even my notions of propriety on a deeply visceral level. It is an abandonment of self-control, at once spiritual and lewdly sexual...*" (emphasis added) (<http://www.salon.com/wlust/1998/06/26mondo.html> (accessed 8 January 2004). This passage would appear to reveal far more about the writer than it does about Thaipusam.

20. The erroneous notion that some of the "more dramatic aspects" of the festival, i.e., the piercing of flesh with rods and hooks, is banned by law within India, appears to have its genesis in Paul W. Wiebe and S. Mariappen's study, *Indian Malaysians: The View from the Plantation* (Delhi: Manohar, 1978), p. 148. This myth is repeated by Hullett, who states that the government of India has outlawed the use of "spikes and other implements" (Hullett, *Thaipusam*, p. 81). Colleen Ward also claims that the festival is banned in India (Colleen Ward, "Thaipusam in Malaysia: A Psycho-Anthropological Analysis of Ritual Trance, Ceremonial Possession and Self-Mortification Practices", *Ethos* 14 [1984]: 324). Finally, Marian Aveling makes the remarkably inaccurate claim that the kavadi ritual forms "no part of Murugan festivals in India" (Marian Aveling, "Ritual Changes in the Hindu Temples of Penang", *Contributions to Indian Sociology* 12, no. 2 [1978]: 192).

21. A psychoanalytic approach is adopted by Elizabeth Fuller Collins, *Pierced by Murugan's Lance: Ritual Power and Moral Redemption among Malaysian Hindus* (Dekalb: Northern Illinois University Press, 1997). My review of this work, which I found reductive, incomplete and occasionally risible, is contained in *Sophia* 40, no. 2 (December 2001): 83–86. Collins' response is found in the same issue. (Elizabeth Fuller Collins, "Of Transgressions: Reply to Carl Vadivella Belle".)

22. Nicholas B. Dirks, *Castes of Mind: Colonialism and the Making of Modern India* (Princeton and Oxford: Princeton University Press, 2001), p. 79.

23. Thus, Evers and Jayarani state that "The worship of Murugan being *only* the son of Siva is less demanding [than the worship of Siva]" (emphasis added). They maintain this was the result of the lack of specialist knowledge among the immigrant Hindus (Hans Dieter Evers and Jayarani Pavadarayan, "Religious Fervour and Economic Success: The Chettiars of Singapore", in *Indian Communities in Southeast Asia*, edited by K.S. Sandhu and A. Mani [Singapore: Institute of Southeast Asian Studies, 1993], p. 864). This shows a comprehensive misunderstanding of Tamil Hinduism and is akin to suggesting that Christians are unsophisticated because they worship Jesus, who is *only* the son of God. (Evers and Jayarani also assert that kavadi-bearing Hindus "mutilate" themselves [ibid., p. 848], a claim that is manifestly untrue.) Hullett also erroneously contends that Murugan is not considered a major god in the Hindu pantheon and ponders why such a "minor" figure has gained such prominence in Singapore and Malaysia (Hullett, *Thaipusam*, p. 71).

24. Thus, for example, in her response to my review of her work, Collins asserts that "the majority of devotees who fulfil vows to Murugan are working-class descendants of the indentured labours who were brought to work in the British colony. These low caste and untouchable labourers…" (Collins, *Of Transgressions*, p. 87). This contains a serious and very basic historical

error. While it is true that the majority of indentured labourers were indeed *Adi Dravidas*, or of low caste, Collins seems unaware that indentured labour, terminated in 1910, provided less than six per cent of total immigration to Malaya. As I will show in Chapters 1 and 3, the far more influential kangany system of recruitment produced a workforce of variegated caste, of whom only about one-third were drawn from *Adi Dravida* castes.

25. Two examples, selected at random from Collins' book, both of which might have been rectified by more careful fieldwork, are as follows: (i) She claims that "Prints of the infant Krishna are frequently used in the decoration of kavadis. Most people seem unaware that the deity represented is Krishna because both Murugan and Krishna are associated with peacock feathers." (Collins, *Pierced by Murugan's Lance*, p. 150). This is simply untenable; any field worker who has spent ten minutes discussing *Puranic* Hinduism with worshippers at Thaipusam would be made aware that devotees have an almost encyclopaedic knowledge of members of the pantheon and their relationship to one another. Malaysian Hindus are vitally aware of both Murugan and Krishna and the easily identified and clearly recognizable motifs distinctive to each deity. (ii) On the same page, Collins continues: "The committee that oversees the Penang Murugan Hill Temple have encouraged the emphasis on the worship of the infant deity by constructing a pond in which the six infant forms of Murugan float on lotus petals." In fact, the committee have made no such encouragement; the pond and the representation of the infant Murugan form part of a well-structured set of iconic symbols which lead the pilgrim from the periphery (Murugan's unstabilized form) to the centre (Murugan triumphant).

26. The issue of trance and the supposed "amnesia" will be discussed in Chapter 7.

27. One obvious example of the Malaysian orientation of Thaipusam is the involvement of non-Dravidian Indians and ethnic Chinese in kavadi bearing.

28. C.J. Fuller, *The Camphor Flame: Popular Hinduism and Society in India* (Princeton: Princeton University Press, 1992), p. xiii.

1

Indians in Malaysia:
The Social and Ethnic Context

The large-scale migration of Indians to Malaya throughout the nineteenth century and the first few decades of the twentieth century led to the creation of a distinctively Malaysian Indian society. One of the most conspicuous features of this community is the sharp division between the minority upper classes — the middle, professional and commercial classes — and a majority working class which comprises over eighty per cent of Indian Malaysians.[1] In general it may be claimed that this disjunction has its origins in the differing circumstances of each class's migration to Malaysia. Thus the descendants of "labour" recruitment — those who were contracted under indenture, kangany or other labour schemes, to work in the plantation estate sector or within government utilities — now make up an underclass which continues to fill a range of labouring and unskilled occupations within modern Malaysia. Conversely, the background of the middle and upper classes can generally be traced to "non-labour" migratory streams; that is, their forbears were those Indians who were appointed to clerical and technical positions in colonial Malaya, or who established themselves in professions and business.[2] Most "non-labour" Indians maintain their social distance from "labour" Indians, and in some instances may even deny all bonds of common ethnicity.[3]

While the earliest Indian labour throughout the colonial period was furnished by transported convicts,[4] the overwhelming majority of Indian workers who arrived in Malaya between 1840 and 1910 were recruited under a system known as indenture. The colonial preference for South Indian labour was informed by an official perspective which viewed the "Madrassi" as docile and easily managed. Indeed, the supposed "cringingly servile" Tamil was portrayed both as an alternative and as a counterweight to the potentially ambitious and assertive Chinese worker.[5] In his landmark study, K.S. Sandhu estimates that in this period a total of 250,000 indentured labourers were contracted to work in Malaya.[6] These were mainly landless agricultural labourers drawn from the lower and *Adi Dravida* (Dalit) castes.[7] The British government terminated the recruitment of Indian indentured labour to Malaya in 1910.[8]

Indenture was initially supplemented and then finally superseded by kangany recruitment. The kangany was a field foreman, a "coolie of standing", a member of a "clean" caste who enjoyed a good reputation, and who was not only charged with the task of recruiting labour to work on estates, but as foreman was required to supervise those he had engaged. The kangany recruited within his own district (*taluk*) of origin in India, thus selecting a workforce composed of those whose customs and traditions he understood.[9] On the basis of available data, Sandhu estimates that between 1865 and 1938 a total of 1,186,717 Indian migrants arrived in Malaya under kangany auspices.[10]

Kangany recruitment produced a far greater flow and a more consistent supply of labour than that achieved under indenture. It also resulted in a far more socially diverse workforce. While approximately one third of kangany labourers were drawn from *Adi Dravida* castes the remainder represented the general spread of Tamil caste groups below Brahman level, including members of higher castes.[11] Kangany recruitment finally ceased in 1938, when, following disputes over wages paid to Indian labour, the Government of India placed a ban on the emigration of assisted labour to Malaya.[12]

Throughout the years leading to World War II, the flow of kangany labour was augmented by two additional migratory streams, namely *independent assisted* and *non-assisted workers*. The former comprised that group of labourers who had volunteered, independent of the kangany system, to enter contractual employment in Malaya, or to whom the Malayan colonial authorities extended financial and other forms of support.

The number of independent assisted workers rose substantially throughout the 1920s, and by 1925 accounted for twenty-eight per cent of the total number of Malayan-funded labourers.[13] Non-assisted migrants were those who funded their own travel and who sought work following their arrival in Malaya.[14] Despite the lack of official support, there was a steady flow of non-assisted migrants from the 1890s onwards.[15]

Throughout this period there were other streams of Indian migration to Malaya. Both government and commercial sectors required the support of a trained English-speaking workforce which possessed a range of specialist skills. This was not immediately available in Malaya, either among the indigenous Malays or the immigrant labouring communities, and thus had to be procured from abroad.[16] The expansion of the Malayan economy attracted other groups — merchants, financiers, skilled labour — who saw personal and professional advantages in working in colonial Malaya. These groups included Ceylonese Tamils (also known in Malaya as "Jaffna" Tamils because of their district of origin), who were recruited by British officials to serve as clerical personnel within the government service and on the estates;[17] educated Malayalees and young professional Tamils; Nattukottai Chettiars, a caste of businessmen and financiers who comprise one of the traditional banking and trading communities of India; Sikh and Punjabi Muslim police and security personnel; and various traders of both North and South Indian background, and including Parsis, Hindus and Muslims.[18]

At the time of *Merdeka* (independence) in 1957, Indians numbered 858,616 people, of which 62.1 per cent were of local birth. Indians constituted 12 per cent of the population.[19] The Federation of Malaya Census Report noted that Indian migration to Malaya had been "of an ephemeral character with approximately 4 million entering and 2.8 million leaving the country between 1860 and 1957". The report further observed that "much of the 1.2 million net immigration appears to have been wiped out by disease, snakebites, exhaustion and malnutrition".[20]

The history of Indians under British colonialism in Malaya was one of oppression and, in the case of the labouring classes, brutalization. Workers recruited under both indenture and kangany auspices were subject to repressive regulation, constant invigilation, and harsh and often capricious discipline. Both systems bore a striking resemblance to slavery in that they established complete domination over the labourer and treated him or her as a mere instrument in the process of production. The rigidity of contractual obligations and the willingness to enforce them stripped the worker of all but a bare minimum of personal rights, denied him or her even the most basic occupational mobility and firmly placed the worker under the absolute control of those who paid his or her wages.[21] The Indian labourer was enclosed in a self-contained and isolated world and subject to a regime of permanent impoverishment and physical and psychological oppression; a regime which discouraged independence of thought or any sense of personal integrity.[22] The labourer and his or her family dwelt in substandard accommodation, both on estates and in government "lines"; lacked proper medical care; was exposed to the risk of disease; was often malnourished; and was subject to a range of social problems, including poor childcare, limited educational opportunities, and a high incidence of alcoholism, gambling, violence and suicide.[23]

Throughout the entire colonial era, the occasional impulses to reform and self-organization, especially those which aimed at general uplift within the broader community, were subject to swift and generally decisive official retaliation. Thus the reformist agenda of the Central Indian Association of Malaya, the first effective Indian political party, formed in 1936, which sought to promote Indian unity and to advance measures to improve the lot of the labouring classes was countered with the implacable hostility and intransigent opposition of the colonial administration.[24] The subsequent Klang Valley strikes of 1941 were resolved, not through negotiation or mediation, but rather through the agency of military force, coupled with mass arrests and deportations.[25] While the wartime politics of Indian nationalism, nurtured during the period of the Japanese Occupation, and largely driven by the charismatic personality of nationalist Subhas Chandra Bose, created an evanescent unity, manifested in the Indian Independence League and its military wing, the Indian National Army, the veterans of both organizations were subject to the vengeful animosity of the returning British.[26] Post-war reform movements such as *Thondar Padai* (Youth/Volunteer Corps) were designated as subversive and subsequently proscribed,[27] while Indian attempts to create a viable trade union movement were defeated by the combined determination of British colonial authorities and the United Malays National Organisation (UMNO) to extirpate sites of perceived leftist radicalism.[28]

Despite their oppressed and brutalized past, Indian Malayans appeared to have every reason to welcome Merdeka in 1957. Independence, it was assumed, would offer the opportunity to participate as fully enfranchised citizens of a relatively prosperous country. The leadership of the Malayan Indian Congress had struck a "bargain" with UMNO and the Malayan Chinese Association (MCA), which, while conceding a suite of Malay privileges and recognizing certain Malay symbols and aspects of Malay culture as the normative template of the new nation, seemed to allow non-Malay communities a chance of educational and vocational advancement and economic reward. Indians were assured that their political representatives enjoyed close relations with the powerful ruling parties of the governing Alliance, and that the structures of the Alliance would guarantee the interests of all citizens, irrespective of ethnic background or class.[29]

However, independence did not result in social or vocational mobility or even relative economic advancement. The bulk of the Indian population continues to constitute an oppressed, exploited and marginalized underclass, lacking political or economic power, and until the rise of the Hindu Rights Action Force (Hindraf) and the election of 8 March 2008, remained seemingly invisible to Malaysian policymakers.

The so-called Malaysian economic miracle, the wealth creation and social mobility which have benefited certain sectors of Malaysian society, have largely bypassed other sectors, including the vast bulk of the Indian community.[30] It is possible to identify four basic causative factors which have contributed to Indian disadvantage. The first is the unending culture of poverty and privation; the unrelenting oppression and marginalization suffered by the wider Indian community; the prolonged brutalization and subjugation of colonialism, followed by post-Merdeka relegation to electoral, economic and political irrelevance. Secondly, Indian leadership, both political and industrial, has been generally uninspired, disunited, often self-serving and largely powerless. Thirdly, Indians in Malaya have lacked both the financial resources or active entrepreneurial skills which might have created a generic commercial or mercantile ethos within the broader Indian community.[31] And, finally, the Indian community remains fissured, rent by long-standing discordancies of caste, regional and linguistic background, but most noticeably split between the Indian educated classes and the working population.[32]

Race and Religion

The general position of the Indian community has been complicated by the "neo-colonial"[33] racial ideologies which have become deeply inculcated in the political and cultural life of contemporary Malaysia. These ideologies had their origins in colonial Social Darwinist racial theories. Colonialist discourse posited an indigenous "Self" as backward, tradition bound, engaged in subsistence agriculture, and requiring protection from the more energetic and predacious "Other".[34] This colonialist construct was inscribed after World War II as a largely defensive ideology of "Malayness",[35] and the concomitant privileging of the claims of those officially proclaimed indigenous,[36] a process aided by the British–UMNO suppression of alternative visions of a more inclusive Malaya.[37] The politics of colonialism, and the reification of an indigene/non-indigene bifurcation, had the effect of continually reinscribing ethnic boundaries, thus reinforcing ethnic polarization and distrust. Malaysian political discourse remains fundamentally structured by issues of "race", and the negotiation of daily life is predicated upon notions of inherent racial difference.[38] Indeed, proposals for greater inclusivity are viewed by many political agents as not only subversive of official ideologies, but also a potential threat to national integrity.[39]

Malay political paramountcy was entrenched in the wake of the traumatic racial riots of 13 May 1969. The UMNO leadership introduced a raft of measures which made it clear that it would tolerate no challenge to its political primacy or that of key Malay institutions of state. The constitutional agreement of 1957 was enshrined as a binding racial contract, and public discussion on a range of issues was prohibited. These included querying the official status of the Malay language, the role and standing of the sultans, the position of Islam as the state religion, and the citizenship rights enjoyed by "immigrant peoples", including their legitimate claims to participate in the administrative and economic structures of the country. Non-Malays would no longer be permitted to question the constitutional "contract".[40] These enactments were supplemented by the introduction of the New Economic Policy (NEP), enunciated within the context of the Second Malaysian Plan of 1971–75 and devised to address the contentious issue of Malay poverty. The NEP was formulated on the premise that the economics of private enterprise and open competition had disadvantaged Malays (as well as some other sections of the population), and that the equitable sharing of the benefits of economic expansion could only be assured by direct government intervention.[41] In essence, the NEP sought through a process of vigorous affirmative action to attain for Malays and other indigenous groups, to be now generically known as *Bumiputeras* (or "sons of the soil"), a thirty per cent share of corporate assets by 1990.

This target was to be subsumed within a policy structure which promoted the dual objectives of the eradication of poverty regardless of race and the elimination of the identification of race with economic function.[42] The UMNO leadership envisaged the NEP as a necessary but strictly temporary measure which would be rescinded once its main objectives had been achieved.[43]

The initial promise that the NEP would eradicate hardcore poverty regardless of race did not translate into practice. It was perhaps inevitable that imperatives dictated by political communalism would triumph over those of social justice.[44] Obligations to the indigent within non-*Bumiputera* communities were easily evaded. The aggregation of "races" as composite wholes meant that average incomes could be used as a template to gauge the fortunes of entire racial communities, thus avoiding a more nuanced approach to identifying overall levels of poverty among the broader Malaysian population.[45]

In the years since the 1969 racial riots and the introduction of the NEP, Malaysia has witnessed a far-reaching and often contentious reassessment of the role of Islam. This has produced an exhaustive and frequently acrimonious debate about the place of Islam within the structures of the modern Malaysian state, as well as a comprehensive re-evaluation of religious practices.[46] Far from proving a unifying force, the redefinition of Islam has revealed deep and sometimes bitter divisions among Malays.[47] The Islamic revival has stimulated parallel renascences in all other religious communities.[48]

The constitutional settlement of 1957 incorporated both Islam and *adat* (custom) into the definition of Malay ethnicity, and enshrined Islam as the official religion of Malaya.[49] However, it was stressed that while no person would be permitted to proselytize "among persons professing the Muslim religion", the Malayan state would be secular and would guarantee freedom of religious belief.[50]

One of the most potent impulses which has underscored the Islamic resurgence has been that of religion as a signifier of Malay identity. While Malays have generally regarded Islam as coterminous with "Malayness",[51] until 1969 religion was merely one of several components of Malay ethnic identity. The constitutional amendments of 1971 and the cultural policies of the same year,[52] clearly established aspects of Malay ethnicity (other than Islam) as the fundamental organizational principles around which the modern Malaysian nation was to be constructed.

In an ethnically charged environment in which notions of Malayness and Malay statecraft were to be regarded as normative, Islam could be regarded as the final bulwark of Malay exclusiveness and thus as a basis for political mobilization.[53] This has become increasingly significant with the displacement of a great body of that which comprised traditional *adat*, often of pre-Islamic and usually Indic origin, and thus discarded as un-Islamic.[54] Within Malaysia the universalism of Islam has been refracted into a particularistic form which may be employed as means to both define and insulate Malayness. While this particularism may be called upon to demarcate Malay Islam from that of other Muslim communities,[55] in relation to other communities Islam becomes a potent ethnic marker, and Islamic symbols, rituals and practices become means of emphasizing and buttressing Malay distinctiveness.[56] In more extreme instances, Islam may be erected as a barrier to interaction and as an expression of superiority to other communities.[57]

The politics of both race and religion were exacerbated during the prolonged prime ministership of Dr Mahathir Mohamad (1981–2003). Adopting a post-dated Social Darwinist concept of "race" and intrinsic racial difference, long abandoned by social scientists,[58] Mahathir promulgated an inflexible ideology of Malay modernism which greatly expanded the Malay political agenda and placed Islam at the centre of Malay politics.[59] In the process, Mahathir transformed UMNO from a grass-roots political organization into a party constructed around networks of politico-economic patronage, cronyism and business interests.[60] Benjamin Barber has observed that when religion enters the political sphere it is invariably employed to advance the politics of nationalism.[61] Mahathir's privileging of the Islamic establishment and the "religious right" drove an aggressive Malay nationalism which deepened ethnic polarization between the putative Malay/Muslim indigene and the non-Malay/non-Muslim "other".[62]

Plantation Culture

In 1993, S. Arasaratnam argued that the shared experiences of working-class Indians from the time of indenture and kangany recruitment had crystallized into a "plantation-oriented culture", representing the worldview of a neglected and marginalized underclass, and characterized by stasis and underachievement.[63] Arasaratnam averred that this culture was marked by meagre educational attainment, low income, a general absence of intergenerational vocational mobility, and burdened by an array of deep-seated and intractable social problems. Moreover, this culture had developed its own paradigmatic impulses which, unless broken, threatened to lock the Indian labouring classes into a permanent underclass.[64]

Scholars have noted that the history of the Indian poor in Malaya/ Malaysia now extends over 170 years, and encompasses up to seven generations of working-class families. Merdeka, greeted with such high expectations, failed to usher in the anticipated rewards. In retrospect it may be viewed as portentous that in order to gain a representative voice for Indians within the ruling structures of an emerging Malaya, the Malayan Indian Congress, the largest Indian political party, was compelled to abandon its policies of inclusive reformism to accord with the ideological agenda of the communally based and conservative UMNO–MCA Alliance.[65] The politics of communalism and the concomitant aggregation of "racial" communities as composite wholes ensured that the problems of the Indian poor would remain submerged and thus ignored.[66] Perceived indifference to the plight of the Indian poor was impressed upon the collective Indian consciousness by the fragmentation of many estates and the summary dispossession of the largely Indian workforces,[67] and the citizenship crisis following the 13 May incident, which threatened many Indians with "repatriation" to India and rendered others stateless.[68] The implementation of the NEP and the consequent contraction of social, vocational, economic and educational opportunities for non-*Bumiputeras* closed potential avenues of advancement to many Indians.[69] The lowly standing of the community appeared to be confirmed by the 2001 Kampong Medan incident, in which organized Malay attacks upon Indians were not only officially attributed to Indian provocation but failed to produce an open investigation, prosecution of any of the instigators, or the payment of compensation to victims.[70]

In recent years there has been a continuous migration of labour from rural to urban areas, a movement initially sparked by fragmentation, and later augmented by mass evictions from estates.[71] The rural–urban migration did not result in any improvement of the economic standing of the Indian working classes, and did not contribute to intergenerational economic or vocational mobility. Indeed, many observers consider that over the past forty-fifty years the condition of the Indian indigent has actually deteriorated.[72] The migration created a large pool of Indian labour, minimally educated and lacking work skills, who were compelled to occupy positions that were basic, repetitive and poorly remunerated, and which offered little or nothing in the way of training or vocational advancement.[73] Indian workers generally found that their wages were insufficient to keep pace with rises in the cost of living. Financial pressures forced most to rent shoddy housing; at best rather inadequate high-rise flats, but often slum or squatter dwellings.[74] The combination of low educational attainment, high unemployment, low-waged work and poor housing has contributed to a spiralling Indian crime rate.[75] It could thus be argued that the plantation culture of chronic underachievement and stagnation, inculcated over generations of subjugation, of subordination to rigid and unyielding control, and physical and psychological oppression which robbed the Indian worker of the qualities of innovation and independence, was now being replicated within urban Malaysia.[76]

Nor have those trapped within the plantation culture been able to look to their more affluent compatriots for leadership and support. In general the social gulf between middle- and upper-class Indians remains as deep and fixed now as it has throughout the entire history of the modern Indian presence in Malaya/Malaysia.[77] Writing in 1993, D. Jeyakumar observed that many middle- and upper-class Indians expressed disgust and shame at the miserable state of the Indian underclass, and "often feel impatient and angry with the Indian poor caught in this subculture of poverty".[78] My own fieldwork suggests that this situation remains largely unchanged.

Hindraf

It is perhaps not surprising that religion was the site from which the Indian underclass launched its challenge to Malaysia's political establishment. While Indians had many causes for resentment — the failure of the Malaysian Indian Congress to represent their interests; the continuing evictions from estates; the disturbing number of Indian deaths in police custody — it was ultimately the perceived excesses of the Islamic authorities and the disrespect shown towards individual Hindus and Hinduism more generally that were to serve as the catalysts for translating long simmering frustrations into action.[79] During a series of well-publicized incidents, Islamic officials seized the remains of individuals whose families identified them as practising Hindus; forced the conversions of, or attempted forced conversions of, people who claimed to be Hindus; and tore asunder long-established families in the name of religion. These episodes, each of which created deep distress and anguish as well as anger within the broader Hindu population (and which engendered anxiety and alarm among Malaysia's non-Muslims), occurred against a backdrop of the repeated destruction of Hindu temples, many of which had served communities of devotees for well over a century.[80]

While the Hindu Rights Action Force (Hindraf) was founded in the period 2003–4,[81] the organization only emerged as a major force within the wider Indian community in 2007. Hindraf's wider significance lay in the fact that its agenda rapidly expanded beyond religious issues to embrace a far broader platform which included demands for structural and economic reforms as well as thorough investigation of systemic failures (for example, custodial deaths). The Indian poor, still socially defined by their ascribed lowly status in terms of a colonially derived racial and vocational hierarchy,[82] seemingly reduced to irrelevance by Malaysian political processes, and often referring to themselves as "forgotten people",[83] as second-class citizens in the land of their birth, were making a statement of intent, a determination to escape from the shackles of the "plantation culture". In this respect it is noteworthy that Hindraf moved beyond Hinduism and that its calls for social justice attracted the involvement of Indians of other religious beliefs.[84] The subsequent abandonment of the ruling Barisan Nasional coalition in the elections of 8 March 2008 was a further gauge of Indian discontent.[85] But it also revealed that the regime of "benign neglect" was no longer to be tolerated, and that henceforth support for Barisan Nasional would be conditional. Indian alienation was acknowledged by incoming prime minister Najib Razak who in addition to offering gestures of goodwill took a series of measures to address Indian concerns.[86]

The reality of an Indian community largely entrapped within a generic culture of poverty and chronic underachievement, and subject to the imperatives of Malay-Muslim discourse, has influenced scholarly discourse regarding the popularity of Thaipusam in Malaysia. As we noted in the Introduction, many accounts, including those of usually perceptive scholars,[87] suggest that participation in the most robust forms of worship, including the kavadi ritual, is restricted to working-class devotees, and forms a wider and perhaps cathartic response to their oppression, and in particular to Malay-Muslim dominance. These claims will be evaluated in later chapters of this book.

Notes

1. C.P. Ramachandran, "The Malaysian Indian in the New Millennium", Keynote Address, The Malaysian Indian in the New Millennium Conference, Kuala Lumpur, May 2002.
2. Ibid.
3. Andrew Willford, *Cage of Freedom: Tamil Identity and the Ethnic Fetish in Malaysia* (Ann Arbor: University of Michigan Press, 2006), p. 210. Willford's observations are confirmed by my own fieldwork.
4. Kernial Singh Sandhu, "Tamil and other Indian Convicts in the Straits Settlements 1790–1873", International Conference of Tamil Studies, Kuala Lumpur, 1966.
5. Kernial Singh Sandhu, *Indians in Malaya: Some Aspects of their Immigration and Settlement* (Cambridge: Cambridge University Press, 1969), pp. 56–58.
6. Ibid., p. 81.
7. Ibid., p. 82.
8. Hugh Tinker, *A New System of Slavery: The Export of Indian Labour Overseas 1830–1920* (London: Oxford University Press, 1974), p. 315.
9. J. Norman Parmer, *Colonial Labor Policy and Administration: A History of Labor in the Rubber Plantation Industry in Malaya 1910–1941* (New York: J.J. Augustin Inc., 1960), pp. 7–9; Sinnappah Arasaratnam, *Indians in Malaysia and Singapore* (London: Oxford University Press, 1970), pp. 18–19.
10. Sandhu, *Indians in Malaya*, p. 96.
11. Arasaratnam, *Indians in Malaysia*, pp. 24–26.
12. Parmer, *Colonial Labor Policy*, p. 213; Selvakumaran Ramachandran, *Indian Plantation Labour in Malaysia* (Kuala Lumpur: S. Abdul Majeed & Co., 1994), p. 68; Sandhu, *Indians in Malaya*, p. 108.
13. Sandhu, *Indians in Malaya*, p. 115; Parmer, *Colonial Labor Policy*, p. 55.
14. Parmer, *Colonial Labor Policy*, p. 55.
15. Ibid.; Sandhu, *Indians in Malaya*, p. 115.
16. Sandhu, *Indians in Malaya*, pp. 67, 122.
17. Arasaratnam, *Indians in Malaysia*, p. 33.
18. Sandhu, *Indians in Malaya*, pp. 117–29; Arasaratnam, *Indians in Malaysia*, pp. 33–35.
19. K.J. Ratnam, *Communalism and the Political Process in Malaya* (Kuala Lumpur and Singapore: University of Malaya Press, 1965), p. 1.
20. *Federation of Malaya Census Report* (Kuala Lumpur: Government Printers, 1957).
21. Tinker, *A New System of Slavery*, p. 17; Lydia Potts, *The World Labour Market: A History of Migration*, trans. Terry Bond (London: Zed Books, 1990), p. 64.
22. D. Jeyakumar, "The Indian Poor in Malaysia: Problems and Solutions", in

Indian Communities in Southeast Asia, edited by K.S. Sandhu and A. Mani (Singapore: Institute of Southeast Asian Studies, 1993), p. 421.

23. Tinker, *A New System of Slavery*, pp. 199, 208–9; Selvakumaran, *Indian Plantation Labour*, p. 57; Ravindra K. Jain, "South Indian Labour in Malaya 1840–1920: Asylum, Stability and Evolution", in *Indentured Labour in the British Empire 1840–1920*, edited by Kay Saunders (London: Croom Helm, 1984), p. 164.

24. In response to representations made by Sir Shenton Thomas, Governor of Singapore, the Undersecretary of State for the Colonial Office on 14 May 1941 approved "firm handling of subversive elements" (London: *Strikes by Indian Labourers*, File L/P&J/8/264, Collection 108/21G, Oriental and India Office).

25. *Negotiations between Indian and Malayan Governments Concerning the Protection of Rights of Indians in Malaya 1939–1941* (London: File L/P&J/8/260, Collection 108/21D, Oriental and India Office); Selvakumaran, *Indian Plantation Labour*, pp. 232–33.

26. Carl Vadivella Belle, *The Development of Indian Political Consciousness in Malaysia: Colonialism, Nationalism and Subhas Chandra Bose*, CSID Paper No. 4 (Hyderabad: Centre for the Study of the Indian Diaspora, University of Hyderabad, 2009); Christopher Bayly and Tim Harper, *Forgotten Wars: The End of Britain's Asian Empire* (London: Penguin Books, 2008), pp. 19, 87; Joginder Singh Jessy, "The Indian Army of Independence" (BA [Hons] Thesis, University of Singapore, 1957–58).

27. Rajeswary Amplavanar, *The Indian Minority and Political Change in Malaya 1945–1957* (Kuala Lumpur: Oxford University Press, 1981), p. 50; K. Nadaraja, "The Thondar Padai Movement of Kedah 1945–1957", *Malaysia in History* 24 (1981), p. 102.

28. Rajeswary, *The Indian Minority*, p. 46; P. Ramasamy, *Plantation Labour, Unions, Capital and the State in Peninsular Malaysia* (Kuala Lumpur: Oxford University Press, 1994), pp. 67–69; Arasaratnam, *Indians in Malaysia*, p. 138.

29. Rajeswary, *The Indian Minority*, p. 199; Mavis Puthucheary, "Indians in the Public Sector", pp. 335–36; Rajeswary Amplavanar-Brown, "The Contemporary Indian Political Elite in Malaysia", p. 238; Chandra Muzaffar, "Political Marginalization in Malaysia", p. 220; all in *Indian Communities in Southeast Asia*, edited by K.S. Sandhu and A. Mani (Singapore: Institute of Southeast Asian Studies, 1993).

30. A national survey conducted in 2013 determined that in order to be "comfortably off", a household required a monthly income of RM3,000. Ninety per cent of Indian households received less than this figure (Datuk Dr Denison Jayasooria, ed., *Malaysian Issues and Concerns: Some Policy Responses* [Batu Caves: Centre for Public Policy Studies/Asian Strategy and Leadership Institute, 2013], p. 242).

31. Selvakumaran, *Indian Plantation Labour*, pp. 306–7; Muzaffar, *Political*

Marginalization, p. 212. For a more recent study, see R. Thillainathan, "A Critical Review of Indian Economic Performance and Priorities for Action", in *Rising India and Indian Communities in East Asia*, edited by K. Kesavapany, A. Mani, and P. Ramasamy (Singapore: Institute of Southeast Asian Studies, 2008).

32. Ramachandran, *The Malaysian Indian*; Jayasooria, *Malaysian Issues*, p. 235.

33. Azly Rahman, "The '*New Bumiputerism*' as Pedagogy of Hope and Liberation: Teaching the Alternative Malaysian Ethnic Studies", in *Multiethnic Malaysia: Past, Present and Future*, edited by Lim Teck Ghee, Alberto Gomes, and Azly Rahman (Petaling Jaya: Strategic Information and Research Development Centre, 2009), p. 454.

34. Sheila Nair, "Colonialism, Nationalism, Ethnicity: Constructing Identity and Difference", in *Multiethnic Malaysia: Past Present and Future*, edited by Lim Teck Ghee, Alberto Gomes, and Azly Rahman (Petaling Jaya: Strategic Information and Research Development Centre, 2009), p. 87.

35. Maznah Mohamad, "Politics of the NEP and Ethnic Relations in Malaysia", in *Multiethnic Malaysia: Past Present and Future*, edited by Lim Teck Ghee, Alberto Gomes, and Azly Rahman (Petaling Jaya: Strategic Information and Research Development Centre, 2009), p. 122.

36. Ong Puay Liu, "Identity Matters: Ethnic Perceptions and Concerns", in *Multiethnic Malaysia: Past, Present and Future*, edited by Lim Teck Ghee, Alberto Gomes, and Azly Rahman (Petaling Jaya: Strategic Information and Research Development Centre, 2009), p. 466.

37. Ahmad Fauzi Abdul Hamid, *Islamic Education in Malaysia*, Monograph No. 18 (Singapore: S. Rajaratnam School of International Studies, 2010), pp. 13–14.

38. Ooi Kee Beng, "Beyond Ethnocentrism: Malaysia and the Affirmation of Hybridisation", in *Multiethnic Malaysia: Past, Present and Future*, edited by Lim Teck Ghee, Alberto Gomes, and Azly Rahman (Petaling Jaya: Strategic Information and Research Development Centre, 2009), p. 456.

39. Lim Teck Ghee, "Introduction: Historical Roots of Identity in Malaysia", in *Multiethnic Malaysia: Past Present and Future*, edited by Lim Teck Ghee, Alberto Gomes, and Azly Rahman (Petaling Jaya: Strategic Information and Research Development Centre, 2009), p. 425.

40. Cheah Boon Kheng, *Malaysia: The Making of a Nation* (Singapore: Institute of Southeast Asian Studies, 2002), pp. 126–27; Ooi Kee Beng, *The Reluctant Politician: Tun Dr Ismail and His Time* (Singapore: Institute of Southeast Asian Studies, 2006), p. 200; A.S. Milne and Diane K. Mauzy, *Politics and Government in Malaysia* (Singapore: Federal, 1978), pp. 81–82.

41. William Shaw, *Tun Razak: His Life and Times* (Kuala Lumpur: Longman Malaysia, 1976), pp. 220–21.

42. Rehman Rashid, *A Malaysian Journey* (Petaling Jaya: Rehman Rashid, 1993), p. 97.

43. Ooi Kee Beng, *The Reluctant Politician*, pp. 215–17.
44. Cheah Boon Kheng, *Malaysia*, pp. 67, 144; Edmund Terence Gomez and K.S. Jomo, *Malaysia's Political Economy: Politics, Patronage and Profits* (Cambridge: Cambridge University Press, 1997), pp. 39–40.
45. Selvakumaran, *Indian Plantation Labour*, p. 310.
46. Zainah Anwar, *Islamic Revivalism in Malaysia: Dakwah among the Students* (Petaling Jaya: Pelanduk, 1987), p. 10; Judith Nagata, *The Reflowering of Malaysian Islam: Modern Religious Radicals and Their Roots* (Vancouver: University of British Columbia Press, 1984), p. 55; Gordon P. Means, *Political Islam in Southeast Asia* (Boulder, CO: Lynne Rienner, 2009), p. 85.
47. Jomo K.S. and Ahmad Shabery Cheek, "Malaysia's Islamic Movements", in *Fragmented Vision: Culture and Politics in Contemporary Malaysia*, edited by Joel Kahn and Francis Loh Kok Wah (Sydney: Asian Studies Association of Australia/Allen and Unwin, 1992), pp. 79–80; Maznah, *Politics of the NEP*, p. 132; Zainah, *Islamic Revivalism*, pp. 88–90.
48. Susan E. Ackerman and Raymond L.M. Lee, *Heaven in Transition: Innovation and Ethnic Identity in Malaysia* (Honolulu: University of Hawai'i Press, 1988), pp. 154–55.
49. Mohamad Abu Bakar, "Islam, Civil Society and Ethnic Relations in Malaysia", in *Islam and Civil Society in Southeast Asia*, edited by Nakamuro Mitsuo, Sharon Siddique, and Omar Farouk Bajunid (Singapore: Institute of Southeast Asian Studies, 2001), p. 61.
50. *Federation Constitutional Proposal, Legislative Council Proposal No. 42 of 1957* (Kuala Lumpur: Government Printers, 1957), pp. 8–9.
51. Mohamad Abu Bakar, *Islam, Civil Society and Ethnic Relations*, p. 63.
52. Lim Teck Ghee and Albert Gomes, "Culture and Development in Malaysia", in *Multiethnic Malaysia: Past Present and Future*, edited by Lim Teck Ghee, Alberto Gomes, and Azly Rahman (Petaling Jaya: Strategic Information and Research Development Centre, 2009), pp. 233–34; Joel S. Kahn and Francis Loh Kok Wah, "Introduction", in *Fragmented Vision: Culture and Politics in Contemporary Malaysia* (Sydney: Asian Studies Association of Australia/Allen and Unwin, 1992), p. 13; John Funston, *Malay Politics in Malaysia: A Study of UMNO and PAS* (Kuala Lumpur: Heinemann Educational Books [Asia] Ltd., 1980), p. 238.
53. Zainah, *Islamic Revival*, pp. 80–81; Nagata, *The Reflowering of Malaysian Islam*, p. 223. Ahmad Fauzi comments, "Given the legally coterminous position between Islam and Malayness in Malaysia, it is hardly surprising that politicians of all divides have manipulated Islam as a political tool to realize their racial agendas" (Ahmad Fauzi, *Islamic Education*, p. 76).
54. Maznah, *Paradoxes of State Islamization*, p. 19; Ahmad Fauzi, *Islamic Education in Malaysia*, p. 76.

55. Nagata, *The Reflowering of Malaysian Islam*, pp. 187–88.

56. Zainah, *Islamic Revivalism*, pp. 80–81.

57. Chandra Muzaffar, *Islamic Resurgence in Malaysia* (Petaling Jaya: Penerbity Fajar Bakti, 1987), p. 30.

58. Ooi Kee Beng, *Done Making Do: 1 Party Rule Ends in Malaysia* (Singapore: Institute of Southeast Asian Studies, 2013), p. 44.

59. Clive Kessler, "The Abdullah Premiership: Interlude or End Game?", in *Awakening: The Abdullah Badawi Years in Malaysia*, edited by Bridget Walsh and James V.H. Chin (Petaling Jaya: Strategic Information and Research Development Centre, 2013), pp. 71–72.

60. Jason Tan, "Malaysian Culture under Abdullah", in *Awakening: The Abdullah Badawi Years in Malaysia*, edited by Bridget Walsh and James V.H. Chin (Petaling Jaya: Strategic Information and Research Development Centre, 2013), p. 410.

61. Benjamin R. Barber, *Jihad Vs McWorld: Terrorism's Challenge to Democracy* (London: Corgi Books, 2005), p. 165.

62. A.B. Sulaiman, *Sensitive Truths in Malaysia: A Critical Appraisal of the Malay Problem* (Petaling Jaya: Strategic Information and Research Development Centre, 2013), p. 298; Andrew C. Wilford, "Every Indian is Burning Inside", in *Awakening: The Abdullah Badawi Years in Malaysia*, edited by Bridget Walsh and James H.V. Chin (Petaling Jaya: Strategic Information and Research Development Centre, 2013), p. 223. Given Mahathir's role in expanding the presence of Islam within Malaysian public life, it is somewhat ironic to note his recent public criticism of the didactic zeal of the Department of Islamic Development Malaysia (Jakim), a body that was created under his leadership (Izra Abdul Rahman, "Dr Mahathir: Jakim Imposing 'its version of Islam'", *The Star*, 20 November 2015).

63. Sinnappah Arasaratnam, "Malaysian Indians: The Formation of an Incipient Society", in *Indian Communities in Southeast Asia*, edited by K.S. Sandhu and A. Mani (Singapore: Institute of Southeast Asian Studies, 1993), p. 193.

64. Jeyakumar, *The Indian Poor*, p. 421.

65. Rajeswary, *The Indian Minority*, pp. 172–75; Sinnappah Arasaratnam, "Political Attitudes and Political Organization among Malayan Indians 1945–1955", *Jernal Sejarah* 10 (1971/72): 5; Muzaffar, *Political Marginalization*, p. 219.

66. Muzaffar, *Political Marginalization*, p. 219.

67. Selvakumaran, *Indian Plantation Labour*, pp. 260–61, 305; Paul W. Wiebe and S. Mariappen, *Indian Malaysians: The View from the Plantation* (Delhi: Manohar, 1978), p. 38; Arasaratnam, *Indians in Malaysia*, pp. 154–56; Muzaffar, *Political Marginalization*, p. 222.

68. Selvakumaran, *Indian Plantation Labour*, pp. 274, 304–5.

69. Rajeswary, *The Contemporary Indian Political Elite*, p. 250.

70. For a full description of the Kampung Medan incident, see Andrew Willford, "Ethnic Clashes, Squatters and Historicity in Malaysia", in *Rising India and*

Indian Communities in East Asia, edited by K. Kesavapany, A. Mani, and P. Ramasamy (Singapore: Institute of Southeast Asian Studies, 2008); S. Nagarajan and K. Arumugam, *Violence against an Ethnic Minority in Malaysia, Kampung Medan, 2001* (Petaling Jaya: Suaram, 2012).

71. Ramachandran, *The Malaysian Indian*; K.S. Susan Oorjitham, "Economic Profile of the Tamil Working Class in Peninsular Malaysia", *Jurnal Pengajian India* 5 (1993), p. 102; Muzafar Desmond Tate, *The Malaysian Indians: History, Problems and Future* (Petaling Jaya: Strategic Information and Research Development Centre, 2008), p. 129. For a detailed analysis of the social impact of mass evictions, see Andrew C. Willford (in collaboration with S. Nagarajan), *Tamils and the Haunting of Justice: History and Recognition in Malaysia's Estates* (Singapore: NUS Press, 2014).

72. This is based on interviews conducted in 2010 and 2011. However, in the mid 1990s, even S. Samy Vellu, leader of the Malaysian Indian Congress, and a Senior Minister in the ruling Barisan Nasional coalition, would claim that "Indians were more marginalized and alienated than ever before" (Gomez and Jomo, *Malaysia's Political Economy*, p. 168).

73. K.S. Susan Oorjitham, *Economic Profile*, p. 102.

74. R. Rajoo, "Indian Squatter Settlers: Rural-Urban Migration in West Malaysia", in *Indian Communities in South East Asia*, edited by K.S. Sandhu and A. Mani (Singapore: Institute of Southeast Asian Studies, 1993), p. 485; K.S. Susan Oorjitham, "Urban Indian Working Class Households", *Jurnal Pengajian India* 4 (1986): 76. For more recent studies, see S. Nagarajan, "Marginalisation and Ethnic Relations: The Indian Malaysian Experience", in *Multiethnic Malaysia: Past Present and Future*, edited by Lim Teck Ghee, Alberto Gomes, and Azly Rahman (Petaling Jaya: Strategic Information and Research Centre, 2009); S. Nagarajan, "Indians in Malaysia: Towards Vision 2020", in *Rising India and Indian Communities in East Asia*, edited by K. Kesavapany, A. Mani, and P. Ramasamy (Singapore: Institute of Southeast Asian Studies, 2008).

75. Jayasooria, *Malaysian Issues and Concerns*, p. 242.

76. Oorjitham, *Economic Profile*, pp. 104–5; Jeyakumar, *The Indian Poor of Malaysia*, pp. 419–20; Oorjitham, *Working Class Indians*, p. 507.

77. Ramachandran, *The Malaysian Indian*.

78. Jeyakumar, *The Indian Poor*, p. 419.

79. K. Kabilan, "The Indian Dilemma: Sucked Up and Spat Out", in *Awakening: The Abdullah Badawi Years in Malaysia*, edited by Bridget Walsh and James V.H. Chin (Petaling Jaya: Strategic Information and Research Development Centre, 2013), p. 198; Willford, *Tamils and the Haunting of Justice*, p. 236.

80. These incidents are detailed in Carl Vadivella Belle, *Tragic Orphans: Indians in Malaysia* (Singapore: Institute of Southeast Asian Studies, 2015), pp. 397–405.

81. Nagarajan, *Marginalization and Ethnic Relations*, p. 387.

82. Rajesh Rai, "'Positioning' the Indian Diaspora: The Southeast Asian Experience", in *Tracing an Indian Dilemma: Contexts, Memories, Representations*, edited by Parvati Raghuram, Ajaya Kumar Sahoo, Brij Maharaj, and Dave Sangham (New Delhi: Sage, 2008), p. 48.
83. Muzaffar, *Political Marginalization*, p. 228.
84. Personal Field Research.
85. Barry Wain, *Malaysian Maverick: Mahathir Mohamad in Turbulent Times* (Basingstoke: Palgrave MacMillan, 2009), p. 329; Ooi Kee Beng, *Arrested Reform: The Unmaking of Abdullah Badawi* (Kuala Lumpur: Research for Social Advancement, 2009), pp. 44–55; James Chin and Chin Huat-Wong, "Malaysia's Electoral Upheaval", *Journal of Democracy* 20, no. 3 (2009): p. 73.
86. Edmund Terence Gomez, Johan Saravanamuttu, and Maznah Mohamad, "Introduction: Malaysia's New Economic Policy: Resolving Inequalities, Creating Difficulties", in *The New Economic Policy in Malaysia: Affirmative Action, Ethnic Inequalities and Social Justice*, edited by Edmund Terence Gomez and Johan Saravanamuttu (Singapore: National University of Singapore/Institute of Southeast Asian Studies, 2013), p. 16.
87. Fred W. Clothey, *Ritualizing on the Boundaries: Continuity and Innovation in the Tamil Diaspora* (Columbia: University of South Carolina Press, 2006), p. 196; Alexandra Kent, *Divinity and Diversity: A Hindu Revitalization Movement* (Singapore and Copenhagen: Institute of Southeast Asian Studies/NIAS Press, 2007), pp. 174, 179.

2

Tamil Traditions and South Indian Hinduism

Most scholars would contend that Common Era India has contained two great and discrete hubs of civilization, each of which served the needs and reflected the aspirations of quite distinct peoples. Burton Stein has termed these hubs "Hindu Aryan India" (centred on the Gangetic Plains/Chambal Basin) and "Hindu Dravidian India" (South India defined as that portion of Peninsular India which falls south of the Karnataka watershed — excluding the modern state of Kerala in the west and the Kistna [Krishna]-Godavari delta in the east). Stein, following other scholars, asserts that the shared social, cultural and political histories of Hindu Dravidian India are such as to constitute it as a recognizable and sufficiently coherent unit for the purposes of study. He identifies the essential acculturating core of this region as the Tamil Plain and its immediate hinterland.[1]

While the origins of the South Indian peoples remains speculative, archaeological evidence confirms that the Peninsula has been continually inhabited since very early times.[2] This culture was given distinctive expression through, inter alia, the development of the Tamil language, which comprises one strand of a discrete linguistic family later known as "Dravidian". The most ancient surviving Tamil writings, located in caves that were once occupied by Jain ascetics, date from the second century BCE and used Devanagari script common among Ashokan inscriptions found in North India. This suggests that even at this early juncture contacts between South India and the Gangetic Plains were well established.[3]

South Indian Hinduism has developed its own distinctive societal mores, modes of spiritual inquiry and systems of philosophical speculation. This chapter will provide a general overview of the development of Tamil Hinduism and highlight some of its most enduring institutions and characteristics. This does not make any pretence to be an exhaustive historical survey, nor does it attempt to document all the detailed inflections of the many Hindu traditions and forms of worship located within the Tamil country (*Tamilakam*). The chapter will demonstrate that the continual reworking of Tamil Hinduism, especially the mutable boundaries of *Agamic* religion, provided multiple sites of particularistic religious expression, ranging from textual, philosophical and *Agamic* forms to those whose cosmologies inhere within the context of ritual and which may not recognise the putative authority of Brahmanic Hinduism. It will trace the emergence of several pervasive features of Tamil Hinduism, namely the Sanksritization/*Agamicization* of goddess (Amman/Devi) worship, the paradigmatic sovereignty of the deity within the temple, the rise of *bhakti* devotion, and the development of Saiva Siddhanta philosophy.

Many scholarly descriptions of Tamil Hinduism posit a functional model structured in hierarchical layers, with *Agamic*/Sanskritic or "Great Tradition" Hinduism at the apex, and supposedly "little" traditions, variously described as folk, village or popular traditions, comprising the subordinate layers, with the purportedly lowest manifestation, spirit worship — the furthest removed from the *Agamic*/Sanskritic ideal — forming the lowest rung. The limitations of such a hierarchical schema have been criticized on various grounds: that it is structured upon unstated caste/*jati* distinctions; that it is a product of a colonialist sociology of knowledge which both privileges and upholds Brahmanic hegemony; and that it fails to recognize or accommodate the crucial importance of regional traditions and historical specifities.[4]

More recent scholarly works have demonstrated that the portrayal of Tamil Hinduism as starkly divided between two fundamental and discrete strands, that is, *Agamic*/Brahmanic orthodoxy as opposed to popular/village Hinduism, is reductive, simplistic and erroneous. Rather, the tradition must be viewed in holistic terms, as a complex continuum, in which unceasing dialogue between various and often antagonistic segments leads to reworking of themes, rituals and belief structures which are then reincorporated and offered to audiences at a range of levels within society. Thus elements of the "classical"/orthodox are reinterpreted to provide significance for lower-caste devotees, while aspects of the "lower" traditions, especially those which belong in the realm of raw *bhakti* movements, are "reformed" (that is, Sanskritized/*Agamicized*) and adapted to classical philosophy and practice, and are accoutred with symbols appropriate to their now elevated standing.[5] The fluidity of Tamil belief structures will become more obvious as we examine the evolution of Tamil traditions.

It has been convincingly argued that the great and enduring socio-religious cultural beliefs, philosophies and institutions of the Tamil peoples were shaped, developed and reinforced throughout the extended period in which the region was under the tutelage of the great dynasties — Pallava (*c*.575–900 CE), Chola (*c*.900–1350 CE), Vijayanagara (*c*.1350–1700 CE) and to a lesser extent the Pandyan (*c*.600–1400) — dynasties which ruled from circa sixth century CE to the early eighteenth century. These processes were necessarily incremental and accumulative, and each dynasty made its own distinctive contribution.[6] However, before exploring the evolutionary trajectory of Hinduism under the dynasties, it is necessary to examine the South Indian concept of the state and the role that the king played in maintaining his realm.

The State and Kingship

The most distinctive feature of the South Indian dynastic polity was its segmentary character; that is, it consisted of bonded social units which might act and operate with or in opposition to other social groupings. According to theories of state located in both *Puranic* and *sastric* sources, society predated political formations so that while states might encompass social collectivities, it was also obliged to protect them. The basic social aggregations consisted of kinship groups (*kula*), local coalitions usually comprising occupational groups of several castes and formed around shared and cooperative interests (*sreni*), alliances based on religious or political affiliations held in common, and territorial or representational bodies (*puga*). Each segment regarded itself as a socially, structurally and morally autarkic unit, and staunchly guarded its own autonomy.[7]

The segmentary states of South India were organized pyramidically from base to apex, consisting at every level of "balanced and opposed internal groupings which jealously clung to their independent entities and privileges and internal governance".[8] Together, these local and supralocal entities expanded upwards towards the kingship which necessarily occupied the very peak of the pyramid.[9]

The great dynastic states of South India and the successor kingdoms ruled by the *Palaiyakkarars* (or "little kings") were thus both contingent and fluid and were reliant on the shared acceptance of the moral authority and sacred persona of the king for their existence. Indeed, textual tradition emphasized the necessity of kingship for the upholding of both moral and social order; it was considered that a society without a king would dissolve into chaos.[10] The king was the ritual apex of the segmentary states, a sacred actor who ruled from a weak centre over a complex system of hierarchical relations. Beyond the core region of his dominions, his writ was largely administrative rather than legislative. His commands and decrees were context specific rather than generic; thus they were addressed to groups and individuals rather than to the population at large, and were subject to modification or revocation according to changed circumstances.[11]

The theoretical framework for the instrumentalities of South Indian kingship was set out in medieval law texts (*dharmasastra*), as well as literary and other works. The *rajadharma*, based on the ancient canons of Aryan kingship,[12] was a body of *dharmic* law (*dharma* defined as action in conformity with the intrinsic universal norm)[13] which enunciated the role and duties of the king. The kingdom was portrayed as a sacred universe in which the raja was the principal and most critical actor.[14] Indeed, the king was clearly identified with the deity. His body was symbolically equated with the kingdom, and conversely the territory of the kingdom reflected his royal person and presence.[15] The king's duty was to rule wisely, to be a worthy representative of the deity, to uphold the moral order, to bestow justice and to ensure prosperity. He was also patron of sacred ritual.[16] However, while the *rajadharma* envisioned the king as a sacred personage, his power in many respects was limited to enforcing moral responsibility (*ksastra*) to the very limits of his territory. The dispensation of divine sanctions and hence dharmic justice (*danda*) was pivotal to the maintenance of his dynastic realm.[17]

Ritual incorporation — based on presentations and the gift — worked to buttress the overarching moral authority of the South Indian king while recognizing the diffusion of social power inherent in a segmentary state. Essential duties of the kingship included the bestowal of generous allocations of productive lands to Brahmans who would study and chant the Vedas and perform ritual services for the king, and the lavishing of funds upon temples and lodging houses for Brahmans and other pilgrims. In return, Brahmans recognized the temporal ascendency of the kingship.[18] The king was also required to generate prosperity throughout the entire kingdom. This was demonstrated by his continuing ability to engage in bounteous presentations to lesser figures — chieftains and others — within the polity.[19] In his bestowal of the gift, grant or honour, the king signified the transfer of some of the sacred essence of his kingship — power, majesty and authority — to the lesser figure of the chieftain. This established a hierarchical relationship which incorporated the chieftain within the overall structure of the kingdom while clearly delineating his role and subordinate status.[20] In accepting the gift or honour, the chieftain (or other nominated recipient), recognized his incorporation, an act which engendered a set of moral obligations to the king.[21] The gift was a political transaction; an exchange which simultaneously devolved limited sovereignty to the chieftain whilst reinforcing the overlordship of the king, thus ritually reiterating the generic hierarchical and social structure of the kingdom. This system of exchange and redistribution of goods and services, known as *jajmani*, and flowing hierarchically from and to the apex, played a crucial and catalytic role in both upholding and maintaining royal authority and in promoting effective lines of communication between the centre and the diverse territories and peoples which comprised the state.[22]

The South Indian king was expected to constantly demonstrate all the attributes of kingship. These included the enactment of the "repeated and continued celebration of rites" engendered by kingship,[23] including royal consecration (*rajasuya*) and installation (*apisekam*). However, throughout the Vijayanagara dynasty, the most elaborate and splendid royal commemoration was the nine-day festival of *Mahavani*, or *Navaratri*, staged in the Tamil month of *Puratacci* (September–October). *Navaratri* fused with another festival known as *ayuta puja*, or the honouring of one's arms, instruments of trade or, in the case of the king, his weaponry.[24] A tenth day added to *Navaratri* for this purpose became known as *Vijayadisami* (the Victorious Tenth: the day of victory).[25] *Navaratri*, permeated by royalty and royal symbology, and ceremonially renewing sovereignty and reinfusing the king and his weaponry with cosmic power for the protection and rejuvenation of the capital city, portrayed the king as the key ritual performer and the catalytic agency upon whom the prosperity and stability of the kingdom depended.[26] The king also exchanged ceremonial gifts and honours with subordinate chieftains and other important figures, all of whom had to be brought to the capital for this purpose.[27] On *Vijayadisami*, the king's royal procession, his court assemblies and ritual worship signified the goddess's regeneration of the cosmos, with the king clearly identified as its conspicuous locus.[28] The festival thus incorporated all the diverse elements of the segmentary state within the framework of a recognized polity, with the capital city as the symbolic universe over which the king ruled.[29]

Sangam and Dynastic Hinduism

Tamil Hinduism can be reliably traced to the poetry collection known as the *Sangam*, which comprises the earliest extant Tamil literature. The *Sangam* is variously dated from 300 BCE to 300 CE, but most scholars now incline towards the early centuries of the Common Era.[30] Tradition asserts that this literature was composed by an academy of poets.[31] The *Sangam* literature not only explicated the sources of early Tamil Hinduism but also revealed the "visible presence of Buddhist and Jain religions".[32] Both religions coexisted with Hinduism and various folk traditions up to and throughout the Pallava and Pandya eras.[33] The *Sangam* gave expression to the main strands of the Brahmanic tradition, namely Vedic, *Smarta* and *Puranic*, which were portrayed as forming a cohensive unitary tradition.[34] The earliest *Sangam* anthologies emphasized the ideal of love (*akam*) combined with the associated virtues including heroism, courage, patronage and generosity.[35] They also highlighted the seminal centrality of the legendary sage Agastya as foundational poet of the first *Sangam*.[36] These poems reflect the varying socio-economic influences prevailing within the Tamil eco-zones (*tinai*), each with its own deity honoured with "intensely humanistic" modes of worship.[37]

Well prior to the *Sangam* period, cultural exchanges between North and South India had inextricably embedded both Vedic and Sanskritic influences within the collocation of indigenous South Indian forms.[38] Indeed, as early as the first century CE, Tamil Hinduism comprised an integration of indigenous and Sanskritic religious, philosophical and cultural forms and symbols, a fusion of influences "so inextricably interwoven as to defy disaggregation into autochthonous interacting phenomena".[39]

The *Puranas* trace their origin to changes within Brahmanism which followed the Mauryan era (that is, after 185 BCE) and developed into full efflorescence by the Gupta era (sixth to tenth centuries CE).[40] The process represented a structured synthesis of the Brahman Vedic tradition and sectarian bardic poetry.[41] In effect, the major currents of folk belief were reinterpreted to accord with Sanskrit "great traditions", thus endowing them with Vedic authority.[42] While this process was an India-wide phemomenon, regional differences and localized traditions assured that the *Puranas* would assume particularistic forms. Thus, in *Tamilakam*, Brahmanic *Puranas* represented an amalgam of Sanskrit and Tamil belief structures influenced by folk, popular and localized sources drawn from the Sangam corpus.[43] The *Puranic* tradition facilitated the spread of Brahmanism to all corners of Tamilakam.[44]

What exactly are *Puranas*? Edwin Bryant states that the Sanskrit term *Purana* signifies "that which took place previously", that is, "ancient lore and legend", and that the *Puranas* consist of:

> a vast repository of stories about kings and royal dynasties; the gods and their devotees; sectarian theologies; traditional cosmologies; popular religious beliefs concerning pilgrimages, holy places and religious rites; yogic practices; information of social and cultural relevance such as caste duties; and even prophetic statements about the future.[45]

The *Puranic* texts are regarded as *smirti* (that which is remembered),[46] and thus a divine revelation, but both composed and transmitted via human instrumentality.[47]

But, while they may consist at one level of detailed "biographies" of the gods and establish and sustain discourses which establish the gods' relationships with one another, that is, a cosmology, on a deeper plane they present the most profound philosophical truths of Hinduism, thus explicating "the ultimate reality of the universe giving expression to that which cannot be discursively experienced".[48] Indeed, most scholars would contend that the *Puranas* comprise the fundamental basis of almost all aspects of modern Hinduism.[49] Professor Champakalakshmi has pointed out that the *Puranas* were employed to underscore Brahmanic norms and subsequently constituted an authoritative basis for the development of specific religious practices and rituals, as well as reinforcing sectarian and regional belief structures. Indeed, continual dialogue between folk and popular elements lead to the emergence of a *"Puranic* pantheon", the major deities of which consisted of variants of Siva and Vishnu, Vedicized gods drawn from localized/folkish traditions.[50]

The Pallava dynasty established the first Brahmanic kingdom in northern *Tamilakam* and ruled much of South India circa 575–900 CE.[51] Under Pallava rule there were a number of significant socio-religious cultural and economic developments within the region. The central thrust of Pallava rule was the adoption of a wholly *Puranic* ideology structured around Vaishnavism and Saivism, and the creation of an enlarged pantheon bolstered by the incorporation of a number of non-Vedic deities.[52] The chosen deity of the Pallavas was *Somaskanda* (a representation of Siva the father, Uma his consort, and Skanda/Murugan as the infant son); a deity which fostered the integration of an array of territorially segmented peoples, many of whom continued to observe pre-Pallavan orthogenetic cultural forms.[53] Other developments included the construction of a series of monumental temples; the foundation of *bhakti* devotional cults; the vigorous promotion of Brahman settlements (*brahmadeyas*) as the focal points of Sanskrit education and culture; the gradual rise of urban centres involved in more elaborate forms of agrarian and commercial organization; and the establishment of sophisticated trade networks that extended as far as the Mediterranean.[54] A key element in shaping the emerging culture of the Pallava era was the forging of close ties between the peasant cultivating classes and the Brahmans. By the ninth century, peasant society had attained pre-eminence in Pallava South India, in the process blunting the influence of territorially segmented organizations. The Pallava era was marked by hostility between the residents of the lowland plains and the putatively dangerous peoples of the hills and dryland plains.[55]

Under the Chola dynasty (*c.*900–1300 CE), a resurgent Hinduism witnessed the eclipse and decline of Buddhism and Jainism. The Cholas united the whole of *Tamilakam* into a single political entity and promoted an overarching ruling culture which permeated the entire region.[56] Hinduism was enlivened and reshaped by intense philosophical speculation, the replacement of sacrificial Vedic rites with religious forms centred upon temple worship and *bhakti* devotion, and the incorporation of localized cults, in particular Tamil *Amman* (goddess worship), into the fabric of *Agamic* Hinduism.[57]

The royal veneration of the deity Siva, which had been practised under the Pallavas, was continued under the Cholas.[58] Indeed the Cholas attempted to consolidate all localized cults and tutelary deities into a major religious order centred on the worship of Siva. This represented a sweeping political manoeuvre designed to gather all independent cults, as well as regional and caste deities, under direct Chola control and to establish a form of ritual sovereignty in which all lesser gods as well as local chiefs would pay homage to the god of both the king and the realm.[59]

The Chola policy of assimilation resulted in the elevation of several longstanding folk deities to full Vedic stature; these were assigned an honoured place within the "great tradition" pantheon. Thus, for example, the god Seyon, or Murugan of the hills (*kurunci tinai*), became identified with Subrahmanya, while Mayon, the black god of the pastoralists (*mullai tinai*), became firmly linked with Krishna. In addition, the *Agamic* injunctions or doctrines were amended or even "reinvented" to allow the inclusion of Tamil village or regional elements within Brahmanic Tamil Hinduism.[60]

The era was also marked by the full emergence and incorporation of goddess (*Amman* or *Devi*) worship into the folds of *Agamic* Hinduism. Within Tamil traditions, female deities had long been central to village, clan and locality worship, including fertility and protection functions.[61] However, a number of goddesses whose roles were both ambivalent and problematic, especially the so-called "fierce" goddesses, were accepted only after their identification as consorts of one of the *Puranic* deities.[62] From the thirteenth century onward, separate shrines were consecrated in *Agamic* temples for the recently elevated female deities.[63]

The religious changes of the late Pallava and Chola eras reflected major social tranformations occurring within the Tamil country throughout this period, in particular the coalescing of Brahman–peasant interests, i.e., those who controlled cultivation and those who through their sacral duties and expertise were able to wield significant ideological power.[64] Thus, the incorporation of folk and tutelary deities, including those whose origins lay in regional or tribal backgrounds, within *Agamic* Hinduism, constituted "a necessary compromise" between Brahman canonists and the economic impetus of non-Brahman peasant castes.[65] Similarly, the *bhakti* attacks on Jainism and Buddhism (described later in this chapter) and the development of the broader devotional tradition were largely the creative handiwork of a Brahman–peasant alliance.[66] The evolving emphasis on temple worship of *Agamic* deities increased the involvement of influential peasant castes, especially those living near to the *brahmadeyas*, within the ritual life of high religious culture.[67] After the twelfth century, leading peasant groups began to establish their own ritual and educational centres. These were influenced by Brahmanic culture and norms and were maintained by non-Brahmans steeped in Sanskritic and *sastric* knowledge. They became important centres of learning and culture within South India.[68] However, although the intercessionary power of Brahmans and their standing as the sole custodians and transmitters of *Agamic* education were weakened, they attained unprecedented levels of secular power. Indeed, Brahmans, *brahmadeyas* and the great temples were key pillars of the *Chola* ideological system of *rajadharma* (kingly dharma).[69]

Stein has argued that it was throughout the period of the Chola dynasty, and especially the two centuries between circa 1000 and circa 1200 CE, that many of the most characteristic forms of agrarian organization were founded, particularly in the Tamil plains and the Kaveri Basin, the heartland of Chola power.[70] During this era the Vellalars, the highest non-Brahman caste, expanded their influence and attained overall control of the riverine and deltaic regions in the south.[71] The essential political unit of the Chola state was the *nadu*, a macro territorial assembly which met ethnic demands as well as fulfilling an economic function.[72]

Between circa 1350 and 1500 CE, a period of transition in South India, bodies of Telegu warriors, the founders of the Vijayanagara dynasty (*c*.1350–1700 CE), gained and consolidated control over much of South India. The Vijayanagara regime successfully checked the encroachment of Muslim invaders from the north, restored and nurtured Hindu culture and institutions, and established a new state which was grounded in military power and was thus martial in character.[73] Unlike its predecessors, the Vijayanagara kingdom was not based in the Tamil core regions — the Coromandel Coast and the Kaveri Basin — but in the comparatively remote Western Deccan.[74]

The Vijayanagara kings introduced a number of new elements into South Indian politics and culture. Their role as defenders of Hindu culture, especially the engagement of the Vijayanagara rulers and their agents as vital *dharmic* actors in state affairs, provided the South Indian polity with a vigorous and radically fresh ideology of governance.[75] In inaugurating a supra-regional peninsular state with an expanded economy and new modes of administrative economy, the Vijayanagara rulers sought to establish an exclusive ideology which both superseded and subsumed regional and localized religious forms. The Vijayanagara kings pursued a vigorous policy of Sanskritization/Vedicization which aimed at reconciling northern Sanskritic and popular southern, Tamil and regional traditions within an overall Vedantic philosophical discourse. While this was often promoted through the agency of the *mathas* (Tamil: *madam*, monasteries), it was also advanced by co-option of the leaders of sects, especially those who might have proven refractory or resistant to the Vijayanagara order.[76] Thus, while many sects within the kingdom continued to worship a local deity possessing his own territorial (*nadu*) attributes, these deities were *Agamicized* and subsequently recognized as a form of Siva. The Vijayanagara Empire continued the Chola practice of consolidating goddess worship as a component form of *Puranic* Hindu culture. Their linkage to accepted *Agamic* gods ensured consistency within entrenched patterns of Siva worship.[77] Throughout this period both the *mathas* and temples emerged as the most obvious focal points for the dissemination of Vijayanagara ideology and thus as centres of religious hierarchy. The emphasis on temple worship provided a moral order which embraced all levels of society — family, *jati*, clan, village and region — and the kingdom itself.[78] The *mathas* served as a link between the temples and the state.[79] Throughout the Vijayanagara era there was an overall increase in the number and frequency of integrative rituals and festivals. The establishment of pilgrimage centres and their linkage into networks of temples/*mathas* elevated them beyond the local context and embedded them within the overarching rubric of Sanksritic India-wide sacred geographical structures.[80]

In 1565 the forces of the Vijayanagara dynasty were defeated by a coalition of five Deccani sultanates, and the capital of the empire was lost.[81] Although Vijayanagara survived into the early seventeenth century, it was steadily supplanted by a series of successor kingdoms ruled by former locality chiefs, the *Palaiyakkarars*, whose rule persisted into, and occasionally beyond, the eighteenth century.[82] Throughout the Vijayanagara era the *Palaiyakkarars* had extended their sub-caste dominance, thus displacing the Vellalar chieftains whose regnancy within the *nadus* had been a major feature of Chola rule.[83] The later *Palaiyakkarar* principalities resulted in the steady, but often sudden, elevation of groups and castes who had previously been regarded as outside the main structures and instrumentalities of state. Thus, for example, the Maravars and Kallars were ultimately transformed from peripheral people, on the margins of Tamil society, into "little kings", and from devout worshippers of folkish deities into responsible rulers, who both promoted and defended Sanskrit culture.[84]

However, while over the periods of the dynasties a number of prominent deities of village or popular traditions were now identified as great gods, accoutred with the precepts of philosophical Hinduism, and subsequently accepted into the corpus of the received *Agamic*/great tradition pantheon, these changes left untouched the great body of village traditions and associated belief structures to which the overwhelming majority of Tamil Hindus subscribed.[85] Indeed, Brahman and *Agamic* authorities refused to consider the incorporation of certain village or "lower" traditions, such as animal sacrifice or "excessively erotic religious customs", within the structures of *Agamic* Hinduism.[86] Adherents of "little tradition" Hinduism thus continued to recognize a hierarchy of superhuman entities consisting of *Puranic* gods, intermediate gods, demons and *bhuta/preta/pey* (spirits).[87] While village Hinduism often borrowed from other sources, including *Agamic* traditions, it retained (and continues to retain) its own autonomy which did not recognize or defer to other sites of religious authority. As Gunther Sontheimer observes, "From the point of view of sects and the Brahman's point of view, the deity may be considered to be just a *bhuta* or inferior godling ... but for actual worshippers *he is central to their life and beliefs*"(emphasis added).[88] This will be further explored later in this chapter.

Caste in South India

Within classical Hinduism the institution of caste is derived from the *Purusa Sakta* (literally Purusa's or primeval man's sacrifice) of the Rig Veda, which divides society into a four-tiered hierarchical reading of *varnas* (or classes); namely the generic categories of:

1. Brahmans: custodians of the sacred word; the teachers and advisors of society;
2. *Ksatriyas*: society's defenders and warriors, kings and administrators;
3. *Vaisyas*: farmers and merchants, those considered central to economic functions;
4. *Sudras*: unpropertied labourers, servants and menials.[89]

In fact, the fourfold *varna* system represents an idealized model which has never been replicated within quotidian Indian Hindu life.[90]

Fundamentally, a caste may be viewed as a discrete and self-encompassing social unit which regulates the conduct of its members according to agreed behavioural norms, disciplining those who breach caste mores and expelling those who commit serious caste transgressions.[91] Birth into a particular caste provides an individual with an ascriptive code of social behaviour which theoretically mandates occupation, diet, customs, social interactions and choice of marriage partner, as well as furnishing the guidelines for patterns of worship.[92] At base, each caste is built around extended kinship, reinforced by endogamous marriage, in conjunction with agreed protocols governing behavioural aspects specific to that group. Ultimate caste boundaries are coterminous with kinship limits.[93]

In fact, in practical terms the main operational unit is *jati*.[94] While *jati* loosely translates as a "kind" or "species",[95] the term is multivalent and may obtain in a variety of settings to group together people who, because of their primary origins, are considered intrinsically alike, in contradistinction to those who because they do not share those origins may be considered fundamentally different.[96] Endogamy ensures that each *jati* functions as an extended kin network and may relate to each member of the wider caste or sub-caste grouping as potential kinsmen to whom in extreme circumstances he/she may turn for aid, succour, welfare or other forms of support.[97] In such a world, miscegenation not only signifies the commingling of categories which ought to be kept separate and distinct, but also represents a threat to the "natural order".[98]

In the earliest *Sangam* period there was no obvious societal hierarchy structured upon the concept of *varna*. Rather, kinship networks comprised the basis of social organization, while the importance of lineage was emphasized in verifying chieftaincies and kingship.[99] Towards the conclusion of the classical *Sangam* era, the poetic canon *Tolkappiyam* separated the population of *Tamilakam* into twelve dialectical subregions and into four distinct categories; namely, Brahman, *Arasar* (or king), *Vanniyar* (or merchant) and *Vellalar* (or peasant). The Vellalars were further divided into two classifications — superior and inferior — the latter comprising farm labourers.[100] In the sixth century CE a basic *varna* hierarchy was established in which ruling families were accorded *Ksatriya* status. This followed the fashioning of suitably striking genealogies in the *psastras* (described as "eulogies ... composed by the brahmanas in return for royal patronage and land grants"). Together, Brahmans and *Ksatriyas* formed the apex of societies. Other, lower-ranked groups were defined in terms of occupational background.[101] Following the *bhakti* movement of medieval South India (see later section), these categories appear to have been recognized for ritual purposes.[102] Other than rulers, the political and social structures of South India were notable for their almost total absence of any caste which could be clearly recognized as *Ksatriya*.[103]

Castes were formed in various ways and under differing circumstances. These ranged from social units that comprised the armature of various kingdoms, to group identities created by the processes of economic change, urbanization, centralization and affiliation.[104] Social hierarchy was defined in terms of the expressed hegemony of dominant classes and delineated according to specific ideologies of social organization and kinship.[105] For rulers, the ritual ranking of society below the *Ksatriya/* Brahman level was viewed as an institutional base for the mobilization and distribution of economic resources, but it also served as an integrative force for social organization and the classification of all social, tribal and ethnic groups.[106]

Ideally, all castes, Brahman and Sudra alike, were required to furnish support for the king, to ensure his ritual purity while he provided order and, through the sacrifice, regenerated the cosmic power of the kingdom.[107] However, the instability inherent within a dispersed and segmentary society meant that, while kingship supplied order, the multiplicity of social units simultaneously resisted the imposition of centralized and universalized creeds.[108]

The construction of caste in Tamil Nadu was further complicated by the vertical division of the social order into the right hand (*valangai*) and left hand (*idangai*), consistent with the Tamil envisionment of a human society homologized into a bifurcated human body possessing a single head (Brahman) and clearly delineated right and left functions.[109] The right hand was associated with primary production and related vocations, whereas the left consisted of occupational groupings of artisans and traders.[110] This division originated with the social crisis of the twelfth century which resulted from the separation of the Saiva–Vaishnava traditions, and these structures were accepted as a paradigm for providing ritual ranking below the level of Brahman/Vellalar for emerging craft and lower agricultural groups.[111] Tamil society was thus segmented into a tripartite caste structure of Brahmans, Vellalars and right/left castes.[112]

These divisions are also reflected in worship patterns. In her study of left- and right-handed castes in Konku, Brenda Beck noted that:

1. Whereas right-handed castes venerated deities who were territorial in character, left-handed devotees worshipped the universal gods of the pantheon, and placed great emphasis on scholarship and scriptural knowledge.[113]

2. Whereas right-handed sectarian loyalties were confined to the Konku region, left-handed castes promoted and sustained a network of

allegiances (including pilgrimage destinations) throughout the entire Tamil country.

3. The ceremonial concerns displayed by right- and left-handed castes tend to correlate to the ritual division of the year into dark and bright halves.[114]

For unexplained reasons the *valangai/idangai* divisions had largely disappeared within South India by the mid-twentieth century and remained only in certain locations.[115]

Dumont has famously argued that caste was the dominant feature of Hindu society and its hierarchies are ineluctably determined by the rigid application of a purity–pollution paradigm shaped and legitimized by a series of unyielding religious precepts. Thus, the ritually pure caste is ensconced at the apex of society, whereas those most polluted form the base, while the remaining castes are horizontally ranked in accordance with their relative calibrated levels of purity.[116] However, Dumont's approach is rejected by most contemporary scholars who argue that the dynamics of inter-caste relations were additionally influenced by a range of factors, most commonly the political and economic power of the dominant caste, in combination with the allocation of ritual roles and functions.[117] Moreover, caste relations were further influenced by the demands of a peasant society which engendered complex lines of economic, political and ritual cooperation, and interdependence between various communities.[118]

Thus, while Brahmans theoretically provided a scriptural reference point for the construction of caste hierarchies[119] and a paradigm for the maintenance of an ideal society,[120] in reality the position of all castes and their relations to one another were highly contingent on the nature of their association with the dominant caste in any locality or territory; that is, the major landholders who by virtue of their political and economic leverage enjoyed a high ritual status.[121] The dominant caste in the Tamil kingdoms was that of the Vellalars, "the highest ranking Sudras in a caste system in which there are neither Ksatriyas nor Vaisyas". Most scholars now consider that the Vellalars both embodied and transmitted high Tamil culture as well as adapting Sanskrit structures and philosophies to the Tamil region. Traditionally, they also worked in cooperation with Brahmans and Brahman institutions.[122]

However, this is not to totally deny the influence of Dumont's purity–pollution paradigm. Ritual considerations continued to modify caste organization, so that although a given caste's final standing was influenced by its localized economic and political reliance upon the dominant caste, it could not be wholly defined in terms of that dependency.[123] Ideally, each caste had its own attributive occupation, which when assembled cumulatively comprised a vocational hierarchy that echoed, albeit in a more complicated format, the theoretical concatenation of the *varna* system.[124] Indeed, an ideal agrarian settlement was believed to require a full array of vocational specialists, representatives of "the eighteen castes".[125] Taking into account the economic and political power wielded by the dominant caste, and locally by each *jati*'s relationship with that caste, in generalist terms the overall hierarchical grading of *jati* and caste depends upon the principle of purity–pollution. Vocational impurity is essentially a physiological state and is ascribed according to a caste's relative proximity to death, as well as the management and curtailment of those substances designated as polluting.[126] In sum, a specified division of labour entails that certain groups are designated to perform the tasks necessary for removal of impurity, so that the ritually pure are left free to fulfil those functions which are necessary for the health of society as a whole.[127] Thus, Brahmans, who occupy a range of "clean" positions, and who observe an extensive array of prohibitions and rituals ensuring that they retain freedom from pollution, remain the "purest" and "highest" caste, whereas *Adi Dravida* castes undertake the "unclean" and ritually polluting occupations and are regarded as the "lowest" castes within South Indian society.[128] While the relative ranking of a caste at either end of the spectrum is undisputed, the placement of other castes within a strict and graduated hierarchy is frequently problematic and elicits numerous disputes over issues involving precedence and relative status within society.

Adi Dravida castes, "the sudra of the sudra",[129] are defined as such because their *toril* ("action" or "duty") closely associates them with the deaths of humans and cows, and they bear the accumulated and indelible pollution (*tittu*) of their vocations.[130] *Adi Dravida* castes consist of *Paraiyars* (drum players, often connected with funerary or exorcism rites), *Pallars* (field labourers), and *Chakkilliyars* (leather workers),[131] and cumulatively comprise eighteen per cent of the Tamil population.[132] In traditional society, *Adi Dravidas* live in their own quarters outside the set boundaries of established communities, and other castes refuse to engage in a range of transactions with them, including the acceptance of food and water, or the exchange of marriage partners.[133] However, while *Adi Dravidas* may be viewed as agents of social disorder, they also play a key role in many village festivals and acts of worship.[134] Many of the self-protective rights which *Adi Dravidas* once possessed were lost as a consequence of land reforms introduced under British colonialism.[135]

In traditional society, caste was an organizational principle, a unit which codified kinship relations and established some protocols of social behaviour, including marriage and intercaste dining. But castes were only one unit within a wider economic and political world, and were by no means the sole form of social identity.[136] Moreover, caste relations were and remain neither fixed nor static, and may over time demonstrate considerable fluidity. Castes have shown a capacity to redefine themselves in terms of function and hierarchical grading. The processes of adjustment may involve splitting, uniting with others of similar ritual status or generic occupational grouping, or changing the caste name and/or nomenclature.[137]

Temples and Kingship in the Tamil Country

The modern understanding of the Hindu temple evolved throughout the period of the great dynasties. The earliest accounts of the art of Hindu temple construction date from the fourth century CE and are contemporaneous with ancient records of *vastu*, the Hindu science of building.[138] From the sixth century onwards in South India the centrality of temple worship to Hindu spirituality was emphasized by the emergence of *bhakti* devotion (see subsequent section), especially the outpourings of the groups of saints known as *Alvars* and *Nayanars*. The *bhakti* tradition identified the temple as a sacred miniature universe and emphasized the great merit which accrued from temple worship.[139]

The *bhakti* stress upon temple worship coincided with other concurrent changes within Tamil society. The most notable was the establishment of *varna* as an organizational principle, and the concomitant identification of the king as a *Ksatriya* (warrior). The ritual significance of the concomitant Brahmana–*Ksatriya* alliance axiomatically located the remainder of society at lower levels. Various groups were subsequently ritually ranked around the temple, which thus served as an institutional base for social integration.[140]

The temple fulfilled a number of roles. Essentially the temple was viewed as a royal palace for the deity ensconsed within, "a paradigmatic sovereign who received respect from a community of devotees and returned resources to temple servants, donors and worshippers".[141] Clothey has observed that the construction of a temple and the investiture of a deity is homologous to the coronation of a king and the delineation of his kingdom.[142] The significance of the deity as sovereign ruler and moral and iconographic centre of the South Indian temple is constantly ritually emphasized. The Tamil word *kovil* means both temple and palace and is derived from the root words *ko* (king/emperor) and *illam* (home).[143] Temple servants are referred to as *paricanankal* (or courtiers of the king), and most of the ritual paraphernalia displayed or worn by temple deities, especially when they undertake temple processions, is identical to that of the royal insignia of human kings. Much of the language addressed to the deity is that of bonded servitude (*atimai*); the deity is constantly referred to by terms (*iriavan, svami, perumal*) that are indicative of universal lordship or sovereignty.[144] The deity as divine sovereign and thus guardian of his devotees and upholder of the universe was paralleled by the idea of the ruler as regal upholder of dharma and protector and controller of the domain.[145]

The temple also served as a recognized arena in which a community of co-sharers was formed within the sight of a particular god.[146] By furnishing a set of symbols which gave expression to concepts concerning authority, hierarchy, reciprocity as well as modes of worship, the temple provided a public forum in which these relations and concepts were articulated and negotiated.[147] A parallel function was the temple's role as a node for the mobilization and redistribution of economic resources within the realm.[148]

The role of the temple as a key integrative force endures within contemporary Hindu society. As well as providing a focus for the religious life of communities, temples play a pivotal role in the intellectual and cultural life of devotees. They not only support and foster artistic activities but are also foremost among Hindu charitable institutions, providing mass feedings and other forms of material succour.[149]

Throughout the period of the dynasties, principles of temple construction were regularized and consolidated within specialist texts, bodies of knowledge known as the *Agamas*. These laid down detailed instructions on the architectural design of temples, provided invaluable astronomical and astrological information, and specified the requisite forms and attributes of icons.[150] Sculpting techniques were regulated by comprehensive canons known as the *silapasastra*, while the actual building was executed in accordance with construction manuals (*vastusastra*).[151]

The *Agamas* developed from the seventh century CE onwards, and reached their definitive form throughout the Vijayanagara era. The *Agamas* reflected the transition from Vedic to *Puranic* Hinduism, and expanded to incorporate the voluminous potentialities supplied by the extensive mythology, including the many and varied exploits of particular deities throughout their cosmic careers,[152] as well as the mythology of regionalized, local and folk traditions.[153] The *Agamas* and *Sastras* were regarded as authoritative and prescribed the explicit form and layout of temples as well as the sanctioned representation of deities. These texts allowed no latitude for individual interpretation;[154] indeed the icon was intended to constitute a validated "written image"; a cultural vocabulary faithfully reproduced in stone.[155]

The incremental innovations in temple construction were reflected in new forms of art, iconography and architecture.[156] Under the Pallavas the transition was made from cut rock to granite construction, a modification initiated in the early eighth century CE by King Rajasimha.[157] The Cholas introduced such characteristics as the multifaceted column (*goparum*) with the projecting square capital.[158] These embellishments, often inspired by the poetic imagery of the *bhakti* hymns,[159] invested temples with "a new sense of imposing power".[160] The Vijayanagara dynasty embraced the ideal of monumentalism in construction, thus foregrounding the ascendant role played by the temple in urban life and the new economy. Temples were expanded to accommodate multiple loci of worship, so that the sanctum sanctorum would often be encircled by a series of outer shrines. The major innovation introduced under Vijayanagara patronage was the huge gateways (*gopuras*) capped on the summit by an emblematic "barrel vaulted" roof form.[161] The style perfected under the Vjiyanagara dynasty remains largely unchanged in modern temple construction.[162]

The temple is regarded as a sacred venue which links heaven and earth, a liminal point of crossing (*tirtha*, or river ford), in which the boundaries between devotee and deity are both permeable and navigable.[163] The temple is visualized as a microcosm of the universe, and is constructed around the principle of the *vastu purusa mandala*. A complex geometric design (*mandala*) is prepared which represents the various anatomical features of the original cosmic man (*Purusa*) from whose body the entire universe was constructed.[164] As Arjun Appadurai explains:

> In the symbol of temple architecture, the various parts of the temple are
> considered parts of the body, not simply the human body, but the divine
> body as well. This physiological analogy, given the biophysical theories of
> Hinduism, is simultaneously a cosmological analogy, so that the temple
> is a cosmic body, that is, the universe conceived of as a body.[165]

The sanctum sanctorum of the temple, a small sanctuary known as the
"womb chamber" (*garbhagriha*) and representing the head, is regarded as
the "kernel and essence" of the temple.[166]

We should note in passing that the temple embodies the Hindu principle
of inner direction: that is the logic of progression from the outer world
of flux, of shapes and forms, to the still transcendence of the centre. The
devotee leaves the outer world and moves through a series of enclosures
which become increasingly laden with sacred energy as he/she approaches
the sanctum sanctorum.[167] Consistent with this movement is the journey
from the light and glare of the open world into the relative darkness and
confined space in which the Truth, like buried treasure, is to be sought.[168]
This principle is also reflected in the fact that while the sanctum sanctorum
radiates energy to all parts of the temple, steps must be taken to protect
the inner truth from negative forces, the impurities of the outer world.
The temple's eight directions are thus protected by external cosmic regents
(*lokapalas*), while lesser or "guardian" deities are installed at the outer
entrances of the temple.[169]

As we have observed, *Agamic* temples are constituted according to
an established corpus of detailed instructions. They are built by specialist
temple architects (*sthapatis*) and are dedicated according to a congery
of elaborate and precise rituals designed to invoke and sustain the
manifestation of the Divine. We have also noted that the rituals associated
with temple construction parallel those of the coronation of a king and
the demarcation of his territory. Ritual acts include groundbreaking
(*pratisha*), installation of the images of the deities, and consecration of the
sacred vessel placed above the sanctum sanctorum shrine (*kumbabishekam*),
conducted over forty days.[170] Following the establishment of the breath of
life (*prana*) within the image, the final part of the installation is the ritualistic
opening of the eyes of the deity. Hinduism places great emphasis upon
the eyes within worship; it is through the eyes that contact between deity
and devotee is exchanged.[171] The temples are subsequently maintained in
conformity with *Agamic* rituals and are conducted by specialists, usually

of Brahman caste, known as *kurukkals* in Saivite temples and *pattars* in Vaishnavite temples. Recognized temple rituals include a series of daily *pujas*, accompanied by the chanting of mantras, the singing of devotional hymns, and the playing of traditional instruments known as *nadaswaram* (shaped rather like a clarinet) and *meelam* (a form of drum). All offerings to deities within the temple are vegetarian.[172]

It should be emphasized that the icon installed within the temple is more than a sculptural stone image; it is nothing less than an emanation of divine power whose central role is to make accessible the world of truth.[173] The icon enables the devotee to envisage the divine in a specific form (*sanguna*); the contemplation of the formless (*nirguna*) is available only to those of advanced spirituality and is thus beyond most worshippers.[174] Indeed, the common Sanskrit word for image is *murthi*, which variously translates as "an embodiment, incarnation"; a "form, body, figure" and "anything which has definite shape and limits".[175] A *murthi* is thus significantly more than a mere portrayal of a deity; it is the divine taking form, a localized realization of the universal, a sentient representation of the formless.[176] The many and seemingly limitless *murthis* of the gods/goddesses reveal both the "multiplicity and oneness of the divine, and they display the tensions and seeming contradictions that are resolved in a single mythic image".[177] The multiple arms and emblems displayed are a feature of many *murthis* and, together with the many poses adopted, indicate the array of powers and attributes which emanate from the particular deity, and which may be worshipped in their own right as a means to realization of the truth embodied within that *murthi*.[178]

Similarly, the sovereignty of the deity obtains at many levels. At base, the *murthi* of the deity is received as more than a mere stone image; in many respects it is envisaged as a person and is, in both philosophical and popular traditions, treated as a fully corporeal, sentient, vital, supra-intelligent and responsive person. Daily rituals will include a series of very intimate acts, including waking, bathing and dressing the deity, offering the deity food, and putting it to sleep at night. At all times the deity will be accorded the deepest veneration. He/she will be woken with soft songs, and throughout the day certain melodies will be offered. The deity will be initially bathed in warm water, and will be dressed and garlanded consistent with season. In addition, gifts will be offered to the deity, who will be mentioned by name.[179] But at a more complex level the temple deity is postulated as ruler of a domain which is ultimately universal. On this plane the theory of iconicity or embodiment presents a dynamic conception of a divinity which is inseparable from the deity portrayed; that is the *murthi* as an emanation, a *sakti* of the god, and thus a "point at which the worshipper perceives the contiguity in the identity of empirical and divine realms".[180] In this sense, throughout the temple ritual the *murthi* and the gods are undifferentiated, and the *murthi* becomes a local point of ever-expanding reality in redefining the universe of which it is the grounded cosmic centre.[181]

It is in this context that the full significance of gifts to the deity — whether of worship, food, service or other offerings — must be understood. Any gift to the deity places the donor (*upakayar*) in a personal and redistributional relationship with the god. The devotee expects a response, and the resultant returns or temple honours (*mariayatai*) are shared with others, namely the temple staff and fellow worshippers. The receipt of temple honours signifies that the devotee has partaken of the paradigmatic royalty of the deity, and has thus, in ultimate terms, shared in the universal redistributive divinity of the polity ruled by the god.[182]

Non *Agamic* and Popular Temples

Non-*Agamic* temples range from well-managed village or urban temples which may incorporate worship of universal *Agamic*/Sanskritic deities and elements of *Agamic* scriptural traditions and *Puranic* mythology through to rudimentary temples, often little more than sheds, devoted to the worship of localized village/tutelary gods or at the most basic level the propitiation and manipulation of spirits. These temples lack scriptural authority for determining iconic representation, and are not constructed or dedicated according to the detailed and precise *Agamic* rites and injunctions.[183] The *murthis* installed are generally made of cement and clay (as opposed to black granite in *Agamic* temples). Worship of deities may not be conducted in accordance with *Agamic* precepts, and is performed by *pantarams* (non-Brahman priests) and *pujaris* (often shaman-diviners). At the village level, worship may be basic and without the complex elaboration of *Agamic* rituals (for example, frequently excluding both *mantras* and devotional hymns, which are integral to *Agamic* worship). In many small shrines, rituals of worship are performed only occasionally, sometimes daily or at even less-frequent intervals. Animal sacrifice may form a part of festival celebrations or be included in prescribed rituals; this differs from *Agamic* Hinduism, which permits only vegetarian options.[184]

The Tamil *Bhakti* Movement

The *bhakti* movement of the Tamil country centred upon the experiences of saints who lived over a three-hundred-year period, beginning in the pre-Pallava era and extending throughout the Pallava dynasty.[185] Although there were up to nine hundred of these people, most of whom resided on the plains of the Kaveri Basin (and who referred to themselves as slaves (*adiyar* or *tondar*) of the Lord,[186] the stories of only seventy-five of this number (sixty-three Saivites [*Nayanars* or "leaders"], and twelve Vaishnavites [*Alvars*, or "those who delve deeply"/"those who are absorbed in the Divine"]) are now commemorated.[187] The *Nayanars* were drawn from varied backgrounds; while many were Brahmans, others were of more modest origins and included both women and Dalits.[188] Four Tamil saints — Appar, Sambandar, Sundarar and Manickavasagar, the "four revered ones" — are regarded as pre-eminent in the Tamil *bhakti* tradition[189] and are often depicted iconically within *Agamic* temples. In the mid twelfth century the stories of the Tamil saints were gathered within a compendium known as the *Periya Purana*.[190] Within Saivism the complete canon, comprising twelve volumes, is known as the *Tirumai*, while the most popular and often sung portion, consisting of seven volumes, is referred to as the *Tevaram*.[191]

Bhakti represented the melding of several distinct influences. Most scholars have highlighted the germinal concepts instilled by the *Bhagavad Gita*, which formalized and inculcated the notion of equality before the Divine, and replaced the path of unyielding asceticism with that of profound devotion, a form of spirituality which bypassed the Brahmanic strictures of ritual, sex and caste to assert the individual's direct experience of the deity.[192] But other major influences included the humanism which had pervaded the Tamil *Sangam* tradition; the individual character of anthropocentric religion; the infusion of mythical narratives; the emotional and sensual character of popular Tamil religion, in particular the ecstatic union with various deities which had long existed within the indigenous South Indian folk religion (especially within the dances of possession/inspiration which had linked worshipper to deity); and finally the Brahmanic/Sanskritic concept of a transcendent and absolute Godhead.[193]

Bhakti spirituality appeared to reflect the needs of the emergent Tamil social order, most notably a dominant peasant caste whose religion was structured around the devotional traditions of the agrarian society of the Coromandel Plain.[194] While *bhakti* represented a rejection of the ritual implications of caste,[195] it was accepted by the Brahmans as a powerful ideological counter to the Sramic religions of Jainism and Buddhism.[196] *Bhakti* emphasized the central role of the temple in devotional religion but also led to the emergence of new forms of religious authority, and in particular the establishment of monastic organizations (*mathas*) among Tamil Saivite Hindus.[197]

The main impact of *bhakti* was to instil within Tamil Hinduism a religious form which provided a means of affirming the value and indeed the primacy of human devotional experience and the individual relationship to the deity.[198] *Bhakti* was thus a path of emotional and sensual worship which forged an intimate personal connection with the Transcendent (often in his/her local embodiment), the impact of which was to remould the psycho-spiritual constitution of the devotee and cast him/her into a condition of "self-transformative flux" which would ultimately lead to awareness of, surrender to, and identification with the deity.[199] Moreover, the way of *bhakti* was open to all; it was not dependent upon birth, caste or asceticism, and was judged by its practitioners as superior to the path of contemplative knowledge (*jnana*) and action.[200]

Upon initial examination it seems difficult, if not impossible, to correlate the practices of *bhakti* with its dual identification with the human and present world as well as the ultimacy of Divine Reality with the ascetic traditions of yoga, involving meditation and contemplation and intrinsically suspicious "of all human cognitions and perceptions ... of all that normally constitutes the psycho-physical entity we think of as a human person".[201] Unlike yoga, the *bhakti* worldview is tragic in the sense that at the moment of revelation the ecstatic experience of the deity produced by pure devotion is both transitory and partial; the fullness of transcendence can never be completely apprehended by human reality. Moreover, our torments must be recognized as the deity's *lila* (Tamil: *vilaiyadal*); that is, the god's mode of relating to the diverse parts of his nature and to the world generally.[202] Yet, both *bhakti* and yoga encompass common goals. Both attempt to reorient consciousness inwards to escape the domination and falseness of the ephemeral forms of the external world, and to achieve experiential knowledge of the permanent core of existence, that which is recognized as Transcendence.[203] A willingness to embrace transformation is implicit within all forms of *bhakti*; the *sadhaka* (aspirant) seeks to sacrifice the self, to sever the bonds of attachment and achieve "a return to primordial essence", thus attaining unity with the universal.[204] The apprehension of mortality and the bestowal of the grace of the Divine through participation in ecstatic rituals which allow the devotee to "lose oneself" in ecstasy, to dissolve one's physical and temporal boundaries to gain a glimpse, however evanescent, of the Eternal, is to use the senses to plumb the Divine, and to gain knowledge, the "Truth beyond reason", which leads toward *moksha* (liberation).[205] Indeed, tantric traditions enjoin their adherents to see "ritual action as being more important than philosophical speculation, and that this ritual action of the internalization of the text, the internalization of tradition and the forming of the self in text specific ways".[206] It is in this sense that *bhakti* may be identified with yoga; it is a discipline which quests for and achieves the same outcomes as those sought through meditation and contemplation.[207]

But *bhakti* also reflects the Tamil insistence on the validity of the soul. Thus, while the soul may be immersed within the Divine and partakes of the Universal, so that in a profound sense it is one with the Divine, yet it continues to retain its authenticity and individual distinctiveness.[208]

Bhakti Spirituality, the *Nayanars* and Transgressive Sacrality

Many scholars have commented on the anti-authoritarianism and antinomianism which appears to permeate much of Tamil Hinduism, both within popular (that is, non-*Agamic*) Hinduism but also, perhaps more surprisingly, within the more extreme behaviour of some of the *Nayanar* saints.

The Tamil *Nayanars* were distinguished by their love (*anpu*) of Siva, whom they transformed from a remote supreme godhead into an accessible deity, a local, almost human, figure.[209] The path of *bhakti* as enunciated by the *Nayanars* is that of full and impassioned engagement with Siva. Though the duality of Siva as both transcendent and immanent pervades their philosophy, many of the most celebrated songs speak of their deity as a familiar and indeed intimate figure — father, brother, friend, child or even lover.[210] The quality which characterizes their devotion is their obsessive single-mindedness, their divine "drunkenness".[211] The *Nayanars* reflect the notion that the nature of divinity is unconfined and transcends all moral categories, that Siva infuses the world with a wild love which ranges beyond the normative societal structures of order and control.[212] Siva's dharma consists of both mild (*manta*) and fierce (*tivira*) aspects. In terms of *bhakti*, Siva's mildness finds expression in such forms as temple service (*cariya*) and ritual service (*kriya*), whereas his fierceness translates into the fanatical and unwavering *anpu* of the *Nayanars*, whose actions frequently violate and transgress societal norms.[213]

At its more extreme, the *bhakti* movement of the *Nayanars* contains violent and impure elements which would appear to contravene many of the fundamental precepts of normative *Agamic* and philosophical Hinduism. Some of the histories of the *Nayanars*, for example, depict expressions of Siva's *anpu* involving the infliction of crude brutalities upon self and others, including close kin.[214] These forms of *bhakti* not only outrage societal values but seem to violate the most sacred ethical codes and belief systems upon which received *Agamic* Hinduism is constructed. Moreover, the actions of the *Nayanars* challenge the understood conventions of spiritual unfoldment; that is, their extremism appears to circumvent the lifetimes of stringently observed and mentored disciplines which are regarded as necessary to guide the committed *sadhaka* on the clearly graduated and incremental pathway to *moksha*. Moreover, the "shocking excesses" of some of the *Nayanars* are often cited as among the most profound and highest manifestations of the Saiva *bhakti* tradition and the subject of "queasy veneration" within Saiva Siddhanta.[215] According to Tamil scholar M.V. Aruncalan, it is Siva himself who must be held responsible for the *Nayanar's* crazed devotion; Siva "intoxicates" his devotees to the point where they no longer retain any shred of self-control. Thus, what is perceived as the deranged and often beserk actions of a group of criminals and lunatics must be understood as behaviour inspired by the Divine; an excess of love, a devotional form of inebriation intentionally created by Siva himself.[216]

To explain, inter alia, the glaring anomalies between the sometimes outré, often bizarre, behaviour of the *Nayanar* saints, adherents of "inferior" *bhakti* and criminal gods and demon devotees on the one hand, and received philosophical doctrines on the other, Sunthar Visuvalingam has posited a doctrine of "transgressive sacrality"; that is, one which violates the established conventions and hierarchies but somehow seems to retain its location, however unlikely, within the fabric of orthodox Hinduism. He maintains that a study of spiritual praxis reveals sets of "complex relations between the mutually interfering categories of pure and impure, the sacred and profane, orthodoxy and heterodoxy, sacrifice and *bhakti*, external ritual and internal yoga, Vedism and Saivism, Brahmanical law and tantric aggression".[217] He argues that trangressive sacrality "acquires a sacred dimension only when it is subordinated to a suprahuman aim which explicitly and through its inscription in a symbolic context, which by paradoxically juxtaposing and especially infusing them with the values of interdictory sacred, charges even the crudest profanities with transcendent significance".[218]

The concept of transgressive sacrality among the *Nayanars* may therefore be summed up as follows. Transgressive sacrality, a form of divine madness, is at once both overarching and unfathomable. Its underlying momentum is generated by a love (*anpu*) controlled by God's actions upon the soul, and is therefore both beyond and unanswerable to normal human moral categories. The ferocious *bhakti* of the more extreme *Nayanars* propels devotees from the periphery, the world of a multitude of forms maintained by a network of binary oppositions, into the undifferentiated centre of the Absolute within which all polarities dissolve. In other words, transgressive *bhakti* Hinduism overcomes orthodox resistance to its zealous extremism by collapsing the deceptively fluid dialectical opposition of pure and impure within the context of an all-encompassing transcendence which both reveals and pronounces its devotional actions as sacred.

Transgressive Sacrality and Popular Hinduism

As with *Nayanars* who breach societal mores, so with some elements of Tamil popular Hinduism. This contains a veritable rogues' gallery of "criminal" gods and demon devotees who deliberately ignore or flout the sacred moral order and prescribed maxims by which *Agamic*/high gods and the devout *sadhaka* (seeker) are guided.[219] The habitual and serious infractions perpetrated by these gods/demons defy established societal philosophical and dietary structures, and threaten to subvert received cosmologies. The exploits of criminal gods and demon devotees are the subject of both oral and written traditions, and are well known among the communities which offer worship to these figures.[220]

At the lowest level, the spirits of the premature dead, that is, those who have died prior to reaching householder status, may assume a malevolent character and create disruption and misfortune. In his study of *virabhadras* ("the children of Siva", from *Virabhadra*, a terrible deity born of Siva's rage), within Andhra Pradesh, David Knipe demonstrates how the spirits of those who have suffered untimely death, usually in childhood, and who are believed to be denied any meaningful place within the Brahmanic-controlled universe of *samsara*, "return" to intrude upon and subvert familial and societal structures.[221]

Tamil Hinduism has devised measures which circumscribe, control and give direction to the antinomianism and disruption created by criminal gods, demon devotees and potentially malignant spirits, and which neutralize threats to cosmic order. Thus, *virabhadras* are restrained through a system of ritualized remembrance and reincorporation in which their wishes are divined and respected and each spirit is allocated an honoured position within continuing family structures and patterns of worship.[222]

As with *virabhadras*, so with criminal gods and lesser godlings. Criminal gods and demons are conquered and subjugated by a theology of *bhakti* which transforms them into submissive devotees of *Puranic* or *Agamic* deities. This often involves their slaying or sacrificial death, and their subsequent incarnation in the sphere of the great gods.[223] Alternatively, or additionally, the powers of lesser entities are localized and their passions are assuaged by appropriate supplications and meat offerings. In all cases they are subject to the commands of, and are restrained by, a higher deity.[224] Indeed, their lowly place in the divine hierarchy may be gauged from their spatial location within the shrine, their lack of precedence in worship, and the nature of offerings made to them.[225] Thus, violent carnivores reside at the border of the shrine, a liminal position infused with danger, ambivalence and uncertainty. These servants conduct essential functions on behalf of the god of the shrine; they face the dangers of the world beyond the shrine, and undertake all necessary violent and polluting acts to protect the god/goddess from contamination, and thus ensure that his/her role as a great and pure deity is not compromised.[226]

The actual subordination of the lesser deity and its retention on the border, its "complete subservience and ontological dependence" upon the deity, reflect the principles of encompassment and hierarchy which obtain within Tamil Hinduism.[227] The inner subsumption of gross outer forms (which also applies between the inner subtle body and the gross outer body which comprise two of the five sheaths which enclose the soul) provides a logic of directional movement; it is the inner, higher and less differentiated which encloses the outer, lower and more differentiated and, having established a hierarchy of forms, reverts to the (controlling) centre. It is thus the subjugated gatekeepers who occupy the outer shrines on the border, and the concentrated power of the higher deity which is located at the heart of the shrine. However, it should be noted that the deity's "residue" or "essence", as it were, may be located within the gross or lower forms, so that the worship of the outer offers the prospect of successive progression to the ultimate encounter with the inner.[228]

But the profoundly democratic principles of *bhakti* devotion operate at other levels as well, and elevate the "transgressive" devotee from his outcast liminal status and ultimately render his "impure" offerings to equal footing with those who perform "higher" forms of devotion. In his studies of the cult of the goddess Draupadi, Alf Hiltebeital has shown how wayward forms of "inferior *bhakti*" directed towards "criminal" or "lesser godlings" and involving alcohol, narcotics and "polluted" forms of possession may be neutralized and subsequently received as expressions of "higher *bhakti*".[229] Thus it follows that *any* devotee who in good faith offers *any* form of sincere devotion to *any* deity will be subject to the ineluctable logic of inner direction, of encompassment and hierarchy noted in the previous paragraphs, and which is intrinsic to Tamil Hindu *bhakti* philosophies.

Saiva Siddhanta

From about the eighth century onwards, Tamil traditions were the subject of intense philosophical speculation. Throughout the Chola period the *brahmadeyas* were responsible for much of this theological inquiry. One major outcome of this conjecture was that henceforth all the great Vedic/ Tamil gods were to be firmly enmeshed in esoteric philosophical schools, and that as a consequence their symbols were dispossessed of their literal meanings and invested with more profound significance (thus, for example, Murugan's lance was no longer regarded as a simple weapon but was rather viewed as a symbol of wisdom and discrimination).[230] While this theorizing resulted in the founding of several distinct schools of religious belief, the most influential and enduring within the Tamil country was the comprehensive body of doctrine known as Saiva Siddhanta. Saiva Siddhanta represented a determination among Tamil philosophers to develop Saivism into a coherent and resilient philosophical tradition.[231] The rise of Saiva Siddhanta accompanied the surge of Saivism which was contemporaneous with Chola rule.[232]

Professor R. Champakalakshmi has demonstrated that Saiva Siddhanta philosophy evolved in three distinct stages, beginning with the large body of hymns (the *Tevaram*) composed by the *Nayanar* saints between the sixth and ninth centuries CE; this was followed by the initiation of the institution of formalized recital (*potikam* singing) of these hymns in ritual worship, which were performed by specialist musicians known as *otuvars* and which from the late ninth century were conducted under royal patronage; and finally the development of *mathas* (monasteries) which played a vital role in the moulding and final redaction of the Saiva Siddhanta canon.[233]

The main body of Saiva Siddhanta was developed between the eighth and tenth centuries CE. Both the Chola and Vijayanagara rulers were anxious to effect a reconciliation between the *Agamas*, which had no standing in orthodox religious literature, and Vedic teachings.[234] The new philosophy incorporated a range of formative influences, including certain Sanskrit texts, the Saiva *Agamas*, and elements of the teachings of the *Siddhas* (non-conformist mendicants who were believed to possess yogic powers), as well as Vedic teachings.[235] The core texts of Saiva Siddhanta were based upon the *Puranas* and stressed the centrality of temple worship.[236] These diverse materials were blended into a cohesive body of philosophical doctrine by the great sage Tirumular, averred to be the original *Siddha* and in hagiographical literature portrayed as a contemporary of the fabled *rishi* Agastya.[237] Tirumular recited the *Tirumantaram*, the great and definitive canonical text which remains the lodestar of all Saiva Siddhantans (that is, those who practice the philosophy of Saiva Siddhanta). Indeed, Tirumular's aphorism *Anbe Sivam* ("God is Love") is considered to encapsulate the absolute essence of the entire philosophical structure of Saiva Siddhanta.[238] Siddhantans regard the *Saiva Agamas* as the consummate explication of the Vedas, and the school of Saiva Siddhanta as the ultimate efflorescence of the Vedic religion.[239]

The Saiva Siddhanta canon extends well beyond the *Tirumantaram* to include the *Saiva Agamas*, the twelve *Tirumurais* (the collected outpourings of the *Nayanar* saints) and the *Tiruttontar Purana*, more commonly known as *Periya Purunam*. These works incorporate the hymns and devotional experiences of the *bhakti* saints, but also anticipate philosophical issues, such as the nature of the soul, sainthood and human destiny, which were to become the subject of further inquiry.[240] While the *Agamas* were largely of Brahman origin, other devotional literature was compiled by a wide array of authors drawn from a range of social and caste backgrounds. Most of the philosophical works of the Saiva Siddhanta school were written in Tamil, and many of those who contributed to the development of the major doctrines of Tamil Saivism succeeded in combining Brahmanic and Sanskritic patterns of thought with non-Brahmanic and popular Tamil belief structures.[241] The doctrines of Saiva Siddhanta were later systematized by Meykander (c.1250) in his Tamil work *Sivajnanabodham*, and subsequently elaborated by his disciple Sivacaraya,[242] regarded by many Tamil commentators as the "true founder of Saiva Siddhanta".[243]

We have already noted, in passing, the part played by *mathas* in the overall development of final Saiva Siddhanta doctrine. Founded throughout the period of *bhakti* saints, these were consolidated institutionally between the eleventh and thirteenth centuries CE. From the twelfth century onwards, there was a substantial increase in the number of Tamil Saiva *mathas* headed by non-Brahman preceptors who involved themselves in the promotion of Saiva Siddhanta. Many of these were formed by members of the Vellalar caste, who, reacting against perceived Brahman exclusivism, played a key role in the overall development of Saiva Siddhanta doctrine. Vellalar run *mathas* were generally more liberal than those of other traditions, and included women, members of other Sudra castes, and tribal participants in religious observances.[244]

Saiva Siddhanta Philosophy: An Overview

Saiva Siddhanta posits three categories of existence; namely, *Pati* (or the Godhead), *pacu* (the soul), and *paca* (the fetters or bondages of ignorance). All of these entities are considered real and eternally enduring. It may be thus assumed that Saiva Siddhanta comprises a system of pluralistic realism; however, this would be to misunderstand the relationship of *Pati* to the other two qualities. The "realness" of *pacu* and *paca* are qualified by their dependence upon *Pati*, the supreme Reality, which dominates and saturates the other two entities. As Swami Siva Adikalaar et al., explain,

> *Pati, Pacu, Paca* — roughly God, the Self and the world … are logically distinct though distinction is not necessarily difference. It is this inherent resistance to monism that gives the system the appearance of pluralism, though this label is misleading — Saiva Siddhanta admits not factual separateness but only cognizable difference between things 'separated' as connoted by the three terms. God is by definition [an] infinite or unlimited being, just as the other ultimates are by definition again, finite and independent beings.[245]

Moreover, the cosmology is invested with a Divine purpose, which is the purification and perfection of souls, so that they obtain knowledge of real and perpetual bliss within the realization of the Godhead.[246]

Pati: As mentioned, *Pati* is the paramount and controlling feature of Saiva Siddhanta cosmology. *Pati* is within and beyond all categories; he is both transcendent and immanent, formed (*sarupa*) and without form (*arupa*), universal in form (*visvarupa*) and unconfined by the universe (*visadhika*).[247] *Pati* is neither sentient (*cit*) or insentient (*acit*).[248] As the Supreme Spirit, *Pati* is the ultimate cause, and is omniscient, omnipotent and omnipresent. He is immersed in both the conditions of infinite life and existence constitutive of the soul's bondage, though in the latter quality he remains unsullied by the imperfections of matter.[249]

The deity's forms and action are manifested through *Sakti* (conscious and eternal energy). Indeed, *Sakti* infuses all aspects of the Divine's nature, and is the intermediary between God's transcendence and immanence. Within the soul, it is *Sakti* which takes the form of Divine Grace (*arul*); the dynamic love and compassion indicative of the *Pati*'s transformative activities upon the soul.[250]

Pati takes many forms and permeates them all; as the *Tirumantiram* makes clear, all gods are functions of the immanent Siva. The explanation for the multitudinous forms of the deity is that while Truth is ultimately One, the paths to the Truth are many and varied. Each form represents a particular aspect of the Supreme Reality, and is thus devised to meet the variegated needs of countless souls.[251] However, each of these forms is perceived as a valid vehicle for worship, as each will ultimately lead the soul to the contemplation of the transcendent Godhead. This "democratic" ethos, consistent with the general thrust of *bhakti*, maintains that any act of worship conducted in good faith will direct the devotee towards the ultimate goal of *moksha*.[252]

Pacu: The term *pacu* refers to the soul in its state of bondage, in its identification with the world.[253] *Pacu* may be translated as "cattle"; as early as the Atharva-Veda, Siva is referred to as *Pasupati*, the Lord of Cattle,[254] and like cattle, the soul in its benightedness is tethered by the rope of *avidya* or spiritual ignorance.[255]

While the soul is intelligent and capable of knowledge, this is restricted and veiled by the impurities (*malas*) to which it is subject.[256] *Pacu* can never stand alone; it is associated either with *paca* or *Pati*. When the soul identifies with matter, it remains sunken in ignorance and concerned with material objects (*a-sat*) and worldly connections. However, when *pacu* is prompted by Divine Grace, it inclines towards *Pati*, and *jiva* (the bound soul) ultimately becomes *mukta* (the liberated soul).[257]

Paca: This refers to the fetters or net that binds or enmeshes the soul.[258] As ordinary rope is made up of three plaited strands, so *paca* comprises three major *malas* (or impurities); namely, *anava* (egoism), *karma* (the consequences of deeds and action), and *maya* (material purpose).[259]

1. *Anava*: Ego consciousness is the most persistent of the *malas*; it is a fetter which envelopes the soul in ignorance and leads it to equate itself with the body, to regard itself as independent and its actions as self-motivated.[260] It causes the soul to identify with the senses and passions, to suffer needlessly from suppressed material wants, to be swayed by superficial and fleeting likes and dislikes, and to express false emotions such as pride, self satisfaction, etc.[261] *Anava* expresses itself differently in each soul, and hence its levels of pervasiveness vary markedly from soul to soul.[262]

2. *Karma*: In this context *karma* encompasses the existential consequences engendered by each of the *pacu*'s actions — that is, those of mind, body and speech.[263] Karma leads the soul through complex patterns of action and reaction, birth and death, and may influence the soul to behave in ways that are detrimental to its welfare.[264]

3. *Maya*: This is the primordial stuff from which all creation is fashioned and which clings to the soul in various ways. It is a lower emanation of power that conceals Siva's grace and envelopes the soul in a world of illusion. From *maya* emerges a hierarchy of thirty-six primal elements, or *tattvas* (states of existence), from which the universe is composed. These states range from the highest forms of knowledge down to the grossest and most dense forms of ignorance. As Flood explains, "The cosmos unfolds in order that souls can experience the results of their actions and ... the *tattva* hierarchy describes that entrapment. Through ritual absorption of the tattvas the soul can become free."[265]

Pati–pacu–paca **and the Destiny of the Soul**: The heart of Saiva Siddhanta philosophy consists of the dynamic interplay between the triangle of

Pati–pacu–paca, and the ultimate destiny of *pacu* in realizing and living within the eternal bliss of *Pati*, which is achieved when the bondages of *paca* are subjugated and dispelled.[266] *Pati* liberates the soul through a process of five activating functions, each of which marks a definitive stage in the *pacu's* unfoldment. These functions are (i) Creation (*aakkal, srishti*), (ii) Preservation/Protection (*sthiti*), (iii) Destruction (*azhitthal, sankaram*), (iv) Concealing grace (*tiropavam*), and (v) Revealing grace (*anugraha; arulal*). These successive functions lead the *pacu* from the inertia and darkness of ignorance through unfolding states of awareness and spiritual illumination to liberation, the ultimate Grace where the *pacu* rests in blissful contemplation of the Divine.[267] The fivefold functions, symbolized in the form taken by Siva and dancing Nataraja, is often referred to as *Pati's* "sport" or "game" (*tiruvilaiyatal* or *lila*). However, despite the ludic connotations of these terms, the *lilas* are neither meaningless, nor do they reflect the caprices or ephemeral whims of the deity. The "games" of the Divine have an ultimate purpose; namely the transformation and release of the *pacu*.[268]

The soul's evolution consists of a progression of repeated births and deaths which culminate in final liberation from bondage. At each birth the soul is furnished with a fresh form or body to provide the array of experiences commensurate with its level of unfoldment. These experiences gradually weaken the dominance of *anava* (ego consciousness), and the mature soul now searches for ways to terminate the cycle of *samsara*, the endless chain of birth, death, and rebirth which immerses it within the impermanence of the phenomenal universe. The mind seeks ways to achieve liberation, and will increasingly turn to spiritual disciplines and worship, including the direction of a guru who, in providing initiation (*diksha*) and the training required, will guide his disciple (*sishya*) towards *moksha* (release).[269]

The soul's maturing cognition of *Pati* is recognized in a fourfold schemata, each level of which characterizes the soul's relationship and engagement with the Divine. These states range from trepidation and hesitation at the most elementary level, to intimate devotional love at the most advanced. The four ways or paths (*margas*) represent a pattern of sequential unfoldment, each *marga* providing a full complement of experience, conditioning and understanding necessary before the *pacu* may progress to the next.[270] These stages are *Chariya* (*Dasa Marga*, the path of service); *Kriya* (*Satputra Marga*, the path of ritualistic worship); *Yoga*

(*Sakha Marga*, the path of comtemplation); *Jnana* (*San Marga*, the path of illumination).[271]

The transformation of souls is the nature of *Pati*, and to abide in the illumination and bliss of the Divine is the soul's destiny. However, the soul's ability to grasp knowledge is developed only when the power of knowing is extended to it; that is, when awakened by the *Pati*.[272] But, in the final analysis, Saiva Siddhanta insists upon the autonomy of the soul. Thus, while *pacu* achieves oneness with *Pati* and is so infused with bliss that it is unaware of the loss of its individuality, it remains a distinct entity, a form which can never become *Pati*. As Zaehner remarks, "just as Siva and Sakti are eternally one and united in substantial love, yet ultimately distinct in that without distinction love is impossible, so is the liberated soul one with and fused in Siva-Sakti, but still distinct in that it knows and loves what it can never altogether become."[273]

Conclusions

The essential contours of modern Tamil Hinduism were shaped throughout the period of the great South Indian dynasties, each of which made their own distinctive contributions to South Indian institutions. These dynasties embraced societies which were characterized by astounding diversity; a heterogeneous population segmented both horizontally and vertically by a medley of ethnicities, regions, occupations, castes and modes of worship, and further complicated by internal movement and migration. These societies were ruled by a ritually incorporative sovereignty, a kingship which reached and controlled the various segments through the establishment of complex reciprocal obligations and supplemented by annual and splendid rituals of cosmic renewal and redistribution.

The Hindu religion which evolved within the dynastic era reflected the profound segmentation of the societies themselves. At the upper level the Ksatriya–Brahman nexus produced great temples and centres of learning. These were replicated by Vellalar and merchant castes, especially as economic changes enhanced the political power of these groups. The history of Tamil Hinduism reads as a continual process of dialogue and redefinition, and in particular the incorporation of "popular" practices and gods, many of whom retained their site-specific characteristics while simultaneously acquiring the title and overarching attributes of one or another of the great *Agamic* deities.

The triumph of Hinduism over the Sramic religions of Jainism and Buddhism created new forms of religious expression, including *bhakti* and Saiva Siddhanta, both of which absorbed significant elements of indigenous folk religions and popular belief structures. *Bhakti* practices became a vehicle for direct cognition of the god, a highly charged and emotional devotion which stressed the validity of the individual experience of the divine and which bypassed the formal ritualism, ceremonialism and disciplines of the orthodox approach to liberation. At its most extreme, *bhakti* countenanced seemingly solipsistic and outwardly bizarre forms which transgressed societal norms and claimed justification in direct experience of the Transcendence. Saiva Siddhanta posits a dynamic relationship between the categories of *Pati–pacu–paca* (God, soul and matter). However, these closely interrelated and overlapping religious forms insist upon the validity and autonomy of the individual soul, and propound a logic of inner movement in which the individual who genuinely and devoutly worships the deity in whatever form he/she perceives him/her, including the outer forms or devolutions of *Pati*/God, will be progressively drawn towards a full realization of Divine Reality. In sum, Tamil philosophies as well as popular belief structures advocate an essential anti-authoritarianism, a "democratic" ethos which recognizes that the inner movement towards Transcendence embraces an infinite range of possibilities and a multitude of forms, and thus that countless paths, often convoluted, even contrary, all in the final analysis lead to the common destination.

Notes

1. Burton Stein, *Peasant, State and Society in Medieval South India* (Delhi: Oxford University Press, 1980), pp. 31–33.
2. R. Champakalakshmi, *Trade, Ideology and Urbanization: South India 300 BC to AD 1300* (New Delhi: Oxford University Press, 1996), p. 93; Burton Stein, *A History of India* (London: Blackwell, 1996), p. 89; Fred W. Clothey, *The Many Faces of Murukan: The History and Meaning of a South Indian God* (The Hague: Mouton, 1978), pp. 15–21.
3. Stein, *A History of India*, pp. 89–90.
4. Nicholas B. Dirks, *Castes of Mind: Colonialism and the Making of Modern India* (Princeton, NJ: Princeton University Press, 2001), pp. 49–52; Vineeta Sinha, *A New God in the Diaspora? Muneeswaran Worship in Contemporary Singapore* (Singapore and Copenhagen: Singapore University Press/NIAS Press, 2005),

p. 28; R. Champakalakshmi, *Religion, Tradition and Ideology; Pre-colonial South India* (New Delhi: Oxford University Press, 2011), p. 9.

5. For a wider description of this process, see Sunthar Visuvalingam, "The Transgressive Sacrality of the *Diksita*: Sacrifice, Criminality and *Bhakti* in the Hindu Tradition", in *Criminal Gods and Demon Devotees: Essays on the Guardians of Popular Hinduism*, edited by Alf Hiltebeital (Albany: State University of New York Press, 1989).

6. See Stein, *Peasant, State and Society*.

7. Ibid., pp. 22–23.

8. Ibid., p. 275.

9. Ibid., p. 23.

10. Gavin Flood, *The Tantric Body: The Secret Tradition of the Hindu Religion* (London and New York: I.B. Taurus, 2006), pp. 76–77.

11. Arjun Appadurai, *Worship and Conflict under Colonial Rule* (Cambridge: Cambridge University Press, 1981), pp. 68–69.

12. Stein, *Peasant, State and Society*, p. 275.

13. Ibid., p. 268.

14. David Dean Shulman, *The King and Clown in South Indian Myth and Poetry* (Princeton, NJ: Princeton University Press, 1985), pp. 18–19.

15. Flood, *The Tantric Body*, p. 43.

16. Declan Quigley, *The Interpretation of Caste* (Oxford: Clarendon, 1993), p. 124; Bernard S. Cohn, *Colonialism and its Forms of Knowledge: The British in India* (Princeton, NJ: Princeton University Press, 1996), p. 113; Flood, *The Tantric Body*, p. 78.

17. Stein, *Peasant, State and Society*, pp. 267–68.

18. Dirks, *Castes of Mind*, pp. 69–70.

19. Nicholas B. Dirks, *The Hollow Crown: Ethnohistory of an Indian Kingdom*, 2nd ed. (Ann Arbor: University of Michigan Press, 1993), p. 134.

20. Ibid., p. 86.

21. Ibid., p. 134.

22. Ibid., p. 31.

23. Carol A. Beckenbridge, "From Protector to Litigant: Changing Relations between Hindu Temples and the Raja of Ramnad", in *South Indian Temples: An Analytical Reconsideration*, edited by Burton Stein (Delhi: Vikras, 1978), p. 78.

24. Ibid., p. 82.

25. Ibid., p. 88; Dirks, *The Hollow Crown*, p. 40.

26. Stein, *Peasant, State and Society*, p. 384; Dirks, *The Hollow Crown*, p. 40; Breckenbridge, "From Protector to Litigant", p. 88.

27. Breckenbridge, "From Protector to Litigant", p. 92; Stein, *Peasant, State and Society*, p. 391.

28. Dirks, *The Hollow Crown*, p. 42.
29. Stein, *Peasant, State and Society*, p. 391.
30. Champakalakshmi, *Trade, Ideology and Urbanization*, p. 36.
31. Clothey, *The Many Faces of Murukan*, p. 15.
32. Champakalakshmi, *Religion, Tradition and Ideology*, p. 13.
33. Stein, *Peasant, State and Society*, p. 64.
34. Champakalakshmi, *Religion, Tradition and Ideology*, p. 14.
35. Ibid., p. 607.
36. Ibid., p. 611.
37. Ibid., p. 14.
38. Stein, *History of India*, pp. 89–90.
39. Stein, *Peasant, State and Society*, p. 51.
40. Champakalakshmi, *Religion, Tradition and Ideology*, p. 87.
41. Cornelia Dimmitt and J.A.B. van Buitenen, *Classical Hindu Mythology: A Reader in the Sanskrit Puranas* (Philadelphia: Temple University Press, 1978), p. 7.
42. Champakalakshmi, *Religion, Tradition and Ideology*, p. 87.
43. Ibid., p. 369.
44. Ibid., p. 88.
45. Edwin F. Bryant, "Introduction", in *Krishna: The Beautiful Legend of God*, Srimad Bhagavata Purana Book X (London: Penguin, 2003), p. xi.
46. As opposed to *sruti* or "that which is heard"; that is divine revelation which is immutable and cannot be adjusted to meet ritual and cultural contexts.
47. Bryant, "Introduction", p. xiv.
48. George Michell, T*he Hindu Temple: An Introduction to its Meanings and Forms* (Chicago: University of Chicago Press, [1972] 1988), p. 20.
49. Bryant, "Introduction", p. xiv.
50. Champakalakshmi, *Religion, Tradition and Ideology*, pp. 10–11.
51. Ibid., p. 503.
52. Ibid., p. 124.
53. Ibid., p. 503; Stein, *Peasant, State and Society*, p. 65.
54. Stein, *Peasant, State and Society*, pp. 64–65, 100.
55. Ibid., pp. 74–75.
56. Champakalakshmi, *Religion, Tradition and Ideology*, pp. 483, 552.
57. Ibid., p. 125.
58. Stein, *Peasant, State and Society*, p. 323.
59. Ibid., p. 331.
60. Ibid., pp. 84–85.
61. Ibid., pp. 237–38.
62. Lynn E. Gattwood, *Devi and the Spouse Goddess: Women, Sexuality and Marriage in India* (New Delhi: Manohar, 1985), p. 185.
63. Stein, *Peasant, State and Society*, p. 237.

64. Ibid., pp. 239–40.
65. Ibid., p. 330.
66. Ibid., p. 331.
67. Ibid., p. 84.
68. Ibid., p. 172.
69. Ibid., p. 352.
70. Ibid., p. 57.
71. Dirks, *The Hollow Crown*, p. 33.
72. Stein, *Peasant, State and Society*, pp. 90, 104.
73. Arjun Appadurai, "Kings, Sects and Temples in South India 1350–1700 AD", in *South Indian Temples: An Analytical Reconsideration*, edited by Burton Stein (New Delhi: Vikras, 1978), p. 57.
74. Dirks, *The Hollow Crown*, p. 35.
75. Stein, *Peasant, State and Society*, p. 383.
76. Champakalakshmi, *Religion, Tradition and Ideology*, pp. 26, 35–36; Appadurai, *Worship and Conflict*, p. 52.
77. Burton Stein, "Temples in the Tamil Country 1300–1750 AD", in *South Indian Temples: An Analytical Reconsideration*, edited by Burton Stein (Delhi: Vikras, 1978), pp. 26–27.
78. Stein, *Peasant, State and Society*, p. 454.
79. Champakalakshmi, *Religion, Tradition and Ideology*, p. 313.
80. Ibid., p. 156; Stein, "Temples in the Tamil Country", pp. 27–28.
81. Stein, *A History of India*, p. 155.
82. Dirks, *The Hollow Crown*, p. 19.
83. Ibid., p. 52.
84. Ibid., p. 71.
85. C.J. Fuller, *The Camphor Flame: Popular Hinduism and Society in India* (Princeton, NJ: Princeton University Press, 1979), p. xi.
86. Stein, *Peasant, State and Society*, p. 85.
87. Michael Moffat, *An Untouchable Community in South India: Structure and Consensus* (Princeton, NJ: Princeton University Press, 1979), p. 219.
88. Gunther Sontheimer, "Between Ghost and God: A Folk Deity of the Deccan", in *Criminal Gods and Demon Devotees: Essays on the Guardians of Popular Hinduism*, edited by Alf Hiltebeital (Albany: State University of New York Press, 1991), pp. 300–301.
89. Klaus Klostermaier, *A Survey of Hinduism* (Albany: State University of New York Press, 1994), p. 334.
90. Ibid., pp. 12–15.
91. J.M. Hutton claims the word "caste" has its origins in the Portuguese word *casta*, signifying "breed", "race" or "kind" (J.H. Hutton, *Caste in India: Its Nature, Functions and Origins*, 4th ed. [Oxford: Oxford University Press, 1969], p. 47).

92. Rajakrishnan Ramasamy, *Caste Consciousness among Indian Tamils in Malaysia* (Petaling Jaya: Pelanduk, 1984), pp. 5–7.
93. Quigley, *The Interpretation of Caste*, pp. 106, 161.
94. Ibid., p. 7.
95. Fuller, *The Camphor Flame*, p. 13.
96. Quigley, *The Interpretation of Caste*, pp. 4–5.
97. Ibid., p. 106.
98. Ibid., p. 141.
99. Champakalakshmi, *Religion, Tradition and Ideology*, p. 236.
100. Moffat, *An Untouchable Community*, p. 36; Stein, *Peasant, State and Society*, p. 107.
101. Champakalakshmi, *Religion, Tradition and Ideology*, pp. 449–50.
102. Stein, *Peasant, State and Society*, pp. 54–55.
103. Ibid., p. 47.
104. Dirks, *Castes of Mind*, p. 66.
105. Ibid., pp. 72–73.
106. Champakalakshmi, *Religion, Tradition and Ideology*, pp. 449–51.
107. Quigley, *The Interpretation of Caste*, p. 139.
108. Ibid., p. 166.
109. Stein, *Peasant, State and Society*, p. 174; Brenda E.F. Beck, *Peasant Society in Konku: A Study of Right and Left Subcastes in South India* (Vancouver: University of British Columbia Press, 1972), pp. 7–8.
110. Stein, *Peasant, State and Society*, p. 177.
111. Champakalakshmi, *Religion, Tradition and Ideology*, p. 103.
112. Ibid., p. 82.
113. Beck, *Peasant Society in Konku*, p. 14.
114. Ibid., p. 56.
115. Dirks, *Castes of Mind*, p. 77.
116. Quigley, *The Interpretation of Caste*, p. 24.
117. Dirks, *The Hollow Crown*, p. 259; Moffat, *An Untouchable Community*, p. 28; Quigley, *The Interpretation of Caste*, p. 137; Beck, *Peasant Society in Konku*, p. 181.
118. Stein, *Peasant, State and Society*, pp. 10–11.
119. Hutton, *Caste in India*, p. 92.
120. Stein, *Peasant, State and Society*, p. 9.
121. Quigley, *The Interpretation of Caste*, p. 11.
122. Dirks, *The Hollow Crown*, p. 247.
123. Quigley, *The Interpretation of Caste*, pp. 160–61.
124. Paul W. Wiebe and S. Mariappen, *Indian Malaysians: The View from the Plantation* (Delhi: Manohar, 1978), p. 69; Fuller, *The Camphor Flame*, p. 14; Quigley, *The Interpretation of Caste*, pp. 163–64.
125. Stein, *Peasant, State and Society*, pp. 10–11.

126. Wiebe and Mariappen, *Indian Malaysians*, pp. 69–70; Rajakrishnan, *Caste Consciousness*, p. 6.

127. Beck, *Peasant Society in Konku*, p. 7.

128. Rajakrishnan, *Caste Consciousness*, pp. 4–5.

129. Quigley, *The Interpretation of Caste*, p. 140.

130. Moffatt, *An Untouchable Community*, p. 111.

131. Ibid., p. 59.

132. Ibid., p. 40.

133. Quigley, *The Interpretation of Caste*, p. 156; Moffat, *An Untouchable Community*, pp. 87–88.

134. Dirks, *The Hollow Crown*, pp. 278–80.

135. Moffat points out that prior to the imposition of British rule, lower castes had certain rights. In cultural terms, the high castes were restrained by fear of the power of lower-caste sorcery. Economically, the non-cultivating high castes were dependent on low caste agricultural labourers, giving the low castes a degree of bargaining power. Politically, the high castes needed the support of low caste retainers in factional disputes. Moreover, low castes could appeal to extra-village royal authority. In addition, low castes had a right to boycott a high caste person who mistreated one of their number. The creation of the new monetarized colonial agricultural economy effectively abolished these rights, thus depriving lower castes of their traditional modes of self-protection (Moffat, *An Untouchable Community*, p. 44).

136. Dirks, *Castes of Mind*, pp. 73–79.

137. Hutton, *Caste in India*, pp. 50, 112. See also Quigley, *The Interpretation of Caste*, pp. 163–64.

138. Michell, *The Hindu Temple*, p. 78.

139. Champakalakshmi, *Religion, Tradition and Ideology*, pp. 16, 153, 601.

140. Ibid., p. 154.

141. James J. Preston. "Creation of the Sacred Image: Apotheosis and Destruction in Hinduism", in *Gods of Flesh, Gods of Stone: The Embodiment of Divinity in India*, edited by Joanne Punzo Waghorne and Norman Cutler in association with Vasudha Narayanan (Chambersburg: Anima, 1985), p. 9.

142. Fred W. Clothey, *Rhythm and Intent: Ritual Studies from South India* (Bombay: Blackie and Son, 1983), p. 195.

143. Kandiah Chelliah, *Hinduism: A Brief Study of It's* [sic] *Origins: Tradition and Practice* (Bukit Berunting: Kandiah Chelliah, 2012), p. 82.

144. Appadurai, *Worship and Conflict*, p. 21.

145. Champakalakshmi, *Religion, Tradition and Ideology*, p. 478; Flood, *The Tantric Body*, p. 82.

146. Stein, *Peasant, State and Society*, p. 454.

147. Appadurai, *Worship and Conflict*, p. 18.

148. Champakalakshmi, *Religion, Tradition and Ideology*, pp. 449–50.

149. Michell, *The Hindu Temple*, pp. 58–60.
150. Ibid., p. 73; Champakalakshmi, *Religion, Tradition and Ideology*, p. 567.
151. Sinha, *A New God*, p. 70; Michell, *The Hindu Temple*, p. 78.
152. Champakalakshmi, *Religion, Tradition and Ideology*, pp. 470–71; Diana L. Eck, *Darsan: Seeing the Divine Image in India*, 3rd ed. (New York: Columbia University Press, 1998), p. 51.
153. Champakalakshmi, *Religion, Tradition and Ideology*, p. 25. In passing it is worth noting that in some Saivite traditions the word *agama* is synonymous with the term *tantra*, that is, "a system of revealed teaching that leads to liberation and power" (Flood, *The Tantric Body*, p. 9).
154. Michell, *The Hindu Temple*, pp. 54, 73.
155. Eck, *Darsan*, p. 52.
156. Champakalakshmi, *Religion, Tradition and Ideology*, p. 24.
157. Michell, *The Hindu Temple*, pp. 133–34.
158. Ibid., p. 145.
159. Champakalakshmi, *Religion, Tradition and Ideology*, pp. 471–72.
160. Michell, *The Hindu Temple*, pp. 145–46.
161. Ibid., pp. 149–51.
162. Ibid., p. 183.
163. Eck, *Darsan*, p. 62; Michell, *The Hindu Temple*, pp. 61–62.
164. Eck, *Darsan*, pp. 59–60.
165. Appadurai, *Worship and Conflict*, p. 22.
166. Michell, *The Hindu Temple*, p. 62.
167. Ibid., pp. 66–70.
168. David Dean Shulman, *Tamil Temple Myths: Sacrifice and Divine Marriage in the South Indian Saiva Tradition* (Princeton, NJ: Princeton University Press, 1985), p. 19.
169. Eck, *Darsan*, p. 59; Michell, *The Hindu Temple*, pp. 74–76.
170. R. Rajoo, "Sanskritization in the Hindu Temples of West Malaysia", *Jurnal Pengajian India* 2 (1984), p. 161.
171. Eck, *Darsan*, p. 7.
172. Rajoo, "Sanskritization", p. 160.
173. Michell, *The Hindu Temple*, p. 20.
174. John Bowker, *Why Religions Matter* (New York: Cambridge University Press, 2015), p. 215. Indeed, the *Vishnu Samhitha* 29.55–57 advises that "Without form how can one contemplate God? On what will the mind focus? If there is nothing to which the mind can attach itself it will drift away from meditation and slip into a state of sleep. The wise, therefore, focus on some form." (ibid.)
175. Eck, *Darsan*, p. 38.
176. Clothey, *Rhythm and Intent*, pp. 195–96.
177. Eck, *Darsan*, p. 38.
178. Michell, *The Hindu Temple*, p. 38.

179. Anand Mishra, "Rituals in Religious Ceremonies of Pustimarga", in *Emotions in Rituals and Performances*, edited by Axel Michaels and Christoph Wulf (New Delhi: Routledge, 2012), p. 101; Stein, *Peasant, State and Society*, pp. 20–21.

180. Norman Cutler, "Conclusion", in *Gods of Flesh, Gods of Stone: The Embodiment of Divinity in India*, edited by Joanne Punzo Waghorne and Norman Cutler in association with Vasudha Narayanan (Chambersburg: Anima, 1985), pp. 163–68.

181. Paul B. Coutright, "On this Holy Day in my Humble Way", in *Gods of Flesh, Gods of Stone: The Embodiment of Divinity in India*, edited by Joanne Punzo Waghorne and Norman Cutler in association with Vasudha Narayanan (Chambersburg: Anima, 1985), p. 46.

182. Appadurai, *Worship and Conflict*, pp. 35–36, 60–61.

183. Sinha, *A New God*, p. 70.

184. Kalimuthu Ramanathan, "Hindu Religion in an Islamic State: The Case of Malaysia" (PhD dissertation, Universiteit Van Amsterdam, 1995), pp. 79–82; Rajoo, "Sanskritization", pp. 160–61.

185. Stein, *Peasant, State and Society*, p. 81; Vidya Dehejia, *Slaves of the Lord: The Path of the Tamil Saints* (New Delhi: Munshiram Manoharlal, 1988), p. 1; Champakalaskmi, *Religion, Tradition and Ideology*, p. 16.

186. Dehejia, *Slaves of the Lord*, p. 1.

187. Ibid., p. 8.

188. Ibid., pp. 15–17.

189. Ibid., pp. 8–9.

190. Ibid., p. 19.

191. Swami Siva Nandhi Adikalaar, K. Loganathan, and S.P. Thinnappan, *Saivite Hinduism* (London: Meikandar Aadheenam, 1994), p. 39.

192. Ibid., pp. 18–21; Bunki Kimura, "Ramanuja's Theory of Bhakti based on the Vedanta Philosophy", in *The Historical Development of the Bhakti Movement in India*, edited by Iwao Shima, Teiji Sakata, and Katsuyuki Ida (New Delhi: Manohar, 2011), p. 51.

193. Clothey, *The Many Faces of Murukan*, pp. 160–61; Champakalakshmi, *Religion, Tradition and Ideology*, p. 55.

194. Stein, *Peasant, State and Society*, p. 81.

195. Siva, Loganathan and Thinnappan, *Saivite Hinduism*, p. 17; Moffat, *An Untouchable Community*, p. 39.

196. Champakalakshmi, *Religion, Tradition and Ideology*, p. 19.

197. Ibid., p. 286.

198. Fuller, *The Camphor Flame*, p. 157.

199. David Dean Shulman, "The Yogi's Human Self: Tayumanavar in the Tamil Mystical Tradition", in *Religon* 21 (January 1991): 51–52.

200. Fuller, *The Camphor Flame*, p. 157; Bryant, "Introduction", p. li.

201. Shulman, "The Yogi's Human Self", p. 52; Clothey, *The Many Faces of Murukan*, p. 101; Lise F. Vail, "Founders, Swamis and Devotees: Becoming Divine in North Karnataka", in *Gods of Flesh, Gods of Stone: The Embodiment of Divinity in India*, edited by Joanne Punzo Waghorne and Norman Cutler in association with Vasudha Narayanan (Chambersburg: Anima, 1985), p. 130.
202. Shulman, *The King and the Clown*, pp. 351–53.
203. Shulman, "The Yogi's Human Self", p. 52.
204. Clothey, *The Many Faces of Murukan*, p. 102.
205. Barbara Ehrenreich, *Dancing in the Streets: A History of Collective Joy* (London: Granta Books, 2007), pp. 60–61; Yoshitsugu Sawai, "Reflections on Bhakti as a Type of Indian Mysticism", in *The Historical Development of the Bhakti Movement in India*, edited by Iwao Shima, Teiji Sakata, and Katsuyuki Ida (New Delhi: Manohar, 2011), p. 25.
206. Flood, *The Tantric Body*, p. 9.
207. Kazuyo Sakaki, "Realization of Inner Divinity: Natha Yogins in the Medieval Bhakti Movement", in *The Historical Development of the Bhakti Movement in India*, edited by Iwao Shima, Teiji Sakata, and Katsuyuki Ida (New Delhi: Manohar, 2011), pp. 131–32.
208. Clothey, *The Many Faces of Murukan*, p. 102.
209. Dehejia, *Slaves of the Lord*, p. 4.
210. Ibid., pp. 14–15.
211. Dennis Hudson, "Violent and Fanatical Devotion among the *Nayanars*: A Study in the *Periya Purunam* of *Cekkilar*", in *Criminal Gods and Demon Devotees: Essays on the Guardians of Popular Hinduism*, edited by Alf Hiltebeital (Albany: State University of New York Press, 1989); Dehejia, *Slaves of the Lord*, p. 65.
212. Shulman, *The King and Clown*, p. 354.
213. Hudson, "Violent and Fanatical Devotion", p. 380.
214. Some examples: Iyarpahai Nayanar, who, when requested, offered his wife to a visiting Brahman devotee, and killed his relatives when they attempted to intervene; Kannappar Nayanar, who placed pork on the *lingam* (aniconic symbol of Siva), thus defiling it, and plucked his eye out to stop the *lingam* bleeding; Murthi Nayanar, who ground his own elbow to provide sandalwood powder for ritual worship; and Chandesvar Nayanar, who cut off his father's feet when he interfered with his devotions (Swami Sivananda, *Sixty-Three Nayanar Saints* (Batu Caves: Sivanandashram, 1980), pp. 43–45, 65–69, 80–81, 88–90).
215. Visuvalingam, "The Transgressive Sacrality", pp. 449–50.
216. Hudson, "Violent and Fanatical Devotion", pp. 385–91.
217. Visuvalingam, "The Transgressive Sacrality", p. 428.
218. Ibid., p. 431.
219. Madeleine Biardeau. "Brahmans and Meat Eating Gods", in *Criminal Gods and Demon Devotees: Essays on the Guardians of Popular Hinduism*, edited

by Alf Hiltebeital (Albany: State University of New York Press, 1989), pp. 30–31.

220. Alf Hiltebeital, "Introduction", in *Criminal Gods and Demon Devotees: Essays on the Guardians of Popular Hinduism*, edited by Alf Hiltebeital (Albany: State University of New York Press, 1989), p. 1. This has been confirmed by my own field research.

221. David M. Knipe, "A Night of the Growing Dead: A Cult of Virabhadra", in *Criminal Gods and Demon Devotees: Essays on the Guardians of Popular Hinduism*, edited by Alf Hiltebeital (Albany: State University of New York Press, 1989), pp. 124–39.

222. Ibid., p. 144.

223. Hiltebeital, "Introduction", p. 1.

224. John M. Stanley, "The Capitulation of Mani: A Conversion Myth in the Cult of Khandoba", in *Criminal Gods and Demon Devotees: Essays on the Guardians of Popular Hinduism*, edited by Alf Hiltebeital (Albany: State University of New York Press, 1989), p. 278.

225. Alf Hiltebeital, "Draupadi's Two Guardians: The Buffalo King and the Muslim Devotee", in *Criminal Gods and Demon Devotees: Essays on the Guardians of Popular Hinduism*, edited by Alf Hiltebeital (Albany: State University of New York Press, 1989), p. 364.

226. David Dean Shulman, "Outcast, Guardian and Trickster: Notes on the Myth of Kattavarayan", in *Criminal Gods and and Demon Devotees: Essays on the Guardians of Popular Hinduism*, edited by Alf Hiltebeital (Albany: State University of New York Press, 1989), pp. 30–31.

227. Ibid., p. 59.

228. Ibid., p. 58.

229. Hiltebeital, "Draupadi's Two Guardians", p. 365.

230. Clothey, *The Many Faces of Murukan*, pp. 28–29.

231. Champakalakshmi, *Religion, Tradition and Ideology*, p. 23.

232. Burton Stein, "Temples in the Tamil Country", p. 26.

233. Champakalakshmi, *Religion, Tradition and Ideology*, pp. 249–52.

234. Ibid., p. 304.

235. Devapoopathy Nadarajah, *The Strength of Saivism* (Kuala Lumpur: Second International Seminar on Saiva Siddhanta, 1986), p. 79; Champakalakshmi, *Religion, Tradition and Ideology*, pp. 253–55.

236. Champakalakshmi, *Religion, Tradition and Ideology*, p. 114.

237. B. Natarajan, "Introduction", in *Tirumantiram: A Tamil Scriptural Classic*, edited by B. Natarajan (Mylapore: Sri Ramankrishna Math, 1991), p. viii.

238. Dehejia, *Slaves of the Lord*, p. 75; Natarajan, "Introduction", p. viii.

239. Clothey, *The Many Faces of Murukan*, p. 90.

240. Devapoopathy, *The Strength of Saivism*, pp. 15–32.

241. Clothey, *The Many Faces of Murukan*, pp. 91–92.

242. Siva, Loganathan and Thinnappan, *Saivite Hinduism*, p. 4.
243. Ibid., p. 32.
244. Champakalakshmi, *Religion, Tradition and Ideology*, pp. 292–303.
245. Siva, Loganathan and Thinnappan, *Saivite Hinduism*, p. 27.
246. Devapoopathy, *The Strength of Saivism*, p. 52.
247. Natarajan, "Introduction", p. viii.
248. Clothey, *The Many Faces of Murukan*, p. 92.
249. Siva, Loganathan and Thinnappan, *Saivite Hinduism*, p. 30; Devapoopathy, *The Strength of Saivism*, p. 52.
250. V. Paranjoti, "The Sakti of God", in *Saiva Siddhanta: An Exploration and Assessment by Scholars the World Over* (Maliladuthuria: Dharmapura Adhinam, 1994), pp. 168–69; Devapoopathy, *The Strength of Saivism*, p. 68.
251. Devapoopathy, *The Strength of Saivism*, pp. 52, 66.
252. As St. Cheraman states, "In whatsoever form/whosoever/in his innermost need/continually visualises him/In that form/He will give/grace." (Quoted in Dehejia, *Slaves of the Lord*, p. 72.)
253. Devapoopathy, *The Strength of Saivism*, p. 54.
254. R.C. Zaehner, *Hinduism* (London: Oxford University Press, 1962), p. 88.
255. Natarajan, "Introduction", p. viii; Flood, *The Tantric Body*, p. 122.
256. Devapoopathy, *The Strength of Saivism*, p. 54.
257. Ibid., pp. 54–55; Zaehner, *Hinduism*, pp. 88–89.
258. Zaehner, *Hinduism*, p. 88.
259. Clothey, *The Many Faces of Murukan*, p. 94. Devapoopathy points out that while there are only three major *malas*, the impurities take a multitude of forms (Devapoopathy, *The Strength of Saivism*, p. 55).
260. Devapoopathy, *The Strength of Saivism*, p. 55.
261. Clothey, *The Many Faces of Murukan*, p. 94.
262. Devapoopathy, *The Strength of Saivism*, p. 55.
263. Ibid., p. 56.
264. Clothey, *The Many Faces of Murukan*, p. 94.
265. Flood, *The Tantric Body*, p. 127.
266. Siva, Loganathan, and Thinnappan, *Saivite Hinduism*, p. 30.
267. S. Shivapadasundaram, *The Saivite School of Hinduism* (Kuala Lumpur: Malaya Arulneri Thirukoottam, [1934] 1975), pp. 60–62; Devapoopathy, *The Strength of Saivism*, pp. 53–54; Paranjoti, "The Sakti of God", p. 169.
268. R.C. Zaehner, *Hinduism*, p. 89; Devapoopathy, *The Strength of Saivism*, p. 53.
269. Devapoopathy, *The Strength of Saivism*, p. 59.
270. Ibid., p. 65.
271. Ibid., pp. 64–65; Natarajan, "Introduction", p. viii.
272. Paranjoti, "The Sakti of God", p. 170.
273. Zaehner, *Hinduism*, p. 89.

3

Colonialism, Colonial Knowledge and Hindu Reform Movements

In the previous chapter we noted that most scholars accept that the developments throughout the period of the great dynasties of South India stamped Tamil Hinduism with characteristics which were to prove both formative and enduring. In order to understand the shape of contemporary reformist impulses within South India, it is necessary to explore the ideologies of British colonial rule in India. These ideologies permeated British scholarship in India and ultimately extended to the subject populations. In the process, "colonial knowledge" profoundly reshaped Indian perceptions of their own culture, society and history, setting in train a series of far-reaching (and in many cases continuing) social and political transformations.[1]

The India over which the British East India Company was to assume control consisted of a segmented population of breathtaking diversity, manifesting in a conglomeration of ethnic, linguistic, regional, caste (*jati*) and religious formations. British orientalist scholarship interpreted this society according to a series of cultural assumptions that were regarded as axiomatic, namely:

1. India was a timeless, static society whose major institutions — caste, religion, despotic rule — were impervious to change and thus largely

immutable. Indian stagnation contrasted with the dynamism and progressivism of Europe.[2]

2. Throughout its entire history, Indian polities had been ruled by theocratic despots (both Hindu and Muslim). This implied that Indians were accustomed to and required the guidance of firm rule. Indeed, the social, cultural and linguistic differences within India inevitably resulted in civil discourse, unrest and conflict, all of which could only be contained by "the strong hand of the British".[3]

3. All of the civilizations which had invaded and conquered India had declined under the twin impact of the intolerable climate and the inevitable degeneration resulting from miscegenation. It followed that if the British were to survive as rulers they had to remain independent of the degraded races which inhabited India.[4]

4. All knowledge of Indian religious customs and law could be derived from ancient texts. It followed that the investigation of original scriptures would uncover the abiding procedures and principles by which Indian society should be regulated. A corollorary of this thesis was that all of India's problems sprang from deviation from and corruption of pristine Vedic ideals. This perspective insisted upon the primacy of Sanskrit as the sacred language of Hinduism.[5]

5. After the Great Rebellion (Indian Mutiny) of 1857–58, caste was viewed as the foundational principle of Indian society. Caste was not only intrinsic to Hinduism but also to the whole of India. Indeed, caste held the key to understanding and hence control of India.[6]

Mosaic Ethnology

In 1785, Sir William Jones, Justice of the Supreme Court of Calcutta, founded the Asiatic Society of Bengal. The Society became the vehicle for the scholarly exploration of Hinduism.[7] Jones believed that the key to understanding India and the discovery of the fixed body of Indian law would be located only by a deep exploration of antique texts, those composed in the "classical languages of India", and in particular those written in Sanskrit.[8] The earliest scriptural and legal texts were considered to be more authoritative than later works, which could be assumed to have been corrupted by accretions, interpretations, deviations and digressions.[9] British orientalist scholarship determined that the *Manu Dharma Sastra* (The Law of Manu) was the original, and thus the most authentic guide to Hindu Law.[10] *Manu*, translated by Jones and published in 1792, and a "chronicle of Brahman dominance", was subsequently enshrined as "the canonical … text for understanding the foundational nature of Indian society", in the process conferring upon it a significance it had never enjoyed in pre-colonial India.[11]

In interpreting Indian languages and culture, Jones employed a methodology of philological analysis which Thomas Trautmann has described as "Mosaic Ethnology".[12] This schema was refracted through a literalist Biblical chronology, based in particular on those events described in Genesis, the first book of the Bible. At this point it was widely accepted among British scholars that Genesis 1.1, the Creation, had occurred some four thousand years before the birth of Christ.[13] But Genesis also relates how the Great Flood, unleashed by God, had been survived by Noah, his three sons, and their families. Furious at the insulting behaviour of his son Ham, Noah had cursed Ham's descendents to eternal servitude to the descendents of the other two sons, Shem and Japheth.[14] In his magisterial study, *The Making of New World Slavery*, Robin Blackburn points out that Biblical scholarship identified Hamitic peoples as possessors of dark skins.[15] Jones duly identified Indians as descendents of Ham and thus fated to subjugation.[16] In accordance with God's wishes, Noah's descendents, all of whom spoke the same language, repopulated the world, but following God's destruction of the Tower of Babel,[17] were dispersed across the face of the globe. Mosaic mythology was thus structured around three basic assumptions, namely that the complete history of Earth was compressed within a few thousand years, that Ham's descendents were destined to labour for those of Shem and Japheth, and that the complete monolingual population of the Earth had been scattered throughout the world from a pristine central point.[18] Mosaic ethnology was viewed as a master narrative of universal history which could be used to connect languages and peoples across the face of the globe, and to explain the interrelationship of diverse peoples.[19]

Early European scholars of Sanskrit had discovered that the language was very similar to ancient Greek and Latin.[20] Jones now postulated that the Sanskrit, Greek, German, Celtic and old Persian languages were closely related, and that Sanskrit comprised an Indian branch of this European "family".[21] He concluded that Sanskrit was a language of great antiquity and that the Vedas had been composed very soon after the destruction of the Tower of Babel.[22] He further asserted that Rama had organized

Indian society, and that India could be viewed as one of the oldest Biblical civilizations, a living museum of what Europe had once been.[23] In recognition of India's standing as a "Biblical" society, Christian tracts began depicting Hindu gods as *avatars* of Jesus.[24]

Jones' views on race and caste were incorporated into the Benthamite scholar James Mill's *History of India*, published in 1817.[25] Mill wrote this work without paying a single visit to India, and without the slightest knowledge of any Indian language. He dismissed Indians en bloc as childlike, superstitious, perfidious and backward. His views on caste were entirely textualist and highlighted the centrality of *Manu Dharma Sastra* in understanding the organizational principles of Indian society. Mill's work was extremely influential in shaping British attitudes towards India.[26]

While Sanskrit was placed within the European family of languages, the studies of Francis Whyte Ellis (1777–1819), the Collector of Madras, revealed a further and discrete group of languages that were primarily located in South India. Although Tamil had absorbed a large number of Sanskrit "loan" words, Ellis postulated that southern languages were the "aboriginal languages" of India which had existed prior to the arrival of Sanskrit.[27] Later, Brian Houghton Hodgson (1848) contended that just as Indians, Persians, Germans, English, Irish and Russians were members of one family (which he named the Iranian), so the Tamilians, Tibetans, Indo-Chinese, Tangus, Mongols and Turks belonged to another family grouping known as the Turanians.[28] Hodgson's work was later complemented by the theories of Max Muller, who postulated the notion of an invading (Japhethic) light skinned "Aryan" race which had vanquished the dark skinned indigenous (Hamitic) race. Muller claimed that in the south the Brahmans ("upon whom the noble stamp of the Caucasian race can be seen") had not displaced the aboriginal peoples, but, rather, had colonized them.[29]

These ideas were further developed by Bishop Robert Caldwell (1814–91). Caldwell asserted that the Dravidian presence preceded the arrival of the Aryans and that the Brahmans, who were the agents of the Aryans, had manipulated and cheated the Dravidians.[30] Caldwell's thesis was wholly driven by his distrust of Brahmans, whom he blamed for the failure of his attempts to evangelize significant sections of South Indian society. Caldwell aimed at nothing less than the creation of "an ethnic identity separate from the rest of India".[31] He proposed the removal of Sanskrit words from Tamil, though again this was a stratagem designed to counter what he interpreted as Brahmanic civilizational influences which were limiting conversions to Christianity. Secretly, Caldwell shared British racial beliefs and regarded South Indians as manifestly inferior to "Aryan" Indians.[32]

Caldwell's views were supported by Arthur de Gobineau, who in 1853 released his highly influential *Essay on the Inequality of Human Races*, described as "the motherlode of all modern racist theories". De Gobineau, foreshadowing Social Darwinism (see below), located race as the central dynamic of world history. According to his theories, all of the world's great civilizations were the product of racial whiteness, and all had declined due to racial intermingling. (The exception was the Germanic race, the last bastian of pure white civilization.)[33] De Gobineau argued that the invading Aryans had devised the institution of caste to preserve their white culture from the contaminating influences of the "aboriginal" population.[34]

Social Darwinism

The theory of language as a conceptual tool to explain the origin of peoples began to unravel in the 1850s. Archeological and geological discoveries clearly demonstrated that both human history and the Earth itself were of far greater antiquity than six thousand years, in the process undermining and ultimately destroying the notion that Biblical timelines and language-derived genealogies were central to the understanding of human history and the interrelationship of societal families.[35] These interpretations were increasingly displaced by Darwinian evolutionary theory and the concomitant acceptance of race as a critical factor in the ranking of human societies.[36] As a consequence, anthropology was to replace history as an analytical tool to decipher the mysteries of India.[37] Inevitably, however, the theoretical vestiges of language and its relationship to civilizational origin were to linger on, melding in unexpected ways with faux-Darwinian racial theories.

The 1859 publication of Charles Darwin's *On the Origin of Species* appeared to cast race as inexorably moulded by biology, thus as "the prime determinant of all important traits of body and soul, character and personality of human beings and nations".[38] Since any given society's racial characteristics ineluctably shaped its culture and outlook, it was now possible to grade all human races within an overarching human taxonomy.[39] Social Darwinism (as this doctrine became known)[40] implied the linear development of Man, a trajectory impelled by "progress" and creativity (both defined according to European perspectives), and survival of the fittest as the critical principle of human organization.[41]

Moreover, Social Darwinism could also be deployed to document the putative weaknesses of races deemed inferior. The reverse of evolution was racial degeneration, the result of unregulated human interaction and, especially, miscegenation. Degeneration explained the phenomenon of "stationary" societies and "uncivilized" peoples, as well as the deterioration and fall of once powerful civilizations and empires.[42]

In certain respects Social Darwinism may have been tailor-made for India, or at least British conceptions of India. British racial theory assigned great weight to the colour of a person's skin in determining their standing; socio-biological status diminished in proportion to the increasing darkness of hue.[43] The "Negroid" features and complexions of the Dravidians marked them out as among the most backward of racial groupings, and thus belonging to a decidedly lower stratum than the Indo-Aryans. Moreover, Social Darwinism insisted on the juxtaposition of a dark-skinned savage in perpetual opposition to the light-skinned bearer of civilization.[44] Within India this necessarily took the form of a prolonged civilizational struggle between the migratory Sanskrit-speaking and highly developed invading Aryans and their "lesser" compatriots, the Dravidian "Aboriginals". Many racial theorists and officials regarded this theory as accepted fact and sought corroborating evidence within the Vedas which would describe this encounter.[45]

British Social Darwinist theories insisted that the Aryans who colonized India in the centuries BCE and who had bestowed the multiple benefits of higher civilization, including the Hindu religion upon the subcontinent,[46] had, despite their noble origins, irrevocably "degenerated", the result of long association and careless miscegenation with the indigenous Dravidians. Indeed, racial decay had proceeded to the point where renewal or regeneration was dismissed as impossible. It followed that political or social reforms designed to uplift the Aryans would fly in the face of the condemnatory verdict passed by both science and history and would thus constitute so much wasted effort.[47]

But the Dravidians were not just racially degenerate. British evolutionary theory also charged them with the long-term contamination and debasement of the superior and upright religion of the Aryans. As we have noted, British orientalist scholarship had determined that the original religion of the Aryans could be uncovered by careful and discriminating study of the ancient Brahmanic texts, which were written in Sanskrit, and which had been validated as "pristine" and "authentic" Hinduism by a whole century of European scholarship. By contrast, the religion of the Dravidians, the "aboriginal" peoples of India, with its perceived lack of scriptural and philosophical underpinnings, was deemed little more than barbarism and a collocation of "material demonologies".[48] Over time, it was opined, the advanced, refined and textual traditions of the Aryans had meshed with the "wholly degrading" religions of the Dravidians to the detriment of the former. Indeed, the Dravidians were held responsible for all the "superstitious abominations" with which modern Hinduism was allegedly studded.[49]

In the late nineteenth century, a novel point of origin was suggested for the Dravidians. It was postulated that South Indians had initially inhabited an imagined continent known as Lemuria, which, in ancient times, had supposedly spanned the entire Indian Ocean before vanishing beneath the waves. The Lemuria connection was first formulated by British zoologist Philip Lutley (1829–1913) and was later popularized by Madam Helena Blavatsky, the co-founder of the Theosophical Society. Lemuria was seen as providing an explanation for the distinct civilizational impulses of the Dravidians, and allowed Tamil "nationalists" to speculate on the many rich glories of the autochthonous society which had supposedly existed before the Tamils had been subjugated at the hands of the treacherous Brahman "colonizers". Although the concept of the sunken continent has long been dismissed by the scientific community as mere fantasy, Lemuria was seized upon by some Tamil commentators, and has in certain circles melded into the foundation mythology of a putatively discrete Dravidian civilization.[50]

Census operations which began in India in 1872 accumulated vast quantities of data which enumerated the population according to a multiplicity of social criteria.[51] The full cumbersome apparatus of Victorian Social Darwinism transformed these data into a complete Indian bio-racial taxonomy which ordered India both vertically and horizontally into a series of overlapping classificatory systems revolving around caste, religion and notions of primary race. This taxonomy enabled the British to exactly locate the cultural and racial status of any individual within the overall structure of what was perceived as the timeless, unchanging Indian social hierarchy. The taxonomy also emphasized the "otherness" of India, a society whose people could only be "known" according to categories which permitted the development and maintenance of colonial authority, and which underscored the intrinsic social and racial distance of Indian society from that of metropolitan Britain.[52]

Caste: The foremost and most basic categorization was caste, which according to Social Darwinist discourse was the basic building block of India's unyielding and immutable social pyramid.[53] The British deciphered caste in terms of the theoretical classificatory systems described in classical Hindu texts.[54] In interpreting these texts, colonial officials placed great emphasis on the primacy of ritual position and clear subordination of lower castes to those of higher status.[55] Caste was seen as the causal factor underlying the deep religiosity of the Hindus, as well as explaining their supposed servility, and was viewed by missionaries (who composed the majority of ethnographies) as a conspiracy foisted upon the Indian population by the "wily" Brahmans.[56] In compiling registers of caste, the demands of political administration often overcame the discipline of evolutionary anthropology, and many caste categories were in effect largely the creation of the Colonial Office.[57]

A major consequence of the colonial caste taxonomy was the institutionalization and expansion of Brahman power. The colonial authorities accepted without reservation the classical description of the *varna* system which firmly installed the Brahmans at the apex and as the custodians of caste hierarchies. The Brahmans had always furnished the majority of literate functionaries of most Indian polities, and thus it seemed obvious for the British to employ them as civil servants. However, the power now at their disposal appeared to greatly exceed that which they had exercised in the pre-colonial era.[58] This naturally affected the way in which Brahmans were viewed by the remainder of the population, and was to ultimately create anti-Brahman social and political sentiment, especially in South India. This will be further explored later in this section.

The British envisaged castes as "tight organic communities socially distinct from all others around them",[59] and theorized that the changelessness of Indian societal structures and the immutablity of caste over the centuries had imbued each caste within its own indelible "essence" shaped by its occupational profile, its standing within the overall hierarchy, and inherent cultural and moral characteristics.[60] Thus it was possible to ascribe to each caste its own unalterable and ineradicable sub-biological character (for example, "criminal", "martial", "degenerate"), which firmly situated the status of the caste and caste members within the overall structure of Indian society.[61]

This view, of caste groups as closed communities, was developed further by H.H. Risley, a leading member of the Royal Anthropological Institute, who claimed that the bond of caste was racial in character. Risley contended that, over the centuries, endogamy had served to enhance physical differences between castes and had inculcated intrinsic racial characteristics within each caste.[62] His anthropometric studies, based on phrenology and the application of nasal measurements,[63] aimed at distinguishing between those castes which belonged to the Aryan "race" and those which were Dravidian.[64] His research was informed by the fact that the term *varna*, as a descriptor of caste categories, could also be translated as colour.[65]

In the process of developing a model of caste hierarchy which faithfully reproduced the *varna* system drawn from classical textual sources, colonial anthropology activated the politics of caste, in particular that of caste mobilization.[66] This accorded with colonial perceptions of caste relations. Indeed, so wedded were British racial ideologies to the comparative imperatives of implacable inter-caste hostility, that when the examination of any given social structure revealed no overt discord, colonial officials felt obligated to contrive the dynamics of opposition and confrontation.[67]

The immediate impact of the British caste taxonomy was to freeze Indian social structures and to arrest the general fluidity which had hitherto prevailed within Indian society.[68] As Washbrook states, the British perspectives "missed the finely honed status differentials within caste, missed the practical openings for social mobility which gave the system flexibility, and above all missed the webs of interdependency which linked members of different castes together in an economic and social structure".[69]

The most significant losers of the colonial juggling and manipulation of the various component groups of India were those now identified as "untouchable". Under the Raj, what had been a localized phenomenon confined to certain areas became institutionalized across India, and especially among the poorest classes within the expanding urban areas.[70]

Religion: The British misunderstood the essential nature of all Indian religious traditions, especially those described as "Hindu". British administrators and scholars reduced the vast, disparate and often conflicting mosaic of cults, deities, sects, ideas and philosophies into a single religion clustered under the unitary fabric of Hinduism.[71] In locating an "essential" Hinduism within a Brahmanic and textual framework, and in relying upon Brahman advice on all matters relating to Hindu culture, law and customary belief, the British authorities effectively discounted the validity and significance of popular manifestations of Hinduism (which were often customary and which expressed their cosmologies through ritual rather than texts). British insistence that India was a stationary, stagnant society led the colonial authorities to disregard the social and historical character of the various Indian traditions and the specific contexts in which each had arisen.[72]

Following M.N. Srinavas (1976), Vineeta Sinha observes that nineteenth-century Indological research and the concomitant admiration shown by European scholars for Indian scriptures and philosophy brought immense pride and satisfaction to educated Hindus. Hence, "Great Tradition" Hinduism was wholly identified with philosophical Hinduism, whereas "Little" or "Village" Hinduism was seen as a lower class/caste phenomenon.[73] As Nicholas Dirks points out, the process of Sanksritization is a legacy bequeathed from colonial anthropology, and it continues to reflect the British inscription of Brahmanic hegemony.[74] Henceforth, despite the fact that these traditions claimed the allegiance of the overwhelming majority of Hindus,[75] for British administrators, village/popular expressions remained mere "deviations"; lesser and bastard offshoots of Brahmanism, the originating and vital source of "pure" Hinduism.[76]

A further product of British colonial anthropology was the envisagement of Hinduism as a bounded religion and thus axiomatically reactive to, and exclusive of, all who fell beyond its compass.[77] The 1872 census established an India which consisted of a Hindu "majority" and a sizeable Muslim "minority".[78] This formed the basis for the British contention that India was divided into two great and implacably antagonistic religious communities, namely those of Hinduism and Islam.[79] According to this perspective, every Indian, by virtue of his/her religious *identity*, inescapably belonged to a religious *community*, and was thus destined to gaze with ingrained distrust and hostility at the other. Religious identity additionally imbued its members with a number of specific inscribed characteristics which reflected the stage of evolutionary development each had reached.[80] This bifurcation of Indian society into two clearly demarcated and mutually antagonistic communities not only ignored the immense cultural pluralism within India,[81] and the huge swathe of liminal religious forms which drew inspiration from both Hindu and Muslim impulses,[82] but also overlooked the fact that Indians had never primarily typecast each other according to religious adherence.[83] Romila Tharpar asserts that the "perception which groups had of each other was not in terms of a monolithic religion, but more in terms of distinct and separate castes and sects along a social continuum".[84]

Hindu reform movements, reacting to British ideologies and the incessant propaganda of Christian missionaries, began the task of reconstructing an idealized Hinduism which was largely the fabrication of Orientalist scholarship. This "neo-Hinduism", which found particular favour among the Brahmans, as well as a minority colonially acculturated elite who were contemptuous of their "backward" compatriots, sought to "rescue" India by retrieving an imagined pristine Hinduism which had supposedly existed in the era of original Sanskrit civilization.[85] This project would necessarily require the suppression of the "dark, feminine and materialistic and sensual religion of the Aboriginal Dravidians" wherever such excrescences appeared.[86] Among the missionaries and their supporters, festivals involving rites of asceticism or ecstatic trance (often mistaken by missionaries and other Europeans for drunkenness) were held to constitute "devil worship" and "demonology",[87] and were thus obvious deviations from the higher Aryan culture of Brahmanic textual Hinduism. Such "crazed" and unrestrained manifestations were ripe for reform or suppression.[88]

In late nineteenth century India, Western-educated elites, mainly Brahmans and upper caste Hindus, taking their cue from the diatribes of Christian missionaries, successfully agitated for the enactment of legislation to ban the practice of hookswinging.[89] This ritual, which was common in Bengal, the Deccan and South India, involved various castes, trance states, and vows offered generally to female and "lower" deities. To these elites, the practice was "a symbol of some of the worst excesses they were determined to leave behind, and their attack on the practice, an expression of their solidarity, not only with each other, but also the new forces they so admired in Western culture". Although there was evidence that hookswinging served to unite villages and that the ritual was believed to promote general well-being, the reformers, using the terminology of British Social Darwinism, declared it "uncivilized", and the festival as that of "the mob" and "the lower orders". In presenting their case against hookswinging, these elites employed the essential arguments most calculated to win the support of missionaries and colonial officials; namely that the practice was not located in Brahmanic culture and was thus unrelated to Aryan/Vedic traditions; was not justified by the *Sastras* of classical Hinduism; and had never involved Brahman participation.

South Indian Reform Movements

Hindu and other reform movements gained particular and enduring strength within South India. For this was the region where colonial ideologies weighed most heavily; the homeland of the "backward" Dravidians who supposedly bore responsibility both for the degeneration of the Aryans and the corruption of the original Brahmanic and Aryan Hinduism. In general, South Indian responses coalesced into three main movements; Neo-Hinduism, "Neo- Shaivism" and Dravidian "nationalism". The latter two movements, in implementing their religious and political schedules, emphasized the primacy of the Tamil language.[90] The major thrust of these reform movements cannot be fully understood without reference to the dynamics of inter-caste politics, animated throughout the period of British rule.

In the previous section I noted that British social evolutionary theories insisted upon the concept of inter-caste conflict as an activating principle of Indian society, to the point that in situations where such rivalry was not immediately obvious, the colonial authorities felt constrained to assume it or even invent it. The declaration by senior members of the Secretariat of the Madras Presidency that the British would look favourably upon appeals directed against caste "aggression" produced a new dimension in local politics. As David Washbrook comments, "Once the language of large scale communal hostility, of broadly defined castes competing against each other had been introduced, there was no end to the number of situations it could be used to describe."[91] The result was a proliferation of caste associations, all of which now demanded that they be accorded recognition for administrative, political and educational purposes.[92]

Within the Madras Presidency, inter-caste conflict took the form of a virulent anti-Brahmanism which was to form the central plank of Dravidian "nationalism". By the end of the nineteeth century, the philological and racial theories of Bishop Caldwell and his strident denunciations of Brahmans had become engrained in both colonial ideology and local political discourse.[93] But the anti-Brahman invective was exacerbated by the emergence of political formations under British rule. As in much of the remainder of India, the British employed Brahmans as integral agents of colonial administration. By 1920 the Brahmans, who comprised a mere three per cent of the population, dominated the bureaucracy, many professions and the politics of the Madras Presidency.[94] However, the attempts of the so-called Mylapore group within the Home League to consolidate Brahman political power were opposed in the 1920s by the non-Brahmans of the recently formed Justice Party. The political rhetoric of the Justiceites was couched in the florid polemics of anti-Brahman discourse, including the claim that Brahmans were not true Dravidians, but represented a wave of "northern invaders".[95]

The anti-Brahman movement had a powerful religious dimension. Many Brahmans supported the concept of neo-Hinduism, which implicitly dismissed South Indian Hindu practices and argued for a return to the supposed traditions of an imagined Aryan textual religion. This project was resolutely opposed by the emerging non-Brahman elites, the class of educated, almost wholly upper-caste professionals and administrators, who sought to establish an identity grounded in the "authentic religion" of the Tamils, and which gloried in the veneration of the Tamil language and the Tamil scriptures. Sumathi Ramaswamy has labelled this movement "Neo-Shaivism".[96]

Neo-Shaivism, the "true" Tamil religion (*tamilar matam*), formulated from Saivite texts and narratives, was centred upon the monotheistic and "rational" worship of Siva, designated the Tamil divinity par excellence. This worship was conducted according to "true" Tamil rituals, by "Tamil" (that is non-Brahman) priests, and using the Tamil language. Neo-Shaivism was structured around several principles; namely, that Saivism was the primordial and "original" religion of all non-Brahman Tamils, and that the tenets of its beliefs were enshrined in Tamil texts; that it was the most ancient religion of India and pre-dated Sanskritic Aryan Hinduism by many centuries; and that Brahmanism and Aryanism had corrupted this pristine religion.[97] The promoters of Neo-Shaivism were determined to restore the religion to its imagined (and exclusively) Tamil effulgence. This, they believed, could only be achieved by identifying and extirpating all Aryan–Sanskritic accretions (especially the traditions of "polytheistic" worship), supposedly imported from North India. The framing and codification of Neo-Shaivism proved a difficult and often contentious task. There were disagreements as to what constituted "pure" Saivism, and the disentangling of the complex linkages and fusions between Tamil and Sanskrit Hinduism, established and sustained over an extended period reaching back well beyond the first century BCE.[98]

But while Neo-Shaivism contested the claims advanced both by British evolutionary anthropology and Neo-Hinduism in connection with Dravidian culture, language and religion, its promoters had no hesitation in accepting colonial propositions about village traditions or non-Agamic Hinduism, which formed the religion of the vast majority of the Tamil population.[99] As Sumathi Ramaswamy has observed, the programme of Neo-Shaivism was "puritanical and elitist ... in its advocacy of vegetarianism and teetotalism and its calls for the excision of 'irrational' customs, and actions and rituals (animal sacrifices, the worship of godlings and the like), which were the very stuff of village and popular religion".[100]

Throughout the early decades following the rise of Neo-Shaivism, its proponents viewed the Tamil religion as merely one variation of the great collocation of discourses which comprised the Hindu tradition, and criticism of Sanskrit, per se, was muted.[101] This changed in the 1920s with the rise of the vehement anti-Brahman rhetoric of the increasingly powerful Justice Party.[102] The moderation of earlier years gave way to the shrill allegations of maleficent Sanskritic–Brahmanic conspiracies designed to denigrate the divinity both of Tamils and the Tamil religion and assertions that Brahmans were not "true Tamils" at all.[103] In 1922 the fervour generated by these polemics led to representatives of depressed castes claiming and receiving official sanction for the — wholly erroneous — title of *Adi Dravida* or "first" or "original" Dravidians.[104] Although, as noted, both Tamil and Sanskrit had been fundamental to institutionalized South Indian Hinduism for many centuries, Neo-Shaivite radicals now demanded that all worship in Tamil temples be conducted in Tamil.[105] The (re)divination of Tamil was embodied in the figure of the rather obscure goddess *Tamiltay*, and various myths attributed her creation to the quintessentially "Dravidian" god Siva, sometimes through the agency of Earth, at other times by the intervention of Murugan, and in further interpretations by the sage Agastya.[106] As Neo-Shaivite claims for the exclusive divinity of Tamil traditions and the Tamil language as the proper and sole vehicle for the conduct of worship increased, so too did the calumniation of Sanskrit, and the denial of its very legitimacy as a language of worship. By the late 1940s, Neo-Shaivite extremists were insisting that Tamil temples be "cleansed" of the "filth" of Sanskrit.[107]

The Tamil ideologies and anti-Brahmanism which found expression in Neo-Shaivism and the political agenda of the Justice Party took on a far more vociferous and aggressive tenor in the atheistic Dravidianism of the Self Respect movement headed by E.V. Ramasami Naicker. Ramasami's social theories, fully incorporating Caldwell's racial theories, posited a separate South Indian racial and hence civilizational identity, and called for the establishment of an autonomous Tamil polity.[108] He identified the enemies of this project as Tamil Brahmans who represented the northern "Aryan invaders" who had subjugated Tamil society with their caste rules and rituals.[109] But Ramasami had no faith in the ideologies of Neo-Shaivism. His atheism led him and his followers to ridicule Neo-Shaivism with the same contempt he evinced towards Hinduism, which he regarded as nothing more than an Aryan–Brahmanic Sanskritic conspiracy designed to destroy Tamil identity and annihilate Dravidian culture.[110] Ramasami also launched fierce attacks on the rituals and practices of popular Hinduism and called for the implementation of a "rational" and essentially modernist political agenda.[111]

Ramasami remained influential throughout the 1930s and 1940s. However, after the formation in 1949 of the Dravida Munnera Kalagam (Dravidian Progress Association, or DMK), which embodied the principal constructs of Dravidian ideologies, the party took steps to distance itself from Ramasami's iconoclasm. The DMK's more inclusive Dravidianism allowed for the exploration of Tamil religiosity, which incorporated both popular and established devotional traditions, including emphasis on the worship of Murugan, within the framework of its cultural policy.[112] In 1967 the DMK won a convincing electoral victory, thus ushering in a period of intense Tamilization (including the renaming of the Madras state, which became Tamilnadu (Tamil Nadu).[113]

The corrosive impact of colonial ideologies in undermining the confidence and self-respect of Indians has been widely recognized.[114] Many scholars have commented on the phenomenon whereby those colonized internalize the central ideology of the colonizers, subsequently refracting back to the colonizers the very preceptions and theories developed by the colonizers about those they rule.[115] The ideologies which permeated British scholarship in India ultimately extended to the subject populations, thus profoundly reshaping the way many Indians envisaged their own culture, society and history. Indeed, many of the key constructs of Empire, so sedulously inculcated by the British, were ultimately accepted by influential sections of the Indian population. Thomas Metcalf has demonstrated how the portrayal of an India deeply sundered between two competing religious communities took root in India.[116] But other critiques of Indian society also gained wide currency, especially among Indian intellectuals. These included perspectives on caste as the foundational principle of Indian society; the Aryan/Dravidian racial divide; on Brahmanism and Sanskrit texts as the sole repository of authentic Hindu culture (with its corollary, the denial of the validity of regional or popular Indian religious forms); on the measurement of Hinduism against perceived and often idealized benchmarks set by Semitic religions (especially Christianity, and more latterly against those established by an imagined modernistic "Western scientific" ethos).[117]

Conclusions

We have noted that the period of British colonialism and British racial ideologies, based upon orientalist readings of Indian history, culture and institutions, produced reactive Hindu reform movements, which in South India attempted to locate and disinter imagined pasts. These consisted of the colonially inscribed neo-Hinduism, which looked to an orientalist-fabricated Aryan-Sanskritic civilization, and two Tamil-oriented movements, Neo-Shaivism and Dravidian "nationalism", both of which sought in radically different ways to recreate a supposed autochthonous Tamil culture free of Sanksritic–Brahmanic accretions. Both condemned, in vituperative terms, indigenous "little" or popular traditions. The debates, commenced by arcane, largely discredited and in many cases all but forgotten colonial discourses, continue to circulate among metropolitan and diaspora Indians (and as we will see, in the following chapter, within Malaysia).

Notes

1. Nicholas Dirks, "Introduction", in Bernard S. Cohn, *Colonialism and its Forms of Knowledge: The British in India* (Princeton, NJ: Princeton University Press, 1996), p. ix.

2. Bernard S. Cohn, *Colonialism and its Forms of Knowledge: The British in India* (Princeton, NJ: Princeton University Press, 1996), p. 79.

3. Ibid., p. 8.

4. Ibid., p. 93.

5. Ibid., pp. 29, 65; Nicholas Dirks, *Castes of Mind: Colonialism and the Making of Modern India* (Princeton, NJ: Princeton University Press, 2001), pp. 38–39; Vineeta Sinha, *A New God in the Diaspora? Muneeswaran Worship in Contemporary Singapore* (Singapore and Copenhagen: Singapore University Press/NIAS Press, 2005), p. 238.

6. Dirks, *Castes of Mind*, pp. 41, 123.

7. William Dalrymple, *White Muslims: Love & Betrayal in Eighteenth Century India* (London: Harper Perennial, 2003), p. 41.

8. Cohn, *Colonialism*, pp. 29–33.

9. Ibid., p. 29.

10. Ibid., pp. 71–72.

11. Dirks, *Castes of Mind*, pp. 34–35.

12. Thomas R. Trautmann, *Aryans and British India* (Berkeley: University of California Press, 1997), pp. 8–9.

13. This timeline was based on the chronology devised in 1650 by Archbishop James Ussher. In his highly influential "Annals of the Old Testament", Ussher calculated that the Creation had occurred at 9 a.m. on 26 October 4004 BCE. Most eighteenth- and nineteenth-century Bibles included a chronology of Biblical events based on Ussher's estimations (Don Gifford, *The Farther Shore: A Natural History of Perception* [London: Faber & Faber: 1990], p. 72).

14. Rajiv Malhotra and Aravindan Neelakandan, *Breaking India: Western Interventions in Dravidian and Dalit Faultlines* (New Delhi: Amaryllis, 2011), p. 39.

15. Robin Blackburn, *The Making of New World Slavery: From the Baroque to the Modern 1492–1800* (London: Verso, 1997), p. 65.

16. Malhotra and Aravindan, *Breaking India*, pp. 39–40.

17. The myth of the Tower of Babel is as follows. Genesis 11:1–9 states that following the Great Flood the entire human population journeyed to one location ("the land of Shinar"), where they began to build a tower which would reach to heaven. God, angered, scattered them across the face of the Earth.

18. Trautmann, *Aryans*, pp. 10–15.

19. Ibid., p. 15; Malhotra and Aravindan, *Breaking India*, p. 40.

20. Trautmann, *Aryans*, p. 6.

21. Ibid., p. 38.

22. Thomas R. Trautmann, *Languages and Nations: The Dravidian Proof in Colonial Madras* (Berkeley: University of California Press, 2006), p. 217.

23. Malhotra and Aravindan, *Breaking India*, p. 167.

24. Wendy Doniger, *The Hindus: An Alternative History* (New York: Penguin, 2009), p. 585.

25. Dirks, *Castes of Mind*, p. 34.

26. Amartya Sen, *The Argumentative Indian: Writings in Indian History, Culture and Identity* (London: Allen Lane, 2005), p. 149.

27. Trautmann, *Languages and Nations*, p. 73.

28. Trautmann, *Aryans*, pp. 158–59.

29. Ibid., pp. 172–75.

30. Malhotra and Aravindan, *Breaking India*, p. 64.

31. Ibid., p. 67.

32. Dirks, *Castes of Mind*, p. 138; Malhotra and Aravindan, *Breaking India*, p. 62.

33. Trautmann, *Languages and Nations*, p. 224.

34. Malhotra and Aravindan, *Breaking India*, pp. 29–30.

35. Gifford, *The Farther Shore*, p. 72; Trautmann, *Aryans*, p. 193. In 1830, Charles Lyall argued that geological evidence pointed to a world significantly older than that estimated by Bishop Ussher. He showed that the Earth's crust had not been directly shaped by the Creation, but rather by the long-term action of wind and water (Karen Armstrong, *The Case for God: What Religion Really Means* [London: Bodley Head, 2009], pp. 233–34).

36. Trautmann, *Aryans*, p. 133; Trautmann, *Languages and Nations*, p. 221.

37. Dirks, *Castes of Mind*, p. 43.

38. Christine Bolt, *Victorian Attitudes to Race* (London: Routledge and Kegan Paul, 1971), p. 9.

39. Charles Hirschmann, "The Meaning and Measurement of Ethnicity in Malaysia: A Study of Census Classifications", *Journal of Asian Studies* 46, no. 3 (August 1987): 568–89.

40. Bolt, *Victorian Attitudes*, pp. 24–26.

41. Ibid., p. 11; Hirschmann, "The Meaning and Measurement", p. 568.

42. Arthur Hermann, *The Idea of Decline in Western History* (New York: The Free Press, 1997), p. 114; Anthony Reid, *Charting the Shape of Early Modern Southeast Asia* (Singapore: Institute of Southeast Asian Studies, 2000), pp. 238–39.

43. Bolt, *Victorian Attitudes*, p. 168.

44. Trautmann, *Languages and Nations*, p. 225.

45. Ibid. By 1891 the Census Report of the Government of India could speak of the Dravidians in the following terms: "This was a race, black in skin, low in stature, and with matted locks, in war treacherous and cunning, in choice of food disgusting, and in ceremonial absolutely deficient. The superior civilization of the foreigner [the Aryan] soon asserted itself, and the lower race had to give way.... The newcomers had to deal with opponents far inferior to themselves in civilization and with only a very rudimentary political organization, so the opposition to be overcome before the Aryan could take possession of the soil was of the feeblest." (Sumathi Ramaswamy, *Passions of the Tongue: Language Devotion in Tamil India 1891–1970* [New Delhi: Munshiram Manoharlal, 1998], p. 26).

46. Romila Tharpar, "Imagined Communities? Ancient History and the Modern Search for Hindu Identity", *Modern Asian Studies* 23 (1989): 218.
47. Thomas R. Metcalf, *Ideologies of the Raj* (Cambridge: Cambridge University Press, 1995, pp. 88–90.
48. Ramaswamy, *Passions of the Tongue*, p. 26.
49. Ibid. Thus, in 1901, Charles Johnstone, a high-ranking Methodist missionary, could write of the Tamils: "To this black race, passionate, magnetic of wild imaginings, we must trace every lurid and demoniac element in the beliefs of India. This is their contribution to the common sum: a combination fitting in the hue of the African voodoo, the Australian cannibal, and the Papuan headhunter." (Bolt, *Victorian Attitudes*, pp. 128–29).
50. Malhotra and Aravindan, *Breaking India*, p. 83.
51. Pieter Van der Veer, *Religious Nationalism: Hindus and Muslims in India* (Berkeley: University of California Press, 1994), p. 19.
52. Ibid; Maria Misra, *Vishnu's Crowded Temple: India Since the Great Rebellion* (London: Allen Lane, 2007), pp. 37–38.
53. David Washbrook, "The Development of Caste Organization in South India 1880–1925", in *South India: Political Institutions and Political Change 1880–1940*, edited by C.J. Baker and David Washbrook (Delhi: Macmillan, 1975), p. 180.
54. Van der Veer, *Religious Nationalism*, p. 19.
55. Washbrook, "The Development of Caste Organization", p. 180.
56. Dirks, *Castes of Mind*, pp. 46–47, 173.
57. Christopher Baker, "Facts and Figures: Madras Government Statistics 1880–1940", in *South India Political Institutions and Political Change 1880–1940*, edited by C.J. Baker and David Washbrook (Delhi: MacMillan, 1975), pp. 222–41; Washbrook, "The Development of Caste Organization", p. 186.
58. Declan Quigley, *The Interpretation of Caste* (Oxford: Oxford University Press, 1993), pp. 124–26.
59. Van der Veer, *Religious Nationalism*, p. 19.
60. Dirks, *Castes of Mind*, p. 181.
61. Metcalf, *Ideologies of the Raj*, p. 127.
62. Dirks, *Castes of Mind*, p. 212.
63. Misra, *Vishnu's Crowded Temple*, p. 51.
64. Trautmann, *Aryans*, p. 191.
65. Dirks, *Castes of Mind*, p. 210.
66. Ibid., pp. 235–36.
67. Washbrook, "The Development of Caste Organisation", p. 181.
68. Ibid., p. 189.
69. Ibid., p. 181.
70. Misra, *Vishnu's Crowded Temple*, p. 34.
71. Tharpar, *Imagined Communities?*, p. 225.

72. Ibid., p. 218.
73. Sinha, *A New God?*, pp. 237–41.
74. Dirks, *Castes of Mind*, p. 253.
75. David Washbrook, "Introduction", in *South India: Political Institutions and Political Change*, edited by C.J. Baker and David Washbrook (Delhi: MacMillan, 1975), p. 7.
76. Metcalf, *Ideologies of the Raj*, pp. 136–37.
77. Dirks, *Castes of Mind*, p. 253.
78. Van der Veer, *Religious Nationalism*, p. 19.
79. Metcalf, *Ideologies of the Raj*, p. 132.
80. Ibid., p. 183.
81. Van der Veer, *Religious Nationalism*, p. 22.
82. Dominique-Sila Khan, *Crossing the Threshold: Understanding Religious Identities in South Asia* (London: Tauris/Institute of Ismaili Studies, 2004), pp. 44–50.
83. Tharpar, *Imagined Communities?*, p. 225.
84. Ibid., pp. 220–21.
85. Ramaswamy, *Passions of the Tongue*, pp. 26–27.
86. Ibid., p. 26.
87. Ehrenreich, *Dancing in the Streets*, p. 157.
88. Stephen Inglis, "Possession and Pottery: Serving the Divine in a South Indian Community", in *Gods of Flesh, Gods of Stone: The Embodiment of Divinity in India*, edited by Joanne Punzo Waghorne and Norman Cutler in association with Vasudha Narayanan (Chambersburg: Anima, 1985), p. 89; Geoffrey A. Oddie, *Popular Religion, Elites and Reforms: Hookswinging and its Prohibition in Colonial India 1800–1894* (New Delhi: Manohar, 1995), pp. 53–54.
89. Dirks, *Castes of Mind*, p. 150. For a full description of the events described in this paragraph, see Oddie, *Popular Religion*.
90. Ramaswamy, *Passions of the Tongue*, p. 25.
91. Washbrook, *The Development of Caste Organization*, p. 190.
92. Dirks, *Castes of Mind*, p. 239.
93. Ibid., p. 238.
94. Ramaswamy, *Passions of the Tongue*, p. 27.
95. Christopher John Baker, *The Politics of South India 1920–1937* (Cambridge: Cambridge University Press, 1976), pp. 27–29.
96. Ramaswamy, *Passions of the Tongue*, pp. 25–27.
97. Ibid., pp. 29–30.
98. Burton Stein, *Peasant, State and Society in Medieval South India* (Delhi: Oxford University Press. 1978), p. 51.
99. Washbrook, "Introduction", p. 7.
100. Ramaswamy, *Passions of the Tongue*, p. 25.
101. Ibid., p. 30.

102. Baker, *The Politics of South India*, pp. 27–32.
103. Ramaswamy, *Passions of the Tongue*, pp. 31–32.
104. Dirks, *Castes of Mind*, p. 240.
105. Ramaswamy, *Passions of the Tongue*, pp. 31–32.
106. Ibid., p. 87.
107. Ibid., p. 139.
108. Ibid., p. 63.
109. Michael Wood points out that in his most violent speeches, Ramasami actually called for the murder of Brahmans (Michael Wood, *The Smile of Murugan: A South Indian Journey* [Harmondsworth: Penguin, 1996], p. 48).
110. Ramaswamy, *Passions of the Tongue*, p. 69. Nicholas Dirks comments: "If it seems peculiar that Caldwell's Christian understanding of South Indian society should be adapted to the purposes of an extreme form of secular ideology, it is even stranger that Caldwell's colonial view of Aryan cultural hegemony should have been converted to the uses of a xenophobic nationalism that substituted Brahmans for Britons, Aryanism for modernity, Sanskrit or Hindi for English, and northern India for Europe." (Dirks, *Castes of Mind*, p. 145.)
111. Baker, *The Politics of South India*, pp. 83–85; Ramaswamy, *Passions of the Tongue*, p. 69.
112. Ramaswamy, *Passions of the Tongue*, pp. 64–70.
113. Ibid., pp. 73–74.
114. Sen, *The Argumentative Indian*, p. 77.
115. Doniger, *The Hindus*, p. 597.
116. Metcalf, *Ideologies of the Raj*, p. 148.
117. Tharpar, *Imagined Communities*, p. 218; Van der Veer, *Religious Nationalism*, pp. 20–21; Ramaswamy, *Passions of the Tongue*, p. 26; Oddie, *Popular Religion*, p. 33.

4

Hinduism in Malaysia: An Overview

The waves of Indian migration which followed the British colonization of Malaya and which continued up until the eve of the Pacific War were accompanied by the re-establishment of Hinduism as a significant minority religion in Malaya.[1] The transplantation and historical evolution of Malaya/ Malaysian Hinduism has occurred in the absence of those traditional points of reference — namely, the religious centres of learning or monastic orders (*mathas*) which had provided a system of scriptural hermeneutics and exegesis, as well as an influential Brahman or dominant orthodox caste — which had such a marked impact upon Hindu structures, belief systems, mythology and patterns of worship in South India.[2] The new arrivals in the estates and workplaces, lacking wider points of reference, tended to automatically reproduce remembered belief structures, practices and mores of the Hinduism of their home regions.[3] Since the majority of Indian immigrants were either indentured or later kangany recruited labourers, the deities worshipped and the rituals associated with that worship largely revolved around the sub-communal norms of behaviour and caste variations of the village of origin.[4] Over time these practices were in some cases reinforced, in others modified, in many more supplemented, by other regional and caste influences introduced to the estates, workplaces and cities of Malaya.[5]

This chapter will provide a general overview of Hinduism as it has evolved in Malaysia. Professor Champakalakshmi has pointed out that religion cannot be isolated as an autonomous domain but must be considered in relation to the specific historical socio-political contexts in which it is implicated.[6] Despite the enduring and formative influences of metropolitan Indian–Malaysian links, and those of more recent intra-diaspora exchanges, and many profound resemblances to practices in the Indian "homeland", Hinduism in Malaysia has followed its own unique trajectory, shaped by the specific historical and other circumstances which attended its importation and adaptation.

In seeking to explore Hinduism in Malaysia, I echo Vineeta Sinha's observation that it is necessary to move beyond fixed theoretical models of Hinduism, and in particular established hierarchical pantheonic Sanskritic/non-Sanskritic ranking, and to locate spheres of actual practice.[7] Hindu belief and rituals in Malaysia are astonishingly heterogenous and involve a wide range of imported practices and traditions which have been subsequently moulded by a multitude of localized factors, including region, caste, ethnicity and class. Over the years various belief structures have interacted in complex and sometimes unexpected ways, often producing outcomes which commingle *Agamic*/Sanskritic and folk religious traditions in fresh, pragmatic and sometimes innovative syncretic forms. Many Malaysian devotees practise a form of worship, which while inclining towards a particular tradition, contains a substantial leavening of other variants and belief structures.

While in this chapter I have accessed a variety of written source materials, much of what follows is also based on my own field research. This involved extensive interviews with temple and religious officials, political functionaries and, of course, devotees.

Caste in Malaysia

In Chapter 1 we noted that the indentured workforce in Malaya was in the main drawn from landless labourers and those dispossessed by agricultural reforms within the Madras Presidency, and consisted largely of members of the *Adi Dravida* castes. Kangany recruitment resulted in major changes in the overall composition of the Indian workforce. The reputation of the kangany, as a member of a "clean" caste and a man who promised to guarantee the welfare of those he recruited, led to a significant increase in the number of labourers who were prepared to relocate to the estates and workplaces of Malaya.[8] While approximately one-third of kangany migrants originated from among the *Adi Dravida* castes, others were drawn from the entire range of non-Brahman castes. Major caste groupings comprised *Vellalar, Goundar* and *Vanniyar*, and included members of landowning and cultivating *jatis*, regarded as among the higher Tamil caste groupings.[9] Kangany recruitment produced a more variegated Indian community within Malayan estates and towns, and thus a greater spread of social behaviours and belief structures.[10]

The absence of a strong Brahman/Vellalar model on the estates and more generally within the social and cultural fabric of the Malayan Hindu community had a profound impact on the evolution and organization of inter-caste dynamics in Malaya/Malaysia.[11] In Chapter 2 we observed that South Indian caste hierarchies were largely structured independently of the prescriptions of *varna*, and while loosely inclining to a purity–pollution paradigm were often fluid and moulded by a variety of localized economic and cultural factors. Within Malayan workplaces and estates the re-creation of known hierarchical rankings was complicated by the ambiguities of regional caste variations which had obtained within the Madras Presidency. Thus, the full reconstruction of the traditional village communities with their stipulated and demarcated frameworks of occupation, order and precedence was clearly impossible within the Malayan settings.[12]

While there was no real possibility of reproducing the totality of caste organization in Malaya and the complete array of distinctive behaviours, diets and ideals of ritual purity as they existed in the home environment, major elements of ritual caste observations were introduced into the social life of Indians in Malaya. Certain caste prohibitions and taboos were adhered to, especially the provision of separate housing and supplies of water for upper castes and *Adi Dravidas*.[13] In general, *Adi Dravidas* accepted the allocation of discrete housing lines and water supplies without protest.[14] Most marriages remained within caste, though some minority *jatis* did not have sufficient numbers in Malaya to sustain the practice of endogamy, and there was a tendency for small *jatis* to be absorbed within the nearest hierarchically ranked generic caste grouping. There was evidence of caste clashes on estates, and caste associations were later formed, including the establishment of *Adi Dravida Sangams* among depressed castes.[15]

Caste distinctions among Indians in Malaya gradually ebbed as the Indian workforce became more settled within Malaya. The slow easing of caste relations was undoubtedly assisted by the fact that within the plantations or workforce contexts, *jati* had no operational significance either as a term or a concept.[16] S. Arasaratnam has suggested that the change in caste relations began in the 1920s when upper-caste leaders, inspired by Gandhian ideologies, offered assistance to *Adi Dravida Sangams*.[17] By the early 1930s officials were noting the softening of caste hierarchies within Malayan social, vocational and religious life. Commenting on the admission of *Adi Dravidas* to the newly opened *Agamic* Mariamman temple in Penang in 1935, J.M. Barron, the Acting Controller of Labour, described it as "a remarkable instance of the growth of a new spirit of [inter-caste] tolerance". However, in an indication that this new lenience was not shared by all Tamil workers, he also noted that on one estate in Province Wellesley, upper-caste labourers complained that *Adi Dravidas* did not evince "the same respectful inferiority as in India".[18] In the same year, K.A. Mukundan, Agent of the Government of India, noted an increase in inter-caste marriages, though he did not elaborate upon which castes were involved.[19] In 1936, C. Wilson, Controller of Labour, opined optimistically that "Caste distinctions are not so strong in Malaya as in India, and the spirit of tolerance is growing.… In time, no doubt, caste distinctions will die in Malaya. A piped water system spells death to caste." However, he also noted that "on estates it is necessary to provide caste men with separate accommodation from the *Adi Dravidas*, though quarrels between the two bodies are not common."[20]

The opening of the Penang Mariamman temples to *Adi Dravidas* in 1935 represented a triumph of Gandhian principles in Malaya,[21] and was followed by an open-door policy in several other temples in Malaya. After World War II, in the wake of the unifying experiences of the IIL/INA and inspired by the anti-caste rhetoric of Subhas Chandra Bose, all temples were opened to *Adi Dravida* devotees. While this measure elicited sustained resistance in India, within Malaya the open-door policy aroused little opposition.[22]

The traditional model of social organization, structured around the fundamental division of Brahman, non-Brahman and *Adi Dravida* castes was replaced in Malaya with two broader, and essentially more generic groupings. While "clean" castes identified themselves as *"Tamilar"* (*uyarntajati*, or higher castes), *Adi Dravida jatis* were known as *"Paraiyar"* (*talntajati*, or lower castes). In general, this basic division, which emerged within the late kangany era, continues to remain valid within Malaya.[23]

The continuing moderation of caste boundaries and inter-caste perceptions has been a prolonged and gradual process among Malayan/ Malaysian Indians. I have noted that the lack of a dominant or Brahman/

Vellalar caste left Malaysian Hinduism without a key principle of social organization, and that estate and workplace arrangements within Malaya removed vocational calling as an ascriptive criterion of caste. Since World War II, a range of economic and educational influences, especially social and occupational mobility, have continued to temper traditional notions of caste and caste hierarchy. Moreover, the post-war politics of communalism, and the stress upon Indian identity vis-à-vis other ethnic groups, have served to cut across prescribed inter-caste modes of communication, and to introduce more cooperative concepts of social organization.[24] While it is generally agreed that many younger Indians tend to be less interested in formal caste relations and notions of putative hierarchy and precedence, my own observations have led me to conclude that these more relaxed attitudes are often theoretical and that caste/*jati* will often be invoked as a causal factor to explain egregious behaviour or individual/inter-family disputes.

However, while caste boundaries have continued to blur, and the perceptions that castes hold of each other have been extensively renegotiated and some aspects of caste behaviour have been relaxed, caste remains a clearly identifiable social phenomenon within Malaysian Indian Hindu life. Enduring caste signifiers centre upon patterns of worship, maintenance of endogamous marriage and the observation of ritual purity and pollution in social interaction. Higher castes continue to regard wedlock with lower castes as socially degrading and deleterious for the entire clan affected by the liaison.[25] Taboos relating to food and diet, and from whom one will accept cooked food, continue to reinforce caste identity; for example, during wedding ceremonies or other occasions requiring mass feedings, the host group will normally employ a higher-caste cook. Among upper castes, especially older members, it is common to discern certain pejorative attitudes regarding the characteristics of lower castes as a group — for example, that they are aggressive, unclean, generally bad mannered, loud and uncouth in behaviour, loose tongued and foul mouthed, and that they eat messily and noisily, etc. Moreover, among higher castes it is often asserted that the membership of Indian criminal gangs consists almost wholly of *Adi Dravida* youth.

In general, caste remains a persistent and resilient form of social identification for many Hindus. Thus, for example, throughout the late 1970s and into the mid-1980s the irruption of caste politics destabilized the MIC, with the formation of rival interest groups coalesced around higher and lower castes.[26] Moreover, as we will see, Hindu reformers and educators offer a model of Hinduism structured around the imagined higher-caste/Brahmanic ideals, and completely stripped of its putative socially unacceptable village/lower-caste accretions. It can perhaps be argued that these groups of reformers represent a new approach to maintenance and indeed reinforcement of upper-caste control of the social and ritual parameters of Malaysian Indian Hindu society.

Caste associations have limited influence in contemporary Malaysia. Upon their formation in the 1920s, *Adi Dravida* caste *sangams* developed mass followings. Most of these were reform oriented, concerned with welfare, education and upliftment.[27] Some, however, became politically aligned with the "Dravidian" ideologies of Ramasami Naicker's Self Respect movement, and served to disseminate the vehement anti-Brahman propaganda associated with pan-Dravidian organizations.[28] In more recent times the membership of such caste associations has become increasingly restricted to poorly educated and lower-caste Tamils. These associations are generally shunned by younger and urban-educated Tamils, and continue to decline in significance.

Malaysian Hindu Temples

In his 1995 study on Hinduism in Malaysia, Ramanathan Kalimuthu estimated that there was an approximate total of 17,000 Hindu temples in Malaysia.[29] Hindu authorities have informed me that there is no reliable mode of calculating the exact number of Hindu temples in Malaysia (despite the pleas of authorities, many temples remain unregistered), but they believe Ramanathan's figure remains a reliable approximation. Temples in Malaysia range across the entire gamut of South Indian tradition, from modest shrines and small temples, often little more than sheds, used for mediumship and worship of guardian/tutelary dieties, to the most elaborate and properly maintained *Agamic* temples. Ramanathan points out that the large number and sheer multiplicity of temples encountered "is clearly a reflection of the diverse practices within the Hindu religion itself. It also reflected the various sub-ethnic divisions based on caste, religion and the orientation of the Malaysian Hindu community."[30]

The Hindus who migrated to Malaya were inspired by two deeply held cultural convictions regarding the construction of temples. The first is that no settlement, village or town is complete for the Hindu unless it has a temple, and that if the locality does not have a temple it is the duty of individuals or the community to construct one. Secondly, it is believed that those who participate in the construction or maintenance of a temple will acquire great merit. The building of temples represented the determination of Hindu immigrants to "sacralise the space in which they now resided" and to inscribe their identity and beliefs on to the new landscape to which they had travelled.[31]

Malaysia's earliest temples were built around regional, caste or sub-caste belief structures imported from the home localities of India. However, as will be discussed, in many instances the deities worshipped and the rituals performed have undergone profound alterations over the years, and the initial specific caste, lineage or regional focus has either been expunged or obscured.

Agamic Temples

Agamic Hinduism was imported to Malaysia by middle and upper class Hindus, in particular the Chettiar and Jaffna Tamil communities. The specific contributions of each of these communities to the development of Malayan/Malaysian Hinduism will be outlined below. As we noted in the previous chapter, *Agamic* Hinduism is based upon scriptural and textual sources, and public worship is conducted in temples dedicated to the great or universal deities of traditional Saivism or Vaishnavism. Temples are constructed in consonance with *Agamic* stipulations. *Agamic* temples are dedicated and maintained according to prescribed rites, and worship is conducted by ritual specialists, usually of the Brahman caste. Brahmans and "clean" castes within Malaysia regard these temples as embodying the absolute ideals of Hindu religious belief and therefore superior in concept and instrumentality to non-*Agamic* or popular temples. A large percentage of *Agamic* temples in Malaysia are dedicated to either Murugan (Subrahmanya) or to Mariamman (Sakti).

The major *Agamic* temples in Malaysia were established by the upper castes. The initial burden of temple construction fell disproportionately on the Chettiar caste, and more latterly upon the Jaffna Tamil community, although professional and commercial classes also contributed towards the establishment of temples.[32] Both the Chettiars and Jaffna Tamils established exemplary models of *Agamic* temple construction, maintenance and worship, which adhered to the scriptural injunctions, rituals, festivals and other specified observances learnt in their respective countries of origin. Brahman *kurukkals* were imported to officiate at these temples.[33] At this point it is important to note that many members of the South Indian middle class who might have been expected to promote *Agamic* worship and to provide leadership in the construction of temples initially distanced themselves from open allegiance to Hindu belief and worship structures, especially in the period leading to World War II. Much of this class, from which the reform movements were to ultimately spring, were acutely conscious of the perceived standing of the Indian community in the eyes of the British and other ethnic communities, and were anxious to establish themselves as a "modern" and "Westernized" community. This necessitated maintaining social distance from other Hindus, especially from the bulk of the labouring classes and their "debased" and supposedly socially embarrassing traditions.[34]

Chettiars

The Nattukottai Chettiars, generally referred to as the Chettiars (but also known as the *Vanikars*, *Nagarathars* or *Chettyars*),[35] are by tradition a Tamil moneylending caste. The Chettiar base in India is centred on the generic territory known as *Chettinad* ("The Land of the Chettiars"), located in the districts of Ramnad and Puddukkottai.[36] The social organization of the Chettiars is based in nine ancestral temples, each of which is owned by one of nine clan groups.[37] The Chettiars are endogamous, and cross-cousin marriage is common. Although the Chettiars were originally a Sudra caste, in more recent times they have made claim to be considered as Vaisyas.[38]

British colonialism provided the Chettiars with an expanded range of trading possibilities both within India and in other colonies, particularly Ceylon, the Straits Settlements and Burma.[39] By the 1790s the first Chettiar business houses, known as *kittingi*,[40] were opened in Penang, and others followed in Melaka in 1808 and Singapore in the 1820s.[41] Throughout the 1820s, as their numbers increased, the Chettiars established formal temples in the style of their homeland in their places of operation. By the end of the nineteenth century the Chettiars had established a chain of *kittingi* and temples within all major economic centres down the west coast of the Malay Peninsula. As they became more firmly established in Malaysia and Singapore, they brought their wives and children to join them.[42]

Murugan, venerated in the specific form of *Thandayuthapani* (the ascetic deity enshrined at Palani, India), is the caste deity of the Chettiars, and his worship permeates all social and business life of the community. As a patron deity, Murugan is held to be honorary chairman of all temple, social and financial meetings, as well as witness in business dealings between Chettiars.[43] The first dealing of the day is always done in Murugan's name, and a nominal sum is registered in the ledger book as expenditure sustained by the deity. An agreed percentage of income (usually about ten per cent) is levied on all Chettiar commercial undertakings and retained as a tithe (*Mahamai*) within an account held in the name of "Chetti Murugan". The funds thus generated are later used for charitable purposes and for temples, festivals and other religious expenses.[44]

Chettiar temples in Malaysia were constructed according to strict *Agamic* precepts and continue to be maintained in conformity with these ideals. These temples are generally regarded as well organized and appear largely free of the vexatious factionalism which is often found among the management committees of many other Hindu temples throughout Malaysia. The general supervision of temple affairs is entrusted to a five-member management committee (or *panchyat*), which is usually elected for a five-year term. Because each temple is regarded as a final arbiter on all religious and social matters affecting the Chettiar community, the *panchyat* also fulfils important mediatory and adjudicatory functions.[45]

Festivals in Chettiar temples are primarily organized around the worship of Murugan. These are invariably well planned and executed. Since Murugan has a number of festival days, particular festivals are allocated to specific temples in different locations, and throughout the calendar year all Chettiar temples will organize at least one major festival (as is the practice in India). However, it should be noted that the spatial distribution of Murugan festivals may also be seen as an attempt to replicate the sacral geography of Murugan worship as found in India. There, as we will more fully observe in the following chapter, specific temples are fused with strategic episodes in the overall chronology of Murugan mythology, from which the festival associated with each of these temples derives its meaning. Thus, within Malaysia/Singapore, for example, Thaipusam is associated with Singapore and Penang, while Chitra Paruvam has become linked to the temple in Telok Intan, in Perak. In the early days the commemoration of the festival calendar provided Chettiars stationed in different localities with regular opportunities to visit each other.

The Chettiars have never experienced the problem of recruiting and retaining temple priests, a matter which has become an issue of perennial concern to many Malaysian temples. This is largely because since the

1950s they have maintained meticulous documentation of temple affairs, and are thus able to justify to immigration authorities the need to import approved temple priests, musicians and temple craftsmen. Moreover, the Chettiar community in India have established an institution in Pallaiyar Patti in Chettinad for the education and training of both Brahman and non-Brahman priests. The Chettiars have also provided handsome donations to *mathas* which train Brahman *kurukkals*. Since the 1980s the Malaysian Chettiars have sponsored several local candidates (including at least two ethnic Chinese, but mainly Tamils of the Vellalar caste) to train as temple priests.[46] The Chettiars are known as good employers, and provide all temple officiants with accommodation and fair remuneration. In return, priests are required to acknowledge members of the Chettiar community, and to offer them precedence throughout all ritualistic and ceremonial occasions.

The perceived exclusivity of the Chettiars and the priority that they accord their own caste, both within their temples and within the overall structures of the festivals which they sponsor, have created resentment among some Malaysian Tamils. Moreover, the economic success of the Chettiars has promoted charges of arrogance, lack of compassion, parsimoniousness and indifference to the sufferings of the broader Tamil community. In recent years the Chettiar community, stung by these criticisms, has made efforts to reach out to other sectors of the Indian Hindu population. Many of the censorious judgements passed on the Chettiar community seem exaggerated and without real foundation. The Chettiars make substantial donations to charities, and are equally generous in their contributions to religious and cultural organizations, scholars and artists. Moreover, as Ramanathan remarks, "no-one can compare to them in terms of the financial resources lavished on the maintenance of temples, since all are financially secure and seem well able to face any challenge in the future".[47]

Ceylonese "Jaffna" Tamils

The culture of the Ceylonese "Jaffna" Tamils contains marked variations from the Tamil culture of mainland India. Distinctive elements include linguistic differences in the use of spoken Tamil, the structure of inter-caste relations, the observation of life cycle ceremonies, and some modes of worship. The overwhelming majority of Jaffna Tamils who migrated to Malaya were members of the authoritative Vellalar caste, who were principally agriculturalists and landowners, and who dominated the middle and upper classes of Ceylonese Tamil society. The Vellalars saw themselves as patrons-in-chief, who were expected to fulfil a kingly role and to conform to the *dharma* specified for those who occupied the highest echelons of society. They ran the temples according to *Agamic* precepts and demanded the compliance of the supporting "clean" castes.[48] The small Brahman caste in Jaffna, numerically insignificant and politically irrelevant, was largely dependent upon the Vellalars for employment within the temples.[49]

Within Malaya the Jaffna Tamils developed an exemplary record for temple building, and wherever a community established itself, the construction of a temple invariably followed. Given the fact that the Ceylonese Vellalars are overwhelmingly Saivite and are steeped in the practices and traditions of *Agamic* Hinduism, these temples were axiomatically dedicated to the major deities — Siva, Ganesha and Skanda-Murugan.[50] Temples were built along the length and breadth of the Malay Peninsula, including at many isolated locations in which Jaffna Tamils were employed (for example, the railway settlement of Kuala Lipis, and the former royal town of Pekan, both in the state of Pahang).[51]

The Jaffna Tamil temples are regarded as well managed and maintained. The community has been careful to establish legally protected temple endowments for the maintenance of these temples, and to devise safeguards which stipulate the conditions under which these funds may be drawn upon. Wherever possible, Jaffna Tamils have attempted to restrict membership of the temple management committees to their own community, though in recent years there has been some relaxation surrounding this issue, especially as the abilities of the educated Indian Tamils have become more apparent. However, Jaffna Tamils have been greatly alarmed by reports of mismanagement of some Malaysian Hindu temples, and are determined to ensure that this does not occur within the temples they have established.

Among some sectors of the broader Hindu community, the Jaffna Tamils have a reputation for exclusivity, which manifests as a perceived condescension towards Indian Tamil Hindus.[52] It is generally acknowledged that Jaffna-managed temples distribute honours to their own community, and that in matters of ritual and worship the *kurukkals* are expected to accord precedence to Jaffna Tamils. The key to this putative clannishness must be explained in relation to their history, and the desire to foster and protect their cultural and religious heritage. Throughout the colonial era, Sri Lankan Hindus were subject to the intense zealotry and persecution of Portuguese Catholicism, which was followed by sustained attacks mounted by Protestant missionaries.[53] Jaffna Tamils normally inculcate religious values among their children at a very early age, and thoroughly verse their adolescents and young people in the beliefs, traditions and rituals of the philosophical school of Saiva Siddhanta. This has produced a depth of expertise within the community which is well placed not only to manage temples but also to hand on to the succeeding generations the traditions of scholarship and cultural accomplishment for which the Jaffna Tamils are renowned. Within Malaya, the tight cultural bonds have been reinforced by intermarriage, though this is now being gradually relaxed among younger members of the community.

Popular Hinduism

C.J. Fuller describes popular Hinduism as "the beliefs and practices that constitute the living 'practical' religion of ordinary Hindus".[54] In Malaysia, village or popular Hinduism is "a religion of pragmatism … based on non-Sanskritic village Hinduism with an admixture of Sanskritic/higher Hinduism".[55] Thus, while popular Hinduism worships village and tutelary gods, and may involve the propitiation or manipulation of spirits, it also incorporates elements of *Agamic* scriptural traditions and *Puranic* mythology, as well as the worship of universal *Agamic*/Sanskritic deities such as Murugan, Ganesha, Lakshmi, Parvati (Sakti), Vishnu and Krishna. The observances and rituals of popular Hinduism are primarily geared towards control of the forces of the mundane world, such as obtaining material blessings and warding off misfortune.[56] However, while some observers posit an inner logic of popular Hinduism which is both self-reflexive and wholly existential, my fieldwork leads me to suggest that popular Hinduism also develops its own soteriological doctrines which incorporate detailed concepts built around eschatology.

Village Deities

These were "brought", in a manner of speaking, to Malaya, mostly by lower-caste Hindus, and re-established in shrines and temples on estates and near labour lines in urban areas. The deities worshipped inevitably reflected the village or region of origin.[57] Many were female and were known as the Mother Goddess (*Uramma*, *Amman* or *Ambal*). These goddesses were habitually parochial, and were responsible for the general welfare of the village, which was regarded as her domain, her sphere of control. The inhabitants of the village were thus her subjects, her devotees who received her protection from the vagaries of temporal life — illness, drought, misfortune — as well as the blessings she saw fit to bestow — prosperity, good health, etc.[58] Village goddesses are invariably agrarian and associated with the elements which cumulatively constitute productivity; namely, earth, plants and fertility. Among the most common forms of Mother Goddess is Mariamman, the goddess of health and rain, who is not only a provider of plenty, but also a protector against contagion, including smallpox.[59]

Rituals of worship of popular deities were constructed around remembered mores of the home village. The temples to such deities were non-*Agamic* in character, and were not built according to *Agamic* rites and injunctions. The *murthis* within the temples are generally made of cement and clay (as opposed to black granite in the *Agamic* temples) and are worshipped according to rites which are not necessarily attuned to *Agamic* precepts. The deities are served by *pantarams* (non-Brahman priests) and *pujaris* (shaman/diviners). In many instances the latter lack formal instruction in the finer details of temple worship, and often relax or ignore customary purity rituals. Worship of village deities may be basic and without the complex elaboration of *Agamic* rituals (for example, frequently excluding both *mantras* and devotional hymns). Indeed, in many of the smaller shrines the relevant worship rituals are occasional, sometimes daily, but in some instances weekly. Animal sacrifice may comprise part of festival celebrations or prescribed rituals; this differs from *Agamic* Hinduism, which permits only vegetarian offerings to deities. Often the constituency of a given village temple will revolve around an extended family and kinship network, or a particular sub-caste/caste alliance, and in many cases the village goddess is regarded as a clan deity.

It is important to note that while these deities are generally worshipped by lower-caste devotees, they are often supplicated by higher-caste and well-educated Hindus. Over the years most of the village deities have become closely associated with, and in some instances have fused identity with, the major Sanskritic deities. Thus Mariamman, while maintaining her village persona in many temples, has in others achieved congruence with Sakti, especially Parvati, wife (consort) of Siva. Indeed, many temples dedicated to Mariamman in this latter capacity contain an image of Murugan, the son of Siva/Sakti.

Guardian or Tutelary Deities (*Gramadevata*)

These deities are normally regarded as under the control of the village goddess, and are often located in the compounds outside her shrine. Where separate temples have been established for these "little" gods, they are usually situated away from the main temples.[60] The function of the guardian deities is to protect their devotees from attack by malignant forces. Although these deities may be benevolent in outlook, especially when propitiated, they are likely to create mischief and wreak vengeance upon those who ignore them. The guardian deities are almost exclusively masculine, and within traditional India were usually local in character. In Malaysia, they are worshipped in non-*Agamic* temples, which are often small, usually constructed of plank and mud walls with zinc roofs. The images are made of cement or clay. Their worship often involves animal sacrifice, and they are usually served by part-time *pujaris*.[61] Some of the guardian deities, especially *Muniandy*, *Aiyannar*, and (formerly) *Muneeswaran* are regarded as protectors of the *Adi Dravida* castes, and are fully identified with lower-caste patterns of worship.

Spirit Worship

Theoretically, the *gramadevata* stand above the realm of spirit worship, but in practice the veneration of village and guardian deities and spirits is frequently interlinked, and often overlaps. Moreover, the fluidity of popular Hinduism, and the ambiguities and porosity of boundaries between the different categories, means that a presence identified by a particular group or generation as a spirit may over time be invested with the qualities of a tutelary or village deity, or even ultimately associated with great *Agamic* deities. Spirits may be divided into three basic categories, namely:

1. *Bhuta*, or potent spirits who have obtained powers which may assist or frustrate the living;
2. *Preta*, or spirits of the departed; and

3. *Pey*, the widely encountered and malevolent ghosts who may create misfortune, illness and distress.

All categories of spirit must be carefully distinguished from *asuras*, the demonic beings found in *Puranic* mythology.[62]

According to popular Hindu belief, the spirit of any human who meets a premature death — whether by suicide, accident, epidemic disease, infant mortality, or childbirth — or otherwise dies unfulfilled (for example, a childless woman), will remain close to and attached to the world of humans, rather than passing into the astral world or the world of the manes.[63] Many Hindu families who have lost a member to untimely death make provision for the "departed" individual by strategically mounting and periodically honouring a framed photograph of the deceased person. This ensures that he/she is constantly remembered, and by being continually reincorporated within familial structures is appropriately placated to compensate for his/her physical absence, and is thus not tempted by neglect to create disturbances within the family as whole. One of the most simple and ubiquitous methods of accommodating a spirit who can create endless mischief and cause great harm is to deify the spirit so that its malevolence can be controlled and turned to the advantage of the living. The *bhuta* — spirits who have thus been elevated — are also able to minimize the danger that *pey* might inflict, and are generally considered benevolent. On the other hand, *preta* are naturally vengeful in character, and may be invoked by practitioners of black magic to visit misfortune upon their enemies.

However, the deification of a spirit is often an arbitrary process. Dumont comments that "often a spirit is malevolent only as long as it lacks a cult; once the cult is provided, it becomes tutelary".[64] This is exemplified by the Tamil tutelary deities *Karuppan* and *Madan*, whose elevation rescued them from their original standing as *pey* and assured them of a regional and caste-based status as guardian deities.[65] Despite deification, both *preta* and *bhuta* may remain volatile and unpredictable, and unless handled carefully may create problems for family, clans and friends.

Spirits are also deified in other ways. Often these are *viras*, heroes who had achieved reputations as great warriors and who died on the battlefield. Thus, the little deity *Madurai Viran*, who was a general of a Madurai Pandyan king, achieved posthumous regional deification, and was worshipped in Malaya/Malaysia as the patron deity of the *Vannar* (laundrymen) caste. In recent years his worship has become more widespread, extending beyond his original regional/caste base.[66] In addition, *Sati Matas*, heroines who voluntarily elect to die on their husband's funeral pyres, may be deified, but this practice is uncommon in Tamil Nadu and unknown in Malaysia. Both *vira* and *sati matas* are employed as clan deities, but many of them ultimately gain a wider circle of devotees and are transformed into tutelary deities.[67]

Many of the shrines dedicated to *bhutas* and *pretas* are located on private or government land, and are often positioned next to trees regarded as possessing inherent spiritual significance. Among Malaysian Hindus, spirit worship is conducted by mediums, some of whom by dint of their reputation — a reputation built on actual or imagined outcomes as gauged by devotees — gain a broad following, including members of higher castes. The majority of mediums "divine" messages from *bhutas/ pretas*, or with the aid of spirits will invoke spirits to settle scores with enemies (either real or perceived), though the placing of curses or plotting misfortune for others is generally considered unethical and the requisite rituals are fraught with danger. Because spirits are former humans, they are believed by some devotees to have a greater understanding of the needs and motivations of ordinary people. However, neither *bhutas*, *pretas* nor *pey* have other than limited and quite specific powers, and as their influence is confined to a fixed domain[68] they can be "overridden", as it were, by appeal to higher deities; that is, village or *Agamic* gods, especially Ganesha and Murugan. Some of the shrines dedicated to *bhutas* and *pretas* may grow into temples as the spirits evolve into tutelary deities, or (more rarely) become associated with the *Agamic* deities of the Hindu pantheon.

Non-*Agamic* Temples

While shrines and minor temples had been constructed on estates and adjacent to urban labour lines throughout the period of indentured labour, the introduction of kangany recruitment was followed by the gradual but inexorable establishment and development of Hindu religious institutions within Malaya.[69] Temples were built either on or near most workplaces and invariably reflected the beliefs prevailing within the village of origin of the labourers who constructed them. As well as providing a symbol of shared Hindu identity, temples became a focal point for community life, allowing the commemoration of all life cycle markers as well as the staging of festivals in accordance with the Hindu calendar.[70]

Plantation Temples

The initial costs associated with the construction of estate temples was usually funded by a management grant supplemented by workers' donations.[71] The management was keen to establish and preserve a settled workforce, and the provision of a temple was often seen as a small price to pay as a means of helping workers adjust to the plantation environment,[72] as well as convincing them that their employers were interested in the welfare of the labour force and their families.[73] Estate temples relied upon two sources of income for financial upkeep; firstly, a small impost levied upon labourers, and secondly, a management grant furnished from the profits of employer-run toddy shops.[74]

As noted, most of the temples constructed reflected the popular beliefs of the villages of origin. However, the entire range of sub-cultural norms and patterns of worship — whether regional, linguistic, caste or lineage — were woven within the totality of the religious life of the estate. It was thus not uncommon for the medium and higher castes of any given estate — Vellalar, Gounder, Kallar, Vanniyar, etc. — to establish a temple dedicated to "universal" deities such as Siva, Ganesha, Murugan or Vishnu, or Mariamman in her capacity as Sakti. Invariably, Mariamman temples contained a shrine to Murugan.[75] Whereas *Agamic* deities were worshipped in non-*Agamic* temples, temples dedicated to village or tutelary deities and patronized by lower castes were generally built away from the main plantation lines. These temples also practised animal sacrifice, usually of goats, buffaloes and chickens, which was not permitted in temples dedicated to universal deities.[76] Nearly all the plantation temples, whether dedicated to universal, village or tutelary deities, were served by *pujaris* (lower-caste temple priests), who often had little knowledge of the inner significance of the rituals they performed, or of the more detailed requirements of temple etiquette.

Plantation temples were administered by a committee known as a *panchyat*. Whereas in India the *panchyat* (literally Council of Five) consisted of the elders of a village and was charged with maintaining general order within the community, this was not the case on the Malayan estates.[77] In general, *panchyats* were used as a tool of the plantation management. The estate managers appointed the *panchyat* membership, generally the clerical staff and the work supervisors (that is, the *kanganies* and the *tindals*), and set the general directions the *panchyat* was expected to follow. The estate manager (*Dorai*) — throughout the colonial era, generally British, and in more recent years, Asian — was regarded as the honorary chairman of the temple, and during festivals was awarded the honour and respect which in India had been reserved for kings and noted dignitaries.[78]

Urban Temples

Most urban non-*Agamic* temples commenced their existence as very basic structures established near labour lines. Many of these began as simple shrines, dedicated to tutelary deities, especially Muniandy and Muneeswaran, but others were more elaborate edifices containing a shrine to Mariamman, usually in her role as a village deity.[79] Often these places were marked by a single religious symbol betokening the presence of a deity. These included the trident (signifying Siva-Sakti) or the *Vel* (the most potent symbol of Murugan). In many cases, more than one shrine was established near a particular worksite. Some of these were shrines set up to supplicate the village deity of a specific family or sub-caste. Over time, many of these shrines and structures developed into temples with established worship patterns which celebrated an anniversary festival and the rounds of festivals pertinent to the deity/deities associated with the temple. The priests who officiated within the temples were often lower-caste *pujaris*, and often mediums or shaman/diviners. The management of the temple sometimes remained under the control of an individual or family who founded the temple, but often it was devolved to a *panchyat* which was usually dominated, in the initial years at least, by a lineage group or a particular caste.[80] The constitution and development of a temple bestowed both status and honour upon the temple founder(s), the management and the priest, and elevated the standing of those involved in these capacities within the context of their immediate social circle and the wider neighbourhood.[81]

Wayside Shrines/Temples

Apart from non-*Agamic* temples already described, there are a large number of rudimentary shrines within Peninsular Malaysia, especially along the West Coast, which appear to have no obvious ownership. These are often constructed adjacent to roads and railway lines, and usually under or next to trees. These shrines, occasionally little more than a box-like structure on the ground, or a tiny shed containing devotional pictures or symbols, have a wide range of origins and purposes. They may have been set up to propitiate *bhuta/preta*, to worship a deity considered too dangerous to supplicate within the home/shrine and/or unacceptable within the local temple, to allow travellers or peripatetic workers to offer worship to a particular deity,[82] or as a result of mediumship or personal inspiration (often in the latter case arising from individual good fortune attributed to the intervention of a particular deity). Occasionally they are established on a site where there has been a fatal accident or particular misfortune, and where the spirits of the departed may be thought to be lingering. Worship at these shrines is normally conducted by an individual or medium/shaman, and is usually observed by a small coterie of devotees, occasionally by only a single family.

Shrines may also be established at the sites of geographic or other natural phenomena considered to have divine associations. Thus, some types of trees are said to contain spirits, while particular rocks and stones are held to embody representational attributes of a given deity. Other phenomena which may inspire shrines include caves, snakes (especially the larger varieties, for example cobras and pythons), anthills, hills and mountains, and streams and rivers (especially the confluence of watercourses). While many of these shrines may exist for no more than a few years, others may survive indefinitely, while still others may attract a regular circle of devotees and gradually make the transition to an established temple (sometimes *Agamicized*), and very occasionally to a recognized pilgrimage centre. Worship linked with natural phenomena has its genesis in animistic belief, and is primarily pursued by lower-caste or less-educated Hindus, but this is by no means invariably the case, and the reputed powers generated by worship at a specific shrine may draw higher-caste or better-educated Hindus. Where a shrine which has its origins in the divine power manifested at a particular locality becomes a pilgrimage centre, the patterns of worship will range across the entire spectrum of Hindu belief structures, sometimes evolving into idiosyncratic and syncretic forms of worship which may fuse elements of village and *Agamic* Hinduism.[83]

Ritual Specialists

There are very few Brahman priests in Malaysia, and most are employed within the *Agamic* temples managed by the Chettiar and Jaffna Tamil communities, as well as in a number of recently "*Agamicized/*

Sanskritized" temples. (This phenomenon will be discussed in later sections of this chapter.) The Malaysian immigration authorities have proven unsympathetic to requests to issue work permits for Brahman *kurrukals* brought from India or Sri Lanka, claiming that the Malaysian Hindus should be training their own temple specialists. (Informants have advised me that no matter how often the situation is explained, Malaysian authorities seem unwilling to accept that (i) *kurukkals* form an hereditary caste; (ii) that very few *kurukkals* migrated to Malaya and (iii) that according to the dictates of *Agamic* religion, certain rituals can be performed only by qualified *kurukkals*.) The employment of *kurukkals* and the justification for their temporary immigration are issues which have been the subject of repeated political representations.

Many temples in Malaysia are served by a sub-caste of non-Brahman priests known as *pantarams*, most of whom undertake a temple apprenticeship which equips them with the rudimentary training required to deal with the ritual contingencies they will encounter in the normal course of their duties. The majority of non-*Agamic* temples are served by *pujaris*, many of whom are part-time priests. The training of *pujaris* varies from comprehensive (in a small minority of cases) to elementary, through to a substantial group who possess a minimum of ritual skills and limited understanding of temple etiquette and management and whose observation of the need for ritual purity in the discharge of temple rites is all but non-existent. Some *pujaris* are mediums or shaman-diviners who are recognized to have skills in worshipping tutelary deities, in controlling *bhuta/preta*, or in divining forecasts and issuing prognostications for individual and familial welfare. For many of this latter group, the rituals associated with formal temple worship are incidental to their mediumship function.

Major Festivals

While colonial accounts contain a number of descriptions of Hindu temples, especially more graphic descriptions of firewalking (*timiti*) and rituals involving "self-torture",[84] they rarely provide details of the name of the festival or document the deities worshipped.

Thaipusam appears to have emerged early in the colonial era as the most widely observed "popular" festival within Malaya, with both Penang and Batu Caves clearly identified as prominent pilgrimage centres.[85]

Murugan/Subramaniam was widely worshipped on the estates, and centres commemorating Thaipusam attracted thousands of devotees from many miles around.[86] By the 1930s, Thaipusam was clearly established as the most important Hindu festival.[87] It is generally agreed that its pre-eminence in the Malaysian Hindu calendar has become more pronounced over the past three decades. Other festivals dedicated to the deity Murugan were also prominent in the Hindu calendar, especially Panguni Uttiram and Masi Magam.[88]

Deepavali was also established as a major festival in the Hindu calendar during the colonial period.[89] However, unlike other parts of India where Deepavali often commemorates Lord Krishna's victory over Naragasuran, Deepavali in Malaya/Malaysia has been observed more as a generalist triumph of good over evil, of light over darkness.[90] While Deepavali is a proclaimed national holiday, the only Hindu festival to have achieved this status, its religious dimension has been diluted to the point where it is often regarded as little more than a day of feasting, open house celebrations and merrymaking.

A further major festival widely commemorated throughout Malaya was the Tamil harvest festival of **Thaipongal**, held over the first two days of the Tamil month of *Tai* (which commences in mid-January). On the first morning, worship is performed and rice is ceremonially cooked with sugar and milk in a pot, timed to boil over the rim of the pot at sunrise. The ground outside the house is carefully decorated with intricate patterns of slaked lime and/or coloured rice (an art form known as *kolam*) and indoors with fresh produce. The second day is given over to the decoration and honouring of animals, though this aspect of the festival is now little observed in Malaysia. Throughout the 1960s, with the rise of Dravidianism, Thaipongal was increasingly celebrated as the secular Tamizhar Tirural (Festival of the Tamils).[91] In recent years the secular observation of Thaipongal has become somewhat muted.

In addition to these observances, the annual festival held in the workplace temple is also regarded as of crucial importance in the ritual life of a given community.[92] The festival is arranged by the temple committee and is seen as an opportunity for united community cooperation and celebration, thus perhaps echoing important integrative village festivals held in India. This was, and remains, of especial significance among the dwindling number of estate communities.[93] Devotees often use this festival as a day of penance or vow fulfilment to the temple deity, often through *timiti* or the kavadi ritual.[94]

The festivals listed above are merely the most prominent of those observed in Malaysia. There are many others, including the important *Agamic* festivals of Mahasivaratri and Navaratri, both established within the Saivite calendar and promoted by Hindu reform movements; Tamil New Year; major festivals for Vishnu and Krishna and Rama (all observed by Malaysia's Vaishnavites); festivals honouring Mariamman and Sakti worship (including "women's" festivals emphasizing the most dramatic aspects of uncontrolled *sakti*, which feature ritualistic abuse and denigration of absent menfolk); and a heterogeneity of other festivals peculiar to the medley of ethnic, caste or sub-caste and regional groupings which make up the Hindu population of Malaysia.[95]

Malaysian Hindu Reform Movements

All of the Hindu reform movements described in the previous chapter — Neo-Hinduism, Neo-Shaivism, the secular Dravidianism inspired by E.V. Ramasami Naicker, and the more inclusive philosophies of the DMK — have taken root in Malaya/Malaysia and continue to shape contemporary reformist impulses. However, these ideologies have been localized in the light of Malaysian conditions and experiences, sometimes producing idiosyncratic and often paradoxical outcomes. Membership and agendas of reformist bodies often overlap in various ways and it is not uncommon to find reformers or religious commentators who combine elements of Neo-Hinduism, Neo-Shaivism and Dravidian ideologies in their discourses. However, it is possible to discern two generic thrusts of reform within Malayan/Malaysian Hinduism; firstly, that of an imagined *Agamic* or Sanskritic Hinduism, consisting of a mainly middle-class membership, which has sought to impose reform from above; and secondly, a more diffuse Dravidianism which has sought to inspire egalitarian change within the sphere of religion and religious observance.[96] However, while over the past century the diverse Hindu traditions which have been transplanted to Malaysia have been exposed to the impulses of reform, unification and modernism, Hinduism in Malaysia remains weakly integrated, and subject to competing and potentially fissiparous influences.

Much of the *Agamic*/Sanskritic reformist programme has been geared towards creating and inculcating the tenets of a "modern" Hinduism which will theoretically improve the public image of the religion in the eyes of the ruling authorities and other ethnic communities. In the process of seeking change, reformers have often shown limited understanding of the ritualistic and customary bases of many practices found within Malaysia, and have repeatedly displayed great insensitivity towards the feelings and beliefs of those whose traditions they wish to refashion. It is not an infrequent experience to encounter Hindu reformers, often profoundly lacking in even the most rudimentary understanding of the fundamental precepts of popular traditions, who denounce the beliefs, practices and experiences of their non-*Agamic* co-religionists in terms strikingly reminiscent of those once used by British administrators and Christian missionaries to describe Hinduism as a whole.

Early Hindu Administration and Reform

In 1906, reacting to the multiplicity of religious forms and mounting evidence of irregularity, disputation and factionalism within temple management committees, the Government of the Straits Settlements passed the Hindu Endowments Board Ordinance which empowered the governor to appoint a board (the Penang Hindu Endowments Board, or PHEB) to manage, where necessary, the affairs of a specified group of Penang temples. For the next fifty years the PHEB continued its work in Penang, and following Merdeka in 1957 was absorbed within the bureaucracy of an independent Malaya.[97] Within Singapore, the creation of a similar board in the 1920s created deep concern among the Hindu population that Europeans (and thus presumably Christians) were being invited by the colonial administration to arbitrate on matters affecting Hindu worship.[98] No other such regularatory bodies were established in the Malay states.[99]

Throughout the 1920s, Hindu groups established *sabhas* and *sangams* in major centres of Indian population throughout the country. Many of these bodies suffered from weak leadership, unstable management and internecine conflict. The multiplicity of organizations meant that there was no central coordinating agency representing Hinduism with which the colonial authorities could deal in arbitrating upon the administration of regional issues. An early reform movement, which emerged in the 1920s, comprising a largely upper-class membership, aimed at creating an acceptable public image for Hinduism. The reformers sought the banning of animal sacrifice, and later the prohibition of *timiti* (firewalking) and the kavadi ritual.[100] From the mid-1930s onwards, many of these bodies amalgamated to form more durable and representative institutions.[101]

Dravidianism

The major impetus to Hindu reformism prior to World War II was the cult of radical Dravidianism launched by the Tamil cultural and political separatist movement, the Self Repect organization, headed by E.V. Ramasami Naicker. As we noted in the previous chapter, Self Respect aimed at restoring and refurbishing an imagined autochthonous Tamil culture which it contended had long been subjugated and adulterated by North Indian, Brahman and Sanskritic influences. Within the religious sphere, the Dravidian movement aimed at eliminating "superstition" and practices which it determined were inconsistent with the "modern" age; of disentangling all Brahmanic and Sanskritic accretions from Tamil belief structures; and of uniting all castes to overthrow the putative Northern Aryan Brahmanic "oppression" of Tamil society.[102] A Tamil Reform Association (TRA) was formed in 1932. The TRA was not only concerned with "modernizing" Hinduism, but planned to uplift Malaysian Hindus "onto a level with other communities in Malaya, so that they would not be looked down upon as backward and archaic". The TRA produced a journal entitled *Reform*, the first issue of which was published in 1936.[103]

A concurrent reform movement, which overlapped with the Self Respect movement, was the *Adi Dravida* caste association, which set up branches across Malaya and developed substantial followings throughout the pre-war years. The movement strove to eradicate blood sacrifices in Hindu worship, to curtail the worship of guardian/tutelary deities and *bhuta/preta*, to cease *tappu* beating by *Paraiyans* as part of Tamil funerary rites, and to push for open-door admission policies at all temples. *Adi Dravida* associations also provided basic tuition classes for members.[104]

The TRA, having suspended operations throughout the Japanese Occupation, resumed its activities following the war. The refusal of estate labourers — particularly younger workers — to unquestioningly accept the reimposition of British authority, created a plantation environment more receptive to the dissemination of the extreme ideologies of the TRA. Many younger workers were now prepared to accept the view that the Hindu temple was a "Brahmanic" institution designed to hoodwink and exploit all other castes, and was thus integral to the system of social control which the "invading" northern Brahmans had "imposed" upon South India.[105]

The TRA campaign aimed at ensuring that reforms within Malayan temples accorded with the programme of "modernization" which had been launched within the Tamil homeland. Initially, the association targeted the practice of animal sacrifice within the context of temple and ritual worship. The suppression of animal sacrifice had been largely successful in Madras, and the TRA conducted a vigorous educational programme within Malaya, which was supplemented by the application of selective pressure on temple managements that refused to ban the practice. This objective met with considerable success; animal sacrifice became less common, though it is still found within some non-*Agamic* temples.

The post-war religious revival among the bulk of the Hindu population was deeply influenced and ultimately shaped by Dravidian ideologies. The preponderance of Tamils within the Hindu population inexorably led to the "Tamilisation" of Malaysian Hinduism.[106] This resulted in the greater use of Tamil ritual in temple worship, the publication of a plethora of devotional material in Tamil, and the establishment of Tamil classes throughout Malaya.[107] The Hindu renascence also resulted in the rediscovery and exploration of all the Tamil arts — literature, Carnatic classical music, the *Bharatanatyam* dance form, and drama, as well as the inauguration of a range of societies dedicated to nourishing these arts and promoting concerts and performances.[108]

Middle-Class Reform

The period of the Japanese Occupation resulted in the cohering of Malaya's major ethnic groups into generic racial blocs, and the development of sharply delineated inclusive–exclusive boundaries. In the Indian case, the community's wartime involvement in the politics of the INA/IIL and concomitant absorption of the leitmotif underpinning the ideology of Indian nationalism — that of India as a great, enduring and incomparably rich civilization — promoted a renewed interest among Malayan Indians in the examination and re-evaluation of their cultural and religious heritage. The latter phenomenon was especially pronounced among middle- and upper-class Indians, many of whom prior to the war had eschewed open adherence to all forms of Hinduism, and had attempted a veneer of "Westernisation" which would publicly distance them from working-class Indians.[109]

Many educated Hindus expressed interest in studying the philosophical basis of Hinduism, especially the teachings of Saiva Siddhanta, but also in reformulating elements of popular Hinduism.[110] Their enthusiasm was reinforced by the visit of a steady stream of swamis and spiritual teachers from Tamil Nadu and Ceylon.[111] These educated strata took a special interest in non-ritualized devotional worship, especially the performance of *bhajan* (the singing of devotional hymns), but tended to eschew, and ultimately lose contact with, the more robust traditions of bhakti worship, such as the performance of *tapas* (austerities), foot pilgrimage (*pada yatra*), or the kavadi ritual.

In the early 1950s, the Hindu revival led to an influx of fresh talent and expertise into the management and administration of temples, as well as the establishment of a number of educational organizations which provided classes in Saiva Siddhanta and *Agamic* ritual worship. These new societies included a number of Hindu youth organizations.[112] Many of these bodies provided outreach services within the broader Indian community. In 1954, major Hindu groups across the country convened an all-Malaya Hindu Conference, which resulted in the inauguration of the Malayan Hindu Sangam.[113] This body has sought to exercise a central role in the affairs of Malaysian Hinduism.

Other philosophical movements inspired by Hindu reformism have had a profound influence, primarily among English-educated and professional, middle-class Hindus. Andrew Willford has pointed out that most of these movements, which he describes as "ecumenical", can trace their origins back to critiques of Hinduism conducted in the mid-nineteenth century among English-educated and higher-caste Bengalis, those "trained in science and logic and believing in a rational plan of national uplift, reform and cultural rejuventation".[114] These later movements were greatly influenced by such prominent philosophers as Sri Ramakrishna, Swami Vivekenanda and Sri Aurobindo, and by the political activism of Mahatma Gandhi. This discourse stressed both the ancient and enduring elements of Hinduism wedded to rational, universalistic and transcendent philosophies, and advocated realization through *bhakti*, yoga and service.

The **Ramakrishna Mission** constructed the Vivekananda Ashram in the largely Indian Kuala Lumpur suburb of Brickfields in 1903. Other ashrams were later opened in Singapore and Penang. The mission promulgated a modernist Vedantic philosophy and brought members of the order to Malaya to teach and offer classes. The mission is very influential within middle-class Hindu circles, especially among non-Tamils. In recent years the mission has constructed a modern centre in Petaling Jaya, where it offers counselling services, organizes charitable works, promotes cultural events and arranges activities for the youth.

A subsidiary organization, the **Divine Life Society**, operates an ashram at Batu Caves. The society was founded by Swami Sivananda, who garnered a reputation for holiness while working as a medical doctor in Malaya in the 1920s. He was known for his extraordinary devotion to his duties, his compassion and his legendary generosity.[115] The ashram offers accommodation to pilgrims and publishes literature on Hinduism, especially that dealing with the more ecstatic significance of the deity Murugan.

The **Shiva Family** was founded by Swami Shatanand Saraswati, one of Swami Sivananda's initiates, following a visit to Malaysia in 1971.[116] The Shiva Family has attracted a largely middle-class, mainly English-educated membership, and is managed by a predominantly Jaffna Tamil and Malayali leadership. The organization teaches a Vedantic-based philosophy and emphasizes the need for service and charity. The Shiva Family holds prayer meetings which incorporate *bhajans* and meditation.

The **Temple of Fine Arts** (TFA) was born out of the Shiva Family. The TFA is a cultural body dedicated to the promotion of worship and contemplation through the study and performance of the arts, principally classical music and dance. The TFA runs a vegetarian restaurant, the *Annalakshmi* (formerly known as the *Devi Annapoorna*), founded in the 1980s, and staffed by volunteer labour. (Initially located in the upper-middle-class suburb of Bangsar, the restaurant later moved to Brickfields.) The TFA also operates the Hamsa-Vahini Travel Agency, which, inter alia, organizes spiritual trips to India, as well as a computing firm.

More recently, caucasian American, Guru Sivaya Subramuniyaswami (1927–2001) and his successor, Sat Guru Bodhinath Veylanswami, have established a small but dynamic following in Malaysia, though their teachings, structured upon a monist form of Saiva Siddhanta, have reached a much wider audience than their immediate body of supporters. Sivaya Subramuniyaswami's theology has been criticized by some Hindus for his use of Christian ecclesiastical terminology (adherents belong to an organization known as the **Saiva Siddhanta Church**), his perceived restrictions on the role of women, and the putative selective scholarship of his order, in particular its sparing usage of *Puranic* mythology.[117]

The Indian guru, the late Sai Baba, has also developed a substantial following in Malaysia. The first Sai Baba bhajan was held in Kuala Lumpur in 1969,[118] and the Malaysian branch of the **Satthya Sai Baba**, with links to the parent ashram in Puttaparthi, India, was established shortly afterwards.

Sai Baba (1926–2011), who claimed to be, and was accepted by his devotees, as an *avatar* (that is, an incarnation of the Divine) of Siva-Sakti,[119] and the possessor of miraculous powers, established a wide and largely middle-class following in Malaysia, with a number of centres in the major cities. His teachings emphasize the primacy of Vedic philosophies encompassing a modernist form of *bhakti*, and highlighting the ideals of selfless service and humility. A youth offshoot, TRAC (Tradition, Religion, Aspiration and Culture), was formed in the 1990s. The Satthya Sai Baba movement has also attracted significant numbers of Chinese participants.

In general, middle- and professional-class Hindu reformers have attempted to project an image of Hinduism as a tolerant, progressive and dignified religion.[120] However, many of these reformers are often beset with acute, and in some instances, chronic, anxieties regarding the perceptions of Hinduism held by Malays, Chinese, and Westerners. Proponents of "great tradition" Hinduism have sought to discourage what they often portray as localized beliefs and practices; that is, those allegedly based on caste, lineage, region and sects. Indeed, a minority of middle-upper-class reform movements have taken extraordinary steps to distance themselves from the more ascetic, stark or ebullient traditions of *bhakti* worship and *Puranic* Hinduism, even to the extent of denying that these rituals and beliefs have any basis in Hinduism at all. Among a small, select group of reformers, the emphasis upon philosophical and scriptural Hinduism, without a countervailing knowledge of the full gamut of Hindu devotional traditions, often produces a rarefied aloofness and a tendency to the rather dogmatic omniscience, which sometimes expresses itself in a vigorous denunciation of those who subscribe to what are resolutely condemned as "lower" forms of belief and worship.

Thaipusam and Reform

Over the years, the "popular" commemoration of Thaipusam has been criticized by various reformers. There have been two major attempts to ban kavadi worship in Malaysia/Singapore. The first of these was launched by the TRA, the second was a somewhat more generalist campaign initiated by the Hindu Sangam of Malaysia.

TRA: In 1938–39, the TRA tried to persuade the colonial government to outlaw both *timiti* and kavadi worship in Malaya.[121] This action formed part of E.V. Ramasami's programme of expunging Dravidian culture of practices not considered "rational". The colonial government, aware of Ramasami's communist affiliations, was not disposed to respond.[122]

Following the war, the TRA actually appealed to the Singapore government to legislate against kavadi worship and *timiti*.[123] The Singapore Hindu Association sought Indian direction on the matter and was "allegedly" advised in July 1949, in a letter signed by a high government (Congress) official, that the proscription of kavadi worship might "lead to the disappearance of piety and religion" in Malaya and Singapore.[124] The existence of this letter was confirmed in a 1995 conversation with a senior *kurukkal* in Seremban who possessed a copy. He stated that "These rascals actually went running off to the British to try to ban a Hindu custom which brought joy and meaning to thousands of devotees. Is such a thing possible? These meddlers were prepared to soil their hands hobnobbing with the colonialists. They were stupid and ignorant men." Several other senior Hindus to whom I spoke in the course of my fieldwork were aware of this letter and the quite explicit advice it contained.[125]

Having failed in their efforts to persuade the colonial authorities to prohibit kavadi worship and *timiti*, the TRA now endeavoured to coerce major temples to comply with their demands.[126] In 1950, the Mariamman and Tank Road temples, responding to TRA insistence, imposed a temporary ban on *aluga* kavadis. This was revoked after the temples were overwhelmed by pressure exerted by wealthy patrons, and by the many requests of devotees wishing to bear kavadis.[127]

Malaysian Hindu Sangam: In 1988 the Malaysian Hindu Sangam issued an extraordinary statement condemning kavadi worship as "an affront to the Hindu religion", a practice which was devoid of scriptural injunction, and which constituted an offence to the human body (which should be regarded as a temple). The statement also claimed that many who undertook the kavadi ritual did so to "show off".[128] In addressing the 1988 Asia Pacific Hindu Conference in Singapore, Sangam President Datuk S. Govindaraj asserted — erroneously — that Thaipusam worship in Malaysia was not only "markedly different" to that found in India, but had "become a horrible spectacle and wild display, competition and exhibition of demonic acts carried to excess that finds no sanction in our *Saistra* [sic]." He spoke further of the "ignorance" of devotees, and the "terrifying techniques of kavadi worship".[129]

Datuk Govindaraj's attack was received angrily by many Hindus, who regarded it as highhanded, unconscionable, and, for a high official of an institution supposedly steeped in the traditions of Hindu culture, almost unbelievable in its nescience. Govindaraj's strictures had no observable impact upon the commemoration of Thaipusam in Malaysia.

In 1991, a minor Hindu organization, the Rudra Devi Samaj of Kuala Lumpur, criticized the kavadi ritual as practised in Malaysia as "un-Hindu". Their objections centred on the sacredness and hence inviolability of the body in Hinduism; the supposed spilling of blood in temple premises; the putative infliction of pain which allegedly ran counter to God's wishes; and the taking of a kavadi as a spectacle rather than as a philosophical action.[130] Respondents countered that the Samaj's censures revealed limited understanding of the traditions of Murugan worship or the role of *tapas* (austerities) and sacrifice within Hinduism; that they ignored empirical evidence which contradicted their assertions (e.g., the absence of both blood and pain is a highlighted feature of the festival); and that they cast gratuitous and insulting aspersions upon the integrity and inner dispositions of devotees.

In reviewing more recent criticisms of Thaipusam, my own fieldwork tends to confirm Andrew Willford's observation that "most of the reformist calls come from higher status Indians or from religious institutions that cater for them", and his suggestion that:

> the reformers are ambivalent about the perceived image of Hindu self-mortification and though they share a theological commitment to Murugan devotions, find that their ambiguous closeness to the working-class expressions of identity is a source of anxiety — a recognized self within that which was thought to have been already "surmounted".[131]

Sanskritization/*Agamicization* in Malaysia

Over the past half century, the process of Sanskritization and/or *Agamicization* has had a major impact on the overall structures of Malaysian Hinduism. In the previous chapter we noted that the process of Sanskritization had privileged textual sources of Hinduism, thus simultaneously inscribing Brahmanic hegemony and downplaying the significance of popular and localized Hindu traditions. Within the metropolitan Indian context, Sanskritization implies the disposal of lesser deities and localized customs, beliefs and patterns of worship, and their subsequent replacement with recognized practices and deities drawn from an imagined "higher tradition" *Agamic* Hinduism.[132] However, Sanskritization operates somewhat differently in Malaysia. In Malaysia it is more common for gods and goddesses to be redefined in terms of their putative relationship to recognized *Agamic* deities, an undertaking which involves their celestial uplift (as it were), and their subsequent relocation within the Hindu pantheon.[133] Thus, a large number of shrines and temples dedicated to village or tutelary deities have been elevated, with the deities being assigned attributes which enable them to be firmly identified with one of the great *Agamic* gods: Siva, Ganesha, Murugan, Sakti (especially Parvati, Lakshmi and Saraswati), Vishnu and, more rarely, Krishna.[134] The rituals and modes of worship associated with the deities also undergo a corresponding revision as befitting the status of deities who are now regarded as *Agamic*. Simultaneously, temples are refurbished and remodelled to accord with *Agamic* precepts.[135]

In the following paragraphs I will provide an example of the phenomenon of Sanskritization/*Agamicization* as it has affected the Raja Rajesvariyamman Temple in Kuala Lumpur, as well as examining the calculated and ritual upgrading of the tutelary deity, Muneeswaran.

Until 1977, the site of the Raja Rajesvariyamman Temple, located in Ulu Kelang, Kuala Lumpur, was occupied by a small temple dedicated to Mariamman in her capacity as village deity. The temple was frequented by Hindu utility and other workers, and the deity was served by a *pujari*. However, throughout the early 1970s the Ulu Kelang region, which had been a combination of jungle, rubber estates and squatter settlements, was comprehensively redeveloped into a largely middle-class suburb. Hindu residents moving into the suburb believed that the temple should be reconstructed to serve the needs of the newly arrived community. The management therefore employed *sthapatis* to refashion the temple so that it observed all *Agamic* requirements. The temple was provided with a name — Raja Rajesvariyamman — which followed the traditions of a similarly named great *Agamic* temple of South India. Two *kurukkals* were engaged from Tamil Nadu to ensure that temple worship and rituals were performed in accordance with *Agamic* precepts. In time, the temple became a noted centre for the teaching and performance of Carnatic classical music as well as *Bharatanatyam* dance, both of which are seen as intrinsic to the culture associated with "great tradition" Hinduism.[136] In the process of *Agamicization*, the identity of the former village temple has not been so much eclipsed as completely expunged, in effect being replaced with a new temple which fully embodies the ideals of *Agamic* Hinduism.

The temples dedicated to the tutelary deity Muneeswaran have undergone a similar process of partial *Agamicization*. Muneeswaran originated as a tutelary deity (*gramadevata*) who was held to engage in nocturnal protective patrols of the village boundary (Tamil: *ellai*). In her major study of the deity, Vineeta Sinha states that he was brought from India to Malaya by railway workers.[137] Until comparatively recently, his identity was fused with that of Muniandy, another tutelary deity. Both were often found standing guard in the temple compounds of village goddesses. Muneeswaran accepted blood sacrifices, and was said to control both *bhuta* and *preta*. He was thus a typical tutelary deity, benevolent when propitiated, but capable of acts of anger and destruction when ignored. Muneeswaran is often depicted as of sturdy, powerful build with dominant, occasionally protruding eyes, a thick moustache, sometimes bearded, bare chested, and sometimes astride a white horse. He is often shown wearing a turban and carrying a walking stick (*dandam*) roughly hewn from the limb of a tree. Within Malaysia he was usually found in small temples constructed of plank and zinc, and portrayed in images made of clay or cement. From the early 1970s, the *pujaris* serving Muneeswaran temples began to insist that the deity was not a lesser "little" god, but rather should be identified with Siva, and that the animal sacrifice being conducted in his temples was actually offered to Muniandy, whose role was specified as that of doorkeeper/custodian to the temple. It was determined that Muneeswaran was born of Siva during the destruction of Daksha's sacrifice[138] (discussed in the next chapter), and that the construction of his name made this association plain: namely the conjunction of *Muni* (great sage) and *Iswara* (Lord).[139] In 1974, a conference was called by the managements of Muneeswaran and Kaliyamman temples. This conference was attended by representatives of thirty-seven (mainly Muneeswaran) temples, who determined, inter alia, that Muneeswaran was a manifestation of the *Agamic* god, Siva, and that as a consequence a number of non-*Agamic* practices, including animal sacrifices, should be discontinued within Muneeswaran temples.[140] Many of these temples have begun to observe the major Siva festival, Maha Sivaratri, as well as other festivals dedicated to Siva, and have introduced other elements of *Agamic* worship into their corpus of temple ritual. The elevation of Muneeswaran led to his distancing from Muniandy, who has, as a consequence, become less prominent, and whose status unambiguously remains that of a tutelary deity.[141]

Agamicization/Sanskritization in India is largely a phenomenon of caste, an attempt to relocate a particular *jati* as a higher social group within the overall caste hierarchy. It is essentially a process of cultural mobilization whereby a specific caste consciously adopts the religious and social practices of higher castes, thus, over time, achieving acknowledgement of a more elevated social status than it was previously accorded. In the course of achieving this revised standing, the social process may involve the clustering and subsequent welding of hitherto fragmented social groups into a new and recognizably integrated social unit.[142] However, Sanskritization/*Agamicization* takes on a somewhat different orientation in Malaysia. While the process also involves projected upwards social mobility and a redefinition of a specific group's cultural status, it is only incidentally a caste-related phenomenon. Rather, with the general weakening of the institution of caste, and the emergence of class as the primary agency for the social organization of Malaysian Hindu society, Sanskritization/*Agamicization* may be interpreted as a form of social striving by which lower-class Indians attempt, by emulating the religious practices observed in the major *Agamic* temples, to identify with middle- and upper-class Hindus.

Viewed in this context, *Agamicization*/Sanskritization may be seen as a lower-class-initiated movement dedicated to reshaping the form and boundaries of Hinduism as an overall ethnic marker. By imposing "higher" and uniform traditions of worship, *Agamicization*/Sanskritization re-images and repositions Hinduism (and by extension all devotees) in the eyes of other ethnic communities, and presents it as a respectable, dignified and cultivated religion.

But while Sanskritization/*Agamicization* results in the introduction of more recognized and higher-status patterns of worship, the process does not result in the loss of cherished village and tutelary deities. They are retained, redefined and accoutred with new and higher attributes which fuse their identities with those of selected *Agamic* deities, and subsequently offered an honoured position within the received Hindu pantheon. The processes of Sanksritization/*Agamicization* has also resulted in the widespread veneration of former village gods and goddesses within the context of the great *Agamic* festivals, as well as other calendrical rituals normally restricted to *Agamic* deities. Thus, for example, throughout Thaipusam, certain devotes will acknowledge Muneeswaran, the former tutelary deity, as none other than Siva, the "father" of Murugan; and in the great *Agamic* festival of Navaratri, celebrating the "feminine" energies of the *Trimurti*, various village goddesses will be identified and worshipped as manifestations of the *Agamic* deity, Sakti.

In Chapter 2 we noted that Great Tradition and popular Hinduism could not be considered totally discrete, and that most devotees observed beliefs, rituals and patterns of worship which incorporated elements from both. The continuing creative dialogue between these traditions provided opportunities for the emergence of "hybrid" syncretized belief structures. Within Malaysia, *Agamicization*/Sanskritization represents a form of this process, in effect the grafting of selected elements of Great Tradition Hinduism upon a reconstituted popular religion.

One of the pronounced syncretic impulses within Malaya, however, has been the "Tamilization" of Hinduism, and the concomitant absorption of other forms of Hinduism, especially the minority Vaishnavite tradition, within the overarching fabric of the majority popular Saivite traditions. Thus one finds Vaishnavite deities, especially Krishna and Hanuman, and to a lesser extent Vishnu, represented within the great Saivite festivals, and the incorporation of some Vaishnavite motifs and scriptures — in particular, the *Bhagavad Gita* — into Malaysian Saivism. Similarly, many of those who adhere to Vaishnavite belief will often incorporate Saivite deities, especially Murugan, into their worship.

The Kerling Incident, Challenge and Renewal

The general response to Islamization has been one of renewal. This has been manifested in such activities as temple construction, increased participation in festivals and exploration of religious traditions. However, the first specific "Islamic" event which acted as a catalyst for these processes was the spate of temple violations which culminated in the so-called Kerling incident. Between December 1977 and August 1978, a small band of young men, university lecturers and students, styling themselves "The Army of Allah", perpetrated a series of nocturnal attacks on Hindu temples, vandalizing statuary, including dedicated *murthis*.[143] A total of twenty-eight temples, most adjacent to the main road between Melaka and Perak states, were desecrated. The raids ceased following an armed clash with Hindu temple guards in the Subramaniar temple in the southern Perak town of Kerling on 19 August 1978. Four young Malays were killed in this exchange.[144] Hindus had been less than impressed with police attempts to apprehend the desecrators and regarded their efforts as both laggardly and half-hearted. Many believed that the protection of Hindu temples was viewed officially as a low priority. Others commented privately that they felt Hinduism had been viewed by extremists as a "soft" target which could be attacked with relative impunity. These perceptions moulded a wider view that the Malaysian government could not be relied upon to guarantee the security and preservation of their Hindu heritage. The Kerling incident thus served as a warning to Hindus that the future of their community was wholly dependent upon their own efforts.[145]

Hindraf

In Chapter 1 we noted the political developments which accompanied the formation of Hindraf. However, it was ultimately the perceived excesses of the Islamic authorities and the general disrespect shown towards major Hindu symbols and Hindu sensitivities which were to prove catalytic in igniting long-smouldering Hindu resentments. Indian frustrations, which had been provoked by the wave of mass evictions from the estates and the concomitant enforced rural–urban migration, were further exacerbated by the systemic denial of social, economic and educational opportunities. This reinforced the marginalization of the working-class Tamil population which comprised the vast majority of the Indian community. The rise of Hindraf followed a series of contentious incidents which included the seizure by Islamic officials of the remains of individuals who had identified themselves as Hindus; actual forced conversions and attempted conversions of people who regarded themselves as practising Hindus and the resultant breakup of established family units; and unwise and gratuitously insulting comments offered by high-level officials which were seen to denigrate Hindus and which were interpreted as confirming their second-rate status in the land of their birth.

However, the undoubted touchstone for Hindu outrage was the wave of temple demolitions which began in the early 2000s, a development which deeply wounded Hindu sensibilities as well as creating a climate of apprehension among all non-Muslim communities. These demolitions were conducted with a patent disregard for the feelings of the communities involved. Often demolition gangs, operating under police protection, wilfully destroyed temple statuary and sacred objects. In a few cases where sites were made available for the relocation of temples, the plots of land were regarded as too small or completely unsuitable (in one instance a plot was sited adjacent to a sewage pond, and in another the plot consisted of land that had recently been used as an abbatoir).

A large proportion of the temples thus destroyed had been established as "plantation temples"; that is, as temples that had originally been constructed on estates which had subsequently been subdivided for housing or industrial development. Many of these temples had operated as sites of worship for more than a century and held deep significance for the communities which had gathered around them. Because these temples had no formal title to the land which they occupied, the authorities were able to claim that they were "illegal" structures. However, the circumstances of their construction, coupled with the extended length of prior occupation and the fact of community ownership would appear to have made such claims both legally and morally problematic.[146] The potential destruction of some hundreds of these community-built and maintained temples created anxiety, distress and ultimately anger among Malaysian Hindus.[147]

As temple demolitions became more frequent, Hindu communities noted that their representations weighed ever more lightly upon the government bureaucracy, and were dismissed with increasing condescension often amounting to open disdain. As the demolitions continued, there were repeated and increasingly dangerous confrontations between the largely Muslim demolition crews and police on the one hand, and Hindu devotees on the other.[148]

Matters reached a crisis point with the demolition of a century-old temple in Shah Alam on 30 October 2007, a week prior to the major Hindu festival of Deepavali. The demolition gang was accompanied by a large contingent of regular and riot police.[149] In the pursuant clash between police and protestors, fourteen devotees were arrested, temple statuary was vandalized and the temple priest was assaulted by police while he attempted to carry sanctified *murthis* from the temple. Security personnel were alleged to have resorted to unnecessary violence, and photographic evidence clearly spotlighted police carrying weapons and pieces of wood and throwing stones at devotees.[150] This incident created local outrage and received international news coverage.

Following the accession of Najib Abdul Razak to the prime ministership on 3 April 2009, his Barisan Nasional government made genuine attempts to reconnect with the Hindu community which had largely abandoned the ruling coalition in the election of 8 March 2008. Najib announced a raft of initiatives to assist the Indian community. In addition, he attended the Thaipusam festival at Batu Caves as a guest of the MIC-linked Sri Maha Mariamman Devasthanam which manages the complex. There is no doubt that Najib's personal efforts, the projection of an emollient disposition, together with the package of economic and educational reforms he unveiled, won him a large measure of goodwill, and did much to reinstil Indian trust in his leadership.

However, Najib's leadership has been punctuated by "Islamic" incidents which continue to prove disheartening and distressing to Malaysia's Hindu community. The most notorious of these was the so-called "Cow's head" episode. In August 2009, a group of Malays, including members of UMNO, protesting against the proposed relocation of a Hindu temple to the suburb of Shah Alam, a Muslim majority area, carried a cow's head to the gates of the (Pakatan) Selangor Government's State Secretariat. Photos released on the Internet clearly showed these demonstrators stamping on the cow's head — a gesture plainly designed to offend Malaysian Hindus. Police took no action throughout this protest.[151] Many Malaysians were shocked when Hishamuddin Hussein, Minister for Home Affairs, met with the protestors, and even appeared to defend their actions.[152] One of the demonstrators later justified his behaviour with the provocative statement, "It's proven historically that this is *Tanah Melayu* — others are categorized as second class citizens."[153] In subsequent talks aimed at reaching a compromise, Muslims shouted down speakers and claimed that the mere presence of a Hindu temple would disturb their prayers. A peaceful protest held by Hindus to condemn racial and religious intolerance resulted in sixteen arrests. To many Hindus, the contrasting reactions of the authorities to the two demonstrations constituted proof that they were indeed officially regarded as "second class citizens".[154]

The Malay Islamic upsurge has been paralleled with a renewed Hindu involvement and exploration of their heritage and traditions. Much of this occurred within the area of temple worship, which has always been viewed as a central facet of Hinduism in Malaysia. Throughout the 1980s there was a sharp rise in the number of temples built. Many shrines and non-*Agamic* temples were reconstructed and dedicated as *Agamic* temples. A further development was the increase in the multi-shrine temples in Malaysia; many temples which were formerly dedicated to a single deity were refashioned to provide shrines for additional *Agamic* gods, even to the extent of some Saivite temples incorporating shrines for Vaishnavite deities. In addition, there has been considerable interest in exploring the philosophical foundations of Hinduism, and in reinterpreting Hindu practices in the light of *Agamic* traditions. This has led to the discouragement of obscure and irrelevant practices, and the discreet jettisoning of some seen as antiquated. The Hindu resurgence has also been obvious in the annually swelling numbers of devotees participating in festivals — both popular and local — and the enhanced "urgency" with which they are commemorated.[155] The intensification of the Hindu revival has produced a more active engagement with the wider world of Hindusm, in particular the attempt to situate Malaysian Hinduism in terms of its relationship both with metropolitan India and the Tamil/Indian *diaspora*.

The Evangelical Challenge

While "Islamic" issues have created widespread unease among non-Muslim communities, this has been rendered more urgent by intense and aggressive proselytization mounted by evangelical Christian sects largely inspired by U.S.-based pre-millennial and chiliastic theology. These fundamentalist groups, a comparatively recent phenomenon,[156] consist of a series of interlinked "militantly anti-modernist Protestant [evangelicals].... a loose, diverse and changing federation of co-belligerents united by their fierce opposition to modernist attempts to bring Christianity into line with modern thought."[157] While these groups are prohibited from campaigning among Muslims (though this does not stop U.S.-based chiliastic websites from depicting Muslims as the Antichrist), they have directed fierce, simplistic and often offensive polemics against adherents of other faiths, including mainstream Christian traditions. Pre-millenialism is informed by literalist interpretations of the Bible, uncomplicated by contextualization or scholarly exegesis, and places undue emphasis upon the imagined prophecies of the Book of Revelation (regarded by most modern scholars as an apocalyptic Jewish commentary on the Roman Empire).[158] Other than a doctrine of imminent eschatology, chiliasm develops no systematic theology of any depth. Rather, it advances its claims through selective and often repetitive Biblical quotes which according to one scholar act as "simplistic solutions to non-religious problems".[159]

A central tenet is a stress on the immediate and spontaneous experiental reality of divine revelation defined wholly in terms of self-redemption.[160] The chiliastic project is conducted in absolutist, indeed Manichean terms, which resolutely divides the world into good versus evil and which thus emphatically denies the validity or even the possibility of the integrity or sincerity of any alternative belief structure.[161] This essentially negative discourse is conducted through the projection of a series of shrill, vitriolic and often meretricious caricatures of other religious beliefs, which traduce foundation mythologies and equate all non-believers with Satan and "devil worship". These movements, supported by U.S. poltical leaders as a core component of U.S. Cold War policy,[162] have attempted to portray themselves as both modern and Western (in opposition to supposed moribund Asian traditionalism), and, more problematically, as embedded within the established Christian theological mainstream. This aggressive campaign, often grounded in "clash of civilizations" rhetoric, has had moderate success within the Chinese and Indian communities, mainly among English-speaking middle classes, especially those who aspire to be identified as "modern" and Westernized.[163]

Conclusions

This chapter has examined the relocation and adaptation of Hinduism — its practices, belief structures, philosophies — within Malaya/Malaysia. It has been noted that this occurred in the absence of two key forces which had played major roles in shaping metropolitan Tamil Hinduism; firstly, the centres of religious learning (*mathas*), and secondly, an influential Brahman or dominant orthodox caste.

The formative period of kangany recruitment produced a variegated caste structure in Malaysia, with about one-third of the population drawn from *Adi Dravida* castes and the majority of the remainder from a range of *Sudra* castes. Although caste as an institution has been renegotiated in Malaysia, it retains its potency in certain facets of Hindu life; for example, in choice of marriage partners, food exchange, and in observation of ritual purity and pollution.

Malaysian Hinduism is remarkably diverse and is marked by a proliferation of religious forms. While *Agamic* Hinduism was imported by middle- and upper-class groups, especially the Chettiar and Jaffna Tamil communities, popular or village Hinduism consisted of practices built around remembered mores. The diversity of temples, ranging from *Agamic* to wayside shrines, reflects the many divisions within the community — those of caste, sub-ethnicity and locality of origin. However, a common feature has been the worship of Murugan, which is practised within nearly all *Agamic* temples, as well as a high percentage of plantation and workplace temples. This phenomenon perhaps accounts for the rapid emergence of Thaipusam as the most widely celebrated Hindu festival in Malaya/Malaysia.

As in Tamil Nadu, Hindu reformist movements have sought to reconfigure the structures and practices of Hinduism. While reformism has assumed a multiplicity of forms, two major influences can be identified; namely, (i) middle-class groups concerned with the imposition of an imagined *Agamic*/Sanskritic Hinduism, and (ii) Tamil bodies, representing a diffuse Dravidianism. Middle-class reformism, which largely emerged after World War II, has proven most selective in its depiction of what can be considered to constitute Hindu belief and ritual, preferring to appeal to wholly textual and scriptural sources. Dravidianism has ranged from emphasis on the introduction and observation of putative Tamil forms of worship through to the more iconoclastic and intolerant radicalism initially championed by Ramasami Naicker's Self Respect movement. As I have noted, both groups have in their own way challenged the validity of current worship patterns displayed at the festival of Thaipusam.

However, the most influential impulses in reformulating Malaysian Hinduism have been those which had produced syncretic outcomes — those which have aligned or fused one form of Hinduism with another. These movements have reworked belief and ritual structures to "Tamilize" Hinduism, to *Agamicize*/Sanskritize village Hinduism, and to incorporate symbols and motifs drawn from *Agamic* Saivite and Vaishnavite traditions into popular forms of worship. The reconstitution of boundaries has resulted in a diversity of "hybrid" Hindu structures.

In recent years it has been possible to discern an incipient and thus inchoate sense of unity among Malaysian Hindus. Thus, while Hinduism in Malaysia remains a concatenation of fluid and potentially kinetic structures, still fissiparous but loosely integrated, its membership has become increasingly aware of its overriding commonality and shared interests. This has been reinforced by the pressures exerted by a resurgent Islam, and in particular the dual shocks of the Kerling incident as well as the sequence of events which led to the emergence of Hindraf. Both indicated to Hindus their own vulnerability. The result has been a renewed exploration of the Hindu heritage and its traditions, in particular the location of Malaysian Hinduism within the context of a wider civilizational arena, embracing both metropolitan India as well as the Tamil Hindu diaspora.

Notes

1. Prior to the arrival of Islam on the Malay Peninsula, Hinduism and Indic civilizational impulses more generally played a crucial role in the formation of political, societal and religious structures within the wider Malay Archipelago. Recent publications which examine this history include Anthony Reid's *A History of South East Asia: Critical Crossroads* (Chichester: Wiley Blackwell, 2015) and *Early Interactions between South and Southeast Asia*, edited by Pierre Yves Manguin, A. Mani, and Geoff Wade (Singapore and New Delhi: Institute of Southeast Asian Studies/Manohar, 2011).

2. Susan E. Ackerman and Raymond M. Lee, *Heaven in Transition: Innovation and Ethnic Identity in Malaysia* (Honolulu: University of Hawai'i Press, 1988), pp. 91, 95.

3. Kalimuthu Ramanathan. "Hindu Religion in an Islamic State: The Case of Malaysia" (PhD dissertation, Universiteit van Amsterdam, 1995), pp. 75–76.

4. Ibid., p. 84.

5. Ravindra K. Jain, *South Indians on the Plantation Frontier in Malaya* (New Haven: Yale University Press, 1970), p. 276.

6. R. Champakalakshmi, *Religion, Tradition and Ideology in Precolonial South India* (New Delhi: Oxford University Press, 2011), p. 12.

7. Vineeta Sinha, *A New God in the Diaspora? Muneeswaran Worship in Contemporary Singapore* (Singapore and Copenhagen: Singapore University Press/NIAS Press, 2005), pp. 3, 84–85.

8. Sinnappah Arasaratnam, *Indians in Malaysia and Singapore* (London: Oxford University Press, 1970), p. 17.

9. Ibid., pp. 24–26.

10. Ravindra K. Jain, "South Indian Labour in Malaya 1840–1920: Asylum, Stability and Involution", in *Indentured Labour in the British Empire 1834–1920*, edited by Kay Saunders (London: Croom Helm, 1984), p. 175; Michael R. Stenson, *Class Race and Colonialism in West Malaysia: The Indian Case* (St Lucia: University of Queensland Press, 1980), pp. 24–26.

11. Jain, *South Indians on the Plantation Frontier*, p. 346; Ackermann and Lee, *Heaven in Transition*, p. 95.

12. Jain, *South Indians on the Plantation Frontier*, pp. 346–47.

13. Arasaratnam, *Indians in Malaysia*, pp. 65–66.

14. Rajakrishnan Ramasamy, *Caste Consciousness among Indian Tamils in Malaysia* (Petaling Jaya: Pelanduk, 1984), p. 13.

15. Arasaratnam, *Indians in Malaysia*, pp. 65–66.

16. Paul W. Wiebe and S. Mariappen, *Indian Malaysians: The View from the Plantation* (Delhi: Manohar, 1978), pp. 69–70.

17. Sinnappah Arasaratnam. "Malaysian Indians: The Formation of an Incipient Society", in *Indian Communities in Southeast Asia*, edited by K.S. Singh and A. Mani (Singapore: Institute of Southeast Asian Studies, 1993), p. 206.

18. J.M. Barron, Acting Controller of Labour, *Annual Report of the Labour Department, 1935* (Kuala Lumpur: Government Press, 1936).

19. K.A. Mukundan, *Annual Report of the Government of India, 1935* (Calcutta: Government of India Press, 1936).

20. C. Wilson, Controller of Labour, *Annual Report of the Labour Department, 1936* (Kuala Lumpur: Government Press, 1937).

21. Arasaratnam, *Malaysian Indians*, p. 206.

22. Arasaratnam, *Indians in Malaysia*, p. 168.

23. Rajakrishnan, *Caste Consciousness*, pp. 15–16.

24. Ackerman and Lee, *Heaven in Transition*, p. 95.

25. Rajakrishnan, *Caste Consciousness*, p. 59.

26. Rajeswary Amplavanar-Brown, "The Political Elite in Malaysia", in *Indian Communities in Southeast Asia*, edited by K.S. Sandhu and A. Mani (Singapore: Institute of Southeast Asian Studies, 1993), pp. 245–47.

27. Rajakrishnan, *Caste Consciousness*, p. 73.

28. Jain, *South Indians on the Plantation Frontier*, p. 346.

29. Ramanathan, "Hindu Religion", p. 95.

30. Ibid.

31. Cynthia J. Miller, "Immigrants, Images and Identity: Visualising Homelands across Borders", in *Tracing an Indian Diaspora: Contexts, Memories, Representations*, edited by Parvati Raghuram, Ajaya Kumar Sahoo, Brij Maharaj, and Dave Sangha (New Delhi: Sage, 2008), p. 296.

32. Arasaratnam, *Indians in Malaysia*, p. 163.

33. Ramanathan, "Hindu Religion", p. 299.

34. Arasaratnam, *Indians in Malaysia*, p. 173.

35. M. Nadarajan, "The Nattukottai Chettiar Community and Southeast Asia", International Seminar on Tamil Studies (Kuala Lumpur, 1966), p. 251.

36. Hans Deiter Evers and Jayarani Pavadarayan, "Religious Fervour and Economic Success: The Chettiars of Singapore", in *Indian Communities in Southeast Asia*, edited by K.S. Sandhu and A. Mani (Singapore: Institute of Southeast Asian Studies, 1993), p. 848.

37. Nadarajan, "The Nattukottai Chettiar Community", p. 253.

38. Ramanathan, "Hindu Religion", p. 97.

39. Ibid., p. 101.
40. Evers and Jayarani, "Religious Fervour", p. 853.
41. Ramanathan, "Hindu Religion", p. 101; Nadarajan, "The Nattukottai Chettiar Community", p. 256.
42. Evers and Jayarani, "Religious Fervour", p. 853.
43. Ibid., p. 856.
44. Ramanathan, "Hindu Religion", p. 100.
45. Ibid., p. 98.
46. Nadarajan, "The Nattukottai Chettiar Community", p. 253.
47. Ramanathan, "Hindu Religion", p. 108.
48. Rajakrishnan Ramasamy, "Indo-Ceylonese Relations in Malaysia", *Jurnal Pangajian India* 4 (1986): 98.
49. Ibid., p. 103.
50. Ramanathan, "Hindu Religion", p. 116.
51. Ibid., p. 122.
52. Rajakrishnan, *Indo-Ceylonese Relations*, p. 103.
53. For an example of Portuguese desecration of a major Hindu temple, see Gannanath Obeyeskere, *The Cult of the Goddess Pattini* (Chicago: University of Chicago Press, 1984), p. 23. Protestant attitudes towards Sri Lankan religions, buttressed by British colonialism, may be revealed by the fact that in 1880, when Major Olcott and Madame Blavatsky of the Theosophy Society visited Ceylon, they discovered that only Christian marriages were regarded as legal by the colonial authorities. Education was dominated by Christian missionaries; there were 805 Christian schools as opposed to a mere four Buddhist schools. Grants to schools were dependent upon a commitment to teach the Bible (Peter Washington, *Madame Blavatsky's Baboon: Theosophy and the Emergence of the Western Guru* (London: Secker and Warburg, 1993), pp. 66–67).
54. Fuller, *The Camphor Flame*, p. 5.
55. R. Rajoo, "Hindu Religious Values and Economic Retardation among the Indian Plantation Workers in Peninsular Malaysia — a Myth or Reality?", *Jurnal Pengajian India* 4 (1986): 44.
56. Ibid.
57. Ramanathan, "Hindu Religion", p. 82; Lynne E. Gattwood, *Devi and the Spouse Goddess: Women, Sexuality and Marriage in India* (New Delhi: Manohar, 1985), p. 138.
58. R. Rajoo, "Sanskritization in the Hindu Temples of West Malaysia", *Jurnal Pengajian India* 2 (1984): 161.
59. Ramanathan, "Hindu Religion", p. 70.
60. Ibid., p. 85.
61. Rajoo, "Sanskritization", p. 161.
62. Fuller, *The Camphor Flame*, p. 50.

63. Ibid., p. 49.
64. Ibid.
65. Ibid.
66. Ramanathan, "Hindu Religion", pp. 202–3.
67. Fuller, *The Camphor Flame*, p. 49.
68. Ibid., p. 51.
69. Arasaratnam, *Indians in Malaysia*, p. 65.
70. Ramanathan, "Hindu Religion", pp. 80–82.
71. Charles Gamba, *The Origins of Trade Unionism in Malaya: A Study in Colonial Labour Unrest* (Singapore: Eastern Universities Press, 1962), p. 307.
72. Arasaratnam, *Indians in Malaysia*, p. 65.
73. Gamba, *The Origins of Trade Unionism*, p. 307.
74. *Report of the Agent of the Government of India, 1932* (Calcutta: Government of India Press, 1933).
75. Ramanathan, "Hindu Religion", pp. 84–85; Arasaratnam, *Indians in Malaysia*, pp. 66–67.
76. Arasaratnam, *Indians in Malaysia*, p. 171.
77. Gamba, *The Origins of Trade Unionism*, p. 309.
78. Ramanathan, "Hindu Religion", p. 84.
79. Ibid., p. 89.
80. Arasaratnam, *Indians in Malaysia*, p. 164.
81. Ramanathan, "Hindu Religion", p. 91.
82. Sinha notes that railway workers established at least fifty shrines dedicated to Muneeswaran along the rail line between Singapore and Ipoh (Sinha, *A New God?*, p. 109).
83. Ramanathan, "Hindu Religion", p. 79.
84. Leopold Ainsworth, *The Confessions of a Planter in Malaya: A Chronicle of Life and Adventure in the Jungle* (London: H.F. & G. Witherby, 1933), p. 81; George Bilainkin, *Hail Penang! Being a Narrative of Comedies and Tragedies in a Tropical Outpost among Europeans, Chinese, Malays and Indians* (Penang: Areca Books, [1932] 2010), pp. 166–71.
85. Wilson, *Annual Report of the Labour Department, 1936.*
86. K.A. Mukundan, *Report of the Agent of the Government of India, 1936* (Calcutta: Government of India Press, 1937); Jain, *South Indians on the Plantation Frontier*, p. 134.
87. Wilson, *Annual Report, 1936*; George Bilainkin provides a generally sympathetic account of Thaipusam in Penang in the 1930s. He notes Chettiar management of the festival, is sceptical of the colonial (and missionary-inspired) shibboleth that participants are drugged prior to entering trance, and expresses unqualified "admiration of the Tamil's courage". (Bilainkin, *Hail Penang*, pp. 172–74).
88. Mukundan, *Report of the Agent, 1936*; Wilson, *Annual Report, 1936.*

89. Ainsworth, *The Confessions of a Planter*, p. 126; Mukundan, *Report of the Agent*, 1936.

90. Jain, *South Indians on the Plantation Frontier*, p. 132; Sri Delima, *As I was Passing* (Kuala Lumpur: Berita, 1976), pp. 152–58.

91. Jain, *South Indians on the Plantation Frontier*, p. 133.

92. Ramanathan, "Hindu Religion", p. 83.

93. Jain, *South Indians on the Plantation Frontier*, p. 276.

94. Ramanathan, "Hindu Religion", p. 84; Arasaratnam, *Indians in Malaysia*, p. 172.

95. For a major, albeit now dated, survey of the major Hindu festivals in Malaysia, see Sinnappah Arasaratnam, *Indian Festivals in Malaysia* (Kuala Lumpur: Department of Indian Studies, 1966).

96. Arasaratnam, *Malaysian Indians*, p. 207.

97. Ramanathan, "Hindu Religion", pp. 177–81.

98. Arasaratnam, *Indians in Malaysia*, p. 164.

99. Information garnered from interviews with temple officials, Kuala Lumpur.

100. Ackerman and Lee, *Heaven in Transition*, p. 96.

101. Arasaratnam, *Indians in Malaysia*, pp. 126–27.

102. Ibid.

103. Ibid., pp. 172–73.

104. Rajakrishnan, *Caste Consciousness*, pp. 73–75.

105. Gamba, *The Origins of Trade Unionism*, pp. 307–8.

106. Arasaratnam, *Indians in Malaysia*, p. 165; Ackerman and Lee, *Heaven in Transition*, p. 97.

107. Arasaratnam, *Indians in Malaysia*, pp. 166–67.

108. Ibid., p. 128.

109. Ibid., pp. 165–66.

110. Ackerman and Lee, *Heaven in Transition*, p. 97.

111. Arasaratnam, *Indians in Malaysia*, p. 167.

112. Ibid., p. 195.

113. Ibid., p. 166.

114. Andrew C. Willford, *Cage of Freedom: Tamil Identity and the Ethnic Fetish in Malaysia* (Ann Arbor: University of Michigan Press, 2006), pp. 129–30.

115. Conversation with the late Dr S.M. Ponniah.

116. Willford, *Cage of Freedom*, p. 169.

117. *Hinduism Today*, April/May/June 2002; interviews with members of the Saiva Siddhanta Church.

118. Alexandra Kent, *Divinity and Diversity: A Hindu Revitalization Movement in Malaysia* (Singapore and Copenhagen: Institute of Southeast Asian Studies/ NIAS Press, 2007), p. 71.

119. In general, Saivite doctrines do not allow for avatars of Lord Siva.

120. Rajoo, "Sanskritization", p. 168.
121. Arasaratnam, *Indians in Malaysia*, pp. 172–73.
122. Christopher John Baker, *The Politics of South India 1920–1937* (Cambridge: Cambridge University Press, 1976), p. 193.
123. Vineeta Sinha, "Hinduism in Contemporary Singapore", in *Indian Communities in Southeast Asia*, edited by K.S. Sandhu and A. Mani (Singapore: Institute of Southeast Asian Studies, 1993), p. 829.
124. Arasaratnam, *Indians in Malaysia*, p. 174.
125. I also discussed this letter with a government-appointed senior temple official in Palani. He responded, "I have no idea why these fellows [that is, Hindu "reformers"] get themselves so heated [about kavadi bearers]. They are not very knowledgeable people." He went on the explain that the kavadi ritual has long been regarded as an integral devotional tradition within the Murugan cultus, and was well established not only in South India but elsewhere throughout the Tamil diaspora (interview February 1998). The advice contained in this letter also foreshadows that conveyed in the early 1970s by Indian officials to Indonesian authorities in connection with a proposal to ban the kavadi ritual in Medan (this will be discussed in Chapter 7).
126. Arasaratnam, *Indians in Malaysia*, p. 174.
127. Sinha, *Hinduism in Contemporary Singapore*, pp. 844–45.
128. *Hinduism Today* 10, no. 3 (April 1988): 8.
129. Dato S. Govindaraj, "Country Report: Malaysia", First Asia-Pacific Hindu Conference, Singapore, 3 April 1988.
130. Fred W. Clothey, *Ritualizing on the Boundaries: Continuity and Innovation in the Tamil Diaspora* (Columbia: University of South Carolina Press, 2006), p. 191.
131. Willford, *Cage of Freedom*, p. 79.
132. Rajoo, "Sanskritization", p. 167.
133. Ibid., pp. 158–59.
134. Ramanathan, "Hindu Religion", p. 81.
135. Rajoo, "Sanskritization", p. 164.
136. Ibid., pp. 163–64.
137. Sinha, *A New God*, p. 165.
138. Ibid., pp. 54–56.
139. Ibid., p. 50.
140. Rajoo, "Sanskritization", pp. 164–65.
141. Sinha, *A New God*, p. 202.
142. Rajoo, "Sanskritization", p. 167.
143. Judith Nagata, *The Reflowering of Malaysian Islam: Modern Religious Radicals and their Roots* (Vancouver: University of British Columbia Press, 1984), p. 127.

144. The sole Malay survivor was a Colombo Plan student enrolled in a medical degree at an Australian university. At this point my duties within the Australian High Commission, Kuala Lumpur, included responsibility for sponsored students. During an extended interview, this student revealed the following sequence of events. He informed me that when the desecrators had entered the temple, the guards had summoned a Malay haji who had returned to the temple and berated the intruders for committing acts that ran counter to the precepts of Islam. In the darkness the desecrators, supposedly mistaking the haji for a Sikh, had attacked him, thus provoking the fatal conflict. Police sources later advised me that there was general confusion surrounding the actual course of events which followed this attack. Significantly, the haji was not called to testify at the subsequent trial of the temple guards, and no reference was made to his presence within the temple.

145. Ramanathan, "Hindu Religion", p. 243.

146. Lim Teck Ghee, "Malaysia's Prospects: Rising to or in Denial of Challenges", in *Multiethnic Malaysia: Past, Present and Future*, edited by Lim Teck Ghee, Alberto Gomes, and Azly Rahman (Petaling Jaya: Strategic Information and Research Development Centre, 2009), p. 486; S. Nagarajan, "Marginalisation and Ethnic Relations: The Indian Experience", in *Multiethnic Malaysia*, p. 378.

147. Andrew C. Willford (in collaboration with S. Nagarajan), *Tamils and the Haunting of Justice: History and Recognition in Malaysia's Plantations* (Singapore: NUS, 2014), p. 38.

148. Andrew Ong, "Hindus Protest Temple Demolition", *Malaysiakini*, 25 May 2006 <http://www.malaysiakini.com.news/51572> (accessed 28 May 2006); S. Nagarajan, "Indians in Malaysia: Towards Vision 2020", in *Rising India and Indian Communities in East Asia*, edited by K. Kesavapany, A. Mani, and P. Ramasamy (Singapore: Institute of Southeast Asian Studies, 2008), p. 386.

149. Lim, "Malaysia's Prospects", p. 487.

150. Andrew Ong, "Temple Row: 12 Freed by Police", *Malaysiakini*, 3 November 2007 <http://www.malaysiakini.com.news/74341> (accessed 5 November 2007).

151. "Malaysian State to Seek New Site for Temple", *Taipei Times*, 7 September 2009 <http://www.tapeitimes.com/news/world/archives/2009/09/07/20003452999> (accessed 9 September 2009).

152. John R. Malott, "The Price of Malaysia's Racism", *Wall Street Journal*, 8 February 2011 <http://www.on.line.wsj.com/article.SB10001424052748704422045761_2966360557634.html> (accessed 28 February 2011).

153. James Chin, "Malaysia and the Rise of Najib and 1Malaysia", *Southeast Asian Affairs*, edited by Daljit Singh (Singapore: Institute of Southeast Asian Studies, 2010), p. 170.

154. Taipei Times, *Malaysian State to Seek New Site for Temple*.

155. Willford, *Tamils and the Haunting of Justice*, p. 74.
156. This movement emerged in the late 1860s. For a description of its origins in the United States, see Matthew Avery Sutton, *American Apocalypse: A History of Modern Evangelicism* (Cambridge, MA: The Belknap Press of Harvard University Press, 2014), pp. 8–46.
157. Ibid., p. xi.
158. See, for example, Jonathan Kirsch, *A History of the End of the World: How the most Controversial Book in the Bible Changed the Course of Western Civilization* (San Francisco: HarperCollins, 2006); Norman Cohn, *The Pursuit of the Millennium: Revolutionary Millenarians and Mystical Anarchists of the Middle Ages* (London: Pimlico, 2004). Most scholars have noted that the apocalyptic interpretation has particular appeal to those who regard themselves as "outsiders" or in some way excluded from mainstream society. Jonathan Kirsch has observed that Revelation is often anticipated by such devotees as a "revenge fantasy" and comments: "The apocalyptic idea … [is] both a balm and a liquor. Today you are oppressed … they are told by the apocalyptic texts but tomorrow your oppression and persecution will end because the whole world will end. And what's more they are encouraged to look forward not only to relief from suffering — a messianic hero and his army of holy warriors will defeat the demonic arch-villain and his army of evil-doers, but also revenge those who made them suffer in the first place." (Kirsch, *The History of the End of the World*, pp. 45–46)
159. Chris McGillion, "Jesus Loves Y'all", Spectrum, *Sydney Morning Herald*, 2 September 2000.
160. Ibid.
161. Sutton, *American Apocalypse*, p. 304.
162. Ibid., p. 311. See also Barbara Victor, *The Last Crusade: Religion and the Politics of Misdirection* (London: Constable, 2005), pp. 59–64.
163. Ackerman and Lee, *Heaven in Transition*, p. 85.

5

Murugan: A Tamil Deity

Cosmic History

The deity Murugan has been closely identified with Tamil religiosity for at least two millennia. Descriptions of Murugan are contained within early Tamil literature, including the substantial corpus of *Sangam* poetry.[1] In his landmark study, *The Many Faces of Murukan — The History and Meaning of a South Indian God*, Fred W. Clothey points out that throughout the *Sangam* period Tamil culture progressively absorbed elements of the Sanskrit culture of the Aryan North. The later portrayals of Murugan reflect the admixture of these northern influences and thus differ markedly from those found within the earlier poetry.[2]

In the earliest phase of *Sangam* literature, Murugan is clearly depicted as a rural deity, and is firmly identified with the *kurinci tinai* (hilly eco-zone) of the Tamil country, and hence the *tinai's* people.[3] The deity is also regarded as the god of the hunt, and indeed Asim Kumar Chatterjee postulates that Murugan may have been the patron god of the Karuvars, or hunting tribes.[4] In this guise, Murugan's enemy is the *cur* (*soor*), a demon who ranges the countryside randomly seeking out and possessing young women.[5] In early literature the *cur* is viewed as an actual physical manifestation whose very presence produces terror. However, over time, the *cur* transforms into the *cura*, whom Murugan defeats in battle, initially with a specially shaped leaf, but later with a leaf-shaped lance. Murugan's intense heroism is portrayed in many love poems.[6] He is clearly identified as a god who generates paroxysms of excitement among girls and young women; indeed he becomes established as the patron of premarital love.[7] He is also represented as a deity both adept at creating and dispelling suffering (*ananku*).[8] The red colour of the god is constantly reiterated, and he is thus known as *Ceyon/Seyon* ("The Red One").[9] Murugan is closely associated with the elephant and the peacock, the latter assuming a major role as the deity's mount.[10]

Throughout the later *Sangam* era — a period of urbanization and the establishment of kings in the Tamil country — Murugan incorporates additional roles and motifs. His identity moves beyond the *kurinci tinai* to gain acceptance in other *tinai* within the *Tamilakam*, namely the forests (*Mullai*), the plains (*Marutum*), the dry and semi-dry zones (*Palai*), and the littoral (*Neital*).[11] Murugan was one of a number of deities elevated into the received pantheon throughout the period of the Pandya and Pallava dynasties. Both dynasties pursued a universalistic and syncretic *Puranic* ideology embracing both Vaishnavite and Saivite motifs, deities and philosophies. Under this ideology, many non-Vedic and non-Brahmanical deities, including mother and folk goddesses and tribal deities, were identified as regional/local variants of the great gods and subsequently absorbed into the higher celestial realms.[12] Clothey suggests that poetical references link Murugan with the deities *Mayon* and *Tirumal*, generally portrayed in pastoral and forest settings, and who are later more generally recognized as Vishnu, especially in his *avatar* as Krishna, the cowherd.[13] He is also closely associated with Siva and Indra, as well as with the ruling echelons — kings, chiefs, warriors — and indeed he is established as the exemplar of wise command and the model against which all kingship is to be judged.[14] In this guise, the deity acquires all the regalia and symbols intrinsic to royal authority.[15] His role as the warrior god results in the establishment of military encampments (*padai veedu*) in other *tinais*.[16] Thus, even by the close of the *Sangam* period, Murugan may be regarded as a composite deity, incorporating various roles and motifs. He is both a bucolic and sylvan god worshipped by diverse rural peoples, as well as an urban deity encompassing the functions of warrior and king. His early and established broad acceptance distinguishes him as a "universal" god within the Tamil country.[17]

Clothey has pointed out that the very earliest literature relating to the deity emphasizes that possession is one of the ways by which the devotee might gain access to Murugan and thus receive his grace (*arul*).[18]

A marked feature of early Murugan worship is the frenzied dance of his devotees, including the priests (*velan*) dedicated to his service, who employ trance states inspired by the god to practice divination and to cure sickness. Later, within the urban context, "women in festive spirit ... wearing *kanci* blooms, dance in streets and in the temple courts of Madurai, zealously adoring him who wears the *katumpu* blossoms".[19] Even at this early juncture, Murugan is a god who inspires possession, ecstatic dancing, and the healing of illness.

Sanskritic Skanda: The God's Northern Presence

In ancient North India, mythology tracing and explicating the deeds and attributes of the deity Skanda gained wide currency throughout the epoch of kingship (that is, roughly between the third and six centuries CE). As in South India, the deity gradually acquires a multiple persona which ascribes to him the vastly diverse roles of warrior, sage, master thief and rogue.[20]

Early references to Skanda are contained within the Great Epics where he is identified as the son of Agni and depicted as the god of war. The youthful sage *Sanatkumara*, later linked to Skanda, appears in the *Chandyoga Upanishad*.[21] Sanatkumara ("Eternal Son") is portrayed as a sagacious and benevolent figure who imparts profound knowledge relating to the mysteries of existence. His youthfulness is seen as an attribute which connects him to the origins of time and primordiality, thus endowing him with an inherent awareness of the meanings of creation. Indeed, in his role of sage, he teaches the Brahman Narada the inner significance of the concept of *atman*, the individual soul which merges with Brahman, the Universal Soul[22] (thus anticipating Skanda's later imprisonment of the god Brahma for his inability to apprehend the *Pravana Aum*, and his subsequent explanation of the inner meaning of the mantra to his father, Siva). But while Sanatkumara is clearly identified with learning and knowledge, he also conveys the ideals of penance and austerities.[23]

The deity Skanda-Karttikeya also features in both the Epics and the *Puranas*. Within the Epics, Karttikeya[24] is repeatedly described as the Sun-God, a role which in earlier Vedic literature was usually assigned to Agni.[25] More commonly, however, Karttikeya is a warrior, a powerful deity whose astounding handsomeness is remarked upon, and who adopts as his mount the peacock, "the most beautiful bird found anywhere in the world".[26] His most frequent weapon is the *sakti*, or lance.[27] However, within the *Puranas*, Karttikeya's role as warrior god is augmented to portray a deity who embodies penetrating learning and wisdom.[28] Clothey has observed that within the context of Epic and *Puranic* mythology, the warrior embraces the dual functions of creation and destruction, entailing responsibility for the maintenance of cosmic *dharma*. Thus, in his defeat of his enemies he preserves, renews or restores universal order. His role as a central pillar of cosmic symmetry elevates Skanda-Karttikeya into the position of a major deity, a high god.[29]

A further and often neglected aspect of Skanda-Karttikeya is his casting in the role of divine lover. In the *Brahma Purana*, the deity is shown as a profligate who is constantly found beguiling and seducing the consorts of the celestials. Understandably upset, the gods complain to Parvati who fruitlessly tries to persuade her son to refrain from a life of dissolution and pleasure. When her cajolery fails, Parvati decides to intervene more directly. Subsequently, whenever Skanda sets out on an amorous adventure, he encounters his mother. Stymied and frustrated, he pauses to reflect, ultimately embracing the path of asceticism. This myth is later repeated in the *Skanda Purana*.[30]

However, as Clothey has pointed out, the most obvious and profound motif of Skanda-Karttikeya mythology within the Vedic tradition is that of divine sonship. The implications of this role are far-reaching and establish the deity's credentials as a great and universal god. In many respects the celestial son is viewed as the embodiment of the father, and not only fulfils the father's cosmological function but also assumes responsibility for many of the specific roles ascribed to the father. Moreover, in early Sanskrit literature the son of a creator partakes of the world's primordiality, that is, the very essence of creation itself, and thus may be perceived as a generator of cosmic order.[31] Throughout the Gupta era, Skanda becomes firmly identified as Siva's son, and thus a member of Siva's family.[32]

Throughout the period of Aryan-Vedic teachings, Skanda thus incorporates a variety of celestial motifs and themes. This composite deity gains the allegiance of many sectors of Northern Indian society, including kings, warriors and religious philosophers. At some point in this era the warrior god fuses with the Brahmanic Skanda, the slayer of the *asuras*,[33] and the sustainer and renewer of cosmic order.[34] Not only does Skanda integrate all of these roles and functions, but as son of Siva he is infused with all of the commanding characteristics of a supreme deity and is thus elevated to the status of a high god in his own right.[35] While he is an auspicious deity who can and does grant boons to his devotees, at the same time he retains the ludic qualities of a rogue deity; as a philanderer, and as *Dhurta*, the patron of thieves.[36] These qualities, as much as those of the great Brahmanic deity, are to remain, sometimes unnoticed, often denied, as authentic voices of the god's multifarious persona.[37]

The Northern–Southern Fusion

By the fourth to fifth Century CE, Skanda of the Epics had become known in South India. By this stage he had made the transition to a pan-Indian god, though his primary northern manifestation as a Sanskritic kingship–warrior god tended to differ from his Tamil orientations. However, the growing influence of Sanskrit and Aryan themes in the South were to be increasingly reflected in the Tamil Murugan. These did not detract from the folkish attributes of the deity; the high Brahmanic god who occupied a prominent position within the established Hindu pantheon continued to coexist with the popular god of the hills, forests and pastoral peoples.[38]

The late *Sangam* works, the *Paripatal* and the *Tirumurukarruppatai* (TMP), fuse Sanskritic and Tamil mythology and create a pan-Tamil geography with specific reference to certain localities and shrines.[39] The TMP represents a transition in Tamil mythology in that it moves beyond the heroic poetry of the earlier *Sangam* era and into the age of *bhakti* (devotional) literature.[40] The TMP incorporates earlier myths of Tamil Murugan, and clearly foreshadows the commingling of this identity with that of the *Puranic* Skanda/Karttikeya.[41] Skanda-Murugan is now identified as a composite deity, and the god is expressly linked to other great deities. Thus, for example, his mother Parvati is shown to be the sister of Vishnu, thus making the latter an uncle of Skanda. Another passage provides the deity with two brides, the celestial *Devesena* (later more popularly known by her Tamil name of *Devayanai*), and the earthly *Valli*, a bride of humble origins. The two brides of Murugan suggest a dual role for the deity; a heavenly and thus transcendent god, and one who in his earthly presence is immanent to his devotees.[42] The implications of the relationship between Murugan, Devayanai and Valli will be explored later in this chapter.

However, the Tamil Skanda-Murugan assumes a vastly different persona from that of the Gupta and pre-Gupta Skanda. The Skanda of the northern tradition is largely a mythological figure. He fulfils a prominent role in the cycle of creation, is familiar with and moves easily in the world of high deities, and is expressly linked to the great celestial motifs — the sun, the stars and God as creator. His covenant with his devotees is that offered by Brahmanic Hinduism — the promise of release, liberation and absorption into the heavenly sphere. His Sanskrit manifestations contrast with those of the more immediate and accessible Tamil Murugan, for although by this juncture Murugan has been accepted as a "high" god with all the characteristics that such a role implies, he retains his earthly aspects, as a god of fertility, of forests and rural life, a deity whose worship is exuberant and frequently sensual, a god depicted as "an extension of joyous humanness".[43]

But while Skanda-Murugan was becoming deeply entrenched within the Tamil country, Skanda was fading from the prominence he had enjoyed in North India. Indeed, in the period following the Gupta era, the worship of Skanda, except that of Karttikeya, who was regarded as a rather minor deity, had all but disappeared in the Aryan regions.[44] Thus Skanda-Murugan was to become almost exclusively a South Indian and especially a Tamil god, and his cultus was to increasingly reflect the religious, philosophical and political permutations of Tamil history and society.

Skanda-Murugan in the Tamil Country

Towards the end of the *Sangam* period, and up until the tenth century, Murugan faded into relative obscurity. Much of this period was marked by the temporary eclipse of Hinduism within the Tamil country, and the momentary ascendency of the more austere religions of Jainism and Buddhism. The seventh century resurgence and the veneration of Siva and Vishnu inspired by the *bhakti* poets and their philosophy of devotion failed to re-establish Skanda as a major deity. While throughout this era he continued to be identified as a son of Siva, he was relegated to the status of a minor god, and his public and ceremonial worship languished.[45]

However, as this era progressed, Skanda-Murugan began to regain his former prominence. The reinstatement of Skanda-Murugan coincided with the inauguration of the Chola era and the concomitant decline of Jainism/Buddhism. Following the re-emergence of Siva and Vishnu as the undisputed leading gods of the South Indian Hindu firmament, the profound implications of Skanda's divine sonship were more widely recognized, while his brother Ganesha also gained extensive acceptance.[46] This period was marked by intense philosophical speculation in the Tamil country, much of it conducted within the *brahmadeyas*, which received substantial royal patronage.[47] The deity Subrahmanya played a considerable role in this process as *gurumurti* (philosophical guru), as did Murugan as the font of the Tamil language, the moulder and teacher of Tamil grammar, and the creative inspiration of Tamil literature and poetry.[48] Indeed, Champakalakshmi observes that the "crystallization of the Murukan cult as that of Skanda-Kartikkeya was one of the most significant aspects of the Tamil Saiva tradition in the early medieval period, that is the sixth to thirteenth centuries AD".[49] The Chola fondness for Skanda in his role as the Skanda *gurumurti*, Subrahmanya, did much to advance this process. Firmly positioned within the Saivite tradition, Skanda's militaristic role gradually receded, and temple iconography increasingly depicted him as a philosopher and guru.[50]

The positioning of Skanda-Murugan as a great Saivite god spawned an accompanying devotional literature in both Sanskrit and Tamil, and an extensive mythology (as exemplified by the *Skanda Purana*).[51] Murugan's "rehabilitation" as a great god was accompanied by a flowering of iconography which celebrated the deity's multifaceted persona and which incorporated most of the elements of his prior background. Several persistent Murugan motifs and symbols were firmly established throughout this period. The depiction of the peacock as Murugan's mount became standard, displacing that of the elephant. In addition, portrayals of Murugan as *San Mukha* (Shanmugan), a six-faced god astride a peacock, became accepted iconography in the Chola era.[52]

However, although Skanda-Murugan's single composite identity had been established, throughout much of the medieval period the inconsistencies between the Sanskrit Skanda and the Tamil Murugan remained obvious. As Clothey has remarked, "Murukan is as fully Tamil in the medieval period as Subrahmanya is Sanskrit."[53] Thus, while at one extreme the high Brahmanic god Skanda-Subrahmanya embodied the ideals of asceticism, renunciation and release, at the other, Murugan, the folk deity, affirmed the fullness and exhilaration of life. It was not until the Vijayanagara era that awareness grew of the intrinsic correspondences between the Tamil and Sanskritic attributes of Skanda-Murugan, and there was a concomitant more general, though never complete, acceptance of the deity in all his diversity. During this period the TMP with its delineation of Murugan's sacred geography and his temples was absorbed into the received Saiva canon.[54]

Since the late nineteenth century, Murugan has been an integral component of the great cultural regeneration which has swept the Tamil country and the Tamil diaspora. Throughout the period leading to the independence of India, the deity had been associated with the revitalization, and indeed the entire spectrum of the Tamil arts, and, as patron of the Tamil language, the publishing and promotion of neglected or forgotten works of Tamil literature and philosophy. The renewed pride in the Tamil heritage took the form of popular movements which emphasized Tamil arts and traditions, and resulted, inter alia, in the renovation of the great temples of the Tamil country.[55]

In the period that followed the attainment of Indian independence, Murugan temples have been opened to *Adi Dravidas*, and the overall improvement of transport in Tamil Nadu has made all Murugan pilgrimage destinations much more accessible to all sectors of the population. The 1967 elections which brought the anti-Brahman Dravidian party (Dravida Munnera Kalagam) to office in the state of Tamil Nadu was followed by a suite of measures which, inter alia, further entrenched Murugan's already powerful presence within Tamil consciousness. Subsequent to the chief minister's declaration that as Palani the deity was "God of the DMK", the government moved to appoint non-Brahman executive officers to all major Murugan temples, attempted to enforce the reciting of *archanai* and the singing of hymns in Tamil, and adopted a series of policies aimed at sweeping away imagined Brahmanic practices and influences. In the five years between 1967 and 1972, annual attendances at all Murugan shrines rose dramatically,[56] and steadily increased over subsequent years.[57] Indeed, Murugan appears to remain the Tamil deity par excellence, a god who reflects the heritage, history, traditions and social backgrounds of all Tamilians, and who, in one form or another, is regarded as accessible to every segment of Tamil Hindu society.

Puranic Mythology

In essence the festival of Thaipusam commemorates the granting of the *Sakti Vel* (cosmic spear, or *Vetrivel*) to Murugan, son of the supreme deity, Siva, by Parvati, Siva's consort, at the outset of Murugan's campaign to defeat the army of *Surapadman*, head of the *asuras* (demons). In this section

I have provided a synopsis of the corpus of *Puranic* mythology which describes the creation of Murugan, delineates his essential identity and records the nature of his victory over the *asuras*.[58] Much of the following account was originally taken from field notes gathered during extensive conversations with senior Hindus and Murugan *bhaktas* (devotees). While the deity is known by many names (e.g., *Muruga/Murugan/Murukan*, *Skanda, Shanmugan, Ceyon, Palani, Subramaniam, Karthikeya, Swaminathan*, etc.), each of which conveys a specific aspect of the deity's multifaceted divinity, unless otherwise stated, I have used the generic term *Murugan* throughout this section.

It is perhaps apposite to offer some brief comments on the term *mythology*. In recent years *myth* has been popularly used in a pejorative sense, as a falsehood, an invented story, at best a widely held but erroneous notion. However, within the sphere of religion a myth is regarded far more positively and more generally as a discursive narrative which mediates human encounters with mystery, and often encapsulates an entire worldview. Myths convey philosophical truths that lie "beyond language and reason" and which cannot be transmitted or accessed by unaided rationality.[59] John Bowker has pointed out that for the bulk of human history, myths had provided profound insights into cosmic realities and our place within and in relation to these realities.[60] Myths also provide the basis for ritualized action within the world; indeed the ritual enactment of mythology is often far more influential than doctrine in imparting understanding of the precepts of a religious tradition. This is especially true of Hinduism.[61]

The mythology pertaining to Murugan opens with the separation of Siva, the most powerful of the gods (*Mahadevas*), from his consort *Uma*. This parting has its origins in an incident which had occurred during Siva's wedding to Uma. Siva had agreed to marry Uma, who had been incarnated as the daughter of *Daksha* (Tamil: *Takkan*), but had unexpectedly vanished during the nuptials. He subsequently carried Uma away as his bride. Incensed, Daksha convened a great sacrifice to which he invited all the gods, with the exception of Siva, about whom he spoke disparagingly, denying that one who was both "naked and deformed" could ever be the Soul of the Universe.[62] Taking the form of *Virabhadra* (Siva as Divine Anger),[63] Siva appeared during the ritual, destroyed the sacrifice, humiliated all the gods present, and slew Daksha. Uma advised Siva that she hated her current incarnation, for as long as she inhabited her present body she would be known as the daughter of Daksha, he who had cursed Siva, the supreme god. Siva advised her to become reincarnated as the daughter of *Himalaya*, the Mountain Lord. She accordingly departed from Siva, and reborn as Parvati performed great austerities (*tapas*) to purify herself and to make herself attractive to Siva as her groom.

Left without Uma, his *Sakti* (Divine Energy personified as female), Siva secluded himself from daily life to devote himself to austerities and meditation. Before his withdrawal, however, he granted substantial boons to three *asuric* (demonic/lower astral) brothers[64] —Surapadman, *Singamukhan* and *Tarakasuran* — including the extraordinary boon to Surapadman that "he would live forever without being killed by anyone ... [that he would] rule the thousand and eight *andams* [most of the worlds] for a hundred and eight [*sic*] *Ugas* [several millions of years]".[65] Surapadman had particularly sought — and obtained — the assurance that he would die only at the hands of a son of Siva. He believed that as the Supreme Yogi, Siva would never beget a son.[66]

The granting of these boons to Surapadman and his two brothers formed an integral part of a long-term *asuric* strategy to gain control of and dominate the universe. This plan had its origins in the birth of a daughter, *Surasai*, to *Atisuran* (also known as *Akhiresa*), the king of the *asuras*. From her early childhood, Surasai was trained in the arts of *maya* (illusion) by *Sukracharya*, the chief *asuric* preceptor. She became thoroughly proficient in all these arts, and thus became known as *Mayai*. The intention of these teachings was to equip Mayai to help avenge the earlier defeat the *asuras* had suffered at the hands of the *devas* (angelic beings).[67]

To further this quest, Mayai was told to transform herself into a beautiful and seductive woman who would beguile *Kashyapar*, a well-known and powerful *rishi* (sage). She was to conceive children with Kashyapar, as it was well known that any offspring of a sage, especially an ascetic who had undergone many penances and austerities, would command powers greater than those wielded by the *devas*. Mayai sought out Kashyapar in the forest where he was deep in meditation. Using her magical powers she transformed the dark and tenebrous forest into an enchanted clearing full of light and colour. Having stirred the interest of the sage, she captivated him with her melodious singing and enthralling dancing. In due course their marriage produced three sons, Surapadman, Singamukhan (with the face of a lion) and Tarakasuran (with the face of an elephant), and a daughter, *Ajamukhi* (with the face of a goat).[68] Kashyapar, as a *rishi*, admonished them to live a virtuous life in accordance with the dictates of righteousness. He attempted to teach his children the basic tenets of Saivite *bhakti* devotion, namely that the aim of the wise is to study the essential deity (*Pati*), the individual being or soul (*pacu*), and the forms of bondage (*paca*) which prevent the soul from attaining knowledge of its true nature and that of God.[69] Those who eschew this path are subject to impurities (*mala*), such as illusion, luxury and pride, and are thus fated to live and die in the world of *samsara* (essentially understood as the cycle of birth, death and rebirth in the phenomenal world). Only righteousness can lead to true knowledge, awareness and bliss. Mayai openly scorned Kashyapar's teachings and instructed her children that the material world was the sole reality, and that power and wealth were of paramount importance. She denied the authenticity of concepts such as *karma*, universal *dharma* or the distinctions between the truth and illusory perceptions (*ahamkara*).[70] After some time Kashyapar realized that his children were firmly ensnared within the web of trickery spun by their mother, and that his advice was proving unavailing. Defeated and disillusioned, he returned to the forest to resume his penance.

Mayai now instructed the children to perform *tapas* (austerities/ purificatory sacrifices) to Siva, so that they might acquire the powers which would enable them to subjugate the world and heavens. The three brothers successfully performed *tapas* of increasing severity, and, as earlier related, were granted innumerable boons, including that of immortality. Once this process was complete they returned to Mayai, and received further tuition from Sukracharya, who taught them to live by the credo:

> *Live to eat, live to enjoy,*
> *Live to destroy, live to deny,*
> *Live to kill, and kill to live,*
> *Pleasure is the goal of life,*
> *Gratify all your desires,*
> *Man is the Supreme God,*
> *There is none higher than he,*
> *Everything here is meant*
> *Only for his enjoyment.*

Armed with the boons bestowed by Siva, the brothers set out to conquer the world. Having vanquished and enslaved their opposition, they began their protracted period of overlordship. Surapadman built a magnificent capital at Mahendrapuri in the south of India, while Singamukhan located his capital Asuram in the north, and Tarakasura built his capital at Emakudaman in the southwest. Their rule involved a complete inversion of cosmic order and was characterized by injustice, torture, persecution, and a total disregard for the path of *dharma*. The moon was prohibited from waxing and waning, the sun was forced to shine throughout the night and was barred from radiating any warmth, and death was abolished. The *asuras* created terror among the celestials and subjected them to countless indignities. *Vayu*, the god of the wind, was made to sweep the streets of the *asuric* city, and *Varuna*, the god of rain, was forced to wash them. Other gods were compelled to fulfil menial and degrading tasks, including taking up the role of fishermen, thus staining their celestial purity with the repeated and *adharmic* destruction of life.

The *devas*, weary of the intense suffering they had experienced under the misrule of the *asuras*, entreated *Kama*, the embodiment of desire, to rouse Siva from his meditations so that he would marry Parvati and produce a son who would destroy the *asuras*. Kama, fearful of the response, dutifully shot his arrows of lust into Siva, who, opening his third eye, the symbol of asceticism (an "anti-erotic force"),[71] burned Kama to ash. While Siva did marry Parvati, as foreseen by the celestials, the union was barren. The gods sent Vayu in the form of a breeze to discover why the marriage had produced no issue, but he was denied entry. Led by Brahma, Vishnu and Indra, the gods approached Siva to ask him for his aid to overturn the *asuric* regime. They found him seated with Parvati. The celestials recounted the many wicked deeds perpetrated by the *asuras*, and told of the perverted and cruel rule of the *asura* Surapadman. Upon hearing of the atrocities of the *asuras*, Siva promised the gods that he would provide his assistance. He also agreed to restore Kama to life, but only as an invisible being. Siva now sprouted five additional heads, and from each of his (now) six heads emitted a divine spark. The seed of Siva, fiery after the long years of austerities,[72] was borne in agony by Vayu and *Agni* (god of fire), and deposited in the Ganges, which, unable to withstand the extreme heat, transported it to Lake *Saravana*, a mystic body of water located in the Himalayas. Each of the sparks subsequently developed into a baby boy, and each was individually guarded and nurtured by one of the six Pleiades maidens (*Krttikas*). Parvati, excluded from the role of mother, cursed the maidens to eternal barrenness. At this point Parvati's anklet broke and each of the nine jewels in the anklet reflected her image on the surface of the lake. Siva commanded these images to come to life, and nine *saktis*[73] emerged from the lake. As Siva's glance fell upon these *saktis*, each was impregnated. The infuriated Parvati cursed the *saktis* to an unnaturally elongated pregnancy. Despairing, the *saktis* sought Siva's intervention, and he insisted that Parvati lift her curse. Each *sakti* produced a fully grown son, who collectively were to provide the nine generals (*Nava Veera*) of Murugan's *devonic* army. The chief of these was *Veerabahu* (individual wisdom and discriminative intelligence). The six babies born of Siva's spark rushed to Parvati and were embraced so that they fused into one being, with six heads and twelve arms, the form of Murugan known as *Shanmugan* or *Arumugan*. The baby was nursed by Parvati and fed milk from her breasts.

We should note in passing that Murugan was born on the new moon day, which in cosmic terms parallels the rising of the sun. Having been suckled by the *Krttika* maidens, Murugan dispatched them into the heavens where they formed a constellation by which time was henceforth to be measured. Indra, king of heaven, proclaimed Murugan Lord of Time and announced that with his birth a new era of cosmic chronometry had begun.[74]

Throughout his brief infancy, Shanmugan displayed extraordinary talents, sometimes engaging in childish acts, reflecting his lack of awareness of his own strength and his intrinsic qualities. Thus "his games and playthings became terrible ones. He piled mountains on top of one another, and upended others. Mt. Meru he dumped into the sea. He damned the waters of the Ganges, changed the orbits of the planets...".[75] But he also successfully tamed a fierce, destructive and terrifying ram which had arisen from a sacrifice conducted by the *rishi* (sage) Narada.[76] However, his most celebrated childhood act was the imprisonment of Brahma. During a visit of the *devas* to Mount Kailas, the celestial abode of Siva, all but one of the gods paid obeisance to Murugan. The exception was Brahma who, obsessed with his superior rank, refused to acknowledge Shanmugan's status as the son of Siva. Murugan waited until Brahma was seated in the hall with the other gods and asked him a series of questions regarding the inner meaning of the mystical symbol, the *Pravana Aum*.[77] When Brahma could not answer, Shanmugan had him beaten and thrown into jail. Siva, alerted to this development, approached Shanmugan, and playfully requested him to explain the significance of this sacred symbol. Dutifully, Shanmugan instructed his father in the mysteries of the *Pravana Aum*.[78]

After his boyhood, and following a period of purificatory asceticism and self-realization at the hilltop retreat of Palani (described in a later section of this chapter), Murugan was presented with the *Vel* by Parvati.[79] Accompanied by Veerabahu, Veerabahu's eight brothers, and the *devonic* army, Murugan left Mount Kailas in the north of India to head southwards to combat the *asuras*. En route, Murugan encountered *Krownchan*, one of the lieutenants of Tarakasuran, attempting in the form of a mountain to block the passage of the *devonic* forces. Murugan destroyed Krownchan with a single blow of his *Vel*. The battle with the *asuric* forces raged for six days and nights, with both Surapadman and Murugan taking a limited role in the early conflicts. The warring sides sought the assistance of the planets; the *devas* enlisted Jupiter (*Brihaspati*) as their planetary preceptor, while the *asuras* looked to Venus (*Shakra*).[80] Ascendency alternated between the *devas* and *asuras* during the course of this great struggle, and neither was able to vanquish the other. Although both armies sustained numerous casualties, through the use of certain powers each side was able to bring their slain comrades back to life. However, whenever the *devas* appeared to be near defeat, the intervention of Murugan assured that they regained the upper hand. Once the *devonic* forces began to control the course of the war, the *asura* Agnimukhan prayed to the goddess *Bhadrakali*[81] to intervene on the side of the *asuras*, but upon encountering Veerabahu, Bhadrakali merely smiled and withdrew from the battlefield.

With the arrival of Murugan and Surapadman, the final phase of the conflict commenced. Realizing the immense power of Murugan, and that defeat in a straight fight was inevitable, Surapadman employed all the illusory stratagems he had been taught by Mayai, assuming the forms of objects, birds and animals. However, Murugan was beyond any delusion, and quickly flushed Surapadman from each of his disguises. Towards the conclusion of the battle Murugan appeared before Surapadman in all his glory,

> ...his own true and eternal form: the cosmos and all of its constituent elements organized hierarchically from the highest (at the head) to the lowest (at the feet) and encompassed in the figuration of a male with one head, and two arms, the transcendent male principle that is identified with *Purusa*, Cosmic Man.[82]

Surapadman was temporarily overcome with Divine Love, but when Murugan resumed the form of Shanmugan (that is, with six faces, twelve arms and twelve eyes), Surapadman converted himself into a massive cannibalistic monster with a thousand arms and a thousand legs, and launched a frenzied attack. Murugan split Surapadman in two with his *Vel*, whereupon the latter escaped into the ocean and became a gigantic mango tree which threatened to smother the world. Murugan cleft this tree with his *Vel*, and Surapadman then took shape as a peacock (*mayil*) and a rooster (*sevai*), both of which charged at Murugan. However, Murugan tamed both with a single, loving glance. To commemorate the defeat of the *asuras*, Murugan ordered that the peacock and the rooster should, respectively, become his *vahana* (mount) and emblem of his standard.[83] Thus, Surapadman, who could not be annihilated, having been granted the gift of immortality by Siva as the result of the austerities he had performed, was finally slain by a son of Siva, and became, in the form of two birds, the transformed and submissive symbols of Murugan's dominance.[84]

This struggle is commemorated in the six-day festival of Skanda Shasti (also known as Kanthashasti) in the month of *Aippaci* (October–November). The main centre in India is the Murugan temple of Tiruchendur in southern Tamil Nadu, mythical scene of Murugan's final battle with Surapadman.

Kamil Zvelebil has pointed out that all Tamil mythology is multivalent, and thus interpretable on several planes; namely, as a story, metaphorically, and as a cosmological expression of metaphysical principles and divine truths.[85] As George Michell comments:

> These [*Puranic*] myths present the collective wisdom of a timeless, anonymous and many-sided civilization and are much more than fanciful "biographies" of the gods. Like the great philosophical systems of India, the myths of Hinduism reveal the ultimate reality of the universe by giving symbolic expression to that which cannot be discursively expressed.[86]

In the following sections I have outlined the major cosmological and metaphysical implications of this mythology, the latter in terms of what it might imply for the evolution and destiny of the individual soul in relation to the Divine.

At the cosmological level, this myth represents nothing less than the process of phenomenal entropy and dissolution and subsequent reconstitution and renewal. The Divine has two essential states. *Being*, the passive, is known as *Siva*; and *Becoming*, the dynamic, is known as *Sakti*. These two states are envisaged as masculine and feminine respectively. Without the feminine aspect, Siva is remote and unknowable, and without the masculine aspect, Sakti has no existence. The entire universe with all its beings is a manifestation of the dynamic Sakti who exercises agency for the restoration of cosmic order.[87] Siva, the supreme effulgence, animates the entire universe of beings and abides within as Spirit. (Within each human, Sakti comprises body [*Deha*], life force [*Prana*], senses [*Indrayas*], mind [*Manas*], intelligence [*Buddhi*] and ego [*Ankhara*]. Siva infuses all these layers with life and spirit.) The tension and interplay between the two polarities results in movement and creation; its absence results in stasis, decay and ultimately destruction.[88] The constantly shifting relationship between Siva/Sakti (that is, between Absolute and Generative power) is constantly emphasized within all Tamil Saivite philosophy, both popular and *Agamic*.

As we have seen, this myth opens with the separation of Siva and Uma, and the withdrawal of Siva into austerities and meditation. Moreover, as the daughter of Himalaya, Parvati also enters into purificatory *tapas* to make herself worthy of Siva. Divided from one another, Siva and Uma/Parvati accumulate the unrelieved and ascetic "heat" which is produced by the practice of *tapas*.[89]

The splitting of Siva/Sakti creates a dangerously and inherently unstable cosmos, one tending to entropy. "Together they are fertile, generative and equilibrating, but apart they are essentially destructive."[90] The *tapas* of the *asuras*, and their acquisition of untrammelled power within the phenomenal universe heralds an inversion of the established cosmic order, the withdrawal of the animating spirit (Siva) and the cessation of adherence to *rita dharma* (rule by divine cosmic law). Within Hinduism the single goddess represents raw and uncontrolled power, essentially undirected and resulting in devastation.[91] The mastery of the *asuras* and the systematic wrecking of the established order indicate the damaging nature of unchecked Sakti. This is further stressed by:

1. Siva's incineration of Kama, thus repudiating both erotic desire and fertility; and
2. The barrenness of Siva's marriage to Parvati.

The story of the *asuras* emphasizes the triumph of absolute materialist desire, of lust without corresponding fertility, of wild and powerful but ultimately unproductive imagination. Mayai represents the very embodiment of unmitigated Sakti, with her employment of illusion to create both cause and effect, and thus to circumvent and deny reality. The army of the *asuras* represents the thousands of forms of the original impurities, namely *avidya* (spiritual ignorance), *kama* and *karma*. The *asuric* inversion of the cosmic order is perhaps most emphatically exemplified in the form of Surapadman's sister, Ajamukhi, whose savage sexuality causes her to rape all the men she meets, who is cannibalistic and who rejects and destroys all categories.[92]

The imploring of the celestials for the restoration of order marks the genesis of cosmic renewal. But the initial phases of this process are attended by fragmentation and implied violence. Reflecting the barrenness of the marriage between Siva and Parvati, Siva sprouts five additional heads and emits six divine sparks from the ascetic eye of each. The emission of the seed, its carriage by Vayu (wind), Agni (fire), and its deposition within the Ganges (water), which finally bears it to Lake Saravana, involves the combination of ether, air, fire, water and earth, the constituent elements of the phenomenal universe. Wendy Doniger O'Flaherty points out that while in human terms asceticism is opposed to sexuality and fertility, within the mythological context *tapas* becomes a most powerful force which generates extreme heat. The seed of an ascetic, especially when placed in water, is the commencing point of many cosmogonic myths.[93] Moreover, the seed produced by an ascetic is inherently dangerous — it can beget great heroes or, more likely, uncontrolled monsters. It must be properly disposed of. For this reason the gods are never born from Parvati or in any natural manner. The image of fire placed in water is used consistently within Hindu mythology to express control of indestructible mass energy.[94] The placing of Siva's seed within Lake Saravana, and the impregnation of the constituent elements with energy and effulgence, the divine essence of Siva, anticipates at microcosmic level the ultimate union and reunification of the dynamic principle of Siva/Sakti. But the tensions which continue to divide Siva/Sakti are evident in Parvati's recalcitrance, her fury at being denied maternal responsibility for the bearing of the six babies, and her cursing of the Pleiades. The breaking of the anklet (a common metaphor for the vagina in South Indian mythology),[95] and the creation of the nine *saktis*, each an activating quality of Parvati, and thus a modification of uncontrolled Sakti, signals a resolution of this phase. The nine gems of the broken anklet collectively comprise *navaratna*, regarded as an auspicious configuration.[96] Each gem and thus each of the *saktis* is associated with one of the nine planets (*navagraha*). The generals thus born of the *saktis* assume the respective qualities of the *sakti* from whom they are delivered, and collectively constitute the beneficent force required to attend and protect the young deity.

Parvati's embrace of the six babies to create a single identity, the six-faced Shanmugan, unifies unmanifested and manifested elements in a single being. The significance of this is underscored by Indra's declaration that Murugan's birth marks the commencement of a new *yuga* (era). But throughout his earliest stages, Shanmugan is unstable and undirected, as demonstrated by the wilful, chaotic and instinctive actions of his childhood, including the beating and imprisonment of Brahma. His spiritual evolution is illustrated by his taming of a wild ram (in some versions a buck goat), both symbols of lust within Hindu mythology.[97] Murugan's instruction of Siva in the intrinsic significance of the *Pravana Aum* indicates a growing awareness of his divine powers, nature and identity. This foreshadows his future role in subduing the *asuras*, the embodiment of rampant materialism exemplified by unrestrained *sakti*. This phase of the deity's unfoldment, together with the spiritual retreat at Palani, culminates with the acquisition of the *Sakti Vel*.

The bestowal by Parvati of the *Vel*, the weapon used to re-establish cosmic harmony, upon (the Siva-created) Murugan represents a manifest fusion of the Divine's absolute and generative powers. Murugan and his *Vel* in conjunction implies "the integrating of dualities in a manner consistent with Saiva thought.... Murugan and his lance are Siva–Sakti, the cosmic pair."[98]

The stabilization of Murugan, his progression to mature spiritual power, proceeds as the divine campaign against the *asuras* unfolds. D. Handelman comments, "the evolution of divinity in this myth is the movement from the lower-order reflexive, a metamorphosis to self-realization that is integral to a deity who encompasses the cosmos in his being".[99] This transformation is complete when Murugan reveals himself as *Purusa* to Surapadman; that is, the primal person who partakes of all the qualities of Brahma.[100] Thus "The true [i.e., Highest] being of Shanmugan is not his furious multiform of six heads and twelve arms, but that of Cosmic Man with one head and two arms.... But the true being of Surapadman is indeed a multiform of one thousand heads that depends on illusion for its existence."[101]

On the *metaphysical* level, the *purana* may be seen as an extended metaphor for spiritual evolution, the destiny of the soul and its ultimate relationship with the Divine (in esoteric terms the alienation of the *jivatnam* [embodied soul] from the *Paramatman* [Supreme Soul] and its return to its source).[102] Once an individual reaches a certain stage of spiritual awakening, there is a desire to renounce superfluities, and to realize Truth. But in the struggle to achieve *moksha* (liberation), the devotee often remains unaware of the power of negative forces of the world, and the magnetism which deluding joys can exercise. The union of the soul with *Advidya* (ignorance of the essential Divine character of the soul) leads to the birth of:

> *Asmita*: ego consciousness (Surapadman);
> *Kama*: ego-motivated desire (Singamukhan);
> *Karma*: ego-motivated selfish actions (Tarakasuran); and
> *Avarana*: veiling power: that which beguiles the soul and leads him/her to fall prey to transient and sensual desires (Ajamukhi).

Indeed the three brothers may be viewed as the three *gunas* (qualities of nature — *sattvas*, *rajas* and *tamas*) which promote ignorance of the intrinsic spirit of the soul and tie the individual to the gross world.[103]

The advice given by the father Kashyapar to his children was to lead a righteous life. However, the code of Mayai, subsequently reinforced by Sukracharya, the *asura* guru, was to exploit the illusionary material world. As has been shown, Surapadman and his siblings ignored the instructions of their father and followed the pathway advocated by their mother. The description of the radically divergent directions available to the offspring represents the inner conflicts, choices and "pulls" experienced by the soul.

The improper use of intelligence to acquire power seems to bestow upon the individual a certain strength, even omniscience, and he/she becomes corrupt, self-centred, forgets the Divine, and exploits his/her knowledge for selfish pursuits. Having been created by Siva in the image of the Divine (*Sura*), the soul falls into the grasp of the lower nature (*Asura*). The description of how Surapadman and his brothers petitioned Siva for certain boons, and their subsequent employment of God-given powers for evil and unworthy ends, illustrates this process.

The "birth" of Murugan is thus recognition of the Yogic Grace extended by Siva. Shanmugan is created by the third eye of Siva, the eye of wisdom which is able to penetrate all illusion. I have observed that the triumph of the *asuras* is ultimately predicated upon Mayai's use of chimera, both as cause and effect, which is fundamental to her success. Mayai (*maya*, or illusion), a lower emanation of Sakti, entraps souls within the beguiling world of appearances, of shapes and forms, thus obscuring the Divine Reality which lies behind the superficial and transitory.[104] The *Vel* represents the highest power of Sakti (*Para-Sakti*), which when employed by Murugan dispels all phenomenal illusion and allows the *sadhaka* (aspirant) to see beyond the magical world created by Mayai. Murugan's acquisition of the *Vel* represents the fusing of *Jnana-Sakti* of Siva (that is, his absolute power of wisdom) and the *Para-Sakti* of Parvati, to form *Yoga-Sakti* (contemplative knowledge). Murugan and his *Vel* are thus identified as the pursuit of pure spiritual knowledge which destroys the *asuras* within man. In sum, therefore, it may be stated that Murugan denotes a synthesis of the ultimate powers of Siva/Sakti, a deity created by the Absolute to destroy the bondages of ignorance imposed by the individual ego, but furnished with means to accomplish this by Parvati. In essence, Murugan may thus be perceived as the principle of Siva–Sakti's action within the substance of the mind.

This is further illustrated by the actual sequence of events surrounding the "birth" of Murugan. I have noted that the divine sparks emanating from Siva's third eye were borne by Vayu (wind) and Agni (fire) to the Ganges, which carries them to a lake (*Saravana Poihai*, or the pond of Saravana). Saravana is encircled by reeds. The depositing of the energy (*tejas*) of effulgence in the world involves a combination of the five principles of creation — ether, air, fire, water and earth. Parvati's embrace of the six babies creates a Being with a single body and six faces. The six heads of the as yet unintegrated deity represent the six attributes which constitute the necessary qualities of the Supreme Lord; namely, *jnana* (wisdom), *vairagya* (dispassion), *bala* (strength), *kirti* (fame), *shree* (wealth), and *aiswarya* (divine powers). They also represent the six advanced *cakras* (or spheres of spiritual energy).[105] Moreover, the six heads also recognize the all-pervading gaze of the Supreme — that is, the four cardinal directions plus up (into the world of the *devas*) and down (into the inner world of devotees).[106] Sakti, as the dynamic force of the universe, thus integrates the Spirit which was six into one, Skanda (the United One) conjoining the Divine Light (Siva), and Life (Sakti), superficially diverse but ultimately experienced by the *Yogi* in essential Oneness. The consignment of sparks within the divine lake may be homologized to the creation of the human soul and the provision of the conditions for its spiritual evolution. The lake itself is thus the human complex, whereas the reeds within the *Saravana Poihai* — impregnated with the Divine effulgence of Siva which animates all six portions of this complex; namely, Body (*Deha*), Life Force (*Prana*), Senses (*Indrayas*), Mind (*Manas*), Intelligence (*Buddhi*) and Ego (*Ahankara*) — represents the web of nerves in the human physical body, the network of life currents known as *nadis* in the vital body, and the thought flows in the astral body. Psychically, the *nadis* become the battleground within the human complex in which the inner war between the *devas* and *asuras* is fought. In this sense the *Vel* and Murugan constitute the essential paradigm for spiritual evolution and the attainment of *moksha*. For, in contemplating the animating life energies with which he/she is composed (*Sakti*-Becoming), the *sadhaka* (aspirant) is led to the discovery of his/her true divine nature (Siva-Absolute) and thus into the intrinsic unity of all existence. Thus the individual (microcosm) is linked to the universal (macrocosm) and is possessed of the full knowledge of the cosmic union of Siva–Sakti, the duality of oneness in perfect dynamic balance.

The petitioning of Siva by the *devas* not only signifies the need to enlist the Yogic forces of God to control the lower nature but also reveals the longing of the aspirant for liberation, for the bestowal of God's Divine Grace. But when the *sadhaka* reaches the stage of asking for Murugan's guidance, he/she is forced to acknowledge:

1. The impulsive power of the lower nature, and the ease with which an individual can succumb to these urges;
2. The need to develop willpower, and to discipline the mind, so that the individual may gain knowledge; and
3. The fact that maleficence and illusion cannot be defeated by an appeal to morality and ethics. Divine grace (*arul*) is necessary to remove him/her from the pull of lower urges, and to develop willpower and cognition. Divine Grace will often be bestowed in the form of a Guru. But Divine Grace is initially offered partially and piecemeal. Throughout the battle with the *asuras* the aspirant gains repeated glimpses of the nature of the Divine, but it is only in the final stages of unfoldment that *arul* is bestowed.

Murugan approached in this form, as the personification of *Yoga Sakti*, who will direct the *sadhaka* to attain perfect victory of lower forces, is known as *Guru-Guhan*, the Divine Preceptor, who dwells within and guides from the Cave of the Heart (*Guhan*: the One who stays concealed within).[107]

In the initial stages of spiritual unfoldment the *sadhaka* is sustained by powerful emotional forces which generate a seemingly invincible supply of willpower. This gathering resolution is symbolized by the destruction of Krownchan, an *asura* who takes the form of a mountain lying in the path of the *devonic* forces, and who represents inertness, laziness, sloth and a crude effort to fulfil instinctive urges, namely hunger, thirst, and sexual desire. At this juncture it appears only a matter of time before the lower forces are routed, and the untroubled mind is permanently installed in the higher *cakras*. But the fervour engendered by the emotions is not durable, and in time the mind will deviate to the urgings of the lower *cakras*. The aspirant is able to call upon two forces in his fight to banish ego-dominated ignorance: Discriminative Intelligence (Veerabahu), and Universal Wisdom (Murugan). The early stages of the battle are fought by Discriminative Intelligence, but at all times the devotee is subject to counter attack by *asuric* forces. The *devonic* and *asuric* forces occupy and operate from the same ground (human consciousness), and employ the same vehicles (human intellect and senses) in mounting their "campaigns". Whenever the *asuras* threaten to overwhelm the *sadhaka*, the Divine intervenes, ultimately weakening the ego. Among the *asuras* who challenge the *devas* are Surapadman's sons:

1. *Banugopan*: (seemingly sophisticated but actually distorted knowledge which denies the existence of Reality; Banugopan also symbolizes the inadequacy of the human intellect as a vehicle to discern the Divine);
2. *Agnimukhan* (the abusive and loud-mouthed crudity which displaces methodical knowledge); and
3. *Hiranyan* (the argumentative force, carping and querulous, but lacking knowledge and withdrawing timorously when directly confronted).

A major enemy of the devotee is the limiting sense of Time and the belief that despite his/her efforts he/she is not making headway towards his/her final destination. The realization that Time is a product of humanity's circumscribed linear conceptions is symbolized by Agnimukhan's summoning of the goddess *Bhadrakali*, embodiment of Time, who upon meeting Veerabahu, the pure form of analytical wisdom, merely smiles and withdraws from the battlefield. Bhadrakali can only be terrifying to those enfeebled by ignorance, but she relinquishes all power over those who have acquired the ageless knowledge which has liberated them from the grasp of Time's narrow constraints.

The most formidable enemy remains the ego. As long as this continues to exist the devotee may be overwhelmed by ignorant and selfish desires. The final battle between Surapadman (ego) and Murugan (Universal Wisdom) represents the ultimate struggle to shatter the ego. Throughout this conflict Surapadman appears in many forms, each of which demonstrates the delusions imposed upon awareness by the sense of ego. Each of these camouflages is uncovered by Universal Wisdom. The diversity of forms assumed by Surapadman has an esoteric explanation. In the course of its evolution the soul has passed through many categories, such as inanimate matter, as well as vegetable, plant, tree, bird and animal life, before taking human form. The ego possesses residues of all past lower existences. Thus, as Murugan repeatedly flushes Surapadman from each of his many disguises, visible and invisible, so the soul is liberated from the remaining pull of the *advidya* (ignorance) of each of these former categories.

As the ego is isolated and its power is gradually blunted, the aspirant gains a brief and fleeting vision of Lord Murugan, representing the Ultimate Wisdom he/she has been seeking. The ego makes one final attempt to reimpose its dominance, but has met Divine Grace, the powerful Sakti force of the Absolute, and is destroyed.

The destruction of the ego is explicitly symbolized in the form of Surapadman's final incarnations. Towards the conclusion of the battle the *asura* becomes a tree, or *maram*. However, it is instructive that this is a mango tree, and that Surapadman seeks refuge in the ocean. Both trees and mangos may symbolize the power of *sakti*; trees represent procreation and fertility, while mangos may symbolize desire and lust. Water is the element of *sakti*, and the oceans are the ultimate element of water's power. Therefore, Surapadman's attempt to take the shape of a mango tree within the ocean, a tree which seeks to smother the world, may be seen as the final dramatic efflorescence of uncontrolled *sakti*. The splitting of the tree produces two birds — the rooster and the peacock — both of which attack Murugan. In classical Tamil, the term *maram* signifies an individual full of *anava* or ego. The two properties which in combination form *anava* are *yaam* (or the "I" of individual assertion) and *ennathu* (denoting the possessive self). *Yaam* is symbolized in the form of a cockerel as it struts around with its chest puffed out, while *ennathu* is seen to be exhibited by the peacock as it vaingloriously spreads its tail feathers. Just as Murugan tames both birds with a single loving glance, and incorporates one as his standard and employs the other as his mount, so he first subdues *anava* and transforms the lower forces of *yaam* and *ennathu* into awareness, so that the soul is forever bound close to him in grace and love.[108]

By homologizing the human body to the cosmos, the *Purana* also resolves the seeming incompatibility between the transcendent Skanda-Murugan, the great Saivite deity, distant and powerful regulator of immense cosmic forces and divine *dharma*, and immanent Murugan, the compassionate and loving deity, intimately connected with the affairs of his devotees. Thus, Murugan sets off to his campaign from Mount Kailas, divine home for Siva in the north of India, and passes through six sacred cities (Tirukedaram, Kashi, Tirukalasti, Tiruvengadam, Chidambaram and Tirupparankunram), before finally vanquishing Surapadman in the extreme south. Esoterically, North is held to symbolize Siva (Being/Absolute), while the South symbolizes Sakti (Becoming/Generative), and the locations in between are various combinations. With the human body as universe, the farthest north is the crown of the head, the far south the soles of the feet, the centre the base of the coccygeal plexus (the base of the spine). The region from head to foot is divided into fourteen sections, representing the fourteen worlds.[109] Human spirituality emerges at the base of the spine, and ascends through psychic centres (the sacred cities), the higher *cakras*. The descent of Murugan from the north in response to the entreaties of the devotee, and the gradual unfoldment of spirituality, overcoming the counter-pull of the seven worlds below the coccygeal plexus, resolves the seeming incongruity of the transcendent/immanent principles on a microcosmic level.

The concept of a universe in dynamic tension, the perennial and constantly shifting relationship between Siva/Sakti, ties all elements and polarities within a unifying framework, indissolubly fuses both macro and micro cosmology (that is the individual/universal), and creates a divine symmetry. This is central not only to Saiva Siddhanta philosophy, but also popular Tamil religious beliefs,[110] and, as we will see in Chapters 6 and 8, finds its full expression in the festival of Thaipusam.

In passing we should note the crucial, indeed indispensable role played by Surapadman within the Murugan mythology. Surapadman enacts the oppositional dynamic which Lewis Hyde has described as that of the "trickster"; that is, a boundary figure who "sits on the cusp of reflexive consciousness",[111] but whose actions — his lying, deception and illusion — perform a catalytic and indeed creative role in precipitating the destruction of the old cosmic order and the reconstitution of the new.[112] Hyde notes that the trickster initially operates at the point of flexibility, the one place of cosmic vulnerability.[113] Thus, Siva who responds to all devotees who perform penance and austerities (*tapas*) to him, *must* acknowledge the intense *tapas* of Surapadman and his brothers and grant them the boons that they seek, regardless of the use to which they intend to put them. Surapadman and his siblings duly invert the cosmic order, signalling atrophy and the collapse of cosmic order. Surapadman's excesses result in the creation of Murugan, the Divine Son who in his vanquishment of Surapadman ushers in a new cosmic era, the *Kali Yuga*. At a metaphysical level, Surapadman's manifestation as the destructive force of ego provides a counterpoint to Murugan's grace, and provides the webs of signification which must be experienced and overcome before the devotee can perceive and attain true awareness. As we have seen, Surapadman's necessary role is recognized in Murugan's incorporation of the rooster as his standard and his adoption of the peacock as his mount (*vahana*).

Murugan's Marriage to Valli

Within the Sanskrit tradition, Skanda is viewed as a celibate ascetic (the eternal *brahmacarin*), married to a single wife, the fair and celestial Devesena (the Army of the Gods). However, within the Tamil traditions, the earliest reference to Murugan's bride is the earthy Valli.[114] Valli, dark complexioned, a native of the Tamil country, is regarded as more fun-loving, even "frivolous", than the seemingly austere Devesena.[115] Among Tamils, Valli is undoubtedly the more popular of Murugan's consorts, and her marriage conveys more profound and immediate philosophical implications to many devotees.[116] This was emphasized by the obvious reverence felt for Valli among the Malaysian devotees whom I interviewed in the course of my fieldwork, and in their determination to explain the significance of the divine marriage. In the following paragraphs, I have outlined the essential mythology surrounding the courtship and marriage of Valli, and have delineated the major inferences of this mythology for Murugan devotees.

Contemporaneous with Siva's creation of Skanda, Mahavishnu, the deity representing the illusive cosmic mind, and clearly identified as brother of Parvati,[117] ejected fierce light through both of his eyes, in the process creating two daughters, called *Amirthavalli* and *Sundaravalli*. The two virgins, having met Murugan at the home of his father, Siva, in Mount Kailas, both fell in love with the deity and declared their determination to be married to him. Both performed severe *tapas* in order to be united with him. Finally, Murugan appeared to both of them and advised that he would marry them after he had defeated Surapadman, the chief of the *asuras*. But the marriages would not take place until both had been reborn. He decreed that each was to have an animal as a mother; Amirthavalli's was to be a heavenly white elephant and Sundaravalli's a doe.

Amirthavalli was duly borne from a white elephant and was known as Devesena, or more commonly by her Tamil name, Devayanai. Devayanai was adopted by Indra, the king of heaven, and raised as his daughter. Following the battle with Surapadman at Tiruchendur, Indra respectfully reminded the victorious Skanda that he had promised to marry Devayanai, now a beautiful young woman. Skanda travelled to Tirupparankunram near Madurai for the wedding. The marriage was conducted according to established Brahmanic rites. Skanda's parents, Siva and Parvati, were in attendance, as was Skanda's elder brother, Ganesha. The parents solemnly blessed their Divine Son and their celestial daughter-in-law.

Sundaravalli's birth was less propitious. She was conceived after the mute sage Shivamuni was distracted from his *tapas* in the forest by the sight of a beautiful doe, which he impregnated with a "lustful" glance.[118] The doe gave birth to a baby girl in a pit underneath the creepers (by tradition, these are sweet yam creepers), and among the tubers. The deer immediately abandoned the child, who was discovered by a Kuruvar hunter chieftain, Nambirajan, reputedly at a location known as Vallimalai, near Chittoor in the Tamil country.[119] (In Sri Lankan recensions, the mythology specifies that Valli was born at Kathirkaman, and Nambirajan is identified as king of the tribal Veddas, a hunting people.)[120] Nambirajan adopted the girl as his own and named her "Valli" (creeper).[121] Upon reaching the age of twelve years she was sent out to guard the millet fields from the beasts and birds. She kept the former at bay with a slingshot and deterred the latter by crying out and throwing pebbles as they attempted to alight on the crops. During this period she was informed by a wandering fortune teller that she was destined to marry Murugan. She yearned for Murugan's presence, and firmly resolved that she would accept no other suitor.

The sweet cries of Valli's voice as she watched over the millet fields reached the ears of the *rishi* (sage) Narada, who hastened to Mount Kailas to advise Murugan of her beauty. Leaving Devayanai in the celestial abode of his parents, Murugan set off for the millet fields. Upon his arrival, he assumed the form of a hunter prince and engaged Valli in conversation. However, when his remarks ventured into the realm of flirtation, Valli raised a cry of alarm, and her father returned with his band of hunters. Murugan immediately transformed himself into a *venkai* tree.[122] The hunters asked Valli how a fully grown tree had so suddenly appeared. Valli responded, "I do not know how it came; it appeared, I think, like magic (*mayam*). I have been trembling at the thought that something that was not here before has sprung up so suddenly."[123] Some informants assert at this point the hunters attempted to fell the tree, but when their best efforts made no impression, they gave up and departed.

After the hunters had withdrawn, Murugan resumed his original form and proposed marriage to Valli. Valli responded that she was a girl of very modest origins: was it not wrong for one so exulted as he to trifle with her in such a flippant manner? Murugan as a hunter prince then disappeared, only to return as an itinerant bangle seller, a function which gave him the license to massage Valli's hands as he fitted his wares on her wrists. Valli, suspecting ulterior motives, was very quick to see through his disguise and to send the "bangle seller" on his way.

Once again, Murugan appeared as a hunter prince. However, with the return of Nambirajan and his retinue, he transformed himself into a decrepit aged ascetic, complete with holy robes, but toothless, grey-bearded, and hunched of back. The old "sage" offered Nambirajan due felicitations and advised him that he wished to bathe in the spring of the mountain which fell under Nambirajan's control. The chief gave the ascetic his permission, and ordered Valli to be companion to the sage. Valli subsequently escorted the sage to the other side of the mountain where the spring was located.[124] When the ascetic complained of hunger, Valli provided him with honey and nuts, though because of his infirmity she was obliged to feed him by hand. The saint then desired to quench his thirst. Valli led him to a spring with the aid of a stick; she held one end and he held the other. When they reached the spring, the saint pretended to fall into the water, and grasping Valli pulled her in after him. Valli was unable to swim, and the aged sage was obliged to rescue her. The frail ascetic was unexpectedly transformed into a handsome young man, who bore Valli to the caves where she was accustomed to churn buttermilk. Here he applied "artificial respiration".[125] Valli was seized with a powerful vision of her marriage to Murugan and the wonder of his embrace, or, in Arumugam's words, "she was seeing Lord Murugan and nothing else. In short, she was in a trance."[126]

At this point Valli became aware that she was being observed by her best friend, who was standing outside the cave, and her trance disappeared. In place she found herself in the arms of an aged saint, who now asked Valli to marry her. Laughing, Valli refused, stating that he was both old and infirm, and that an elderly ascetic should not be lusting after young women. In return the old sage responded that he had been merely joking with her.

Murugan pondered over the failure of his wooing, and suddenly realized that he had neglected to enlist the aid of his brother, Ganesha (*Maha Ganapati*, Remover of Obstacles). Almost instantly, Ganesha appeared in the form of a "huge, black tusker",[127] and resoundingly trumpeted the *Pravana Aum*. Terrified, Valli rushed back into the arms of the aged ascetic and implored his protection. The sage replied that he would ensure her safety on the condition that she agreed to wed him. Distraught, Valli agreed, whereupon the sage approached the elephant, held up his palm and asked the elephant to leave. The "tusker" immediately departed. Turning to Valli, the saint reminded her of her promise to marry him. By now completely distressed, Valli put her hands to her ears to block out the old man's voice. As she did so, she heard the sound of the *Pravana Aum* within. Confused, and suspecting trickery, Valli censured the old man for joking with her. The sage merely laughed and replied, "Oh ho, Valli, you have already learned how to joke with the real joker himself, and as such you are now fit and matured enough for the yoke of Divine Union."[128]

According to most Malaysian informants, the courtship ends with Valli's recognition of the wild elephant as Ganesha. The deity then reappears as a divine white elephant, which Valli worships and supplicates for his aid to marry Murugan. In response, the white elephant picks Valli up in his trunk, and then places her in the arms of the aged ascetic who now reveals himself as Murugan. Ganapati appears before Murugan and Valli, and agrees to conduct their marriage. He blesses them both, and promises to be with them forever.

However, other more extensive versions have Valli returning to the millet fields after her encounter with the deity. Her companion notices her change in manner. Murugan subsequently enlists the aid of her companion by threatening the extreme measure of mounting the *matal* hobbyhorse and parading through the streets of the village if he is denied access to Valli; the companion agrees to assist and thus acquiesces in the secret trysts between the sage/deity and Valli.[129]

Following the harvest, Valli returns to the village where she frets for Murugan. Fearing that she is unwell, her foster parents lock Valli in their hut. They subsequently consult a woman medium, but she is possessed by the *cur*, the demon of the mountain slopes. The Kuravar then hold a ritualistic dance (*veriyattal*) for Murugan. The deity descends, and through visions and other signs makes it clear that he took possession of Valli while she was tending the millet, but that her malady will be cured if he is worshipped. Valli instantly recovers as praises are offered to Murugan.

Murugan searches for Valli in the fields, but failing to find her the lovelorn deity wanders the mountain, finally pausing outside Nambirajan's hut. Observing him, Valli's companion urges him to elope with Valli, and the two lovers flee from the village. Murugan then marries Valli in secret. The following morning the Kuravar, finding Valli gone, send out an armed search party. Happening upon the couple, the Kuravar fire volleys of arrows at Murugan, but at a single crow of the rooster on his banner, they all fall down slain. Valli is distressed, and, at Narada's urging, Murugan restores them all to life.[130] Nambirajan now insists that the couple be married according to orthodox rites. The wedding is duly held, and Siva, Parvati and all the gods are present to extend their blessings to the couple.[131] Murugan ties the *tali*, the Tamil wedding necklace that binds the bride to her husband. Murugan then bears Valli to Tirutanni, in modern-day northern Tamil Nadu, and then to his celestial dwelling in the *Kanta Mantaram* (the sacred mountain of Skanda), where, with Valli seated on his auspicious right side, and Devesena (*sic*) on his left, he works to protect the universe.[132]

Murugan and His consorts: The Implications

The mythology surrounding Devayanai and Valli conveys a comprehensive array of symbolic messages and motifs, as well as a substantial corpus of metaphysical and ontological conclusions integral to the Murugan cultus. Indeed, so vast is the topic that a full and detailed interpretation and explanation of the mythology's significance lies beyond the scope of this book. In the following paragraphs I have highlighted some of the major themes and philosophical implications of the divine marriages.

Firstly, the marriages fuse Saiva and Vaishnava motifs. By his marriage to the daughters of Vishnu, Murugan may be identified as more than Siva's son and nephew to Vishnu; he is now the deity's son-in-law.[133] Indeed, in some versions, accepted among sections of the Malaysian Hindu population, Murugan's bride Valli is a daughter of Krishna, himself an incarnation (*avatar*) of the recognized father, Vishnu-Tirumal.[134]

Secondly, the marriage to Valli further confirms Murugan's identity as a Tamil deity. While the celestial Devayanai (Devesena) is imported from the Aryan north, the Sanskritic universe of Indra and the gods, Valli is indigenous, a product of the southern soil, and integrated into the agricultural pursuits of the region.[135] Moreover, she hails from an exceedingly modest background; she is born among the Kuravar hill people, raised by a hunter chieftain and his wife, and is sent to work in the fields.[136] However, her origins prove no barrier to her union with the Divine, and indeed her significance is underscored by her placement at the (auspicious) right-hand side of Murugan.[137]

Thirdly, Murugan's two brides reflect his constant movement through an array of cosmic possibilities and potentialities. The deity is now viewed on the one hand as the transcendent Skanda, restorer of cosmic *dharma*, and re-creator and ruler of the cosmos. On the other, he is perceived as Murugan, immanent deity who is close to and vitally concerned with the affairs of his devotees. In the following paragraphs I will draw upon the work of D. Handelman,[138] as well as adding observations of my own.

Saiva Siddhanta philosophy and popular Tamil belief structures posit a cosmos which is in constant flux and transformation. This flux, resulting from the dynamic tension and constantly shifting relationship between Siva and Sakti, produces a never-ending succession of symmetrical and asymmetrical states.[139] Indeed, as observed earlier in this chapter, the attainment of an absolute balance between these two principles would result in cosmological stasis and universal disintegration and entropy.

Saivism posits three ontological principles or categories within the phenomenal cosmos; namely, in order of hierarchical descent, Siva, Sakti, and *asura* (or "demonic").[140] Siva is the foundation of all creation and permeates all levels of the hierarchy. While any given category can reconstitute itself at still lower levels in the hierarchy, it cannot move to higher levels without upsetting the cosmic balance. Thus, Sakti can and does create *asuras*, and manifests on lower planes as *maya*, but Sakti cannot become Siva (although Siva can absorb Sakti back into his own being). The *asuras*, at the base of the hierarchy, cannot encompass higher categories without causing destruction and chaos.[141]

It follows, then, that the deity can "descend" into a deflection of himself, or into multiple or lesser forms (*saktis*). As Vanamali comments: "God [Siva] implies unconditional freedom. He has the freedom to assume any form he likes. To limit him to one form alone is the failing of the human mind. The universe of innumerable forms is an expression of God's freedom to take on any form he chooses."[142] Thus, the great Siva who manifests in such "pure" forms as *Parasivam* (Absolute Reality), or the sublime *Nataraja* (Lord of the Cosmic Dance), may at lower levels appear in such terrifying guises as *Bhairava* (the Terrible), who delights in destruction, or *Bhutesvara* (Lord of the Elements), who "haunts graveyards and places of cremation, wearing serpents round his neck and skulls for a necklace, attended by troops of imps and trampling on rebellious demons."[143] But Siva can reconstitute himself in totality by ascending hierarchically through these manifestations. (We should note, in passing, that the devotee who continually worships the substratum, as it were, which constitutes the very essence of the devolved Siva *in any manifestation*, is similarly able to progressively achieve knowledge of Siva in his fullness.) In a like manner, Sakti can move through a succession of aspects — such as *jnana sakti* (knowledge), *kriya sakti* (action) and *iccha sakti* (desire, volition) — which can reassemble themselves as Sakti, consort of Siva. But no principle or category can surmount its natural place in the hierarchy, that is, at the level at which it was ordered or at which it entered existence, without disconnecting or fragmenting the agglomeration of elements that form the higher realms of encompassment.[144]

To summarize thus far: The cosmos depends upon constant movement. At one extreme, absolute control by Siva results in total subsumption of all creation within him, the cessation of all existence, and the cosmic stasis of *mahapralaya*; at the other, total dissolution of inclusion leads to cosmic decomposition, disintegration and chaos. Handelman has suggested that the genius of South Indian cosmology is the role of triads, which both encourage and explain shifts and permutations as the various elements interact with one another. Murugan and his consorts Valli and Devayanai represent such a triad. The deity mediates between his two wives, while the latter relate to Murugan and each other. As the relationship between the three constantly shifts, so do the circumstances of the deity. This dynamism produces a broad and complex array of points of intersection, each of which represents a cosmic possibility.[145] The marriages of Murugan enable us to resolve the seeming dilemma posed by the deity's polarity as both a transcendent and immanent deity.

Skanda weds the celestial Devayanai following the defeat of the *asuras*. The marriage observes the paradigmatic conventions of phenomenal Tamil society. Devayanai is the ideal wife for a transcendent god. She embraces the quality of *karpu*; that is, she is chaste and pure. However, this marriage and Skanda-Murugan's withdrawal to the celestial spheres renders him remote and isolated from his devotees. His seclusion in the heavens results in a slowing of cosmic activities, which if left unchecked would create stagnation and ultimately degradation.[146]

Conversely, Valli is associated with vigour and the quickening of cosmic movements. In esoteric terms Valli may be viewed as the *jiva* (soul) which is separated from its source. The birth is the product of the desire for Divine Union; Shivamuni, the dumb sage, represents Vishnu, her father, who impregnates the deer (*Lakshmi*), his consort, for whom he is filled with longing. Valli is born in the dark forest (representing *tamas*, or ignorance), but reveals her determined spirituality with her resolution to marry none other than Murugan. This is demonstrated by her dedication in guarding grain; as Vanamali observes, "She keeps the catapult of discrimination (*viveka*) in her hands and shoots the pebbles of dispassion (*vairagya*) at the birds that come to disturb her spiritual practice."[147]

As Murugan pursues Valli, he assumes a number of exceptional attributes: he becomes a trickster, a prankster, a master of evanescent guise. However, should Murugan remain continually with Valli in the phenomenal world, his continued immanence would result in the loss of transcendence, which invests in him the properties required for cosmic rulership.[148] The collapse of transcendence would lead to cosmic decay and disintegration.

In sum, the triad of Skanda-Murugan, Devayanai and Valli provides a schema for cosmic organization apposite for a deity who is constituted from and combines within himself the inherently dynamic tension of the principles of Siva–Sakti. The reciprocal mediation between each point of the triad, and the other two members, implies the incessant movement of the deity along a finely graduated continuum of cosmic potentialities ranging between the polarities of transcendence and immanence.

Finally, the mythology has profound implications for the modalities of worship within the Murugan cultus. For while, at base, both consorts symbolize the conventionalities of Saiva Siddhanta and popular Tamil belief structures, that is, the soul (*pacu*) liberated from the bondages of ignorance (*paca*) and united with God (*Pati*),[149] the routes by which this objective are attained are vastly different. The marriage mythology suggests, inter alia, the limits of orthodoxy in achieving knowledge of the Divine; indeed, it underscores the dictum that while conventional religion might be understood as the elevation of man to god (Devayanai), *bhakti* impels the descent of god to man.[150]

Devayanai's marriage to Murugan follows the conventions of Tamil society. Her wedding is solemnized according to accepted formalities, and precedes a proper conjugal life.[151] She thus symbolizes *kriya sakti*, the path of action and motivation,[152] and thus of established modes of devotional worship conducted within the framework of received *Agamic* rites.

In contrast, the deity's relationship with Valli is imbued with the Tamil concept known as *kalavu*; that is, premarital love undertaken without regard for the niceties and formal obligations of societal mores. Valli thus symbolizes *iccha sakti* (desire/volition) in terms that equate to human understanding and experience of this quality; that is, worship of the Divine, not through ritual and scriptural study, but rather through "ecstasy and self-abandonment.... [however] Self-abandonment in Hinduism is associated with lack of control, and consequently with danger and defilement in general."[153]

While Valli is resolute in her determination to marry Murugan, it must be underscored that it is the deity who pursues Valli, just as the pure-hearted and committed devotee is rewarded by the god's engagement and union with the soul. In this regard the episode involving the *matal* hobbyhorse assumes special significance. The *matal* hobbyhorse was a device employed by lovesick young men to shame their adored. However, in the writings and songs of the *bhakti* poets, the *matal* hobbyhorse becomes a metaphoric convention to portray the longing of the soul for union with the deity, which is thus made to appear as a hard-hearted or indifferent woman. In the myth of Valli, the *bhakti* perspective is inverted; the god is male, and the threat to mount the *matal* hobbyhorse, an act of abasement and humiliation, is to drive the devotee to union with the deity.[154] But even without this incident, Murugan's behaviour is revealed as deceptive and feckless, and heedless of accepted societal standards and norms of respectability.[155]

The marriage of Murugan and Valli exemplifies the very essence and final goal of *bhakti* spirituality, "the immediate spontaneous union of the soul with the Divine".[156] However, the pathway to the marriage is convoluted. Skanda-Murugan does not reveal his identity at the outset, but rather approaches Valli in a series of disguises. In so doing he tests the strength of her vow that she intends to marry Murugan and no other. Although the deity ultimately weds Valli, his true identity is revealed only at the moment of immediate union. His advances to Valli and the different forms he adopts are indicative of his divine play (*lilas*), and reveal Murugan as a trickster, the honourable rogue who leads the aspirant through the experiential world until he/she is relieved of all illusions and is fully prepared for the encounter with Divine Reality.[157] The meaning is made explicit in Murugan's comments to Valli, when, in his guise as the old sage, having tricked Valli into marriage, he commends her on having learned to deal with the "real joker", and that she is now ready for the "yoke of Divine Union".[158]

The premarital trysts and ultimate union with Valli symbolize the disorder which attends the apprehension of the Divine, and the overwhelming power which accompanies this process. However, Valli's lowly status suggests that the modest, self-effacing and the subservient are capable of responding to and discerning the divine,[159] though in ways that might not necessarily fall within the prescribed corpus of recognized ritual *Agamic* worship. At this point it is worth remarking that the mythology of Valli infers that the transcendent Skanda appears to devotees in whatever form he chooses to manifest himself, and even though this may be a guise or illusion, the aspirant who truly reveres the divine who inheres in that form, however unconventional that may be, and however removed from accepted *Agamic* depictions, will, through the love and mercy of the deity, attain ultimate knowledge of and union with the Reality and Truth that is Skanda-Murugan.[160]

The Kavadi Ritual

Undoubtedly one of the most dominant motifs of Thaipusam in Malaysia, and that which invariably receives the greatest publicity, is the bearing of kavadis. The kavadi ritual and the asceticism which is a necessary concomitant of this practice are both infused with meaning and given shape by interlinked episodes which occurred during the period of Murugan's spiritual maturation, and which culminated in Parvati's bestowal of the *Vel*. These are outlined in the following paragraphs.

Murugan's period of renunciation followed the loss of a competition with his elder brother, the elephant-headed Ganesha. The *Purana*, ever popular among Malaysian Hindus, and often recited in temples and reiterated with variations in public storytelling, is as follows. One day the sage Narada, regarded as the source of many disputes, visited the Siva family. He left a large and especially succulent mango (in some versions a pomegranate) with Siva and Parvati. Narada emphasized that because this was the fruit of cosmic wisdom, it could not be cut in two.[161] Siva and Parvati therefore proposed to offer the fruit as a reward to whomever of their sons was the quicker to travel around the world. Murugan immediately mounted his peacock and vanished over the horizon. Ganesha, on the other hand, realizing that he was no match for Murugan in a straightforward race, reflected, then bathed, prostrated before his seated parents, circumambulated them, and demanded the mango. When questioned by his parents as to why he would claim the prize when he had yet to even begin his journey, Ganesha explained that in performing this action he had not only encircled the world, but the entire cosmos, for did not his parents contain the all-encompassing Siva–Sakti duality, together with all Truth, Will and Action?[162] Siva and Parvati, pleased with his answer, gave him the fruit. When Murugan returned he was deeply upset to discover Ganesha devouring the mango. Told the reason, he vowed to renounce the world. Angrily he accused his parents of deception, and of violating the hallowed tenets of *varna dharma* (family dharma).[163] He removed his sacred thread, shaved his head, and, wearing only a loincloth and holding a *sannyasin*'s staff, bade farewell to his parents. Although Parvati pleaded with him, and Siva forbade him to leave, saying, "Why do you renounce the world? You are *Palam ni*" (the fruit),[164] meaning that he was already the Truth he intended to seek (that is, the embodied soul [*jivatman*] and the Supreme Soul [*paramatman*] are one),[165] Murugan refused to listen. He retired first to the Krownchan Mountain, then to the district now known as Palani,[166] where he pursued yogic disciplines and realized the Truth within (the inner fruits of his *tapas* — austerities and meditations). Thus, according to *Puranic* lore, Ganesha is supplicated by those who wish to partake of the proper enjoyments of the fruits of the world, whereas Murugan is worshipped by those who eschew material benefits in favour of ascetic spirituality and the fruits of liberation.

It was while Murugan was at Palani that he encountered and vanquished the *asura Idumban*. This engagement is summarized in the following paragraphs.

Agastya, a Vedic *rishi* (sage), journeyed to Mount Kailas in the Himalayas, the earthly abode of Siva, to offer worship to both Siva and Sakti. His devotion was rewarded when they appeared on the hills known, respectively, as *Sivagiri* and *Saktigiri*. Siva subsequently instructed Agastya to deliver Saivite wisdom embodied within the two hills to Potikai in South India, which Siva planned to make his southern abode, and his seat of worship.[167] He commanded: "Go to the South. Take with you all that I have taught you; the skill of communication, the secrets of astronomy and medicine; the arts and music; the science of agriculture and animal herding; the fundamentals of philosophy; skills in warfare, sacred love and essentials of sacrifice. Take it all."[168]

Agastya approached an *asura*, Idumban, to undertake this task. Despite Idumban's background, Agastya believed that the demon was sufficiently trustworthy to execute this commission. Idumban was initially at a loss as to how he might carry the hills, but he discovered the *danda* (staff) of Brahma standing above the hills.[169] Using the Divine serpents of the earth in place of ropes, Idumban tied each hill to the end of the *danda*, which thus became a shoulder pole, with the weight evenly distributed.[170] This became the prototypical kavadi. Near the forest at a site now known as Palani, Idumban tired and set down the hills while he rested. When he attempted to resume his journey, he found that the hills were stuck to the ground. Upon ascending the slopes, he discovered a youth clad only in a loincloth, holding a staff and "shining like a thousand suns".[171] This youth claimed the hills as his own. In the subsequent fight, Idumban was killed. Both Agastya and *Idumbi* (Idumban's wife) interceded on Idumban's behalf, and Murugan restored Idumban to life. The now transformed Idumban requested that he remain forever at the portal of Murugan's shrine as a *Divarapala*, or guardian. Murugan instructed him, "You will stand watch at the foot of the hill. But since you brought Sivagiri and Saktigiri on a shoulder pole, all who henceforth worship me with *kavati* will first worship you."[172]

The myth incorporates a number of recurring motifs common to Saivism, but the major implications may be summarized as follows:

1. The two hills were a gift from Siva, and were delivered to South India through the agency of Agastya, mythical civilizer and bringer of culture to Tamil Nadu.[173]
2. The two hills constitute Siva/Sakti, the cosmic duality, and thus the entirety of creation, from which Murugan was both born and provided with the means to fulfil his role as the vanquisher of the *asuras*.
3. The hill on which the Palani temple now stands is that claimed by Murugan from the faithful *asura*, Idumban.[174]

In metaphysical terms, the mythology implicitly conveys the transformative powers of asceticism, spiritual retreat and yogic disciplines. Tricked on the most fundamental level by Ganesha, who has the insight to recognize the inner truth of a literal direction and to apply this to his ultimate benefit, Murugan determines to renounce the world and family life, disobeys his father and mother, and retires to self-imposed exile in Palani where he pursues his quest of realizing the truth within. It is significant that Murugan initially repairs to the Krownchan Mountain. As we noted earlier, Krownchan is recognized as the quintessential embodiment of *tamas* (the *guna*, or quality which promotes laziness, inertness and crude fulfilment of basic desires) which must be overcome before true spirituality can be attained. However, when Idumban arrives he bears the two hills representing Siva–Sakti and containing the totality of Saivite wisdom, the true fruits of liberation. Recognizing this, Murugan claims the hills as his own, his spiritual destiny. But Idumban, the *asura*, remains a barrier between Murugan and his goal of spiritual enlightenment. Idumban must be vanquished; he represents in metaphorical terms the remnants of uncontrolled *sakti*, the superimposed ego which identifies self with the impermanent body which must somehow be transformed before Murugan can stabilize into full self-reflexivity. Idumban's "death" is that of the ego, the "cloak of mortality".[175] The subsequent combat, annihilation of Idumban and his rebirth represents the new depths of knowledge garnered through the period of intense yogic asceticism which enables the deity to dispose of the Idumban within, and to symbolically convert this burden into a spiritual asset — a guard who stands ready to defend him from external forces.

The kavadi thus becomes a metaphor for spiritual change. In esoteric terms the pole of the kavadi symbolizes the internal axis which links the *muladhara cakra* (at the base of the spine and representing the opening of spirituality) at one end to the *sahasrara cakra* (at the crown of the head and representing spiritual illumination/realization) at the other. In this regard it is significant that Idumban is first aware of the radiance of Murugan only when he has set his load on the ground, that is, at the foot of the deity, and begins to ascend the hill. The subsequent fight, annihilation and rebirth represent the spiritual battle which results in recognition, transformation and final liberation.

On its most obvious level, the Idumban myth provides a paradigmatic model for a specific form of ritual worship involving temporary renunciation, the asceticism of pilgrimage, the catalytic experiences of trance and kavadi bearing as a means for the relief of psychic burden, as well as the fruits of fresh self-discoveries resulting from an encounter with the deity, which can then be taken forward into the post-Thaipusam mundane life. Idumban, who conveys a kavadi, is subdued, and following his encounter with the deity is transformed into an exemplar of devotion. Idumban's experience may thus be emulated by the individual aspirant. Clothey remarks that "All devotees who bring the *kavati* or submit to the god on the hill-top are thought to be re-enacting the example of that primordial devotee, all of whose malevolence and simple-mindedness was taken from him in that act of worship."[176] Those who worship with kavadi bearers are, like Idumban, psychically transmuted, and are relieved of the burden of ignorance through the burden of the divine. In sum, the kavadi ritual is explained and justified in terms of the Idumban myth, and has become a popular mode of worship in localities where Murugan is considered a major deity.[177] It is this concept which underlies the principle of worship at Thaipusam. By placing his/her psychic burden at the feet of Murugan, the aspirant publicly demonstrates the wish to be freed from the yoke of those burdens.

Murugan: Sacred Geography

The sacred geography of the Murugan cultus essentially comprises the six camps[178] or sites (collectively known as the *aaru padai veedu*), each of which is linked to particular episodes in his divine career, and which cumulatively embrace the major corpus of mythology which encompasses the deity.[179] In modern times these centres firmly identify Murugan with the ethno-linguistic state of Tamil Nadu, thus simultaneously emphasizing the deity's "Dravidian" associations and sacralizing the region in which the temples are located.[180] Clothey has pointed out that the temple at Tiruttani, near the northern border of Tamil Nadu, together with Palani, near the western edge of the state, and Tiruchendur, on the southeast coast, collectively form a triangle which roughly encloses the Tamil country.[181]

While the location of five of Murugan's centres are undisputed, many Tamils hold that the sixth site is every other shrine dedicated to Murugan (Clothey points out that the Tamil expression is *kunratal*, translating as "every hill upon which the god dances").[182] However, Patrick Harrigan argues that there are five *padai veedu*, and the sixth sacred site must be understood in metaphysical terms. He contends that the number six relates to Skanda-Murugan's origins as the six divine sparks which emanated from Siva's forehead and which later coalesced into *Sanatkumara* (or Perpetual Youth). In his role as *Sanmukha* (Shanmugan), the six-faced Skanda-Murugan represents the Lord of Space incorporating the six cardinal directions, that is East, West, North, South, up and down; "The Unmoved Mover abiding as a conscious presence at the source and center of the matrix of infinite possibilities."[183] The six sites thus constitute the fullness of Skanda-Murugan, each site comprising one facet of the deity, and thus one essential cosmological function. As Clothey has demonstrated, the six sites collectively serve to cosmicize and sacralize the Tamil country. Thus, "Tamil Nadu becomes a microcosm with six *cakras* even as the human frame is a microcosm in the symbol-system of yoga, and the temple is a microcosm in the symbol-system associated with temple ritual."[184]

Each of the five major pilgrimage centres embodies a mythological event within the Murugan cultus, and this prescribes a range of ritual behaviours germane to the particular chapters of his cosmology. The five centres are:

1. **Swamimalai**: Approximately eight kilometres from Kumbakonam and standing on the banks of the Kaveri River, often regarded as the "Ganges of the South". The location where the youthful Murugan punished Brahma and subsequently at Siva's request revealed to him the meaning of the *Pravana Aum*.

2. **Palani**: About sixty kilometres from the city of Madurai. The locality where Murugan retired to realize the Truth (or fruits) within, following his "race" with Ganesha, and where he subsequently defeated and transformed the *asura* Idumban.

3. **Tiruchendur**: Located in the Tirunelvi District on the Bay of Bengal. This temple marks the site of Murugan's final battle with the *asura* Surapadman, when the latter entered the ocean as a giant mango tree and threatened to smother the world.

4. **Tirupparankunram**: About eight kilometres from the city of Madurai. This temple is held to be the site of Murugan's marriage to Devayanai, adopted daughter of Indra, king of heaven.

5. **Tiruttani**: situated on the northern border of Tamil Nadu, approximately one hundred kilometres north of Chennai. This site is regarded as the location from where Murugan conducted his courtship of his second wife, Valli, and later wed her. Tiruttani also marks the spot where Murugan instructed the sage Agastya in Tamil, thus recognizing Murugan's role as patron and mentor of Tamil literature and founder of Saiva Siddhanta.[185]

Ritual Chronometry and the Murugan Cultus

Sacred chronometry, the measurement of time against cosmic rhythm, enables devotees to synchronize beliefs and ritual behaviours to the movement of bodies which are both extraterrestrial and supramundane. The calibration of time not only makes the cosmic rhythm more immediately understandable, but also allows the determination of important units of time into significant periods when certain ritual observances are regarded as appropriate and access to the deities more negotiable. Clothey describes these moments as "tempocosms", units of time which represent "points of access to a larger dimension of existence".[186] Thus, festivals with their enclosed and prescribed ritual behaviours are fixed to coincide with important tempocosms. Taken collectively, these tempocosms provide the devotee with a cyclical cosmology, a vision of the world which imposes calendrical order, but simultaneously representing the possibility of both ritual and thus actual transcendence over the tyranny of linear time.[187]

Put simplistically, Tamil chronometry can be explained in terms of the daily cycle in relation to two much larger and concentrically arranged measurements of time; namely, the lunar month and the solar year. The *daily cycle* is divided into a schedule of sacred hours (*tirukkalam*) which are homologized to the deity's existential life. Thus the dawn is associated with the commencement of the deity's life and the creation of the cosmos. The growth of cosmic dynamism (and of the deity's powers) reaches its peak at midday (*mattyanam*), which also marks the finalization of the daylight ritual observances. The afternoon–evening round concludes with the "ritual of the bedchamber", in which the deity retires for the evening.[188] The *lunar cycle* is divided into twenty-seven units (asterisms, or *nakasastras*) marked by conspicuous stars or star groups.[189] The fortnights within the lunar month — the "bright cycle" when the moon is waxing, and the "dark" cycle when the moon is waning — are each calibrated into fifteen *tirthis*, or stages. The full moon (*pournami*) is regarded as especially momentous, and is commemorated in all Saivite temples. The *solar cycle* is divided into twelve monthly segments, which are calculated, in the main, against the moon's movements in relation to the *nakasastras*. Tamil months commence with the day in which the sun "enters" the new sign of the zodiac. The entire year represents a day in the life of the gods, and the deity's cosmic cycle is carefully calculated against a complex and graduated chronometry. Only when the cycles of months, *nakasastras*, *tirthis*, and ritual hours have been assigned a weighted significance, can tempocosms or points of cosmological access be regarded as established.[190]

The Murugan cultus has intricate associations with the notion of cosmic time. Thus, within the epic the *Mahabharata*, Skanda is born on *amavsaya* (new moon day), when the sun and the moon are conjoined. As we have seen, Indra, king of heaven, declares Skanda to be Lord of Time and his birth to inaugurate a fresh chronometric era.[191] In popular belief, Murugan is associated with the regularity of the seasons, and is not only responsible for ushering in the rains but is also linked to the blossoming of certain trees.[192]

Clothey has demonstrated how ritual worship of Skanda-Murugan is comprehensively embedded in notions of cosmic time. The majority of Murugan festivals fall in the six months of the year between the winter and summer solstices, thus homologizing to the "pre-dawn" and "morning" of the deity's "cosmic day". Thaipusam is fixed by the *nakasastra pucam* which falls on or near the full moon day in the month of *Tai* (January–February) and is homologized to *piratakkalam*, or the post-dawn early morning hours of the deity's "cosmic day", a time when the deity is moving towards the very height of his power and vigour. The presiding star is the planet *Brihaspati* (Jupiter), which is considered beneficient, and which during the mythological battle with the *asuras* was enlisted as a preceptor of the *devonic* forces.[193] Within Tamil traditions, and in particular those of the Murugan cultus, the full moon implies the attainment of complete maturity and authority, the total control of faculties and capabilities. The asterism of Thaipusam is that of *tantapani*, which consists both of the staff of asceticism (and symbolic of the conquest of ignorance and malevolence) and that of *danda*, that is royal and military leadership. Murugan is known as *Tantayutapani* at Palani and is represented as an ascetic.[194] This sacred chronometry unambiguously echoes events in the deity's cosmology. Murugan has angrily departed southwards from the family home at Mount Kailas to seek the inner fruits of knowledge and wisdom at Palani, and in living as a renunciant he has conquered the inner passions. He has destroyed the demon Idumban, relieved him of his burden, and has converted him to both disciple and perpetual gatekeeper. Parvati's presentation of the *Sakti Vel* represents the final stage of this transformative period, and heralds his readiness to meet the *asuric* forces in battle.

Conclusions

This chapter has examined the Murugan cultus from its dual origins in Tamil folk traditions and northern Sanskritic religion. This section identified a wide array of roles accorded to Skanda-Murugan, ranging from that of possessive deity to high Sanskritic god. The fusion of northern–southern motifs produced a composite deity whose complex persona enabled him to reach every segment of South Indian society, and with the rise of Dravidian "nationalism" located him as the quintessential Tamil deity. Murugan's sacred geometry and the chronology of the Murugan cultus further establishes both cosmic and sequential links with *Tamilakam*, and provides a range of propitious ritual moments and concomitant behaviours favourable for communication with the deity.

We have also traced the multivalent significance of the *Puranic* mythology surrounding Murugan's receipt of the *Sakti Vel*. I have suggested that the acquisition of the *Vel* symbolizes the unification of the principles and powers of Siva–Sakti within the form of Murugan. Cosmologically, the myth embraces themes of phenomenal dissolution and entropy and subsequent reconstitution and renewal; that is, the collapse and restoration of cosmic order. In metaphorical terms the mythology may be viewed as an extended metaphor for the spiritual evolution of the individual and his/her ever-changing perception of the Divine. Overall, the mythology underlines the perennial and constantly shifting relationship between Siva–Sakti, and thus emphasizes a universal order in profound and dynamic tension which may oscillate between chaos and control — the violence and disorder of cosmic inversion, and hierarchical reconstitution and penetrating illumination which accompanies restoration. The mythology assembles all cosmological constituents and polarities within a unified framework, one which indissolubly fuses both macro and micro cosmology, thus creating a Divine symmetry which is central not only to Saiva Siddhanta philosophy but also to popular belief structures. The homologizing of body to cosmos resolves the seeming incompatibility of the transcendent Skanda and the immanent Murugan, thus constituting the cosmic drama as an internal and individual struggle, while simultaneously offering the prospect of knowledge of and ultimate unity with the Transcendent. Finally, the divine marriages to Devayanai and Valli suggest possibilities of spiritual unfoldment within the Murugan cultus, ranging from the conventionalities of formal worship and strictly observed orthodox disciplines, to the more idiosyncratic and even transgressive *bhakti* exemplified by Murugan's wooing of Valli. In this way Murugan meets all individual potentialities and offers every devotee from the highest to the lowest, from the soul deep in yoga to the most simple and unsophisticated *bhakta*, the ultimate promise of illumination, knowledge and release. Finally, the *Puranic* mythology also incorporates the description of Murugan's encounter with the *asura* Idumban, which not only underscores the transformative power of asceticism and yogic disciplines but also furnishes a legitimating model for the kavadi ritual.

Notes

1. Fred W. Clothey, *The Many Faces of Murukan — the History and Meaning of a South Indian God* (The Hague: Mouton, 1978), p. 15.
2. Ibid., pp. 23–24.
3. R. Champakalakshmi, *Religion, Tradition and Ideology: Precolonial South India* (New Delhi: Oxford University Press, 2011), p. 127.
4. Asim Kumar Chatterjee, *The Cult of Skanda-Karttikeya in Ancient India* (Calcutta: Puthi Pustak, 1970), p. 63.
5. Clothey, *The Many Faces of Murukan*, p. 26.
6. Ibid., p. 130; Champakalakshmi, *Religion, Tradition and Ideology*, p. 377.

7. Chatterjee, *The Cult of Skanda-Karttikeya*, p. 63.
8. Clothey, *The Many Faces of Murukan*, p. 126.
9. Chatterjee, *The Cult of Skanda-Karttikeya*, p. 63.
10. Clothey, *The Many Faces of Murukan*, pp. 26–32; Kamil V. Zvelebil, *Tamil Traditions on Subrahmanya-Murugan* (Madras: Institute of Asian Studies, 1991), p. 87.
11. Champakalakshmi, *Religion, Tradition and Ideology*, p. 468.
12. Ibid., p. 128.
13. Clothey, *The Many Faces of Murukan*, p. 34.
14. Champakalakshmi, *Religion, Tradition and Ideology*, p. 128.
15. Clothey, *The Many Faces of Murukan*, pp. 34–35.
16. Ibid., p. 128; Champakalakshmi, *Religion, Tradition and Ideology*, p. 198.
17. Clothey, *The Many Faces of Murukan*, p. 128.
18. Fred W. Clothey, *Ritualizing on the Boundaries: Continuity and Innovation in the Tamil Diaspora* (Columbia: The University of South Carolina Press, 2006), p. 196.
19. Clothey, *The Many Faces of Murukan*, p. 34.
20. Chatterjee, *The Cult of Skanda-Karttikeya*, pp. 2–6.
21. Vanamali, *The Lilas of the Sons of Siva* (New Delhi: Aryan Books International, 2008), p. 106.
22. Clothey, *The Many Faces of Murukan*, pp. 49–50.
23. Chatterjee, *The Cult of Skanda-Karttikeya*, p. 6.
24. So named because he was attended by the *Krttikas*, or Pleiades (see later sections).
25. Chatterjee, *The Cult of Skanda-Karttikeya*, p. 24.
26. Ibid.
27. Ibid., p. 101.
28. Ibid., p. 24.
29. Clothey, *The Many Faces of Murukan*, pp. 47–48.
30. Ibid., p. 107.
31. Ibid., pp. 146–47.
32. Chatterjee, *The Cult of Skanda-Karttikeya*, p. 48.
33. Clothey, *The Many Faces of Murukan*, p. 54.
34. Ibid., pp. 59–60.
35. Ibid., p. 61.
36. Chatterjee, *The Cult of Skanda-Karttikeya*, p. 4.
37. Patrick Harrigan, "Dionysius and Kataragama: Parallel Mystery Cults", *Journal of the Institute of Asian Studies* 14, no. 2 (March 1997): 1–3.
38. Clothey, *The Many Faces of Murukan*, pp. 62–63.
39. Champakalakshmi, *Religion, Tradition and Ideology*, p. 90.
40. Ibid., p. 201.

41. Ibid., p. 128.

42. Clothey, *The Many Faces of Murukan*, pp. 64–65.

43. Ibid., pp. 70–71.

44. Ibid., p. 73; Chatterjee, *The Cult of Skanda-Karttikeya*, p. 42.

45. Clothey, *The Many Faces of Murukan*, pp. 73–75.

46. Ibid., pp. 76–77.

47. Burton Stein, *Peasant, State and Society in Medieval South India* (New Delhi: Oxford University Press, 1980), p. 42.

48. Clothey, *The Many Faces of Murukan*, p. 85.

49. Champakalakshmi, *Religion, Tradition and Ideology*, p. 129.

50. Clothey, *The Many Faces of Murukan*, pp. 76–79.

51. Ibid., p. 85.

52. Ibid., pp. 77–79.

53. Ibid., pp. 109–10.

54. Champakalakshmi, *Religion, Tradition and Ideology*, p. 16.

55. Ibid., pp. 114–15.

56. Ibid., p. 116.

57. Personal field research.

58. There are a number of variations on the mythology surrounding the Skanda-Murugan cultus. However, most Malaysian Hindu authorities would concur with the essential points as contained in this section. A simplified account of this *Purana* appears in my earlier work, *Towards Truth: An Australian Spiritual Journey* (Kuala Lumpur: Pacific Press, 1992), pp. 222–37.

59. Karen Armstrong, *The Case for God: What Religion Really Means* (London: Bodley Head, 2009), p. 34.

60. John Bowker, *Why Religions Matter* (New York: Cambridge University Press, 2015), p. 254.

61. Gavin Flood, *The Tantric Body: The Secret Traditions of Hindu Religion* (London: I.B. Taurus, 2006), p. 70.

62. Cornelia Dimmitt and J.A. von Buitenen, eds. and trans., *Classical Hindu Mythology: A Reader in the Sanskrit Puranas* (Philadelphia: Temple University Press, 1978), p. 174.

63. Swami Harshananda, *Hindu Gods and Goddesses* (Madras: Sri Ramakrishna Math, 1981), p. 79.

64. *Puranic* traditions assert that Siva is obligated to reward all devotees, including demons, who worship him with *tapas* (austerities).

65. Arumugam Rasiah, *Kataragama: Divine Power of Kathirkaman and Methods of Realization* (Sithankerny: Holiday Ashram, 1981), p. 4.

66. Vanamali, *The Lilas*, p. 115.

67. Hindu conceptions of creation and destruction revolve about extensive periods or ages of the universe known as *yugas*. Saiva Siddhanta and popular

Tamil belief structures view the universe as in a state of constant flux, with a continuous dynamic tension between *asuras* and *devas*. As we will see, the creation of Murugan corresponds with the inauguration of the current age, the *Kaliyuga* (Fred Clothey, *Rhythm and Intent: Ritual Studies from South India* [Bombay: Blackie and Son, 1983], p. 48).

68. Vanamali, *The Lilas*, p. 139.
69. D. Handelman, "Myths of Murugan: Asymmetery and Hierarchy in South India", *History of Religions* 27, no. 2 (1987): 140.
70. Ibid., p. 150.
71. Wendy Doniger O'Flaherty, *Siva, the Erotic Ascetic* (London: Oxford University Press, 1973), p. 249.
72. Ibid., p. 265.
73. Ibid.
74. Clothey, *Rhythm and Intent*, p. 48.
75. Handelman, "Myths of Murugan", p. 140.
76. Clothey, *The Many Faces of Murukan*, p. 82.
77. Saivite Hinduism emphasizes that all creation ultimately emanates from sound. Aum (sometimes spelled "Om") is regarded as the basic or primal sound (*Pravana Aum*). "Aum" is chanted as a preparatory or purificatory mantra (Vanamali, *The Lilas*, p. 15).
78. Clothey, *The Many Faces of Murukan*, p. 82.
79. Among Malaysian Hindus, Murugan is nearly always understood to have received the *Vel* from Parvati, and indeed is depicted as doing so at Batu Caves. However, some *Puranas* portray Siva arming Murugan with the *Vel* (see, for example, Handelman, "Myths of Murugan").
80. Vanamali, *The Lilas*, p. 150.
81. Bhadrakali: "Auspicious-Power-of-Time" (Alain Danielou, *The Myths of Gods of India* (Rochester: Inner Traditions International, [1964] 1991, p. 287). C.J. Fuller recounts that the fierce Kali is subdued and becomes the benevolent Bhadrakali after losing a dancing competition with Natarajah (Siva) (C.J. Fuller, *The Camphor Flame: Popular Hinduism and Society in India* [Princeton: Princeton University Press, 1992], p. 199).
82. Handelman, "Myths of Murugan", p. 143.
83. We should note that while Murugan rides the elephant, the symbol of royalty and divine kingship, into battle, once he has vanquished Surapadman the peacock serves as his mount. Clothey suggests that the substitution commemorates Murugan's unequivocal victory over all his foes and his now unchallenged cosmic superiority (Clothey, *The Many Faces of Murukan*, p. 186).
84. Ibid., p. 117.
85. Zvelebil, *Tamil Traditions*, pp. 4–5.

86. George Michell, *The Hindu Temple: An Introduction to its Meanings and Forms* (Chicago: University of Chicago Press, [1977] 1988), p. 20.

87. Champakalakshmi, *Religion, Tradition and Ideology*, p. 142.

88. Dimmitt and von Buitenen, *Classical Hindu Mythology*, p. 252.

89. Handleman, "Myths of Murugan", p. 137.

90. Ibid.

91. Dimmitt and von Buitenen, *Classical Hindu Mythology*, p. 226.

92. Handelman, "Myths of Murugan", p. 149.

93. O'Flaherty, *Siva*, p. 41.

94. Ibid., pp. 267–70, 286.

95. Handelman, p. 129.

96. Ibid., p. 140.

97. O'Flaherty, *Siva*, p. 128.

98. Clothey, *The Many Faces of Murukan*, p. 193.

99. Handelman, "Myths of Murugan", p. 135.

100. Dimmitt and von Buitenen, *Classical Hindu Mythology*, p. 35.

101. Handelman, "Myths of Murugan", p. 149.

102. Vanamali, *The Lilas*, p. 150; Flood, *The Tantric Body*, p. 28.

103. Rahul Kabade, *Sri Muruga: Legend, Short Stories and Worship* (Wembley: Sri Muruga Publications, 2012), p. 25.

104. Bowker, *Why Religions Matter*, pp. 92–93; Flood, *The Tantric Body*, p. 126.

105. Vanamali, *The Lilas*, p. 105. *Cakras* are "vortices of psychic energy … they do not 'exist' as such in the 'physical' matter but may be considered vital centres, regulators of higher psychic and spiritual forces which condition all physical responses." (Kamil Zvelebil, *The Poets of the Powers* [London: Rider and Company, 1973], p. 41). The *cakras*, or higher spiritual centres, are symbolically located along the spine.

106. Kabade, *Sri Muruga*, p. 125.

107. Manuel Moreno, "God's Forceful Call: Possession as Divine Strategy", in *Gods of Flesh, Gods of Stone: The Embodiment of Divinity in India*, edited by Joanne Punzo Waghorne and Norman Cutler with Vasudha Narayan (Chambersburg: Anima, 1985), p. 117.

108. Doniger O'Flaherty points out that the peacock is often used as a motif to denote eroticism in India (O'Flaherty, *Siva*, p. 167). In this way Murugan may be viewed as subduing and controlling the forces of lust, desire and greed, all products of untrammelled *sakti*.

109. These centres and their locations are as follows: Lower Centres: *patala* (soles of feet: characterized by murder and malice); *mahatala* (feet: characterized by absence of conscience); *rasatala* (ankles: characterized by selfishness); *talatala* (calves: characterized by prolonged mental confusion); *sutala* (knees: characterized by retaliatory jealousy); *vitala* (thighs: characterized by raging

anger); *atala* (hips: characterized by fear and lust). Chakras: *muladahara* (base of the spinal column: characterized by the opening of spirituality); *svadhishthana* (genitals: characterized by reason); *manipura* (navel: characterized by willpower); *anahata* (cardiac plexus: characterized by direct cognition); *vishuddha* (throat: characterized by divine love); *ajna* (third eye [pineal gland]: characterized by divine sight); *sahasrara* (crown: characterized by realization / illumination) (Sivaya Subramuniyaswami, *Dancing with Siva: Hinduism's Contemporary Catechism* [Concord: Himalayan Academy, 1993], pp. 699–700).

110. Handelman, "Myths of Murugan", p. 151.
111. Lewis Hyde, *Trickster Makes the World: Mischief, Myth and Art* (New York: North Point, 1998), p. 56.
112. Ibid., p. 176.
113. Ibid., p. 256.
114. David Dean Shulman, *Tamil Temple Myths: Sacrifice and Divine Marriage in the South Indian Saiva Tradition* (Princeton, NJ: Princeton University Press, 1980), p. 275.
115. Clothey, *The Many Faces of Murukan*, p. 138.
116. Shulman, *Tamil Temple Myths*, p. 275.
117. Arumugam, *Kataragama*, pp. 8–9.
118. Shulman, *Tamil Temple Myths*, p. 275.
119. Clothey, *The Many Faces of Murukan*, p. 83.
120. Arumugam, *Kataragama*, p. 10.
121. Handelman, "Myths of Murugan", p. 154.
122. The *venkai* tree is closely associated with Murugan, and indeed in earlier traditions the leaf of this tree comprises the original lance (*vel*) with which Murugan defeats the demon *cur* (Clothey, *The Many Faces of Murukan*, pp. 191–92).
123. Shulman, *Tamil Temple Myths*, p. 275.
124. In the Sri Lankan recension, the spring is replaced by the *Menik* (River) Ganga at Kataragama.
125. Arumugam, *Kataragama*, p. 105. Arumugam is being rather coy. In fact the eroticism of the Murugan–Valli courtship is emphasized within many variations of the story (personal field research).
126. Arumugam, *Kataragama*, p. 22.
127. Ibid., p. 24.
128. Ibid., p. 25.
129. Shulman, *Tamil Temple Myths*, p. 277. The matal hobbyhorse was made of the jagged edges of the Palmyra tree and was a public device used by young men to shame their beloved into marriage, but it resulted in the rider being regarded as a fool and a laughing stock.
130. Ibid., p. 278.

131. Handelman, "Myths of Murugan", p. 155.
132. Clothey, *The Many Faces of Murukan*, p. 84.
133. Ibid.
134. Shulman, *Tamil Temple Myths*, p. 283; personal field research.
135. Shulman, *Tamil Temple Myths*, pp. 281–82.
136. Clothey, *The Many Faces of Murukan*, p. 84.
137. Shulman, *Tamil Temple Myths*, p. 282.
138. Handelman, "Myths of Murugan".
139. Ibid., p. 151.
140. Ibid., p. 167.
141. Ibid., p. 168.
142. Vanamali, *The Lilas*, p. xxix.
143. Alain Danielou, *Hindu Polytheism* (New York: Bollingen Foundation, 1964), p. 196.
144. Handelman, "Myths of Murugan", p. 168.
145. Ibid., pp. 168–69.
146. Ibid., p. 160.
147. Vanamali, *The Lilas*, p. 158.
148. Handelman, "Myths of Murugan", p. 160.
149. Clothey, *The Many Faces of Murukan*, p. 85.
150. Chihiro Koiso, "The Bhakti in Tukarami's Abhangas", in *The Historical Development of the Bhatki Movement in India — Theory and Practice*, edited by Iwao Shima, Teiji Sakata, and Katsuyuki Ida (New Delhi: Manohar, 2011), p. 197.
151. Handelman, "Myths of Murugan", p. 154.
152. Shulman, *Tamil Temple Myths*, p. 282.
153. Handelman, "Myths of Murugan", pp. 154–55; see also Vanamali, *The Lilas*, p. 158.
154. Shulman, *Tamil Temple Myths*, p. 282.
155. Handelman, "Myths of Murugan", p. 155.
156. Shulman, *Tamil Temple Myths*, p. 282.
157. Patrick Harrigan, "Sacred Geography in the Cult of Skanda-Murugan", *Journal of the Institute of Asian Studies* 15, no. 2 (March 1998): 47.
158. Arumugam, *Kataragama*, p. 25.
159. Shulman, *Tamil Temple Myths*, pp. 280–81.
160. Or, as Vanamali remarks, "all spiritual seekers, no matter what form they worship, will eventually reach the same goal" (Vanamali, *The Lilas*, p. 44).
161. Ibid., p. 153.
162. Clothey, *The Many Faces of Murukan*, p. 117. In some variations the prize is not the fruit but rather marriage. In these versions Murugan returns to find Ganesha married to *Siddhi* (power and accomplishment, or perfection;

that is, realization of the Self) and *Buddhi* (intellect of the disciplined mind) (Zvelebil, *Tamil Traditions*, p. 30). These brides, together representing spiritual illumination and control, underscore the significance of the mango as a metaphor for the fruit of spiritual knowledge.

163. Used in this sense to refer to family *dharma* as opposed to *rita dharma* (universal dharma). Many accounts indicate that Murugan was annoyed with his own lack of insight that prevented him from discerning the truth which was so obvious to his brother.

164. Clothey, *The Many Faces of Murukan*, p. 118.

165. Vanamali, *The Lilas*, p. 153.

166. Somalay, *Palni: The Hill Temple*, 2nd ed. (Palani: Sri Dhandayuthapani Swami Devasthanam, 1982), p. 13.

167. Agastya is typically associated with Siva. According to legend, the many southerners who journeyed to Mount Kailas to witness Siva's marriage to Parvati had requested that Siva provide them with a sage. Siva chose the dwarf Agastya (Klaus L. Klostermaier, *A Survey of Hinduism* [Albany, State University of New York Press, 1994], p. 294). Alain Danielou states that Agastya means Mover-of-Mountains, or Mover-of-Unmoving (Danielou, *Hindu Polytheism*, pp. 322–23).

168. Kandiah Chelliah, *Hinduism: A Brief Study of It's* [sic] *Origins, Traditions and Practice* (Bukit Beruntung: Kandiah Chelliah, 2012), p. 200. Kandiah relates that, along with every sentient creature in the cosmos, Agastya had journeyed to Mount Kailas to hear Siva give a discourse on yoga. As a result the world was seriously out of balance. Realizing the gravity of the situation, Siva asked Agastya to journey to the south to restore the cosmic equilibrium (Ibid., pp. 200–201).

169. P.V. Jagadisa Ayyar, *South Indian Shrines* (New Delhi: Asian Educational Services, 1982), p. 476.

170. Jagadisa Ayyar states that "when he (i.e. Idumban) was at a loss to know how to lift them, the *Danda* or stick of Brahman stood over the hillocks, while the snakes of the earth served in place of ropes to enable him to carry them". P.V. Jagadisa Ayyar, *South Indian Customs* (Madras: Asian Educational Services, [1925] 1989), p. 138.

171. Zvelibil, *Tamil Traditions*, p. 32.

172. Ibid.

173. This myth is not universally accepted, and indeed is firmly rejected by some Dravidian nationalists (vide: Sumathi Ramaswamy, *Passions of the Tongue: Language Devotion in Tamil Nadu 1891–1970* [New Delhi, Munshiram Manoharlal, 1998]). However, many Malaysian Hindus accept the role of Agastya, and indeed some even claim that the sage visited the Malay Peninsula and is buried in an undisclosed site on Kedah Peak.

174. Clothey, *The Many Faces of Murukan*, pp. 119–20.
175. Vanamali, *The Lilas*, p. xvi.
176. Clothey, *The Many Faces of Murukan*, p. 120.
177. Zvelebil, *Tamil Traditions*, p. 32.
178. Many scholars have highlighted the significance of the number six in the Murugan cultus. Thus, to take some examples, Shanmugan has six faces, the six babies are nursed by the six *Krttikas*, Murugan has the ability to see in six directions, he journeys through six camps, in his war against the *asuras* he has six main abodes, he fights for six days against Surapadman, he leads his devotees through the six *cakras* above the *muladhara cakra*, etc. (Kabade, *Sri Muruga*, pp. 125–26).
179. Harrigan, "Sacred Geography", pp. 38–39.
180. Clothey, *The Many Faces of Murukan*, p. 117.
181. Ibid., p. 123.
182. Ibid., p. 117.
183. Harrigan, "Sacred Geography", pp. 38–39.
184. Clothey, *Rhythm and Intent*, p. 34.
185. Clothey, *The Many Faces of Murukan*, pp. 116–29.
186. Clothey, *Rhythm and Intent*, p. 47.
187. Ibid.
188. Ibid., pp. 49–51.
189. Ibid., pp. 60–61.
190. Ibid., pp. 76–79.
191. Ibid., p. 48.
192. Ibid.
193. Neelvani A/P Thanabalan, *Taipucam in Malaysia: An Analysis of a Hindu Festival (A Case Study of Batu Caves, Selangor)*, Jabatan Antropologi dan Sosiologi, Universiti Malaya, 1987–1988; Vanamali, *The Lilas*, p. 128.
194. Clothey, *The Many Faces of Murukan*, p. 138.

6

The Phenomenology of Thaipusam at Batu Caves

In the previous chapter we examined the mythology surrounding the deity Murugan — his creation, his spiritual maturation, his acquisition of the *Vel*, and his defeat of the *asuric* army headed by the demon Surapadman. It specifically noted his adaptation and emblematic role as a quintessentially Tamil deity. As we have observed, the festival of Thaipusam commemorates a specific and determining event in the deity's cosmology, namely Parvati's bestowal of the *Vel* upon Murugan as the weapon he will use to defeat the *asuric* army. This chapter will examine the conduct of the festival of Thaipusam at Batu Caves, located outside Kuala Lumpur. While Batu Caves is the major Malaysian centre in which Thaipusam is commemorated, there are other significant pilgrimage sites, both in Peninsular and East Malaysia, where the festival is observed.[1]

The first section will trace the founding and development of Batu Caves as Malaysia's foremost Murugan pilgrimage site. It will also detail the current layout of the caves compound. This not only contains the main shrine to Murugan, but also incorporates a number of supplementary temples, an administrative building, a cultural complex including a museum (*Muzium*) and a gallery, a Tamil school and retail outlets.

The following section will explore the overall structure of the festival. This will emphasize the chariot procession from the Sri Maha Mariamman

Kovil (temple) to Batu Caves, the ceremonial visit of the deity Murugan to his Batu Caves shrine, the installation of the Golden *Vel* in his mountaintop temple, and his subsequent return to his main abode in central Kuala Lumpur. The section will emphasize the centrality of the chariot procession and its general linkages to the rituals associated with South Indian kingship.

The final section focuses upon the kavadi ritual as one of the defining features of Thaipusam at Batu Caves. Many scholars have pointed out that myths only reveal their potency and inner truths, their "transformative capacity to reveal the ways in which the invisible is enfolded within the visible", when they are re-enacted within ritual.[2] The previous chapter examined the mythology of Idumban, outlining the legitimating model for the kavadi ritual and highlighting the transformative power of asceticism and yogic disciplines. This section describes some of the many forms that kavadi worship may take, and suggests that while kavadis may be borne for deities other than Murugan, the associated ritual nearly always falls within the received Murugan paradigm. This section also traces the involvement of the individual devotee through the processes of taking a vow, preparatory fasting, the catalytic function of trance (*arul*), the bearing of the kavadi and the post-Thaipusam return to society.

Batu Caves: An Overview

The first official celebration of Thaipusam in Malaysia was held at Batu Caves, outside Kuala Lumpur, in 1892.[3] Batu Caves, a limestone massif approximately thirteen kilometres north of the city centre, was accidentally discovered in 1878 by William Hornsby, an American naturalist, while on a hunting expedition.[4] The site gained popularity with British residents of Kuala Lumpur, who conducted candlelight explorations of the caves.[5] In the 1880s, K. Thambusamy Pillai, who had migrated from India to Singapore in 1872,[6] and who had subsequently become a prominent and wealthy contractor in Kuala Lumpur as well as leader of the Indian community,[7] had a dream in which Maha Mariamman directed him to establish a temple within the Batu Caves, dedicated to her son Murugan.[8] Accordingly, he visited the caves in 1891 with some associates and members of his workforce and cleared the largest cave. A *vel*, the symbol of Murugan, was implanted in the cave.[9]

In passing we should note that although Hindu *murthis* and temples are consecrated, and complex rituals are performed to invoke the deity, other sites are considered inherently sacred, especially those which seem to appear spontaneously. These are regarded as *svayambhu* (or "self-born").[10] Thus, mountains are considered to link heaven and earth, and caves are regarded as the equivalent of the *sanctum sanctorum* of a temple; conversely, the *sanctum sanctorum* of a temple may be viewed as a "cave" within the symbolic mountain.[11] We will return to this point in Chapter 8.

Following the placement of the *vel*, a steady stream of Hindu devotees was attracted to the shrine. In response, Thambusamy, together with friends and employees, made the cave more accessible by constructing simple steps and by clearing the area near the base of the shrine. An attempt by the British District Officer of Kuala Lumpur to bar public access to the shrine and to remove the *vel* was referred to the courts, which decided in favour of devotees.[12] The first Thaipusam followed in 1892. In 1920 the *vel* which marked the site of the shrine was replaced by a *murthi* (image) of Murugan.[13]

From the outset the festival was associated with the Sri Maha Mariamman Kovil Devastanam, located on Jalan Tun H.S. Lee, in the centre of Kuala Lumpur. This link developed as follows. The temple, now the richest in Malaysia, was first constructed in the 1870s as a rudimentary non-*Agamic* shrine dedicated to the tutelary deity Mariamman, and was frequented by Kuala Lumpur's growing Indian workforce. The temple was enlarged in the 1880s under the leadership of Kayarohanam Pillai, who was accorded the status of village headman. In 1887 his son, K. Thambusamy Pillai, transformed the temple from a shed and attap edifice into a brick and mortar building.[14] In the process, the non-*Agamic* Mariamman, a meat-eating deity, was replaced with the *Agamic* or celestial goddess, Maha Mariamman, Mother Sakti, identified as a form of Parvati.[15] In 1889 the temple held its first *Kumbabishekam* (the ritual sanctification and purification of the entire temple, often involving renovation and renewal as well as the formal installation of the deities).[16]

K. Thambusamy's leadership of the Sri Maha Mariamman Kovil Devastanam and his active sponsorship of the Murugan shrine at Batu Caves made it virtually inevitable that the Batu Caves Sri Subramanya Swami Kovil would fall under *devastanam* control. Within several years Thaipusam became a significant festival at Batu Caves.[17] The connection with the *devastanam* established by the founder was consolidated, and the *devastanam* assumed responsibility for the management of Batu Caves and organization of Thaipusam. In 1889 the *devastanam* acquired control of the popular Court Hill Sree Ganesha Temple in central Kuala Lumpur. The *devastanam* remained under the unchallenged direction of the Pillai sub-caste until 1924, when the broader Hindu community attempted to establish public management over the temple.[18] These measures were not successful until 1930 when a court hearing ruled in favour of public control.[19] This ensured, inter alia, that the festival of Thaipusam as commemorated at Batu Caves would be coordinated by representatives of the entire Kuala Lumpur Hindu community rather than being left under the organizational direction of a specific caste. Over the years the Sri Maha Mariamman Kovil has become one of the wealthiest and most influential temples in Malaysia.[20]

From the very beginning the festival of Thaipusam at Batu Caves was modelled upon modes of ritualistic worship observed in South India, especially those associated with the great temple complex at Palani, one of the main Murugan pilgrimage centres in South India. Batu Caves as a site combined a number of motifs intrinsic to the Murugan cultus, including caves, mountaintop retreats, and wilderness (as Batu Caves was then regarded: the site was comparatively remote from Kuala Lumpur, and surrounded by dense jungle; the complex has now been enveloped in encroaching suburbia).

In 1940 the *devastanam* acquired an additional seven acres of land to allow for further development. A Tamil-medium school was established within the caves' precincts.[21] Since World War II, the Batu Caves complex has been extensively redeveloped. By the late 1940s the caves had become the pre-eminent pilgrimage site in Malaya, and the *devastanam* aimed at fostering a social, cultural and religious environment which would accommodate the needs of the gathering Hindu revival in Malaya, most particularly the renewed focus on the worship of Murugan. The *devastanam* set out to create a centre which would incorporate all the major symbols and themes of worship found within the Murugan cultus in the Tamil country. In recent years the *devastanam* has made efforts to provide for the needs of North Indian Hindus, especially those who subscribe to Vaishnavite traditions.

The entire Batu Caves complex covers several hectares, incorporating the limestone outcrop which rises dramatically from the riverine plains north of Kuala Lumpur, together with the immediate surrounds. The complex contains the caves, a couple of hectares of lawns, spiritual and commercial buildings, statues, and a Tamil-medium primary school managed by the *devastanam*.[22] The gateway to the complex opens out on to a nearby road, Jalan Batu Caves, which links the eponymous Jalan Ipoh and Jalan Kuantan (Ipoh and Kuantan Roads). About five hundred metres west of the gateway lies the *Sungai Batu* (Rocky River), a river which was once used for ceremonial bathing throughout Thaipusam. In the past decade, due to the increasingly polluted state of the river, special bathing sites have been constructed along the banks for the use of devotees. A railway station, until recently reserved for the service of tourist and festival traffic, but now linked into the main suburban rail network, lies to the immediate west of the complex.

In describing the temples, complexes and surrounds at Batu Caves, it should be borne in mind that Tamil Hindu shrines are regarded as symmetrical representations of their divine hierarchy, as well as constituting an *axis mundi*. The shrine as a whole is thus considered ordered and patterned, and in contradistinction to the disorder and chaos that reigns beyond its borders. The gates of the shrine represent a boundary for the worshipper. Thus, any approach to the shrine will guide the supplicant from the confusion and disarray of the mundane world to the divine order which prevails at the heart of the shrine.[23] The approaches to Batu Caves reflect this ordered transition.

Outside the main entrance to the caves, the visitor passes a row of stalls which retail religious items, in particular garlands and flowers, which might be required by the worshipper. Until 2002, the formal entrance to the Batu Caves complex comprised a pair of large gates decorated with the figures of peacocks, the mount of Murugan. These were replaced with an elaborate stone architrave, which was officially opened on 27 December 2002. The architrave contains as its centrepiece statuary depicting Murugan with his consorts, Devayanai and Valli. Other figures include Ganesha and Maha Mariamman, with Idumban as gatekeeper at the end of the architrave. Within the complex a thoroughfare runs approximately three hundred metres from the gateway to the base of the stairway which leads to the master cave (sometimes known as the Cathedral or Main Cave but more often referred to as the Temple Cave). The final stretch of this thoroughfare is barred to vehicular traffic.

In recent years the compound to the west of the thoroughfare has been extensively redeveloped. The school lies close to the entrance, and a refurbished *Mandapam* (ceremonial hall) is sited about midway between the gateway and the foot of the steps to the caves. The *utsava murthis* (festival images) of Murugan and his consorts, together with the chariot, are housed within the *Mandapam* throughout the Thaipusam festival. The redesigned double-storied Batu Cave headquarters of the Sri Maha Mariamman Kovil Devastanam, which was officially opened on 27 January 2009 by Tan Sri Datuk R. Nadarajah, chairman and trustee of the *devastanam*, sits immediately adjacent to the roadway. The older building contained an upper-story balcony upon which temple officials and invited dignitaries sat, both to view the constant stream of kavadi bearers and to make speeches. A statue of K. Thambusamy Pillai, founder of the *devastanam*, and originator of Thaipusam at Batu Caves, is located in the courtyard outside the office complex. In the distance, along a pathway which leads to railway stations, there are two recently constructed Vaishnavite temples. One of these is dedicated to the monkey deity Hanuman. A huge fifteen-metre statue of the god sits at the entrance to the temple. The other temple is dedicated to the deity Rama.

On the east side of the roadway, several *asrama* (spiritual centres/retreats) have been established (including the Malaysian headquarters of the Divine Life Society), as well as a row of commercial enterprises, including restaurants, and shops dealing in religious artefacts, souvenirs, and light refreshments.[24] A number of these outlets are run by non-Hindus, many of whom have limited knowledge of Hinduism, temple activities, or even the significance of Batu Caves to Malaysia's Hindu community. One of these buildings contains a theatre which shows films of the history of the caves. (The film I viewed on 26 February 2010 — and remaining in circulation in 2014 — was notable for its effusive praise of the current *devastanam* management. It also made the fallacious claim that Malaysia was the only nation outside India which celebrated the festival of Thaipusam.) A large parking bay located behind the shops caters to the coaches of visitors and tourists.[25]

The limestone outcrop contains a myriad of caves, including two large (upstairs) caves and several, much smaller (downstairs) caves. In addition there are literally hundreds of minor caves and passageways, but these are not open or even accessible to the public, and can be reached only by specialist climbers. The Temple Cave, in which the Murugan shrine is situated, is an enormous elevated limestone configuration (the roof of the cave rises over one hundred metres above the floor), with a yawning southern entrance, and a substantial hollow at the extreme north. The cave is accessed via the main stairway. Just over halfway up the steps, and lying to the west of the stairway, a pathway leads off to the other large cave, the Dark Cave. For many years this cave, which extends deep into the outcrop, and is celebrated for its stalactites and stalagmites, and rare fauna, including certain varieties of bats and non-venomous albino snakes, was declared off limits to the public after blasting operations linked with quarrying was considered to have made the cave dangerously unstable. Under qualified guidance this cave may now be toured by members of the public. Until the early 1980s, the entrance to the Dark Cave could be reached by means of a haulage winch (cable railway) which ran alongside the main steps. (The temple at Palani in South India also features a cable railway which transports devotees to the top of the hill.) The cable railway was shut after inspections revealed it to be unsafe. The station and all operating apparatus were subsequently dismantled. In recent years Najib Razak, Malaysian prime minister, promised funds to reconstruct the cable railway. However, subsequent engineering reports concluded that reconstruction was not feasible and that the limestone base would not provide reliable support for either the cable car or the supporting machinery.[26]

The Temple Cave is reached by a steep stairway consisting of 272 steps. These steps are divided into sixteen flights, each separated by a landing. The stairway, which inclines slightly to the right for the final three flights before the summit, is split into three passageways, each bounded by a stone wall of approximately one metre in height. On Thaipusam day the outer passageways are meant for the use of the ascending and descending traffic, while the central section is theoretically reserved for kavadi bearers and their retinues. Each year these dividing walls are painted immediately prior to Thaipusam. Prior to 1920 there were no stairs, and devotees were compelled to climb the hill face to reach the Temple Cave. In that year a single stairway was constructed. This was duplicated in 1939, and in 1975 the third corridor was added. (A fourth passageway is currently under construction.)

Immediately to the left of the base of the stairway lies a temple complex with a series of shrines devoted to Ganesha, Meenakshi (modelled on the famous Sri Meenakshi shrine in Madurai, South India),[27] Parvati, and Siva as Sri Somasundereswara (in the form of a *lingam*). Murals within each temple illustrate relevant *Puranic* mythology. The approach to the Ganesha temple features an elongated wall which displays the major Murugan temples in South India together with appropriate iconography for each cosmic locality. Until the 1980s the Ganesha shrine was little more than a rather modest *murthi* sited at the foot of a tree. Although the deity had rudimentary protection from the elements, devotees were required to stand in the open. The temple formed part of the major upgrade of the caves complex undertaken throughout the late 1980s to the early 1990s.

Opposite the Ganesha temple, and across the main pathway, stands a temple dedicated to the *Navagraha* planets. A Siva temple, featuring the deity in the form of a *lingam*, is immediately adjacent. The latter temple replaced a site formerly occupied by the grave of a *sadhu*/holy man who was believed to have achieved *mahasamadhi* (liberation) at Batu Caves. Following his internment, an emanation appeared above the grave which to many devotees resembled the outline of a *sadhu* meditating in the lotus position. This site was levelled by the temple management to make way for the current shrine. In the process, the earthen impression of the saint was erased, outraging many Hindus who regarded the site as inviolable. Numerous commentators have suggested to me that this development reflects the spiritual immaturity and lack of knowledge which prevails among the current *devastanam* management.[28] Both the *Navagraha* and Siva shrines are comparatively recent developments.

Adjacent to the steps, on the right-hand side, is a towering statue of Murugan, which at over forty metres in height comprises the largest representation of the deity in the world, and completely dominates the immediate approaches to the caves. While the Murugan statue is a source of pride for most Hindus, its construction did not meet with universal acclaim. However, even its harshest critics concede that the colossus must be viewed within the context of the series of Malaysian mega-projects inspired by former Prime Minister Mahathir, but more significantly that it represents a Hindu response to the increasing pressures of Islamization.

A concrete architrave spans the base of the stairway. The obverse aspect of the architrave, the side facing devotees about to ascend the steps, has as its central motif a statue of Shanmugan, the six-faced youth, seated on his *vahana* (mount), the peacock, and accompanied by his consorts Valli and Devayanai, though it also contains an image depicting Valli's fright at being confronted by the "wild" elephant Ganesha, Murugan's older brother, in his disguise as an uncontrolled tusker. The reverse aspect features Murugan's marriage to Valli. Another architrave with further statuary stretches across the top of the stairway and shows Murugan's marriage to Devayanai in the presence of the celestials (thus, one symbolically climbs from Murugan's marriage to the earthy Valli at the foot of the stairs to the world of the celestials at the top).[29] Immediately outside the Temple Caves, to the left of the ascending devotee, is a statue of Surapadman in the process of being split in two by the *Vel*, the peacock and cockerel at his feet. This imagery, a prominent episode in the Skanda Purana, regarded as a crucial symbol to devotees and in particular kavadi-bearing pilgrims, is now largely obscured from public sight by the recent inappropriate and ill-considered siting of a new kiosk. To the right, as one proceeds from the top of the stairway, and against the eastern wall of the Temple Cave, there is a small shrine to Idumban, gatekeeper of Murugan's shrine (who thus fulfils his function as guardian of the Sri Subramanya Kovil, which lies within).

The stairway ends some little distance above the absolute floor of the Temple Caves. Two flights of steps, located on either side of the cave, link the upper level of the cave with this floor. These steps are divided into up and down traffic ways. The central portion of the cave adjacent to these steps is railed off from the general public. At the central junction, facing devotees approaching the main shrine, stands a large figure of Murugan and his *Vel*.

The main shrine, dedicated to Murugan, is located in a minor recess, a mini cave as it were, at the northern end of the western wall. Outside this aperture, a small *murthi* of Ganapati enclosed by a miniature demarcation wall stands upon a bed of mosaic tiles. The *sanctum sanctorum* is reached via several tiled steps, so that the officiating *pantaram*[30] must climb to perform all obeisances.[31] The *murthi* is a small image in the form of Murugan as the renunciant Palani, and is backed by a large *Vel*.

The cave opens into a huge hollow at the northern end. This is reached by several steep flights of roughly finished concrete steps, which rise from the cave floor and are divided into lengthwise sections by rudimentary handrails. These steps are often wet with seepage and are potentially hazardous for the aged and infirm. The hollow is roughly circular in shape and is enclosed by a series of sheer rock walls which rise all but vertically to the sky above. Groups of monkeys cavort on the walls. Although the hollow opens to the sky, it admits very little direct sunlight. A further temple, devoted to Murugan and his consorts Devayanai and Valli (that is, Murugan in his fully stabilized form), has been constructed on the floor of the hollow. This represents an attempt to recreate within this single complex the sense of Murugan as a totality, Murugan in all his forms. A *murthi* of Siva as *Nataraja*, the Divine Dancer, has been built against the northern wall.[32]

In recent years, and in particular in the period since 2000, a number of additional statues depicting mythological episodes within the cosmology of the Murugan cultus have been installed within the Temple Cave. These consist of the following:

Along the western wall of the Temple Cave:
1. An image of Murugan, having received the *Vel* from Parvati, being blessed by both Siva and Parvati.
2. Depictions of (a) the sage Agastya praying to Siva and Parvati, prior to the removal of the two hills, Sivagiri and Saktigiri, to South India, and (b) Murugan the renunciant, following his loss of the race with Ganesha around the world.

Within the hollow:
A portrayal of the incident in which the young Murugan imprisons Brahma after his failure to explain the meaning of the *Pravana Aum*, and subsequently becomes the teacher of his father, Siva, by instructing him in the mysteries of the mantra.

Along the eastern wall of the Temple Cave:
1. At the very foot of the stairs leading to the hollow, statuary showing Murugan blessing the erstwhile *asura*, Idumban.
2. Statuary of Murugan in his final stabilized form with his consorts Devayanai and Valli.
3. A depiction of events which accompany the race between Ganesha and Murugan, for which the prize is a mango, and which precedes the latter's ill-tempered departure for Palani.
4. Murugan as *Thandayuthapani* within the cave at the top of the stairs, with representations of forms of kavadi worship.

In Chapter 8 I will suggest that these additions have been positioned with little regard for the concept, held by the original trustees, of a Hindu pilgrimage as a sequential and chronological recreation of a carefully structured and layered journey from mundane time and space — that of the *Kaliyuga* — to the metaphysical centre (or *axis mundi*) where the devotee may expect a direct encounter with the deity Murugan.

Two of the three main downstairs caves are now enclosed within a new commercial development called Cave Villa. An admission fee of fifteen ringgit is now charged. This has, in effect, converted the main downstairs area into something approaching a religious theme park, though attempts have been made to combine the more obvious commercial aspects with the features that mark the caves as a major pilgrimage centre.

The entrance itself consists of a rather kitschy admission hut, ostensibly designed to resemble the entrance to a minor cave, with turnstiles allowing visitors both ingress and egress. The security staff who formerly controlled visitor traffic and who were noted for their general surliness and studied rudeness appear to be no longer in evidence, and have been replaced with far more responsive personnel who are prepared to interact with visitors and to answer questions.

The main gardens are reached by a concrete pedestrian causeway which zigzags across a small ornamental lake. For many years the waters of this lake were stagnant, discoloured and often noisome. Occasional attempts to restore the lake to its idealized state were invariably defeated, usually within weeks, by the huge volume of rubbish casually deposited by visitors. The degraded condition of the lake had been a sore point with senior Hindus for many years. Over the past few years the lake has been completely transformed; the water is clean and aerated, full of Japanese *koi* fish, and planted with water lilies and lotuses. Man-made waterfalls cascade into the lake, not only creating a striking visual impact, but endowing the area with a sense of vibrancy and motion.

The main gardens are now well maintained with cultivated lawns set within attractive surrounds. A large number of poultry, including ducks, chickens, turkeys and guinea fowl, wander the compound. There is an enclosure for the peacocks, which are to be found at most Murugan shrines. A food court and restaurant serving both North and South Indian food as well as souvenirs abuts the gardens. Directly opposite there is a stage for cultural performances. The rather breathless (and poorly produced) pamphlet issued by Cave Villa[33] promises regular performances of Indian classical dance, but during my visits I have seen nothing more adventurous than a group of seemingly bored dancers rehearsing rather hackneyed Bollywood-style routines. The area also features a children's playground and a sanctuary for exotic tropical birds.

There are three main downstairs caves, two of which are enclosed within the Cave Villa precincts. The most prominent of these is the Art Gallery, which is roughly S-shaped. In recent years the cave and its surrounds have been comprehensively refurbished. The renovated gallery was officially opened on 19 March 2008. The approach to the gallery features two statues, one of a large recumbent *veena* (a stringed musical instrument and, among other things, a symbol of the goddess Saraswati, patroness of the arts, science and learning), and the other of a five-legged bull, once resident within the Batu Caves compound (the fifth leg, atrophied, emanates from the bull's left shoulder). Within the entrance "hall" of the cave, a wall is devoted to photos of kavadi bearers.[34] At the base of the entrance is a *murthi* of Ganesha attended by the two saints Sundarar and Sereman Perimul, as envisaged in the praise poem *Vinayakar Agaval* (Call to Vinayakar) written by St. Avvaiyar,[35] the celebrated circa sixth to eighth century Tamil *bhakti* saint. The *murthi* is set against a backdrop of jungle scenery, which was animated by running water; both familiar motifs of Ganesha worship. However, when last examined the water feature had ceased operating. The interior of the cave, gently illuminated with coloured lights, contains representations of mythology drawn from Saivite and Vaishnavite traditions. These are portrayed by dioramas consisting of both statuary and paintings. The main section features well-known scenes taken from the Skanda Purana and follows the sequential cosmology of Murugan. This includes Parvati praying to the *lingam*[36] (i.e., Sakti longing for union with the Absolute, thus symbolizing the conjoining of the Manifest and the Unmanifest); the *Saravana Poihai*, that is, the six babies resting on lotuses in the Divine Lake and watched over by the celestial maidens; the divine youth Murugan interrogating Brahma (who, significantly, is daubed with the Vaisnavite *tilak*);[37] Murugan instructing Siva in the mysteries of the *Pravana Aum*; the story of the mango;[38] Murugan setting out to destroy Surapadman and the *asuras* (all portrayed as terrifying monstrosities). Other Murugan imagery includes Murugan's marriage to his consort Devayanai; the deity's wooing of Valli, aided by his brother Ganesha; Murugan's marriage to Valli; and Murugan (in the guise of a young cowherd) conversing from a *naval* tree with the saint Avvaiyar after throwing fruit to her.[39] The totality of the Murugan cultus, that is, Murugan in all his forms, is clearly integrated within these dioramas with the sacred geography of Murugan's mythological history in the Tamil country, and the final diorama, Murugan "the shining one", shown at the top of Batu Caves steps receiving homage from kavadi bearing devotees, explicitly links all of these sites and mythological episodes to Murugan's presence at the caves, thus clearly designating Batu Caves as a pilgrimage centre wherein Murugan may be encountered. In another diorama, Siva is depicted in the form of *Nataraja*. Vaishnavite imagery focuses upon the *dasavataras* of Vishnu (that is, the ten embodiments of Vishnu); Vishnu as *Naraya* resting on his great serpent bed, *Sesa*; and Krishna instructing Arjuna the charioteer, a duologue which is central to the *Bhagavad Gita*. A further diaorama, placed somewhat surprisingly among the Murugan exhibits, shows Krishna dancing on the head of the snake *Kaliya* following Krishna's victory over the snake.[40]

The temple custodians have made an attempt to provide interpretative signage for exhibits. Unfortunately, these consist of plastic inserts which are easily removed from their holders, and much signage is completely missing. Other signs have been transferred from their rightful place to other locations, producing unintentional incongruities; thus, on the days of my most recent visit, explanatory signage delineating the various *avatars* of Vishnu was sited in front of a diorama which displayed Murugan's marriage to Valli. In general, the extant signage is both confused and confusing; it is not contextualized and fails to provide a linking, let alone coherent, narrative. Moreover, it reveals limited and often misleading scholarship, the result of inadequate research.

The second cave houses the *Muzium*, formerly known as the Art Gallery, and originally opened on 7 January 1973 by Tan Sri Manickavasagam, a former minister of labour and manpower, and erstwhile president of the Malaysian Indian Congress. In recent years this has been refurbished, and the new *Muzium* was officially re-opened on 27 January 2008. The *Muzium* contains statuary representing precepts taken from the *Tirukural*, St. Tiruvalluvar's great ethical work consisting of a body of aphorisms delivered in rhyming couplets,[41] as well as the statues of the main Saiva *bhakti* saints (Appar, Sundarar, Manickavasagar and Sambandar); and depictions of formative mythological episodes in Tamil Hinduism. Prior to the restoration there were complaints that the tablets containing the verses of the *Kural* were in classical Tamil, an arcane form of the language which bears little resemblance to contemporary demotic Tamil. While attempts have been made to provide interpretative signage, this suffers the same defects as those of the Art Gallery. Many captions are missing, and others are grievously misplaced and bear no relationship to the exhibits they are supposedly interpreting.[42] Frequently the annotations also show signs of deficient scholarship; thus, for example, a feature purporting to identify great figures in Hinduism lists Indian nationalist Subhas Chandra

Bose, who, despite following the teachings of Sri Vivekananda, was an avowed secularist.[43]

An interior cave, leading from the *Muzium*, plays home to a modest reptile enclosure, known as Reptiles Galore. This contains collections of endangered species of crocodiles, lizards, frogs, snakes and tortoises. Many Hindus have pondered on the relevance or indeed the appropriateness of a facility such as this within a major Hindu pilgrimage centre. During my most recent visit a python was in the process of devouring a live chicken, while nearby a cage was full of rabbits waited to be fed to other animals. The Cave Villa pamphlet advertises demonstrations by "our famous snake charmers", but I could find no evidence of scheduled performances.

The third and final downstairs cave, and outside the Cave Villa enclosure, known as the Ramayana Gallery, was officially opened on 15 January 1995, by Dato Seri Dr Samy Vellu, at that stage president of the Malaysian Indian Congress. This is devoted to large-scale murals and statuary depicting noteworthy episodes from the Epic. The opening of the gallery marked an attempt to make the Batu Caves complex relevant to Malaysia's Vaishnavite Hindus, especially those of North Indian origin, and to emphasize the overarching and thus inclusive religious allegiance and rich heritage which supposedly forms a unifying leitmotif among Malaysian Hindus.

Thaipusam: Basic Structure

Thaipusam officially commences with the early morning departure of the chariot bearing the *utsava murthi*[44] of Lord Murugan from the Sri Maha Mariamman Kovil to travel to his home in the mountains. Formerly the departure was at 6:30 a.m, but due to the increasingly chaotic traffic conditions in central Kuala Lumpur, the time of the departure has been successively rescheduled for ever-earlier hours. For some years the chariot left between midnight and 1:00 a.m., but in 2014 the departure was further wound back to 10:00 p.m.

At this juncture it should be noted that the procession of the deity is grounded in South Indian kingship rituals. A polity which lacks a king possesses no appropriately constituted hierarchy, is no long viable, and will quickly descend into chaos.[45] Lawrence Babb points out that:

> In traditional South Indian ritual the processional idiom often serves as a means for the expression of socio-spatial relationships. The procession is

an occasion in which the deity, or rather a portable extension of it, emerges from the temple to journey through the community in which the temple is associated. The imagery is royal; the god or goddess becomes a king or a queen, carried forth to survey his or her dominions and to receive offerings or homage from loyal subjects.[46]

In return the devotees are rewarded with *darsan* of the deity (that is, the sight or vision of the God). However, as we have previously noted, *darsan* as a concept connotes a mystical or "inner vision" and implies reciprocity in that the deity also perceives the devotee.[47]

The departure is preceded by an early morning puja (*visakha puja*),[48] and a special *abishekam* (bathing) in which the *utsava murthi* is successively bathed with water, milk, tender coconut water, ghee, honey, sugar cane juice, *vibhuti* (sacred ash),[49] sandalwood paste, rosewater, and *panccamirtam* (a sweet dish made of five fruits, ideally mango, jackfruit, bananas, grapes and oranges, plus brown sugar water). The *kurukkal* (Brahman temple priest) then recites 108 verses of mantras (in Tamil). A curtain is then drawn while the *utsava murthi* is dressed, adorned with silk, gold and diamonds, and garlanded. The dressing requires considerable skill; the vestments and garlands must not only highlight the majesty of the deity but must maintain their immaculacy and freshness throughout the hours spent in the heat of the journey to the cave.[50]

Immediately prior to this ritual, the throng of devotees who have remained overnight at the temple is augmented by a steady stream of arrivals. Out on the roadway, beyond the temple precincts, thousands more devotees wait expectantly. To a visitor, the atmosphere feels tense, electric, expectant. As the *kurrukal* sings the final invocation prior to revealing the clothed *murthi*, the crowds press forward. The curtain is drawn back, revealing the ornamented Murugan, ready to commence his regal journey. Hundreds of women prostrate on the floor, while all the men press their palms together, their arms extended above their heads.

Occasionally the drawing back of the curtains may be a signal for cases of spontaneous trance. During my 1981 visit, a woman standing next to me was thus "possessed". This state was heralded with a deep sigh, a gentle rocking, which gave way to a slow dreamlike and controlled trance. Arms stretched horizontally, hair unbound, and largely ignored by the crowd around her, the woman remained in a trance for about ten minutes until a *kurrukal* applied *vibhuti* to her forehead.[51] Each year there are invariably several such cases, mostly women, and not always so controlled or peaceful, within the temple.

Once the curtain is opened the *utsava murthi* is offered *alankara deepam* (the showing of the light of a special lamp to one who is garlanded, that is, a god, king or extremely auspicious guest). The *kurrukal* then presents a succession of silver instruments to the deity, all symbols of his kingship. These normally include the *kudai* (umbrella), *visiri* (fan), *alavdham* (leaf), *venjamaran* (another form of fan), *kodi* (flag) and *kannadi* (mirror). As these items are offered the *kurrukal* recites the 108 names of Murugan. An *otuvar* (hymn singer)[52] then performs some verses from the *Teveram*, a corpus of sacred hymns compiled by the Saivite saints. Following this the *kurrukal* offers a tray of flowers to the *utsava murthi* while reciting the deity's 108 names. He then performs an *arati* (display of camphor flames to the deity), and offers flames to the devotees together with *prasadam* (sanctified substances, often food, but also involving other substances, and offered to devotees at the end of worship).[53] On this occasion the *prasadam* consists of *vibhuti, tirttam* (blessed water), *kumkum* (a red powder made of turmeric and lime), sandalwood paste and flowers. However, generally by this time the temple has become so crowded that only a small section of the crowd receives the flames and *prasadam*.

The *utsava murthi* of Murugan, together with his consorts Devayanai and Valli, plus the *Vel*, are mounted on a *mayil* (peacock shrine), before being lifted on wooden poles and carried clockwise within the temple precincts for three circuits. This circumambulation is accompanied by temple musicians playing the *nadaswaram*[54] and drums. Although James Kirkup's description dates from Thaipusam circa 1963, it remains remarkably apposite:

> amid great musical agitation, the glittering, shivery shrine with its three tiny golden figures degged and tagged with jewels, dappled with charms and swathed in flowers, a miracle of gold and silver, and crystal dangling dewdrops and ribbons of embroidered cloth with a large panel of flowered lemon silk billowing behind, is lifted on to two stout long poles and borne on a dozen men's naked shoulders. There is a man holding a fringed, salmon pink umbrella on a six-foot handle high over the sacred image. He walks immediately behind it.[55]

The *utsava murthis* are now installed in the temple's magnificent ornate silver chariot, which waits outside the temple on the roadway. Almost unnoticed, the *kurukkals* retire to the temple. A further *arati* is performed, water sprinkled, and a coconut smashed, before the chariot begins its journey. The elevation of Murugan into the chariot is the signal for sustained jostling among the assembled devotees for favourable vantage points to gain *darsan* of the deity. Normally at this point a handful of devotees are overcome by emotion and weep openly.

The chariot (*ratham*), an elaborate construction, about eight metres in height, was intricately carved from teak and plated with silver at a cost of 350,000 Malaysian ringgit.[56] The silver chariot, which was officially inaugurated in a special ceremony held at Batu Caves on 21 January 1983, replaced an older carved *ratham* which had been used for many years and which remains stored at the temple. The silver *ratham* is decorated with jewellery and is adorned with flags, tinsel and bunting. Figurines include ceremonial horses, and minor deities facing in the four main directions.[57] The interior, dome and spire are brightly illuminated. Power is supplied by a mobile generator which follows behind the chariot as it makes it way to the cave. Religious music is played through a public address system.

Until 2000 the chariot was symbolically drawn by relays of yoked oxen. The oxen were freshly scrubbed and decorated for the occasion. Their horns were painted, and they were then garlanded and caparisoned with richly coloured ceremonial cloth. In point of fact, the oxen's role was largely emblematic; the bulk of the load was borne by volunteers who scrambled enthusiastically to secure a place at one of two lead ropes by which the chariot was drawn. The jostling for favoured positions was occasionally vigorous, and sometimes led to minor affrays, as the tardy and latecomers were elbowed aside. Pulling the chariot is regarded as an honoured form of ritual service to the deity, and many of those who attached themselves to the lead ropes remained with the chariot throughout its journey to Batu Caves (a passage which in those days might have taken seven to eight hours).

In 2000 the management of the *devastanam* replaced the oxen and the lead ropes with a small tractor. This decision, which was unannounced, and apparently taken only hours before the festival, caught devotees by surprise. Many would-be volunteers had waited immediately outside the temple for lengthy periods — some overnight — to gain initial access to lead ropes. The *devastanam* later issued a press release stating that the use of oxen to pull the chariot had been discontinued in response to allegations of abuse levelled by animal welfare groups, but in future years the oxen would symbolically accompany the chariot to preserve the traditions associated with the festival.[58]

Despite the early start, a large crowd (police estimates usually settle on between 150,000 and 200,000, but unofficial sources place the figure up to 400,000)[59] turns out to accompany the chariot on the processional route. The crowd following the chariot normally stretches over several city blocks (and, indeed, is well over a kilometre in length). There is no doubt that in recent years the number of devotees following the chariot has substantially increased. All segments of Hindu society are represented, and prominent political figures can be seen walking with those of more modest backgrounds. Family groups predominate, crocodiles of young women with their hands clasped or upon each other's shoulders in order to maintain contact within the dense crowd, small babies and young children carried by their parents, older women dressed in richly coloured saris, with younger women and female adolescents increasingly likely to be clad in so-called Punjabi suits, many men formally attired in *dupa* (silk cream-coloured prayer shirts), but more likely to be seen wearing Western-style trousers rather than the *vesthis* that are all but de rigeur in major temples in South India.

In the past decade, Indian youth gangs, adherents of a youth "style" derogatorily dismissed as a "gangsta" sub-culture, a hybrid *Weltanschauung* largely inspired by an awkward amalgam of an imagined Western popular culture and the heroes (and anti-heroes) of violent Tamil films, have begun to assemble near the chariot's departure point, and to reassemble at selected meeting places along the route. These groups — as yet low in number — at most totalling two hundred young men, and sometimes containing children as young as eleven or twelve years of age (my observations reveal no female membership) — tend to limit their activities to those of the "seen and being seen" variety, namely creating undue noise, whistling, insulting passersby, and directing offensive comments to young women. Some are obviously drunk, and whenever they move from one site to another they leave behind a pile of empty beer bottles. The presence of these groups has proved an annoyance and a source of chagrin to many Hindus who wish to preserve the integrity and solemnity of Thaipusam.[60]

Over the years the route followed by the chariot has varied considerably, depending upon road upgrades or major construction works within Kuala Lumpur. However, the route travelled in 2014 was as follows: Jalan Tun H.S. Lee, Jalan Pudu, Jalan Tun Perak, Leboh Ampang, Jalan Ampang, Jalan Munshi Abdullah, Jalan Dang Wangi, Jalan Raja Laut, Jalan Sultan Ismail, Jalan Perhentian and Jalan Ipoh.

The chariot makes rapid progress through the neon-lit inner streets, past blocks of modern offices, brilliantly illuminated shopping emporia and recently constructed tourist hotels. Often tourists, alerted by management and staff, spill out from hotels on to the footpaths to take the obligatory photographs, an authentic splash of local colour for their personal albums or websites. Occasionally the press of the crowd sets off car alarms, their signals fading into the general backdrop as the procession passes.

The chariot is preceded by a plethora of youth and other religious groups, representing a spectrum of Hindu society (and including in recent years such non-Saivite groups as ISKCON and Brahma Kumaris), many singing *bhajans* or chanting; by musicians, including temple *nadaswaram* players and drummers; dance groups; and several kavadi-bearing devotees.

A feature of the procession is the performance of the *kolattam* dance by numerous youth groups. Elizabeth Collins describes the *kolattam* as follows:

> The dancers form two circles, one inside the other, so that each dancer faces a partner. The dancers in the inner and outer circles move in opposite directions. They mark the rhythms of the dance with the stamp of their feet emphasized by the jangle of bells worn around their ankles, and the clack of their sticks which are hit together or on those of a partner in patterns signalled by the troupe leader. The dancers may also jump over and between the sticks of other dancers, which are hit on the ground and against each other in complex rhythms at very fast tempo. The dance requires that each dancer precisely regulate his or her movements in accord with the whole group in an ever changing pattern.[61]

In South India, *kolattam* is traditionally danced by young girls, but in Malaysia it is performed by both boys and girls, and occasionally men and women.

The swelling of crowd numbers over recent years has been paralleled by an increase of *kolattam* groups, dance troupes, the latter including members of various dance academies (often featuring young participants), a highly professional talented transgender ensemble whose sensitive performance of the famed *mayil* (peacock) dance — a dance closely associated with Murugan — is invariably well received, and a lion dance (normally enacted by Chinese dancers, but in this case performed by young Indian men). Musicians include drum groups and *meelam* performers (generally consisting of a range of drummers and percussionists together with a singer who directs the other musicians).

The crowd is guided by torch-bearing marshals selected by the *devastanam*, who work in conjunction with the police (who in turn direct traffic and minimize likely bottlenecks), and the Federal Reserve Unit. The strong security presence is ostensibly to prevent disorder among the crowd, but it also acts as a (unspoken) deterrent against the potentially disruptive activities of religious extremists of other communities. The deployment of largely Malay (and hence Muslim) security forces is well publicized by Malaysian politicians and the Malay media, and is often cited as an example of inter-communal cooperation.

In passing, it is worth noting that over the past couple of years the rather stiff and taciturn interactions which hitherto existed between devotees and security personnel have become far more relaxed. It is now common to see members of the *thaneer panthals* (described below) offering security personnel food and drinks and for devotees to converse and even joke with individual officers. As little as three to four years ago such informality would have seemed all but unimaginable.

The logistics of the procession are complex and require considerable organization. This involves the *devastanam* in planning and negotiations for months in advance of Thaipusam. Authorities with which the *devastanam* must liaise include the Malaysian Indian Congress, the civic administration (especially the Municipal agencies), the police and the Federal Reserve, *Tenaga Nasional* (the national electricity company), the Red Crescent, and a host of volunteer and voluntary organizations which will assist with a diversity of tasks, including preparing and polishing the chariot, the provision of food, medical aid, and the care of lost children. *Tenaga Nasional* assigns workers who will cut and disconnect low-slung wires which may impede the progress of the chariot, and auxiliary teams who will repair the wires and reconnect supplies immediately after the procession has passed. (In recent years the decreasing number of such connections has vastly reduced the electricians' workload.) In addition the *devastanam upayams* (or endowments)[62] will furnish a variety of services to devotees, including subsidizing the cost of rail between Kuala Lumpur and Batu Caves, and the supply of items of worship, especially coconuts, sandalwood paste, *vibhuti*, etc.[63]

Along the route, individual devotees, various religious bodies and Hindu representatives of various organizations and commercial firms have erected *thaneer panthals* (special stalls which supply food, drink and other products and services). In recent years these have become far more numerous and considerably more elaborate and well organized. These distribute packets of food as well as drinks to the crowd, including curried chickpeas, noodles, sweet foods, packaged fruit juices, coffee and milk-based drinks, tender coconut juice and fresh water. In addition, some individuals and religious organizations may offer food and other items without the effort of setting up a *thaneer panthal*. Some also issue religious tracts and magazines. In the past two to three years, groups of politicians have stationed themselves at strategic points to convey their best wishes to passing devotees.

Between the chariot's departure and its arrival at Batu Caves, there are usually several cases of spontaneous trances, mainly among women. Some dance wildly, their hair unbound, knocking into or stamping on other people, oblivious to their general surroundings. Others sink into gentle trances, adopting stylized gestures often seen on temple *murthis*. All are subdued by applications of *vibhuti* to the forehead.

Once it is clear of the immediate inner city, the chariot makes frequent stops at *thaneer panthals* and at locations where clusters of devotees, normally family groups, have gathered. This allows devotees to receive the *darsan* of the deity, and to present trays of offerings — generally fruit, coconuts, incense, garlands, cloth and betel leaves and nuts — which are passed up to the *pantarams* seated in the chariot, formally tendered to the deity, and returned to devotees as *prasadam*. Infants are also passed up to the chariot to receive Murugan's blessings, and are returned, often with the wide-eyed wonder of the very young, or in floods of tears, to their parents. The significant increase in crowd numbers and the recent proliferation of *thaneer panthals* has resulted in continual halts in the procession.

While the chariot is stationery, devotees fulfil vows by smashing coconuts before it. The frequency of coconut breaking and the number of coconuts offered has markedly increased in recent years. The smashing of coconuts has many meanings in the Saivite worldview. However, the most common explanation it that the coconut symbolizes the human head, and its fragmentation represents the obliteration of the ego and the realization of the Divine within. According to this thesis, the outer husk of the coconut represents *maya* (the illusive nature of the world), the inner fibrous matter becomes *karma* (action and its fruits), the coconut shell is *anava* (ego), the white matter represents *Paramatman* (the Divine), the coconut water the ambrosial bliss that union with God produces, the three "eyes" at the apex of the coconut represent the two physical eyes of man and the inner mystic eye of Siva which must be opened within before unity with the Divine may be attained. A devotee who smashes a coconut before a *murthi* of a deity is in fact engaging in a recognized devotional ritual which implores the deity to bestow upon that individual the blessings of spiritual unfoldment and liberation.

As the chariot makes its way through the streets, Chinese storeowners, office workers and factory hands emerge to offer obeisance. Many morning motorists supplicate as they pass by. In recent years, volleys of fireworks have become a feature of the chariot procession. These are set off at a number of points and form intricate coloured patterns against the night sky.

In addition to these ad hoc stops, the chariot halts at two prominent temples along the route, both situated on Jalan Ipoh — namely the Sri Thandayuthapani Kovil, owned and managed by Kuala Lumpur's Chettiar community, and the Sri Paranjothy Vinayagar temple, founded by the "Jaffna" Tamil community. At both locations, simultaneous *arati* are performed to the enthroned *utsava murthi* and to the presiding deity within the temple. Large numbers of devotees attempt to place themselves in a convenient position to obtain *darsan* of this event, which is considered extremely propitious. In recent years, procession organizers have begun acknowledging the several temples dedicated to village deities which lie en route, including a prolonged stop at the Kaliamman Kovil at the fourth mile of Jalan Ipoh; formerly the chariot did not pause at these temples.

The chariot's frequent halts, especially after daybreak, and as the warmth, then heat of the gathering sun becomes obvious, occasionally lead to tensions between some of those escorting the chariot, many without any means of deflecting the harsh sunlight, and the marshals, themselves obeying the directives of the *pantarams* ensconced within the chariot, whose first duty is to ensure the dignity of the procession and to allow as many people as possible to obtain *darsan* of the deity. (In point of fact, the *pantarams* are constantly at work, and the heat within the enclosed confines of the chariot is probably significantly greater than that endured by devotees.)

The general increase in crowd numbers and the growing frequency of stops en route means that the arrival time of the chariot at Batu Caves has over the years become successively later, and a journey which formerly took a maximum of ten hours may now stretch to fifteen hours or even longer. Upon reaching the caves, Murugan and his consorts are transferred to a special platform within a downstairs shrine, the New Swami Mandapam, and *puja* and *archanai* (in this instance a more elaborate *puja* involving chanting of the deity's names) are performed. Later, the Golden *Vel* from the chariot is ceremonially presented to the head *pantaram* of the Sri Subrahmanya Swami Koyil, who carries the *Vel* to the top of the hill and places it in the Murugan shrine within the Temple Cave. Towards evening, usually at about 4:00 p.m., the Chairman of the Sri Maha Mariamman Koyil Devastanam will raise the ceremonial flag, a kingship ritual which proclaims that Murugan is now officially in residence in his Batu Caves palace, and declares the festival officially open.

On Day Two of the festival the *utsava murthi* of Murugan is borne to the nearby river for *abishekam* (ritual bathing). However, the bulk of the day is devoted to formal acts of worship and service. While the attention of the vast crowd is focused upon the vibrant spectacle of the several thousand devotees who bear kavadis (described in the following section), there are others who meet their spiritual obligations in less obvious ways. These may include *annathanam* (serving free meals); distributing cool drinks (especially *moor*, diluted milk curd);[64] constructing, manning or making a substantial contribution to a *thaneer panthal*; serving in religious organizations (which may include the circulation of tracts, answering questions on religious issues, or providing spiritual counselling; or the provision of religious entertainment at stipulated times (e.g., *Bharatanatyam* performances or dramatic representations of selected *Puranas*). In addition, personnel from the St. John Ambulance Brigade and the Red Crescent (including, in recent years, Malay Muslim medical staff) are on hand to treat the inevitable casualties, mainly cases of fainting, heat stroke and fatigue, as well as the handful of more serious injuries, including heart attacks or strokes, which are invariably reported each year.

Many parents choose Thaipusam as an auspicious day upon which to shave the hair of young children. *Chaulum* (head shaving) is regarded as one of the essential rituals associated with infancy.[65] Although ideally head shaving is conducted by the child's father, in practice this is usually entrusted to any one of a number of specialist barbers who are present for the occasion. Other devotees may elect to have their heads shaved as a form of penance. Hair is believed to accumulate pollution, and its removal thus rids the child/devotee of any unwanted form of contamination; in the case of infants, *chaulum* assists in cleansing the child of the pollution garnered during and since birth. The shaven heads of both young children and adult devotees are anointed with sandalwood paste, which is viewed as purifying as well as cooling. (The shaving of hair is closely associated with practices observed at the South Indian Murugan shrines, especially those at Tiruchendur and Palani.)

The second day of Thaipusam is easily the most crowded. Thaipusam is now a public holiday in five states (Selangor, Penang, Negri Sembilan, Perak and Johor), and was declared a public holiday in the Federal Territory in 2008.[66] In 2014, Kedah proclaimed Thaipusam a public holiday on an experimental basis. (Whether this foreshadows a permanent declaration remains to be seen.)[67] The fact that it is now a holiday within the adjacent states has undoubtedly made it easier for some outstation devotees to travel to Batu Caves for Thaipusam. Prior to the festival, hundreds of pilgrims and their families — mainly hailing from outlying areas — arrive at Batu Caves in chartered buses. Most of these camp within the compound precincts. Thousands of others arrive via the subsidized special train services which run between Kuala Lumpur and suburban areas to Batu Caves,[68] while others take advantage of dedicated bus services and (in former years) outstation taxis. The number of people present at Batu Caves on Thaipusam day is estimated by the local media to be well in excess of one million people. While the overwhelming majority are Hindus, usually in family groups, there are also many sightseers, especially Malaysians of other ethnic groups (including increasing numbers of Malays).

There are also large numbers of foreign tourists, brought to the caves by tourism operators to imbibe a slab of authentic "Oriental" culture. While there have been complaints about those tourists who treat the entire festival as a sort of extended sideshow, a mere divertissement staged expressly for their entertainment, the majority are well behaved. Indeed, many younger Western tourists appear overwhelmed and often deeply moved. Some approach devotees who have fulfilled their vows to ask questions and to seek further information. Attempts by tourism companies to promote Thaipusam as a "gape and wonder" spectacle have been discouraged by the Malaysian authorities.[69]

The festival is also an occasion for political opportunism. Political patronage has always been a prominent aspect of Thaipusam at Batu Caves. Prior to *Merdeka*, a high colonial official would visit the caves on this day, and be received by executive members of the *devastanam*. This tradition is now continued by the Malaysian government, which in most years is represented by a prominent cabinet minister (occasionally by the deputy head of government). However, in recent years the prime minister

Najib Razak has been received as distinguished guest (the previous prime ministerial visit was that of Datuk Hussein Onn in 1978 — there was no such visit throughout the Mahathir era). The visit recognizes Hinduism as a component religion of Malaysian society, but also implicitly acknowledges the *devastanam* as the organizing authority of Thaipusam in Kuala Lumpur, and by extension the leading role taken by the *koyil* in the religious life of Malaysian Hindus. The prominence accorded to *devastanam* officials is also displayed in another very public way. This involves the bestowal of the garlands (*malais*) worn by the *utsava murthi* throughout the ritual period, together with the vestments which adorn the deity, upon the leading patrons. They are also given priority in receiving both *prasadam* and the water (*tirttam*) spiritualized by contact with the deity.

The temple management committee of the Sri Maha Mariamman Koyil Devastanam has traditionally used Thaipusam as a forum for aspiring politicians, especially those seeking a springboard to careers within the Malaysian Indian Congress (MIC), a component party of the ruling Barisan Nasional coalition.[70] The current chairman, Tan Sri Datuk R. Nadarajah, is closely associated with the MIC and more particularly with former leader Datuk S. Samy Vellu. The chairman of the *devastanam* is thus in a strong position to dispense patronage on Thaipusam day, and carefully selects those whom he invites to speak to the largest Indian audience in Malaysia, and those who are dubbed sufficiently important to sit with him in the front row of the upper-storey balcony of the *devastanam* headquarters. The intrusion of politics into Thaipusam, in particular the snubbing or suppression of influential Hindus whose views do not accord with MIC policies and priorities, has led to much criticism within the broader Hindu community.

The festival is also a magnet for wandering religious hucksters, many with bogus spiritual pedigrees, who appear on Thaipusam day to sell magical cures, miracle potions, charms and the dubious quality of their psychic insights.

At night, as the last kavadis are borne, elements of the crowd turn their attention to entertainment, in particular a sideshow alley which includes merry-go-rounds, mini Ferris wheels, and fun palaces. They also frequent the rows of stalls which are set up in selected areas within the compound. The stalls, in 1999 numbering 656,[71] are allocated by *devastanam* officials in accordance with the results of a lottery draw which also determines the actual physical location of each stall.[72] Many of these stalls have little connection with religious observance. Commercial operators seize the opportunity to retail a huge variety of (non-religious) items, including trinkets, gifts, popular CDs and DVDs, as well as the paraphernalia associated with the cult figures of Tamil cinema.[73] Stallholders who intend to supply free medical services, free food and drinks, and devotional services (including religious counselling) are usually provided with sites free of charge.[74]

The funfair and retail stalls have been the subject of increasing criticism within the broader Hindu community, which views the intrusion of marketplace moneymaking and the crass frivolity of a sideshow alley as debasing and detracting from the solemnity of the festival. Senior Hindus have long argued that stalls should be restricted to the provision of essential or welfare services or the retailing of religious items. In recent years the more generic stallholders have been permitted to trade for several days beyond Thaipusam, thus underscoring what many perceive as the increasing commercialization of Thaipusam and Batu Caves generally.[75]

The departure of the crowds at the conclusion of Day Two leaves as a residue piles of unsightly rubbish and pools of stagnant water, often openly attended by rats and other vermin. It usually takes cleaners a fortnight — sometimes longer — to restore the compound to its regular state. Over the years there has been sustained criticism of the lack of adequate facilities for garbage disposal, and the fact that food is more often than not distributed in environmentally unfriendly containers. In recent times volunteers have made sustained attempts to organize rubbish collections and to minimize wastage, which seems to be an inevitable concomitant of the charitable distribution of food and beverages.

Day Three of Thaipusam is devoted to the return journey of Murugan and his consorts to the Sri Maha Mariamman Koyil. In previous years the Golden *Vel* would be removed from the Temple Cave shrine between 8:00 and 9:00 a.m. and carried down the stairs and restored to the *utsava murthi* within the *Mandapam*. After a brief *puja*, Murugan and his consorts would be installed within the silver chariot. The chariot would then leave Batu Caves. Several thousand people would be present at this ceremony, and a comparatively small number of people would accompany the chariot on the initial phase of its return journey. Because of traffic restrictions, the procession would halt in the Sentul area, about five kilometres from the centre of Kuala Lumpur. (For many years Sentul was one of the most concentrated Indian suburbs in Kuala Lumpur, with a large working-class Tamil population historically associated with the nearby railway workshops and processing factories. In recent years Sentul has been extensively redeveloped, and the Indian nexus has largely disappeared.) The *utsava murthi* would be removed from the chariot and placed in a temporarily consecrated area on a nearby *padang* (field), where it would be guarded throughout the day by temple authorities and selected youth groups. Occasional visitors would pay homage and perform extemporized *pujas*. At 4:30 p.m. there would be further pujas and *archanai* to Murugan, and at 6:30 the *utsava murthi* would be reinstalled to recommence its journey to the Sri Maha Mariamman Koyil.

While the Golden *Vel* is still removed from the Temple Cave shrine between 8:00 and 9:00 a.m., it now remains with the *utsava murthi* in the *mandapam* throughout the day. At about 5:00 p.m., following *pujas* and *archarnai*, the *utsava murthi* is placed in the chariot, which begins its return journey to the Sri Maha Mariamman Kovil. Attendance swells as the procession gathers momentum. Crowd numbers are roughly equivalent to those which accompany the chariot on its outward journey. Released from the pressures imposed by rush-hour traffic, the civic authorities allow the chariot a more leisurely return, and stops are frequent. The atmosphere at night, with the illuminated chariot and the large crowd escorted by torch-bearing marshals, seems even more intense than that of the Day One departure. The chariot is preceded by religious groups performing *bhajans*, dancers, *kolattam* groups, and temple musicians. As the chariot makes its way back to Kuala Lumpur, there are usually several more cases of trances. Once again, security is provided by police and the Federal Reserve Unit.

As with the outward journey, the chariot makes numerous stops to allow devotees to pay homage to the deity. During these pauses considerable numbers of coconuts are smashed, fireworks are detonated and family groups offer trays and babies for blessing by the deity.

In previous years the chariot would reach the Kovil at about 1:00 a.m., but in the past few years the arrival time has been as late as 4:00 a.m. The *utsava murthi* of Murugan and his consorts are taken from the chariot and carried into the temples on long poles, an arrangement which reminds the observer of a palanquin. As the young men bearing the *utsava murthi* reach the inner temple, they stop, and for a few minutes walk on the spot with a stylized swaying motion. The general explanation is that when a god goes abroad he must be entertained with a dance, but in India informants advised that the action is a ritual closely associated with kingship, the bearers imitating the movement of an elephant, the traditional mount of royalty.

Murugan and his consorts are reinstalled within the temple with a series of welcoming rituals and *pujas*. The atmosphere within the temple is one of highly charged emotion, and there are several more cases of spontaneous trances. With the deity's return, the formal aspects of Thaipusam are now at an end.

The Kavadi Ritual

Undoubtedly one of the dominant motifs of Thaipusam in Malaysia, and that which invariably receives the greatest publicity, is the bearing of kavadis. In recent years there has been a huge increase in the number of devotees who undertake worship in this way. In 1978, when I first witnessed Thaipusam, press estimates placed the number of kavadi bearers at between 500 and 600,[76] but by 1997 the total exceeded 10,000 at Batu Caves, while over 50,000 devotees carried *paal kudam* (ritualized milk pots) to the shrine in the cave.[77] These numbers have been sustained over subsequent years.

As we noted in the previous chapter, kavadi bearing, and the asceticism which is a necessary concomitant of the ritual, are both justified and given shape by the *Puranic* mythology which describes Murugan's loss of the competition for the mango to his brother Ganesha, his subsequent renunciation of the world and his retreat to Palani, and his slaying and later restoration of the *asura*-turned-devotee Idumban. For the individual devotee the mythology suggests a model for ritual worship — temporary renunciation, the asceticism of pilgrimage, the catalytic experiences of trance and kavadi worship as a means for the relief of psychic burdens and the fruits of fresh discoveries resulting from an encounter with the deity, which can then be taken forward into post-Thaipusam mundane life.

To most Malaysian Hindus the word "kavadi" connotes "burden" (P.V. Jagadisa Ayyar suggests the word is a combination of *kavu* and *adi*, meaning "the vow made to walk the distance to the place of pilgrimage on foot").[78] At Batu Caves there is no single uniform style of kavadi; indeed, these may range in complexity from the basic and functional to those which are elaborate and highly ornate. However, there are several unifying motifs falling within the gamut of kavadi worship. Firstly, in bearing a kavadi, the devotee, in emulating Idumban, is submitting to the will of a specified deity (as will be discussed, not all kavadis in Malaysia are borne for Murugan). Secondly, the kavadi is perceived as a "shrine in miniature"[79] containing the god himself, so that the devotee may apprehend himself/herself in the manner of a *vahana* (mount) whom the deity actually "fills" or "embraces" during the period of trance, and whom the votary will thus symbolically bear to the shrine within the caves. Thirdly, devotees will carry a gift of milk to be presented to Murugan and which upon the completion of the kavadi ritual will be poured over the *murthi* within the cave. A popularly accepted explanation for this latter requirement is that milk, a sacred product of Mother Cow (*Ma*), symbolizes fertility, purity and prosperity.[80] More detailed explanations will be considered in Chapter 8.

The simplest kavadi is undoubtedly the *paal* (milk) kavadi. This consists of a small wooden pole surmounted by an arch. The kavadi may be decorated with peacock feathers, margosa leaves, flowers and other materials. This type of kavadi is the norm among members of the Penang Chettiar community, and is often recommended as the "approved model" by senior Malaysian Hindus. This was also the type of kavadi carried by the Brahman group with which I undertook a *pada yatra* (foot pilgrimage) in India in 1998 (see Chapter 7).

The most luxuriant kavadis are the *aluga* (beautiful) kavadis (also known at Batu Caves as *mayil*, or peacock kavadis). The central feature of the *aluga* kavadi is a platform on which the *murthi* of the deity is placed. A series of arches are connected to the platform, all of which may be decorated with ribbons, flowers and peacock feathers. The deity may be shaded by an umbrella. The shrine is fixed above the devotee's body by means of an aluminium framework which is secured to a metal belt which extends around the waist. Shoulder pads cushion the (sometimes considerable) weight of the kavadi, and foam padding is placed under the belt. The kavadi is further adorned by a series of light chains or fine rods, numbering up to 108,[81] which are attached to the torso by small hooks (shaped like fish hooks, but without the barb).[82]

A frequently encountered kavadi is the *vel* kavadi, lengthy spears with a lance head at one end, a lime at the other. These are pushed through the cheeks.[83] During the 1970s and early 1980s there was a tendency for *vel* kavadis to become longer by the year, until many exceeded five metres. Temple authorities considered these elongated spears dangerous to devotees, their supporters and onlookers, and the product of vanity and braggadocio rather than of genuine spirituality. Restrictions on the size of *vel* kavadis were imposed in the mid-1980s.

Among the other forms of kavadi commonly found at Batu Caves are the *puspha* kavadi, made of flowers, and the *karumbu* kavadi, a simple burden of sugar cane, carried by couples who have recently been granted a child, usually after a long period of barrenness, and in response to prayers and supplications. The baby is carefully secured in a sling of yellow cloth which is hung from the sugar cane. The husband bears the front of the cane, the wife the back.

Some devotees shoot paper arrows. Various explanations are offered for this, including (i) that votaries identify themselves with Idumban, who prior to his resuscitation and transformation was well versed in archery; (ii) that this represents an increasing emphasis among Malaysian devotees upon the military aspects of Murugan's powers;[84] or that worshippers are shooting *vels*.[85] (This latter interpretation was not supported by the devotees whom I interviewed. One pointed out that this would be dangerous as it would seem to presume upon the power which was exclusively Murugan's domain.) However, it is generally understood that *Kama*, the God of Love, is associated with flower arrows,[86] and who, as we have seen in the previous chapter, is restored to life when Siva agrees to assist the *devas*, thus foreshadowing the processes associated with cosmic renewal, including creation and fertility. Kama's other attributive symbol is the sugar cane, which has obvious implications for the *karumbu* kavadi described in the previous paragraph.[87]

A handful of generally older devotees walk on stilts. Others abase themselves by rolling the distance to the foot of the stairs leading to the Temple Cave. However, these latter forms of worship have become increasingly rare at Batu Caves over the past twenty years.

As mentioned, not all kavadis are borne for Murugan. Indeed, a whole collocation of deities are informally acknowledged at Thaipusam. Kavadis are carried in honour of other Saivite deities (Ganapati, Parvati, Siva), Vaishnavite deities (principally Krishna, Rama and Hanuman), village and guardian deities such as Muneeswaran, Muniandy, Madurai Viran, Aiyannar, Kaliamman, and Durga, and even lesser spirits. One deity who has in recent years gained prominence among Malaysian Hindus is Ayappan.[88] The honouring of "little" deities and spirits has elicted criticism from some Hindus who observe or claim to observe

Agamic traditions, but in general these idiosyncrasies are tolerated, albeit under sufferance.

There is a range of other, barely tolerated kavadis. The most frowned upon kavadis are those of devotees who engage in modes of worship aimed at the supplication of "village" or "little" deities. Overwhelmingly these devotees are young, male and of working-class or estate background. Until the practice was banned at Batu Caves, devotees who were possessed by the village deity *Madurai Viran* were often borne standing on sharp *parangs* (large bladed knives, often shaped like oversized cutlasses). Supporters held the *parangs* at each end and the devotee, who engaged in bouts of ritual "marching" on the upturned blades, balanced himself by placing his outstretched arms on his supporters' shoulders. Very occasionally these devotees "wore" daggers, which were passed through the upper arms. *Muneeswaran*- and *Muniandy*-possessed devotees may pull *ter* kavadis, that is, wooden chariots, which are drawn by means of ropes attached to large hooks which are pressed into their backs (often these are symbolic chariots which are "anchored" by a friend who walks behind and exerts sufficient pressure to keep the ropes taut so that the devotee is still conveying an actual "burden").[89] Because of logistical difficulties in ascending the cave steps, some of these devotees will terminate their pilgrimage at the downstairs Swami Mandipam. Usually, Muneeswaran/ Muniandy devotees wear brightly coloured turbans, will smoke cheroots (cigars), speak in harsh, rasping voices, and some will drink beer, and twirl ropes with which they occasionally whip themselves. Vineeta Sinha points out that Muneeswaran, when seen as "fierce, aggressive and dynamic",[90] has an especial appeal to certain young males who are often perceived by other Hindus as "boisterous, dramatic and superficial in their devotions".[91] These devotees are often viewed unfavourably and their actions and general demeanor are seen as discrediting the festival and more generally Hinduism itself.[92] Votaries who bear kavadis for *Kali* or *Durga* (in their destructive "village" manifestations) will often cut their tongues to produce the obligatory mouthful of blood consistent with popular iconic representations.

In the 1980s, under considerable pressure from reformist Hindus, temple authorities introduced restrictions on all these forms of worship within the Temple Cave, though devotees were permitted to proceed to the foot of the stairs. In practice, for several years little was done to stop these pilgrims from making their way to the main shrine. In 1995, however, the chairman of the *devastanam* banned whips, *parangs*, spears of greater than one metre length and the placing of *kumkum* (red powder) on the tongue (to produce the symbolic bloodiness of a meat-eating goddess), claiming that these were antithetical to the true spirit of Thaipusam.[93]

Condemnation has also been directed against those who are regarded as overtly exhibitionist or frivolous in their modes of worship. Thus, for example, in 2009 two young Penang men who carried kavadis decorated in the respective colours of, and featuring the logos of, the Liverpool and Manchester United soccer clubs, created a storm of outrage. Both were all but universally condemned for traducing the spirituality of the festival and for making a mockery of Thaipusam.[94]

In 2014 the Malaysian Hindu Sangam issued a pamphlet, *Thaipusam Festival Guide for Hindu Temple* [sic] *and Devotees*, which outlined both acceptable and non-acceptable modes of worship. Practices designated as objectionable included "flying" and *ter* (chariot) kavadis; kavadis which incorporated non-religious motifs or which were "decorated horribly"; devotees bearing swords, tridents or whips, or consuming cheroots or alcohol; dressing as Muneeswaran, Madurai Viran, Kali or Katteri; applying kumkum powder to the tongue; and the singing of rap or cinema music. Moreover, the pamphlet also stipulated that those smashing coconuts should "break only a small number of coconuts". The *sangam* indicated that those who followed proscribed practices would not be permitted to fulfil their vows.[95]

This pamphlet was issued without consultation with the Sri Maha Mariamman Devastanam, which is responsible for the organization and management of Thaipusam at Batu Caves. Thus, in attempting to assume a regulatory role, the *sangam* was clearly exceeding its authority. In response, Tan Sri Datuk Nadarajah, *devastanam* chairman, reminded the *sangam* that his organization planned and oversaw the festival. He also pointed out that practices which had been tolerated for decades could not be eliminated overnight, and that education of devotees would produce more favourable long-term outcomes than outright prohibition. Many devotees claimed that in attempting to ban certain forms of kavadis and the worship of "lesser" deities, the *sangam* was actively discriminating against participants of a working-class background. Moreover, it was argued that both "flying" and "chariot" kavadis were well accepted in India and Sri Lanka as legitimate expressions of worship, and that as Muneeswaran was identified as a form of Siva, father of Murugan, the *sangam*'s strictures revealed a gap in its spiritual knowledge. Devotees also complained that strictures on the smashing of coconuts represented a fundamental misunderstanding of the nature of vow fulfilment and the sacred contract negotiated between devotee and deity.

This spiritual eclectism displayed at Thaipusam reflects important processes under way in the formulation of a distinctive Malaysian Hindu tradition. These include syncretization, in particular "Sanskritization/ *Agamicization*" and "Tamilization" (both discussed in Chapter 4). It should be noted that homage to "foreign" or "lesser" deities is nearly always permeated with the rituals, and falls within the received framework of the established paradigms of the Murugan kavadi ritual.[96]

Most kavadi bearers also take to miniature *vels*, about skewer length, one of which is pushed through the tongue, the other through the cheeks. This indicates, firstly, that the pilgrim has temporarily renounced the gift of speech, taking a vow of silence (*mauna*)[97] for the duration of the bearing of the kavadi (the vow of silence is a common feature of pan-Hindu asceticism, and will be discussed more fully in Chapter 8), so that he/she may concentrate more fully upon Murugan (or another selected deity), and secondly that the devotee has passed wholly under the protection of the deity (or Idumban as gatekeeper to Murugan), who will not allow him/her to shed blood or suffer pain. By permitting the *vel* to pierce the flesh, the aspirant is also signifying the transience of the physical body as opposed to the enduring power of truth.

The individual decision to bear a kavadi may be prompted by a number of considerations, including penance, spiritual unfoldment, overcoming unfavourable *karma*, or all of these, but in most cases it is taken to honour a vow. Stereotypically, those fulfilling a vow have entered a reciprocal contract with Murugan, a sort of "cosmic bargaining", as it were, in which they have agreed to bear a kavadi if a certain request is fulfilled (for example, recovery from illness, the conception and successful delivery of a child, reconciliation within a family). Vows may be taken for periods of one, three, or five years, or for life, though a three-year vow appears to be the most common. The factors which influence an individual to take a vow are highly varied, and many spring from personal circumstances, or those of a member of an immediate family (for example, it is not uncommon for a votary to bear a kavadi for a sick relative, especially one who is permanently incapacitated or is suffering a terminal illness). Often those who take kavadis are inspired by spirit mediums who advise them of psychic or spiritual misfortunes, contracted in this or past lives, which have cast a blight upon them personally, or upon their families.

At Batu Caves, kavadi bearers are drawn from the entire spectrum of Malaysian Hindu society. Indeed my own fieldwork corroborates the observation made by Ervin et al., who indicated that the subjects of their study "ranged in age from 12 to over 50 and were equally divided as to sex. They came from all socio-economic levels, and educational backgrounds, and included unemployed youths, college students, labourers and businessmen."[98] Thaipusam, ostensibly a Tamil festival, now draws Hindus from every regional background, as well as Sikhs, members of Malaysia's miniscule Sinhalese community, and Chinese devotees.[99]

Those who would bear a kavadi must enter what is in effect a period of renunciation and asceticism, several weeks of ritual purification which will prepare them for their encounter with the deity. This involves cessation of many daily activities as well as adherence to certain disciplines. Collectively, these observances place the devotee outside the normative boundaries of life as a *grihastya* (householder), and temporarily into the category of *sannyasin*. We should note in passing that these restrictions and disciplines in effect signify removal from mundane time and space and are preparatory for the *tirtha yatra* (literally "ford" or "crossing place"; more esoterically, a journey to the metaphysical "centre"),[100] and are consistent with the broader patterns of pan-Hindu pilgrimage paradigms. This issue will be discussed in Chapter 8.

Purification observations include fasting (a vegetarian diet, excluding eggs, and preferably restricted to one meal each day), eating and drinking from utensils reserved for their specific use (and including cups and plates), refraining from tobacco, liquor and stimulating drinks (some devotees extend this to include cola and caffeine-based beverages), abjuring sexual relations and contact with menstruating women, sleeping on the floor in a ritually clean environment on a cloth of yellow or white, ceasing cutting of hair or shaving, maintaining calm and equanimity in everyday dealings, in particular eschewing lying, cheating, using foul or abusive language, or quarrelling, especially in the face of provocation. At the commencement of their fasts, most devotees will place a string of sacred beads around their necks. These beads will be used in devotions involving chanting or recitation (*japa*). Generally the beads are *rudraksha* seeds, taken from the Blue Marble Tree (*Eleo Carpus Ganitrus*), which is regarded as sacred by Saivites, but beads made of other substances — *tulasi* (basil) or sandalwood seeds or clear crystals — are also permitted. The devotee should not be tarnished with the pollution of recent birth or death within the family (in the case of the death of an immediate relative, pollution is held to last for a period of twelve months). In theory the devotee should wake each morning at 5:00 a.m., break his/her fast with a drink of water or milk containing *tulasi* (basil) leaves, a plant considered sacred, and frequently used in ritual offerings,[101] and having bathed in cold water, should pray, recite mantras, and meditate. He/she should also pray three times a day. However, the exigencies of modern life militate against strict observance of this latter requirement, and most devotees perform their private meditations as and when they can. Ideally, these purificatory rites should extend over forty-eight days, but many devotees observe lesser periods, and experienced participants may fast for as little as seven days. Most aspirants will follow the guidance of a spiritual director, usually an older male. Prior to Thaipusam some devotees may move into a temple or another acknowledged holy place for the final few days of their fast.

The ability to enter trance, and more particularly to acquire the specialized trance (*arul*) which denotes the presence of Murugan, requires both training and habituation.[102] Many intending kavadi bearers attend what is known as a trial trance. Trial trance, sometimes known as trance training, is usually conducted in a single session, but sometimes over a number of sessions, within the small suburban or village and estate temples. These sessions are often directed by the resident *pantaram* or *pujari* (a non-Brahman temple priest), with the assistance of other recognized local spiritual leaders. Trial trance has several intertwined aims. Firstly, it allows the leader to assess the progress of the individual devotees, and to encourage those who have made little or minimal headway, secondly to identify and if possible modify idiosyncratic trance behaviour (if necessary, to decide upon strategies to contain devotees whose trance states are likely to create problems at Thaipusam), and thirdly, to teach devotees the art of achieving and sustaining trance, especially in the face of the distractions they will experience on Thaipusam day when the trance state and bodily piercing which follow must be undertaken in the full — and for some, perhaps intimidating — glare of public scrutiny.

The *pujari*/spiritual leader (hereafter referred to generically as the *leader*) assembles the group for which he (or occasionally she) will be responsible up to a week prior to Thaipusam, when it may be expected that most devotees will have been fasting for at least two to three weeks.

The group, which may number as many as thirty people, will include experienced kavadi bearers as well as several complete beginners. The leader will commence the session with the obligatory invocation to Ganesha, who, as Ruler of Obstacles and Lord of Beginnings, fulfils the liminal role of mediator between the material and divine worlds, and without whose permission and blessing, no undertaking, whether minor or major, can hope to succeed.[103] Supplications to Murugan and/or other deities follow. The leader may speak to the group, emphasizing the special bonds that exist between them, the sanctity of their vow, and the need for cooperation and support at all times. He will then signal to the musicians, generally drummers, singers and individuals playing hand cymbals (*jalrah*). These will perform a selection of kavadi songs, alternating the pace and rhythm according to the instructions of the leader. Devotees generally stand with eyes closed, concentrating in an attitude of reverential prayer. The leader will gesture an experienced member of the group to the front, gently rock him/her back and forth, hand held firmly on the devotee's head, until trance is achieved (sometimes within as little as five to ten seconds). He will then summon other members of the group, one by one. Each member will supplicate to the leader by touching his/her hands on the leader's feet. Sometimes group members achieve spontaneous trances and have no needs of the ministrations of the leader. Others, especially novices, may experience real difficulty in attaining trance, and may require the special and sometimes prolonged attention of the leader and his assistants. This may include concentrated chanting at the devotee, increasing the volume, tempo and proximity of the drumming, touching the head with a *vel*, cutting a lime above the devotee's head (the latter measure is designed to remove impurities and/or negate the influence of malign spirits), or placing the novice alongside an experienced and already entranced devotee (generally one of mature years and of composed or at least equable disposition). Very occasionally a novice is unable to achieve any trance at all, despite the vigorous efforts of the leader and his assistants. Failure to reach trance may elicit social disapproval by implying that the devotee is unworthy to participate in this form of worship, but this assumption is by no means axiomatic. Often it is attributed to a lack of readiness for this level of spiritual commitment, or is taken as an indication that he/she is meant to pursue other avenues of spiritual unfoldment. Very rarely the leader will comprehensively rebuke a person whom he regards as "bluffing" or "playing the fool", and will accuse him/her of failing to observe all the requirements of fasting, or behaving as a fraud or "time waster" (i.e., someone who had no real intention of fulfilling a vow).

The leader identifies individual quirks and the peculiarities of any given devotee's trance states, and may work to modify his/her behaviour prior to Thaipusam. Simon et al. document one such example:

> On three different occasions, adolescent girls used the trance dance as the time out from ordinary social expectations to play out a kind of family psychodrama: they behaved like obstreperous adolescents *vis-à-vis* their guru "father". One was a 20 year old, who, during the first training sessions, swept into the centre of the room, wearing a defiant expression, posturing, demanding the guru's attention, pulling at the hair and shoulders of other devotees who were having difficulty entering trance, and generally making a nuisance of herself. A number of times the guru entered the shrine and returned with a *vel* which he offered to push into her tongue. Each time she indicated "not ready". Once he brought out a long steel pole of the type to be used to pierce the cheeks and once a whip. He appeared to be threatening to bring her into line. As the nights of trance training proceeded, this girl became less and less obstreperous, until by Thaipusam day her trance was calm, controlled and orderly.[104]

The range of trance states varies considerably. Some devotees are gripped by possession trances,[105] usually involving wild and sometimes aggressive dancing. Other possession states present in stylized iconic movements, while others dance gently, arms outstretched, smiling serenely. The leader moves through the group, quiet, dignified, impressive, in control (though not always; occasionally he or one of his assistants is overtaken by a spontaneous trance). When he judges that an individual devotee has been in trance for a sufficient period (generally anywhere between two to fifteen minutes), he terminates the state with a firm application of *vibhuti* to the forehead over the pineal gland (site of the "third" or inner eye). With more intractable cases he may accompany this by blowing on the devotee's head. This measure is also taken to control the inevitable outbreaks of spontaneous trances among some of the onlookers. (Unauthorized trance states may denote investment by lesser deities and even spirits, and are supressed as soon as they arise.) Generally the devotee brought out of trance will slump, his/her knees will buckle, and he/she may be assisted to sit down for a period of recuperation. Often he/she will be offered drinks (usually water, sometimes the water of a tender coconut), and his/her legs will be massaged to prevent cramping. Frequently, after a few minutes the devotee will re-enter trance, and the leader or one of his assistants will once again be required to apply *vibhuti*. Some individuals may enter trance four or five times, and the exasperated leader may banish him/her to the corner of the temple, where he/she is theoretically out of harm's way.

The training prepares the devotee for managing, sustaining, and varying trance behaviour over extended periods. These skills will be necessary on Thaipusam days when significant demands will be made on the votary, including the necessity of attaining trance in a crowded public environment and in the presence of curious onlookers, subsequently remaining still for the time required for the insertion of *vels* and the fitting of the kavadi, as well as exercising control during the inevitable delays en route to the caves. Trance training also promotes devotee awareness of external cues such as signals and directions from his/her supporting retinue.[106]

Several days prior to Thaipusam, many groups will hold a special puja for *Sakti*, often specifically identified as Parvati, but sometimes as Maha Mariamman, as mother of Murugan, acknowledging her role as bestower of the *Vel*.

On Thaipusam eve, aspirants gather at prearranged sites, either at one of the temples within the nearby Indian settlement, or at designated meeting places on the lawns within the Batu Caves compound, or along the riverbank adjacent to the caves complex. Devotees will generally be dressed in yellow clothes with red edgings (both colours traditionally associated with Murugan),[107] shorts or *vesthis* for men, saris or "Punjabi" suits (consisting of a loose *baju* [shirt] and slacks) for women. On Thaipusam day, devotees will also wear anklets which jingle rhythmically as they dance, and some will attach small bells to their kavadis and belts.

Over the next few hours, in an atmosphere increasingly charged with anticipation and exhilaration (perhaps tempered in the case of novices with an all too tangible foreboding), devotees will complete a final set of purification rites. These will include some or all of the following. Firstly, a propitiatory *puja* to Ganesha will be offered (this itself may incorporate a cluster of elaborate observances, but usually consists of an invocation followed by a call for the blessing of the enterprise). Next there is a prolonged *arati* (showing of camphor flame) to all deities present. The flame is subsequently offered to all devotees and to onlookers. Each devotee is then asked to stand next to a coconut, upon which a block of camphor is placed. When this is lit, the devotee carries the coconut and burning camphor to the leader, who smashes it violently upon a strategically located rock. This action is held to symbolize the fiery cleansing of impurities (burning camphor) and the fracturing of the hard shell of the ego (*anava*) to realize the sweetness of inner truth. Success is indicated when the coconut breaks into three or more pieces. A series of *bhajans* (devotional hymns, generally with a call and response refrain) are then sung, and if the group boasts the services of an accomplished singer, he/she may be called upon to render several songs drawn from the highly specialized and musically intricate Murugan repertoire. Later there may be a final trial trance. After this the devotees are summoned one by one to the group leader. He/she is then asked if he/she realizes the full significance of the vow that has been taken, that a turmeric coloured thread is about to be tied round his/her right wrist, and that from that time onwards he/she will not be permitted to leave the temple or designated sacred area until he/she is fitted with the kavadi. (This period may be a matter of minutes or hours, depending upon the circumstances.) The thread is then tied. The devotee may be subsequently fed a handful of chickpeas and saffron rice cooked in the temple, offered to the deities and distributed as *prasadam*.

In many of these groups, some of these preliminary rites may be fulfilled either at the home shrine or in the local temple prior to the journey to Batu Caves. Other groups bypass most of these rites and observe only the propitiatory *puja* and the thread tying.

In the meantime there are occasional disturbances among the onlookers, mainly in the form of spontaneous trance states, sometimes of a superficially alarming nature. These are often heralded with screams, shouts or wild and extravagant dancing. Tamil Hindus recognize and categorize a wide array of trance states, but only one — *arul*, betokening the grace of the deity — is sought and desired throughout Thaipusam. Spontaneous trance states which grip individuals who have neither fasted nor undertaken the elaborate purification rituals or the requisite trance training may represent the unwanted intrusion of disruptive lower deities, or even malign spirits, and are therefore usually quelled at the earliest opportunity.[108]

Immediately prior to the final set of pre-kavadi rituals, the aspirant takes a ceremonial purifying bath. Ideally this will involve immersion in a river, or, if this is not possible, dousing in water taken from a river. Puranic mythology deems rivers among the holiest of places, and bathing within them is regarded as spiritually purifying.[109] In addition, bathing in water deemed sacred celebrates and to some extent re-enacts the birth of

Murugan.[110] However, the Sungai Batu has been declared too polluted for general use, and participants who have gathered along the riverbank will use the specially constructed bathing facilities. Bathing is done while fully clothed. The devotee takes at least three full buckets/dippers of running water and tips these over the crown of the head. Devotees universally report that the water seems abnormally cold, and most manifest this with bouts of shivering, gasping and spluttering. The participant is then daubed with the standard Saivite markings of *vibhuti*.

In the meantime, kavadis are set up in an altar-like arrangement on the ground. Banana leaves are placed in front of the kavadis, and fruit, including limes, coconut, betel leaves and nuts, as well as incense and camphor, are carefully arrayed along the leaves. A sacred fire consisting of selected woods and camphor is lit, and the pungent yet fragrant smoke is used to purify the milk pots which are fixed to the kavadis. This is accomplished by passing the milkpots over the fire, after which they are filled with milk (with painstaking attention paid to purity). The pots are then sealed with yellow cloth, which is passed over the mouth of the vessel and secured around the rim. The final *puja* follows. The incense is lit, the limes cut, and the religious leader lights the camphor on a tray and performs an *arati* to the kavadi. This is now fully sanctified as a shrine. At this point, and this point only, are both devotee and kavadi considered fully prepared for the journey to the shrine within the Temple Cave.

The devotee is then put into a trance. He/she concentrates on the deity while those gathered round chant *"Vel! Vel!"* ("Spear! Spear!"), *"Vetrivel!"* ("The Cosmic/Victorious Spear") or *"Haro Hara"* ("Praise to the Lord"), all chants pertinent to the worship of Murugan.[111] Further stimulation may be provided through music, especially drumming, and incense may be waved in the devotee's face. The onset of the trance state (*arul*) is obvious to all bystanders, and is marked with a host of visible bodily signals, which may include trembling, exaggerated facial contortions, flickering eyes, buckling at the knees, etc. It is at this point that the kavadi is fitted and the *vels* inserted, often accompanied by shouted invocations to Idumban, servant to Murugan, to remove the pain that the aspirant might otherwise be expected to withstand.[112]

The leader works quickly, inserting the first *vel* through the cheeks, initially pinching the skin at the point of entry (normally about twenty-five to thirty millimetres back from the corner of the lips), then pushing the *vel* through the flesh, guiding it with his fingers to the opposite cheek, pinching the inner skin before pushing it to the outer cheek. The pinching is believed to make the skin more malleable. Normally fifty to seventy-five millimetres of the *vel* extrudes from each side of the face. (A similar process is followed with the large *vel* kavadis, except that a banana is used to lubricate the spears, and up to a metre of the rod extrudes from each side.) The leader then asks the devotee to show his/her tongue. He guides the second *vel* carefully and deliberately through the fleshy part of the tongue about twenty-five to forty millimetres from its tip. He then applies *vibhuti* to the tongue. As the insertions are performed the leader's assistants and the aspirant's supporters gather round him/her and chant loudly and close to the devotee's ears. This entire operation is usually accomplished within ninety seconds. If the devotee is to bear an *aluga* kavadi, he/she will now be invited to step inside the framework. The metal belt is secured over the foam padding worn as a protective girdle by the devotee; the kavadi, which may weigh between twelve to thirty-five kilograms, is checked and adjusted to ensure the even distribution of weight upon the devotee's shoulders (small foam pads will be placed under points of contact on the shoulders to prevent rubbing of the metal frame on the exposed skin), and the hooks, numbering up to 108, are inserted into the torso. More inventive *pujaris* and their assistants will organize the hooks to form a pattern upon the torso, but this is not considered essential. Once again the process is undertaken quickly and efficiently. The leader dusts the torso with *vibhuti*. The devotee will then be requested to stand up and move the kavadi about. This is to allow the leader to check that all hooks are firmly in place, and that there thus can be no danger to the devotee's retinue or members of the public from flying or unsecured hooks. It will be seen from this account that the trance state is not so intense or all-encompassing as to preclude communication, in particular the ability to respond to instructions and requests for basic information.

The achievement of an appropriate trance (*arul*) is the fulcrum upon which the entire pilgrimage revolves. The entire period of fasting and the associated *tapas* and other disciplines have been designed to prepare the devotee psychically and spiritually for this "moment of truth", where he/she is able to prove himself/herself worthy of receiving Divine Grace (*arul*), which will allow him/her to bear the kavadi in a sanctified state.

Inevitably one or two devotees fail to achieve trance. These aspirants are usually spared any insertions, and are presented with *paal* kavadis and instructed to proceed to Temple Cave. Occasionally, the moment of presentation provokes the hitherto unattainable trance state.

As with trial trance/trance training, disassociation states among participants vary extensively, ranging from mild trance states to full-blown possession. Ervin et al. claim that the trance is typically followed by amnesia.[113] This is not the experience of the overwhelming majority of kavadi bearers with whom I have been associated and others whom I have interviewed. In most cases the violence of the initial trance state recedes and is replaced by a condition the devotee reports as a form of "supercharged" awareness — "operating at a higher level" is a frequent comment. In this state the devotee is cognizant of all that is happening around him/her and is able to respond positively to practical directions given by the retinue escorting him/her, but feels himself/herself to be functioning at a heightened level of awareness removed from mundane consciousness. This has also been my own experience. The issue of trance will be discussed more fully in Chapter 8.

The kavadi having been fitted, devotees set off to their destination surrounded by an escorting group who urge the devotee on with chanting, and ideally either the renditions of a recognized corpus of kavadi songs known as *kavadi-c-cindu*,[114] or from the book of hymns known as *Tiruppukal*. (Although it is officially frowned upon, many groups chant devotional lyrics, often extemporized, to secular music, usually popular songs taken from Tamil cinema.) The kavadi bearer may be accompanied by a hired musical group, either temple musicians, or more frequently bands of part-time musicians consisting of drummers, percussive instrumentalists and a vocalist. These vary in quality, from the accomplished to the decidedly amateur. The bearer's supportive group forms a protective ring around the kavadi worshipper. Members of the accompanying group will carry drinking water and a stool upon which the devotee is seated at regular intervals while his/her legs are massaged to prevent cramping. Frequently the organized groups of kavadi bearers will set off together. Along the route the devotee will engage in a ritualized dance known colloquially as the "kavadi" dance, based upon the *asura* Idumban's swaying movements as he bore the hills, which were to become the future abode of Murugan, slung on a pole.[115] Lakshmanan claims that the kavadi dance "when performed with vigour and quick movements produces in spectators a feeling of exultation and a temptation to keep in step with the rhythm and the dance".[116] The kavadi dance also reflects the long history of the dance as an integral form of Murugan worship and his role as Lord of the Dance.[117] Many devotees twirl their kavadis in athletic and awe inspiring displays. As Babb comments, "The springy arches of the aluminium kavadis make a splendid sight as they leap up and down in time with the bearer's movements."[118]

During the 1980s, senior Hindus expressed anxiety about the intrusion of non-*Agamic* music and dancing at Thaipusam. One of their particular targets was the use of so-called "bongo" drums, played mainly by working-class/estate youths. These are long tapered metal drums, capped with goatskins. The drums are beaten with sticks, both on the skin and along the side, sometimes by as many as three youths acting in concert, who often produce rhythms of extraordinary complexity. In recent years claims were made that the drums were not of Indian origin, and thus alien to Hindu worship. However, my fieldwork indicates that this is incorrect. Both oral testimony and pictorial records reveal that these drums were long associated with Thaipusam, both at Batu Caves and in Penang.[119] Moreover, the drums are known in Tamil Nadu, where they are played by members of the *Paraiyar* caste (an *Adi Dravida* caste),[120] and used in exorcism and certain types of funerary rites. It can be assumed, therefore, that the decision to ban these drums (and drummers) was based on issues of caste rather than music. Commentators have informed me that the arbitrary and preemptory ban excluded the active participation in Thaipusam of literally hundreds of young men, in the process transforming them into often resentful, and sometimes restive, spectators.

Unwelcome innovations have included the use of whistles to regulate dancing, the singing of film and popular songs, and the performance of disco, rap or breakdancing. Measures have been taken to restrict or ban these adjuncts, which are viewed as unseemly and detrimental to the integrity of the festival.

While devotees may commence bearing kavadis from midnight onwards, the vast majority of kavadis are borne between 7:00 a.m. and 1:00 p.m. Raymond Lee contends that the period between 11:00 a.m. and 1:00 p.m. is regarded as especially auspicious because the sun is at its highest and the penitent not only gains additional merit from enduring the increased heat of the sun but also enjoys the opportunity to perform sun worship.[121] I have not encountered this explanation, at least not in this form. However, in more arcane forms of Tamil Hinduism, the sun god *Surya* is recognized as *Aditya*, the leader of the *devas*, as *Divakara*

("He who brings dawn") and as *Baskaran* ("He who creates light") and as a central figure among the *Navagrahas*,[122] while in some *Puranas*, Murugan is compared to Surya at dawn, "arising in the midst of red clouds".[123] The most common response is that the gathering day symbolically parallels the growth to maturity of Murugan's powers, and thus represents the most propitious time to complete vows to this deity during Thaipusam. This latter view is consistent with the established chronometry of South Indian Hinduism.[124]

The devotees make their way, often through considerable congestion, from the riverbank across the recently elevated roadway which passes over the river and railway lines, rejoining Jalan Batu Caves near the roadway leading to the caves. (Prior to the construction of the roadway, devotees walked across the Jalan Batu Caves bridge to the gateway. Occasionally, all kavadi traffic would be halted by the arrival or departure of passenger trains, special services which run throughout the festival period.) Once the devotees enter the caves precincts they are guided into a roped-off lane which is theoretically reserved for the exclusive use of kavadi bearers and their supporters, and allows free access to the cave steps. The laneway is often clogged with kavadis, and progress may be slow. Stimulation for the spectator at this point may be intense to the point of overwhelming; an auditory overload consisting of hundreds of drums, *nadaswaram*, chanting, the blare of commercially recorded kavadi songs pumped out at full volume through several public address systems, the incomprehensible drone of official speakers (seated on an official dais above the approach to the cave steps), the press of the crowd, the colour and movement of many kavadis, the gathering heat and the swirling dust stirred by thousands of feet.

Some supporting retinues may carry limes, which at certain points along the route are cut into four and thrown in different directions. This action is performed to propitiate malevolent beings which may be encountered at certain localities and which may hinder the kavadi bearer's progress.

Nearly all interviewees report that once they reach the foot of the 272 steps leading to the Temple Cave, they feel a sense of "urgency", a "pull" towards the shrine which invigorates their dancing. This "pull" escalates as they ascend the steps, enter the cave and progress towards the main shrine.

Conditions within the Temple Cave, large as it is, are usually even more chaotic than those prevailing immediately downstairs. The cave is densely thronged with visitors, and the steps leading from the cave to the hollow are packed with onlookers who have taken the best vantage points for viewing the arrival of the kavadi bearers. The flights of stairs leading to the shrine are often wet and slippery, and the kavadi worshippers and their entourages must exercise considerable care in descending. The natural half-light of the cave is further dimmed with the combined impact of camphor smoke,[125] incense and dust. At night, coloured lights throw a patchy illumination. The cave resonates with the echoes of chanting and of stamping feet. Recent improvements to drainage within the caves ensures that the cave floor immediately adjacent to the shrine is now largely free of the souring milk, which prior to remedial work in 1999–2000 used to pond until it was ankle deep. The line of beggars who used to gather along the west wall of the cave to ply their trade are no longer in evidence, and although peripatetic mendicants continue to mingle with the crowd, their numbers are considerably reduced.

As the devotee reaches the area immediately outside the railing of the main shrine, he/she supplicates to the *murthi* within. Many, overcome by emotion, weep openly. The milk, borne in the pot slung from the kavadi, is passed to one of the *pantarams* working within the shrine,[126] and poured over the Golden *Vel*. The spiritual leader of the group, or one of his delegated assistants, who has accompanied the party of kavadi bearers to the cave, sits the devotee on a stool, removes the hooks from his/her body, dusts his/her torso with *vibhuti*, and assists him/her from the kavadi. This is then entrusted to a volunteer (recruited by the bearer), who will convey the kavadi either back to the point of origin, or to a designated storage area.[127] Having extricated the devotee from the kavadi, the leader or assistant then removes the miniature *vels* from the tongue and cheeks (some devotees report a minor "burning" sensation, not amounting to pain or discomfort, as the *vel* is taken from the tongue), and applies *vibhuti* to the points of penetration within the mouth. The devotee is then brought out of the trance state. Occasionally, stubborn cases are offered limes to chew; this is thought to assist in terminating any residual vestiges of trance.

The reaction of the devotees to the cessation of trance is mixed. Some stagger, near to collapse, exhausted by the enormous expenditure of physical and psychic energy, and need the immediate support of members of their retinue. A few seem dazed and disoriented and may require additional applications of *vibhuti* to discontinue persistent symptoms of disassociation. Others seem overcome by their experience, and walk away from the shrine (or shuffle, as the pressing crowd allows little free movement) in a state which they later describe in terms of retrospective amazement and awe. Nearly all devotees return to the point of origin or an agreed meeting place for a vegetarian meal.

In 2014 new arrangements were made for the reception of kavadis at the main shrine, with separate entrances for devotees bearing *paal kudam, pal* kavadis and *mayil/aluga* and other large kavadis. This was introduced with the aim of reducing waiting times and hence congestion near the shrine. Instead, this innovation had the reverse effect and resulted in dangerous levels of crowding in the immediate vicinity of the shrine, and a severe crush among devotees and observers exiting the cave.

On the third day after bearing a kavadi, the devote attends an Idumban *puja*, known colloquially (in English) as the "breaking of fast" ceremony. The ritual formally concludes the period of temporary renunciation/ asceticism entered into by the devotee. A special offering is made to Idumban, which normally includes a number of food items — cooked chicken (sometimes sacrificed in a temple or home-based ritual by male devotees, very rarely is this done by females; the sacrifice of animals by women is generally frowned upon),[128] fruit, eggs and sweets, as well as liquor and cheroots. These are laid on a banana leaf on a makeshift altar, generally placed at the corner of the home, and often located outdoors. A camphor flame is passed over the offering, acknowledging for some Idumban's protection throughout the ordeal of bearing a kavadi, for others the symbolic role of Idumban as gatekeeper to Murugan. Another banana leaf of "pure" food is placed at the other end of the altar. This is subsequently blessed and the devotee and others perform consecutive *aratis*, commencing with the most senior members and concluding with the most junior. The flames are passed by each devotee before the deities within the home shrine, and are subsequently offered to all present. The bearers then serve food and drink to all who have assisted in the fulfilment of his/her vow and present gifts, which may include a cash donation, clothes, fruit or sweets to the religious dignitary who offered guidance and direction throughout the period of fasting and later presided over or performed the purification and kavadi rituals. The devotee is now formally released from the period of renunciation, is "returned" to society, and may resume his/her normal lifestyle.

The atmosphere at the Idumban *puja* may best be described as a blend of reverence, good humour and subdued triumph. Devotees swap anecdotes about fasting, the experience of trance and kavadis, while those who have taken a kavadi for the first time may now freely admit to the difficulties of fasting and the apprehension and perhaps fear they felt upon being confronted with the actuality of trance and bodily mortification. Photographs and videos shot on Thaipusam days may be shown, to the accompaniment of cries of recognition, banter and pithy witticisms. The occasion is underscored by an almost palpable undercurrent of group satisfaction and accomplishment, and understated appreciation of the united achievement of goals which not only benefit the individual but also the wider community of friends, relatives, supporters, and to a lesser extent all fellow believers.

Because Idumban *puja* is held to honour a formal *asura* and may involve both animal sacrifice and liquor, it is considered non-*Agamic*, and thus somewhat disreputable by some reformist Hindus.

Notes

1. Thaipusam is also observed in many other centres, including Penang, Ipoh, Johor Bahru, Sungai Patani, Muar and Maran, and increasingly among the small Indian communities stationed in the major East Malaysian cities. The Chettiar-managed festival in Penang will be described in the following chapter. At the Ipoh festival, large numbers of the minority Telegu community — traditionally Vaishnavites — bear kavadis in accordance with the Murugan tradition.

2. Gavin Flood, *The Importance of Religion: Meaning and Action in Our Strange World* (Chichester: Wiley-Blackwell, 2012), p. 65; Karen Armstrong, *The Case for God: What Religion Really Means* (London: The Bodley Head, 2009), p. 17.

3. Ramanathan Kalimuthu, "Hindu Religion in an Islamic State: The Case of Malaysia" (PhD dissertation, Universiteit Van Amsterdam, 1995), p. 144.

4. Ibid., p. 217.

5. J.M. Gullick, *The Story of Kuala Lumpur 1857–1939* (Singapore: Eastern Universities Press, 1983), p. 68.

6. Fred W. Clothey, *Ritualizing on the Boundaries: Continuity and Innovation in the Tamil Diaspora* (Columbia: University of South Carolina Press, 2006), p. 177.

7. Gullick, *The Story of Kuala Lumpur*, p. 105.

8. Neelvani A/P S. Thanabalan, "Taipucam in Malaysia: An Analysis of a Hindu Festival (A Case Study of Batu Caves, Selangor)" (Jabatan Antropologi dan Sosiologi, Universiti Malaya, 1987–88).

9. Ramanathan, "Hindu Religion in an Islamic State", pp. 143–44.

10. Diane L. Eck, *Darsan: Seeing the Divine Image in India*, 3rd ed. (New York: Columbia University Press, 1998), pp. 54–55.

11. Ibid., pp. 62–63.
12. Ramanathan, "Hindu Religion in an Islamic State", p. 144.
13. Neelvani, "Taipucam in Malaysia". As with many foundational accounts in Malaysia, there is also a populist variation, which, despite lack of documentation, has achieved wide currency. This runs as follows: Following the discovery of the caves, Indian labourers were detailed to gather loads of bat dung, which were to be used as fertilizer. One day the labourers discovered a *vel* within the cave and began acts of worship to Murugan. The British Advisor to the Sultan of Selangor, perturbed by this development, ordered the removal of the *vel*. He was warned by headman K. Thambusamy Pillai that this action would create grave personal difficulties in his life. When this scenario eventuated, the Advisor turned to Thambusamy for counsel as to how he might resolve the problems he was facing. He was instructed to break a coconut and to pray to Murugan for forgiveness. The Advisor followed Thambusamy's direction, restored the *vel*, and preserved the area surrounding the caves as the temple compound. A variation of this account is repeated as fact in Rahul Kabade, *Sri Muruga: Legend, Short Stories and Worship* (Wembley: Sri Muruga Publications, 2012), pp. 100–103.
14. Ramanathan, "Hindu Religion in an Islamic State", p. 142.
15. K. Dharmaratnam, *Elements of Hinduism* (Kelang: Percetakan Naathan, 1987), p. 17.
16. Kalaiyarasi A/P Gurusamy, "Hinduism: The History of Sri Maha Mariyamman Kovil Devastanam" (Class Exercise, Jabatan Antropologi dan Sosiologi, Universiti Malaya, 1987/88).
17. Information provided through interviews with temple officials, Kuala Lumpur.
18. Gullick, *The Story of Kuala Lumpur*, p. 106.
19. Kalaiyarasi, *Hinduism*. The board to whom the court granted authority was largely composed of members of the Thevar caste (see Clothey, *Ritualizing on the Boundaries*, p. 177). Thevars continue to constitute the majority of the *devastanam*.
20. Ramanathan, "Hindu Religion in an Islamic State", p. 140.
21. Clothey, *Ritualizing on the Boundaries*, p. 178.
22. Kalaiyarasi, *Hinduism*.
23. David Dean Shulman, *Tamil Temple Myths: Sacrifice and Divine Marriage in the South Indian Saiva Tradition* (Princeton, NJ: Princeton University Press, 1980), pp. 23–25.
24. For some years the sale of beer and non-vegetarian foods in at least two of the food stores was the subject of sustained criticism by many Hindus. These practices now seem to have ceased.
25. A constant stream of tourist buses arrives daily. The intrusions of mass tourism have been a matter of deep concern to many Hindus. For while

Hindus regard Batu Caves as a sacred site, and are thus sensitive to issues involving ritual purity and pollution, some tourism operators primarily promote the caves as a natural wonder, and only incidentally as a Hindu pilgrimage site. This approach results in what many Hindus regard as offensive behaviour, including shouting and laughter in the vicinity of the shrines, inappropriate dress, smoking and the occasional consumption of alcohol in the caves, and unauthorized photography of devotees, especially those in meditation. The *devastanam* management has attempted to minimize inappropriate conduct within the Temple Cave by means of signage at the foot of the stairs, but it is doubtful that this has had more than a cursory impact. While Hindus may grumble about the incursions of foreign tourists, nearly all are aware that had it not been for the intervention of the Malaysian tourist authorities, Batu Caves would have undoubtedly been destroyed by uncontrolled quarrying. The quarrying, conducted by a Chinese-owned and managed company, had been located on the far side of the outcrop. The company showed no signs of yielding to the pleading of Hindu authorities or government spokesmen, including the former prime minister, Datuk Hussein Onn, who, during his speech at Thaipusam in 1978, urged Hindu leaders to explore every legal avenue possible to halt the quarrying. Operations were finally brought to an end after action taken by the Malaysian tourism authorities.

26. Personal correspondence. The prime minister's announcement received extensive coverage, especially in the Tamil press.
27. Eck, *Darsan*, p. 73.
28. The history of this *sadhu* is as follows: The holy man, who was believed to have formerly been the postmaster at Ipoh, arrived at the caves with a cow. He informed temple officials that he intended to remain at the site and meditate. His needs were simple; he required a bottle of milk per day, which would be supplied by the cow. He selected a spot within the cave, where he meditated for hours at a time. Informants advised me that in those days this required considerable courage, as the cave was infested with snakes and scorpions. One day the cow died, and upon ascending the stairs, temple officials discovered the *sadhu*'s bottle of milk untouched, and nearby the saint himself, obviously deceased and locked in the lotus position. He was buried at the foot of the hill and a simple shrine was constructed around his grave. Shortly afterwards a formation appeared above the burial site, which to devotees was an earthen manifestation of the *sadhu* meditating in the lotus position.
29. This will be more fully discussed in Chapter 8.
30. *Pantaram*: A caste of non-Brahman priests. It should be noted that the service of the deity by non-Brahman priests is consistent with practice at the main temple in Palani.

31. It is held that the devotee must always ascend to worship Murugan. Fred Clothey points out that Murugan shrines other than the main South Indian centres are generically known as *Kunratal* (or, "every hill on which the god [Murugan] dances") (Fred Clothey, *The Many Faces of Murukan: The Meaning and History of a South Indian God* (The Hague: Mouton, 1978), p. 117.

32. Nataraja is regarded as the dynamic symbol of the universe in constant cosmic flux; Siva as Creator, Preserver/Protector, Destroyer, Siva who conceals and reveals his Grace (the properties of rest and release). (Devapoopathy Nadarajah, *The Strength of Saivism* [Kuala Lumpur: Second International Seminar on Saiva Siddhanta, 1986], pp. 80–81.)

33. *Cave Villa Batu Caves Malaysia: Experience Culture and Diversity* (Batu Caves: Jaya Krishna Holdings, n.d.). Copy acquired in May 2012. Apart from an abnormal number of typographical and grammatical errors, the pamphlet suggests that the *Puranic* mythology represented within the caves, generally understood as metaphorical, records actual "events that took place thousands of years ago in the history of Hinduism".

34. It is worth noting, in passing, that the majority of these photographs feature examples of kavadis explicitly condemned as unacceptable by the Malaysian Hindu Sangam in their 2014 pamphlet *Thaipusam Festival Guide for Hindu Temple* [sic] *and Devotees*. This pamphlet will be discussed later in this chapter.

35. St. Avvaiyar encapsulates both the power and unconventionality of *bhakti* devotion. A woman of *Panar* (lower caste) birth, she eschewed beauty and the security of a good marriage in favour of premature age, plainness and a life of devotion and service (especially to those of lower birth). Her "dream" is regarded as a profound meditation and realization of Ganesha, who promised that he would personally transport her to eternally remain with Siva upon Mount Kailas. The *Vinayakar Agaval* is one of the most frequently quoted praise poems to Ganesha.

36. Most scholars contend that the *lingam* had its origins in phallic worship among the inhabitants of the Indus Valley civilization. However, this association is often denied, especially by Hindus who are sensitive to Western perceptions of their religion, in particular the concept of a cosmic universe symbolized by the union of the *lingam* with the *yoni* (vagina, a symbol of Sakti/Parvati). The *lingam* is more commonly worshipped as Siva as unmanifest Reality, i.e., Siva beyond time, form and space, his "formless form", which is both immanent and transcendent. (Devapoopathy, *The Strength of Saivism*, pp. 66–67.)

37. The dubbing of Brahma with Vaishnavite markings "subtly" indicates the superiority of the Saivite path; i.e., that a Vaishnavite requires instruction by a Saivite. Moreover, Murugan is wrongly portrayed as holding the *Vel*, which, in point of fact, at this stage of his cosmological history he is yet to receive.

38. Once again Murugan is depicted with the *Vel*, which is bestowed only after his fight with Idumban at Palani.

39. This myth celebrates a battle of wits between Murugan and the fabled saint, which ends with Murugan promising to grant her the "fruit" of a long life without hunger, pain and disease (Kamil Zvelebil, *Tamil Traditions of Subramanya-Murugan* [Madras: Institute of Asian Studies, 1991], p. 27).

40. Cornelia Dimmitt and J.A.B van Buitenen, eds. and trans., *Classical Hindu Mythology: A Reader in the Sanskrit Puranas* (Philadelphia: Temple University Press, 1978), pp. 114–16.

41. The *Tirukural*, composed by St. Tiruvalluvar, a weaver (and thus of humble birth), is regarded as the ethical centrepiece of Saiva Siddhanta philosophy (see Satguru Sivaya Subramuniyaswami, *Weaver's Wisdom: Ancient Precepts for a Perfect Life* [Himalayan Aacademy: Hawaii, 1999]).

42. Thus, an aphorism extolling the virtues of family life is incongruously placed in front of a king brandishing a sword; when I visited in February 2014, this blunder had been in situ, apparently unnoticed, for well over four years.

43. Many senior Hindus are deeply critical of the *devastanam* management, which is held to be more concerned with politics and financial returns than with spiritual issues. While most critics will concede that over the years there have been marked improvements at Batu Caves, they contend that these have often been marred by lack of appropriate research and but poorly informed by spiritual knowledge or inquiry.

44. *Utsava murthis*: These are special *murthis* which are used throughout festivals. The installed and consecrated *murthi* is regarded as permanent, and is not removed from the temple. These festival images are almost invariably made of bronze, a convention which dates back to the Chola era (R. Champakalakshmi, *Religion, Tradition and Ideology: Precolonial South India* [New Delhi: Oxford University Press, 2011], p. 482).

45. C.J. Fuller, *The Camphor Flame: Popular Hinduism and Society in India* (Princeton, NJ: Princeton University Press, 1992), p. 106.

46. Lawrence A. Babb, *Thaipusam in Singapore: Religious Individualism in a Hierarchical Culture*, Department of Sociology Working Paper No. 49, University of Singapore (Chopmen, 1976), p. 14.

47. Eck, *Darsan*, p. 3.

48. Neelvani, "Taipucam in Malaysia".

49. *Vibhuti* is the ash recovered from burnt cow dung and is used extensively in Hindu worship, especially for sacred markings upon devotees. This ash is believed to possess healing, cleansing and purifying qualities.

50. Ute Husken, "One Nine-Yard Sari, Two Elephants and Ten Sips of Water: Rituals and Emotions at a South Indian Hindu Temple", in *Emotions, Rituals*

and Performances, edited by Alex Michaels and Christoph Wulf (New Delhi: Routledge, 2012), p. 122.

51.   The *vibhuti* is applied on the forehead over the pineal gland, which is regarded as the site of the mystical third eye. The third (inner) eye is believed to open at the onset of yogic insight, thus lifting the aspirant to a new stage of spiritual unfoldment. The application of *vibhuti* may be thus seen as a means of control and, in cases of unauthorized or premature trance, of restraint.

52.   By tradition the *otuvar* (chanter of hymns) is a member of the *vellalar* (non-Brahman) caste, who is required to mediate between the deity and his devotees. He is normally allowed the freedom to improvise, except on festival days when he is required to adhere to a specified repertoire (Champakalakshmi, *Religion, Tradition and Ideology*, pp. 107, 216–17).

53.   The showing of the flame transmits the power and benevolence of the deity, which is absorbed by the devotee through the fingertips and eyes. It also signifies the mutual vision of deity and devotee (Fuller, *The Camphor Flame*, p. 73).

54.   The *nadaswaram* is an instrument resembling a clarinet. In public processions it is usually performed in relays, with one *nadaswaran* player succeeding another. Often a skilled *nadaswaram* player will revisit the themes of those who immediately preceded him, and embellish them with elaborate variations. Most temples employ *nadaswaram* players and drummers who not only perform for the temple deity but will be engaged for weddings, house dedications, etc.

55.   James Kirkup, *Tropic Temper* (London: Collins, 1963), p. 252.

56.   Every major temple has its own chariot (*ratham*) which is used during festivals or on ceremonial occasions to convey the deity in procession. The cost of the *ratham* was announced during its formal inauguration, at which I was present.

57.   Minor or guardian deities often face in four different directions to protect a temple or chariot from malign and thus polluting influences.

58.   Taken from local press accounts. In 2004 an attempt was made to introduce two horses and riders to escort the chariot to the caves. However, these plans were hastily abandoned after one horse, badly frightened, consistently misbehaved, refusing to settle, rearing and threatening to bolt. Given the large crowd crammed within the confined environs outside the temple entrance, and the consequent inability of people to take evasive action, it seems remarkable that no one was seriously injured. Shortly afterwards, both horses were removed from the procession.

59.   These figures are hard to verify. However, sources within the *devastanam* estimated the crowd as up to 400,000 people at the 2012, 2013 and 2014 chariot processions.

60. Over the past few years the *devastanam* has liaised with police to control and where necessary remove troublemakers. The intervention of the temple authorities was regarded as essential; the police were reluctant to act unless they had the full backing of the Hindu community. The presence of plain-clothed police has acted as a major deterrent to the "infiltration" of unruly elements into the crowd.

61. Elizabeth Fuller Collins, *Pierced by Murugan's Lance: Ritual, Power and Moral Redemption among Malaysian Hindus* (Dekalb: Northern Illinois University Press, 1998), p. 68. While Collins claims that the dance is based upon or resembles "stylized combat", Hindu dance masters and teachers have informed me that *kolattam* has its origins in a traditional game played by young Tamil girls. This view is supported by Lakshmanan Chettiar (Lakshmanan Chettiar, *The Folklore of Tamil Nadu* (New Delhi: National Book Trust, 1973), pp. 159–60).

62. *Upayam* are participatory groups, sometimes consisting of a family but more often the Hindu members of a given company or a trade/commercial organization, which assume responsibility for performing certain rituals or administering/funding particular aspects of festival or temple life (Clothey, *Ritualizing on the Boundaries*, p. 70).

63. Raymond M.L. Lee, "Taipucam in Malaysia: Ecstasy and Identity in a Tamil Hindu Festival", *Contributions to Indian Sociology* 23, no. 2 (1989): 320.

64. Milk curd is considered an advisable element of any vegetarian Hindu's diet. It is also viewed as a "cooling" substance, as opposed to the "heat" of asceticism. The issue of "heating" and "cooling" will be discussed in Chapter 8.

65. P.V. Jagadisa Ayyar, *South Indian Customs* (New Delhi: Asian Educational Services, [1925] 1989), pp. 51–52.

66. Ooi Kee Beng, *Arrested Reform: The Unmaking of Abdullah Badawi* (Kuala Lumpur: Research for Social Advancement, 2009), p. 27.

67. "Kedah to get Thaipusam holiday?", 14 July 2013 <www.thestar/com.my/News/Nation/2013/07/14/Kedah-to-get-Thaipusam--holiday> (accessed 7 August 2013).

68. Lee, "Taipucam in Malaysia", p. 320.

69. A senior Malaysian minister, to whom I was introduced in 1982, informed me that the Malaysian authorities strongly opposed the "human zoo" approach to tourism, and made every attempt to ensure that the cultural integrity of religious and belief systems were respected. This stance has remained in force.

70. Kalaiyarasi, *Hinduism*.

71. *The Star*, 29 January 1999. Current figures are unavailable, but are believed to be in excess of this number.

72. Lee, "Taipucam in Malaysia", p. 321.

73. In recent years certain stalls have actually retailed items which promote other religious traditions and have openly sold or distributed printed materials which are critical of Hinduism.

74. Lee, "Taipucam in Malaysia", p. 321.

75. I experienced a side effect of this commercialization during a 2013 visit to the Hanuman temple a few days after Thaipusam. Immediately outside the temple two competing retailers of Bollywood songs attempted to outdo each other, each with loudspeakers turned to maximum volume. As a consequence, devotees within the temple were unable to hear the chanting of the *Pattar*, and the earsplitting noise rendered concentration/meditation impossible.

76. Figure taken from personal diary and derived from local press coverage.

77. *The Star*, 24 January 1997.

78. Jagadisa, *South Indian Customs*, p. 136.

79. Babb, *Thaipusam in Singapore*, pp. 8–9.

80. Neelvani, "Taipucam in Malaysia".

81. The number 108 is considered very significant in Saiva philosophy. Both Murugan and Ganesha are considered to have 108 attributive names, and many religious treatises are presented in 108 sections.

82. The making of kavadis is often an expensive undertaking, and *aluga* kavadis in particular may require considerable outlays for timber, hooks, chains, peacock feathers (which are usually imported from India), and other materials. However, once constructed a kavadi may be used for several years, requiring but minor refurbishment before each Thaipusam. Specialist kavadi makers (usually *pujaris* or members of small temples) often rent kavadis to devotees, frequently letting the same kavadi to up to three individuals over the course of a festival, depending upon the time and place each person plans to take the kavadi. The kavadis will often be transported to the caves by the manufacturer, thus sparing the devotee the logistical ordeal of ferrying such a bulky and unwieldy item to and from the crowded environs of Batu Caves. *Paal* kavadis are significantly less expensive than *aluga* kavadis, more easily transported, and many are donated to the *devastanam* after the pilgrimage for the use of other and often more needy devotees. In recent years rental prices for kavadis have risen sharply.

83. Babb (*Thaipusam in Singapore*, p. 9) claims that *vel* kavadis are not regarded by Singapore devotees as "traditional", and postulates that they may have been introduced to the Hindu community via the agency of Chinese mediumship. (Indeed, during my visit to Singapore in 2000, I was advised that *vel* kavadis had been banned in Singapore on the basis that they do not comprise part of the recognized Murugan tradition.) Senior Malaysian Hindus made similar comments to me during the course of my fieldwork. However, this form of

kavadi is well known in Tamil Nadu, and photographs within lesser Murugan temples, especially near Nagercoil in the extreme south, show devotees bearing these kavadis. Indeed, temple officials not only confirmed that *vel* kavadis have had a lengthy history in *Tamilakam* but also speculated that Indians may have introduced this form of religious expression to Chinese mediums.

84. Alexandra Kent, *Divinity and Diversity: A Hindu Revitalisation Movement in Malaysia* (Singapore and Copenhagen: Institute for Southeast Asian Studies/ NIAS Press, 2007), p. 180.

85. Lee, "Taipucam in Malaysia", p. 325.

86. Champakalakshmi, *Religion, Tradition and Ideology*, p. 176.

87. Kama's ensign is the fish (Champakalakshmi, *Religion, Tradition and Ideology*, p. 177). This forms a feature of some kavadis.

88. The cult of Ayappan has taken root among sections of the Malaysian Hindu population over the past twenty-five to thirty years, and a number of Malaysian Hindus have participated in the annual pilgrimage to the deity's abode at Sabrimalai in the Western Ghats, Kerala. An extended account of this pilgrimage is described and analysed by E. Valentine Daniel, who journeyed with a party that included members of all castes (E. Valentine Daniel, *Fluid Signs: Being a Person the Tamil Way* [Berkeley: University of California Press, 1984]).

89. However, these kavadis are found in both India and Sri Lanka. See Madelaine Biardeau, "Brahmans and Meat Eating Gods", in *Criminal Gods and Demon Devotees: Essays on the Guardians of Popular Hinduism*, edited by Alf Hiltebeital (Albany: State University of New York Press, 1989), p. 21; Arumugam Rasiah, *Kataragama: Divine Power of Kathirkamam and Methods of Realization* (Sithankerny: Holiday Ashram, 1981), p. 41.

90. Vineeta Sinha, *A New God in the Diaspora? Muneeswaran Worship in Contemporary Singapore* (Singapore and Copenhagen: Singapore University Press/NIAS Press, 2005), pp. 181–82.

91. Ibid., p. 163.

92. Ibid.

93. Neelvani lists several other types of kavadis other than those described in the text. Most are not common in Malaysia or are found in a modified form, while some are now very rare even in India. The supplementary list is as follows: *Maccha Kavadi*: A fisherman will put a fish into a pot and carry it to the shrine (Neelvani claims that this is only found at Palani, but I have seen this motif decorating *aluga* kavadis in Penang); *Mayil Kavadi*: Made entirely of peacock feathers. However, quite often the term *mayil* (peacock) and *aluga* are used interchangeably in reference to kavadis, perhaps reflecting the extensive use of peacock feathers as decoration on most kavadis; *Pannir Kavadi*: A kavadi featuring scented water; *Agni Kavadi*: Kavadi in the form of a pot containing

burning charcoal and wood covered with *veppillai* leaves. Neelvani notes that this is recommended for those recovering from illness; *Sandhana Kavadi*: Wet sandalwood paste moulded into the shape of a *Gopuram* (temple tower) and carried on the head; *Kalasha Kavadi*: A kavadi consisting of a milkpot decorated with flowers, leaves and sometimes limes (at Batu Caves, flowers are usually red and yellow — colours associated with Murugan — normally the blossoms of *kantal, venkai, katampu* or lotus); *Pallava Kavadi*: Made of beads such as *rudraksha* (Neelvani, "Taipucam in Malaysia").

94. *The Star*, 9 February 2009.

95. Malaysian Hindu Sangam, *Thaipusam Festival Guide*.

96. It should be noted, in passing, that many of the heterogenous collection of deities worshipped at Thaipusam are in some way connected to Murugan (or are claimed to be so). Thus, certain *Agamic* deities such as Vishnu and Krishna are popularly represented as related to Murugan through his marriage to the celestial Devayanai, whereas some non-*Agamic* traditions explicitly identify specific village deities as local manifestations of Murugan.

97. *Mauna* is a common discipline among Hindu ascetics. Indeed, there are devotees (usually older men and women, and generally occupying positions of spiritual leadership) who take a vow of total silence for the entire period of the Thaipusam festival. This is regarded as the spiritual equivalent of carrying a kavadi.

98. Frank R. Ervin, Roberta M. Palmour, Beverly E. Pearson Murphy, Raymond Prince, and Donald C. Simons, "The Psychobiology of Trance: Physiological and Endocrine Correlates", *Transcultural Psychiatric Review*, no. 25 (1988): 269.

99. The group with which I have been associated throughout my own pilgrimages has over the years included the following vocational/social groupings: a Malaysian government senator, his sons and daughters, the son of a leading cabinet minister, lawyers, merchants, university lecturers, the registrar of a university, family members of one of Malaysia's largest trading houses, nurses, taxi drivers, rubber tappers, labourers, housewives, elderly widows, university students, office workers, female secondary students, and an aged female renunciant (now deceased). While in ethnic terms this group is predominantly Tamil (including Jaffna Tamils), it has also included members of the Chinese, Telegu, Malayalee, Sikh, Gujarati, Punjabi, Marathi and Sinhalese communities. The group, comprising at its maximum a total of between fifty and sixty devotees, has been equally divided by sex.

100. Fuller, *The Camphor Flame*, p. 205.

101. Lee, "Taipucam in Malaysia", p. 328.

102. Clothey, *Ritualizing on the Boundaries*, p. 196.

103. Champakalakshmi, *Religion, Tradition and Ideology*, p. 136.

104. Ronald C. Simons, Frank R. Ervin, and Raymond Prince, "The Psychobiology

of Trance: Training for Thaipusam", *Transcultural Psychiatric Research Review*, no. 25 (1986): 261. At a trial trance I attended, one devotee manifested a vehement Hanuman trance. This became obvious when he literally ran up a nearby coconut palm in the temple compound, bit through coconut husks with his teeth, and shook the crown and trunk of the tree with a powerful violence that one would never have suspected from a person of such slight stature. When he threatened to rain coconuts on to the roof of the temple, the *pujari* coaxed him down from the tree with an offer of a tray of bananas and jackfruit. Once the devotee had descended the *pujari* quickly terminated the trance. The *pujari* later informed me that he marked this young man as potentially disruptive and had advised his assistants to keep him under firm control on Thaipusam day.

105. For the puposes of convenience, I am here using a simplified version of Gilbert Rouget's classification of trance, thus (i) "possession" trance: a form of trance which leads the devotee to acquire a different personality, either of a god or a spirit who has taken complete control of the subject, and (ii) "inspiration trance": where the votary is invested by the deity which then exercises a form of controlling coexistence over the devotee. (Gilbert Rouget, *Music and Trance: A Theory of the Relations between Music and Possession* [Chicago: University of Chicago Press, 1985], p. 26). Various states of trance will be discussed more fully in Chapter 8.

106. Colleen Ward, "Thaipusam in Malaysia: A Psycho-Anthropological Analysis of Ritual Trance, Ceremonial Possession and Self Mortification Practices", *Ethos* 12 (1984): 321.

107. Clothey, *The Many Faces of Murukan*, pp. 171–80. However, these colours may vary. Ayappan and Muneeswaran worshippers will often be dressed in black. Some of these devotees will wear turbans traditionally associated with kingship.

108. Gavin Flood, *The Tantric Body: The Secret Tradition of Hindu Religion* (London: I.B. Taurus, 2006), p. 88. Saivite Hindus list trance states according to a carefully graduated hierarchical ranking, ranging from divine grace (*arul*) down to the lowest categories embracing demonic possession. Hysteria is usually described in terms of psychic disorder. Collins (*Pierced by Murugan's Lance*, pp. 112–14) claims that the trances attained by women and lower castes are often dismissed by members of higher castes as constituting no more than possession by lesser spirits. I have rarely encountered this view, either in Malaysia or India. Indeed the entire *bhakti* tradition would militate against such an approach. It has been my general experience that the trance states of women and lower-caste devotees have been accorded equal status with those of higher-caste males. The issue of trance will be discussed more fully in Chapter 8. However, as an example of an unwanted and intrusive

trance, I cite the following: In 1985, several male devotees, including this writer, were confronted by an entranced teenage girl performing a corybantic and blatantly seductive dance. She was rapidly brought out of trance and removed from the scene by embarrassed relatives. I was later informed that the girl had been possessed by an *apsara* (celestial nymph, often employed by higher deities to divert ascetics or holy figures from their meditations and *tapas*). I met this young woman — a demure, studious and extremely proper schoolgirl — at her home two weeks later. Although she had been informed of her sensuous display, she had no recollection of the events leading to the trance, nor her actual experience of the trance state.

109. Dimmitt and Buitenen, *Classical Hindu Mythology*, p. 251
110. Fred W. Clothey, *Rhythm and Intent: Ritual Studies from South India* (Bombay: Blackie and Son, 1983), p. 40.
111. Neelvani, "Taipucam in Malaysia".
112. Alfredo Roces,"A Matter of Mind Over Matter", *Geo* 3, no. 4 (1981): 86.
113. Ervin et al., *The Psychobiology of Trance*, p. 267.
114. Lakshmanan, *The Folklore of Tamil Nadu*, pp. 162–63.
115. Ibid. In both her doctorate thesis and her book, Collins claims that the kavadi dance is based upon the mating dance of the male peacock (Collins, *Pierced by Murugan's Lance*, p. 74). This claim is unsourced. I have been unable to locate any reference, either oral or textual, which would substantiate this claim, and senior Hindus and temple authorities, both in Malaysia and India, to whom I put this claim, reacted with bemusement, scorn and occasionally outrage.
116. Lakshmanan, *The Folklore of Tamil Nadu*, pp. 162–63.
117. Zvelebil, *Tamil Traditions*, pp. 33–35.
118. Babb, *Thaipusam in Singapore*, p. 10.
119. Ooi Cheng Gee, *Portraits of Penang: Little India* (Penang: Areca Books, 2011), p. 152.
120. Rajakrishnan Ramasamy, *Caste Consciousness among Indian Tamils in Malaysia* (Petaling Jaya: Pelanduk, 1984), pp. 6, 41, 100. Although at the time it was denied by *devastanam* authorities, several of whom themselves claim lower-caste allegiance, the forbidding of *Paraiyar* drumming appeared to be a measure which was specifically directed at banning the practices of an *Adi Dravida* caste.
121. Lee, "Taipucam in Malaysia", p. 326.
122. M. Rajantheran, K. Sillalee, and R. Viknarasa, *An Introduction to Hinduism: A Religious Text for Hindu Students* (Taman Petaling: Malaysian Hindu Sangam, 2012), p. 33.
123. Vanamali, *The Lilas of the Sons of Shiva* (New Delhi, Aryan Books, 2008), p. 130.

124. Clothey, *Rhythm and Intent*, pp. 49–51.
125. The burning of camphor by persons other than *pantarams* was banned in the Temple Cave in 2002.
126. The *devastanam* recruits *pantarams* from all over Malaysia to serve at the caves throughout Thaipusam (Lee, "Taipucam in Malaysia", p. 321).
127. It is important that this task be undertaken by someone other than the devotee. Apart from the fact that by the time of their arrival at the shrine most devotees are physically spent and would thus find it difficult to summon the energy to return the kavadi, it would be considered to negate the whole purpose of the pilgrimage should the devotee convey the kavadi back to the point where he/she commenced his/her pilgrimage — it would be perceived as akin to withdrawing the offering made by the devotee. Similarly, if for various reasons a devotee is unable to bear the kavadi the entire distance, he/she must find a replacement — however extemporized — who will carry the kavadi the remaining distance to the shrine.
128. However, this does not mean it does not occur. In 1978, I was invited to attend a breaking of fast ceremony in a small village temple near the Kuala Lumpur suburb of Damansara. This was conducted by a female medium on behalf of a large number of kavadi bearers, both men and women, whom she had guided throughout Thaipusam. During the course of the Idumban puja her daughter slaughtered several chickens, which were cooked and offered to Idumban, and subsequently to devotees.

7

Other Thaipusams

This chapter provides an overview of the commemoration of Thaipusam (or other Murugan-linked festivals) and the related incidence of kavadi worship in a variety of settings, within both metropolitan and diaspora Tamil Hindu societies. In the process it will comprehensively demonstrate that festivals of Thaipusam (or related festivals) honouring the deity Skanda-Murugan, and involving kavadi rituals, are not only widely encountered within Tamil Hindu society but in fact form a central component of the religious identity of Tamil Hindu communities, both within metropolitan India and in the broader Tamil diaspora. The cultural significance of Murugan worship and the related kavadi ritual is particularly emphasized by the examples of Fiji, where *bhakti* practices clearly demarcate South Indian religiosity against a backdrop of indigenous Fijian and North Indian pressures; of the Seychelles, where the recent construction of a Hindu temple and introduction of kavadi worship have fuelled a Tamil cultural and religious revival; and Medan, Indonesia, where the controversial banning of the kavadi ritual instilled a deep sense of cultural deprivation among Tamil Hindus.

In general there are several common elements found in all Murugan festivals:

1. A chariot procession organized by the controlling temple or religious body in which the *utsava murthi* is paraded and displayed to the

community over which the deity exercises regnancy. (Only in two of the localities surveyed — the Seychelles and Kataragama, Sri Lanka — is the chariot ritual absent. However, as will be shown, Hindus within the Seychelles have only in recent years inaugurated the commemoration of Thaipusam as a major festival, and the community is still in the process of developing many of the key symbols of Tamil Hinduism. At Kataragama the chariot ritual is replaced by a procession involving Skanda-Murugan in the form of a *yantra*, that is, a mystical diagram employed to represent aspects of various deities, most commonly *sakti* powers, and closely identified with healing in Tamil traditions.)[1] The chariot ceremonial is structured around the royal symbolism and kingship (in this context it should be noted that in the Brahman *pada yatra* described later in this chapter, members of the pilgrimage party bore all the insignia of kingship). While Murugan is typically symbolized by the *Vel*, his kingship at Palani, and thus in Thaipusam generally, is characterized by the *danda*, or staff.

2. Various forms of worship with kavadis, typically preceded by a vow requiring a period of asceticism, including *tapas* (austerities) and fasting. The kavadi ritual generally involves an induced trance state or state of altered consciousness, and often includes bodily mortification.

3. Formal recognition of the *asura*-turned-devotee Idumban. This is not only incorporated in the very act of carrying a kavadi but also in the related dance, based on Idumban's gait as he bore the twin hills from the Himalayas to Palani.

4. Other forms of ritualized service to the Hindu community as a whole. This most typically involves mass feedings (*annathanam*), or manning or constructing a *thaneer panthal* (a stall devoted to providing food, drinks or religious materials).

It should be noted that this study is by no means exhaustive. Thaipusam and Murugan-related festivals are celebrated in numerous other locations, including long-established diaspora communities (e.g., Reunion, Myanmar, Mumbai, Kolkatta), as well as other sites to which Tamils have recently migrated (e.g., North America, Europe, Australia).

Penang: The Malaysian Alternative

Thaipusam in Penang follows the same basic format as that of Batu Caves, namely that of a three-day festival commemorating the bestowal of the *Sakti Vel* upon the deity Murugan, beginning and ending with a chariot procession and involving acts of ritual fulfilment. As with Batu Caves, Thaipusam in Penang attracts large numbers of devotees, with crowds in 2014 estimated at 400,000 and the number of kavadi bearers at approximately 16,000.[2]

However, there are important differences in the conduct and rituals of the two festivals. In this section I have concentrated on the points of departure between Penang and Batu Caves, which include (i) Chettiar management of the festival; (ii) ritual forms of non-Chettiar kavadi worship and the demography of worshippers; (iii) the emphasis on coconut smashing as a form of vow fulfilment; and (iv) the importance of *thaneer panthals* as a form of *bhakti* devotion. These are elaborated in the following paragraphs.

Chettiar Management of Thaipusam

The formal structure of Thaipusam in Penang is organized by the Nattukottai Chettiar community. (The role of the Chettiar community in the promotion and maintenance of *Agamic* Saivite Hinduism and their worship of Murugan has been discussed in Chapter 4.) The Chettiars view Thaipusam both as a time of vow fulfilment and of service to the entire Hindu community.

The opening ritual within the Chettiar community is a *pongal* ceremony,[3] which is conducted in the Kovil Veedu, Georgetown, on the afternoon prior to the departure of the silver chariot. A *homa* fire[4] is prepared using sacred woods, a brass pot is placed on the fire, and milk and rice are added to the pot. At the moment the milk boils over the rim of the pot, conches are blown and bells are rung. The *pongal*, dedicated to Ganesha, is considered necessary to remove all barriers to the staging of the festival and to ensure its success.

The entire community gathers in the temple for the purificatory ceremonies held for those votaries, exclusively male, who have elected to bear kavadis throughout Thaipusam. The intending kavadi worshippers are dressed in plain *vesthi* and are seated in a designated area within the temple. The kavadis, all of orthodox *paal* design, and richly decorated with clusters of peacock feathers tied at both ends of the arch, are set in a semicircle in front of the alter dedicated to the *utsava murthi*. Following *bhajans*, the temple priest performs a *puja* to the *utsava murthi*, after which each kavadi is sanctified. There are sporadic trances among intending kavadi devotees as this process proceeds. The community as a whole now circumambulates the kavadis, which have now been, in effect, transformed into mobile altars dedicated to Murugan. *Prasadam* and *vibhuti* are distributed to the kavadi bearers, who in turn redistribute these items to the broader community. A further *puja* is performed to the *utsava murthi*, and the ritual items of kingship are displayed to the deity.

The following morning the chariot leaves from the Kovil Veedu to make its way to the Nagarathaar Nattukottai Chettiar Thandayudapani Temple in Jalan Waterfall (a distance of approximately twelve kilometres; the trip may take anything up to fourteen hours). The Chettiar kavadi bearers file out of the temple and take their places in front of the community's silver chariot. At about 6 a.m., escorted by temple patrons and management, and accompanied by musicians — drummers and *nadaswaram* players — the *utsava murthi* is borne outdoors and, after oblations conducted in front of a huge crowd, is installed within the bullock-drawn chariot.

The kavadi bearers will precede the chariot for its entire journey. In contrast to nearly all other Malaysia kavadi devotees, the Chettiars do not affix milk pots to their kavadis. Fleshly mortification and the use of *vels* are both eschewed. The votaries walk the complete distance in silence, but engage in periodic bursts of ritualistic dancing, occasionally involving trance states. Devotees take turns in bearing the kavadis, and when one bearer tires he merely hands the kavadi to another member of the community. Several of the Chettiar pilgrims whom I interviewed compared their worship to that of "menial servants to a mighty king"; like courtiers in a royal household, they were bound by notions of service, duty and obedience, which were tempered with ideals of reciprocity.

The chariot, which proceeds without illumination on its outward journey from the Kovil Veedu, makes slow progress. There are frequent stops to allow devotees to present trays to the deity, which are returned to their owners as *prasadam*, to display their babies for blessing, and to enable worshippers to gain *darsan* of the deity. Unlike Kuala Lumpur, where municipal authorities insist on the chariot's rapid passage from the central business district, in Penang there are no such pressures, and the chariot halts whenever sufficient devotees have gathered, and for as long as is required to complete all transactions with worshippers. Various *kolattam* troupes accompany the chariot, while Indian and Chinese devotees smash enormous numbers of coconuts in the path of the chariot.

At about 12:30 p.m. the chariot reaches the Sri Muthumariamman Temple on Jalan Dato Keramat. A simultaneous *arati* is performed to the deity within the temple and to the *utsava murthi* within the chariot. Led by musicians, officials emerge from the temple bearing a tray shaded by an umbrella and containing cloth, fruit and a garland. This is presented to the *utsava murthi* through the agency of the priests on the chariot. The Chettiar kavadi bearers now enter the temple, where they take a period of rest.

After a substantial break the chariot resumes its journey, finally reaching the Nagarathaar Nattukottai Thandayudapani Temple in Jalan Waterfall at about 8:40 p.m. The exhausted kavadi bearers now enter the temple. The *utsava murthi* is officially greeted and escorted to the temple gateway, where all the insignia of kingship are displayed. Murugan then proceeds into the temple and, amidst a congery of welcoming rituals, is formally installed. The ceremony concludes at about 10:00 p.m. Murugan is now in state and is considered ready to meet kavadi devotees as they pay homage en route to the Arulmigu Bala Thandayudapani Temple (more commonly known as the Hilltop Temple), the entrance to which is located a short distance further along Jalan Waterfall.

The following day — Thaipusam — large numbers of kavadi pilgrims will enter the temple, circumambulate the courtyard, and pay allegiance to the *utsava murthi*. For much of the day the temple is crowded with devotees, both Indian and Chinese, and many sightseers, including Western tourists. Following a midday *puja*, the Chettiars begin cooking food in large pots. The Chettiar community is initially fed, and then other devotees are provided with meals in successive mass sittings throughout the afternoon.

At 6:30 p.m. the (ethnically Chinese) chief minister of Penang, his family, and members of the Cabinet and their spouses, are received at the temple by leaders of the Chettiar community. The chief minister will be conducted to the *sanctum sanctorum*, where an *arati* will be performed, and he will be marked with *vibhuti* and *kumkum* powder by the head temple priest, presented with vestments taken from the *utsava murthi* and garlanded. He and other guests are also presented with fruit taken from the altar. In this way the Chettiar community offers official hospitality and homage to the political leadership on behalf of the Hindus of Penang, and is officially acknowledged as the sponsoring group within the Hindu community, on the occasion of Thaipusam at least.[5]

The reception of the official guests will be followed by mass feedings (*annathanam*) of all devotees who visit the temple and request a meal.

Members of the Chettiar community will work throughout the day and well into the night to cook and distribute food for up to ten thousand devotees.

As pointed out, the Chettiar temple, and by extension the role of the Chettiars, is also implicitly acknowledged by the majority of kavadi bearers within the Hindu community,[6] who divert from their pilgrimages to the Arulmigu Bala Thandayudapani Temple to circumambulate the main shrine of the Chettiar temple and receive the *darsan* of the deity.

At midnight the *utsava murthi* will be mounted on a palanquin, and ceremonially paraded around the temple. The deity will then be placed within his "chambers", ritually bid farewell, and the curtains will be drawn. Murugan is then considered to have retired for the night.

At 7:30 a.m. a *pongal* is conducted within the temple followed by a *puja* to the *utsava murthi*. The Chettiar kavadi bearers now circumambulate the temple, many in a state of deep trance. Each devotee is presented to the deity and formally relieved of his burden. Breakfast is then served to the kavadi bearers and to members of the Chettiar community.

At 6:30 p.m. that evening, farewell *pujas* are conducted to the *ustava murthi*. Accompanied by torch bearers, musicians and temple officials, the *utsava murthi* is escorted from the temple, and, as dusk becomes night, is reinstalled in the chariot. The chariot is now brilliantly illuminated for the return journey (the general explanation is that Murugan has now received the *Vel* and burns with the full complement of his powers, whereas on his outward journey he was yet to receive the *Vel*). With a large and swelling crowd in attendance, the chariot now begins its return journey. Once again it will make frequent stops for devotees, and more coconuts will be smashed in its path (though not on the same scale as that which marks the outward journey). The chariot arrives at the Kovil Veedu in Georgetown at about 8 a.m. The *utsava murthi* is taken from the chariot and, after a set of welcoming rituals, is borne into the temple. The ceremony is completed at about 8:40 a.m.

A challenge to Chettiar orthodoxy and oversight of the temple is mounted in the form of a village ritual conducted on the night prior to the return of the chariot. This is a "folk" celebration of the marriage of Murugan to Valli. The marriage ceremony commences but is interrupted by a staged sneeze, following which the presiding *pujari* declares that the marriage is now rendered inauspicious and must be abandoned — Murugan, who already has one wife, must return to his temple in Georgetown. The next attempt at marriage will be set for a year's time. This ensures that

Thaipusam will be held the following year.[7] This ritual has no obvious equivalent at Batu Caves.

The Chettiar organization of Thaipusam has resulted in social tensions within sections of the broader Hindu community, in particular dissatisfaction at what has been perceived as Chettiar arrogance in the management of Thaipusam. In the late 1980s, general discontent with Chettiar sponsorship led to large numbers of devotees boycotting Thaipusam and transferring their allegiance to the festival of *Panguni Uttiram*, held in April–May.[8] The boycott led to greater intra-community liaison and concessions to other Hindu groups.

Non-Chettiar Kavadi Worship

While the kavadi ritual is a central feature of Thaipusam in Penang, the demography of those who bear kavadis and the modes of worship differ in certain respects from those found at Batu Caves. These differences are outlined in the following paragraphs.

In the previous chapter I noted that at Batu Caves it is common to find kavadi bearers originating from all segments of the Hindu population. While in Penang most strata of Hindu society are represented among the ranks of those taking kavadis, the majority of those who engage in the ritual appear to be younger men falling within the eighteen to thirty-year-old age group, and of working-class background (this does not axiomatically designate them as belonging to the lower castes; as demonstrated in Chapter 1, many working-class and estate Indians are of neither lower caste/*Adi Dravida* background). The number of women who take *vels* and bear kavadis, both in absolute terms and as a percentage of total kavadi worshippers, is significantly lower than that at Batu Caves.

As with Batu Caves, kavadi bearing takes many forms. However, orthodox *paal* kavadis and *aluga* kavadis are encountered less frequently. Most *aluga* kavadis are of flimsy construction (made of foam plastic and other lightweight materials) and occasionally break before the devotee reaches his/her destination. The classic *mayil* (peacock) adornment, which is such a feature of the decoration of *aluga* kavadis in Kuala Lumpur, is all but absent in Penang. While some *aluga* kavadis incorporate colours traditionally linked to Murugan worship (red, yellow, green, or red and white in combination — the Tamil "primary colours"),[9] most feature other colours — purple, white, black, orange — not generally associated with the Murugan cultus at Batu Caves. Many kavadis contain shrine motifs which are markedly different from those observed in Kuala Lumpur (e.g., a few feature symbols of the *Aum*, or the *Naga* [snake] of Siva, while some Chinese devotees bear kavadis dedicated to deities found within Chinese religious traditions).

The most common form of kavadi is a *paal kudam* (milkpot), taken with or without *vels*, and carried on the head or shoulders of the devotee. This appears to be the preferred form of worship for women kavadi bearers. Another form of kavadi is the hanging of small milk pots (numbering up to 108), which are secured to the torso and arms on small hooks. Sometimes these are sufficiently numerous to obscure the entire upper body. Other devotees carry numbers of limes in a similar manner. *Vel* kavadis are also common in Penang, but less obtrusive than those found at Batu Caves. Many younger men pull "chariot" or *ter* kavadis (that is, hooks which are attached to the backs of devotees and "anchored" with nylon ropes by a friend who walks behind and is responsible for keeping the ropes taut). Still other devotees walk in nailed shoes, or roll for a specified number of times around the concrete courtyard within the Thandayudapani Temple complex (this latter practice involves both male and female votaries). However, the forms of worship associated with lesser or "small" deities — such as Kaliamman, Muniandy and Madurai Viran — are found less frequently in Penang, the result of "active discouragement" by festival organizers.

In addition to the standard *vels* taken through the tongue and cheeks, most kavadi-bearing devotees also take three tiny *vels* which are inserted into the middle of the forehead above the "third eye". These *vels* are left on the altar at the Hilltop temple. Informants advised me that the *vels* are to remind the devotee of Siva, Parvati and Murugan.

Unlike Batu Caves, kavadi bearers do not begin their journey from one recognized focal point, but start out from a number of localities across Georgetown, generally specified temples. They bear kavadis along public roadways, thus sharing carriageways with (often heavy) vehicular traffic. Many walk considerable distances (sometimes up to ten kilometres) before they reach the core sacral areas near the Thandayudapani Temple in Jalan Waterfall. Probably because of the distances covered, the devotees do not dance so energetically as those in Kuala Lumpur. Kavadi bearers dance in short bursts, mainly to amplified music emanating from the *panthals*. Many aspirants do not wear anklets, and there is little chanting, and an almost complete absence of professional musicians along the route.

When they reach the Chettiar temple, worshippers leave the road to circumambulate the shrines and to pay homage to the *utsava murthi*. Upon emerging from the temple, members of the supporting retinue accompanying each kavadi bearer will smash a coconut upon which a square of burning camphor has been placed. They will then proceed along the roadway to the compound containing the Arulmigu Bala Thandayuthapani (Hilltop) Temple.

This compound covers several hectares. A Ganesha temple is situated a short distance within the main gateway. Further on, at the foot of the stairs, is located a small shrine to Idumban. From there on a stairway snakes its way to the recently reconstructed Hilltop Murugan temple. The compound also contains some well-tended gardens, and a scattering of miscellaneous buildings and pavilions.

Once the devotee enters the compound, he/she pauses outside the downstairs Ganesha temple, and if the size and manoeuvrability of his/her kavadi permits will enter and circumambulate the *sanctum sanctorum*. (This is impossible for those bearing *aluga* or other large kavadis.) Devotees then proceed to the Idumban shrine at the foot of the stairway, where they pay obeiscence and formally request his permission and blessing to proceed to the hilltop Murugan shrine. A lime given to the devotee at the outset of his/her journey is offered to Idumban, a coconut is smashed, and the devotee is presented with a fresh lime to surrender to Murugan. The votary then ascends the five hundred steps to the temple. At the summit the pilgrim is assisted from his/her kavadi, the milk pot is taken from the kavadi by the temple *kurukkal* and the milk is poured over the deity, the *vels* are removed and the devotee brought out of trance and encouraged to offer prayers. He/she then proceeds downstairs where he/she distributes small packets of cooked food (usually chick peas) to passers-by. As at Batu Caves, the votary will offer a *puja* to Idumban on the third day after bearing a kavadi, during which he/she will be released from his/her vows of asceticism and symbolically "returned" to society.

Elements of "village" Hinduism appear to intrude more openly into the non-Chettiar kavadi ritual in Penang. There appears to be significantly less attention paid to the *Agamic* and purificatory rites which accompany kavadi bearing at Batu Caves, and most of the preliminary rituals are either abbreviated or neglected. Many votaries commence their journeys from non-*Agamic* "village" temples. All kavadi bearers are given a lime to carry (seen as "cooling", thus countering the heat of asceticism),[10] and the supporting group will smash coconuts and cut limes at auspicious points along the route to propitiate or counteract malevolent spirits or harmful "little deities" which otherwise might impede or cause misfortune to devotees.

Coconuts as Vow Fulfilment

Although coconuts are smashed in the path of the chariot in Kuala Lumpur, the numbers are considerably smaller than those demolished in Penang. In 2014, press estimates indicated that a combined total exceeding two million coconuts were supplied for breaking in the path of the chariot as it made its way to and from the Chettiar Thandayudapani Temple.

While coconut shattering is a recognized mode of sacrificial worship among both Chinese and Indian devotees, Chinese votaries seem to outnumber Indians, both in terms of those who employ coconut smashing to fulfil vows and the total number of coconuts broken. Chinese devotees claim that the destruction of coconuts in such huge numbers "cleanses the path of Lord Murugan". Nearly all devotees who smash coconuts, whether Chinese or Indian, do so to complete a vow.

The logistics and organization associated with the distribution of coconuts in Penang are considerable. Drops are made by local contractors at agreed destination points along the route the chariot will take, with the names of purchasers clearly marked. As the chariot approaches, the devotee (or groups of devotees) will step forward and smash the coconuts on the roadway. As piles of coconuts are destroyed, municipal workers move in to clear the debris from the road and thus allow the smooth passage of the chariot.

In recent years there has been some controversy about the demolition of coconuts on such a huge scale. In 1997 an official of the Hindu Sangam suggested that devotees content themselves with smashing a single coconut, and that they donate the balance of the money they would have spent on coconuts to a recognized charity. This aroused accusations that the official was out of touch with Hindu sentiment, and that he did not understand the nature of Saivite vow fulfilment.[11]

In 1998 the campaign against the smashing of coconuts gathered momentum with the unprecedented, unsought and widely resented intrusion of the Consumers Association of Penang (CAP), which complained about the supposed "pollution" and "waste" linked with the practice. In response, many Hindus claimed, with considerable justification, that the CAP was meddling in matters which pertained to private religious sentiment, that in criticizing Hinduism they were settling upon a "soft" target, and they would be neither sufficiently willing nor adventurous to offer similar animadversions of Muslim or Christian festivals. In 1999, Mr R. Rajendran, deputy president of the Malaysian Hindu Council, warned the CAP against commenting on an issue which was a private matter between individuals and their deity.[12]

Thaneer Panthals in Penang

The construction of *thaneer panthals* is a distinguishing feature of Thaipusam in Penang. Although *panthals* are found both en route to Batu Caves and at the caves themselves, they are largely viewed as functional, a place to offer service, rather than as edifices which are designed to reflect the beauty and spirit of *bhakti* devotion. There are fewer *panthals* at Batu Caves, and those constructed do not match the range of services of those provided in Penang.

The *panthals* are constructed by groups who band together immediately after Thaipusam to plan for the next festival. These groups represent temple associations, youth or service organizations, or more frequently the Indian (and Chinese) staff of local and multinational firms which donate funds.

The *panthals* are erected along the main routes that kavadi bearers follow. They are assembled using lightweight materials (the substructure is generally an aluminium framework which is bolted together), and are usually put in place in the forty-eight hours prior to Thaipusam and are removed just as quickly once the festival is complete. Most contain "walls" of palm and banana fronds, reminders of jungle or remote shrines. These *panthals* offer food, drink, and sometimes religious tracts, as well as seating to the general public. These services are provided either free of charge or at a nominal sum. Proceeds are donated to a particular temple or charity. They also tend to the needs of passing kavadi bearers by providing water for drinking and bathing, and stools upon which the bearer may sit while his/her legs are massaged.

Most of the *panthals* have electricity supplies and feature lightshows, sometimes of extraordinary sophistication, and modern sound systems which are used to play religious music. A devotional altar dedicated to a particular deity is incorporated midway along the frontage of the *panthal*.

Deities thus honoured include Durga, Mahamariamman, Lakshmi, Siva/ Parvati and Muneeswaran, and occasionally Chinese deities such Kuan Yin (Goddess of Mercy), but most commonly Ganesha and Murugan. Many of these altars are painstakingly and intricately designed, and feature potted plants, subdued lighting, foundations, mock waterfalls and motifs peculiar to the deity to whom the altar is dedicated (for example, a common theme is Ganesha set against a jungle backdrop, or Murugan against a background of layered peacock feathers). A *yantra*, always multicoloured and generally of considerable complexity, is painted on the roadway in front of the shrine. Some of these *yantras* remain visible for weeks afterwards.

The *panthals* are staffed by volunteers who have worked throughout the year to plan the design and logistics of the *panthal*, and to raise the funds necessary to support the project. These volunteers are recognized as fulfilling the path of both *bhakti yoga* and *karma yoga*, or the idea of selfless service. The construction of a shrine, however temporary, also incorporates the concept of the sacred vow of temple building, which is viewed by many Hindus as an act of *bhakti* at least equivalent to, or as an accepted alternative to, bearing a kavadi.

Penang: Some Observations

In general it may be stated that the devotional current of Thaipusam in Penang is broader and more diffuse than that of Batu Caves, where devotion and vow fulfilment is largely focused upon the kavadi ritual. In Penang, *bhakti* may take several publicly recognized forms; for example, coconut smashing, or serving in a *thaneer panthal*, as well as the ascetic path of kavadi worship. While kavadi bearing remains a key component of Thaipusam, both within the Chettiar and wider Hindu communities, rites involving the mortification of flesh are far more likely, *though by no means exclusively*, to be concentrated among younger working-class males than is the case at Batu Caves. This may be the result of Chettiar organization and the provision of a "model" and thus socially approved ways of bearing kavadis, as well as the ready availability of alternative methods of vow fulfilment. It should also be noted, in passing, that criticisms of kavadi worship made by Hindu "reform" movements, which appear to be stronger and better organized in Penang than elsewhere throughout Malaysia, may have an influence on the modes of kavadi worship and the demographic profile of kavadi devotees.

The generally more relaxed and receptive environment in which Thaipusam is conducted in Penang may be due to the Chinese demographic and political supremacy in that state, reinforced by widespread Chinese participation in all aspects of the festival. This not only cushions the Malay-Muslim/non-Malay-non-Muslim cleavage so immediately evident in other parts of Malaysia, but also ensures societal acceptance of Thaipusam as integral to Penang's cultural fabric.

However, while Thaipusam in Penang appears to be better organized and superficially more harmonious than the festival at Batu Caves, there is underlying tension and dissent. Resentment of the key role taken by the Chettiar community in the organization and management of Thaipusam, as well as the persistence of discreet and often agonistic religious traditions, indicate the perpetuation of social fissures and divisions.

India

My research has led me to conclude that the kavadi ritual is a popular form of worship within South India, especially Tamil Nadu and Kerala, that it falls under the rubric of recognized *bhakti* traditions of worship, and that most forms of the kavadi ritual found in Malaysia reproduce, almost unchanged, established Indian patterns. Indeed, the official description of a kavadi published in a book prepared under the auspices of the Arulmigu Dhandayuthapani Temple, Palani, could have easily referred to many of those borne at Batu Caves; namely, "An ornamental piece of semi-circular bent wood decorated with pictures of Muruga, carried by ardent devotees in fulfilment of vow with skewers stuck in the body, cheek or tongue in voluntary mortification of the flesh."[13] Morever, my research indicates that the kavadi ritual is not, as claimed by some observers, exclusive to the socially deprived or lower castes, but is found in all castes.

Most colonial descriptions of *bhakti* religious practices in South India were recorded through the jaundiced, disdainful and uncomprehending perspectives of British Christian missionaries. Thus, Henry Whitehead, the Anglican Archbishop of Calcutta, dismissed village festivals as "gloomy and weird rites for the propitiation of angry deities and the driving away of evil spirits".[14] He contended that all trance states are accompanied by "devil music" and "the usual devil dancing".[15] Likewise, L.S.S. O'Malley dismissed Subrahmanya as a "minor god", a mere son of Siva, and wondered at the attention paid to him within the Madras Presidency.[16]

Nevertheless, he recognized the crucial role of festivals in making Hinduism a vital religion to the average devotee. Both Whitehead and O'Malley observed and recorded examples of self-mortification; Whitehead refers to a Telegu festival where devotees pushed "silver pins" through their cheeks,[17] of hook swinging accompanied by the insertion of *vels*,[18] and a firewalking ceremony he witnessed at Bangalore.[19] O'Malley speaks of a "strange exhibition of self-mortification" at "Palni", including the insertion of *vels* and mouth locks,[20] devotees harnessing themselves by means of hooks to the heavy temple cars, and the practice of hook swinging, the latter banned by the Madras Government in 1935.[21]

In his descriptions of the major sites of pilgrimage associated with the Murugan cultus, Clothey lists two at which forms of kavadi worship similar to those conducted in Malaysia are held. The first of these is at Tirupparankunram, nine kilometres from Madurai, where Murugan is believed to have married Devayanai.[22] The festival of *Vaikasi Visakam*, held in the Tamil month of *Vaikasi* (May–June), when the star of *Visakam*, the natal star of Subramaniam, is in the ascendant,[23] draws crowds, predominantly peasants, from the regions adjacent to the temple. These devotees "parade through the streets of Madurai towards Tirupparankunram on the climatic day of the festival, many of them bearing kavadis, pulling carts hooked to their backs, carrying vessels of milk to be used in *apisekam* or walking in a pit of coals in the temple grounds".[24]

The temple at Palani, long associated with the traditions of healing,[25] stages several major and a number of minor festivals which incorporate "nearly all forms of worship and the entire ritual common to Tamil Nadu".[26] The major festivals are Panguni Uttiram, which attracts half a million people and about fifty thousand kavadi bearers, significantly more than the other leading festival, Thaipusam, which is attended by about a hundred thousand people and ten thousand kavadi bearers.[27] While many journey to the hilltop temples, others pilgrimage to the Periyanayaki Amman temple, which is essentially a Murugan temple, though it contains other shrines as well. The Indian tourist authorities describe the kavadi ritual in the following, rather breathless terms, singularly reminiscent of the accounts provided by Christian colonial writers:

> To the uninitiated Thaipusam is a stunning, totally unexpected assault on the senses. Hair raising sights of human bodies covered in hooks, which anchor huge Kavadis (ritualistic yokes) balanced on heads and cheeks

pierced with small spears, wooden tongues and arrows [sic]. The most
elaborate Kavadis can weigh as much as 80 pounds, a platform ornately
decorated with peacock feathers, Christmas [sic] decorations, even plastic
dolls ... the yellow robed "Bhaktas" coming from several different places
dance their way through the streets to reach the Muruga Sannidhi to the
accompaniment of music, both instrumental and vocal. Many strangely
and ghastly [sic] traditions, like the lips pierced with mini silver lance,
and locking of the mouth with metal ring to maintain perfect silence
and drawing of makeshift chariot with its chain hooked into the back of
devotees strike the eye of the spectator during this festival.[28]

During a 1998 interview with a very senior priest at Tiruchendur, a major
Murugan temple, located on the seashore in the Tirunelvi District in
the Bay of Bengal, and the mythical site of Murugan's final battle with
Surapadman, I was told of the kavadi bearing which occurs at the festival
of Chitrai Puruvum, which is held at Tiruchendur during the Tamil month
of *Chitrai* (April–May). Although this festival celebrates Murugan in the
totality of his powers and his bestowal of the gift of immortality, it is
also commemorated as a form of ancestor worship.[29] Chitrai Puruvam
incorporates the kavadi ritual, including the use of *aluga* kavadis, similar to
those borne at Thaipusam in Malaysia. The kavadis are taken by members
of all castes, including some Brahmans, though they are mainly carried
by devotees drawn from Sudra castes.

While the kavadi ritual is found at the main pilgrimage centres, it is
also located within numerous temple communities across South India.
Madeleine Biardeau records kavadi bearing at a Kallar festival held to
honour Mariamman and Aiyanar.[30] The Kallars take kavadis in honour of
Kattavarayan, who is regarded as Mariamman's son and the first of her
bodyguards, and is clearly identified as a form of Murugan. These "human
sacrifices" included "*alaku*" kavadis, which involved the penetration of
needles under the skin of those who were obligated by a vow, the *paal*
kavadi, a stick carried on the shoulder with a pot of milk at each end, and
the *ter* kavadi, a chariot drawn from a rope or hooks.[31]

On the basis of information provided to me throughout my fieldwork,
I suspect that Biardeau's observations are replicated at many sites
throughout Tamil Nadu and Kerala. Certainly, when I showed my
Malaysian kavadi photographs to members of the party with whom I
undertook a *pada yatra* (or foot pilgrimage — see succeeding section), to
swamis and officials in *asramas*, to temple priests, and to other individuals

whom I encountered, I was continually met with descriptions of similar patterns of worship, usually, but not always, associated with Murugan. At several temples, both in Tamil Nadu and Kerala, I was shown prominently displayed photographs of devotees bearing kavadis, often combined with firewalking (*timiti*). A major temple near Nagercoil in the extreme south of Tamil Nadu included photographs of worshippers with their cheeks transfixed with spears. Repeated and careful questioning of a wide and varied range of informants drew the consistent response that the kavadi ritual was a recognized form of *bhakti* religiosity which reached members of all castes, but rarely Brahmans, who tended to avoid body piercing (however, it was emphasized that there were always exceptions). Of the total array of behaviours associated with worship at Thaipusam in Malaysia, only knife walking was viewed as a "village" form of worship, largely restricted to *Adi Dravida* castes, and normally held in honour of Durga (in her village form), or Kaliamman, one of the more fierce manifestations of the meat-eating goddess. This form of worship was regarded as unacceptable among Sudras, let alone Brahman castes, and was not permitted at *Agamic* temples.

India: A Brahman Thaipusam

The following provides an overview of a 1998 Thaipusam *pada yatra* (or foot pilgrimage) undertaken by a party of Smartha Brahmans, and which I was invited to join. The seven-day yatra commenced in the Brahmans' home city of Palakkad, Kerala and culminated in the kavadi ritual and worship of Murugan at Palani on Thaipusam day.

The Palakkad Brahman community was mainly of Tamil origin, having migrated to the area from the Tamil country a couple of centuries earlier. Although the majority of the community were educated as professionals, a sizeable minority were business people, mainly caterers.[32] While all members of the community spoke Malayalee, and many of the younger generation lacked fluency in Tamil, all were steeped in the traditions of Murugan worship.

Our pilgrimage party consisted of approximately thirty-five devotees, all male, and aged predominantly between twenty and fifty-five, though several were significantly older, and a couple of younger devotees were in their late teens. The party included a small group who had returned from various work stations — Mumbai, Kolkatta, Delhi, Patna — to make the *yatra*. While the majority of the party consisted of Smartha Brahmans, the minority (twenty per cent of the party) were Sudras of various caste backgrounds.

The pilgrimage required extensive organization. Because the party of Brahmans were unable, for reasons of purity related to their caste, to rely upon securing appropriate food en route to Palani, they were obliged to take their own victuals, as well as cooking utensils, so that they could prepare their own meals. The party not only packed sufficient food for its own requirements but also loaded additional supplies which allowed it to cater for mass feedings (*annathanam*) of other pilgrims, travellers and villagers, irrespective of caste, religion or social status. The provisioning and victualling of the pilgrimage participants required considerable logistical support, and the party was accompanied by a lorry, a mini bus and a "jeep" (four-wheel drive). On the day prior to our departure, a body of cooks was kept busy washing and preparing vegetables, scouring utensils, and packing items which were checked off against an exhaustive master list which had been prepared several weeks earlier.

(i) Initiation Rituals

The *pada yatra* formally commenced with a *homa* ceremony conducted at 4 a.m. on the first day of the pilgrimage. The *homa*, dedicated to Ganapati (Ganesha), had two clear objectives:

1. To formally request the deity to remove all obstacles to the conduct of the *pada yatra*.
2. To ritually empower a chosen member of the pilgrimage party to act as Kavadi Master throughout the period of the *pada yatra*.

The appointment of the position of Kavadi Master bestows both power and a heavy load of responsibilities upon the person who is installed in this office. His status provides him with almost total authority over logistical and organizational matters throughout the pilgrimage. Following his empowerment, his word is law until the pilgrimage is complete, and due deference is paid to him and the sacred office he represents. However, the authority he now wields obligates him to ensure that the physical and psychological needs of all members of the pilgrimage party are met. This encumbers him with a significant workload, which does not cease until every member of the party is asleep at night.

A further ceremony, the *Kavadi Muttirai Nirattal*, was held in the temple between 7:00 and 9:30 a.m. The ceremony has as its main object the dedication and purification of the kavadis, and formal initiation of the pilgrims who are to bear them. Following this ritual, the kavadis are considered sacred instruments, intrinsically pure. In contrast, the pilgrims, who, despite their status as temporary renunciants, remain in contact with many of the polluting agents of daily life, and must be regularly and ritually re-purified.

Essentially, the *Kavadi Muttirai Nirattal* consists of the following sequence of events: Each *sadhaka* (aspirant) is taken before the Kavadi Master, and prostrates himself before him and before the *murthi* of Murugan. A sacred thread is then tied around the pilgrim's right wrist. Under the guidance of the Kavadi Master, small calico bags are filled by the aspirant with jaggery and sweet mixes, into which coins are inserted. The bags are then secured at the top and affixed to a kavadi, ready to be borne the entire 120 kilometres to Palani. Each participant also pays the Kavadi Master a sum (in this instance, 150 rupees), which is to assist in defraying any expenses he might incur in fulfilling his duties throughout the pilgrimage. After the entire group had been presented to the Kavadi Master, and to the deity, there was a session of chanting, *bhajan* and dancing, all accompanied by drums and hand cymbals, employed for rhythmic effect. The music appeared to provoke several cases of trance, both among participants and male and female observers.

Most of the kavadis were of the same basic design as that which in Malaysia is known as the *paal* kavadi; that is, a decorated wooden arch which is carried on the shoulder. Many of the kavadis were of elegant construction, made of carved wood; in many cases, teak. The motifs upon the kavadi included a range of *Agamic* deities (including Murugan and Ganapati) in various phases of their cosmological history, together with their respective *vahanas* (or carriers; the peacock for Murugan, the rat for Ganapati). The kavadis were decorated with the ritual emblems of kingship, as well as peacock feathers and bells. Some of the thicker wooden kavadis were very heavy, and the one silver kavadi — which every devotee was expected to bear at some point throughout the *yatra* — exceedingly so. Some of the kavadis had been used over many pilgrimages; indeed, I was informed that several were between sixty and 120 years old. The kavadis thus confer a sense of shared tradition within the community, and one of the more elderly pilgrims recounted to me the distinguished figures among the Palakkad Brahmans who had borne these kavadis. In addition to the kavadis, the party also bore the staff (*danda*) which is the defining symbol of Murugan at Palani, as well as the various insignia of kingship, plus the paraphernalia associated with Skanda the warrior. I noted a far more casual relationship between the pilgrim and the carrying of kavadis than is the case at Batu Caves; if a devotee tired while bearing the kavadi, he simply passed it on to another member of the party.

(ii) Ritual Incorporation (Days 1–2)

Early that evening, and accompanied by lantern bearers and musicians, the pilgrimage party embarked on the ritual parading of the kavadis around the town; that is, to the main temples and the homes of members of the Palakkad Smartha Brahman community. At each home, devotees were acknowledged by householders, music was played, and the kavadi dance performed. The ranks of the pilgrimage party were temporarily swollen by the addition of several teenage boys, and by several young unmarried women who also bore the kavadis and participated in the dancing. The procession did a full circuit of the outposts of the Brahman quarters. Worshippers returned to the *mandapam* (ceremonial community hall) at about 9:00 p.m. The entire procession had taken several hours. The kavadis were then stored in a clean area on mats and stretches of carpet which had been set out for this purpose.

Most of the second day was spent in taking the kavadis to the homes of those members of the Smartha Brahman community who resided outside the Palakkad Brahman quarters, but within the general town environs. Throughout the morning and into the evening we were received at a succession of devotee's houses. At each stop, the kavadis were neatly stored in a ritually cleansed area, and usually upon mats or carpet. A brief *puja* was conducted to the kavadis (and sometimes a *bhajan* as well) prior to our recommencement. The route we followed in meeting these obligations was very indirect, and we covered an estimated thirty kilometres zigzagging between various houses. By nightfall we had reached the limits of the Palakkad district.

(iii) On the Road: Days 3–5

The next three days were spent in travelling the approximately 120 kilometres between Palakkad and Palani. Each day followed a roughly typical routine, which I have sketched in the following paragraphs.

Early in the morning the Brahmans would rise to conduct certain caste-related rituals, which the non-Brahman minority were not expected, and indeed not permitted, to participate in. The rituals were considered intrinsic to the maintenance and obligation of duties imposed at the time of initiation; that is, with the bestowal of the sacred thread.

The cooks would then commence work, either in preparing breakfast or coffee and chai. The remainder of the party would be woken with a shout of *"Haro Hara"* ("Praise to the Lord"). All meals would be served on a banana leaf laid in front of each individual as we sat crossed legged on the concrete floor. The food was ladelled by a succession of cooks from stainless steel utensils. We ate using our fingers, right hand only. Generally the food consisted of rice, *vadai* or *thosai*, with vegetables and a curry sauce.

Normally the party would set out in the pre-dawn cool (one morning as early as 4:00 a.m). We would walk through the dawn into the morning sun, generally reaching our destination in the late morning. The party was required to walk barefooted the entire distance. For several members of the group, the hot, uneven and stony roads were a source of agony, producing blisters, cramps and muscle strain. It was also a stipulation that all pilgrims wear a *vesthi* (generally of white or orange; typically the colours linked with renunciation) and walk bare-chested.

When we reached the morning's destination we would perform all ablutions, including bathing, and wash our clothes and lay them out to dry. We would then perform *bhajans* prior to lunch. These were drawn not only from the Murugan repertoire but were also addressed to other deities, including Ganesha, Devi and Krishna. I was informed that "All are within One", and that while the pilgrimage was devoted to Murugan, and in particular to that phase of the deity's cosmology as embodied in Palani, it was perfectly permissible to make other deities the object of veneration.

Following lunch, most members of the party would take a couple of hours sleep, thus avoiding the worst of the afternoon heat. At about 4:00 p.m. the group would be woken by shouts of "chai", and served tiffin. Another *bhajan* session would precede the afternoon's journey. About an hour prior to sunset, kavadis would be allocated, and we would walk through the twilight and into the brilliant light of the waxing moon. Often we strode along heavily populated streets and over roads bristling with long-distance and local traffic — trucks, buses, cars, bullock carts, bicycles and the ubiquitous three wheelers. I noted that the appearance of a kavadi procession did not elicit more than passing interest from the general public.

During the evening we would stop at a prearranged locality for dinner, before undertaking further travel. Generally we would cease walking between 11:00 p.m. and midnight. Overnight accommodation was invariably spartan, and we slept on mats on concrete floors.

The party generally fitted two other rituals into the daily routine. The first was the kavadi dance, sometimes involving trance states, which was usually performed in a temple visited en route, and the second was a mass feeding. At some point, generally in the evening, the cooks would prepare additional food, and travellers and passers-by would be invited to eat. The non-Brahmans did not participate either in preparing or serving food for these mass feedings.

On the third day the Kavadi Master presented all members of the party with a khadi *vesthi* (of dull orange, a colour considered appropriate for pilgrimages). I was informed that these *vesthi* are never distributed at the outset of a pilgrimage, but rather after all members of the party have endured the first days of the *pada yatra*. They are thus received by those who have demonstrated their seriousness and commitment and their determination to see the pilgrimage through to its conclusion.

As the pilgrimage progressed the party appeared to gain considerable cohesion, though it remained clearly understood that this was a *yatra* organized and managed according to Smartha Brahman mores. However, members of the group freely cooperated with one another, and an atmosphere of geniality, often accompanied by quips and humorous exchanges, infused the *pada yatra*, even when pilgrims were weary, hungry, or in acute discomfort. A senior member of the group explained the daily regime of the pilgrimage in these terms:

> During the *yatra* we are spiritual brothers united by a common sense of obligation and devotion. We walk together, we sing and chant together, we eat together seated on the floor — none must be above his brother — we sleep together, we bathe together, we surrender all our blisters and pain in the love of the One, we suspend all privileges of rank and wealth, our common poverty and pursuit of the Divine bind us.

During the first days of our pilgrimage our route took us through a number of villages situated off the main roads. Invariably the villagers offered us drinks, often the milk of tender coconuts. Villagers also placed coins in the kavadis to be borne by devotees to Palani.

(iv) In Palani (Days 6–7)

When we arrived at Palani at the end of the fifth day of the pilgrimage, we were lodged in a retreat, owned and maintained by the Smartha Brahman community. Two days were spent in preparatory rites prior to our ascent to the hilltop temple.

Palani contains several prominent temples, of which the hilltop temple on the top of the Sivagiri hill, the abode of Lord Dhandayuthapani, is the most famous. However, there are also other temples within the town itself, including the Kulandai Velayudaswami Temple, sited at a locality known as Thiru Avinankudi. The temple's presiding deity is Murugan seated on a peacock. Devotees bathe in the enclosures outside the temple, which are considered symbolic of the Saravana Lake in which the seed of Siva was deposited and where the six babies were merged into one by Parvati's embrace. The bathing therefore represents the ritualized purification necessary before approaching the *sanctum sanctorum*. Accordingly, on the morning of the sixth day, we visited this temple, bathed and made our way through to the shrine where a special *abishekam* and *arati* were performed for the pilgrimage party.

We then moved to the courtyard of the temple, where the party set up a portable kitchen and continuously cooked food, which was served to all who requested it. Every member of the group was required to participate, and I spent about an hour serving food to devotees within the temple. Later, when I asked why I was not permitted to assist in the mass feedings but was required to do so on this occasion, I was informed that the former fell within specific Brahman caste duties (service to others) and could not be devolved to non-Brahmans, whereas the feedings within the temple were an intrinsic component of pilgrimage rituals, and were regarded as necessary service preparatory to the encounter with the deity.

On the evening of the sixth day, the entire pilgrimage party, bearing kavadis, undertook a circuit of the road which runs round the base of the hill containing the Dhandayuthapani Temple, a distance of about four kilometres. Our departure was preceded by a ritual purification ceremony, and worship was also offered to the kavadis. An abbreviated *bhajan* session followed, and the Kavadi Master allocated kavadis to those nominated/ entitled to bear them.

Our circuit of Palani Hills took nearly three hours. Our group stopped at frequent intervals to sing *bhajans* and kavadi songs, and to perform the kavadi dance. Several members fell into a vigorous twirling dance, keeping the kavadi balanced on the back of their necks and shoulders without holding on to it in any way with their hands — a feat that was emulated by some devotees in other pilgrimage groups. Most of our party, however, followed the usual kavadi routine: the swaying dance which replicated the movements of Idumban as he bore the weight of the twin hills to South India. Several devotees attained trance.

On the morning of the seventh day the pilgrimage party assembled for an hour's chanting, designed to repurify our kavadis, followed by a further hour's *bhajan* prior to our kavadi procession to the Kulandai Veylayudaswami Temple. The Kavadi Master again allocated kavadis to members of our group. We were accompanied by several musicians — *nadaswaram* players and drummers.[33] We made our way through the streets of Palani, describing a complete circumnambulation of the temple, before entering the portals. Several of our group achieved a trance state. The entry hall of the temple contained a party of devotees who were beating large drums, shaped rather like European timpani, and of similar timbre. The drummers used thick, club-like sticks to maintain a series of complex rhythms which were almost overwhelming in their intensity.[34]

The organizers of our pilgrimage party had arranged for a special *abishekam* to be performed to the presiding deity as a prelude to the following day's ascent to the hilltop temple. The *abishekam* complete, we bore our kavadis back to the retreat, where they were once again stored within the designated "clean" area.

(v) Thaipusam: Day 8

On the morning of Thaipusam all members of the pilgrimage party were active by 6:30 a.m. About an hour after breakfast there was a preliminary ritual in which the kavadis were allocated to members of the party. The kavadis were then moved to the front of the retreat. A lengthy *bhajan* session followed, once again accompanied by temple musicians.

Our kavadi group set off at about 9:00 a.m., initially making our way through the streets of Palani to the "lower" temple. The streets were crowded with other groups of kavadi bearers, representative of many regions of Tamil Nadu and Kerala. As with the previous day, our party described a complete circumambulation of the Kulandai Velayudaswami Temple, before undertaking formal worship within. This complete, we made our way to the foot of the stairway leading to the Dhandayuthapani Temple, where amid considerable congestion, we reassembled as a group. At a signal from the Kavadi Master, we began climbing the 697 steps. The ascent to the summit was accomplished very quickly, with many of the devotees literally running up the stairs.

When we reached the area outside the covered walkway (enclosed with wire), which led into the main shrine, the Kavadi Master and a couple of nominated assistants took the bags which we had borne on the kavadis from Palakkad and piled them on a yellow cloth which they had spread on the ground for this purpose. We were instructed to make our way to the entrance of the walkway. We were required to purchase tickets to the "expedited" laneway which would enable us to gain direct *darsan* of the deity. As we entered the walkway the bags taken from the kavadis were passed over the top to us, together with small brass pots of milk (*paal kudam*). Upon reaching the main shrine these bags were passed to the non-Brahman priests who serve the deity in the hilltop temple. As the milk was poured over the deity it was re-collected in pots via a small out-pipe at the base of the shrine, and returned, as *prasadam*, to us. We were allowed a full two minutes to gain *darsan* of the deity for whom we had conducted the entire pilgrimage.

During the descent, members of the group paid obeisance to Idumban, whose shrine is situated approximately halfway down the hill. Although acknowledgement of Idumban is a formal requirement of any kavadi worshipper, in the case of this party this obligation appeared to be lightly observed. This simple action marked the formal termination of the entire pilgrimage. Later that day the majority of the party returned to Palakkad in the back of a lorry.

(vi) Other Observations

During the *pada yatra*, I observed other pilgrims making the journey to Palani. Many of these devotees later participated in the Thaipusam rituals conducted at the Periyanayaki Amman temple, described in the previous section. It was only when our pilgrimage party reached the main road which runs from Coimbatore to Palani that I began to envisage the scale of the mass pilgrimage which occurs each Thaipusam. Thousands of people were on the road, ranging from solitary pilgrims who bore a kavadi in total silence, to near entire villages encompassing populations ranging from young children to elderly men and women. The sheer exuberance of these pilgrimage parties was totally unexpected — many passed us singing, others dancing, still others chanting. I was advised that some of these pilgrims would walk over two hundred kilometres from their home villages to Palani.

While many of the devotees wore green apparel, others were clad in yellow and red, the same colours that are typically found among kavadi bearers at Batu Caves. I was informed that the colours reflected regional rather than caste variations; green was more likely to be worn by devotees hailing from non-riverine and hills districts, whereas the yellow–red combination was more generally associated with long-established riverine and/or urban communities.

At night most of these parties set up camp alongside the road, groups of men, women and children seemingly oblivious to the constant traffic — both human and motorized — which passed between one and thirty metres from where they slept. I was advised that over the years all *yatra* groups develop a detailed corporate knowledge of their route, and form relationships with traders, shopkeepers, temple custodians and householders who assist with food, water, and logistics. However, nearly every pilgrimage group will have secured accommodation in Palani well in advance, knowing full well how crowded the city becomes throughout any festival. Much of this accommodation is caste based and maintained and operated by *jati* associations.

In Palani the roads were frequently crowded with kavadi parties representing different locality groups, and sometimes specific *jati* groups. When I asked about the Perianayaki Amman commemorations, I was advised that those who bore *aluga* kavadis could not be distinguished by caste or region alone; many of those who worshipped in this way would also make their way to the hilltop temple. In other words there was no set or "approved" pattern of kavadi worship: the practices adopted were fluid and tended to be shaped more by tradition and inclination than by prescribed caste or region-based modalities.

Many pilgrims continued to arrive as our group departed Palani; indeed numbers seemed to have remained constant since the time of our arrival. It was explained that within South India, and particularly at Palani, Thaipusam is regarded as a ten-day festival, whereas in Malaysia the fulfilment of the kavadi ritual is generally condensed into a thirty-six-hour period.

(vii) Pilgrimage: A Rationale

The rationale behind the concept of *pada yatra* was outlined to me in the following terms: Smartha Brahmans worship six emanations of the Divine; that is, what can be ultimately termed Reality or God. These emanations are Siva, Sakti (Devi), Vishnu, Suraya, Ganapati and Subrahmanya. Put simply, each of these manifestations prefigures a path that the individual will elect to follow, but at base each represents a certain useful albeit rarefied fabrication, a distillation of Truth which will direct the mind towards certain ritualistic practices and spiritual disciplines. The fact that the chosen *ishta devata* (the devotee's favourite deity) is a "fabrication" does not make the manifestation "unreal"; rather, it allows the concentration of (latent) Awareness upon a specific aspect of Reality (*Saguna*, or form) which will gradually unlock the secrets of the Absolute (*Nirguna*, or formless). Thus, the major task or duty of the spiritually advanced individual is the pursuit of yogic practices, with the aim of meditation upon, contemplation and realization of, and ultimate absorption in, the Infinite. Those who have elected to worship Subrahmanya (Murugan) will learn to understand intrinsically all of the emanations of the underlying Reality represented by the deity; that is, the truths embodied by Skanda-Murugan in all his forms. This spiritual wisdom destroys the limitations imposed by the human mind in interpreting and determining the many forms of the One. Experiential knowledge leads the *sadhaka* beyond the constraints of categorization, language and human reason, to contemplation, and finally to *moksha* when the *jiva* (human soul) becomes Siva (Reality); that is, the worshipper is one with the object or Reality of his/her veneration.

Given this backdrop, a pilgrimage may be regarded as a metaphor for the entire process of spiritual discovery; a crossing point (*tirtha yatra*) from the mundane world to another state of consciousness. Every action within the pilgrimage is a calculated step on the journey towards the *axis mundi*; it is also a passage which simultaneously reorients the *sadhaka* from the outer world to the inner. The rituals — for example, the separation from the mundane, the removal from the familiarity of the community, the surmounting of the senses, especially pain, as one travels towards the centre, the final presentation of the physical/psychic burden to the deity — represents a series of carefully graduated steps which open the devotee to a range of cosmic possibilities. In supervening the routines of daily life, the pilgrimage rearranges the senses, and forces the individual to confront truth, and ultimately Truth itself. Of course, *moksha* will not be attained by every individual on every pilgrimage; the *sadhaka*'s level of spiritual development will influence his/her relationship to the deity, and hence his patterns of worship. But at the very least the *pada yatra* will erase the boundaries formally demarcated by mundane consciousness, and involve the devotee in several days of focused *bhakti* religiosity which will inspire fresh awareness. This will occur irrespective of whether the *sadhaka* is at the earliest stages of his/her awakening (in which case his/her modes of worship are likely to be rudimentary, unsophisticated and even crude), or the most advanced stages of unfoldment (represented by those who have entered advanced meditation or deep yogic contemplation of the deity). These notions of pilgrimage will be explored in the following chapter.

Singapore

Indians began arriving in Singapore following the British acquisition of the island in 1819.[35] In 2005 Indians numbered 309,300 people, or about 8.7 per cent of the total population.[36] This figure has been boosted by a more-recent influx of skilled migrants.[37] In 2000 Hindus aged fifteen years or above totalled 99,904 people and constituted about 4 per cent of Singapore's population aged over fifteen years.[38] Hinduism in Singapore embraces a diversity similar to that encountered in Malaysia, with the religion fragmented by divisions reflecting ethnicity, caste and lineage.[39] While the overwhelming majority of ethnic Indians were recruited as labourers, and continue to be employed in working-class occupations, a growing minority, especially among recent arrivals, belong to the technical, commercial and professional classes.[40] Over the years Tamil has gained importance as a lingua franca of Singapore's Indians, resulting in the decline of the languages of minority Indian communities.[41]

On the basis of fieldwork conducted between July 1973 and July 1974, Lawrence Babb concluded that kavadis were borne on three main occasions in the ritual life of Singapore's Hindus — Thaipusam, Panguni Uttiram and the annual firewalking (*timiti*) festival at Sri Mariamman Temple in South Bridge Road.[42] Thaipusam was the largest festival featuring the kavadi ritual, and probably the most important Hindu festival celebrated in Singapore.[43] There is significant evidence that Thaipusam has continued to increase in popularity since Babb completed his fieldwork. Temple officials interviewed by the author advised that the number of kavadi bearers had roughly doubled over the past thirty years.

The Thaipusam festival in Singapore essentially covers two days, the first largely devoted to the formalities of a chariot procession, organized and managed by the Republic's Nattukottai Chettiar community, and the second Thaipusam day itself, given over to rituals of vow fulfilment. While Thaipusam is commemorated at most Murugan temples, the focal point is the Chettiar's Thandayuthapani Temple, in Tank Road, constructed in 1869, and generally known as the Chettiar temple.[44]

On the second day, devotees bearing kavadis begin emerging from temples at about dawn.[45] Most kavadi bearers commence their pilgrimage from the Sri Srinavasa Perumal Temple in Serangoon Road, and carry their kavadis to Thandayuthapani Temple.[46] Devotees take kavadis for a diversity of reasons, but mainly to fulfil a vow, for healing within the family, or thanks for a petition answered by the deity.[47] While the most simple offering is a *paal kudam*, many devotees bear *paal* or *aluga* kavadis.[48] Most kavadi devotees also take three *vels*; a small *vel* which is passed through the skin of the forehead representing the mystical third eye,[49] another through the tongue and a third through the cheeks.[50] Many votaries are organized within temple or lineage groups and are guided by a recognized leader, often a spirit medium.[51] Worshippers achieve trance prior to the fitting of kavadis, with their retinue of supporters chanting to remove the pain as the *vels* and hooks are inserted.[52] In recent years there has been a significant increase in the numbers of non-Indian participants in Thaipusam.[53]

Over the years Thaipusam in Singapore has been subject to two major reformist pressures, firstly that of the Dravidian movement, and more recently that exerted by official bodies entrusted to manage Hindu affairs within the republic.

One of the avowed aims of the the Tamil Reform Association (TRA), which established a *Kalagam* in Singapore in 1932, was to "cleanse" Hinduism.[54] The TRA's attempts to ban the kavadi ritual were described in Chapter 4. The TRA and other related Dravidian organizations continued to exercise a major influence over Singapore Tamils until the 1960s, when a new generation of locally educated Hindus began to articulate concerns that were more specifically Singaporean in content.[55]

After gaining independence in 1965, the Singapore Government guaranteed religious freedom. However, in 1972 the government qualified this assurance with the dual stipulation that religions were required to be contemporary in outlook, and that their practices should aim to unify rather than divide the country. This declaration reflected the government's determination to ensure that religions did not intrude into the political sphere.[56]

Two quasi-governmental bodies are responsible for Hinduism in Singapore — the Hindu Endowment Board (or HEB), founded in 1905 as part of the Mohammaden and Hindu Endowment Board and charged with the administration of the major Hindu temples and the management of principal Hindu festivals; and the Hindu Advisory Board (or HAB), initially founded in 1915 by the colonial government to advise on matters relating to Hinduism. Both are entirely staffed by professionals, who have been anxious to remould Hinduism into a "modern" and largely textual religion; one which is allegedly more acceptable to the general public.[57] As Vineeta Sinha has explained, "the HEB and HAB are perceived by the Hindu lay public to be government bodies and are often seen as conduits through which the government is able to channel the expression of Hinduism in a certain direction".[58] Both the HEB and HAB have actively discouraged elements of popular Hinduism, especially those seen as "superstitious" and "primitive", as well as more emotional expressions of *bhakti*.[59]

Throughout the 1970s there was considerable debate about the need for musical accompaniment of the kavadi ritual at Thaipusam. Youths using "non-musical" instruments and alleged to be dancing "garishly" were viewed as diminishing the sacredness of Thaipusam.[60] In 1979 the HEB, having consulted the Ministry of Social Affairs, announced a raft of conditions which would henceforth apply to the commemoration of Thaipusam. These included a ban on musical instruments and a prohibition on dancing by those comprising the retinue of any kavadi bearer. Devotional Indian music was to be permitted only within temple compounds. Despite the objections of many Hindus, who argued that it was "traditional to have classical music accompany the kavadi bearers on their annual penance",[61] the ban on music and dancing was reaffirmed in 1981, and has never been revoked.[62]

Sri Lanka

While the kavadi ritual occurs at many Hindu temples within Sri Lanka,[63] the best-known instance of the kavadi ritual takes place at the Asala festival held annually in July–August at the major pilgrimage centre of Kataragama in southern Sri Lanka. The Asala festival commemorates Skanda's marriage to Valli, which is symbolized by the ritual journey of the deity in his *yantra* form to the shrine of Valli.[64] The Kataragama temple is sacred to Buddhists, Hindus and Muslims, and also attracts some Christian pilgrims.[65]

Kataragama is held to be the Sri Lankan location where the deity wooed and wed the damsel, Valli. The essential mythology attending this event is outlined in Chapter 5. The marriage is held to embody the very essence of *bhakti* spirituality, "the immediate spontaneous union of the soul with the divine".[66]

At Kataragama, Skanda-Murugan is viewed by his Tamil devotees as Kantali, "the reality transcending all categories without attachment, without form, standing alone as the Self".[67] The representation of Murugan claimed to be worshipped at Kataragama (claimed, because it is never displayed to the public), is not a conventional murthi or icon, but rather a six-pointed mystical *yantra* engraved upon a metal plate.[68]

At Kataragama, worship with kavadis is held to symbolize the soul's attempts to find union with the deity. The kavadi represents the human body inhabited by the devotee, the product of all the actions committed in this and other lives. The deity enshrined on the kavadi is illustrative of the god who resides within the devotee; in other words, the Supreme Reality sought by the aspirant. Two milk pots are secured to the kavadi — one represents the bad actions committed by the devotee; the other, good actions. Cumulatively, both comprise the metaphorical "burden" which is submitted by the kavadi bearer upon reaching his/her destination.[69] The kavadi is also recognized as a mode of invoking the powers of healing, and as a means of fulfilling vows.[70]

As in Malaysia, all devotees are expected to perform *tapas* before engaging in the kavadi ritual. These include prescribed fasting, and, at Kataragama, bathing in the Manik Ganga, adjacent to the complex, immediately prior to bearing the kavadi. Arumugam Rasiah lists several types of kavadi considered acceptable at Kataragama. These include the milk and dancing kavadis (equivalent to the Malaysian *paal* kavadi); *sedil* and chariot kavadis (both classified as *ter* kavadis in Malaysia); hanging kavadis (where a devotee is borne on a pole to which he is affixed by hooks and chains; the practice made its appearance in Sri Lanka in the 1940s); and the carrying of babies in temporary cradles slung from sugar cane.[71] Additional penances included rolling around the temple, a practice known as *anga pira thadchanai*, and indicating complete submission to the Lord; carrying pots full of burning camphor; or engaging in firewalking.[72] Among participating Hindus the bearing of a kavadi remains an austere ritual, potent with inner significance. All sections of Tamil society participate in various forms of the kavadi ritual.[73]

South Africa

The Hindu population of South Africa is largely descended from those Indians who were recruited to work as indentured labourers in the British colony of Natal during the latter part of the nineteenth century. This workforce was largely drawn from the Madras Presidency and from North East India.[74]

Hinduism in South Africa finds expression in ritual life, which includes the annual commemoration of a round of calendrical festivals. Kavadi bearing features prominently in the major festival observed by Tamil-speaking Hindus. The principal kavadi festivals are Thaipusam, Panguni Uttiram and Chitrai Paravum, celebrated respectively in the months of *Tai* (January–February), *Panguni* (March–April) and *Chitrai* (April–May.)[75] The July kavadi festival, held in about sixty temples throughout Durban, attracts large numbers of worshippers, and the mass celebration is believed to promote Hindu solidarity.[76]

Of these, Thaipusam is the most popular kavadi festival. More South African Hindus observe this festival than any other, and participation continues to increase, especially among younger Hindus. As in Malaysia, Thaipusam is commemorated as the occasion on which Parvati presented Murugan with the *Sakti Vel*, "the lance like symbol of spiritual knowledge and incisive discrimination".[77]

Fiji

The Hindu population of Fiji is mainly descended from the immigrant labourers who were recruited to Fiji between 1879 and 1916 to work in sugar and other plantation industries. A total of 60,965 adults migrated to Fiji, with about 93 per cent originating from North India (Uttar Pradesh, Bihar and Bengal), with the remainder drawn from the Madras Presidency. Of this number, about 85 per cent were Hindus, while 13 per cent were Muslims.[78] Most of the North Indian migrants were drawn from the middle-order agricultural castes.[79] Few of these labourers, who were known as *girmityas* (derived from the English word "agreement", referring to the workplace contract),[80] returned to India at the expiration of their period of indenture.[81]

As in Malaya, the system of indenture was run under a regime of extraordinary harshness. The hierarchical racial structures imposed by the British colonial overlords, which placed the Indians at the absolute base, was imposed with unrelenting rigidity.[82] The conditions of indenture, which totally defined Indians in terms of their function as units of labour, produced a brutalizing and demoralizing effect upon the workforce.[83]

While Indians made important economic and vocational advances, especially after World War II, and indeed became integral to the development of the South Pacific economy, their successes aroused the fears of native Fijians. From the outset the Fijians had viewed the Indians as "invaders",[84] and by the 1940s were advocating the formal repatriation of all Indians lest Fiji be converted into a "little India".[85] In 1963 the colonial government neutralized this perceived threat by enshrining Fijian establishment,[86] a manoeuvre designed to protect indigenous institutions and to ensure Fijian political control in perpetuity.[87]

Throughout their brief history in Fiji, Indian Hindus have relied upon their religion as a means to counter hegemonic discourse, and as a means of resisting the dominant political and social authority (initially of British colonialism, and in particular Christian missionaries,[88] and more latterly of rampant indigenous Fijian racial chauvinism),[89] as well as furnishing a cultural mode which signifies identity, integrity and authenticity. As such, the celebration of religion within the public arena may be regarded as a form of social statement, which not only speaks in the enclosed code of its devotees, but also sends broader and unambiguous messages to indigenous Fijians.[90]

In her study of firewalking among Indian Hindus in Fiji, Carol Henning Brown points out that throughout the earlier periods of the Indian experience in Fiji, South Indians constituted an excoriated and spurned minority, and had to struggle to retain their languages and culture against North Indian encroachment.[91] Firewalking thus became an agonistic demonstration of South Indian culture; an exhibition of Tamil spirituality which constituted a clear declaration to North Indians, and then as firewalking was increasingly taken up by the latter, to ethnic Fijians.[92]

Thaipusam has been celebrated in Fiji since the establishment of the Periyal Kovil on the banks of the Nandi River by a devotee, Ramasami Pillai, who hailed from Singaranandapur Village, in the Salem District of the Madras Presidency. The *kovil*, which has been upgraded over the years, and is now known as the Siva-Subramaniya Temple, remains the focal point for Thaipusam in Fiji.[93] The first kavadi was borne in 1920 by a devotee, Ambu Nair, who undertook a *pada yatra* of ninety kilometres to the temple. Thaipusam was initially celebrated as a ten-day festival, attracting Hindus from throughout Fiji, many of whom travelled to Nandi by boat to participate.[94] In recent years Thaipusam has become the largest Hindu festival in Fiji. During Thaipusam, daily *pujas*, *abishekams* and *homa* are conducted within the temple, while kavadis are borne around the temple by hundreds of devotees, usually in family groups.[95] The kavadi ritual includes piercing by *vels* and the pulling of *ter* kavadis. The temple chariot containing the *utsava murthi* of Murugan, Devayanai and Valli is paraded each night through adjacent neigbourhoods, stopping at all Hindu homes to allow offerings to be made.[96] Indeed, some Hindus, ex-Fijian nationals, but now resident in other countries, return to Fiji for this festival.[97] Thaipusam is also celebrated at Murugan temples located in Tagi Tagi, Koronbu and Navua. Worship with kavadis is also a feature of the festival of *Panguni Uttiram*, which is the other major Murugan festival observed in Fiji.[98]

The Seychelles

Thaipusam within The Seychelles provides an instance of the recent introduction of the kavadi ritual to a Hindu community, and its subsequent fostering as a quintessential ingredient, if not a distillation, of Tamil Hindu culture.[99]

The Seychelles is a small, multi-ethnic island located in the Indian Ocean, approximately a thousand miles from India. The total population is 81,000, overwhelmingly concentrated on the main island of Mahe, which also contains the capital, Victoria. The Tamil-speaking population in 2001 was approximately 3,500 people (or roughly four per cent of the total population). Tamil traders, especially from the Kaveri delta, were active in The Seychelles well before the arrival of European colonial powers, and exploited the native timber, which was exported to Pondicherry. The Tamil community became established in The Seychelles from 1864 onwards, and by 1901 numbered 332 families. The community has largely been involved in business enterprises.

The Tamil community was slow to develop its own cultural and religious institutions, and early attempts to commemorate festivals were both spasmodic and abortive. In 1984, 120 years after the establishment of a permanent Tamil community in The Seychelles, a group of devotees gathered together to establish The Seychelles Hindu Koyil Sangam. This body, buttressed by substantial donations from the community, purchased land in the centre of Victoria, and subsequently constructed a "traditional" temple, the Arul Mihu Navasakhti Vinayagar Temple, which was dedicated in May 1992. Although the presiding deity was Ganesha, supplementary shrines were established for other deities, including Murugan, Nadarajah and Durga. The temple became the focal point for a Hindu cultural and religious resurgence.

The Thaipusam festival was first commemorated in 1993. During the inaugural year the kavadi procession was restricted to the courtyard of the temple. A total of sixteen devotees took kavadis. By 1999 the festival followed a processional route along the public highway, and involved fifty-one kavadi bearers. A troupe was engaged from Tamil Nadu to provide appropriate temple music, believed to assist in the process of promoting trance and easing the ritual of insertions, and ritual specialists, skilled in the fitting of hooks and *vels*, were imported from India to officiate throughout the festival. The festival has attracted wide coverage within the local media. Thaipusam concludes with a common lunch (*annathanam*) in which the entire community participates.

Thaipusam in The Seychelles commemorates Murugan's marriage to Valli (thus replacing the standard explanation of Thaipusam as a commemoration of Parvati's bestowal of the *Sakti Vel* upon Murugan). The mythology of Idumban and the original kavadi does not feature; here the kavadi is envisaged as a form of karmic axis, with the milk pot balanced at one end representing the good deeds the devotee has performed, whereas the milk pot balanced at the other end represents the individual's evil deeds. In approaching the deity the devotee does not ask to be relieved of the burden of ignorance, as is the case elsewhere, but rather appeals for forgiveness for evil deeds as well as blessings for the good actions he/she has performed. The festival is seen as embodying values and traditions that are integral to Tamil culture and identity.

Mauritius

The earliest Tamil migrants to Mauritius arrived in the eighteenth century, during the period of French colonization. Most of these immigrants were artisans and traders.[100] Throughout the nineteenth century this population was augmented by the arrival of thousands of South Indian labourers who were imported to work on sugar estates. While earlier groups of settlers constructed temples according to *Agamic* rites, estate Indians built their own places of worship and commemorated the festivals they had known in their homeland.

By 1960 there were approximately 110 Tamil temples established on Mauritius, of which thirty were dedicated to Murugan. While many of the remaining *kovils* were consecrated Amman or Siva temples, all contained Murugan shrines. Worship with kavadis is conducted at all Tamil temples throughout Mauritius.

Although the full round of calendrical festivals is commemorated in Mauritian temples, the major deity worshipped is Murugan, and festivals dedicated to him are marked with particular fervour. Of these, Thaipusam has emerged as the central Tamil Hindu festival, and its observance has assumed national significance. Rituals of worship are consciously modelled on those of Palani, India. Mauritius Tamils consider the Murukan Kovil de Garde Mountain as the local equivalent of Palani.

For many Mauritian Tamils, Murugan has assumed a central and definitive significance in articulating and asserting Tamil identity. The kavadi ritual, involving ecstatic trance states is seen as integral to his worship. Indeed, Khevasan Sornum remarks, "Frenzy is possible and indulged in unashamedly ... by ... the kavati carrier. The individual man or woman can enjoy the experiences of divine tremors, especially when hearing devotional hymns and concentrating upon the Lord."[101]

Thaipusam features a chariot procession and the offering of trays to the deity within. Devotees smash coconuts in the path of the chariot. Votaries participating in kavadi bearing observe ten days of disciplined fasting, which involves a vegetarian diet of food prepared within the home, abstinence from alcohol and sexual relations, avoidance of weddings and funerals, and sleeping on a mat on the floor. The kavadis borne by Mauritian aspirants are similar to those taken in Malaysia, and include the piercing of tongues and cheeks with *vels*, the carrying of *vel, aluga* and *ter* kavadis, and *paal kudam*. Other devotees sleep on beds of nails, and walk upon nail slippers. A lemon is attached to all kavadis and borne to the shrine. Many of those who are afflicted with illness, lie on the ground and allow kavadi bearers to pass above them.

In recent years visiting religious specialists from India have begun advising Mauritian Hindus on rituals and doctrinal matters, and providing religious education for the young. Public participation in religious festivals has continued to increase annually. Mauritian Hindus migrating to Europe, North America and Australia have shown their determination to maintain the kavadi ritual as an integral part of the panoply of their religious traditions.

Medan, Indonesia

The history of Tamil immigration to North Sumatra echoes that of Malaya; namely, a largely unskilled and mainly Tamil workforce recruited to work in the plantation economy (in this case, tobacco) and on public works.[102] In the early 1990s the Tamil population numbered about eighteen thousand, most of whom lived in poverty. Over time the Telegu minority have been acculturated into the majority community, which continues to remain structured according to caste.

Since World War II, various associations have been founded to promote and preserve Tamil culture. Most Tamils maintain their cultural values through a process of active identification with the Tamil populations of adjacent areas. Many listen to Tamil radio programmes broadcast from Malaysia and Singapore, watch Tamil cinema, and continue to acquire Tamil cassettes and DVDs from both countries.

The early plantation labourers constructed temples to the deities known from their homelands. These included Mariamman, Murugan, Kaliamman and Muneeswaran.The most important temple is the Sri Mariamman Kovil, constructed in 1884 and dedicated to Mariamman. This temple contains shrines to Palaiyar (Ganesha) and Murugan. However, Tamil Hindus continue to support two other major temples: the Kaliamman Temple and the Thanduyudapani Temple. Some years ago the Indonesian government, through the Religious Affairs Department, Jakarta, appointed the Devastanam of the Sri Mariamman Temple as the official representatives of the entire Tamil community in North Sumatra. This was despite the fact that none of the remaining fifteen temples in Medan was willing to accept this temple's authority on religious matters.

The Hindu community celebrated all major calendrical festivals according to an annual schedule furnished by the Sri Maha Mariamman Kovil of Kuala Lumpur. Over the years, *timiti* (firewalking dedicated to Draupadi Amman) and Thaipusam emerged as the most prominent festivals, with Thaipusam assuming an ever-increasing centrality to the spiritual life of Medan's Tamil Hindus. The festival featured both the kavadi ritual and a chariot procession. Devotees would bathe in the Barbura River, the main watercourse of Medan, adjacent to the Kaliamman Temple, and subsequently bear their kavadis to the Sri Mariamman Kovil.

In 1973 the Chairman of the Sri Mariamman Temple, Marimuthu Pillai, a multi-millionaire patriarch of an influential family which owned textile mills in Java, proposed a ban on kavadi bearing at the temple. Marimuthu contended that Hindus in Medan were now Indonesian Hindus and should accordingly emulate the Balinese Hindus, even though the two groups belong to entirely different traditions. Marimuthu also contended that self-mortification practices "degraded" Tamils in the sight of other Indonesians and reinforced their status as "aliens".[103] In 1974 the ban was extended to all temples and publicly celebrated festivals, and was enforced with the assistance of local police.[104]

Members of the *Adi Dravida* castes who too openly expressed opposition to the ban were subsequently detained by *Kopkamtib*, the branch of the Indonesian military which exercised responsibility for the maintenance of internal security. It was strongly believed that many of these arrests followed denunciations (including anonymous letters) circulated by the administration of the Sri Mariamman Temple. This coercion effectively silenced a number of prominent members of the Tamil community who might otherwise have been expected to publicly oppose the ban.

The ban deeply divided the community, and especially disturbed the large *Adi Dravida* working class, which considered that throughout the years since their initial migration from India they had gradually lost the accretions of a great and rich Hindu tradition, and that kavadis and other ritual forms of worship were all that were left to them to commemorate their Tamil Hindu identity. Members of the Tamil community contended that the process of enforced Indonesian acculturation was driven by the restricted views of the officially recognized "reform" group associated with the management of the Sri Mariamman Temple, who had demonstrated their willingness to arbitrarily suppress long-established traditional forms of cultural expression and worship. Many hundreds of Medan Hindus subsequently paid annual visits to Penang each Thaipusam to participate in traditional worship in Malaysia.

Conclusions

This chapter clearly demonstrates the interrelated phenomena of Murugan worship, Thaipusam and/or similar festivals, and that kavadi rituals involving trance or dissociative states, often including fleshly mortification, are found widely within the world of Tamil Hinduism and indeed constitute powerful, generally accepted and enduring expressions and symbols of Tamil *bhakti* religiosity and cultural identity.

Both colonial records and contemporary accounts reveal that the kavadi ritual is found at many sites throughout South India, and is particularly associated with the *bhakti* worship of the deity Murugan. This is confirmed by my own field observations, which also indicate that worship with kavadis is found among most sectors of the South Indian Hindu population. This often involves fleshly mortification (including, at least on some occasions, members of Brahman castes). These rituals and forms of *bhakti* religiosity are thus firmly grounded in metropolitan traditions and have accompanied Tamil Hindus to various locations within the Tamil diaspora. The geographically scattered communities which commemorate Murugan worship and Thaipusam (and/or related festivals) show wide variations in terms of their representative social, economic and political standings, and include affluent merchant communities (e.g., The Seychelles) and societies in which Tamils enjoy considerable political power (e.g., Mauritius).

These conclusions clearly shatter two assumptions so commonly advanced by scholars and observers of Thaipusam in Malaysia and Singapore; namely:

1. That Thaipusam as practised in Malaysia is banned in India; and
2. That kavadi worship is restricted to lower castes or *Adi Dravidas*, and constitutes a basic village ritual.

The description of the Brahman *pada yatra* firmly locates Thaipusam and the kavadi ritual within the overarching framework of the Hindu pilgrimage tradition, with its inherent formalities of ritual separation from mundane routines as a prelude to the journey, both physical and metaphysical, to the *axis mundi*, for the encounter with the deity. The pilgrimage is conceived as an experiential catalyst which, inter alia, interrupts everyday notions, thus opening the devotee to a range of fresh cosmic potentialities which redefine the individual's relationship to the deity and move him/her indefinably closer to the reality of *moksha*. This ritual will be more closely examined in the following chapter.

Notes

1. Klaus K. Klostermaier, *A Survey of Hinduism* (Albany: State University of New York Press, 1994), pp. 286–87; Lakshmanan Chettiar, *The Folklore of Tamil Nadu* (New Delhi: National Book Trust, 1973), p. 65.
2. These figures are based on press estimates. The number of kavadi bearers seems to be extraordinarily high, especially when compared to figures at Batu Caves. However, it is impossible to gauge a more accurate calculation. Many devotees bear their kavadis throughout the night, including the early hours of the morning, in order to avoid the heat of the day, and in particular the foot-burning bitumen roads.
3. *Pongal*: boiling of rice and milk in a pot. This ritual is quintessentially associated with the Tamil harvest festival *Tai Pongal* (Lakshmanan, *The Folklore of Tamil Nadu*, pp. 104–5), but may also represent a ritual conducted to Lord Ganesha as Remover of Obstacles.
4. *Homa* Fire: This is a fire offering, a ritual in which the deity is supplicated through the medium of fire, which is usually set in a sanctified pit.
5. The chief minister also usually visits other major (non-Chettiar controlled) temples. However, in dining at the Chettiar temple, he implicitly recognizes overall Chettiar management and direction of Thaipusam and, more generally, of Hinduism in Penang.
6. However, a small minority of kavadi bearers refuse to enter the temple, thus rejecting Chettiar sponsorship and (implied) authority.
7. This ritual appears to be based on village ceremonies found in certain parts of Tamil Nadu. The festival of *Panguni Uttiram*, conducted in *Agamic* temples, commemorates Murugan's marriage to Valli (in some centres Devayanai and in others both Devayanai and Valli), and is held on the full moon day of the Tamil month of *Panguni* (March–April) (Gomathi Thiruvasagam, *Book of Festivals* [Kuala Lumpur: Saiva Siddhanta Mandram, 1992], p. 42).
8. Kalimuthu Ramanathan, "Hindu Religion in an Islamic State: The Case of Malaysia" (PhD dissertation, Universeit Van Amsterdam, 1995), p. 108.
9. Brenda Beck, "Colour and Heat in South Indian Ritual", *Man* 4 (1969): 554–58.
10. The issue of heating and cooling will be discussed in the following chapter.

11. Vow fulfilment at Thaipusam occurs within the context of pilgrimage, of stepping outside the boundaries of the mundane. Pilgrimage involves asceticism, self-denial, sacrifice and devotion. Coconut smashing has long been regarded as an accepted form of vow fulfilment. Devotees point out that the smashing of a single coconut is a routine temple ritual, which is also performed during anniversaries and other quotidian commemorations, and thus cannot be regarded as vow fulfilment.
12. *New Straits Times*, 30 January 1999.
13. Somalay, *Palni: The Hill Temple of Murugan*, 2nd rev. ed. (Palani: Sri Dhandayuthapani Swami Devasthanam, 1982), p. 71.
14. Henry Whitehead, *The Village Gods of India* (Calcutta: Association Press, 1921), pp. 46–47.
15. Ibid., p. 119.
16. L.S.S. O'Malley, *Popular Hinduism: The Religion of the Masses* (London: Cambridge University Press, 1935), p. 7.
17. Whitehead, *The Village Gods*, p. 29.
18. Ibid., p. 76.
19. Ibid., p. 79.
20. O'Malley, *Popular Hinduism*, p. 102.
21. Ibid., pp. 103–4.
22. Fred W. Clothey, *The Many Faces of Murukan — The History and Meaning of a South Indian God* (The Hague: Mouton, 1978), p. 126.
23. Gomathi, *The Book of Festivals*, p. 5.
24. Clothey, *The Many Faces of Murukan*, p. 126.
25. Ibid., p. 119.
26. Ibid., p. 120.
27. Somalay, *Palni*, pp. 27–29. Correspondence with associates in India suggests that these figures have markedly increased in recent years.
28. <http://www.indiatravelportal.com> (accessed July 2003; unchanged in August 2010).
29. Gomathi, *Book of Festivals*, p. 3.
30. Madeleine Biardeau, "Brahmans and Meat Eating Gods", in *Criminal Gods and Demon Devotees: Essays on the Guardians of Popular Hinduism*, edited by Alf Hiltebeital (Albany: State University of New York Press, 1989), pp. 20–21.
31. Ibid.
32. Brahman food is regarded as high-quality cuisine, and because it is ritually pure it may be consumed by all castes. It is thus in constant demand for weddings, temple ceremonies and other ritual and social functions.
33. An element of play and competition pervaded the relationship between the Brahmans and the (low-caste) drummers. As the Brahmans performed an increasingly complex set of songs, they would deliberately alter the tempo

and rhythms in an attempt to confuse the drummers. Each variation was met with immediate grins as the drummers effortlessly accommodated the revised structure.

34. The drumming was so pervasive, that when drinking water from a bottle I could feel the vibrations through the plastic, and in holding the bottle in front of me I could see the water in a state of semi-agitation. I was informed that these drummers were members of a *jati* related to the Chettiar/Mudialiar castes, and that the drumming signified the mustering of Murugan's army of *devas* prior to the battle with the *asuric* army of Surapadman. The ritual of impassioned drumming is maintained for hours, indeed for most of Thaipusam day. The devotees are replaced at regular intervals by fresh "shifts" of drummers, so there is no break in continuity.

35. Kernial Singh Sandhu, "Indian Immigration and Settlement in Singapore", in *Indian Communities in Southeast Asia*, edited by K.S. Sandhu and A. Mani (Singapore: Institute of Southeast Asian Studies, 1993), p. 774.

36. G. Shantakumar and Pundarik Mukhopadhya, "Demographics, Incomes and Development Issues amongst Indians in Singapore", in *Rising India and Indian Communities in East Asia*, edited by K. Kesavapany, A. Mani, and P. Ramasamy (Singapore: Institute of Southeast Asian Studies, 2008), p. 568.

37. Asad-ul Iqbal Latif, "From Mandalas to Microchips: The Indian Imprint on the Construction of Singapore", in *Rising India and Indian Communities in East Asia*, edited by K. Kesavapany, A. Mani, and P. Ramasamy (Singapore: Institute of Southeast Asian Studies, 2008), p. 561.

38. Vineeta Sinha, *A New God in the Diaspora? Muneeswaran Worship in Contemporary Singapore* (Singapore and Copenhagen: Singapore University Press/NIAS Press, 2005), p. 25.

39. Vineeta Sinha, "Hinduism in Contemporary Singapore", in *Indian Communities in Southeast Asia*, edited by K.S. Sandhu and A. Mani (Singapore: Institute of Southeast Asian Studies, 1993), p. 828.

40. Latif, "From Mandalas to Microchips", pp. 561–62.

41. A. Mani, "Indians in Singapore", in *Indian Communities in Southeast Asia*, edited by K.S. Sandhu and A. Mani (Singapore: Institute of Southeast Asian Studies, 1993), p. 802.

42. Lawrence A. Babb, *Thaipusam in Singapore: Religious Individualism in a Hierarchical Culture*, Department of Sociology Working Paper no. 49 (Singapore: University of Singapore, 1976), p. 8.

43. Ibid., p. 5.

44. Hans Deiter Evers and Jayarani Pavadarayan, "Religious Fervour and Economic Success: The Chettiars of Singapore", in *Indian Communities in Southeast Asia*, edited by K.S. Sandhu and A. Mani (Singapore: Institute of Southeast Asian Studies, 1993), p. 854.

45. Alfredo Roces, "A Matter of Mind Over Matter", *Geo* 3, no. 4 (1981): 88.

46. Arthur Hullett, "Thaipusam and the Cult of Subramaniam", *Geo* 3, no. 4 (1981): 79.

47. Ibid., p. 86.

48. Babb, *Thaipusam in Singapore*, p. 9.

49. Roces, "A Matter of Mind over Matter", p. 86.

50. Babb, *Thaipusam in Singapore*, p. 9.

51. Ibid.

52. Roces, "A Matter of Mind Over Matter", p. 87.

53. Sinha, *A New God*, p. 3.

54. Sinha, "Hinduism in Contemporary Singapore", p. 829.

55. Mani, *Indians in Singapore*, pp. 796–97.

56. Sinha, "Hinduism in Contemporary Singapore", pp. 826–27.

57. Ibid., pp. 831–39.

58. Ibid., p. 834.

59. Sinha, *A New God?*, p. 37.

60. Sinha, "Hinduism in Contemporary Singapore", p. 832.

61. Ibid.

62. Interviews with temple officials.

63. Arumugam Rasiah, *Kataragama: Divine Power of Karthirkaman and Methods of Realization* (Sithankerny: Holiday Ashram, 1981), p. 38.

64. Donald K. Swearer, "The Kataragama and Kandy Asala Peraharaj: Juxtaposing Religious Elements in Sri Lanka", in *Religious Festivals in South India and Sri Lanka*, edited by Guy R. Welbon and Glen Yocum (Delhi: Manohar, 1978), p. 301.

65. Hilda K. Link, "Where Valli meets Murukan: 'Landscape' Symbolism in Kataragama", *Anthropos*, no. 92 (1997): 91.

66. David Dean Shulman, *Tamil Temple Myths: Sacrifice and Divine Marriage in the South Indian Saiva Tradition* (Princeton, NJ: Princeton University Press, 1980), p. 281.

67. Swearer, "The Kataragama and Kandy Asala Peraharaj", p. 302.

68. Patrick Harrigan, "Sacred Geography and the Cult of Skanda-Murugan", *Journal of the Institute of Asian Studies* 15, no. 2 (March 1998): 39.

69. Arumugam, *Kataragama*, p. 38.

70. Ibid., p. 39.

71. Ibid., pp 40–44.

72. Ibid., pp. 44, 85.

73. Swearer, "The Kataragama and Asala Peraharaj", p. 302.

74. R.R. Pillai, "The Kavati Ritual as a Paradigm of Hindu-Religio-Expression", *Journal of the Institute of Asian Studies* 13, no. 2 (March 1996): 74.

75. Ibid.

76. Personal correspondence.
77. Personal correspondence. For a detailed description of the kavadi ritual at the *Panguni Uttiram* festival at the Civa Cupprimaniyar Temple at Brake Village, Tongaat, north of Durban, in Natal Province, see Pillai, "The Kavati Ritual".
78. Henry Srebrnik, "Indo-Fijians: Marooned without Land and Power in a South Pacific Archipelago", in *Tracing an Indian Diaspora: Contexts, Memories, Representations*, edited by Parvati Raghuram, Ajaya Kumar Sahoo, Brij Maharaj, and Dave Sangha (New Delhi: Sage, 2008), p. 77.
79. Brigadier V. Lal, "The Wreck of the Syria", in *The Indo-Fijian Experience*, edited by Subramani (St. Lucia: University of Queensland Press, 1979), pp. 27–28.
80. John D. Kelly, *A Politics of Virtue: Hinduism, Sexuality and Countercolonial Discourse in Fiji* (Chicago: University of Chicago Press, 1991), p. 1.
81. Ahmad Ali, "Indians in Fiji: An Interpretation", in *The Indo-Fijian Experience*, edited by Subramani (St. Lucia: University of Queensland Press, 1979), p. 8.
82. Ibid., p. 5.
83. Kelly, *A Politics of Virtue*, p. 29; Walter Gill, *Turn Left at Tombstone* (Adelaide: Rigby, 1970), p. 65.
84. Ahmad Ali, "Indians in Fiji", p. 4.
85. Pia Manoa, "Across the Fence", in *The Indo-Fijian Experience*, edited by Subramani (St. Lucia: University of Queensland Press, 1979), p. 187.
86. Ahmad Ali, "Indians in Fiji", p. 17.
87. Manoa, "Across the Fence", p. 205.
88. Kelly, *A Politics of Virtue*, pp. 207, 245.
89. Srebrnik, *Indo-Fijians*, pp. 85–87.
90. Carol Henning Brown, "Tourism and Ethnic Competition in a Ritual Form: The Firewalkers of Fiji", *Oceania* 54 (1984): 241.
91. Ibid., p. 224.
92. Ibid., p. 225.
93. R. Ponnu S. Goundar, "Murugan Worship in Fiji" <http://www/murugan. org/research/goundar.htm> (accessed 28 September 2003).
94. Ibid.
95. *Hinduism Today* 10, no. 3 (April 1988).
96. *Hinduism Today* 17, no. 4 (April 1995).
97. Interviews with ex-Fijian devotees in various Australian locations.
98. Goundar, *Murugan Worship in Fiji*.
99. This section was compiled on the basis of information kindly supplied by Mr Vijayaratnam Sivasupramaniam of The Seychelles. See also V. Sivasupramaniam, *Decade of Growth: Seychelles Arul Mihu Navasakthi Vinayaga Temple 1992–2002* (Seychelles: V. Sivasupramaniam, 2003).
100. This section is partially based on Khevesan Sornum's paper, "The Murukan Cult in Mauritius: Essence of Tamil Ethnic Identity", Second International

Conference on Skanda-Murukan, Port Louis, 24–28 April 2001. The paper is also found at <http://www.murugan.org/research/sornum.htm>. The section also draws upon email correspondence with Mauritian Hindu devotees conducted in 2013–14.

101. Khevesan, *The Murukan Cult*.

102. This section draws upon the scholarship of A. Mani, and in particular his "Indians in North Sumatra", in *Indian Communities in Southeast Asia*, edited by K.S. Sandhu and A. Mani (Singapore: Institute of Southeast Asian Studies, 1993).

103. Presumably, in reaching this judgement, Marimuthu was fully aware that Balinese Hindus also engage in public rites which involve both trance states and self mortification. See Nina Epton, "Kris Dancing in Bali", in *Trances*, edited by Stuart Wavell, Audrey Butt, and Nina Epton (Kuala Lumpur: Antara Book Company, 1988).

104. Mani points out that the ban proceeded against an extraordinary sequence of events:

    (i)   The committee which endorsed Marimuthu's proposal had earlier worked enthusiastically to promote traditional festivals, and had even invited Tamil Hindu priests from Malaysia to visit and advise on how best these might be conducted.

    (ii) The officer in charge of the Hindu Affairs at the Ministry of Religion in Jakarta (a graduate of the Benaras Hindu University, India) had studied Hindu behaviour in North Sumatra. He sought advice from officials at the Indian Embassy, Jakarta, who responded that in their opinion the kavadi ritual might well fall under the rubric of traditional Hinduism.

    (iii) Certain Hindus did not hesitate to accuse the chairman of bad faith; that is, "selling" religion for personal profit, and the temple administration which had so nimbly shifted position as "having changed their views …[to accord with those of the chairman]… in order to gain economic rewards". (More affluent members of the Tamil community who supported the ban were fully aware of the economic and other benefits which might flow to members of an officially recognized "indigenous" religion. (Mani, "Indians in North Sumatra", pp. 80–81)

8

Thaipusam Considered:
The Divine Crossing

This chapter will explore the kavadi ritual at Thaipusam through the structures of the Tamil Hindu pilgrimage ritual. This will examine theoretical notions of pilgrimage and the implications for the individual participant. The chapter will also investigate how Hindu ritual performs its work, and how it enables the devotee to affect a paradigm shift in the circumstances of his/her mundane existence through an appeal to and interaction with the Divine. This process involves substantial modification and transformation, which must be undertaken at a ritually propitious moment. At Thaipusam this follows the installation of the king-deity Murugan in his mountaintop palace, and his consequent readiness to grant audience to his devotees. The chapter looks at asceticism and change, the liminality of trance and its application as an agent of transformation at Thaipusam, and the multivalent symbology of the journey to the caves. Finally, this chapter makes reference to the Idumban *puja*, in which the devotee is restored to society, as well as the heat–colour paradigm.

At this juncture it may be germane to offer some basic observations regarding the role, function and potentially catalytic power of religious ritual. In the previous chapter we noted that ritual is the enactment of myth, in effect testing the validity and inner truth of that myth.[1] The anthropologist Arnold van Gennep postulated that ritual fell into three distinct phases, namely:

1. A phase of separation in which the devotee withdraws from mundane routines into "sacred time" (that is, time outside the quotidian) and embarks upon a period of preparation for the main phase of the ritual.
2. A transformative phase in which the individual is in a state of "betwixt and between". Victor Turner has famously described this phase as that of liminality, a period in which the receptive devotee, freed from the mundane, experiences new perceptions of reality and in which the mind will "proliferate new structures, new symbols, new metaphors".
3. A reincorporative phase in which the individual, newly transmuted, is returned to quotidian routines.[2]

Recent neuroscientific research suggests that ritual strongly blends reason and emotion at crucial moments within our lives, in effect "rewiring" our experiences and perceptions of the world and our place within it.[3] At its most powerful, ritual will transmit more compellingly than doctrine the essential truths of a tradition, and more importantly, by fusing ritual with text, will enable the devotee to "live" the broader truths of that tradition, and thus participate in those truths.[4]

However, the impact of ritual is dependent upon its overall structure and content, and in particular the balance achieved along a continuum running between the oppositional poles of emotion and reason. Following A. Hocart, Anne de Sales points out that rituals which fall at either extreme of this spectrum will lose their efficacy. Thus a ritual which has been subject to over-rationalization (one that, in de Sales' words, is "controlled by the dry minds of the elite") will become empty, sterile and devoid of meaning, whereas one which is simply the product of raw emotions will succumb to populist fervour and hysteria. To be fully effective a ritual must maintain its evolutionary flexibility combined with the "healthy emotion" of its origins.[5]

Rituals admit the seeker into a particular worldview, and not only address basic existential questions but provide a sense of identity.[6] But rituals do more than operate on an individual level; they embrace a community of co-believers, and ensure that the collective wisdom and traditions bequeathed from the past are preserved and transmitted to the rising generation.[7] Rituals extend beyond the provincial level and signal allegiances and a sense of shared identity to similar believers in other localities. In the case of migratory communities, they provide a sense of shared heritage, an enduring link which reaches not only to the country of origin, the metropolis, but also to other members of the broader diaspora.[8]

Pilgrimage: The *Tirtha Yatra*

Within the Hindu tradition, pilgrimage is known as a *tirtha yatra*, that is, a round journey or *yatra* to a "ford" or crossing place (*tirtha*).[9] While rivers are identified as the holiest places in *Puranic* mythology, and some *tirthas* may actually consist of river crossings, the term may be more literally interpreted to incorporate any pilgrimage centre, any one of a broad range of liminal median locations, symbolic and spiritual "fords", in which the boundary between human and divine worlds is both permeable and negotiable.[10] In the most general sense, then, a pilgrimage may be viewed as a return journey to a destination (or "crossing place") where deities normally transcendent are both immanent and accessible.[11]

Pilgrimages are regarded as intrinsically different from visits to village temples or shrines. Local temples and shrines are regarded as appropriate venues for routine worship, general transactions between devotee and deity, and the resolution of standard problems of life, especially wellbeing and happiness.[12] However, many of these shrines and temples are dedicated to the celebration of village or district-specific gods and spirits, frequently of human origin, "whose worship …[is]… susceptible to manipulation rather than adoration".[13] Even when the presiding deity of a village or district temple or shrine is a member of the recognized *Agamic* pantheon, it will be regarded as a secondary dwelling for a god (or goddess) whose sacred geography locates his/her "essential abode" elsewhere.[14] In sum, local places of worship do not offer the efficacy or power of the great pilgrimage centres. Nor does a visit to the local or district shrine require either the effort or the disruption to societal routines involved in undertaking a *tirtha yatra*, or deliver the merit (*punya*) that the pilgrimage earns the devotee.[15]

A pilgrimage centre may be conceptualized as an *axis mundi*, a central and crucial pivot of the universe which is considered outside mundane time and space, even though it is a visible site on earth as well.[16] The shrine is idealized as a ritually ordered universe, and the gatekeeper marks the point of transition from the outside world — a place marked by the chaos, sorrow and flux of the *Kaliyuga* (current age) — to the otherworldly shrine. The ritual ordering of the universe within the shrine thus creates a structured ideal which is in diametric opposition to the disorderly world that exists beyond the shrine's boundaries. The heart of the shrine is suffused with sacred power which is a dense and patterned representation of ritual symbolism.[17] The shrine is viewed as a microcosm of creation in its entirety, the centre of the universe, the one location that is linked to other worlds.[18]

Vineeta Sinha has pointed out that Hindus have well-developed concepts of what might be termed "ritual/sacred spaces" and has shown how these relate to broader notions of divinity, and in specific focal points where a particular deity has manifested.[19] Hindu pilgrimage sites thus have their genesis in scenes of mythological action involving a particular formative phase of a deity's cosmology, or settings for demonstrations of that deity's power or benevolence. This event will be incorporated in what Alan Moronis has described as a "foundation narrative"; that is, an account which simultaneously fixes certain deeds of the deity at a given geographical location at a specific point in time, but also situates these deeds within the context of a philosophical tradition — eternal and thus outside the constraints of linear time — with which the deity is associated. The essential elements of the myth which establishes the nexus between deity and site now proclaim the locale a place where the devotee may anticipate an encounter with the god or goddess.[20] Over the years the veracity of the locale as a place of pilgrimage will be continuously reinforced by the occurrence and recounting of the "miracles" which will substantiate both the deity's presence and his/her willingness to implicate himself/herself in the affairs of his/her devotees.[21]

Localization of mythic action is an especially conspicuous feature of Tamil *Puranas*, and pilgrimage sites are firmly linked to a specific phase of the deity's history. Deities are thus often rooted in a particular territory which is rightfully owned by them, and thus considered to be their province. Territoriality is their characteristic trait, and linkage to a particular event within the overall mythology means that a god of a given location will have a distinctive manifestation, even though he may bear the same name as the same god at another pilgrimage site.[22] Just as localization establishes a nexus between place and mythic action, so it determines and prescribes the forms of ritual worship considered appropriate at a given venue.[23]

Despite the multiplicity of pilgrimage sites in South India, each shrine is viewed as the centre of the universe, an *axis mundi*, the one ordered site that is directly linked to the world of the deities. Cumulatively, these localities provide a sacred geography which not only chronicles the actions and manifestations of a particular deity, but is spatially related to the others in an integrated system of religious topography. Thus each pilgrimage site comprises a node of a wider and unified symbolic domain which embraces the totality of a given deity, and allows the devotees to retrace the narrative and cosmology of his/her object of veneration.[24] As Moronis remarks, "Pilgrimage places as sites where the divine has manifested itself are therefore acknowledged as points on earth especially suited for approach to the deity, for here the immanent deity has 'proven' to be accessible."[25]

Pilgrimage centres are often important focal points for a given sect, cult or tradition, drawing votaries from a wide area; in the case of very important pilgrimage sites (for example Varanasi), from all over India.[26] Frequently they are institutional systems in their own right, containing temples, priests, and sometimes *mathas* and/or *asrama*, and delineating the conventions of symbolic behaviour considered proper for the worship of a particular manifestation of the deity. As such they are often central points for the propagation and dissemination of the orthodox forms of a specific cult.[27] The authoritative ritual symbolism situated with the sacred zones of the pilgrimage sites is constantly animated by the presence and actions of the continual crowds of devotees, together with sacramental specialists, normally priests and related officiants.[28]

Hindu pilgrimage centres are often associated with noteworthy geographical features; indeed, prominent natural landmarks are almost invariably imbued with mythology and folklore.[29] Dolf Hartsuiker has commented that:

> The Hindus inhabit an enchanted land where the Divine makes its presence known in a multitude of forms: mountains, rocks, boulders, stones, oceans, rivers, lakes, wells, trees and human beings. And as if that is not enough the Divine manifests itself in "self-created" and man-made sculptures and images in hymns and songs.[30]

Pilgrimage sites are especially linked with water and mountains;[31] indeed, a Tamil precept suggests that a *yatra* invariably commences in a river and ends in a mountain.[32] Caves are also a recurring feature image in Hindu belief, functioning both as a place of retreat and as an abode for the gods.[33] Mountains are often homologized to the Hindu temple and are viewed as symbolically linking heaven and earth, while caves are regarded as the physical equivalent of the temple *sanctum sanctorum*, the source of the temple's divine power.[34]

While pilgrimage sites may be linked to geographic features, and as a sacred destination draw people from a wide area, in esoteric terms pilgrimage sites may be homologized to the inner *tirthas* within the human body, so that a *yatra* is recognized as a journey to the deity within.[35] Thus, theoretically, the enlightened Hindu may participate in a pilgrimage without actually leaving home, just as the worshipper may revere a deity within his/her body conceived as a temple.[36] And just as each shrine is identified with the centre of the universe, so the hidden centre of each human — the heart, concealed source of life which sustains each body — is viewed as the internal shrine, which, like the pilgrimage centre, is linked to the infinite shrine.[37] Indeed, while Hindu texts may praise the outer pilgrimage, they simultaneously recognize that the primary basis for truth, purity and *moksha* lies within the votary.[38]

As we have noted, the *yatra* entails a ritualized visit to a location where the deity is recognized as immanent and thus approachable. This will involve a period of intense preparation for the forthcoming encounter with the deity, in which the votary is detached from the societal routines of the mundane world and focuses upon cultivating the selfless devotion which ideally should permeate the entire pilgrimage.[39] This detachment will require the temporary adoption of an ascetic code of behaviour more typically associated with the *sannyasin*, or renunciant. Indeed, pilgrimage is often envisaged as a substitute for *sannyasa*/renunciation, a view consistent with Saivite *bhakti* philosophy, which highlights the importance of human experience in perceiving divinity.[40] The chief behavioural characteristics of a renunciant are indifference to both family and caste origins, the rejection of personal property, and the ceaseless and single-minded determination to seek and unite with the deity. This goal may be achieved through the exhaustive practice of *tapas* (austerities), yogic disciplines, or ecstatic *bhakti*. However, while the pilgrim may, for the duration of the *yatra*, conform to the ideal of renunciation, the path of asceticism is to be regarded as a passing phase to be measured in weeks or months rather than in terms of the lifetime vows to be taken by the *sannyasin*. Ascetic practices will ideally involve a minimum regime of sexual continence, a vegetarian diet (and generally no more than one meal a day), sleeping on the floor/ground, and going barefoot, and may require additional observations, depending on the ritual behaviour associated with the pilgrimage centre and the deity ensconced within. Moreover, in furthering compliance with the ascetic ideal, the pilgrim should, upon leaving home, dispense with his/her birth given identity (that is, ties of caste, status, familial associations), in order to devote wholehearted attention to the aims, processes and outcomes of the *yatra*.[41] Collectively, these *tapas* comprise the "fire" necessary for ritual and psychic purification, the cleansing of mundane pollution, which ensures that the pilgrim is in the requisite state of readiness necessary for the contemplation of the deity.[42]

While the pilgrimage is symbolic of the journey of the embodied soul towards *moksha* (enlightenment and release), which remains the central premise of the Hindu life,[43] devotees are aware that a single *yatra* does not necessarily result in personal liberation. However, while the devotee knows that a *yatra* may not result in the attainment of *moksha*, the pilgrimage is regarded as a step on the road of dharma (*dharmasastra*), which will at least bring the devotee closer to this goal. A person who in good faith repeatedly undertakes a *yatra* will penetrate beyond symbolism and uncover the special truths which inform the *yatra*.[44] Moreover, in the process the *tirtha yatra* ultimately becomes a means towards fording "the great flood of *samsara*" (i.e., the cycle of birth and rebirth).[45]

However, while mindful of the ultimate goal of *moksha*, most pilgrims approach the *tirtha yatra* with more practical goals in mind.[46] Thus, at one level the pilgrimage may be seen as a form of cosmic bargaining, a studied reciprocity in which a devotee makes a sacrifice which constitutes an appeal to the deity's benevolence and is acknowledged and rewarded by him/her. Put succinctly, the pilgrim employs or trades his/her devotion to seek the deity's intervention in his/her mundane worldly affairs.[47] Oral traditions emphasize that the devotion, correct disciplines, and ritual actions dedicated to the deity must bear fruit.[48] The two complimentary elements of the pilgrimage are the vow made by the devotee and the subsequent proof delivered by the deity. As Gold comments, "Schematically a pilgrim promises to make a certain offering if he receives a certain boon; the deity won't fulfil the prayer without the vow; the pilgrim is not accountable for anything if he does not get his proof."[49] While open grasping after the fruits of a vow may draw societal censure, their careful pursuit through the studied discipline of a vow contingent upon pilgrimage, an accepted and proven means of attaining the blessings of the deities, is both righteous and justified.[50] It will be seen that the fulfilment of a vow, in particular the suspension of societal routines in favour of the temporary adoption of an ascetic mode of behaviour that involves the renunciant in some form of *tapas*, also embodies the concept of penance. Indeed, the fulfilment of *dharma*, the attaining of merit (*punya*), and the divine assistance in managing or mitigating the vast *karmic* forces of life, often lie at the very heart of the pilgrim's *yatra*.[51] In sum, while the pilgrimage is a form of *bhakti* which will aid the votary's spiritual evolution and bring him/her closer to release (*mukti*), the devotee's motive is for assistance in the mundane world, a material benefit which will soften and rearrange the frequently overwhelming *karmic* forces which buffet humanity, and manifest as sickness, creation, destruction, etc.[52] But while for most devotees the aim of the pilgrimage may consist of the attainment of tangible material benefits, it must be emphasized that at heart, every *yatra* constitutes a personal search for a relationship with the deity, and that great stress is placed upon the qualities of humility, faith, submission and devotion.[53] As Moronis notes: "Pilgrimage, being a compound of rituals, is an especially effective performance for attaining the boons of deities because of its merit producing and purificatory effects."[54]

But the journey is a mere prelude to a deeper sense of self-sacrifice.[55] The climacteric act of the pilgrimage is the presentation of the aspirant to the deity.[56] As the pilgrim passes the gatekeeper of the shrine, he/she enters an idealized zone, increasingly laden with structured symbolism and dense with esoteric meaning. Indeed, these images and symbols, situated as they are within the essential abode of the deity, the *axis mundi*, are endowed with concentrated power and exceptional significance, being far more "pure", condensed, and charged with both meaning and energy, than those variants located elsewhere.[57] Within the sacred centre, the aspirant, unimpeded by the distractions of mundane life, is free to communicate with the immanent deity. But the perception is not one-sided. While the devotee gains the *darsan* of the deity, in the deepest sense, ideally "the scalding sight of God which disrupts the senses and rearranges them on a higher level",[58] the deity also observes the aspirant.

Indeed, the encounter with the deity is one of free-flowing and transformative symbiosis. It is a convention of pilgrimage that the devotee should not arrive empty handed, that he/she should have brought with him/her an offering considered suitable for surrender to the deity installed within the *axis mundi*. This may be a physical offerings — fruit, milk, selected foodstuffs, flowers, sacralized water, etc. — or it may consist of a psychic offering, for instance, ritualized worship consonant with the deity's cosmology (for example, firewalking for Draupadi, the kavadi ritual, or hair shaving for Murugan).[59] At the presentation before the deity, both parties release what they can offer in unqualified volume; the pilgrim his/her devotion, and the deity his/her *darsan*.[60] The devotee thus establishes a reciprocal relationship with the deity which involves a mutual transfer of energies, the extension of the deity's benevolence and blessing upon the devotee, the augmentation of the spiritual energy of the deity. The *murthis* within pilgrimage centres, the embodiments of divinity, thus act, as Hartsuiker so aptly remarks, as both "accumulators" and "conductors" of spiritual energy.[61] In general, the mutual transfer between deity and devotee will be more intense within the greater, more popular and thus more powerful pilgrimage centres where constant crowds of votaries and the concomitant flow of devotees magnify the overall exchange of energy levels.[62]

The encounter complete, the devotee begins the journey home. The homecoming and the redistribution among others of the power, the "imbued leavings" acquired through the act of pilgrimage, is an essential part of the *yatra*.[63] The impact of the encounter with the deity upon the devotee and the special qualities imparted by gaining *darsan* of the deity is the central and defining fulcrum around which the entire pilgrimage is structured, and the proof may be read by others in the qualities the returning pilgrim can both display and offer. Thus, in the Rajastani village where she undertook her fieldwork, Gold observed that the returning pilgrims were traditionally received as deities.[64]

Upon return the pilgrim is released from his/her temporary vows of asceticism, and is free to resume daily societal routines. This release may be authorized by a special ceremony which marks the conclusion of the pilgrim's *yatra*, and symbolically returns him/her to the folds of conventional society. But the processes of pilgrimage, the combined impress of the powerful and catalytic disciplines of austerities, sacrifice and worship, have left the pilgrim transformed. The devotee has stepped outside the mundane world to enter the structured and sacred realm of the Divine, and has experienced at first hand the power imparted by the

Divine within the shrine. As Shulman remarks, "Through his contact with the power of the shrine, the pilgrim brings to the sphere of his usual activity a new sense of order and control."[65]

In sum, then, the pilgrimage may be viewed as a journey from the periphery, from the mundane world of the *Kaliyuga*, to the centre, the *axis mundi*, where direct communication can be made with the immanent deity. Pilgrimage deals with a wide variety of motives, and furnishes a structure which accommodates them all. While the pilgrimage provides the votary with both material reward (*bhukti*) and release (*mukti*), the goals of most South Indian pilgrims are essentially practical in that the worshipper seeks the deity's intervention and assistance to weather or mitigate the karmic forces of everyday life. Pilgrimage is an act of devotion which stresses the qualities of humility, faith and submission, and highlights the aspirant's willingness to undergo rigorous austerities and sacrifice in the service of the deity. In turn, the pilgrim knows that the deity will acknowledge and respond to that devotion.

Batu Caves: A Malaysian Pilgrimage Site

I have noted that Hindu pilgrimage sites contain a number of explicitly distinguishing features. These include:

1. A foundation mythology which clearly establishes a nexus between deity and locality; and
2. An expectation that the normally transcendent deity will prove immanent and accessible to his devotees, at least during certain ritually prescribed festive periods, and that the deity will repeatedly demonstrate his/her willingness to involve himself/herself in the affairs of his/her devotees, even to the extent of deploying his/her "miraculous" powers.

We also noted that pilgrimage sites are often associated with prominent geographical landmarks, including mountains, rivers and caves. Indeed, a combination of these factors may lead to a locality being regarded as intrinsically sacred, or *svayambhu* (self born).[66]

In the previous chapter we outlined the foundation mythology which located Batu Caves as a site of Murugan worship. To recapitulate: In 1891, K. Thambusamy, a prominent member of the Kuala Lumpur Hindu community, had a vision of the deity Maha Mariamman in which he was instructed to establish a shrine to her son, Murugan, within the Cathedral (now Temple) Cave. He duly placed a *vel*, a symbol of Siva–Sakti, within the cave, a cue for other Hindus to visit the site and offer worship. Orders issued by the British District Officer, Kuala Lumpur, directing that the *vel* be removed, and prohibiting admission to the cave, were successfully contested in court. The ruling, a clear victory for Hindus over the otherwise seemingly illimitable power of the colonial authorities, was to many devotees clear proof of Murugan's presence in the cave.[67] The first Thaipusam was celebrated in the caves in 1892.

As we observed in the previous chapter, the Batu Caves locale contained a number of motifs which were integral to the Murugan cultus in South India, including caves, mountaintop retreats, an adjacent river and wilderness. Moreover, the general grandeur of Batu Caves, especially the imposing dimensions of the Temple Cave, made it a fitting domain for the great and regal *Agamic* deity, Murugan. Over the years the site has been developed into a major pilgrimage centre incorporating all of the dominant symbols and themes of worship associated with Murugan in the Tamil country. Batu Caves has been transformed from a simple shrine consisting of a single *vel* into the paramount Murugan complex in Malaysia, complete with temples, administrative and commercial premises, an interpretative *Muzium* and Art Gallery, and a central stairway leading into the Temple Cave. In recent years the opening of the Ramayana Cave and the unveiling of a large free-standing statue of Hanuman has represented an attempt to increase the complex's relevance to the minority Vaishnavite community. Nevertheless, Batu Caves remains a site comprehensively dedicated to the cultus of Murugan and the Saivite tradition in which the deity is enmeshed. The addition to the complex of a gigantic statue of Murugan, proudly proclaimed by the Sri Maha Mariamman Devasthanam as the largest in the world, merely underscores this fact.

While the religious life of Batu Caves is continuous, with a daily schedule of *pujas*, as well as life cycle ceremonies conducted on behalf of the constant stream of devotees and visitors, there is no doubt that Thaipusam is the dominant festival in the ritual year, and overwhelmingly so. We have observed that the festival now annually draws over one million people to Batu Caves, and that thousands of entranced devotees bear kavadis to the main shrine in the Temple Cave. Throughout Thaipusam the power and presence of Murugan is conspicuously displayed. In theory, each of the kavadi-carrying devotees has been overtaken by the divine trance state known as *arul*, representing investment or possession by the deity. These adepts seem charged with a superhuman power which enables them to demonstrate extraordinary feats of strength and endurance, and to pierce their flesh with hooks, spears and *vels* without evincing pain or shedding any blood. They subsequently recount to family and friends details of their encounters with the deity and the divine forces which they experienced while bearing the kavadi. And each year there are reports, often well publicized, of the deity's benevolence; of the power of Murugan to heal chronic and even terminal illnesses, or the sudden and necessary adjustments in quotidian life, explicable only in terms of Murugan's direct intervention. For many Malaysian Hindus, Murugan's presence at Batu Caves is a fact of life, one which is proven beyond any shred of reasonable doubt, and his blessings are clearly and unmistakably bestowed upon the thousands of devotees who flock each Thaipusam to worship him.

Ritual Worship

In Chapter 5 I noted how the conjoined myths of Palani, the renunciant, and the death and transformation of Idumban provide the leitmotifs of kavadi worship at Thaipusam. To briefly restate them, this sequence of events commences when, at the urging of the sage Narada, Murugan and Ganesha embark upon a race around the world for the prize of a mango. The more literally minded Murugan is outwitted by the knowledgeable Ganesha, who adopts the simple expedient of circumambulating his parents, thereby not only encompassing the world but also the entire cosmos, the Siva–Sakti duality, and all the truths contained within. Ganesha is awarded the mango, the fruit of pure knowledge. Furious at this outcome, Murugan renounces the world, and repairs first to Krownchan, and thence to Palani, where he conquers his inner passions and realizes the Truth within. While at Palani, Murugan meets and vanquishes the *asura* Idumban, who is proceeding southwards on a sacred commission to deliver two hills to South India. Idumban is slain but is restored to life after both the sage Agastya and the *asura*'s wife Idumbi appeal to Murugan. Murugan directs that the resurrected and now spiritually awakened Idumban stand guard as a perpetual gatekeeper at the boundary of his shrine, and proclaims that all who worship Murugan in the modality exemplified by Idumban will henceforth acknowledge the *asura*-turned-devotee. After this encounter Murugan returns to Mount Kailas, where Parvati presents him with the *Sakti Vel*, preparatory to his campaign to defeat the *asuric* army and to restore cosmic order.

This mythology merges several motifs common to the Murugan cultus, and to Hinduism generally: namely, the dispelling of illusion; the fruit (*pala*) of Truth (quite clearly represented by the mango); renunciation, asceticism, and the power of *tapas* (spiritual disciplines); the death of ignorance and a rebirth in awareness following an appeal to the Lord. These are all symbolically united within the principal *murthi* in Palani, one of the main Murugan shrines in India, where the deity is portrayed as holding a *danda*, or staff, representing asceticism, military leadership and the royal justice of kingship. There are also other cosmic possibilities, some of which I will pursue later in this chapter. For the moment I merely wish to note that the mythology combines the themes of renunciation, asceticism, and knowledge within a prescribed form of devotional worship, the kavadi ritual. All of these are commemorated in ritual worship at Thaipusam in Palani, and are reproduced at Batu Caves.

Kingship and Thaipusam

In Chapter 2 I noted that South Indian kingship provided the ritual and unifying centre of a sacred realm, consisting of societies segmented by the pronounced diversity of ethnicity, region, caste and localized interests. The king ruled this society in accordance with the precepts of *dharmic* law, or *danda* (described by Dumont as "a kind of immanent power of justice, more or less identical with dharma").[68] I also showed that the king was required to perform public rites which clearly and continually established his association with the Divine and which unequivocally affirmed his sovereignty, and in particular situated him as the pivotal locus and dynamic agency upon whom the prosperity and well-being of the kingdom depended. The kingship rituals thus symbolized cosmic renewal and regeneration, and the monarch was explicitly identified as the principal moral and sacral performer in this process.

Professor Champakalakshmi has demonstrated how the symbology which attended South Indian kingship was expressly imbricated within the *Agamic* tradition, thus becoming a canonical base for all temples. The deity was equated to the king and became the ruler of his territory, the guarantor and upholder of *dharma* and, in return for their devotion, the regal protector of his subjects.[69] This symbology was extended through the *bhakti* tradition to incorporate both temple rituals and the conduct of festivals.[70] I would suggest that Murugan's kingship is unmistakably demonstrated in these terms throughout the entire festival of Thaipusam.

The linkage between the divine and royal sovereigns is made explicit by the festive parading of the deity in the temple chariot.[71] It is thus apposite that Thaipusam commences with the royal procession of the king-deity Murugan, who leaves his temple-palace (*kovil*), the Sri Maha Mariamman temple in Kuala Lumpur, for his mountaintop abode in Batu Caves. As observed in the previous chapter, prior to his departure he is offered a series of propitiatory and supplicatory rites; he is bathed and dressed in rich robes, he receives the *alankara deepam*, or showing of the light to one who is garlanded, in this instance as the king-deity, all the symbols of kingship are displayed to him, and he and his consorts are borne around the temple-palace on a *mayil* (peacock) palanquin, before being installed in the *kovil*'s silver chariot, a vehicle betokening his power, dignity and majesty.

The chariot procession signifies Murugan's sovereignty over his ritual domain, the diverse segments of the Hindu population of Malaysia. Throughout the journey to the caves, he sits in regal splendour in the silver chariot, drawn (even if now, symbolically) by a selected retinue of subjects, constantly attended by his *pantarams* (or temple servants), and escorted by officials, musicians, torchbearers, dance troupes, and representatives of all major Hindu organizations, as well as a vast concourse of devotees drawn from the entire spectrum of Malaysian Hindu society, all of whom have turned out to pledge their allegiance. En route, the chariot makes repeated stops to allow the king-deity to receive the homage and supplication of groups of devotees. In return he offers his *darsan*, with its promise of divine protection and the upholding of universal *dharma*.[72]

Upon his arrival at his mountain abode, Murugan and his consorts are enthroned in the downstairs shrine, the New Swami Mandapam, where devotees may offer worship. However, his Golden *Vel*, the instrumental symbol of his regal divine authority, is borne to the shrine upstairs, an action which exemplifies Clifford Geertz's observation that "the progress of Indic-Hindu kings affirms the association with transcendence by the bestowal of ritual signs upon their territory, thus making their kingdom almost physically part of them".[73] The transfer of the Golden *Vel*, the regenerative symbol of cosmic power, to the shrine within the Temple Cave, and the subsequent raising of the temple flag, the royal standard, signals that the king-deity is now in state in his mountain palace, and that he will receive those votaries who wish to submit personal appeals for his Divine jurisdiction. For a full thirty-six hours devotees may now approach the king-deity for a personal audience in the knowledge that their entreaties and pleas, properly framed within the context of prescribed ritual supplication, will be fully received and acknowledged by a responsive and compassionate monarch.

At the conclusion of this period, the Golden *Vel*, the symbol of regal authority, will be removed from the Batu Caves temple-palace and restored to the deity, the *utsava murthi*, in the New Swami Mandapam. He will then depart for his permanent *kovil*-palace in central Kuala Lumpur. Once again he will be accompanied by officials, musicians and various ritual servants. He will be greeted and enthroned with a congery of welcoming and installation rituals appropriate to his kingship.

In Chapter 2 I demonstrated that South Indian kingship was sustained by a form of ritual incorporation known as *jajmani*, a system of exchange of gifts and service which flowed hierarchically, initially from the apex to lesser chieftains and leaders, and then through a complex network of reciprocities to all groups within the pyramidical and segmentary society. I would suggest that the redistributive principle embodied in *jajmani* applies in the transactions which occur throughout Thaipusam, and is clearly discernible at a number of levels. At its most straightforward it may be seen in an uncomplicated exchange between those who offer simple devotion or service in return for *darsan* of the deity. At another level this exchange functions between those who tender offerings to the deity which are returned charged with his energy. But I would submit that it is the kavadi bearers who participate in the most intimate form of *jajmani* with the king-deity. For in offering themselves and their very bodies as objects of devotion, they are publicly pledging their most profound loyalty and submission. In return the monarch offers some of the sacred essence of his kingship, namely protection, beneficence, and direct intervention in their lives. In this way the votary forges a personal relationship with the deity, one which recognizes the divine justice of his sovereignty, his *danda*, the blessings of which are in the most special sense unique to each individual.

Also in Chapter 2 I observed that the Navaratri festival, the main ceremonial of Vijayanagara kingship, ritually renewed the monarchy, re-established its divine character, and revived incorporative ties with all elements of the segmentary society within the overall structures of a clearly demarcated kingdom. Within Navaratri, the capital city became a symbolic universe over which the monarch claimed dominion. I would argue that Thaipusam fulfils a similar function among Malaysian Hindus. Murugan's annual visit to Batu Caves reaffirms his sovereignty over his domain, and reinfuses his mountaintop palace with the cosmic energy of his presence. Throughout his stay he clearly displays his majesty, redistributive power and his kingly dispositions. He commands the avowed allegiance of all the leading figures of his realm. Murugan is indubitably identified as king-deity whose overlordship is ritually acknowledged in a myriad of ways, ranging from simple worship to acts of service, and finally to those which betoken explicit servitude. The festival commemorating the bestowal of the *Sakti Vel*, the weapon instrumental in enabling Murugan to display his full array of cosmic powers, is the largest Hindu festival in Malaysia, and clearly, albeit temporarily, unites the various (and sometimes antagonistic) segments of a richly diverse community under the overarching power of his ritual sovereignty.

Rites of Separation

In order to understand the transformative changes which occur throughout the processes of pilgrimage, it is first necessary to provide a basic description of the notions of substance and inter-substantial relationships which lie at the very heart of Tamil culture, and which govern the Tamil devotee's dealings with his/her deity.

In his comprehensive study of the Tamil cultural worldview, E. Valentine Daniel describes a creation myth which is based upon the distribution and hierarchical ranking of substance (as the fundamental universal material) and substances. According to this mythology, all differentiated manifest forms in the universe have evolved from a single primordial source, an "unmanifested and equilibrated substance".[74] While the causal factors which produced the "first" movement or action (*karman*) remain unexplained, what is known is that all substances which can be located within the universe possess their own intrinsic properties, each of which contains inscribed codes of action. Each entity is made of substances which in combination assign certain dispositions which cumulatively constitute the "headwriting" (*talai eluttu*) or intrinsic qualities allocated to that entity at the time of its creation, and which constrain it to behave consistently with its innate properties. This constitutes the inherent nature or *dharma* of a particular being which inter alia prescribes patterns of conduct appropriate to that phase of its existence.[75] At the end of its life the entity will be evaluated against the *karma*, both good and bad, generated by its actions, and will subsequently reincarnate with a new set of dispositions (or headwriting) precipitated by its prior history.[76]

Each entity within the universe is unique in terms of its substantial composition, and is subject to its own peculiar array of intersubstantial stresses. The proper proportioning of substances within the body is integral to the latter's continuing vitality and indeed its functionality.[77] But the constant exchange of bodily substances with other entities is an ever-present threat to any given body's well-being.[78] All manifest forms, including humans and even gods, must strive to conserve or restore equilibrium to their body substances. Daniel contends that all everyday actions, including the most mundane, are geared towards maintenance and restitution of equilibrium. This is a necessarily complex process, involving both care and caution.[79] An excess of any form of action, whether good or bad, threatens the stability of the entity, and may also effect that of other entities. If this excess is sufficiently severe, it may even disrupt the cosmic order.[80]

It is the constant interplay between forces, the unremitting flow of exchanges which produces incessant universal flux, and the transformations attending these exchanges are its concomitant.[81] But because the universe is, as it were, a closed system, this flux is dependent upon a perpetual cycle which orders the creation, decay, destruction and re-creation of all entities, and the new must therefore be fashioned from the substantial remnants of the old.[82]

The uniqueness of all categories and entities extends to human beings; humankind is ineluctably variegated, and each person is in the most profound sense an individual. While human behaviour and conduct may be guided on the broadest level by the expectations and conventions which inform a specific culture, on the individual level there can be no single moral schema or set of psychological or physical applications which obtain across the entire spectrum of humankind.[83] The headwriting of any particular person consists of a coded substance which is welded to the body substance at the time of birth (some commentators suggest at the time of conception).[84] The headwriting allocated to a created human being will be moulded by his/her past actions, and will be influenced by the deeds of relatives, and those of other agents, including friends and chance acquaintances.[85] (Conversely, the actions of the individual will have consequences for families, friends, and even entire communities.)[86] This headwriting will exercise a controlling leverage over the individual until such time as the soul casts off the gross and subtle bodies of the particular incarnation. The substance of a person is a coherent amalgam; the qualities (*kunams*) pervade the entity holistically, and cannot be split into psychological or physiological components. The *kunams* are highly resistant to change.[87]

The fact that every human being is endowed with a unique composite substance produces a Hindu worldview which is highly idiosyncratic. Each individual has a singular complement both of substances and the framework which govern its combinations. The resultant quest for personal equilibrium is necessarily determined by the search for those substances which prove compatible with his/her bodily substance.[88] Because each individual remains vulnerable to the circumstances of place, time and space, as well as all substances with which he/she comes into contact, the Hindu outlook is especially sensitive to the body's intimate relationship and interaction with both the immediate and wider environment.[89]

Integral to personal equilibrium is the regulation and maintenance of the proper balances between hot and cold. Within Tamil culture the designation of hot and cold is both relative and situational, and varies among individuals, groups of individuals (for example, *jati*/kinship networks), localities and cultures.[90] This includes foodstuffs; thus, what might be regarded as "heating" by one individual or *jati* might be deemed neutral or even "cooling" among others.[91] However, citrus and products of the cow are generally regarded as cooling; it is my observation that alcohol is widely regarded as heating.[92]

The health of an individual is regulated by three bodily humours; namely, phlegm (*kapam*), bile (*pittam*) and wind (*vayu*). Of these, phlegm is cold and dominant throughout youth, bile is hot and linked to middle age, and wind is neutral and associated with old age.[93] While every human contains a number of hot and cold attributes, the appropriate individual level will depend upon his/her *kunam* (coded substance or headwriting.)[94] An individual's well-being is related to maintaining the hot and cold balance appropriate to his/her *kunam*, and illness is attributed to excessive heat or unnatural cold. (Specific bodily states, often connected with sexuality, are invariably associated with heat. Thus, both puberty and pregnancy are regarded as times of heat, and sexual intercourse is regarded as heating.)[95]

The heat/cold polarity implies a nexus between any given substance and its inherent energy. Thus, while coldness connotes inertness and inanimation, heat suggests dynamism and movement.[96] And, indeed, within the Hindu schemata, heat is ineluctably associated with transformation, including processes involving the mixing and transmutation of substances. These processes include rites of passage and life crisis cycles. Both hot and cold are connected with particular colours; thus black and red are viewed as "hot", while green and white are seen as "cold".[97]

Two qualities inhere within the *kunam* (headwriting) which pervade the created human. These are *yokam* (translated variously as luck, fortune and destiny) and *viti* (or fate), both of which influence the final form the *kunam* takes.[98] Although the *kunam* complex (*kunam-yokam-viti*) is regarded as permanent and thus immutable, in reality all substances are in incessant flux, and under certain conditions the *kunam* is subject to modification.[99] Indeed, the *kunam* complex may prove malleable and ultimately controllable by the combined application of *mati* (discrimination, judgement and intelligence), *muyatcci* (right efforts) and *karmam* (proper effort supported by right actions). These qualities (*karmam-mati-muyatccii*) are collectively known as the *karmam* complex.[100] The *karmam* is an integral component of the body substance. Valentine Daniel points out that several Hindu traditions, including Saiva Siddhanta, use the analogy of *karma* as fruit (*pala*). Thus, when a given *karmam* or *karmic* residue is realized, it is said to have ripened (*palikkum* or *parukkum*). Saiva Siddhanta, following the Upanishads, situates *karmic* residue in the innermost body (*kanjuga sariram*) of the five bodies, thus clearly identifying it as a fundamental body substance.[101]

In order to instigate the desired changes to the *kunam* complex, the *karmam* complex must be set in motion; it must be released from its potentiality and converted to kinetic form. This may be achieved in a number of ways, including sacrifices, pilgrimages, vows, offerings, *pujas*, prayers or individual *sadhana* or disciplines.[102] It is emphasized, in both pan-Indian epics and localized stories, that destiny may be softened and reshaped by personal heroic action, comprising disciplines and inner strength which cumulatively overcome the perceived fixity of fate and character.[103]

While on one level the *karmam* complex (the actor's actions) is distinguished from the *kunam* complex (his/her bodily state, fortune and fate), the very moment of differentiation weds action to actor, thus modifying the *kunam* complex. As Valentine Daniel notes, this seeming paradox emphasizes the action–actor principle so pronounced in Hindu culture.[104]

However, the application of *karmam* to *kunam* is affected by the age we live in, the *kaliyuga*, where degenerative forces are in the ascendant and, at the personal level, greed (considered the root of all suffering), turpitude, wrongdoing and decadence may be regarded as normative.[105] Among Tamils, all creative actions are fraught with pain, vulnerability and danger, and expose the actor to the grave risk of deterioration and the perils of chaos.[106] The individual thus striving to change his/her *kunam* complex must therefore not falter, and must demonstrate great resolution merely to sustain personal equilibrium against the forces of dissolution and entropy which prevail in the phenomenal universe. Indeed, the energy expended in attempting to rectify or "turn around" a deficient *kunam* complex must, in practical terms, be double that of the momentum generated by that *kunam* complex before any perceptible progress can be registered.[107]

In sum, the Tamil's efforts to attain substantial compatibility and arrest personal instability are thwarted by the seemingly irresistible forces of cosmic flux, the ceaseless interplay of substances. The decision to embark upon a pilgrimage is to select a ritual, one that is regarded as extremely powerful, which will generate a new form of knowledge, and thus control.[108] The exact nature of this knowledge will be discussed later in this chapter. But we should note that all religious ritual, when properly observed, is regarded as transformative; it has the power to reshape the aspirant's identity and to move him/her beyond his original condition.[109] The power of pilgrimage is manifestly increased when combined with what Clothey has termed a "tempocosm", or a calendrical moment (such as a designated religious festival), which opens the possibility of access to deeper cosmic realities.[110] For the moment, I wish to examine agencies by which potential pilgrims divine the need to undertake a pilgrimage.

Divination

While some Hindus may decide of their own volition, based on internal experiences (for example, meditation), to undertake a given propitiatory ritual, often to ameliorate or neutralize problems or conditions which might seem to the outside observer as trivial or inconsequential, mere vagaries of life, many will seek the advice of a person whose experience and reputation has designated him/her as qualified to divine a person's *dharma* and *karma*, and to chart an appropriate array of responsive choices. This is accomplished through a process of identification and assessment of an individual's *kunam* and *karnam* complexes, and fusing the two to form a new *kunam* complex.[111]

One way of locating the cause of problems and situating them within a definitive pattern is through consultation with an astrologer. Among Tamils, astrology, "an interpretative art ... firmly shaded in its nuances", is regarded as a blueprint for life, and astrological advice is often sought before making any decisions of importance, especially those involving significant life choices.[112] As Judy Pugh comments, "the world reflected in astrology is a unitary field in which reciprocal relations of all entities is a fundamental axiom, and the ceaselessly patterned timing of the heaven's images a determination of events and conditions in the realms of human action".[113] The heavenly bodies, including the planets (*graha*), constellations (*rasi*) and the asterisms (*nakasastras*), all are held to have a major impact upon the individual, and their configuration at the time of birth is inscribed within the created human as headwriting, that is, as the *karmic* residue accumulated through prior existences.[114] Birth is the key point at which *karma* is made visible, and at which the *kunam* or dispositions of the person may be assessed.[115]

Many Hindus, including some well-educated in *Agamic* beliefs, will consult a medium, "a person who acts as an agency of communication between the people of this world and the denizens of another. More specifically, the Hindu mediums ... provide in their own persons the means by which ordinary people may converse with the deities of the Hindu pantheon."[116] Usually, mediums are men (though in Malaysia there are several well-known female mediums),[117] mainly of modest and unprepossessing circumstances, who initially received their power during a formative and sometimes traumatic encounter with the deity, normally at a tender age. Often the medium is "claimed" by a particular god or goddess with whom he/she communicates exclusively.[118] During consultation, which will sometimes be on a one-to-one basis, or at other times within a crowded temple setting, the medium will be possessed, and while in trance will issue a diagnosis of the individual's condition, a prognosis for the future, and prescribe appropriate corrective measures.[119]

Lawrence Babb has argued that mediumship is best viewed as a constituent element within the broader framework of speculative Hinduism; that is, one which contemplates the perennial and overarching issues of *dharma*, *karma* and *samsara*. In order to locate the source of a particular problem, the actor is progressively led from the circumstances of the particular, towards an exploration of the general, to situate misfortunes within a wider canvas, one which is

> less the consequences of specific, discoverable and thus correctable omissions and errors, and more the symptoms of the general moral conditions of the experiencing self. And this general condition in time is referred to a past which is normally hidden, and implies a future that while obscure, is within the long term control of the individual.[120]

In effect, then, the medium assists the individual to identify a *karmic* pattern which relates his/her personal situation to a higher concept of responsibility and authority, thus linking individual behaviour to conceptions of personal *dharma*.[121]

While a wide range of divinatory rituals exist within popular Hinduism, including the ritual of flowers,[122] clairvoyance and personal fortune telling, it has been my experience, at least within Malaysia, that more serious problems are divined through the agencies of astrology and mediumship.[123] Both are geared to explaining an individual's situations in terms of the legacy of his/her past (that is, the actor's *karma*), a past which can be modified by appropriate actions taken in the present, thus resulting in a higher degree of understanding and control of the future.

The process of divination, whether undertaken personally or via the agency of mediums/astrologers, will always result in recommended measures of corrective action to be taken by the aspirant. In cases involving the malign influences of persons, ghosts, angry demons or little gods, the appropriate response will usually consist of propitiation, including *pujas* and placatory rituals.[124] However, more serious or intractable diagnoses, especially those involving major *karmic* adjustment, will require more drastic measures. The individual may be directed to perform one of an array of votive activities which may range from mild austerities to rituals of penance including pilgrimage, firewalking or kavadi bearing.[125]

A vow (*vrata* or *nerttikkatan* in Tamil) is a form of contract with the deity, and consists of a personal resolution made by the individual to the god to perform a designated action, either to repay the deity for prayers and supplications answered, or in anticipation of their fulfilment.[126] Vow fulfilment has a lengthy history in Tamil Hindu practice, and falls within the received *bhakti* tradition. The taking of a vow is firmly predicated on the assumption that the deity is obligated to recognize a particular penitential action, and to reward the devotions of the aspirant.[127] A vow, especially one involving the rites of penance, is viewed as especially efficacious in resolving or softening *karma*, and in transforming one's life path; that is, discerning and living in accordance with the principles of individual *dharma*.[128] The merit or reward accrued by this devotion, while the result of a compact between aspirant and deity, may produce *karmic* outcomes for others with whom the devotee is associated, including spouse, children and other kin.[129]

Devotees who intend to undertake a pilgrimage must observe a period of austerities regarded as necessary to cleanse him/her of impurities preparatory to the encounter with the deity. Within the Hindu worldview, impurity (or pollution) is an inescapable condition of mundane existence, and invariably accrues from the fundamental daily routines, including eating, elimination, sex, bodily effluvia and, within the broader family, the processes of birth and death. These spiritual disciplines — the dietary restrictions, special prayers, sleeping on the floor, refraining from losing one's temper, etc. — are viewed as a form of purification in that they concentrate the devotee's mind on the forthcoming pilgrimage, and reorient consciousness away from the sphere of the commonplace, quotidian household life, to contemplation of the Divine. Moreover, the disciplines imposed during the period of the vow are believed to produce beneficent results, including nullification of at least some of the *karma* which created the necessity to make the vow in the first place.[130] Purity is regarded as an essential prerequisite for any consequential communication with the deity, and this condition is more pronounced for devotees intending to perform rituals to any of the Sanskritic/*Agamic* deities.[131]

Valentine Daniel argues that all restrictions throughout the preparatory interval of asceticism are subordinate to, and in the final analysis complementary to, the ban on sexual activity. He states that the principle aim of the pilgrim is to progressively overcome the five senses (*intriyas*) — namely sight, hearing, smell, taste and ultimately touch/feeling in the blissful awareness of the Divine. However, it is well known that sexual intercourse is the prime example of sensations, produced by the *mei* (the organ that reacts to the sense of touch and feeling). It is also known within Indian thought that semen is regarded as the essence of all bodily substances, just as ghee is the essence of all foodstuffs. The retention of sexual fluids (or *intiriams*; the term also refers in a generic sense to the five senses) is considered essential to attaining a state of ascetic purity and generating and sustaining *tapas*.[132]

We have earlier noted that pilgrimage is regarded as a substitute for the taking of *sannyasin* and the concomitant vows of total and life-long renunciation. However, the period of austerities removes the pilgrim from his/her status as a householder and temporarily installs him/her within the ranks of renouncers, or *sannysasins*. The importance of this issue cannot be overstated. The *sannyasin* is regarded as a pivotal figure in the overall Hindu worldview. By renouncing the world, symbolically shedding his/her links with family, friends, property and residence by officiating at his own funerary rites, the *sannyasin* plies the lonely ascetic path which aims at the acquisition of transcendental knowledge and the permanent release from the transmigratory cycle (*samsara*).[133] But it may well be that the pathways of the *sannyasin* and the householder constitute "an existential choice between the life of the spirit and the life of the body",[134] and that while householders accord renunciants (including pilgrims) deep respect,[135] the principle embodied in renunciation clashes in practical terms with the entrenched Hindu belief in the importance of family and descendants.[136]

This dichotomy is at least partially resolved within the ritual of pilgrimage, in which for a short while the devotee ceases to be a householder (*grihastya*) and is placed among the ranks of the *sannyasins*. The votary thus becomes, even for a brief period, a revered cultural archetype, the renunciant, and is exposed during this interval to the path of asceticism, and to at least some of the specialist knowledge which is a concomitant of this state. But while pilgrimage embraces temporary renunciation, it eschews the permanence of *sannyasa*, thus remaining consistent with the established Saivite ideal of a complete and integrated life in which human nature in its totality is explored and valued. Moreover, the worldly orientation of *bhakti*, with its emphasis on the fullness of human life, both subverts and militates against anything other than transient renunciation.[137]

To summarize: The individual's attempts to achieve and maintain substantial reality and compatibility have been obstructed by the nature of the cosmos; namely, the world's unceasing flux and the perpetual movement of substances. He/she has discerned, either through personal effort (meditation, intuition) or through the agency of divination (for example, astrology, mediumship or related rituals) that he/she (or someone within the immediate family circle) has a major problem or condition, which may be variously described as *karma*, misfortune, ill-health, an imbalance of humours, an excess of hot or cold, etc., which requires a resolution which will effect a permanent life change (or, in other words, the *kunam* complex must be modified, thus requiring the activation of the *karmam* complex). He/she has made a vow to perform a specialist congery of ritual actions which collectively constitute a pilgrimage, and has undertaken the requisite period of fasting and asceticism, thus temporarily relinquishing the role of householder in order to enter the ranks of renunciants, or *sannyasins*. At this point the devotee is now ready to embark upon the prolonged physical and metaphysical journey to the *axis mundi*, the location where the deity will be immanent and accessible.

Pilgrimage: The Divine Crossing

The devotee's intention is to affect a change in his/her personal circumstances which will produce a state of substantial equilibrium and equipoise. This will require the development of a new form of knowledge, one which transcends the inferior analytical knowledge which belongs to the distinctions and categories of the differentiated mundane world. This new knowledge will be experienced rather than logically understood, and will consist of the inculcation of the reality of undifferentiated Oneness, the impartation of deeper awareness of the fundamental and underlying existential substantial unity, including the nature of the devotee's innermost being, the *Atman*, where movement is replaced by stillness and the quotidian by Transcendence. The pilgrimage is a powerful ritual which disrupts equilibrium and sets new forces in motion; it is a *karmam* which will eventually lead the votary to experience this essential knowledge (*vidya*).[138] However, we should note in passing that the word "eventually" here is the key qualifier; very few Hindus would assert that one pilgrimage on its own would be sufficient to induce such a radical transformation in spiritual consciousness.[139]

The pilgrims experience a long and uncomfortable journey to the main shrine; a journey which consists of a continuous succession of ascetic experiences that will generate *tapas* (austerities).[140] As related in the previous chapter, the Brahman pilgrimage group with which I undertook a *pada yatra* to Palani regarded every action within the pilgrimage as a calculated step in the path towards the *axis mundi*. But it was more than a physical journey; it was a metaphor for the entire process of spiritual discovery, a crossing point from the world of the quotidian to another state of consciousness, one which progressively reorients the *sadhaka* (seeker) from the outer world to the inner. In this sense, then, the pilgrimage may be regarded as soteriological; it is constant movement away from ignorance and illusion (*avidya*) towards *moksha*, that totality of knowledge (*vidya*) in which all polarities and differentiations are dissolved.[141]

Ideally the *tirtha yatra* requires the successive subdual of the eight *ragas*, or attachments to experience or desire, including attachment itself.[142] As earlier noted, the five senses (or *intriyas*) — hearing, smell, sight, speech, hunger/thirst — all which merge into tactility or feeling (touch) — must also be quelled. The organ which absorbs and responds to touch is known as *mei* in Tamil and refers to the entire body (known as *sarira* in Sanskrit), the two outermost body sheaths. When the *mei* is acquiescent, the sensations of discomfort and pain, which are inevitable components of pilgrimage, are checked, and replaced with awareness of love. However, because the vanquishing of the *ragas* and *intriyas* and the final victory over the *mei* are prolonged processes, this feeling of love generally occurs only in the last stages of pilgrimage.[143]

But there are other qualities known as the *kunams* (*gunas*) which are called into play throughout the rite of pilgrimage. These *gunas* are:

1. *Tamas* (darkness): Qualities associated with biological necessity and consisting of inaction, lethargy, mental torpor, crude thoughts, baseness, density and resistance.
2. *Rajas* (passion): Typically these qualities are dominated by transitory or overriding emotions; the individual is aware of these emotions, which are often involuntary. *Rajas* consist of physical activity, the energy that furnishes strength, movement, emotion and vitality.
3. *Sattva* (lightness): Actions in the *sattva* state are selected by the individual, are guided by insight and are directed towards a higher goal. They consist of mental activity, enlightenment, translucence, the higher qualities which create patience, compassion and all other virtues.

In general, *tamas* are identified with night, *rajas* with twilight and *sattva* with day.[144] All humans are composed of varying combinations of these three qualities, though they exist in all entities in different proportions, and each may dominate in any one human at given periods of time.[145] However, the ritual of pilgrimage will disturb the basic equipoise to which the individual inclines, overcoming the personal stasis of matter, and inducing new potentialities.[146]

Valentine Daniel records that throughout the commencing stages of the pilgrimage in which he undertook fieldwork, most participants were dominated by *tamas*; they were dull, unresponsive and languorous. However, after an initial period the *tamas* were replaced by *rajas*, and the same participants reported feelings of freshness, clarity and animation. This transformation was also symbolically recognized in my own Indian *pada yatra*, when on the third day ceremonial *vesthis* were issued to all those who remained in the pilgrimage party; in other words, those who had surmounted the period of *tamasik* inertia. *Rajas* are in turn overtaken by *sattva*, stimulated by the growth of unexpected and often intense perceptions. *Sattva* strengthens towards its zenith at the moment that pain is replaced by love.[147]

The rise of *sattva*, the cumulative feelings of love, provide the devotee with a powerful awareness, however evanescent, of the unmistakable presence of the deity, and the bestowal of *vidya*, or pure knowledge. As Daniel movingly writes of his own pilgrimage group:

> In the formulation of the great Hindu tradition, this …[the vanquishment of *avidya*],… is seen as the merging of the *atman* with the universal soul or *brahman*. Such a formulation by humble pilgrims (especially the unschooled ones), though not entirely absent, was certainly not prevalent. Of those pilgrims I walked and talked with however, none failed to express — even in the most inarticulate of ways — the experiences of having lost their identity and individuality, even if it had been only for a fleeting moment. This sense of union was often not expressed in words (quite appropriately so), but in states of trance. These moments of loss of self-consciousness and even consciousness were later referred to as the purpose and highest point of their entire pilgrimage — if not their entire life.[148]

Modifying Behaviour: Thaipusam

The general sequence of events outlined in the preceding sections is common to most devotees who make a vow to take a kavadi during Thaipusam at Batu Caves.

1. The aspirant identifies a major problem which adversely affects him/ her or a member of his/her wider family. The problem may involve failing of health, childlessness, family disputes, or other deep-seated complications.
2. Divination of the source of the problem follows, whether personally (through means such as meditation, intuition, or revelation) or via consultation (astrology, mediumship), and will lead to an acknowledgement that the matter can only be resolved through some form of appeal to, or propitiation of, a greater force.
3. The devotee will then take a vow to Murugan (or another god), indicating that he/she will bear a kavadi or perform some penitential act at Thaipusam, which will either follow the deity's answering of his/her entreaties or will anticipate their fulfilment.
4. The vow demonstrates that the devotee, in seeking resolution, is responding to a higher authority, and thus attempting to situate the problem within the context of a wider cosmology, one ultimately involving the principles of *karma*, *dharma* and *samsara* (often described under the rubric of "fate" or "destiny"), and knowledge of the Divine.

(i) Fasting

At an agreed period prior to the fulfilment of his/her Thaipusam vow, generally twenty-eight days before, but in some cases as little as seven days and in others up to forty-two days, depending upon the relative experience of the intending votary, the aspirant commences a process of ritual purification, a disengagement with quotidian society, known colloquially among Hindu Malaysians as "fasting". In fact, despite the appellation, fasting involves more than a series of dietary restrictions. As we earlier discussed, fasting entails the withdrawal from a large number of mundane activities, and compliance with a demanding regime consisting of a strictly vegetarian diet, abstention from alcohol and nicotine, cessation of all sexual activity, sleeping on the floor, avoiding all contact with menstruating women, as well as a stringent round of additional spiritual obligations. The initiation of fasting may be marked by a special inauguration ritual, usually a *puja* conducted within the temple, but sometimes within the home shrine. Within India this interval is generally more intense than the fasting observed in Malaysia, and may include restrictions on the apparel worn by votaries, and the homes they may frequent and functions they may perform.[149]

(ii) Tamas

Many of the votaries interviewed over the years reported difficulty in managing the first few days of fasting. They expressed that the challenge was not so much with the process of physical withdrawal which accompanied the cessation of normal householder life but the unexpected changes that were an adjunct of this passage. Many experienced adverse psycho-physical sensations, including weariness, blankness, irritability and mental confusion, in particular discontinuous thought processes. This mental and spiritual stodginess is characteristic of the *tamasik* state.

(iii) Rajas

After a certain period, generally ranging from the third to tenth day within the fasting period, many devotees were aware of a sudden and unexpected surge of energy, a freshness, buoyancy and clarity of thought which represented vital, often novel, and generally far more comprehensive ways of envisioning the world and existential life. These impulses were often accentuated as the fast continued. For experienced pilgrims the "energy" often set in within a couple of days after the commencement of fasting. This displacement of the torpor and disordered thought processes with a sense of confident energy and dynamism represents the rise of the *rajasik* state.

(iv) Sattva

We have noted that *sattva* is reached when pain is vanquished by love. It may therefore be postulated that the *rajasik* state becomes *sattvik* on the attainment of the trance state — the condition known as *arul* — on Thaipusam day. This is categorically demonstrated by the events that follow. Firstly, in allowing the *vel* to penetrate the tongue, the devotee renounces the gift of speech and embraces the state of *mauna* (silence), a renunciatory vow common to certain sages and *sannyasins*. But, more crucially, in permitting mortification of the flesh, the devotee also displays his/her triumph over pain, and thus simultaneously over the *mei*, the organ of touch which produces the sensation of pain.

It follows that in Thaipusam in Malaysia, the hardships and austerities which are in India a concomitant of the physical journey to the pilgrimage shrine, and the knowledge which is acquired throughout this process, are condensed into the period of fasting, and most significantly the concentrated albeit abbreviated period of trance known as *arul*. It will be thus seen that the successful induction of the trance state is the fulcrum around which the success of the entire pilgrimage revolves. It is to this subject that we will now turn our attention.

Trance and Thaipusam: Trance as *Tirtha*

Trance states, as a mode of religious experience, while often viewed with deep disdain, suspicion and even hostility within the post-Enlightenment West,[150] are embraced in a broad array of societies,[151] where they form a widely recognized if not universally accepted pathway to direct cognition of the nature of divinity and the world of the spirits.[152] However, it is worth noting that despite Western scepticism, trance and related dissociative states of widely differing character have in the past been, and indeed continue to be, practised in the "West". For example, Gilbert Rouget has shown that religious-inspired trance was known in Ancient Greece, where it was termed, inter alia, *theoleptos*, a form of divine madness in which it was believed the frenzied subject was seized by the deity.[153] R.A. Knox has demonstrated how recurrent manifestations of the phenomenon of "enthusiasm" have punctuated the history and indeed the development of Western Christianity,[154] while I.M. Lewis has drawn attention to the medieval cult of Tarantism.[155] In more recent times trance and dissociation have been found among groups and movements as dissimilar as charismatic Christian sects, the 1960s Western "counterculture" with its sanctioning of "mind altering" drugs and the cult of psychedelia,[156] the habitués of rock concerts,[157] and the Greek fire-walking adepts of the Anasetenarides Christian sect.[158]

The literature which researches the subject of trance, dissociative and related states is broad and varied, and often reaches differing conclusions on the nature and outcomes of the phenomenon. While some discrepancies have revolved around preferred nomenclatures and systems of classification, others constitute fundamental points of disagreement on more basic issues. Many accounts have become sidetracked by ill-informed speculation on the authenticity of observed trance states. As I.M. Lewis aptly observes, "the majority of anthropological writers on possession have been equally fascinated by richly dramatic elements, enthralled — one might also say — by the more bizarre and shamanistic exercises, and absorbed in quite pointless debates about the genuineness (or otherwise) of trance states".[159] Indeed, Lewis rightly insists that scholars must allow non-Western cultures to speak for themselves, and they must avoid (or at least exercise severe caution) in interpreting such trance states according to Western concepts of "truth" or against Western benchmarks.[160] He also warns against the reductive deployment of psychoanalysis as a tool to explain trance states, especially mediumship and shamanism, stressing that it is often "so contrived and at social variance with facts that it can have little significance or value".[161]

Despite the range of approaches to this phenomenon, it is possible to identify several key themes which are advanced by most scholars as integral to trance states.

1. Trance states lead the participant away from normal consciousness into new forms of awareness. These overcome learned behaviour and install fresh conceptions and understanding, sometimes radically discontinuous from the patterns of consciousness which precede the trance state. Trance temporarily overthrows the routine logic and knowledge which govern quotidian consciousness and which would normally quash radical new forms of experiential awareness.[162]

2. Trance states vary enormously, and range from possession trance, in which the spirit or deity assumes full control of the subject, to more complex states which produce mystical exultation. At their most intense these latter forms of trance constitute what Abraham Maslow has described as "peak experiences", in which the subject is saturated and often psychically transformed by profound states of awareness.[163] Mystical trance, the delving beyond reason to probe the nature of divine truth,[164] often allows the individual to dissolve established personal boundaries and to perceive, even in evanescent form, the prospect of eternity and immortality.[165] Alexandra Kent has suggested that such peak-trance states comprise "the most intense refractions of divinity into individualized form".[166]

3. However, trance states, while capable of producing intense mystical experiences, are not necessarily beneficial, and may, in some instances, result in episodes which prove destructive to the subject, and may

even be psychotic in character. Thus, Felicitas Goodman's study of glossolalia (vocalization in trance) among Apostolics of Yucatán, Mexico, revealed a community torn by violence, reckless charges of misconduct and Satanic possession, sightings of the Devil, self-impoverishment, predictions of the immanence of the Second Coming, disillusionment and alienation.[167] Certain trance states may be deployed to attain dispositions which are "demonic" or "psychotic" in character; the outcomes are dependent upon the nature and range of stimuli used to induce trance and the context in which the relevant rituals are performed.[168] Barbara Ehrenreich has pointed out that secular carnivals devoid of a religious climax tend to result in behaviour that is "ugly", "brutish" and "insensate".[169]

4. Trance states are provoked by exposure to specific stimuli and are shaped by the total cultural environment to which the subjects belong.[170] Indeed, Sheila Walker contends that the power of culture over participants is so marked as to affect all aspects of trance behaviour, including physiological constituents, thus making it difficult to "distinguish exactly what the [underlying] neurophysical influence is".[171]

5. Neither hypnotic states nor hysteria may be regarded as full trance states. Hypnosis, a Western invention, is a condition subject to direct manipulation and specific instruction, "an impure concoction of trance and role playing", while hysteria is an uncontrolled state in which the subject enacts his/her fantasies.[172]

6. Trance is often, but by no means exclusively, located among disadvantaged groups, especially the poor and women, and thus may, under certain circumstances, be utilized as a role-playing stratagem to counter or mitigate the circumstances of their oppression.[173]

7. Trance is more likely to occur among less-formally structured religions. Tightly controlled religions are less likely to tolerate trance. Among loosely organized religions, of which Hinduism is a prime example, while ecstatic ritual might be permeated with elements common to that culture, its symbols often convey a plethora of different meanings to individual participants.[174] Moreover, rituals involving trance have a levelling effect which does not recognize rank and which bypasses the special claims of elites; as Ehrenreich points out, the deity may elect to act through a "lowly shepherdess as readily as a queen".[175]

Throughout the remainder of this chapter, I intend to follow the general categorization of trance states developed by Gilbert Rouget. Rouget firmly rejects the concept of altered states of consciousness, which he regards as too broad and imprecise to capture or enclose the fundamental essence of the trance state.[176] He views trance as a change in the structure of individual consciousness which makes the subject "susceptible of being invaded by an emotional event that submerges …[his/her] normal states and leads to hysteriform behaviour".[177] Rouget claims that there are three basic states of mystic trance, though he cautions that the vagueness and subjectivity of received trance experience produces an array of states which are not readily subsumed within these categories. In focussing on individual mystic trance states which involve complex relationships between devotee and deity, Rouget classifies states as follows:

1. Possession Trance: A force in which the subject's personality is overtaken by that of a god, spirit, genius or ancestor.
2. Inspiration Trance: In which the subject is imbued with the deity or a force originating with the deity. However, while the deity does not dominate as in the case of possession trance, but rather establishes a form of coexistence with the devotee, he/she still exercises control over the subject.
3. Communal Trance: In which the relationship between the divinity and subject is conceived as an encounter. This may be experienced as a form of communion-revelation and illumination. Communal trance does not involve any form of possession or embodiment by any spirit or deity.[178]

Both possession and inspiration trance states are of especial relevance to this discussion.

Inducing Trance

The trance state is induced by a series of culture-specific stimuli or prompts that the participants recognize as a structured sequence which leads devotees from mundane consciousness to the world of the gods. Often this comprises a pattern which is learned by the aspirants in training sessions or in a specifically convened initiation ritual in which the religious officiant carefully instructs the adept in the chronology of stimuli/symbology and in the appropriate responses these should elicit.[179] This period of procedural apprenticeship results in an "irreversible modification of the person's relations with himself, with divinity, and with society".[180] The behaviour learned through the training and/or initiation will be subsequently replicated within the context of the religious festival.

As we have observed, most scholars agree that trance states, as learned experiences, and ineluctably culture specific, are inexorably guided and shaped according to the milieu in which they arise. The cultural background not only provides an interpretative framework which infuses the trance states with meaning but also furnishes the symbols necessary for psychological reinforcement of the experience. Thus, even characteristics of the investing or possessing deity will be expressed in culturally relevant forms.[181] However, while the influence of culture is paramount in moulding trance, it is pertinent to note that additional factors such as human creativity and intellect are brought into play. As a consequence, trance outcomes are anything but uniform and may vary widely from one individual to another.[182]

Music and dance are all but universally associated with the induction of trance. Music in this context is not necessarily the product of a disciplined art form, but rather "any sonic event that is linked with this state, that cannot be reduced to language … and that displays a certain degree of rhythmic or melodic organization".[183] This broad definition makes allowance for a wide range of aural phenomena, including chant, handclapping and improvized instrumentation.[184] But music on its own does not induce trance. Its function is to furnish an ambient psychological setting in which ritual may do its work, all the while sending a series of coded signals, sound bearing meaning, to which the devotee responds "physiologically, psychologically, affectively and aesthetically".[185]

Trance states invariably result in dancing. The music performed and the ritual is inexorably intertwined with the dance; indeed the dance may be regarded as a spatial inscription of the "possession music".[186] But while the dance may highlight the devotee's symbiosis with the deity, and thus comprise an integral component of the trance experience, it also converts the votary into a performer and the ritual into sacred theatre. Thus Rouget comments, "it is through the music that the group provides the entranced person with the mirror in which he can read the image of his borrowed identity and it is the music that enables him to reflect this identity back to the group in the form of a dance".[187] In actively responding to the music, the devotee exteriorizes the relationship between deity and subject and transmits it to all observers — other adepts, fellow believers and spectators — messages regarding the power and character of the possessing deity. Moreover, the evolving nature of the dance signifies to religious observers and others the progress and depth of that relationship.[188]

Trance: The Individual Impact

While the trance state produces immediately observable psycho-physiological changes in behaviour, it may also result in profound and deep-seated psychic–spiritual impacts upon subjects, which sometimes prove life altering.

The main apparent alterations which follow the induction of trance are physiological, and may be readily detected by even casual onlookers. These include pronounced changes in emotional expression and a loss of self-control which may produce trembling, shaking, facial distortions and involuntary muscular spasms and twitching.[189] Psychological changes are less noticeable, but their impact on the individual are even more marked and far reaching. These include disruption of normal thought processes; disturbances to concentration, attention, memory and judgement; disorganization of the subject's sense of time and place; changes to the subject's body image (thus, for example, the body may be directed to assume the public demeanour and personal characteristics of the possession deity or spirits); and the impressive, occasional breathtaking, augmentation of the subject's ability to perform unusual actions (for example, to resist pain, to withstand fatigue, to undertake feats of Herculean strength).[190] But, more importantly, the adept enters a state of sustained liminality or marginality.[191] During this phase normal perceptions become distorted, and the devotee may be subject to feelings of rejuvenation or hypersensibility. The eclipse of mundane consciousness allows normally occluded dimensions of awareness to impinge upon phenomenal awareness. These may allow the ingress and absorption of an array of fresh mental constructs, "the possibility that new, special orientations may be constructed at profound levels without recourse to the logic, knowledge and critical functions of the usual reality orientation".[192]

Often these changes in meaning and awareness suggest or invoke perceptions of powerful spiritual experience, frequently weighted with the impress of the ineffable.[193] At their most esoteric, these perceptions may promote a sense of impending or actual mystical union with the deity; however, because of the ephemeral nature of the trance state, the condition of penetrating awareness is necessarily transitory.[194] However, as William James has observed, mystical experiences are more convincing, more immediate and real than those possessed by the logic of rational intellect.[195] Moreover, such experiences are intrinsically noetic; they are perceived as states of knowledge, and often possess a veracity and vitality which surpass those learned through the agency of mundane consciousness.[196] At their most intense, these experiences may be so powerful as to be life changing; equivalent in their impact to the forces which impel religious conversion. Those who have had such experiences often express their good fortune, their gratitude, as well as their intense feelings of indebtedness to the deity.[197]

But the successful involvement in a trance-related ritual produces other outcomes as well. These include the freedom to act in ways that are not available to devotees within their allotted societal role, and which indeed may in some instances contradict the norms of quotidian life.[198] Ironically, the self-sacrifice and behavioural constraints accepted by the devotee as the preconditions for participation in a specified ritual, and the overt surrender of the ego which is preludial to entry to the trance, provide the devotee with the heightened freedom required to enact his/her spiritual acclimatization within the public arena.[199]

At the same time the involvement of the individual in a public ritual trance places the devotee under considerable societal pressure. The votary's ability to successfully complete the ritual may result in an elevation of his/her social status. The capacity to attain and sustain trance is an open test of his/her spiritual credibility, a very public confirmation that the deity has chosen the aspirant as a worthy vehicle for possession or investment.[200] On the other hand, failure to fulfil his/her allotted role may demonstrate or be interpreted as spiritual inadequacy. It may connote lack of preparation for the encounter with the deity, especially inattention to the necessary preliminary procedures, or more tellingly that the devotee has been deemed spiritually unequal to the task demanded by the deity.[201]

Amnesia and Trance

Many of the commentators who have studied trance have remarked upon the amnesia which supposedly accompanies this state. Thus, Rouget claims that trance is characterized by total amnesia,[202] while Simons et al. maintain that devotees at Thaipusam experience amnesia.[203] Collins emphatically asserts that "The vast majority of devotees who perform ritual vow fulfilment involving piercing the body relate that they retain no memory of the trance experience".[204] However, in contrast, Colleen Ward finds that most devotees are able to recollect and comment upon their dissociative experiences.[205] My own extensive research supports Ward's conclusions. In conducting interviews among votaries at Batu Caves, Penang and in Singapore and India, I have found that the overwhelming majority of subjects, most of whom had engaged in acts of bodily mortification, had vivid and compelling recollections of their trance states. Many were able to describe in pellucid detail the sequence of events which had accompanied the onset of trance and the experiences and insights which followed. Even among the small minority who could remember little of their kavadi *yatra*, most were able to recall at least some of the events between their initial trance state and their arrival at the shrine in the cave. (Most of the latter groups were among those who were gripped by possession trances involving investment by non-*Agamic* or guardian deities.)

Trance and Thaipusam

Hinduism has a long history of trance as an integral paradigm of worship and as a means of encountering the Divine. In South India this medium was well established by the time of the Sangam era.[206] The central conception of trance/possession is understood not in terms of the state per se, but rather as a vehicle for absorbing or internalizing the meaning of the text — both oral and written — of a specific ritual, and thus, by extension, the myth that informs that ritual. This entails the devotee's investment by the deity, the consequent divinization of the body, and its entextualization to accord with the tradition, the underlying rationale of the ritual.[207]

In the previous chapter I noted that votaries and their spiritual mentors aimed at invoking an esoteric trance condition known as *arul*, in which the deity invests the devotee and temporarily infuses the subject with a mystical awareness of his presence. M.D. Muthukumarasamy states that while *arul* literally translates as "grace", its deeper meaning is more fully understood as "a fluid state of the body and consciousness where both have become conduits and sites for a divine energy to descend and communicate".[208] *Arul* is a multifaceted phenomenon, and is expressed in many different forms, ranging from tumultuous vigour to comparative calm, often fluctuating between these two extremes.

I earlier observed that while most participants bear kavadis to fulfil vows to Murugan, a substantial minority of kavadi worshippers pay homage to other deities, ranging from *Agamic* gods through to village gods and goddesses, tutelary deities, and even spirits. Given the extraordinary multiplicity of deities worshipped at Thaipusam, and the social and ethnic heterogeneity of the participants, we might reasonably anticipate observing an extensive array of trance states, displaying not only the entire spectrum of trance behaviour, but also incorporating the characteristics of the medley of deities for whom kavadis are borne. And, indeed, the divergent nature of scholarly analysis of trance outlined above is replicated, as it were, in the melange of trance states observed at Thaipusam at Batu Caves. Research reveals a gamut of trance states ranging from straightforward and uncomplicated possession, in which the aspirant is "seized" by the deity and subsequently manifests his/her dominant or more conspicuous traits, through to more complex behavioural patterns consistent with those states Rouget has categorized as "inspirational" trances and which Maslow describes as "peak experiences". Indeed, the comprehensive lack of uniformity merely serves to underscore Rouget's dictum that "in the field of human behaviour no law can be verified other than with a fairly wide margin of uncertainty".[209]

In the previous chapter we noted that Tamil Hinduism recognizes an extensive and variegated range of trance states. At their lowest and most dangerous level these involve possession by malevolent spirits and treacherous *asuras*, and must either be suppressed or contained through appropriate propitiation. In general it is agreed that the trance states involving the great *Agamic* gods — Siva, Parvati, Vishnu, Murugan, Krishna, Saraswati, etc. — are both "higher" and more powerfully illuminating than those attained through the worship of "lesser" deities. However, given the shifting structures of Malaysian Hinduism and the anti-authoritarian discourse which informs *bhakti* devotionalism, this assertion cannot be regarded as axiomatic. In Chapter 4 I noted that the processes of *Agamicization*/Sanskritization have identified certain non-*Agamic* deities — for example, Muneeswaran and Kali, Mariamman and Durga (in their village forms) — as manifestations of the great *Agamic* gods. Given these circumstances, the devotees who are entranced by those non-*Agamic* deities might (and indeed do) emphatically affirm the equivalence of their trance states to those bestowed upon the votaries of *Agamic* gods. Moreover, *bhakti* philosophies strenuously assert the intrinsic experiential validity and autonomy of individualist devotion, and thus reject societal assessment on the basis of outer markers (for example, caste or the sex of devotees), or of the adoption of arcane or even bizarre forms of worship (such as those which violate prescribed norms). Finally, *bhakti* clearly recognizes the transformative power of persistent and virtuous ritual devotion, and the eventual rewards which must accrue to those who are zealous in their worship. Thus, a devotee who with a pure and open heart completes a ritual for a lesser non-*Agamic* deity may be viewed as embarking upon his/her own transmogrative path, a journey which over the passage of time will ultimately result in the development of a higher consciousness and awareness of a union with the great *Agamic* deities.

I have argued that aspirants actively seek the state of *arul*. However, at Batu Caves there is one small (and extremely controversial) "transgressive" group which quite deliberately promotes "demonic/lower order" possession prior to the ascent to the caves. I shall discuss the phenomenon of the demon devotee later in this chapter.

Inducing Trance

We have noted that the induction of trance leads the aspirant beyond quotidian consciousness; that the attainment of trance is often learned behaviour; that it is culture specific; that the trance state is initiated via a series of sub-rituals; and that these rituals are accompanied by music and dance.

The induction of trance at Thaipusam conforms to this pattern. The devotee approaches the festival after weeks of fasting, during which he/she has endured privations, performed *tapas* and concentrated his/her mind on the ritual which will result in a direct experience of the Divine. He/she is aware that the attainment of trance is a necessary precondition for the successful bearing of a kavadi and the painless and bloodless insertion of the *vels* and hooks within the body. As noted in Chapter 6, many of the aspirants will have attended sessions of trance training where their progress was assessed and their ability to achieve and sustain trance was put to the test. On Thaipusam day the devotee will gather with his/her particular group, either at the river bank outside the Batu Caves complex or in one of the small temples within the nearby Indian settlement. The votary will be clad in the requisite *vesthi*, shorts, sari or a Punjabi suit, usually made of yellow cloth and trimmed with red. He/she will be wearing anklets accoutred with small bells. He/she will undergo all the preliminary rituals, including a *puja* to Ganesha, and the purification of the kavadi that he/she is to carry. All the cultural "prompts" and stimuli now in place, the leader and group's attention will turn to inducing trance. The retinue surrounding the votary will chant, music will be played, and perhaps hymns or songs will be performed, percussive instruments will be hit rhythmically, and incense passed under the devotee's face. As mentioned in Chapter 6, the eventuating trance is obvious to all bystanders, and is dramatically demonstrated by a range of bodily signals. This indicates to onlookers that the deity has invested the devotee who has entered the state of *arul*. At this point the *vels* will be inserted, the kavadi fitted, the devotee and his/her retinue will depart for the Temple Cave. En route the aspirant will perform the kavadi dance, emulating the swaying motion of Idumban as he bore the hills to the south of India.

For many devotees the violent impact of the initial trance is replaced by a calmer plateau state in which the devotee is aware of his/her surroundings, is able to respond to directions, and is able to interact with members of his/her retinue as they guide him/her towards the caves. My interviews with devotees suggest that while the early emphatic trance indicates the arrival and presence of the deity, it is the plateau phase that follows which imparts fresh awareness, the array of abstruse experiences that Ralph Waldo Emerson describes as ecstatic, "the very keynote of religious experience",[210] and which comprise the very heart of the religious ritual. The "superhuman" energies expended by devotees are obvious and are demonstrated in the ability to bear an unaccustomed weight while encumbered with hooks, chains and *vels*, to engage in a vigorous dance, and to climb the steep flights of steps which lead to the Temple Cave.

All of those interviewed indicated that the experience had been manifestly positive, that "messages" — some explicit, others subtle and recondite — had been transmitted during the course of bearing the kavadi, and that these messages would change the way devotees conducted their lives and the way in which they viewed the world. Many older Hindus recounted their own kavadi pilgrimages in terms of awe, and several claimed that the experience had transformed their lives. Timothy Beardsworth has claimed that "In the affective experience, the subject's *own emotions* contribute fundamentally to what he sees. It is a different order of experience — the pre-objective. He does not observe, he responds: and his response colours what he seems to see."[211] But to the devotees I have interviewed, these episodes were real, immediate, urgent and profound; they were authentic mystical experiences of great intensity and power, often the most penetrating interludes in their religious life. In the deepest sense, these equated to the "peak experiences" described by Maslow.

Thaipusam and "Failure"

All devotees, especially first-time aspirants, are under considerable pressure to "perform" at Thaipusam. However, this pressure is often ameliorated throughout the period of fasting by the careful instruction and reassurance provided by religious teachers and influential elders within the temple community, and by the active support extended by friends and family. Trance training may also provide much-needed confidence. However, these measures can only go so far, and the final hours leading to the encounter with the deity, the actual "moment of truth" when *arul* descends, are often fraught with anxiety. As Babb states, the trance state is of great significance to the individual devotee:

> ... more than any other ritual phenomenon, trance fuses public and private truth. It is public in the sense that the devotee's special religious status is visible to all; divine favour can be seen in his demeanour and in his apparently miraculous ability to penetrate his flesh without pain and bleeding. It is private in the sense that the devotee has a truly personal encounter with God...[212]

Inability to reach trance on Thaipusam day, which according to my own observations affects only a handful of devotees, will generally be attributed to one of three causes:

1. The failure to properly observe the requirements of fasting.
2. Spiritual unworthiness; that is, for some reason the deity chooses not to possess or invest the subject.
3. The subject is not ready for the spiritual commitment demanded of participants at Thaipusam, or is required to pursue other forms of spiritual disciplines.

However, while the inability to realize trance will cause acute discomfort for the intending votary, and may earn social disapproval, this does not necessarily follow, especially in instances where the participant is very young. Of more serious moment, however, is the undisputed fact that the prospective votary has been unable to fulfil a vow to the deity, and that an extremely significant transaction remains incomplete. In these cases the devotee is advised to seek spiritual counselling and to find ways of discharging his/her unfulfilled debt to the god.

Trance: The "Demon Devotee"

At this point it is apposite to discuss the role of the transgressive devotee at Thaipusam, the votary who plies, or who is alleged to ply, an unorthodox path, and who ostensibly eschews well-accepted and established rites. The "demon devotee" typically worships a renegade deity or spirit, one which makes no pretence of respecting the recognized moral order and is openly subversive of all received authority. These peripheral figures seem to be largely attractive to the weak and the downtrodden, and their domination of the lowest ranks forms a double protest: firstly, on the part of the deity/ spirit against the cosmology which renders them as outcasts, and secondly on the part of the devotees against the secular/religious authorities who relegate them to the base of society. The intertwining of outcast gods/spirits and recalcitrant adherents provides a public demonstration of the reputedly dangerous powers which the deity/spirit invests in this otherwise scorned or oppressed segment of society.[213] However, the effectiveness of this protest depends on the overall societal acknowledgement of the minatory forces symbolized throughout the period of oppression.[214] Moreover, the leaders of these groups will almost inevitably be subject to intense public ostracism, and their powers will often be discredited or checked by accusations of black magic or witchcraft.[215]

In discussing the issue of the demon devotee at Thaipusam, it is first necessary to resolve the status of two groups, namely women and lower-class devotees, who some observers have designated as "lesser" worshippers; that is, votaries whose experiences can never be considered to be on the same rarefied level as those of upper-caste male devotees.

Gananath Obeskeyere has made the claim that as Murugan became "Brahmanized" his identity was inexorably fused with the higher-caste mores of purity and pollution, a process which rendered him beyond possessing women, whom Obeskeyere asserts are regarded as intrinsically impure. According to this viewpoint, the trance states of women must denote possession by lesser gods and spirits.[216] This contention is not supported by my own observations in Malaysia or India, or among the "Jaffna" Tamils whom I interviewed both for my doctoral dissertation and in the course of preparing this book. On the contrary, it was repeatedly emphasized that such an attitude would be contrary to the ideals of *bhakti* worship, as well as the more general philosophies of Saiva Siddhanta. It was further pointed out that several prominent and well-established female mediums in Malaysia claimed inspiration from Murugan. Finally, the story of Murugan's enthrallment of Valli and the fact that Thaipusam celebrates Parvati's granting of the *Sakti Vel*, the instrumental means by which Murugan achieved domination over the *asuras*, were cited as evidence of the elevated status of women within the Murugan cultus.

In the case of *Adi Dravida* devotees, some commentators aver that their ambiguous spiritual status is the result of their putative continual contact with lower deities and the world of spirits (especially potentially malevolent spirits such as *bhuta* and *pey*), relationships which render them "*supposedly weaker in mental and spiritual terms*" (emphasis added).[217] Certainly my fieldwork reveals that many members of higher castes fear the ability of *Adi Dravidas* to manipulate these forces, and that mediums, shamans and exorcists dealing with godlings and dangerous spirits are usually (though not inevitably) drawn from their ranks. However, while I have encountered pejorative attitudes towards *Adi Dravidas* in Thaipusam rituals (most often from Hindu reformers, especially when worship is directed towards village or "little "deities), it is by no means ubiquitous, nor even widespread. Indeed, most *Adi Dravidas* interviewed reported little overt discrimination throughout the course of their involvement at Thaipusam, although several stated that they felt their experiences were devalued in comparison with those of upper castes. However, the democratizing influence of *bhakti* at Batu Caves is pronounced, especially in the conduct of a ritual such as the *tirtha yatra*, when in theory all notions of caste are suspended and the equality of pilgrims is emphasized. Thus, if a devotee conducts his/her worship in accordance with received norms, his/her participation will generally be considered of commensurate moment to that of other votaries.

At Batu Caves the greatest public animus is reserved for the small group of "transgressive" devotees; that is, those aspirants who quite deliberately flout the fundamental norms of the purity–impurity dichotomy, and who either worship dangerous spirits or who identify themselves with *asuric* or demonic forces, and who drink alcohol and engage in other so-called "left-handed" activities. In fact, interviews with a number of these devotees, most of whom were young males of *Adi Dravida* castes, revealed that none were left-handed in the sense of belonging to the school of *kulavarna tantra* — that is, "spiritual advancement ... achieved by means of the very things which are the causes of man's downfall"[218] — nor were any adherents of the sorts of *sakta tantra* cults described by Sir John Woodroofe.[219]

The rationale which informs their worship is straightforward, and is summed up in the following selected comments: "We have fasted, we have observed all restrictions."; "Surapadman, Singamukhan, Tarakasura and all the other *asuras* behaved badly, even Idumban was a demon, and yet they were all rescued by Murugan. We can hope for the same."; "We hurt no-one. God alone will decide whether our actions are right. God helps those who admit they are ignorant and in need of assistance. It is not for others to decide how we should behave." A highly respected Malaysian Hindu, a venerated elder with a wide range of social, political and religious contacts, told me, "These people are among the misunderstood Hindus. They are on the whole modest, humble and decent. Their path is a sort of modified, heavily diluted left-handedness, a pathway more widely trodden and better understood in India than in Malaysia." Indeed, as noted in Chapter 2, "inferior" *bhakti* may be transformed and subsequently offered as "higher" *bhakti*.[220] These "transgressive" devotees appear to be a Malaysian example of this phenomenon.

Beyond Trance: The Pilgrimage

In this section I trace the devotee's progress to the shrine following the attainment of trance. As we have seen, the votary has now completed his/her period of purificatory fasting; he/she has bathed prior to undergoing the congery of rituals prior to the induction of the trance state and subsequent fitting of the kavadi. The aspirant now sets out on a short but intense journey, densely laden with the ritual symbolism drawn from the Murugan cosmology. The journey re-enacts, even if inexactly, the spiritual genesis, stabilization and triumph of the deity Murugan, and foreshadows the progressive enlightenment of the devotee and thus the final destiny of his/her soul.

In fact the metaphorical journey began the day the votary commenced fasting. In Chapter 5 I noted that Murugan's first military manoeuvre following the acquisition of the *Vel* resulted in the slaying of the *asura* Krownchan, who had taken the form of a mountain attempting to block the passage of the devonic army. Krownchan represents the *tamas*, the forces of inertia, torpor and sloth. We have seen that the *sadhaka* has already vanquished *tamas* throughout the period of fasting.

Bearing the kavadi, a miniature shrine containing the deity himself, and in the state of *arul* in which he/she has been invested by the god, the entranced devotee now makes his/her way from the riverbank or Indian settlement to the entrance of the Batu Caves complex. En route the votary, surrounded by his/her retinue, performs the kavadi dance, the swaying movements of the *asura* Idumban, as under commission from the sage Agastya he bore the twin hills Sivagiri and Saktigiri to South India.

The devotee reaches the *gopuram* (represented by an ornate architrave) which marks the entrance to the Batu Caves complex, where he/she crosses the boundary which divides the outside world of the *Kaliyuga*, the world of chaos and sorrow, from the demarcated and patterned universe within. It is generally held that only at this juncture does the pilgrim's "essential" journey commence, and that he/she begins that stage of the odyssey which moves backwards in time and into the primordial Self.[221]

The pilgrim now makes his/her way along the roped-off lane reserved for kavadi worshippers towards the flight of steps which lead to the Temple Cave. However, even before climbing the first step, the devotee passes a series of sequentially structured symbols, all of which relate to the early phases of Murugan's cosmic history:

1. On his/her right the votary will pass the temple dedicated to the *navagraha*, the nine planets. This recollects the creation of the nine *saktis* following the breaking of Parvati's anklet, each of whom is associated with one of the *navagraha*. The sons subsequently born to the *saktis* assumed the characteristics of the planet to which he is respectively linked, and collectively protect the young deity and later accompany him and his generals on his campaign against the *asuric* army.

2. On his/her left immediately prior to reaching the stairway, the pilgrim will pass a Ganesha temple, emphasizing the deity's relationship to Murugan as older brother, and his role as *Maha Ganapati*, the Ruler of Obstacles, without whose blessings no undertaking can expect to be successful. This landmark also acknowledges Ganesha's role as the mediator of the liminal border between material and divine worlds, and

more specifically as the controller of the *muladhara cakra*, representing the entry point into the realms of higher spirituality.[222]

3. Behind this temple lies a further temple dedicated to Maha Mariamman, Murugan's mother, thus recalling firstly Parvati's presentation of the *Sakti Vel* at the outset of his campaign to vanquish the *asura*-king Surapadman, thus restoring cosmic order, and secondly the foundation mythology of the Batu Caves shrine (as we have seen, it was Mariamman who first directed that worship be offered to her son in Batu Caves).

4. To the right of the base of the stairway stands the Murugan colossus, an unambiguous symbol signifying that Batu Caves is the deity's provenance, his major Malaysian home, and premier pilgrimage site.

5. On reaching the stairway the devotee will pass under an architrave, the centrepiece of which is the deity depicted as Shanmugan, seated on his *mayil vahana* (peacock mount), together with his consorts, Devayanai and Valli. Shanmugan represents the early multiform of Murugan, the unstabilized deity united into One by the embrace of Parvati. He is at the earliest stage of his cosmic career and is yet to attain his destined effulgence as *Purusa*, or Cosmic Man. It will also be recollected that during Murugan's wooing of Valli, his descent from the celestial abode of Mount Kailas to the jungle surrounds of Valli's village is marked by his reversion to the multiform Shanmugan, thus representing his immanence to all sincere devotees.

6. This theme is further developed by the motifs contained on the reverse side of the downstairs architrave, which depicts Murugan's marriage to the dark and earthy Valli, the adopted daughter of the hunter chief and an indigenous child of the soil. Valli symbolizes the power of *bhakti*, the forces of ecstasy and self-abandonment, and thus the unconventional, flexuous pathway the devotee must take in dispelling illusion and attaining realization of the deity's divine identity.

The Stairs: Towards Stabilization

Having passed under the downstairs architrave, the votary now climbs the 272 steps which lead him/her to the Temple Cave. While metaphorically Hinduism envisages spiritual unfoldment as a symbolic ascent towards the mountain peak of enlightenment (*moksha*),[223] in the case of Murugan worship there is an actual physical climb which embraces two additional and intertwined *puranic* themes; namely (1) the mythology of the Murugan–Devayanai–Valli triad, and (2) that of Murugan's campaign against the army of the *asuras*.

Murugan–Devayanai–Valli: We have noted that the reverse side of the downstairs architrave (that is, the side facing the steps) depicts the marriage of Murugan and Valli. The architrave which surmounts the top of the steps shows Murugan wedding his other consort, the fair Devayanai, the daughter of Indra, king of the gods. This ceremony is conducted according to orthodox Brahmanic rites, and in the presence of the celestials. The marriage symbolizes the unification of God and soul, congruent with the established precepts and conventions of spiritual enlightenment; that is, correct observance of appropriate rituals, proper conduct and spiritual disciplines, all leading to *moksha*. In this context it will be recollected that Murugan weds Devayanai only after he has achieved his final victory over the *asuras* and has restored harmony to the cosmos. Devayanai thus represents finality, order, stability and transcendence.

The steps which form a pathway between the two architraves suggest that both metaphysical journeys — that of orthodoxy (Devayanai) and that of *bhakti* (Valli) — will ultimately reach the same destination. But they also represent the widely accepted doctrine that *bhakti* precedes knowledge.[224] In this sense each of the 272 steps taken by the devotee as he/she climbs to the summit is illustrative of any one of an infinitude of cosmological potentialities produced by the constantly shifting axis of the Murugan–Devayanai–Valli triad, as the deity repeatedly moves between immanence (Valli) and transcendence (Devayanai). But the two architraves also reinscribe Hindu conceptions of cosmic hierarchy in which the diversified and multiform (Shanmugan) occupies a lower position than the unified (the stabilized Murugan) who transcends all differences.[225]

The Battles with the *Asuras*: But in climbing the stairs, the devotee also symbolically re-enacts the great war between the *devas* and the *asuras*. As I outlined in Chapter 5, Murugan descended from the celestial abode at Mount Kailas to conduct his military campaign against Surapadman's forces. I noted that by homologizing the battlefield to the human body, the mythology is internalized and the conflict between Murugan and the *asuras* becomes a spiritual quest to subdue *anava* (ego). As we have seen, this homology collapses the seeming incompatibility between the deity who is both transcendent and immanent. In this context the mounting of the stairs represents the ascent through the "lotuses"; that is, the *cakras*, the series of spiritual centres figuratively located along the spine. Hindus hold that the force of *kundalini* (or primordial power), depicted as a serpent, "uncoils" as the aspirant progressively moves towards his/her final spiritual goals, travelling up the *susumna nadi* (the central psychic current within the spinal column), activating each of the six "lotuses" (i.e., *cakras*) in succession before reaching the seventh *cakra* (*sahasrara*), located in the crown and signifying ultimate wisdom.[226] Or, as Iwao Shima comments, "The *Kundalini, prana* [vital energy/life force] in her hand, ascends the stairway of the sky and climbs the steps of the *susumna*."[227] (I observe in passing that the two main energy channels which complement the *susumna nadi* are [i] the *ida nadi* [Valli], also known as Chandra [moon], and portrayed as feminine, located on the left side of the body, which flows downward and conveys physical–emotional energy, and [ii] the *pingala nadi* [Devayanai], also known as *Surya* [sun], portrayed as masculine, located on the right side of the body, which flows upward and conveys intellectual–mental energy.[228] The tension and dynamic interplay of Siva–Sakti is thus intimately conjoined within the multitude of processes that collectively comprise spiritual unfoldment.)

The rise through the *cakras* is symbolically and collectively underscored by the location of Ganesha's temple at the foot of the stairs, the lower architrave featuring the unstabilized Shanmugan, contrasting with the celestial Murugan at the summit, a deity who has fulfilled his prescribed cosmic role and attained his full array of powers. We have already commented on Shanmugan and his eventual effulgent destiny as *Purusa*, Cosmic Man, the slayer of Surapadman. As we have noted, Ganesha is considered to control entry into the realm of the seven *cakras*, and is himself seated upon and permeates the *muladhara cakra*, symbolically sited at the base of the spine, which governs memory, space and time. Murugan initiates the devotee into yogic powers which move the devotee beyond the *muladhara cakra* and into the pull of the six higher *cakras*. As the devotee moves progressively towards a spiritual enlightenment, he/she will successively pass through the following *cakras*: *svadhisthana* (below navel) — reason; *manipura* (solar plexus) — willpower; *anahata* (heart centre) — direct cognition; *visuddha* (throat) — divine love; *ajna* (third eye) — divine sight; finally reaching the *sahasrara cakra* at the crown of the head, betokening spiritual illumination. Each of the *cakras* equates to one of the heads of the six-faced Shanmugan, and the ascent culminates in the fullness of the stabilized Murugan, the United One, vanquisher of Surapadman, and possessor of yogic wisdom.[229] The stairway as a whole thus encapsulates Murugan's campaign and the final triumph over the *asuras*, and each step therefore represents movement towards conquering *maya* (illusion), *malas* (impurities), *anava* (ego), and *avidya* (ignorance), and thereby acquisition of *vidya* (pure knowledge) and *moksha* (enlightenment and release).

The Temple Cave

At the entrance of the cave the votary will encounter two further iconic depictions, symbolizing Murugan's triumph over the *asuras*, and the dispelling of *anava*, or ego-dominated ignorance. Both reflect the deity's profound and transformative spiritual power.

On the devotee's left he/she will pass statuary showing Murugan's *Vel* splitting the *asura*-king Surapadman into two prior to his final defeat and conversion into two avian forms in which he permanently serves Murugan; namely the *mayil* (peacock), which becomes his *vahana* (mount), and the rooster which is inscribed upon his standard. The slaying of Surapadman not only concludes the campaign against the *asuras* but also clearly demonstrates the subjugation of *anava*, which is now converted into blissful awareness of the deity. (The pilgrim's view of this statue, regarded as an essential marker on the route to the final destination, is now all but obliterated by a thoughtlessly placed kiosk.)

On the right the devotee will pass a shrine to Idumban, the defeated and transformed *asura* who now permanently remains at the border of the Swami Subrahmanya Kovil as guardian gatekeeper of the inner temple. Idumban represents the destruction of ignorance, the transformed awareness of the nature of divinity and the role of perennial service as a form of worship. His defeat at the hands of the renunciant god at Palani also provides a prominent mode of ritual worship, the bearing of a kavadi.

As the devotee enters the cave, immediately prior to the steps which lead to the cave floor he/she will pass a large statue of Murugan with his *Vel*, that is, Murugan as "the shining one", the god triumphant, totally integrated and in possession of his full complement of cosmic powers. The entry to the cave marks a critical threshold for all votaries. In Chapter 2 we observed that all Tamil Hindu philosophies and belief structures posit a direction of inner movement, a progression from the outer world of forms to the centre where the undifferentiated Oneness is encountered in the perfect stillness and silence of transcendence. Thus the undifferentiated *atman* lies at the metaphorical centre of the five body sheaths, and truth is discovered only by constant probing and penetration of layer after layer of impurity and illusion. In the same chapter I also noted that the Hindu temple is homologized to the body. Within Tamil temples the central shrine (*garbhagriha*: literally, "womb chamber") is considered the "heart"; a small enclosed area which draws the devotee inwards from the outer world, "away from the sun and harsh shadows of the day into a dark and magical world for a purely personal transaction".[230] Entry to the cave is thus symbolic of the search for final truths; a sequential progression from light into darkness and from the expanse of the outdoors to an enclosed and confined space.[231] As noted in Chapter 6, the *murthi* of Murugan is located within an aperture at the northern wall of the Temple Cave; as it were, a cave within a cave. At Batu Caves this is doubly significant: as I have observed, one of Murugan's attributional names is Guru-Guhan, the divine preceptor who dwells within and issues wisdom from the cave of the heart. This entry to the cave symbolizes the final stage of the *sadhaka*'s search for Truth, the passage from ignorance to enlightenment.

But this is more than outer symbolism. As we have seen, the logic of inner movement also applies to the Hindu pilgrimage; it is a *tirtha yatra* (a divine crossing) which takes the adept from the border to the metaphysical centre. The same logic will direct that, just as Murugan/Guru-Guhan sits at the heart of the cave, so does the heart of Truth lie within the votary, and the heart within the human body becomes the shrine where purity and *moksha* may be realized. At this moment all paradoxes are resolved: Murugan's battle with the *asuras*, indeed, his entire cosmology, is internalized, and all polarities — the dynamic tension of Siva–Sakti, the illusory divisions between differentiated and undifferentiated, the outer and the inner, transcendence and immanence — collapse.

The votary proceeds to the main shrine to perform a final dance before the deity. The god and the adept exchange energies; the votary pours forth all the emotion of his/her devotion, still encumbered by the kavadi he/she has borne for the Lord, a public admission of his/her ignorance, the votary stands as if psychically naked before the deity. Thus the "burden" has been carried from the periphery through a series of symbolic thresholds to the inner world, where Murugan is encountered in his supreme majesty, and is laid at his feet. In return the deity offers his *darsan*, his blessings, the transformative spiritual energy that emanates from his eyes. The milk is taken from the kavadi and tipped over the Golden *Vel*, the symbol of Murugan's authority and kingship, which has been transferred from the deity's permanent *koyil* (palace) in Kuala Lumpur to the caves for the duration of the festival. The subject will then be removed from the kavadi, the *vels* will be extracted, and he/she will be brought out of trance. The formal exchange between devotee and deity is now at an end; the contract is fulfilled.

(As I mentioned in Chapter 6, over the past few years a number of additional statues and diaromas have been installed within the Temple Cave. These have been placed without any obvious regard for the chronological and sequential unfoldment of the ritual symbolism which is believed to be a necessary concomitant of the pilgrimage experience.)

Rites of Reincorporation

In Chapter 6 we noted that on the third day after Thaipusam the votary attends an Idumban *puja*, which not only honours the former *asura* but also releases the devotee from his/her adoptive and temporary role as *sannyasin*. He/she is thus symbolically restored to society and resumes the mundane routines of a householder.

But the devotee has changed, and the person who returns to society is not the same individual who commenced fasting some two to six weeks previously. As we have seen, the pilgrimage is conceived of as an experiential catalyst, which, inter alia, disrupts everyday notions, thus opening the adept to a range of cosmic possibilities which will reshape his/her relationship to the deity, and move the votary indefinably towards *moksha*. By bearing a kavadi at Thaipusam, the pilgrim has been exposed to new forms of knowledge, has encountered the deity in all his fullness, has been relieved of a measure of *karma*, and has been infused with new energies. He/she thus brings to quotidian life a fresh sense of purpose, control and direction, a renewed appreciation of his/her religion, and all that this implies. The devotee now stands, in psychic terms, on a more elevated plateau, representing the transformation and equipoise he/she has sought; a temporary resolution which will equip him/her spiritually, as well as in the conduct of the subsequent mundane life to which he/she is returning.

Throughout the pilgrimage the aspirant has been assisted by a close supporting retinue of relatives and friends, as well as his/her spiritual advisor, all of whom were present during the intimate and reactive meeting with the deity. This is now acknowledged by the adept, who serves his/her supporters with food and drink. The palpable feelings of group satisfaction, of a significant undertaking now complete, not only pervades the entire Idumban *puja* but also confirms a complex of shared interests and emotions that survive into quotidian life.

Afterword: Colour, Heat and Cold in Thaipusam

Earlier in this chapter we noted that red and white are the primary Tamil colours. We also observed that red is a hot colour and that white is considered cool. Brenda Beck explains that while white represents stability, freedom from pollution and general well-being, it is also associated with purity and linked to ritual cooling substances, including water and milk. Red on the other hand is a colour of ambiguity and uncertainty. Although it is often used to show health and vitality, it may also be identified with human blood. In this connection it may be used to express pollution, conflict and even death. However, red and white in combination are regarded as auspicious and progenitive.[232]

Beck contends that the majority of South Indian rituals are conducted in units of three, consisting of an initial event, a climax and a conclusion. She further asserts that these can be expressed in terms of colours, and that stage one and three will always be white, while stage two is invariably red.[233] If we assume that South Indian rituals are designed to move an individual from a given state to a more desirable condition, we must deduce that the central stage of the ritual, the red state, is that in which the transition is affected. And, indeed, red is associated with extraordinary or innovative occurrences, and with the processes of transformation.[234] If we link red/white with heating and cooling, we can conclude that any Tamil ritual will be constituted in a three-stage structure, comprising white–cool/red–hot/white–cool. While heat is implicated in the transformation of substances, and thus forms the central and decisive element within major rituals and ceremonies, if left uncontrolled, red–heat can prove dangerous and destructive. Tamil rituals thus seek to surround and contain red–heat with white–cool.[235] I would suggest that the red–hot/white–cool dichotomy is in clear evidence throughout Thaipusam.

The festival opens with the raising of the flag (*koti*) within the Batu Caves compound. The flag raised at Batu Caves consists of a red-painted rooster (Murugan's standard) against and enclosed by a white background (thus the red–hot is surrounded by white–cool).

On the *individual* level, the devotee's fasting, asceticism and generation of *tapas* is a period of prolonged and unrelieved heating. The ascetic is one who quells his earthly desires, especially his sexual passions. These energies are directed inwards and are transmuted, igniting a spiritual "fire" within. All heat is extremely dangerous if not properly controlled.[236] While the renunciant manipulates his/her heat to produce spiritual outcomes, at Thaipusam the adept's red–heat is controlled within the parameters of approved and tested ritual behaviours.

The votary's heat is at its most pronounced, and thus at its most dangerous, during the interval immediately preceding trance, and throughout the period of *arul*. We have noted that devotees usually wear clothes which incorporate Murugan's colours: yellow (a cool colour) with red trimmings. Prior to taking the kavadi, the devotee is cooled by a ritual bath. (In Chapter 6 we noted that nearly all devotees report that the water in which they bathe is experienced as preternaturally cold; an indication, perhaps, of the aspirant's superheated condition.) The state of *arul* is regarded as a red–hot condition and must be carefully contained and directed. However, some cooling agents are employed — the *vels* and spears are often lubricated with bananas, citrus is often supplied to the votary (or cut above his/her head), and *vibhuti* (holy ash) is applied to the torsos of those bearing *aluga* or other large kavadis. All of these measures are regarded as cooling (indeed, as we have seen, *vibhuti* is used by the *pujari* and his assistants to suppress unwanted and potentially intrusive trance states). However, despite these white–cooling measures, it is generally acknowledged that the "crossing" which follows the "moment of truth", that is, the attainment of *arul*, is accompanied by a steep rise in the red–heat of the aspirant.

When the devotee reaches the shrine in the cave and is presented to Murugan — a potential exchange of red–heat spiritual energies — the milk the devotee has borne on the kavadi is poured over the Golden *Vel* to help "cool" the deity. As noted earlier in this chapter, the *murthis* within the shrine are regarded as accumulators and conductors of energy. Throughout a major festival such as Thaipusam, when countless numbers of worshippers express their adulation, and thousands are engaged in intimate transfers of substantial power with the deity, there is a huge risk that the god will overheat, with unpredictable and possibly dire consequences. Milk is regarded as something more than a mere white cooling agent; it is *amirtha* (the light of the moon), the symbol of knowledge and immortality. The act of pouring this substance is thus not only a "cooling" act; it restores to the deity some of the spiritual power he expends as he bestows *darsan* upon the devotee.[237]

Following the presentation of his/her psychic burden, which is symbolically laid at the feet of the deity, the devotee is brought out of trance (a white–cooling action), dusted with *vibhuti* (cooling), and *kumkum* (red–heating) is applied to his/her forehead. Those who show reluctance or difficulty to emerge from trance are offered limes (cooling) to chew. The subsequent Idumban *puja* is a white–cooling ritual in which the devotee terminates his/her period of red–heating asceticism and is returned to society.

In very basic terms, the schema outlined by Beck, and strongly supported by my own research, as applied to Thaipusam, might be displayed as follows:

1. Original state of white: Mundane life.
2. Red/heat: Vow/asceticism/fasting/*arul*/pilgrimage.
3. New state of white: Idumban *puja*/return to society.

In this context, stage two, that of red–heat fire, represents the period of transformative liminality which separates the white–cool phases which enclose the ritual.

The above is a very elementary discussion of a complex issue, and does not delve into the many white–cool/red–heat permutations which might be uncovered by a closer examination of the festival as a whole. However, in a very general sense, this section does demonstrate the essential red/white correspondences which obtain throughout Thaipusam.

Conclusions

This chapter has examined Thaipusam in terms of the Tamil Hindu ritual of pilgrimage, the *tirtha yatra* (or divine crossing), a journey from the periphery to the *axis mundi*, or centre, a location where a given deity is both immanent and accessible. In this sense the movement from outer to inner pilgrimage is consistent with the logic of inner direction found in Tamil Hindu philosophies and belief structures. We have noted that pilgrimage is a ritual which, while conducted for reasons which may, on occasion, appear superficially mundane, also produces spiritual outcomes. Batu Caves is a recognized Malaysian pilgrimage centre with a well-established foundation mythology and a prescribed corpus of ritual behaviours. However, as I have noted, these ritual behaviours occur only when the king-deity is in residence at his mountaintop *kovil*; that is, when he makes his annual regal procession from his Kuala Lumpur palace, and the symbol of his royal authority — the Golden *Vel* — is installed within the shrine in the cave. In a sense the rites of kingship establish the wider boundaries of the Thaipusam festival, and the ritual incorporation of the king-deity's segmentary population also encompasses the period when the kavadi ritual — the personal supplication to the deity — is regarded at its most efficacious.

In examining Tamil approaches to the rite of pilgrimage, we have explored the South Indian understanding of substance movement, and in particular the concept of head writing and what this internal code implies for the individual. We have noted that the *kunam* complex may be modified by the appropriate supplication of the *karman* complex, resulting in the formation of a new *kunam* complex. The need to move from one state to another — a personal repositioning towards greater equipoise and control — may be divined internally or through an agency, and may be effected by a number of prescribed rituals, one of which is pilgrimage.

The decision to embark upon a pilgrimage (in the case of the devotee at Thaipusam to bear a kavadi) is followed by the votary making a vow, a form of contract in which he/she agrees to undertake a pilgrimage in return for a tangible benefit bestowed by the deity. The period prior to the pilgrimage is marked by a stipulated interval of asceticism in which the aspirant withdraws from mundane societal routines and assumes the role and persona, at least in part, of a *sannyasin*, a revered Hindu cultural archetype.

This chapter has also examined trance as a mechanism for totally extricating the devotee from the realm of the quotidian, and thus proving a new form of consciousness in which sub-rituals can suggest, induce and enhance direct communication with the Divine. *Arul* is a defining category of trance which represents the descent of the deity, and his "filling" or "embracing" of the votary. I have postulated that *arul* forms the core phase of Thaipusam, and plunges the devotee into an ecstatic and noetic liminality, in which he/she is exposed to the deity's power, and "messages" and knowledge are transferred.

Beginning with the initiation of fasting, the pilgrim commences a journey which is saturated with the symbology of the Murugan cultus, and which contains within its structures the essential corpus of Murugan mythology. The period of asceticism sees the subdual of the *tamas* (forces of inertia which impede spirituality) and the rise of *rajas* (activity, energy), which are in turn displaced by *sattva* (pure consciousness) which arrives at the moment of *arul*; a crucial and pivotal point in which pain is quelled and replaced by love. The devotee then begins an intense journey which re-enacts many of the significant and formative events within the Murugan cosmology — the deity's early history, the presentation of the *Vel*, his triumph over the *asuras*, his full stabilization, his divine marriages, his ultimate rule as the powerful Skanda-Murugan, enclosing and embracing all cosmic powers and offering the potentiality of transcendence. But the homologization of the body and the cosmic fuses external and internal rituals and symbolism, so that in the most profound sense the aspirant adumbrates and symbolically fulfils his/her own metaphysical journey to the centre, climaxing with the entry to the Temple Cave, where all theoretical oppositions and paradoxes of the outer world collapse and the votary is presented to the deity. The devotee submits his/her burden to Murugan, and the deity extends his blessings and bestows his *darsan*. The adept is returned to the mundane routines of society following the Idumban *puja*, but is transformed; he/she brings to the quotidian sphere a new and more elevated sense of purpose and control.

Finally, this chapter touched upon the use of colour and heat in Hindu ritual, and demonstrated that Thaipusam as practised in Malaysia conforms to the white–red–white/cool–heat–cool sequences common to Tamil ritual.

Notes

1. Karen Armstrong, *The Case for God: What Religion Really Means* (London: Bodley Head, 2009), p. 3.
2. Lewis Hyde, *Trickster Makes This World: Mischief, Myth and Art* (New York: North Road Press, 1998), p. 130; Birgitt Rottger-Rossler, "The Emotional Meaning of Ritual", in *Emotions in Rituals and Performances*, edited by Axel Michaels and Christoph Wulf (New Delhi: Routledge, 2012), pp. 42–43.

3. John Bowker, *Why Religions Matter* (New York: Cambridge University Press, 2015). See also Rottger-Rossler, "The Emotional Meaning of Ritual", pp. 52–53.

4. Gavin Flood, *The Importance of Religion: Meaning and Action in our Strange World* (Chichester: Wiley-Blackwell, 2012), p. 112; Fred W. Clothey, *Rhythm and Intent: Ritual Studies from South India* (Bombay: Blackie and Son, 1983), p. 161.

5. Anne de Sales, "Ritual Virtuosity, Emotions and Feelings in Shamanic Rituals in Nepal", in *Emotions in Rituals and Performances*, edited by Axel Michaels and Christoph Wulf (New Delhi: Routledge, 2012), p. 163.

6. Alexandra Kent, *Divinity and Diversity: A Hindu Revitalization Movement in Malaysia* (Singapore and Copenhagen: Institute of Southeast Asian Studies/ NIAS Press, 2004), p. 128; Flood, *The Importance of Religion*, p. 105.

7. Axel Michaels and Christoph Wulf, "Emotions in Rituals and Performances: An Introduction", in *Emotions in Rituals and Performances*, edited by Axel Michaels and Christoph Wulf (New Delhi: Routledge, 2012), p. 15.

8. Cynthia J. Miller, "Immigrants, Images and Identity: Visualising Homelands across Borders", in *Tracing an Indian Diaspora: Contexts, Memories, Representations*, edited by Parvati Raghuram, Ajaya Kumar Sahoo, Brij Maharaj, and Dave Sangha (New Delhi: Sage, 2008), p. 284.

9. Anne Grodzins Gold, *Fruitful Journeys: The Ways of Rajasthani Pilgrims* (Berkeley: University of California Press, 1988), p. 4.

10. Cornelia Dimmit and J.A.B. van Buitenen, eds. and trans., *Classical Hindu Mythology: A Reader in the Sanskrit Puranas* (Philadelphia: Temple University Press, 1978), pp. 251–52; E. Alan Moronis, *Pilgrimage in the Hindu Tradition: A Case Study of West Bengal* (Delhi: Oxford University Press, 1984), p. 49; Diana L. Eck, *Darsan: Seeing the Divine Image in India*, 3rd ed. (New York: Columbia University Press, 1998), p. 64.

11. Moronis, *Pilgrimage in the Hindu Tradition*, p. 280.

12. Gold, *Fruitful Journeys*, p. 36.

13. Ibid., p. 136.

14. Ibid., pp. 195–96.

15. Ibid., pp. 136–37.

16. C.J. Fuller, *The Camphor Flame: Popular Hinduism and Society in India* (Princeton, NJ: Princeton University Press, 1992), p. 208.

17. Moronis, *Pilgrimage in the Hindu Tradition*, pp. 209–10.

18. David Dean Shulman, *Tamil Temple Myths: Sacrifice and Divine Marriage in the South Indian Saiva Tradition* (Princeton, NJ: Princeton University Press, 1980), p. 55.

19. Vineeta Sinha, *A New God in the Diaspora? Muneeswaran Worship in Contemporary Singapore* (Singapore and Copenhagen: Singapore University Press/NIAS Press, 2005), p. 92.

20. Moronis, *Pilgrimage in the Hindu Tradition*, pp. 204–5.
21. Ibid., pp. 228–29.
22. Shulman, *Tamil Temple Myths*, p. 40; Moronis, *Pilgrimage in the Hindu Tradition*, p. 112.
23. Moronis, *Pilgrimage in the Hindu Tradition*, pp. 42–45.
24. Fuller, *The Camphor Flame*, p. 209.
25. Moronis, *Pilgrimage in the Hindu Tradition*, p. 280.
26. Fuller, *The Camphor Flame*, p. 208.
27. Moronis, *Pilgrimage in the Hindu Tradition*, pp. 42–45.
28. Ibid., p. 213.
29. George Michell, *The Hindu Temple: An Introduction to its Meanings and Forms* (Chicago: University of Chicago Press, [1977] 1988), p. 68.
30. Dolf Hartsuiker, *Sadhus: The Holy Men of India* (London: Thames and Hudson, 1993), p. 79.
31. Dimmitt and van Buitenen, *Classical Hindu Mythology*, p. 251; Michell, *The Hindu Temple*, p. 69.
32. Manuel Moreno, "God's Forceful Call: Possession as Divine Strategy", in *Gods of Flesh, Gods of Stone: The Embodiment of Divinity in India*, edited by Joanne Punzo Waghorne and Norman Cutler in association with Vasudha Narayanan (Chambersburg: Anima, 1985), p. 109.
33. Michell, *The Hindu Temple*, p. 69.
34. Eck, *Darsan*, p. 62.
35. Gold, *Fruitful Journeys*, p. 295.
36. Fuller, *The Camphor Flame*, p. 209.
37. Shulman, *Tamil Temple Myths*, p. 41.
38. Gold, *Fruitful Journeys*, p. 296.
39. Ibid., p. 137.
40. R. Champakalakshmi, *Religion, Tradition and Ideology: Precolonial South India* (New Delhi: Oxford University Press, 2011), p. 238.
41. Gold, *Fruitful Journeys*, pp. 5–6.
42. Ibid.; Shulman, *Tamil Temple Myths*, p. 18.
43. Hartsuiker, *Sadhus*, p. 10; Vanamali, *The Lilas of the Sons of Shiva* (New Delhi: Aryan Books International, 2008), p. 253.
44. Vanamali, *The Lilas*, p. 253; Gold, *Fruitful Journeys*, p. 263.
45. Eck, *Darsan*, p. 64.
46. Moronis, *Pilgrimage in the Hindu Tradition*, p. 60.
47. Shulman, *Tamil Temple Myths*, pp. 18–19.
48. Gold, *Fruitful Journeys*, pp. 6–7.
49. Ibid., p. 187.
50. Ibid., pp. 6–7; Moronis, *Pilgrimage in the Hindu Tradition*, p. 67.
51. Moronis, *Pilgrimage in the Hindu Tradition*, p. 225.

52. Ibid., pp. 221–26; Gold, *Fruitful Journeys*, p. 262; Fuller, *The Camphor Flame*, p. 214; Shulman, *Tamil Temple Myths*, pp. 18–21.

53. Moronis, *Pilgrimage in the Hindu Tradition*, p. 226.

54. Ibid., p. 67.

55. Ibid., p. 224; Shulman, *Tamil Temple Myths*, p. 18.

56. Eck, *Darsan*, p. 3.

57. Moronis, *Pilgrimage in the Hindu Tradition*, p. 209.

58. Thomas Keneally, *Three Cheers for the Paraclete* (Ringwood: Penguin [1969] 1984), p. 42.

59. Carl Gustav Diehl, *Instrument and Purpose: Studies on Rites and Religions in South India* (Lund: C.W.K. Gleerup, 1956), p. 253; personal field research.

60. Gold, *Fruitful Journeys*, p. 188.

61. Hartsuiker, *Sadhus*, p. 79.

62. Moronis, *Pilgrimage in the Hindu Tradition*, p. 213.

63. Gold, *Fruitful Journeys*, p. 188.

64. Ibid., p. 253.

65. Shulman, *Tamil Temple Myths*, p. 26.

66. Eck, *Darsan*, pp. 54–55; Clothey, *Rhythm and Intent*, p. 13.

67. Interviews with trustees, Batu Caves.

68. Burton Stein, *Peasant, State and Society in Medieval South India* (Delhi: Oxford University Press, 1980), pp. 267–68.

69. Champakalakshmi, *Religion, Tradition and Ideology*, pp. 474–78.

70. Ibid., p. 481.

71. Ibid., p. 489.

72. Ibid., p. 478.

73. Clifford Geertz, *Local Knowledge: Further Essays in Interpretative Anthropology* (New York: Basic Books, 1983), p. 125.

74. E. Valentine Daniel, *Fluid Signs: Being a Person the Tamil Way* (Berkeley: University of California Press, 1983), pp. 3–5.

75. Alexandra Kent, *Divinity and Diversity*, p. 63.

76. Sheryl B. Daniel, "The Tool Box Approach of the Tamil to Issues of Moral Responsibility and Human Destiny", in *Karma: An Anthropological Inquiry*, edited by Charles F. Keyes and E. Valentine Daniel (Berkeley: University of California Press, 1983), pp. 27–28.

77. Daniel, *Fluid Signs*, pp. 5–6.

78. Moreno, "God's Forceful Call", pp. 119–20.

79. Daniel, *Fluid Signs*, pp. 5–6. Thus, for example, diet must be appropriately regulated, and a balanced meal must contain a total of six qualities — sweet, sour, salty, bitter, astringent and hot (Gabriella Ferro-Luzzi Eichinger, "Ritual as Language: The Case of South Indian Food Offerings", *Current Anthropology* 18, no. 3 (1977): 511.

80. Wendy Doniger O'Flaherty, *Siva: The Erotic Ascetic* (London: Oxford University Press, 1973), p. 282. The breaching of *dharma* (a process known as *adharma*) results not only in the creation of adverse individual *karma* but may also disrupt the social order and by extension the cosmic order, and in the most extreme cases may lead to chaos (Kent, *Divinity and Diversity*, p. 63).

81. O'Flaherty, *Siva*, p. 316.

82. Ibid., pp. 282–83; Stephen Inglis, "Possession and Pottery: Serving the Divine in a South Indian Community", in *Gods of Flesh, Gods of Stone: The Embodiment of Divinity in India*, edited by Joanne Punzo Waghorne and Norman Cutler in association with Vasudha Narayanan (Chambersburg: Anima, 1985), p. 99.

83. Daniel, *Fluid Signs*, pp. 70–71.

84. Daniel, *The Tool Box Approach*, p. 33; Kandiah Chelliah, *Hinduism: A Brief Study of It's* [sic] *Origins, Traditions and Practice* (Bukit Berunting: Kandiah Chelliah, 2012), p. 130.

85. Daniel, *The Tool Box Approach*, p. 28.

86. Fuller, *The Camphor Flame*, pp. 224–25.

87. Daniel, *The Tool Box Approach*, pp. 31–33.

88. Daniel, *Fluid Signs*, pp. 70–72.

89. Ibid.; Sudhir Kakar, *Shamans, Mystics and Doctors: A Psychological Inquiry into India and its Healing Traditions* (Delhi: Oxford University Press, 1982), p. 234.

90. E. Valentine Daniel, "Karma Divined in a Ritual Capsule", in *Karma: An Anthropological Inquiry*, edited by Charles F. Keyes and E. Valentine Daniel (Berkeley: University of California Press, 1983), p. 84.

91. Ibid., p. 86.

92. Brenda E.F. Beck, "Colour and Heat in South Indian Ritual", *Man* 4 (1969): 561.

93. Ibid., p. 562; Daniel, *Karma Divined*, p. 86.

94. Daniel, *Fluid Signs*, p. 182.

95. Beck, "Colour and Heat", pp. 561–62.

96. Lawrence A. Babb, *The Divine Hierarchy: Popular Culture in Central India* (New York: Columbia University Press, 1975), p. 236.

97. Daniel, *Fluid Signs*, p. 182.

98. Ibid., p. 197.

99. Daniel, *The Tool Box Approach*, pp. 35–36; Kandiah Chelliah, *Hinduism*, p. 130.

100. Daniel, *Karma Divined*, p. 95.

101. Daniel, *Fluid Signs*, p. 212.

102. Ibid., p. 149.

103. Brenda E.F. Beck, "Fate, Karma and Cursing in a Local Epic Milieu", in *Karma: An Anthropological Inquiry*, edited by Charles F. Keyes and E. Valentine Daniel (Berkeley: University of California Press, 1983), p. 79.

104. Daniel, *Fluid Signs*, p. 210
105. Dimmitt and Von Buitenen, *Hindu Mythology*, pp. 22, 41.
106. Inglis, "Possession and Pottery", p. 99.
107. Daniel, *Fluid Signs*, p. 203.
108. Ibid.
109. Clothey, *Rhythm and Intent*, pp. 6–7.
110. Ibid., p. 18.
111. Daniel, *Fluid Signs*, pp. 221–22.
112. Michael Wood, *The Smile of Murugan: A South Indian Journey* (Harmondsworth: Penguin, 1996), p. 29.
113. Judy F. Pugh, "Astrology and Fate: The Hindu Muslim Experiences in Karma", in *Karma: An Anthropological Inquiry*, edited by Charles F. Keyes and E. Valentine Daniel (Berkeley: University of California Press, 1983), p. 132.
114. Ibid., p. 134; Fuller, *The Camphor Flame*, p. 251.
115. Pugh, *Astrology and Fate*, p. 135.
116. Lawrence A. Babb, "Hindu Mediumship in Singapore", *Southeast Journal of Social Science* 2, nos. 1–2 (1974): 31.
117. For a comprehensive description and analysis of a female Malaysian medium, see Andrew C. Willford, *Cage of Freedom: Tamil Identity and the Ethnic Fetish in Malaysia* (Ann Arbor: University of Michagan Press, 2006), pp. 237–60.
118. Babb, *Hindu Mediumship*, p. 32.
119. Throughout my years in Malaysia, and during subsequent fieldwork, I witnessed several medium sessions in various locations. During one such session the medium, who was possessed by Ayappan, and who had never met me previously, issued a detailed prognostication which was startlingly accurate.
120. Lawrence A. Babb, "Destiny and Responsibility: Karma in Popular Hinduism", in *Karma: An Anthropological Inquiry*, edited by Charles F. Keyes and E. Valentine Daniel (Berkeley: University of California Press, 1983), p. 177.
121. Ibid., pp. 176–79.
122. Beck, "Colour and Heat", pp. 553–56; Daniel, *Fluid Signs*, pp. 221–22.
123. However, I have also seen mediums use aura forecasting, and rituals involving flames.
124. Babb, "Destiny and Responsibility", p. 174.
125. Lawrence A. Babb, *Thaipusam in Singapore: Religious Individualism in a Hierarchical Culture*, Department of Sociology Working Paper No. 49, University of Singapore (Chopmen, 1976), p. 15; Beck, *Karma, Fate and Cursing*, p. 71.
126. Babb, *Thaipusam in Singapore*, p. 15; Moreno, "God's Forceful Call", p. 104.
127. Susan S. Wadley, "Vrats: Transformers of Destiny", in *Karma: An Anthropological Inquiry*, edited by Charles F. Keyes and E. Valentine Daniel (Berkeley:

University of California Press, 1983), p. 156; Fred W. Clothey, *Ritualizing on the Boundaries: Continuity and Innovation in the Tamil Diaspora* (Columbia: University of South Carolina Press, 2006), p. 196.

128. Wadley, "Vrats", p. 147.
129. Ibid., pp. 158–59.
130. Ibid., p. 147.
131. Babb, *The Divine Hierarchy*, pp. 293–94.
132. Daniel, *Fluid Signs*, pp. 274–75; O'Flaherty, *Siva*, p. 42.
133. Fuller, *The Camphor Flame*, p. 17.
134. O'Flaherty, *Siva*, p. 73.
135. Fuller, *The Camphor Flame*, p. 17; Daniel, *Fluid Signs*, p. 248.
136. O'Flaherty, *Siva*, p. 68; Gavin Flood, *The Tantric Body: The Secret Tradition of Hindu Religion* (London: I.B. Taurus, 2006), p. 45.
137. Champakalakshmi, *Religion, Tradition and Ideology*, p. 228.
138. Daniel, *Fluid Signs*, pp. 236–37; Kandiah, *Hinduism*, p. 139.
139. Vanamali, *The Lilas*, p. 253.
140. Shulman, *Tamil Temple Myths*, p. 18.
141. Daniel, *Fluid Signs*, p. 270.
142. K. Sivaraman, *Saivism in Philosophical Perspective: A Study of the Formative Concepts, Problems and Methods of Saiva Siddhanta* (Delhi: Motilal Banarsidass, 1973), pp. 239–42, 637. The remaining seven *ragas* are *kaman* (lust or desire), *krodam* (jealousy), *lobam* (greed, avarice), *moham* (presumptuousness, pride), *matsaryam* (arrogance), *titiksa* (translated by Valentine Daniel as "the fixing of one's mind on a single object", or — in a pejorative sense — "persistence"), and *dambam* ("flamboyance" or "showiness") (Daniel, *Fluid Signs*, p. 270).
143. Daniel, *Fluid Signs*, pp. 270–74.
144. Bowker, *Why Religions Matter*, p. 122; Dimmitt and Von Buitenen, *Classical Hindu Mythology*, p. 146.
145. Sivaya Subramuniyaswami, *Dancing with Siva: Hinduism's Contemporary Catechism* (Concord: Himalayan Academy, 1993), p. 727; Daniel, *Fluid Signs*, pp. 275–76.
146. Kandiah, *Hinduism*, p. 139.
147. Daniel, *Fluid Signs*, p. 275.
148. Ibid., pp. 285–86.
149. Personal fieldwork; Daniel, *Fluid Signs*, pp. 247–48.
150. Barbara Ehrenreich, *Dancing in the Streets: A History of Collective Joy* (London: Granta Books, 2007), pp. 4–7. Indeed, Eva Amos points out that stereotypically the Western understanding of trance is as "a violent act of invasion and possession of the body" (Eva Ambos, "Emotion and Healing Rituals in Sri Lanka", in *Emotions in Rituals and Performances*, edited by Axel Michaels and Christoph Wulf [New Delhi: Routledge, 2012], p. 127).

151. Charles T. Tart, "Introduction", in *Altered States of Consciousness*, edited by Charles T. Tart (New York: Wiley, 1969), p. 2.

152. I.M. Lewis, *Ecstatic Religion: An Anthropological Study of Spirit Possession and Shamanism*, 2nd ed. (London: Penguin, 1989), p. 57.

153. Gilbert Rouget, *Music and Trance: A Theory of the Relations between Music and Possession* (Chicago: University of Chicago Press, 1985), p. 189.

154. R.A. Knox, *Enthusiasm: A Chapter in the History of Religion* (Oxford: Clarendon Press, 1950).

155. Lewis, *Ecstatic Religion*, p. 57.

156. Ibid., p. 39.

157. Rouget, *Music and Trance*, p. 241; personal observation.

158. Rouget, *Music and Trance*, p. 275.

159. Lewis, *Ecstatic Religion*, p. 227.

160. Ibid., p. 24.

161. Ibid., p. 174. An example of this is provided by Elizabeth Fuller Collin's claim that the piercing of the "phallic" tongue with the *vel* may represent "symbolic castration". Collins asserts that the action may represent the nullifying of the Oedipal complex, and thus reassures "the powerful representatives of the father — the god, high-caste leaders and political leaders — that the rebellious sons are not a threat" (Elizabeth Fuller Collins, *Pierced by Murugan's Lance: Ritual Power and Moral Redemption among Malaysian Hindus* (Dekalb: Northern Illinois University Press, 1997), pp. 145–46). However, this explanation is both self-referential and tendentious. Firstly, Collins makes no mention of the concept of *mauna* (or silence), which is the most common explanation offered by the devotees themselves. Secondly, the statement does not reflect the reality that penetration of the tongue extends to many high-caste men. Finally, it conveniently ignores the large number of women who take *vels* through their tongues, and seem to have no place in this Oedipal schemata.

162. Ronald E. Shorr, "Hypnosis and the Concept of the Generalised Reality Orientation", in *Altered States of Consciousness*, edited by Charles T. Tart (New York: Wiley, 1969), pp. 246–47.

163. Abraham Maslow, *Religions, Values and Peak Experiences* (Harmondsworth: Penguin Books, [1964] 1976), p. 63.

164. Yoshitsugu Sawai, "Reflections on Bhakti as a Type of Indian Mysticism", in *The Historical Development of the Bhakti Movement in India: Theory and Practice*, edited by Iwao Shima, Teiji Sakata, and Katsyuki Ida (New Delhi: Manohar, 2011), p. 20.

165. Ehrenreich, *Dancing in the Streets*, pp. 60–61.

166. Kent, *Divinity and Diversity*, p. 136.

167. Felicitas Goodman, "Apostolics of Yucatan: A Case Study of the Religious

Movement", in *Religion, Altered States of Consciousness and Social Change*, edited by Erika Bourguignon (Columbus: Ohio State University Press, 1973), pp. 210–15.

168. Arthur J. Deikman, "Deautomization and the Mystic Experience", in *Altered States of Consciousness*, edited by Charles T. Tart (New York: Wiley, 1969), p. 43. Thus, for example, in October 1980 a group of entranced Muslim radicals, believing themselves invulnerable to bullets and acting under the leadership of a self-proclaimed Cambodian visionary, a recent convert who claimed to be the Mahdi, embarked on a frenzied assault on a police station in Batu Pahat, Johore. This attack resulted in eight deaths and twenty-three injuries (Judith Nagata, *The Reflowering of Malaysian Islam: Modern Religious Radicals and Their Roots* (Vancouver: University of British Columbia Press, 1984, p. 127).

169. Ehrenreich, *Dancing in the Streets*, p. 93.

170. Lewis, *Ecstatic Religion*, p. 16; Ehrenreich, *Dancing in the Streets*, p. 17.

171. Sheila Walker, *Ceremonial Spirit Possession in Africa and Afro-America: Forms, Meanings and Functional Significance for Individuals and Social Groups* (Leiden: Brill, 1972), p. 80.

172. Shorr, "Hypnosis", p. 248.

173. Lewis, *Ecstatic Religion*, p. 24.

174. Ehrenreich, *Dancing in the Streets*, p. 17; Kandiah, *Hinduism*, p. 153.

175. Ehrenreich, *Dancing in the Streets*, p. 44.

176. Rouget, *Music and Trance*, pp. 16–17.

177. Ibid., p. 322.

178. Ibid., p. 26.

179. Walker, *Ceremonial Spirit Possession*, pp. 55–56; Rouget, *Music and Trance*, p. 46.

180. Lewis, *Ecstatic Religion*, p. 16.

181. Walker, *Ceremonial Spirit Possession*, pp. 55–56, 80.

182. Ehrenreich, *Dancing in the Streets*, p. 17.

183. Rouget, *Music and Trance*, p. 63.

184. Ibid.

185. Ibid., p. 119.

186. Ibid., p. 117.

187. Ibid., p. 325.

188. Ibid., p. 117.

189. Arnold M. Ludwig, "Altered States of Consciousness", in *Altered States of Consciousness*, edited by Charles T. Tart (New York: Wiley, 1969), pp. 13–16.

190. Ibid; Rouget, *Music and Trance*, p. 14.

191. Ehrenreich, *Dancing in the Streets*, p. 11.

192. Shorr, "Hypnosis", pp. 245–47.

193. Ludwig, "Altered States", pp. 13–16; Ehrenreich, *Dancing in the Streets*, pp. 60–61.
194. William James, *The Varieties of Religious Experience* (Glasgow: Collins, [1902] 1960), p. 367.
195. Ibid., p. 87. See also Yoshitsugu, "Reflections on Bhakti", p. 20.
196. James, *The Varieties of Religious Experience*, p. 367.
197. Maslow, *Religious Values*, pp. 66–75.
198. Esther Pressel, "Umbinda in Sao Paulo: Religious Innovation in a Developing Society", in *Religion, Altered States of Consciousness and Social Change*, edited by Erika Bourguignon (Columbus: Ohio State University Press, 1973), p. 312.
199. Walker, *Ceremonial Spirit Possession*, p. 84.
200. Jeanette H. Henney, "The Shakers of St. Vincent: A Stable Religion", in *Religion, Altered States of Consciousness and Social Change*, edited by Erika Bourguignon (Colombus: Ohio State University Press, 1973), pp. 255–56; Ronald C. Simons, Frank R. Ervin, and Raymond H. Prince, "The Psychobiology of Trance: Training for Thaipusam", *Transcultural Psychiatric Review* 25 (1988): 250.
201. Simons et al., "The Pyschobiology of Trance", p. 250; Colleen Ward, "Thaipusam in Malaysia: A Psycho-Anthropological Analysis of Ritual Trance, Ceremonial Possession and Self-Mortification Practices", *Ethos* 12 (1984): 325.
202. Rouget, *Music and Trance*, pp. 9–10.
203. Simons et al., "The Psychobiology of Trance", p. 263.
204. Elizabeth Fuller Collins, "Of Transgressions: Reply to Carl Vadivella Belle", *Sophia* 40, no. 2 (December 2001): 89.
205. Ward, "Thaipusam in Malaysia", p. 322.
206. Flood, *The Tantric Body*, p. 87.
207. Ibid., p. 88.
208. M.D. Muthukumarasamy, "Trance in Fire Walking Rituals of Goddess Tiraupati: Temples in Tamilnadu", in *Emotions in Rituals and Performances*, edited by Axel Michaels and Christoph Wulf (New Delhi: Routledge, 2012), p. 140.
209. Rouget, *Music and Trance*, p. 305.
210. Robert D. Richardson, *Emerson: The Mind on Fire* (Berkeley: University of California Press, 1995), p. 353.
211. Timothy Beardsworth, *A Sense of Presence* (Oxford: The Religious Experience Research Unit, Manchester College, 1977), p. 12.
212. Babb, *Thaipusam in Singapore*, p. 19.
213. Lewis, *Ecstatic Religion*, p. 127.
214. Ibid., p. 96.
215. Ibid., pp. 121–22.
216. Gananath Obeyeskere, "The Firewalkers of Kataragama: The Rise of Bhakti

Religiosity in Buddhist Sri Lanka", *Journal of Asian Studies* 37 (1978): 417; see also Collins, *Pierced by Murugan's Lance*, pp. 112–14.

217. Fuller, *The Camphor Flame*, p. 240.

218. Stuart Wavell, "Through the Fires of Existence to the Needles of Eternity", in *Trances*, edited by Stuart Wavell, Audrey Butt, and Nina Epton (Kuala Lumpur: Antara Book Company, 1988), p. 147.

219. Sir John Woodroffe, *Shakti and Shakta: Essays and Addresses on the Shakta Tantrashastra* (Madras: Ganesh & Co., 1920).

220. Alf Hiltebeital, "Draupadi's Two Guardians: The Buffalo King and the Muslim Devotee", in *Criminal Gods and Demon Devotees: Essays on the Guardians of Popular Hinduism*, edited by Alf Hiltebeital (Albany: State University of New York Press, 1989), p. 365.

221. Shulman, *Tamil Temple Myths*, p. 18. Or, as Gavin Flood comments, "to trace the route back through the cosmos to its divine source or the point in which the disembodied self became entangled with matter" (Flood, *The Tantric Body*, p. 28).

222. Champakalakshmi, *Religion, Tradition and Ideology*, p. 136.

223. Michell, *The Hindu Temple*, p. 70.

224. Champakalakshmi, *Religion, Tradition and Ideology*, p. 148.

225. Kent, *Divinity and Diversity*, p. 8.

226. Vanamali, *The Lilas*, p. 100.

227. Iwao Shima, "Jnanesvar's Interpretation of the Bhagava-gita I–VI", in *The Historical Development of the Bhakti Movement in India: Theory and Practice*, edited by Iwao Shima, Teiji Sakata, and Katsuyuki Ida (New Delhi: Manohar, 2011), p. 191.

228. Vanamali, *The Lilas*, p. 151.

229. Ibid., p. 105.

230. Wood, *The Smile of Murugan*, p. 73.

231. Michell, *The Hindu Temple*, p. 70.

232. Beck, "Colour and Heat", p. 558.

233. Ibid., p. 556.

234. Ibid., p. 554.

235. Shulman, *Tamil Temple Myths*, p. 94.

236. Beck, "Colour and Heat", p. 565.

237. Shulman, *Tamil Temple Myths*, pp. 101–3.

Conclusions

In the Introduction I argued that many scholars who had written about Thaipusam in Malaysia had constructed interpretations of the festival and the associated forms of worship (especially the kavadi ritual) which suggested their own rationales for Thaipusam. It was contended that each of these analyses was superficially convincing, but when subject to close examination relied upon ethnographies that were far from complete. In treating Thaipusam as *sui generis*, these scholars had failed to situate either the festival or the kavadi ritual within a sufficiently broad cultural or comparative framework. The main objective of this study has been to closely examine Thaipusam from the "inside", as it were, and to trace the layers of meaning and the recondite vocabularies of this multifaceted and complex festival in terms of its continuing relevance to Malaysian Hindus. In the following paragraphs I will conclude that Thaipusam at Batu Caves, far from being a cultural aberration, a product of time, place and the peculiar circumstances of Hindu Malaysians, is constructed from deep-rooted elements of South Indian culture, and can only be fully comprehended by locating it within Tamil history, philosophies and belief structures, and in particular those associated with the Tamil deity Murugan.

The Indian population in Malaysia can be traced to two major streams of migration; namely, those recruited to serve as a labour force within the colonial economy, and a minority of technical, professional and business migrants attracted by the economic opportunities offered in British Malaya. Labour recruitment produced a variegated population consisting of the general spread of castes below the Brahman level. Skilled and professional migrants included an influential Chettiar merchant/moneylending class,

Jaffna Tamils, as well as Malayalees, North Indians, Sikhs and professional and artisan Tamils. The Indian population was characterized by a clear social and vocational chasm between the middle-upper class and the labour force, the former dedicated to maintaining their distance from the despised "coolies". The social divisions between middle-upper class and working Indians established by the conditions of colonial labour and non-labour migration remain as fixed and potent in contemporary Malaysia as they were in pre-war Malaya.

Since Merdeka, Indian political social and economic weaknesses have been repeatedly exposed, especially in the period following the implementation of post-1969 economic, educational and cultural policies designed to increase social and economic opportunities for Malays. In recent years the position of the labouring community as a marginalized underclass has become entrenched, and the "plantation culture" of poverty, underachievement and social stasis has been transferred from the estates and reproduced within Malaysian towns and cities.

Since 1969, Malaysia has been dominated by Malay-Muslim powerbrokers who have refused to tolerate any challenge to their hegemony, or to the major assumptions which underpin their modernist and nationalist project. This has been accompanied by a process of Islamization which has effectively reinforced ethnic boundaries by emphasizing the essential Malay-Muslim/non-Malay-non-Muslim dichotomy which divides Malaysian society. The rise of a sharply contested Islam, and the challenge of an aggressive evangelical Christianity have spurred a renewal in all other religious traditions. Malaysia remains a nation fragmented by multiple sites of particularistic resistance that exist below the level of nationalist discourse.

The defining characteristics of Tamil society and Hinduism were shaped throughout the period of the great South Indian dynasties, the Pallava, Chola and Vijayanagara kingdoms which cumulatively ruled the Tamil country between circa the sixth and eighteenth centuries CE. These were societies of astonishing diversity and movement, embracing heterogeneous populations divided by ethnicity, region, language, caste and *jati*. These segmentary societies were held together by a ritual kingship whose rule took the form of an incorporative moral authority derived from the deity. Kings were obliged to respect and protect the social-political formations which collectively constituted their realms. The monarch's authority was both activated and reinforced by a flow of gifts and honours from and to the centre, which transferred some of the king's divine authority to the empire's principal chiefs and leading authorities and bound them and the sovereign in ties of mutual obligation. The Vijayanagara kings also convened annual festivals of great splendour in which the monarchs and their empires were ritually reinfused with cosmic energies and the sovereign's intimate relationship with the deity was emphasized.

Tamil Hinduism reflected the bewildering diversity which constituted South Indian society, collectively comprising a multitude of forms ranging from Brahmanic/Sanskritic philosophical Hinduism to countless indigenous and localized sects. The study of Tamil Hinduism reveals no distinctive or categorical demarcation between the boundaries of great tradition *Agamic* Hinduism and systems of popular belief, but rather demonstrates a continuum of overlapping, interlinked and porous religious forms which have historically informed and influenced each other. High Sanskritic/ *Agamic* culture was disseminated through the agency of the *brahmadeyas*, often in alliance with Vellalars, and later through the *mathas* (monasteries). Continual revision of *Agamic* Hinduism resulted in the incorporation and recognition of many local or indigenous deities (including the folkish Murugan), who were identified with the high Sanskritic gods, as well as making provision for goddess (*Amman*) worship. However, the vast majority of Tamil Hindus continued to worship according to local or popular traditions.

The great Hindu revival towards the conclusion of the Pallava era produced new religious forms. One of these was *bhakti* Hinduism, which insisted upon the equality of souls before the deity, and which embraced and affirmed the validity of a multitude of possibilities for approach to the deity, including simple devotion, as well as forms of transgressive and ostensibly "inferior" *bhakti*. Another was the influential philosophy of Saiva Siddhanta, which emphasized the triangular relationship of *Pati–pacu–paca*. Both movements overlapped, not only with each other, but also with popular forms of Tamil Hinduism.

Tamil Hinduism was characterized by its anti-authoritarianism, its powerful assertion of the primacy and validity of the individual's relationship with the deity. Tamil Saivite traditions posit a universe in eternal flux and movement in which gods and humans constantly interact and in which the underlying organizational principle is based upon the dynamic tension of Siva–Sakti and the continually shifting relationship between these polarities. Moreover, they advance a logic of inner direction which insists that whatever god is worshipped, in whatever form that god inheres, and whatever the modality of worship, the sincere devotee will be led from the outer world — the periphery, the world of forms and oppositions — to the inner unity where the primordial and transcendent deity may be realized.

Colonial rule in British India embraced new ideologies of governance informed by orientalist scholarship, especially that of evolutionary anthropology, which propounded theories of inherent socio-biological qualities inscribed by racial origin. The British envisaged a timeless and unchanging India structured according to the clearly demarcated and immutable categories of caste, religion and primary race. Many of these ideas were to gain currency among Indians themselves, especially the newly Westernized administrative and professional classes. British theories ultimately influenced three major "reform" movements in South India; namely, neo-Hinduism which sought to recreate an imagined pristine Sanskritic-"Aryan" Hinduism; Neo-Shaivism, which aimed at reformulating an authentic Tamil Hinduism stripped of its supposed Brahmanic-Sanskritic accretions; and Dravidianism, which looked to the re-establishment of an autochthonous and "pure" Tamil culture which had putatively existed prior to a supposed Aryan-Brahman "invasion" that had subjugated *Tamilakam* and imposed "alien" cultural forms. Dravidian ideologies ranged from the atheistic radicalism of E.V. Ramasami's iconoclastic Self-Respect movement to the more moderate Dravidianism of the DMK.

Hinduism was reproduced within Malaya/Malaysia without two of the major features — a Brahman or dominant orthodox caste, and the *mathas* or institutions of learning — which had influenced and shaped religious forms within metropolitan South India. The kangany system of recruitment, which provided a socially diverse labour force within Malaysian plantations and workplaces, was indirectly responsible for the introduction of an array of regional, localized and caste-based forms of worship into Malaya. While many estate or workplace temples were dedicated to village or locality gods, middle-level castes established temples for the worship of *Agamic* deities such as Mahamariamman/Parvati, Siva, Murugan, Ganesha, Vishnu and Krishna. However, the full tradition of *Agamic* worship was introduced to Malaya by the Chettiar caste and by "Jaffna" Tamils. Both groups founded temples constructed, dedicated, managed and maintained according to *Agamic* rites. These temples also commemorated a round of calendrical rituals and festivals congruent with

Agamic prescriptions and injunctions. In the years following the Pacific War there was a pronounced Hindu revival and a renewed middle-class interest in Tamil arts and culture, as well as philosophical Hinduism, especially Saiva Siddhanta. Although Hindu reform movements in Malaya/Malaysia echoed many of the sentiments of those bodies active in the Tamil heartland, these were overshadowed by the processes of far-reaching syncretism, *Agamicization*/Sanskritization, the fusing of Saivite and Vaishnavite motifs and the general Tamilization of Hindu forms. These continue to reconfigure the Malaysian Hindu landscape. While the impact of caste and caste organization in Malaysia has generally weakened, many caste-specific deities have retained their potency, although syncretism has linked them and sometimes blended their identities with one or another of the great *Agamic* deities.

The current Hindu renewal in Malaysia has undoubtedly been given impetus by three basic stimuli. The first is the charged ethnic-religious discourses which shape Malaysian politics and culture, and in particular the pressures exerted by Malay-Islamic dominance. The second is the aggressive challenge mounted by evangelical Christian movements, and their often overt contempt for Hindu culture and traditions. The third is the powerful influence of Dravidian ideologies, which emphasize the genius and singularity of Tamil culture, and which not only continue to resonate within the Tamil heartland but which have also percolated to all sections of the Tamil diaspora. Religion is an increasingly potent force among Malaysia's Hindus. This has been evidenced by escalating participation in ritual worship, especially during major festivals, and in temple refurbishment and construction. Nowhere is this more obvious than in the worship of the Tamil deity Murugan, which finds its most powerful public expression in the festival of Thaipusam.

The deity Skanda-Murugan reflects and encompasses Tamil history, culture and religion. Over the centuries the deity absorbed an array of attributes and functions, including those which had their genesis in South Indian folk traditions, *Puranic* mythology, Sanskritic philosophies and scriptural Hinduism. Throughout the Chola period the Sanskritic-*Agamic* Skanda became fused with the Tamil folk deity Murugan. His extensive range of roles and duties — incorporating high philosophical god, warrior king, god of possession and healing, patron of Tamil language and literature, rogue deity who was both philanderer and patron of thieves — make him immediately accessible to all sectors of the variegated Tamil society.

His marriages to the celestial Devayanai and the earthy Valli underscore the extraordinary range of cosmic potentialities which embrace orthodox forms of progressive and incremental spiritual unfoldment, as well as the unconventional and convoluted schema of *bhakti* worship, a path which may rupture societal norms. In the contemporary Tamil milieu, which privileges Dravidian traditions and ideologies, Murugan is the Tamil god par excellence. His mythology emphasizes his intimate and continuing engagement with the Tamil heartland, while his chronometry provides a series of propitious moments for his direct and ritual worship.

The festival of Thaipusam commemorates Parvati's bestowal of the *Sakti Vel* upon the Siva-created deity Murugan prior to his battle with the demon-king Surapadman, under whose leadership the *asuras* had inverted cosmic order. While this mythology applies on many levels, in essence it may be read as a statement of phenomenological dissolution, entropy and subsequent reconstitution and renewal, and secondly as a charter for individual spiritual unfoldment and liberation. In this context, Murugan and the *Vel* represent the unification of the principles of Siva and Sakti, the Absolute force and its generative energies in perfect synchrony. Batu Caves, the main Malaysian centre at which Thaipusam is commemorated, became a site dedicated to the veneration of Murugan and the Murugan cultus after an influential Hindu had a vision which instructed him to offer worship to the deity in the Main (later Temple) Cave. The first Thaipusam at Batu Caves, based on the mythology and rituals observed at the major South Indian pilgrimage centre of Palani, was conducted in 1892. Batu Caves was subsequently developed into the largest pilgrimage centre for Murugan within Malaysia, complete with shrines, *asrama*, statuary, interpretative centres, offices and commercial premises. The festival of Thaipusam is enclosed within kingship rituals, which commence with the departure of the king-deity, Murugan, from his permanent *kovil*-palace, the Sri Maha Mariamman Temple in Kuala Lumpur, to his mountaintop palace at Batu Caves, where his symbol of authority, the Golden *Vel*, is installed within the main shrine of the Temple Cave. The major form of ritual worship throughout Thaipusam, the bearing of kavadis, is derived from the esoteric applications of two conjoined *Puranic* myths — the mango/Palani myth and the Idumban myth — which not only emphasize themes of asceticism, renunciation, self-discipline, the generation of *tapas* (austerities), and the search for the Truth or inner fruits (*pala*) within, but also provide an approved, and indeed divinely sanctioned, mode of worship. The kavadi ritual, including acts of bodily mortification, cuts across divisions of caste, sect, class, regional background, ethnicity and sex, to reach all segments of the Hindu population, as well as some members of other religious traditions.

The study of Thaipusam and the kavadi ritual throughout various locations both within metropolitan India and a number of Tamil diaspora societies reveals common patterns of worship. These include the following essential elements:

1. A chariot procession in which the *utsava murthi* of the deity is ceremonially paraded before the population which recognizes his regal-divine authority.
2. Various forms of the kavadi ritual, involving vow taking, a period of asceticism, trance states or altered states of consciousness, often including acts of bodily mortification. Kavadi bearing is found throughout various castes and *jatis*, and includes instances of Brahmanic bodily mortification.
3. Formal recognition of the *asura*/devotee Idumban. This is incorporated into Thaipusam and related festivals in various ways; firstly through the act of bearing a kavadi, secondly by performing the kavadi dance, thus emulating the laboured movements of the *asura* as he bore the twin hills to South India, and finally in a formal *puja* releasing devotees from their vows of asceticism and returning them to the folds of quotidian society.
4. Other forms of ritual service, most frequently involving manning a *thaneer panthal* or participating in an *annathanam* (mass feeding).

This comparative study situates Thaipusam at Batu Caves in a broader cultural framework, and clearly demonstrates that the festival as conducted in Malaysia contains typical and normative elements which are readily found within Murugan festivals both in Tamil Nadu and in diaspora locations. Inter alia, this comparative study undermines the social deprivation theory advanced by some scholars in connection with Thaipusam at Batu Caves; that is, that the ritual behaviours of participants are an internalized mimesis or cathartic social protest against the conditions of their marginalization and oppression. The comparative study also lays to rest the canard that Thaipusam as practised at Batu Caves is banned in India.

The kavadi ritual at Thaipusam constitutes a pilgrimage, a *tirtha yatra*, or divine crossing, which in metaphysical terms moves from the periphery, the world of forms, to the *axis mundi*, the centre, where a normally transcendent deity is both immanent and accessible. The pilgrimage site itself is ordered and patterned and exists in an oasis of timelessness beyond the confusion and disorder of the *Kaliyuga*. Batu Caves forms such a pilgrimage venue within Malaysia.

A devotee who undertakes a pilgrimage often does so in response to a discernible condition which requires rectification or alleviation. In esoteric terms this is seen as a modification of his/her uniquely coded body substance, a ritual which will activate the *karman* complex, and thus alter the semi-permanent *kunam* complex, shifting the devotee into a fresh state of awareness offering greater equipoise and control. The process of pilgrimage involves the votary taking a vow to a given deity, which is followed by prescribed rites of asceticism that allow the devotee to attain the requisite state of inner purity necessary for this encounter. During the period of fasting the aspirant perceives of himself/herself, temporarily at least, as a *sannyasin*, a renunciant, a revered Hindu archetype. Throughout the pilgrimage the inner qualities or *gunas* are roused, resulting in the votary progressing from a state of *tamas* (characterized by inertia and resistance), through a *rajasik* phase (typified by movement and energy), to the phase of *sattva*, where the *sadhaka* (aspirant) experiences intense perceptions. *Sattva* normally replaces *rajas* when the pain of the pilgrimage is overcome by love. Within the context of Thaipusam, *tamas* is superseded by *rajas* throughout the period of fasting, while *sattva* is experienced at the onset of the trance state (*arul*) and the fitting of the kavadis, which clearly and publicly reveals the conquest of pain.

Trance states may take a number of forms, but at Thaipusam only one trance is sought or desired, that of *arul*, a state of grace in which the devotee is "filled/embraced" by the deity. However, *arul* may manifest in many ways, ranging from full-scale possession to inspirational trance states where the deity invests the consciousness of the votary. It is throughout this period of trance that the devotee receives noetic "messages" which impart knowledge of the deity. Often these "messages" permanently alter his/her worldview.

In bearing a kavadi the votary embarks upon a metaphysical journey that encompasses the entire cosmological history of the deity Murugan. This commences with the violence of his creation and the bestowal of the *Vel*, and continues with the conversion of Idumban, the defeat of the *asuras*, the isolation and destruction of Surapadman, the deity's full stabilization, and his marriages to his consorts. The homologization of the body to the cosmos ensures that this divine crossing is replicated within the devotee, representing the unleashing of the *kundalini* spiritual force and its rise through the *cakras* to the human crown, the seat of full illumination. The outer–inner dichotomy collapses when the votary enters the Temple Cave and is presented to the deity, and the world of paradoxes and oppositions is temporarily replaced by awareness of the immanent deity. On the third day after Thaipusam, the pilgrim attends an Idumban *puja* in which he/she is released from his/her vows and returned to quotidian life. But the devotee brings to this mundane realm a new sense of control and fresh forms of knowledge, the fruits (*pala*) of the encounter with the deity.

Wendy Doniger O'Flaherty has observed that "Myths come alive in the context of history, ritual or philosophy and the social law. Hidden somewhere in the maze is the key to the Hindu worldview, startling, fascinating and complex."[1] This comment is most certainly applicable to the festival of Thaipusam, which operates along lines of significance which provide layers of meaning to individuals and groups, and which speaks to many different audiences.

We have seen that the festival commemorates the bestowal of the *Sakti Vel* upon the deity Murugan. The worship of Murugan throughout the festival dramatizes and re-enacts the entire cosmology of the deity, which is offered to devotees on a variety of levels, ranging from the noetic knowledge imparted to entranced individuals, to generalized knowledge of Murugan as powerful king-deity.

But the festival of Murugan cannot be neatly extricated from the cultural context in which he is implicated. Thaipusam in Malaysia comprises nothing less than a public celebration of Malaysian Hinduism which reproduces condensed codes of Tamil history and culture, as well as displaying an extensive repertoire of philosophies and belief structures. This celebration may be seen in acts as diverse as the kingship ritual which re-establishes the monarch-deity's sovereignty over his domain, and transforms the mundane into the Divine, and the period of asceticism/fasting in which devotees are temporarily converted to the socially approved state of *sannyasin*.

One of the most profound cultural statements offered by Thaipusam is the open commitment, admittedly often grudging and conditional, to the diversity of religious traditions evinced within the festival. These range from Sanskritic/*Agamic* modes through a number of variants influenced to differing extents by Saiva Siddhanta, village Hinduism, and examples of transgressive worship. All, however, are permeated with the ethos of *bhakti*, covering a gamut of forms from classical *bhakti* to more dramatic expressions of worship. I have shown that Tamil Hinduism insists upon the equality of the soul before the deity, and the autonomy and validity of devotional worship, even when this is conveyed in idiosyncratic forms. According to this perspective, while there may be socially approved models of worship with kavadis, there can be no one verifiably "correct" way of performing the ritual, and the devotee who offers worship, however singular, with a pure heart, will be subject to the same inner directional force, and will ultimately reach the same destination as the votary who strictly adheres to *Agamic* precepts.

The insistence on Thaipusam as a heterogeneous and even conflicting medley of ideals, motivations and religious forms, coexisting within the broad paradigms established by the rituals of Murugan worship, constitutes a vigorous assertion of the segmentary traditions set by Tamil history, religious ideals and beliefs, as well as categorically signalling their continuing relevance in contemporary Malaysia. The festival thus sends a number of clear statements, not only to devotees and the general Hindu community but also to a series of external audiences.

Firstly, it offers a firm rebuke to Hindu reformers, those who condemn the festival, express scepticism about the motivations and dispositions of its practitioners and deny the validity of their spiritual experiences. By exhibiting the continuing strength and power of Malaysian Hinduism in all its forms, Thaipusam issues a categorical rejection of the demands of those who would "disenchant" Hinduism by disavowing its rich collocation of rituals, gods and cosmologies in favour of a monochromatic world of textual or hermeneutic religion.

Secondly, Thaipusam disseminates agonistic signals to non-Hindus. The huge crowds, the public chariot procession, the elaborate organization, the extensive publicity, the full societal involvement, all speak of the determination of Malaysian Hindus to retain their cultural and religious traditions as a living force, while asceticism, trance states, kavadis and bodily mortification clearly demonstrate the discipline and inner strength required by the devotees of a powerful and miraculous god who will protect his votaries from pain, even while bestowing his blessings.

Thirdly, Thaipusam speaks to the Tamil/Hindu heartland. It makes a clear statement about a proud, shared and continuing heritage, common membership of the great, rich and enduring civilization, which not only includes metropolitan India but also the wider diaspora. This broad message also incorporates an agonistic subtext. It states to Malays and Chinese that, just as they have sought religious forms and inspiration from external civilizational impulses, and just as they claim allegiance to a wider religious community, so too do Hindus owe their genius to a broader cultural canvas, a religion which has moved from its metropolitan origins to become truly global.

Thaipusam rapidly emerged as the most popular and widely observed Hindu festival in the years following the commencement of modern Indian migration to colonial Malaya. It has survived challenges, most notably the attempts of the Tamil Reform Association and the Malaysian Hindu Sangam to either ban the festival or to restrict the permitted modes of worship. The continuing relevance of Thaipusam to Malaysian Hindus is beyond question. This is clearly demonstrated by the annually increasing crowds who attend the festival, and the expansion in the number of devotees who bear kavadis. Thaipusam remains the largest and most consistent expression of Hindu identity in Malaysia. While worship coalesces around the quintessentially Tamil deity, Murugan, the festival provides a stable forum for the public articulation of the concatenation of religious forms and belief structures which collectively comprise Malaysian Hinduism, and offers public space for the contributions made by both high and low status groups. Thaipusam has over the years developed its own paradigmatic impulses which have stimulated the evolution, expression, aggregation and negotiation of the Hindu presence and identity in Malaysia. Given the centrality of Thaipusam to Malaysian Hinduism it is not unreasonable to suggest that this process will continue.

Note

1. Wendy Doniger O'Flaherty, *Siva: The Erotic Ascetic* (London: Oxford University Press, 1973), p. 1.

Glossary

aaru padai veedu	the six camps or sacred sites of Lord Murugan
abishekam	ritual bathing of the *murthi* during a *puja*
Adi Dravida	literally "first" or "original" Dravidians; Dalits or depressed castes
advidya	spiritual ignorance
Agamas	literally "that which has come down"; a body of texts regarded as revealed, and consisting of mythology, ritual and philosophy
aluga	beautiful
Alvars	the twelve Vaishnavite Saints, contemporaneous with the Saivite *Nayanars*
Amman	a generic name for a mother goddess
anava	egotism; the principal impurity which enmeshes the soul
annathanam	a mass feeding
arati	showing a camphor flame before the image of a deity, normally in the context of a *puja*
archanai	a form of worship devoted to a specific *murthi*, and by extension to the deity
arul	divine grace
asrama	an ashram, a spiritual retreat
asuras	demons
bhajan	singing of devotional hymns
bhakti	the cultivation of devotion; devotional Hinduism
bhuta	spirits which possess specific powers
brahmadeyas	Brahman settlements, specifically sites of Sanskrit learning, culture and philosophical speculation
cakras	centres of spiritual energy, symbolically located along the spine
darsan	auspicious sight of the *murthi* during a *puja*

devas	gods
dharma	a specific code of conduct intrinsic to a given entity
garbhagriha	literally "womb chamber", the *sanctum sanctorum* of a Hindu temple
gramadevata	a lesser "village" deity, often a village goddess
gunas	the three qualities of Nature, namely *sattva*, *rajas* and *tamas*
jalrah	hand cymbals
jati	a particular lineage which sits within the overall caste structure
Kaliyuga	the current age, considered to be degenerate (*yuga*: epoch; *kaliyuga* is thus literally the age of Kali)
karma	the consequences of actions, both good and bad; the outcomes of all actions can occur within this or subsequent lives
kolattam	a complex dance performed with sticks; in South India traditionally danced by girls
kovil (koyil)	a Hindu temple
ksatriyas	the second highest caste of the *varna* system, representing the warrior caste
kumbabishekam	a ceremony conducted to dedicate deities during temple consecration
kundalini	the spiritual power, typically depicted as a serpent, which symbolically uncoils to travel up the spinal column to successively activate the *cakras*
kurrukals	Brahman priests in the Saivite tradition
lilas	the play of the Divine
lingam	the aniconic form representing the formless Siva
Mahadeva	the supreme deity, Siva, or more generically one of the other high gods/goddesses
malas	the impurities which bind the soul
mantras	"sacred chant"; formulaic words constituting an inner truth
marga	a pathway; a stage of spiritual development
matha (Tamil: *madam*)	a monastery
mauna	silence, often in the form of a vow
maya	illusion (in the broadest sense of the term)
meelam	a kind of drum
moksha	liberation from the cycle of *samsara*
mukti	release from the cycle of birth, death and rebirth
murthi	the image of the deity

nadaswaram	a woodwind instrument, shaped like a clarinet
Nayanars	The sixty-three Tamil Saivite saints who composed the hymns which make up the sacred work, the *Tirumurai*
nirguna	God beyond form and time
paal kudam	a milk pot
paca	matter, the fetters or bondages of ignorance
pacu	the individual soul
pada yatra	a foot pilgrimage
Palaiyakkarars	"little kings", the monarchs of the series of states which succeeded the Vijayanagara dynasty
pantaram	a non-Brahman trained priest
Pati	The Supreme Lord, the Godhead
pattars	Brahman priests in the Vaishnavite tradition
pey	a malevolent spirit, a ghost of the dead
prasadam	food offered to the deity, sanctified and then returned to devotees
preta	spirits of the departed
puja	a ritual of formal worship
pujari	a non-Brahman priest
Purana	compendia of myths and religious philosophy
rajas	the intermediate of three qualities (*gunas*) or strands of Nature; embracing the characteristics of passion, energy, desire
rishi	a sage possessing great spiritual power
sadhaka	a spiritual seeker, an aspirant
sadhu	a wandering holy man
Sakti Vel	the *Vel* given by Parvati to Murugan
sakti	divine power envisaged as feminine (as *Sakti*, the term refers to the Goddess, often as the consort of Siva)
samsara	the ceaseless cycle of birth, death and rebirth
Sangam (Cankam)	traditionally the colloquium of poets who established Tamil literature; more recently a term used to denote a Hindu peak body
sanguna	God worshipped in a specific form and with specified qualities
sannyasin	an ascetic renunciant
sattva	the first quality (*guna*) of Nature: the higher characteristics of translucence, harmony, balance
sishya	the disciple of a guru
sudras	the fourth caste of the *varna* system; those who, in theory, form the caste of labourers and other menials

svayambhu	holy images or places that have appeared spontaneously
Tai	the Tamil month (January–February) in which Thaipusam is held
tamas	the third of the qualities (*gunas*) of Nature: the dense characteristics of darkness, ignorance, sloth
tapas	performance of spiritually directed austerities
tattvas	the thirty-six primal states of existence from which the universe is composed
thaneer panthal	stalls which provide food, drink and other forms of service
timiti	ritual fire-walking
tinai	a traditional eco-zone of the Tamil country
tirtha yatra	pilgrimage
utsava murthi	the festival image of the deity
vahana	the animal that serves as a god's mount
vaisyas	the caste that in theory comprises the land-holding and merchant castes
varna	the theoretical system of caste; one of four categories of caste
vastu	the Hindu science of building and construction
vel	spear, lance
vellalars	the highest non-Brahman Tamil caste
Vetrivel	the cosmic spear
vibhuti	the sacred ash used in ritual worship
vidya	spiritual knowledge
vira	a deified hero
yantra	a mystical diagram

Bibliography

Ackerman, Susan E. and Raymond L.M. Lee. *Heaven in Transition: Innovation and Ethnic Identity in Malaysia*. Honolulu: University of Hawai'i Press, 1988.

Adikalaar, Swami Siva Nandhi, K. Loganathan, and S.P. Thinnappan. *Saivite Hinduism*. London: Meikandar Aadheenam, 1994.

Ahmad Ali. "Indians in Fiji: An Interpretation". In *The Indo-Fijian Experience*, edited by Subramani. St. Lucia: University of Queensland Press, 1991.

Ahmad Fauzi Abdul Hamid. *Islamic Education in Malaysia*, Monograph No. 18. Singapore: S. Rajaratnam School of International Studies, 2010.

Ahmad Mustapha Hassan. *The Unmaking of Malaysia: Insider's Reminiscences of UMNO, Razak and Mahathir*. Petaling Jaya: Strategic Information and Research Development Centre, 2007.

Ainsworth, Leopold. *The Confessions of a Planter in Malaya: A Chronicle of Life and Adventure in the Jungle*. London: H.F. & G. Witherby, 1933.

Ambos, Eva. "Emotion and Healing Rituals in Sri Lanka". In *Emotions in Rituals and Performances*, edited by Axel Michaels and Christoph Wulf. New Delhi: Routledge, 2012.

Appadurai, Arjun. "Kings, Sects and Temples in South India 1350–1700 AD". In *South Indian Temples: An Analytical Reconsideration*, edited by Burton Stein. New Delhi: Vikras, 1978.

———. *Worship and Conflict under Colonial Rule*. Cambridge: Cambridge University Press, 1981.

Arasaratnam, Sinnappah. "Malaysian Indians: The Formation of an Incipient Society". In *Indian Communities in Southeast Asian*, edited by K.S. Sandhu and A. Mani. Singapore: Institute of Southeast Asian Studies, 1993.

———. "Political Attitudes and Political Organization among Malayan Indians 1945–1955". *Jernal Sejerah* 10 (1971/72).

———. *Indian Festivals in Malaysia*. Kuala Lumpur: Department of Indian Studies, 1966.

———. *Indians in Malaysia and Singapore*. London: Oxford University Press, 1970.

Armstrong, Karen. *The Case for God: What Religion Really Means*. London: The Bodley Head, 2009.

———. *The Spiral Staircase: A Memoir*. London: Harper Perennial, 2005.

Arumugam Rasiah. *Kataragama: Divine Power of Kathirkaman and Methods of Realization*. Sithankerny: Holiday Ashram, 1981.

Aslan, Reza. *No God but God: The Evolution and Future of Islam*. London: Heinemann, 2005.

Aveling, Marian. "Ritual Changes in the Hindu Temples of Penang". *Contributions to Indian Sociology* 12, no. 2 (1978).

Azly Rahman. *Dark Spring: Essays on the Ideological Routes of Malaysia's GE-13*. Petaling Jaya: Strategic Information and Research Centre, 2013.

———. "The 'New *Bumiputeraism*' as a Pedagogy of Hope and Liberation: Teaching the Alternative Malaysian Ethnic Studies". In *Multiethnic Malaysia: Past, Present and Future*, edited by Lim Teck Ghee, Alberto Gomes, and Azly Rahman. Petaling Jaya: Strategic Information and Research Centre, 2009.

Babb, Lawrence A. "Destiny and Responsibility: Karma in Popular Hinduism". In *Karma: An Anthropological Inquiry*, edited by Charles F. Keyes and E. Valentine Daniel. Berkeley: University of California Press, 1983.

———. "Hindu Mediumship in Singapore". *Southeast Asian Journal of Social Science* 2, nos. 1–2 (1974).

———. *Thaipusam in Singapore: Religious Individualism in a Hierarchical Culture*, Department of Sociology Working Paper No. 49. Singapore: University of Singapore, 1976.

———. *The Divine Hierarchy: Popular Culture in Central India*. New York: Columbia University Press, 1975.

Baker, Christopher. "Facts and Figures: Madras Government Statistics 1880–1940". In *South India: Political Institutions and Political Change 1880–1940*, edited by C.J. Baker and David Washbook. Delhi: MacMillan, 1975.

Baker, Christopher John. *The Politics of South India 1920–1937*. Cambridge: Cambridge University Press, 1976.

Baker, Christopher and David Washbrook, eds. *South India: Political Institutions and Political Change 1880–1940*. Delhi: MacMillan, 1975.

Baldiserra, Fabrizia. "Emotions in Indian Drama and Dances". In *Emotions in Rituals and Performances*, edited by Axel Michaels and Christoph Wulf. New Delhi: Routledge, 2012.

Barber, Benjamin R. *Jihad vs McWorld: Terrorism's Challenge to Democracy*. London: Corgi Books, 2005.

Barron, J.M., Acting Controller of Labour. *Annual Report of the Labour Department, 1935*. Kuala Lumpur: Government Press, 1936.

Bayly, Christopher and Tim Harper. *Forgotten Armies: The Fall of British Asia*. Cambridge, MA: The Belknap Press of Harvard University Press, 2004.

———. *Forgotten Wars: The End of Britain's Asian Empire*. London: Penguin, 2008.

Beardsworth, Timothy. *A Sense of Presence*. Oxford: The Religious Experience Research Unit, Manchester College, 1977.

Beck, Brenda. "Colour and Heat in South Indian Ritual". *Man* 4 (1969).

———. "Fate, Karma and Cursing in a Local Epic Milieu". In *Karma: An Anthropological Inquiry*, edited by Charles F. Keyes and E. Valentine Daniel. Berkeley: University of California Press, 1983.

Beck, Brenda E.F. *Peasant Society in Konku: A Study of Right and Left Subcastes in South India*. Vancouver: University of British Columbia Press, 1972.

Beckenbridge, Carol A. "From Protectors to Litigant: Changing Relations between Hindu Temples and the Raja of Ramnad". In *South Indian Temples: An Analytical Reconsideration*, edited by Burton Stein. Delhi: Vikras, 1978.

Belle, Carl Vadivella. *The Development of Indian Political Consciousness in Malaysia: Colonialism, Nationalism and Subhas Chandra Bose*, CSID Paper No. 4. Hyderabad: Centre for the Study of the Indian Diaspora, University of Hyderabad, 2009.

———. "Forgotten Malaysians? Indians and Malaysian Society". In *Tracing an Indian Diaspora: Contexts, Memories, Representations*, edited by Parvati Raghuram, Ajaya Kumar Sahoo, Brij Maharaj, and Dave Sangha. New Delhi: Sage, 2008.

———. "Hindu Resurgence in Malaysia". In *Rising India and Indian Communities in East Asia*, edited by K. Kesavapany, A. Mani, and P. Ramasamy. Singapore: Institute of Southeast Asian Studies, 2008.

———. *Towards Truth: An Australian Spiritual Journey*. Kuala Lumpur: Pacific Press, 1992.

———. *Tragic Orphans: Indians in Malaysia*. Singapore: Institute of Southeast Asian Studies, 2015.

Berger, Peter L. *Adventures of an Accidental Sociologist: How to Explain the World without Becoming a Bore*. New York: Prometheus, 2011.

Biardeau, Madeleine. "Brahmans and Meat Eating Gods". In *Criminal Gods and Demon Devotees: Essays on the Guardians of Popular Hinduism*, edited by Alf Hiltebeital. Albany: State University of New York Press, 1989.

Bilainkin, George. *Hail Penang! Being a Narrative of Comedies and Tragedies in a Tropical Outpost among Europeans, Chinese, Malays and Indians*. Penang: Areca Books, 2010.

Blackburn, Robin. *The Making of New World Slavery: From the Baroque to the Modern 1492–1800*. London: Verso, 1997.

Bolt, Christine. *Victorian Attitudes towards Race*. London: Routledge and Kegan Paul, 1971.

Bourguignon, Erika, ed. *Religion, Altered States of Consciousness and Social Change*. Columbus: Ohio State University Press, 1973.

Bowker, John. *Why Religions Matter*. Cambridge: Cambridge University Press, 2015.

Brown, Carol Henning. "Tourism and Ethnic Competition in a Ritual Form: The Firewalkers of Fiji". *Oceania* 54 (1984).

Bryant, Edwin F. "Introduction". In *Krishna: The Beautiful Legend of God (Srimad Bhagavata Purana Book X)*. London: Penguin, 2003.

Bunki Kimura. "Ramanuja's Theory of Bhakti as a Type of Indian Mysticism". In *The Historical Development of the Bhakti Movement in India: Theory and Practice*, edited by Iwao Shima, Teiji Sakata, and Katsuyuki Ida. New Delhi: Manohar, 2011.

Case, William. "Corruption Unplugged under Abdullah". In *Awakening: The Abdullah Years in Malaysia*, edited by Bridget Welsh and James V.H. Chin. Petaling Jaya: Strategic Information and Research Development Centre, 2013.

Champakalakshmi, R. *Religion, Tradition and Ideology: Precolonial South India*. New Delhi: Oxford University Press, 2011.

———. *Trade, Ideology and Urbanisation: South India 300 BC to AD 1300*. New Delhi: Oxford University Press, 1996.

Chatterjee, Asim Kumar. *The Cult of Skanda-Karttikeya in Ancient India*. Calcutta: Puthi Pustak, 1970.

Cheah Boon Kheng. *Malaysia: The Making of a Nation*. Singapore: Institute of Southeast Asian Studies, 2002.

Chihiro Koiso. "The Bhakti in Tukarami's Abhangas". In *The Historical Bhakti Movement in India: Theory and Practice*, edited by Iwao Shima, Teiji Sakata, and Katsuyuki Ida. New Delhi: Manohar, 2011.

Chin, James. "Malaysia and the Rise of Najib and 1Malaysia". *Southeast Asian Affairs 2010*, edited by Daljit Singh. Singapore: Institute of Southeast Asian Studies, 2010.

Chin, James, and Chin-Huat Wong. "Malaysia's Electoral Upheaval". *Journal of Democracy* 20, no. 3 (July 2009).

Chin, James V.H. "'Doing the Invisible': A Conversation with Tun Abdullah Ahmad Badawi". In *Awakening: The Abdullah Years in Malaysia*, edited by Bridget Welsh and James V.H. Chin. Petaling Jaya: Strategic Research and Development Centre, 2013.

———. "It Had to Happen: The Chinese Backlash in the 2008 General Elections". In *Awakening: The Abdullah Badawi Years in Malaysia*, edited by Bridget Welsh and James V.H. Chin. Petaling Jaya: Strategic Research and Development Centre, 2013.

Clothey, Fred W. *The Many Faces of Murukan: The History and Meaning of a South Indian God*. The Hague: Mouton, 1978.

———. *Rhythm and Intent: Ritual Studies from South India*. Bombay: Blackie and Son, 1983.

———. *Ritualizing on the Boundaries: Continuity and Innovation in the Tamil Diaspora.* Columbia: University of South Carolina Press, 2006.

Cohn, Bernard S. *Colonialism and its Forms of Knowledge: The British in India.* Princeton, NJ: Princeton University Press, 1996.

Cohn, Norman. *The Pursuit of the Millennium: Revolutionary Millenarians and the Mystical Anarchists of the Middle Ages.* London: Pimlico, 2004.

Collins, Elizabeth Fuller. "Of Transgressions: Reply to Carl Vadivella Belle". *Sophia* 20, no. 2 (December 2001).

———. *Pierced by Murugan's Lance: Ritual Power and Moral Redemption among Malaysian Hindus.* Dekalb: Northern Illinois University Press, 1997.

Comber, Leon. *Templer and the Road to Independence: The Man and His Time.* Singapore: Institute of Southeast Asian Studies, 2015.

Coutright, Paul B. "On This Holy Day, in My Humble Way". In *Gods of Flesh, Gods of Stone: The Embodiment of Divinity in India*, edited by Joanne Punzo Waghorne and Norman Cutler in association with Vasudha Narayanan. Chambersburg: Anima, 1985.

Cutler, Norman. "Conclusion". In *Gods of Flesh, Gods of Stone: The Embodiment of Divinity in India*, edited by Joanne Punzo Waghorne and Norman Cutler in association with Vasudha Narayanan. Chambersburg: Anima, 1985.

D'Alpuget, Blanche. *Turtle Beach.* Ringwood: Penguin, 1981.

D'Cruz, J.V. and William Steele. *Australia's Ambivalence towards Asia.* Clayton: Monash University Press, 2003.

Dalrymple, William. *White Mughals: Love and Betrayal in Eighteenth Century India.* London: Harper Perennial, 2004.

Daniel, E. Valentine. *Fluid Signs: Being a Person the Tamil Way.* Berkeley: University of California Press, 1984.

———. "Karma Divined in a Ritual Capsule". In *Karma: An Anthropological Inquiry*, edited by Charles F. Keyes and E. Valentine Daniel. Berkeley: University of California Press, 1983.

Daniel, Sheryl B. "The Tool Box Approach of the Tamil to Issues of Moral Responsibility and Human Destiny". In *Karma: An Anthropological Inquiry*, edited by Charles F. Keyes and E. Valentine Daniel (Berkeley: University of California Press, 1983).

Danielou, Alain. *Hindu Polytheism.* New York: Bollingen Foundation, 1964.

———. *The Myths of Gods of India.* Rochester: Inner Traditions International, [1964] 1991.

De Sales, Anne. "Ritual Virtuosity: Emotions and Feelings in Shamanic Rituals in Nepal". In *Emotions in Rituals and Performances*, edited by Axel Michaels and Christoph Wulf. New Delhi: Routledge, 2012.

Dehejia, Vidya. *Slaves of the Lord: The Path of the Tamil Saints.* New Delhi: Munshiram Manoharlal, 1988.

Devapoopathy Nadarajah. *The Strength of Saivism*. Kuala Lumpur: Second International Seminar on Saiva Siddhanta, 1986.

Dharmaratnam, K. *Elements of Hinduism*. Kelang: Percetakan Naathan, 1987.

Diehl, Carl Gustav. *Instrument and Purpose: Studies on Rites and Religions in South India*. Lund: C.W.K. Gleerup, 1956.

Diekman, Arthur J. "Deautomization and the Mystic Experience". In *Altered States of Consciousness*, edited by Charles T. Tart. New York: John Wiley, 1969.

Dimmitt, Cornelia, and J.A. van Buitenen, eds. and trans. *A Reader in Sanskrit Puranas*. Philadelphia: Temple University Press, 1978.

Dirks, Nicholas. *Castes of Mind: Colonialism and the Making of Modern India*. Princeton, NJ: Princeton University Press, 2001.

———. "Foreword". In *Colonialism and its Forms of Knowledge: The British in India* by Bernard S. Cohn. Princeton, NJ: Princeton University Press, 1996.

———. *The Hollow Crown: Ethnohistory of an Indian Kingdom*, 2nd ed. Ann Arbor: University of Michigan Press, 1993.

Doniger, Wendy. *The Hindus: An Alternative History*. New York: Penguin, 2009.

Eck, Diana L. *Darsan: Seeing the Divine Image in India*, 3rd ed. New York: Columbia University Press, 1998.

Ehrenreich, Barbara. *Dancing in the Streets: A History of Collective Joy*. London: Granta Books, 2007.

Eichinger, Gabriella Ferro-Luzzi. "Ritual as Language: The Case of South Indian Food Offerings". *Current Anthropology* 18, no. 3 (1977).

Epton, Nina. "Kris Dancing in Bali". In *Trances*, edited by Stuart Wavell, Audrey Butt, and Nina Epton. Kuala Lumpur: Antara Book Company, 1988.

Ervin, Frank, Roberta M. Palmour, Beverly E. Pearson Murphy, Raymond Prince, and Ronald C. Simons. "The Psychobiology of Trance: Physiological and Endocrine Correlates". *Transcultural Psychiatric Review* 25 (1988).

Evers, Hans Deiter and Jayarani Pavadarayan. "Religious Fervour and Economic Success: The Chettiars of Singapore". In *Indian Communities in Southeast Asia*, edited by K.S. Sandhu and A. Mani. Singapore: Institute of Southeast Asian Studies, 1993.

Farish A. Noor, "The Discursive Construction of the Image of Prime Minister Abdullah as the 'Sleeping PM'". In *Awakening: The Abdullah Badawi Years in Malaysia*, edited by Bridget Welsh and James V.H. Chin. Petaling Jaya: Strategic Information and Research Development Centre, 2013.

Federation Constitutional Proposal, Legislative Council Proposal No. 42 of 1957. Kuala Lumpur: Government Printers, 1957.

Federation of Malaya Census Report. Kuala Lumpur: Government Printers, 1957.

Flood, Gavin. *The Importance of Religion: Meaning and Action in Our Strange World*. Chichester: Wiley Blackwell, 2012.

———. *The Tantric Body: The Secret Tradition of Hindu Religion*. London: I.B. Tauris, 2006.

Fuller, C.J. *The Camphor Flame: Popular Hinduism and Society in India*. Princeton, NJ: Princeton University Press, 1979.

Funston, John. *Malay Politics in Malaysia: A Study of UMNO and PAS*. Kuala Lumpur: Heinemann Educational Books (Asia), 1980.

Gamba, Charles. *The Origins of Trade Unionism in Malaya: A Case Study in Colonial Unrest*. Singapore: Eastern Universities Press, 1962.

Gattwood, Lynn E. *Devi and the Spouse Goddess: Women, Sexuality and Marriage in India*. New Delhi: Manohar, 1985.

Geertz, Clifford. *Local Knowledge: Essays in Interpretative Anthropology*. New York: Basic Books, 1983.

Genn, Celia A. "The Chistiyya Diaspora: An Expanding Circle". In *Tracing an Indian Diaspora: Contexts, Memories, Representations*, edited by Parvati Raghuram, Ajaya Kumar Sahoo, Brij Maharaj, and Dave Sangha. New Delhi: Sage, 2008.

Gifford, Don. *The Farther Shore: A Natural History of Perception*. London: Faber & Faber, 1990.

Gill, Walter. *Turn Left at Tombstone*. Adelaide: Rigby, 1970.

Gold, Anne Grodzins. *Fruitful Journeys: The Ways of Rajasthani Pilgrims*. Berkeley: University of California Press, 1988.

Gomez, Edmund Terence and Johan Saravanamuttu, eds. *The New Economic Policy in Malaysia: Affirmative Action, Ethnic Inequalities and Social Justice*. Singapore: NUS/Institute of Southeast Asian Studies, 2013.

Gomez, Edmund Terence, Johan Saravanamuttu, and Maznah Mohamad. "Introduction: Malaysia's New Economic Policy: Resolving Horizontal Inequalities: Creating Difficulties". In *The New Economic Policy in Malaysia: Affirmative Action, Ethnic Inequalities and Social Justice*, edited by Edmund Terence Gomez and Johan Saravanamuttu. Singapore: NUS/Institute of Southeast Asian Studies, 2013.

Gomez, Edmund Terence and Jomo K.S. *Malaysia's Political Economy: Politics, Patronage and Profits*. Cambridge: Cambridge University Press, 1997.

Goodman, Felicitas. "Apostolics of Yucatan: A Case Study of the Religious Movement". In *Religion, Altered States of Consciousness and Social Change*, edited by Erika Bourguignon. Columbus: Ohio State University Press, 1973.

Govindaraj, Dato S. "Country Report: Malaysia". First Asia-Pacific Hindu Conference, Singapore, 3 April 1988.

Gray, John. *Black Mass, Apocalyptic Religion and the Death of Utopia*. London: Allen Lane, 2007.

Gullick, J.M. *The Story of Kuala Lumpur 1857–1939*. Singapore: Eastern Universities Press, 1983.

Gutschow, Niels. "Aggression with Obscenity: The Annual Annihilation of Evil Spirits on Occasion of the New Moon in August in Bhaktapur, Nepal". In *Emotions in Rituals and Performances*, edited by Axel Michaels and Christoph Wulf. New Delhi: Routledge, 2012.

Handelman, D. "Myths of Murugan: Asymmetery and Hierarchy in South India". *History of Religions* 27, no. 2 (1987).

Harper, T.N. *The End of Empire and the Making of Malaya*. Cambridge: Cambridge University Press, 1999.

Harrigan, Patrick. "Dionysius and Kataragama: Parallel Mystery Cults". *Journal of the Institute of Asian Studies* 14, no. 2 (March 1997).

———. "Sacred Geography in the Cult of Skanda-Murugan". *Journal of the Institute of Asian Studies* 15, no. 2 (March 1998).

Harshananda, Swami. *Hindu Gods and Goddesses*. Madras: Sri Ramakrishna Math, 1981.

Hartsuiker, Dolf. *Sadhus: The Holy Men of India*. London: Thames and Hudson, 1993.

Harvey, Jonathan. *Music and Inspiration*. London: Faber and Faber, 1999.

Henney, Jeanette H. "The Shakers of St. Vincent: A Stable Religion". In *Religion, Altered States of Consciousness and Social Change*, edited by Erika Bourguignon. Columbus: Ohio State University Press, 1973.

Hermann, Arthur. *The Idea of Decline in Western History*. New York: The Free Press, 1997.

Hiltebeital, Alf, ed. *Criminal Gods and Demon Devotees: Essays on the Guardians of Popular Hinduism*. Albany: State University of New York Press, 1989.

———. "Draupadi's Two Guardians: The Buffalo King and the Muslim Devotee". In *Criminal Gods and Demon Devotees*, edited by Alf Hiltebeital. Albany: State University of New York Press, 1989.

———. "Introduction". In *Criminal Gods and Demon Devotees: Essays on the Guardians of Popular Hinduism*, edited by Alf Hiltebeital. Albany: State University of New York Press, 1989.

Hiroaki Ikebe. "Some Sources of Madhva's Bhakti Theory". In *The Historical Development of the Bhakti Movement in India: Theory and Practice*, edited by Iwao Shima, Teiji Sakata, and Katsuyuki Ida. New Delhi: Manohar, 2011.

Hirschmann, Charles. "The Making of Race in Colonial Malaya: Political Economy and Racial Ideology". *Sociological Forum* 1, no. 2 (Spring 1986).

———. "The Meaning and Measurement of Ethnicity in Malaysia: A Study of Census Classifications". *Journal of Asian Studies* 46, no. 3 (August 1987).

Hudson, Dennis. "Violent and Fanatical Devotion among the *Nayanars*: A Study in the *Periya Puranam* of *Cekkilar*". In *Criminal Gods and Demon Devotees: Essays on the Guardians of Popular Hinduism*, edited by Alf Hiltebeital. Albany: State University of New York Press, 1989.

Hullet, Arthur. "Thaipusam and the Cult of Subramaniam". *Geo* 3, no. 4 (1981).

Husken, Ute. "One Nine-Yard Sari, Two Elephants and Ten Sips of Water: Rituals and Emotions in a South Indian Hindu Temple". In *Emotions in Rituals and Performances*, edited by Axel Michaels and Christoph Wulf. New Delhi: Routledge, 2012.

Hutton, J.M. *Caste in India: Its Nature, Functions and Origins*, 4th ed. Oxford: Oxford University Press, 1969.

Hyde, Lewis. *Trickster Makes the World: Mischief, Myth and Art*. New York: North Point Press, 1998.

Inglis, Stephen. "Possession and Pottery: Serving the Divine in a South Indian Community". In *Gods of Flesh, Gods of Stone: The Embodiment of Divinity in India*, edited by Joanne Punzo Waghorne and Norman Cutler in association with Vasudha Narayanan. Chambersburg: Anima, 1985.

Iwao Shima. "Jnanesvar's Interpretation of the Bhagava-gita I–VI". In *The Historical Development of the Bhakti Movement in India: Theory and Practice*, edited by Iwao Shima, Teiji Sakata, and Katsuyuki Ida. New Delhi: Manohar, 2011.

Iwao Shima, Teiji Sakata, and Katsuyuki Ida, eds. *The Historical Development of the Bhakti Movement in India: Theory and Practice*. New Delhi: Manohar: 2011.

Jagadisa Ayyar, P.V. *South Indian Customs*. Madras: Asian Educational Services, [1925] 1989.

———. *South Indian Shrines*. New Delhi: Asian Educational Services, 1982.

Jain, Ravindra K. "South Indian Labour in Malaya 1840–1920: Asylum, Stability and Involution". In *Indentured Labour in the British Empire 1840–1920*, edited by Kay Saunders. London: Croom Helm, 1984.

———. *South Indians on the Plantation Frontier in Malaya*. New Haven: Yale University Press, 1970.

James, William. *The Varieties of Religious Experience*. Glasgow: Collins, [1902] 1960.

Janakey Raman Manickam. *The Malaysian Indian Dilemma: The Struggles and Agony of the Indian Community in Malaysia*. Klang: Janakey Raman, 2010.

Jayasooria, Datuk Dr Denison, ed. *Malaysian Issues and Concerns: Some Policy Responses*. Batu Caves: Centre for Public Policy Studies/Asian Strategy and Leadership Institute, 2013.

Jessy, Joginder Singh. "The Indian Army of Independence". BA (Hons) dissertation, University of Singapore, 1957–58.

Jeyakumar, D. "The Indian Poor in Malaysia: Problems and Solutions". In *Indian Communities in Southeast Asia*, edited by K.S. Sandhu and A. Mani. Singapore: Institute of Southeast Asian Studies, 1993.

Jomo K.S., ed. *Rethinking Malaysia*. Kuala Lumpur: Malaysian Social Science Association, 1999.

Jomo K.S. and Ahmad Shabery Cheek. "Malaysia's Islamic Movements". In *Fragmented Vision: Culture and Politics in Contemporary Malaysia*, edited by Joel Kahn and Francis Loh Kok Wah. Sydney: Asian Studies Association of Australia/Allen and Unwin, 1992.

Kabade, Rahul. *Sri Muruga: Legend, Short Stories and Worship*. Wembley: Sri Muruga Publications, 2012.

Kabilan, K. "The Indian Dilemma: Sucked Up and Spat Out". In *Awakening: The Abdullah Badawi Years in Malaysia*, edited by Bridget Welsh and James V.H. Chin. Petaling Jaya: Strategic Information and Research Development Centre, 2013.

Kahn, Joel and Francis Loh Kok Wah, eds. *Fragmented Vision: Culture and Politics in Contemporary Malaysia*. Sydney: Asian Studies Association of Australia/ Allen and Unwin, 1992.

——. "Introduction". In *Fragmented Vision: Culture and Politics in Contemporary Malaysia*, edited by Joel Kahn and Francis Loh Kok Wah. Sydney: Asian Studies Association of Australia/Allen and Unwin, 1992.

Kakar, Sudhir. *Shamans, Mystics and Doctors: A Psychological Inquiry into India and its Healing Traditions*. Delhi: Oxford University Press, 1982.

Kalaiyarasi A/P Gurusamy. "Hinduism: The History of the Sri Maha Mariyamman Kovil Devastanam". Class Exercise, Jabatan Antrologi dan Sosiologi, Universiti Malaya, 1987–88.

Kandiah Chelliah. *Hinduism: A Brief Study of It's* [sic] *Origins: Tradition and Practice*. Bukit Berunting: Kandiah Chelliah, 2012.

Katsuyuki Ida. "The Concept of Bhakti in the Tantric Tradition". In *The Historical Development of the Bhakti Movement in India*, edited by Iwao Shima, Teiji Sakata, and Katsuyuki Ida. New Delhi: Manohar, 2011.

Kazuyo Sakaki. "Realization of Inner Divinity: Natha Yogins in the Medieval Bhakti Movement". In *The Historical Development of the Bhakti Movement in India*, edited by Iwao Shima, Teiji Sakata, and Katsuyuki Ida. New Delhi: Manohar, 2011.

Kelly, John D. *A Politics of Virtue: Hinduism, Sexuality and Countercolonial Discourse in Fiji*. Chicago: University of Chicago Press, 1991.

Kent, Alexander. *Divinity and Diversity: A Hindu Revitalization Movement in Malaysia*. Singapore and Copenhagen: Institute of Southeast Asian Studies/NIAS Press, Singapore, 2007.

Kesavapany, K., A. Mani, and P. Ramasamy, eds. *Rising India and Indian Communities in East Asia*. Singapore: Institute of Southeast Asian Studies, 2008.

Kessler, Clive. "The Abdullah Badawi Premiership: Interlude or End Game?". In *Awakening: The Abdullah Badawi Years in Malaysia*, edited by Bridget Welsh and James V.H. Chin. Petaling Jaya: Strategic Information and Research Development Centre, 2013.

Keyes, Charles and E. Valentine Daniel, eds. *Karma: An Anthropological Inquiry*. Berkeley: University of California Press, 1983.

Khevesan Sornum. "The Murukan Cult in Mauritius: Essence of Tamil Ethnic Identity". Second International Conference on Skanda-Murukan, Port Louis, April 2001.

Kirkup, James. *Tropic Temper*. London: Collins, 1963.

Kirsch, Jonathan. *A History of the End of the World: How the Most Controversial Book in the Bible Changed the Course of Western Civilization*. San Franciso: HarperSanFranciso, 2006.

Klostermaier, Klaus. *A Survey of Hinduism*. Albany: State University of New York Press, 1994.

Knipe, David M. "A Night of the Growing Dead: A Cult of Virabhadra". In *Criminal Gods and Demon Devotees: Essays on the Guardians of Popular Hinduism*, edited by Alf Hiltebeital. Albany: State University of New York Press, 1989.

Knox, R.A. *Enthusiasm: A Chapter in the History of Religion*. Oxford: Clarendon Press, 1950.

Lakshmanan Chettiar. *The Folklore of Tamil Nadu*. New Delhi: National Book Trust, 1973.

Lal, Brigadier V. "The Wreck of the *Syria*". In *The Indo-Fijian Experience*, edited by Subramani. St. Lucia: University of Queensland Press, 1979.

Latif, Asad ul-Iqbal. "From Mandalas to Microchips: The Indian Imprint on the Construction of Singapore". In *Rising India and Indian Communities in East Asia*, edited by K. Kesavapany, A. Mani, and P. Ramasamy. Singapore: Institute of Southeast Asian Studies, 2008.

Lee Kim Heng. "Forging Interethnic Cooperation: The Political and Constitutional Process Towards Independence 1951–1957". In *Multiethnic Malaysia: Past, Present and Future*, edited by Lim Teck Ghee, Alberto Gomes, and Azly Rahman. Petaling Jaya: Strategic Information and Research Development Centre, 2009.

Lee, Raymond L.M. "Taipucam in Malaysia: Ecstasy and Identity in a Tamil Hindu Festival". *Contributions to Indian Sociology* 23, no. 2 (1989).

Lewis, I.M. *Ecstatic Religion: An Anthropological Study of Spirit Possession and Shamanism*, 2nd ed. London: Penguin, 1989.

Lim Teck Ghee. "Introduction: Historical Roots of Identity in Malaysia". In *Multiethnic Malaysia: Past, Present and Future*, edited by Lim Teck Ghee, Alberto Gomes, and Azly Rahman. Petaling Jaya: Strategic and Information Development Centre, 2009.

———. "Malaysia's Prospects: Rising to or in Denial of Challenge?". In *Multiethnic Malaysia: Past, Present and Future*, edited by Lim Teck Ghee, Alberto Gomes, and Azly Rahman. Petaling Jaya: Strategic Information and Research Development Centre, 2009.

Lim Teck Ghee and Alberto Gomes. "Culture and Development in Malaysia". In *Multiethnic Malaysia: Past, Present and Future*, edited by Lim Teck Ghee, Alberto Gomes, and Azly Rahman. Petaling Jaya: Strategic Information and Research Development Centre, 2009.

Lim Teck Ghee, Alberto Gomes, and Azly Rahman, eds. *Multiethnic Malaysia: Past Present and Future*. Petaling Jaya: Strategic Information and Research Development Centre, 2009.

Link, Hilda K. "Where Valli meets Murukan: 'Landscape' Symbolism in Kataragama". *Anthropos*, no. 92 (1997).

Ludwig, Arnold M. "Altered States of Consciousness". In *Altered States of Consciousness*, edited by Charles T. Tart. New York: John Wiley, 1969.

Malaya: Strikes by Indian Labourers. London: Oriental and India Office File IOOR/L/P&J/8/264, Collection 108/21G.

Malhotra, Rajiv and Aravinda Neelakandan. *Breaking India: Western Interventions in Dravidian and Dalit Faultlines*. New Delhi: Amaryllis, 2011.

Mani, A. "Indians in North Sumatra". In *Indian Communities in Southeast Asia*, edited by K.S. Sandhu and A. Mani. Singapore: Institute of Southeast Asian Studies, 1993.

———. "Indians in Singapore". In *Indian Communities in Southeast Asia*, edited by K.S. Sandhu and A. Mani. Singapore: Institute of Southeast Asian Studies, 1993.

Manoa, Pia. "Across the Fence". In *The Indo-Fijian Experience*, edited by Subramani. St. Lucia: University of Queensland Press, 1979.

Maslow, Abraham. *Religions, Values and Peak Experiences*. Harmondsworth: Penguin Books, [1964] 1976.

Maznah Mohamad. "Politics of the NEP and Ethnic Relations in Malaysia". In *Multiethnic Malaysia: Past Present and Future*, edited by Lim Teck Ghee, Alberto Gomes, and Azly Rahman. Petaling Jaya: Strategic Information and Reseach Development Centre, 2009.

McGillon, Chris. "Jesus Loves Y'all". *Spectrum, Sydney Morning Herald*, 2 September 2000.

Means, Gordon P. *Political Islam in Southeast Asia*. Boulder, CO: Lynne Reinner, 2009.

Metcalf, Thomas R. *Ideologies of the Raj*. Cambridge: Cambridge University Press, 1977.

Michaels, Axel. "Performative Tears: Emotions in Rituals and Ritualized Emotions". In *Emotions in Rituals and Performances*, edited by Axel Michaels and Christoph Wulf. New Delhi: Routledge, 2012.

Michaels, Axel and Christoph Wulf, eds., *Emotions in Rituals and Performances*. New Delhi: Routledge, 2012.

———. "Emotions in Rituals and Performances: An Introduction". In *Emotions in Rituals and Performances*, edited by Alex Michaels and Christoph Wulf. New Delhi: Routledge, 2012.

Michell, George. *The Hindu Temple: An Introduction to its Meanings and Forms*. Chicago: University of Chicago Press, [1972] 1988.

Millar, Cynthia J. "Immigrants, Images and Identity: Visualising Homelands across Borders". In *Tracing an Indian Diaspora: Contexts, Memories, Representations*, edited by Parvati Raghuram, Ajaya Sahoo Kumar, Brij Maharaj, and Dave Sangha. New Delhi: Sage, 2008.

Milne, R.S., and Diane K. Mauzy. *Politics and Government in Malaysia*. Singapore: Federal Publications, 1978.

Mishra, Anand. "Interplay of Emotions and Rituals in Religious Ceremonies of Pustimarga". In *Emotions in Rituals and Performances*, edited by Axel Michaels and Christoph Wulf. New Delhi: Routledge, 2012.

Misra, Maria. *Vishnu's Crowded Temple: India Since the Great Rebellion of 1857*. London: Allen Lane, 2007.

Moffat, Michael. *An Untouchable Community in South India: Structure and Consensus*. Princeton, NJ: Princeton University Press, 1979.

Mohamad Abu Bakar. "Islam, Civil Society and Ethnic Relations in Malaysia". In *Islam and Civil Society in Southeast Asia*, edited by Nakamuro Mitsuo, Sharon Siddique, and Omar Farouk Bajunid. Singapore: Institute of Southeast Asian Studies, 2001.

Moreno, Manuel. "God's Forceful Call: Possession as Divine Strategy". In *Gods of Flesh, Gods of Stone: The Embodiment of Divinity in India*, edited by Joanne Punzo Waghorne and Norman Cutler in association with Vasudha Narayanan. Chambersburg: Anima, 1985.

Moronis, E. Alan. *Pilgrimage in the Hindu Tradition: A Case Study of West Bengal*. Delhi: Oxford University Press, 1984.

Mukundan, K.A. *Annual Report of the Agent of the Government of India, 1935*. Calcutta: Government of India Press, 1936.

———. *Report of the Agent of the Government of India, 1936*. Calcutta: Government of India, 1937.

Muthukumaraswamy, M.D. "Trance in Firewalking Rituals of Goddess Tiraupati Amman: Temples in Tamilnadu". In *Emotions in Rituals and Performances*, edited by Axel Michaels and Christoph Wulf. New Delhi: Routledge, 2012.

Muzaffar, Chandra. *Islamic Resurgence in Malaysia*. Petaling Jaya: Penerbity Fajar Bakti, 1987.

———. "Political Marginalization in Malaysia". In *Indian Communities in Southeast Asia*, edited by K.S. Sandhu and A. Mani. Singapore: Institute of Southeast Asian Studies, 1993.

Nadaraja, K. "The Thondar Padai Movement of Kedah 1945–1957". *Malaysia in History* 24 (1981).

Nadarajan, M. "The Nattukottai Chettiar Community and Southeast Asia". International Seminar on Tamil Studies, Kuala Lumpur, 1966.

Nagarajan, S. "Indians in Malaysia: Towards Vision 2020". In *Rising India and Indian Communities in East Asia*, edited by K. Kesavapany, A. Mani, and P. Ramasamy. Singapore: Institute of Southeast Asian Studies, 2008.

———. "Marginalisation and Ethnic Relations: The Indian Malaysian Experience". In *Multiethnic Malaysia: Past, Present and Future*, edited by Lim Teck Ghee, Alberto Gomes, and Azly Rahman. Petaling Jaya: Strategic Information and Research Development Centre, 2009.

Nagarajan, S., and K. Arumugam. *Violence against an Ethnic Minority in Malaysia: Kampung Medan*. Petaling Jaya: Suaram, 2012.

Nagata, Judith. *The Reflowering of Malaysian Islam: Modern Religious Radicals and their Roots*. Vancouver: University of British Columbia Press, 1984.

Nair, Sheila. "Colonialism, Nationalism, Ethnicity: Constructing Identity and Difference". In *Multiethnic Malaysia: Past Present and Future*, edited by Lim Teck Ghee, Alberto Gomes, and Azly Rahman. Petaling Jaya: Strategic Information and Research Development Centre, 2009.

————. "Constructing Civil Society in Malaysia: Nationalism, Hegemony and Resistance". In *Rethinking Malaysia*, edited by Jomo K.S. Kuala Lumpur: Malaysia Social Science Association, 1999.

Natarajan, B. "Introduction". In *Tirumantiram: A Tamil Scriptural Classic*, edited by B. Natarajan. Mylapore: Sri Ramakrishna Math, 1991.

Neelvani A/P Thanabalan. "Taipucam in Malaysia: An Analysis of a Hindu Festival (A Case Study of Batu Caves, Selangor)". Class Exercise, Jabatan Antropologi dan Sosiologi, Universiti Malaya, 1987–88.

Negotiations between India and Malaya Concerning the Rights of Indians in Malaya February 1939 – June 1942. London: Oriental and India Office File IOOR/L/P&J/8/260, Collection 108/21/C.

Netto, Anil. "Great Expectations, Unrealised Dreams: Human Rights and Abdullah Badawi". In *Awakening: The Abdullah Years in Malaysia*, edited by Bridget Welsh and James V.H. Chin. Petaling Jaya: Strategic Reseach and Development Centre, 2013.

O'Flaherty, Wendy Doniger. *Siva: The Erotic Ascetic*. London: Oxford University Press, 1973.

O'Malley, L.S.S. *Popular Hinduism: The Religion of the Masses*. London: Cambridge University Press, 1935.

Obeyeskere, Gannanath. *The Cult of the Goddess Pattini*. Chicago: University of Chicago Press, 1984.

————. "The Firewalkers of Kataragama: The Rise of Bhakti Religiosity in Buddhist Sri Lanka". *Journal of Asian Studies* 37 (1978).

Oddie, Geoffrey A. *Popular Religion, Elites and Reform: Hookswinging and its Prohibition in Colonial India*. New Delhi: Manohar, 1995.

Ong Puay Liu. "Identity Matters: Ethnic Perceptions and Concerns". In *Multiethnic Malaysia: Past, Present and Future*, edited by Lim Teck Ghee, Alberto Gomes, and Azly Rahman. Petaling Jaya: Strategic Information and Research Development Centre, 2009.

Ooi Cheng Gee. *Portraits of Penang: Little India*. Penang: Areca Books, 2011.

Ooi Kee Beng. *Arrested Reform: The Unmaking of Abdullah Badawi*. Kuala Lumpur: Research for Social Advancement, 2009.

————. "Beyond Ethnocentrism: Malaysia and the Affirmation of Hybridisation".

In *Multiethnic Malaysia: Past Present and Future*, edited by Lim Teck Ghee, Alberto Gomes, and Azly Rahman. Petaling Jaya: Strategic Information and Research Development Centre, 2009.

———. *Done Making Do: 1Party Rule Ends in Malaysia*. Singapore: Institute of Southeast Asian Studies, 2013.

———. *The Reluctant Politician: Tun Dr Ismail and His Time*. Singapore: Institute of Southeast Asian Studies, 2006.

Oorjitham, K.S. Susan. "Economic Profile of the Tamil Working Class in Peninsular Malaysia". *Jurnal Pengajian India* 5 (1993).

———. "Urban Indian Working Class Households". *Jurnal Pengajian India* 4 (1986).

Paranjoti, V. "The Sakti of God". In *Saiva Siddhanta: An Exploration and Assessment by Scholars the World Over*. Maliladuthuria: Dharmapura Adhinam, 1994.

Parmer, Norman J. *Colonial Labor Policy and Administration: A History of Labor in the Rubber Industry in Malaya 1910–1941*. New York: J.J. Augustin, 1960.

Parvati Raghuram. "Representations, Contestations of/in the Indian Diaspora". In *Tracing an Indian Diaspora: Contexts, Memories, Representations*, edited by Parvati Raghuram, Ajaya Kumar Sahoo, Brij Maharaj, and Dave Sangha. New Delhi: Sage, 2008.

Parvati Raghuram and Ajaya Kumar Sahoo. "Thinking 'Indian Diaspora' for Our Times". In *Tracing an Indian Diaspora: Contexts, Memories, Representations*, edited by Parvati Raghuram, Ajaya Kumar Sahoo, Brij Maharaj, and Dave Sangha. New Delhi: Sage, 2008.

Parvati Raghuram, Ajaya Kumar Sahoo, Brij Maharaj, and Dave Sangha, eds. *Tracing an Indian Diaspora: Contexts, Memories, Representations*. New Delhi: Sage, 2008.

Pillai, R.R. "The Kavati Ritual as a Paradigm of Hindu-Religio-Expression". *Journal of the Institute of Asian Studies* 13, no. 2 (March 1996).

Potts, Lydia. *The World Labour Market: A History of Migration*. Translated by Terry Bond. London: Zed Books, 1990.

Pressel, Esther. "Umbinda in Sao Paulo: Religious Innovation in a Developing Society". In *Religion, Altered States of Consciousness and Social Change*, edited by Erika Bourguignon. Columbus: Ohio State University Press, 1973.

Preston, James J. "Creation of the Sacred Image: Apotheosis and Destruction in Hinduism". In *Gods of Flesh, Gods of Stone: The Embodiment of Divinity in India*, edited by Joanne Punzo Waghorne and Norman Cutler in association with Vasudha Narayanan. Chambersburg: Anima, 1985.

Pugh, Judy. "Astrology and Fate: The Hindu Muslim Experiences in Karma". In *Karma: An Anthropological Inquiry*, edited by Charles F. Keyes and E. Valentine Daniel. Berkeley: University of California Press, 1983.

Puthucheary, Mavis. "Indians in the Public Sector". In *Indian Communities in*

Southeast Asia, edited by K.S. Sandhu and A. Mani. Singapore: Institute of Southeast Asian Studies, 1993.

Quigley, Declan. *The Interpretation of Caste*. Oxford: Clarendon Press, 1993.

Rai, Rajesh. " 'Positioning' the Indian Diaspora: The Southeast Asian Experience". In *Tracing an Indian Diaspora: Contexts, Memories, Representations*, edited by Parvati Raghuram, Ajaya Kumar Sahoo, Brij Maharaj, and Dave Sangham. New Delhi: Sage, 2008.

Rajakrishnan, R. "Indo-Ceylonese Relations in Malaysia". *Jurnal Pengajian India* 4 (1986).

Rajakrishnan Ramasamy. *Caste Consciousness among Indian Tamils in Malaysia*. Petaling Jaya: Pelanduk, 1984.

Rajantheran, M., K. Sillalee, and R. Viknarasa. *An Introduction to Hinduism: A Religious Text for Hindu Students*. Taman Petaling: Malaysian Hindu Sangam, 2012.

Rajeswary Amplavanar. *The Indian Minority and Political Change in Malaya 1945–1957*. Kuala Lumpur: Oxford University Press, 1981.

Rajeswary Amplavanar-Brown. "The Contemporary Indian Political Elite in Malaysia". In *Indian Communities in Southeast Asia*, edited by K.S. Sandhu and A. Mani. Singapore: Institute of Southeast Asian Studies, 1993.

Rajoo, R. "Hindu Religious Values and Economic Retardation among the Indian Plantation Workers in Peninsular Malaysia — a Myth or Reality?". *Jurnal Pengajian India* 4 (1986).

———. "Indian Squatter Settlers: Rural-Urban Migration in West Malaysia". In *Indian Communities in Southeast Asia*, edited by K.S. Sandhu and A. Mani. Singapore: Institute of Southeast Asian Studies, 1993.

———. "Sanskritization in the Hindu Temples of West Malaysia". *Jurnal Pengajian India* 2 (1984).

Ramachandran, C.P. "The Malaysian Indian in the New Millennium". Keynote Address, The Malaysian Indian in the New Millenium Conference, Kuala Lumpur, May 2002.

Ramanathan, Kalimuthu. "Hindu Religion in an Islamic State: The Case of Malaysia". PhD dissertation, Universiteit Van Amsterdam, 1995.

Ramasamy, P. *Plantation Labour, Capital and the State in Peninsular Malaysia*. New York: Oxford University Press, 1994.

Ramaswamy, Sumathi. *Passions of the Tongue: Language Devotion in Tamil India 1891–1970*. New Delhi: Munshiram Manoharlal, 1998.

Ratnam, K.J. *Communalism and the Political Process*. Kuala Lumpur: University of Malaya Press, 1965.

Rehman Rashid. *A Malaysian Journey*. Petaling Jaya: Rehman Rashid, 1993.

Reid, Anthony. *Charting the Shape of Modern Southeast Asia*. Singapore: Institute of Southeast Asian Studies, 2000.

Report of the Agent of the Government of India, 1932. Calcutta: Government of India Press, 1933.

Richardson, Robert D. *Emerson: The Mind on Fire*. Berkeley: University of California Press, 1995.

Roces, Alfredo. "A Matter of Mind over Matter". *Geo* 3, no. 4 (1981).

Rottger-Rossiter, Birgitt. "The Emotional Meaning of Ritual". In *Emotions in Rituals and Performances*, edited by Alex Michaels and Christoph Wulf. New Delhi: Routledge, 2012.

Rouget, Gilbert. *Music and Trance: A Theory of the Relations between Music and Possession*. Chicago: University of Chicago Press, 1985.

Sadanori Ishitobi. "Theories of Salvation in the Tengalao and Vadagalai Schools". In *The Historical Development of the Bhakti Movement in India: Theory and Practice*, edited by Iwao Shima, Teiji Sakata, and Katsuyuki Ida. New Delhi: Manohar, 2011.

Said, Edward. *Orientalism: Western Conceptions of the Orient*. London: Penguin, 1991.

Sandhu, K.S. and A. Mani, eds. *Indian Communities in Southeast Asia*. Singapore: Institute of Southeast Asian Studies, 1993.

Sandhu, Kernial Singh. "Indian Immigration and Settlement in Singapore". In *Indian Communities in Southeast Asia*, edited by K.S. Sandhu and A. Mani. Singapore: Institute of Southeast Asian Studies, 1993.

———. *Indians in Malaya: Some Aspects of their Immigration and Settlement*. Cambridge: Cambridge University Press, 1969.

———. "Tamil and other Indian Convicts in the Straits Settlements 1790–1873". International Conference of Tamil Studies, Kuala Lumpur, 1966.

Sangha, Dave. "The New Indian Diaspora". In *Tracing an Indian Diaspora: Contexts, Memories, Representations*, edited by Parvati Raghuram, Ajaya Kumar Sahoo, Brij Maharaj, and Dave Sangha. New Delhi: Sage, 2008.

Saravanamuttu, Johan. "The Great Middleclass Debate: Ethnicity, Politics or Lifestyle". In *Multicultural Malaysia: Past, Present and Future*, edited by Lim Teck Ghee, Alberto Gomes, and Azly Rahman. Petaling Jaya: Strategic Information and Research Development Centre, 2009.

Sarrukkai, Sundar. "Rituals, Knowledge and Method: The Curious Case of Epistemological Sanskritization". In *Emotions in Rituals and Performances*, edited by Axel Michaels and Christoph Wulf. New Delhi: Routledge, 2012.

Saw Swee-Hock. "Population Trends and Patterns in Multi-Racial Malaysia". In *Malaysia: Recent Trends and Challenges*, edited by Saw Swee-Hock and K. Kesavapany. Singapore: Institute of Southeast Asian Studies, 2006.

Selvakumaran Ramachandran. *Indian Plantation Labour in Malaysia*. Kuala Lumpur: S. Abdul Majeed & Co., 1994.

Sen, Amartya. *The Argumentative Indian: Writings in Indian History, Culture and Identity*. London: Allen Lane: 2005.

Shantakumar, G. and Pundarik Mukhopadhya. "Demographics, Incomes and Development Issues among Indians in Singapore". In *Rising India and Indian*

Communities in East Asia, edited by K. Kesavapany, A. Mani, and P. Ramasamy. Singapore: Institute of Southeast Asian Studies, 2008.

Shaw, William. *Tun Razak: His Life and Times*. Kuala Lumpur: Longman Malaysia, 1976.

Shivapadasundaram, S. *The Saivite School of Hinduism*. Kuala Lumpur: Malaya Arulneri Thirukootam, [1934] 1975.

Shorr, Ronald E. "Hypnosis and the Concept of the Generalised Reality Orientation". In *Altered States of Consciousness*, edited by Charles T. Tart. New York: John Wiley, 1969.

Short, Anthony. *The Communist Insurrection in Malaya 1948–1960*. London: Frederick Muller, 1975.

Shulman, David Dean. *The King and Clown in South Indian Myth and Poetry*. Princeton, NJ: Princeton University Press, 1985.

———. "Outcast, Guardian and Trickster: Notes on the Myth of Kattavarayan". In *Criminal Gods and Demon Devotees: Essays on the Guardians of Popular Hinduism*, edited by Alf Hiltebeital. Albany: State University of New York Press, 1989.

———. *Tamil Temple Myths: Sacrifice and Divine Marriage in the South Indian Saiva Tradition*. Princeton, NJ: Princeton University Press, 1985.

———. "The Yogi's Human Self: *Tayumanavar* in the Tamil Mystical Tradition". *Religion* 21 (January 1991).

Sila-Khan, Dominique. *Crossing the Threshold: Understanding Religious Identities in South Asia*. London: I.B. Taurus/The Institute of Ismaili Studies, 2004.

Simons, Ronald C., Frank R. Ervin, and Raymond H. Prince. "The Psychobiology of Trance: Training for Thaipusam". *Transcultural Psychiatric Review* 25 (1988).

Sinha, Vineeta. *A New God in the Diaspora? Muneeswaran Worship in Contemporary Singapore*. Singapore and Copenhagen: Singapore University Press/NIAS Press, 2005.

———. "Hinduism in Contemporary Singapore". In *Indian Communities in Southeast Asia*, edited by K.S. Sandhu and A. Mani. Singapore: Institute of Southeast Asian Studies, 1993.

Sivananda, Swami. *Sixty-Three Nayanar Saints*. Batu Caves: Sivanandashram, 1980.

Sivaraman, K. *Saivism in Philosophical Perspective: A Study of the Formative Concepts, Problems and Methods of Saiva Siddhanta*. Delhi: Motilal Banarsidass, 1973.

Sivasupramaniam, V. *Decade of Growth: Seychelles Arul Mihu Navasakthi Vinayaga Temple 1992–2002*. Seychelles: V. Sivasupramaniam, 2003.

Somalay. *Palni: The Hill Temple*, 2nd ed. Palani: Sri Dhandayuthapani Swami Devasthanam, 1982.

Sontheimer, Gunther. "Between Ghost and God: A Folk Deity of the Deccan". In *Criminal Gods and Demon Devotees: Essays on the Guardians of Popular Hinduism*, edited by Alf Hiltebeital. Albany: State University of New York Press, 1991.

Srebrnik, Henry. "Indo-Fijians: Marooned without Land and Power in a South Pacific Archipelago". In *Tracing an Indian Diaspora: Contexts, Memories, Representations*, edited by Parvati Raghuram, Ajaya Kumar Sahoo, Brij Maharaj, and Dave Sangha. New Delhi: Sage, 2008.

Sri Delima. *As I was Passing*. Kuala Lumpur: Berita, 1976.

Stanley, John M. "The Capitulation of Mani: A Conversion Myth in the Cult of Khandoba". In *Criminal Gods and Demon Devotees: Essays on the Guardians of Popular Hinduism*, edited by Alf Hiltebeital. Albany: State University of New York Press, 1989.

Stein, Burton. *A History of India*. London: Blackwell, 1996.

———. *Peasant, State and Society in Medieval South India*. Delhi: Oxford University Press, 1980.

———. "Temples in the Tamil Country 1300–1750 AD". In *South Indian Temples: An Analytical Reconsideration*, edited by Burton Stein. Delhi: Vikras, 1978.

Stenson, Michael R. *Class, Race and Colonialism in West Malaysia: The Indian Case*. St. Lucia: University of Queensland Press, 1980.

Subramani, ed. *The Indo-Fijian Experience*. St. Lucia: University of Queensland Press, 1979.

Subramuniyaswami, Sivaya. *Dancing with Siva: Hinduism's Contemporary Catechism*. Concord: Himalayan Academy, 1993.

———, ed. *Weaver's Wisdom: Ancient Precepts for a Perfect Life*. Hawaii: Himalayan Academy, 1999.

Sulaiman, A.B. *Sensitive Truths in Malaysia: A Critical Appraisal of the Malay Problem*. Petaling Jaya: Strategic Research and Information Development Centre, 2013.

Sutton, Matthew Avery. *American Apocalypses: A History of Modern Evangelicism*. Cambridge, MA: The Belknap Press of Harvard University Press, 2014.

Swearer, Donald K. "The Kataragama and Kandy Asala Peraharaj: Juxtaposing Religious Elements in Sri Lanka". In *Religious Festivals in South India and Sri Lanka*, edited by Guy R. Welbon and Glenn Yocum. Delhi: Manohar, 1978.

Tan, Jason. "Malaysian Culture under Abdullah". In *Awakening: The Abdullah Badawi Years in Malaysia*, edited by Bridget Welsh and James V.H. Chin. Petaling Jaya: Strategic Information and Reseach Development Centre, 2013.

Tart, Charles T., ed. *Altered States of Consciousness*. New York: Wiley, 1969.

———. "Introduction". In *Altered States of Consciousness*, edited by Charles Tart. New York: Wiley, 1969.

Tate, Desmond Muzafar. *The Malaysian Indians: History, Problems and Future*. Petaling Jaya: Strategic Information and Research Development, 2008.

Thapar, Romila. "Imagined Communities? Ancient History and the Modern Search for Hindu Identity". *Modern Asian Studies* 23 (1989).

Thayaparan S. *No Country for Righteous Men and Other Essays in a Culture of*

Offendedness. Petaling Jaya: Strategic Information and Research Development Centre, 2014.

Thillainathan, R. "A Critical Review of Indian Economic Performance and Priorities for Action". In *Rising India and Indian Communities in East Asia*, edited by K. Kesavapany, A. Mani, and P. Ramasamy. Singapore: Institute of Southeast Asian Studies, 2008.

Thiruvasagam, Gomathi. *Book of Festivals*. Kuala Lumpur: Saiva Siddhanta Mandram, 1992.

Tinker, Hugh. *A New System of Slavery: The Export of Indian Labour Overseas 1830–1920*. London: Oxford University Press, 1974.

Trautmann, Thomas R. *Aryans and British India*. Berkeley: Yale University Press, 1997.

———. *Languages and Nations: The Dravidian Proof in Colonial Madras*. Berkeley: University of California Press, 2001.

Uthayakumar, K. "Marginalization of the Indians in Malaysia". Copy emailed to the author on 6 April 2010.

Vail, Lise F. "Founders, Swamis and Devotees: Becoming Divine in North Karnataka". In *Gods of Flesh, Gods of Stone: The Embodiment of Divinity in India*, edited by Joanne Punzo Waghorne and Norman Cutler in association with Vasudha Narayanan. Chambersburg: Anima, 1985.

Van der Veer, Peter. *Religious Nationalisms: Hindus and Muslims in India*. Berkeley: University of California Press, 1994.

Vanamali. *The Lilas of the Sons of Shiva*. New Delhi: Aryan Books, 2008.

Victor, Barbara. *The Last Crusade: Religion and the Politics of Misdirection*. London: Constable, 2005.

Visuvalingam, Sunthar. "The Transgressive Sacrality of the *Diksita*: Sacrifice, Criminality and *Bhakti* in the Hindu Tradition". In *Criminal Gods and Demon Devotees: Essays on the Guardians of Popular Hinduism*, edited by Alf Hiltebeital. Albany: State University of New York Press, 1989.

Von Scheve, Christian. "Collective Emotions in Rituals: Elicitation, Transmission and a 'Matthew Effect'". In *Emotions in Rituals and Performances*, edited by Axel Michaels and Christoph Wulf. New Delhi: Routledge, 2012.

Wade, Geoff. *The Origins and Evolution of Ethnocracy in Malaysia*, Working Paper Series 112. Singapore: Asian Research Institute, National University of Singapore, April 2009.

Wadley, Susan S. "*Vrats*: Transformers of Destiny". In *Karma: An Anthropological Inquiry*, edited by Charles F. Keyes and E. Valentine Daniel. Berkeley: University of California Press, 1983.

Waghorne, Joanne Punzo and Norman Cutler, eds., in association with Vasudha Narayanan. *Gods of Flesh, Gods of Stone: The Embodiment of Divinity in India*. Chambersburg: Anima, 1985.

Wain, Barry. *Malaysian Maverick: Mahathir Mohamad in Turbulent Times*. Basingstoke: Palgrave MacMillan, 2009.

Walker, Sheila. *Ceremonial Spirit Possession in Africa and Afro-America: Forms, Meanings and Functional Significance for Individuals and Social Groups*. Leiden: Brill, 1972.

Ward, Colleen. "Thaipusam in Malaysia: A Psycho-Anthropological Analysis of Ritual Trance, Ceremonial Possession and Self-Mortification Practices". *Ethos* 14 (1984).

Washbrook, David. "The Development of Caste Organization in South India 1880–1925". In *South India: Political Institutions and Political Change 1880–1940*, edited by C.J. Baker and David Washbrook. Delhi: MacMillan, 1975.

———. "Introduction". In *South India: Political Institutions and Political Change*, edited by C.J. Baker and David Washbrook. Delhi: MacMillan, 1975.

Washington, Peter. *Madame Blavatsky's Baboon: Theosophy and the Emergence of the Western Guru*. London: Secker and Warburg, 1993.

Wavell, Stuart. "Through the Fires of Existence to the Needles of Eternity". In *Trances*, edited by Stuart Wavell, Audrey Butt, and Nina Epton. Kuala Lumpur: Antara Book Company, 1988.

Wavell, Stuart, Audrey Butt, and Nina Epton, eds. *Trances*. Kuala Lumpur: Antara Book Company, 1988.

Welsh, Bridget. "Enabling and Empowering of Malaysians". In *Awakening: The Abdullah Badawi Years in Malaysia*, edited by Bridget Welsh and James V.H. Chin. Petaling Jaya: Strategic Information and Research Development Centre, 2013.

Welsh, Bridget and James V.H. Chin, eds. *Awakening: The Abdullah Badawi Years in Malaysia*. Petaling Jaya: Strategic Information and Research Development Centre, 2013.

Whitehead, Henry. *The Village Gods of India*. Calcutta: Association Press, 1921.

Wiebe, Paul W., and S. Mariappen. *Indian Malaysians: The View from the Plantation*. Delhi: Manohar, 1978.

Willford, Andrew C. *Cage of Freedom: Tamil Identity and the Ethnic Fetish in Malaysia*. Ann Arbor: University of Michigan Press, 2006.

———. "Ethnic Clashes, Squatters and Historicity in Malaysia". In *Rising India and Indian Communities in East Asia*, edited by K. Kesavapany, A. Mani, and P. Ramasamy. Singapore: Institute of Southeast Asian Studies, 2008.

———. "Every Indian is Burning Inside". In *Awakening: The Abdullah Badawi Years in Malaysia*, edited by Bridget Welsh and James V.H. Chin. Petaling Jaya: Strategic Research and Development Centre, 2013.

Willford, Andrew C., in collaboration with S. Nagarajan. *Tamils and the Haunting of Justice: History and Recognition in Malaysia's Plantations*. Singapore: National University of Singapore, 2014.

Wilson, Bernard. "Meta Mobilis: The Case for Existence in K.S. Maniam's *Between Lives*". In *Tracing an Indian Diaspora: Contexts, Memories, Representations*, edited by Parvati Raghuram, Ajaya Kumar Sahoo, Brij Maharaj, and Dave Sangha. New Delhi: Sage, 2008.

Wilson, C., Controller of Labour. *Annual Report of the Labour Department, 1936*. Kuala Lumpur: Government Press, 1937.

Wood, Michael. *The Smile of Murugan: A South Indian Journey*. Harmondsworth: Penguin, 1996.

Woodroofe, Sir John. *Shakti and Shakta: Essays and Addresses on the Shakta Tantrashastra*. Madras: Ganesh, 1920.

Wulf, Christoph. "Memory, Mimesis and the Circulation of Emotions in Rituals". In *Emotions in Rituals and Performances*, edited by Axel Michaels and Christoph Wulf. New Delhi: Routledge, 2012.

Yoshitsugu Sawai. "Reflections on Bhakti as a Type of Indian Mysticism". In *The Historical Development of the Bhakti Movement in India*, edited by Iwao Shima, Teiji Sakata, and Katsuyuki Ida. New Delhi: Manohar, 2011.

Zaehner, R.C. *Hinduism*. London: Oxford University Press, 1962.

Zaharom Nain. *Rhetoric and Realities: Critical Reflections on Malaysian Politics, Culture and Education*. Petaling Jaya: Centre for Studies of Communications and Culture/Strategic Information and Research Development Centre, 2013.

Zainah Anwar. *Islamic Revivalism in Malaysia: Dakwah among the Students*. Petaling Jaya: Pelanduk, 1987.

Zvelebil, Kamil V. *The Poets of the Powers*. London: Rider, 1973.

———. *Tamil Traditions on Subrahmanya-Murugan*. Madras: Institute of Asian Studies, 1991.

Index

About the Author

Carl Vadivella Belle obtained a Bachelor of Arts degree at the Australian National University, Canberra. Between 1976 and 1979 he served in the Australian High Commission, Kuala Lumpur. He has maintained a long-term interest in Malaysian social, political, religious and political issues, especially Hinduism in Malaysia and the history and traditions of Malaysia's Indian population. His doctoral dissertation, "Thaipusam in Malaysia: A Hindu Festival Misunderstood?" was accepted by Deakin University in 2004. He has also acted as principal consultant to several television and radio productions focussing on the festival of Thaipusam as it is practised at Batu Caves, Kuala Lumpur. Dr Belle was appointed Inaugural Hindu Chaplain at the Flinders University of South Australia in 2005. He has lectured extensively on both Malaysian politics and society, and on South Indian Hindu traditions, as well as wider religious issues, and has published numerous papers on these topics. His earlier work, *Tragic Orphans: Indians in Malaysia*, also published by ISEAS, in 2015, constitutes a comprehensive general history of the modern Indian presence in Malaysia.

The statue of Lord Murugan at the foot of Batu Caves steps. Note the crowd on the steps. This continues throughout the entire period of the Thaipusam festival. © Krisztian Gal. Reproduced with permission.

Preparing for Thaipusam: Batu Caves on a night leading up to the festival.
© Kahan Singh Gill. Reproduced with permission.

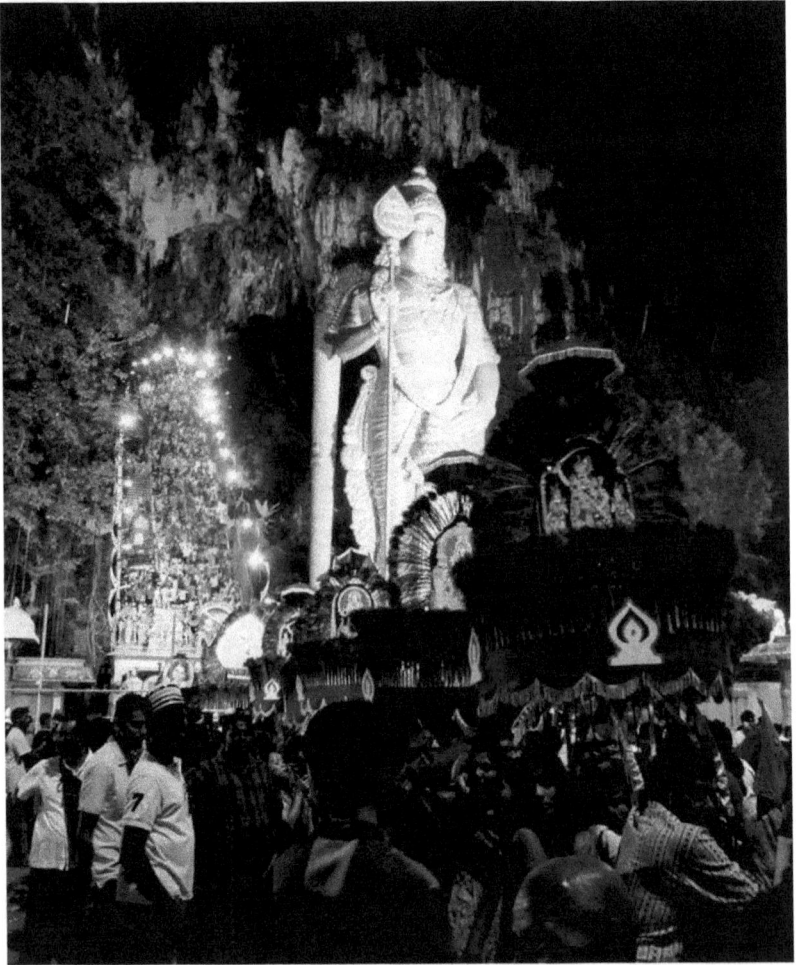

Thaipusam at Night: A series of *mayil* (peacock) kavadis are being borne towards the Batu Caves steps. © Krisztian Gal. Reproduced with permission.

Altar within the chariot and the priests. © Jayaganesan Kangris.
Reproduced with permission.

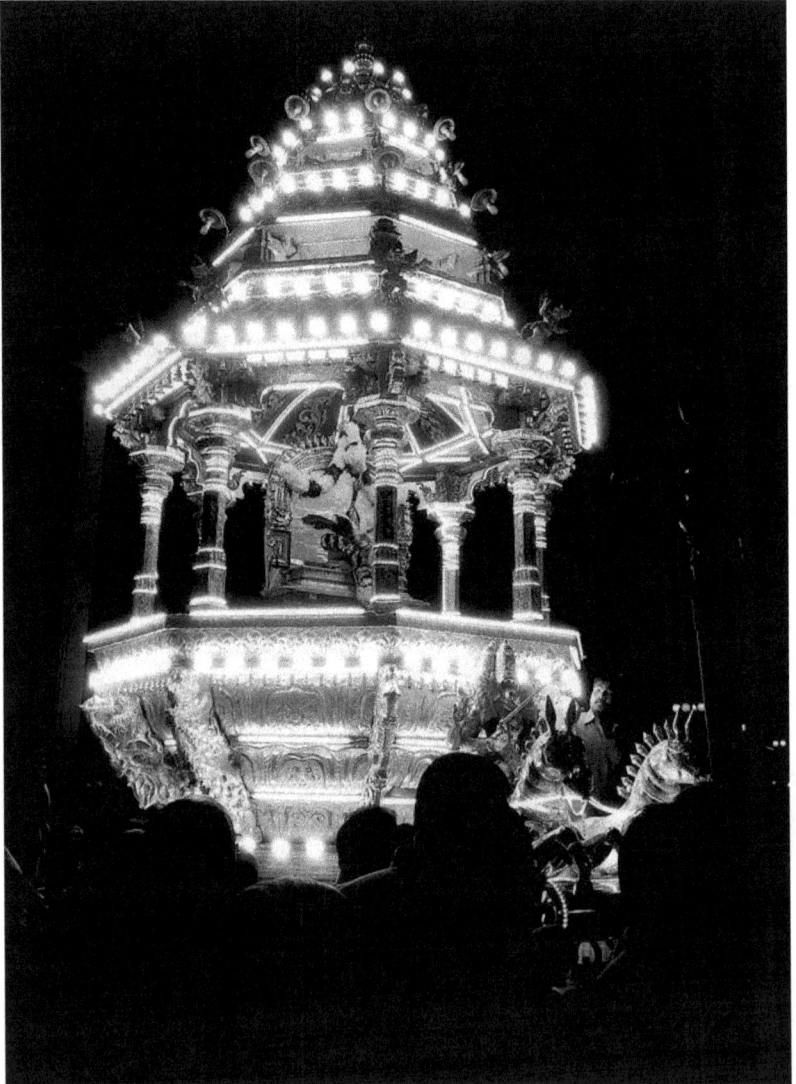

Chariot at night. © Jayaganesan Kangris. Reproduced with permission.

Preparing the kavadi altar – each kavadi has its own altar.
© Krisztian Gal. Reproduced with permission.

Altar setup. © Eric Lafforge. Reproduced with permission.

A devotee preparing for trance. The surrounding crowd demonstrates the public scrutiny each devotee must endure and the pressures to attain trance.
© Krisztian Gal. Reproduced with permission.

Devotees preparing to enter trance. © Kahan Singh Gill. Reproduced with permission.

A devotee at the onset of the state of trance (*arul*).
© Krisztian Gal. Reproduced with permission.

An entranced devotee undergoing the insertion of a *vel*. This one is being pushed through the cheeks. © Krisztian Gal. Reproduced with permission.

Devotees at Batu Caves. © Kahan Singh Gill. Reproduced with permission.

A Chinese devotee with a *ter* kavadi. The assistant holds the rope taut while the bearer makes his way to the shrine in the caves. © Krisztian Gal. Reproduced with permission.

Author with kavadi. © Eric Lafforge. Reproduced with permission.

Batu Caves statue of Murugan. © Kahan Singh Gill. Reproduced with permission.

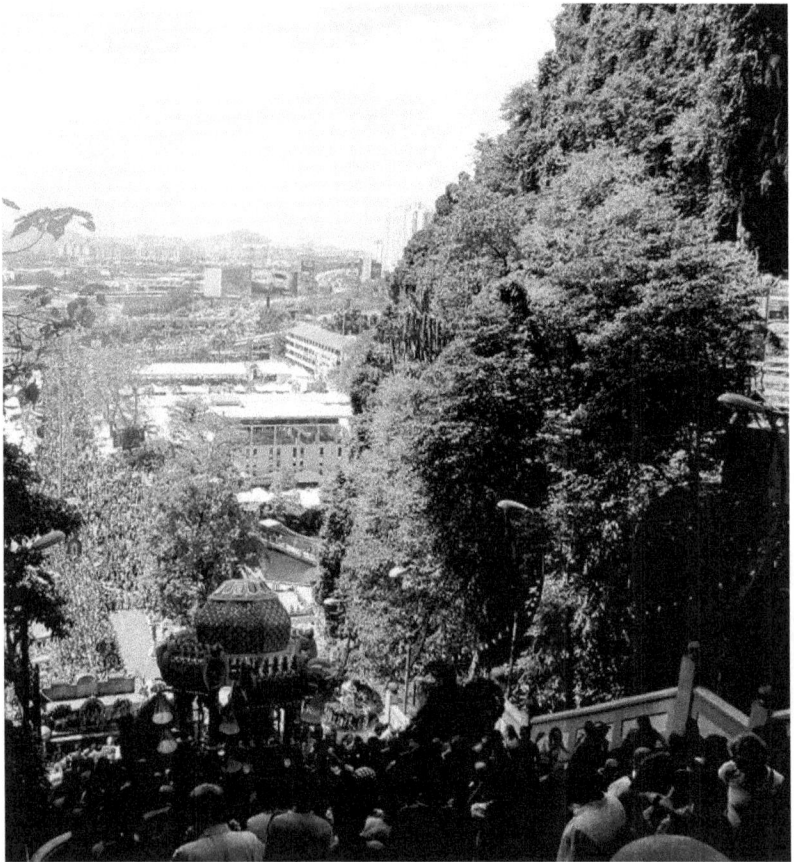

A crowd scene taken from the top of Batu Caves steps. Over a million people attend Thaipusam at Batu Caves each year. © Krisztian Gal. Reproduced with permission.

Sri Vivekananda Ashram, Brickfields, Kuala Lumpur: A landmark in Malaysian Hinduism.

Statuary depicting Murugan and his consorts. From left: Valli, Murugan and Devayanai. (Taken at the newly opened Om Sri Maha Nageswari Temple, Puchong, south of Kuala Lumpur.)

An image of Murugan with the sage Agastya. (Taken at the newly opened Om Sri Maha Nageswari Temple, Puchong, south of Kuala Lumpur.)

Chettiars with the
Silver Chariot, Penang.
Postcard circa 1910.

Thaipusam in Penang. Postcard circa 1940.

www.ingramcontent.com/pod-product-compliance
Lightning Source LLC
Chambersburg PA
CBHW072041020426
42334CB00017B/1346